Frontispiece. The temple of Yahweh at Mount Nebo (see pp. 235-238).

PUBLICATIONS OF THE STUDIUM BIBLICUM FRANCISCANUM No. 1

THE MEMORIAL OF MOSES ON MOUNT NEBO

PART I. THE TEXT

BY

SYLVESTER J. SALLER, O. F. M.

PRINTED BY THE FRANCISCAN PRESS
JERUSALEM
1941

EX PARTE NOSTRA NIHIL OBSTAT QUOMINUS IMPRIMATUR

P. ALBERTUS GORI, O.F.M.,
Custos Terrae Sanctae,

Hierosolymis, die 30 Septembris, 1941.

IMPRIMATUR

Sacerdos GABRIEL SUEDAN,
Censor Delegatus,

Hierosolymis, die 7 Octobris, 1941.

PREFACE

The excavations at Siyâgha (Mount Nebo) were undertaken primarily as part of the program of the Studium Biblicum Franciscanum, which aims at giving both professors and students every opportunity of becoming thoroughly acquainted with the Land of the Bible. The undertaking was made possible only by the far-sighted policy and by the whole-hearted cooperation of the authorities of the Custody of the Holy Land; to these as well as to the generous benefactors of the Custody we are above all others deeply indebted and sincerely grateful. But we wish to use this opportunity of thanking also all others who have in any way contributed towards the success of this enterprise.

The present publication aims at giving a complete and accurate report of all the discoveries which were made at Siyâgha (Mount Nebo); their relation to other discoveries is indicated wherever possible. Circumstances oblige us to publish the treatise on pottery by Father Hilary Schneider, O. F. M., (see pp. 21 f.) separately; we venture to hope that the printing of that treatise will not be postponed very long; everything else is treated here. All the proofs were read by the writer, by Rev. Father Bonaventure Simon, O. F. M., Discreet of the Custody of the Holy Land, and by Mr. J. Calis of the Franciscan Press; Fathers D. Baldi, B. Bagatti, J. Dowling, G. Stol and others willingly assisted whenever required. In fact, we found such hearty cooperation from all sides that we find it difficult to express our appreciation adequately. As a token of our gratitude we dedicate this work to our superiors, benefactors and friends.

The Feast of Moses on Mount Nebo,
September 4th, 1941,
Jerusalem.

CONTENTS

PART I

PART II

LIST OF ILLUSTRATIONS IN THE TEXT

LIST OF ABBREVIATIONS

AASOR	*Annual of the American Schools of Oriental Research*
ACB	*Altchristliche Basiliken und Lokaltraditionen in Südjudäa*, 1918, A. Mader
Aetheria	See pp. 330 f.
AJA	*American Journal of Archaeology*
Antioch	*Antioch on the Orontes: I. The Excavations of 1932*, edited by G. W. Elderkin, 1934; II. *The Excavations of 1933-1936*, edited by R. Stillwell, 1938
AP	*Arabia Petraea: I. Moab*, 1907, A. Musil
APES	American Palestine Exploration Society
ARP	*Archaeological Researches in Palestine during the years 1873-4*, I-II, 1896, Clermont-Ganneau
ASG	*Antike Synagogen in Galilaea*, 1916, H. Kohl & C. Watzinger
BASOR	*Bulletin of the American Schools of Oriental Research*
Beih. ZATW	*Beiheft zur Zeitschrift für die alttestamentliche Wissenschaft*
Bethléem	*Bethléem, Le Sanctuaire de la Nativité*, 1914, H. Vincent et F.-M. Abel, O. P.
Beth-Shan	*Publications of the Palestine Section of the Museum of the University of Pennsylvania:* III. *Beth-shan Excavations 1921-3, The Arab and Byzantine Levels*, 1931; IV. *A Sixth Century Monastery at Beth-shan (Scythopolis)*, 1939; both by G. M. FitzGerald
BRL	*Biblisches Reallexikon*, 1937, Kurt Galling
BSP	*Biblia Sacra Polyglotta* I, 1660, Brianus Waltonus
BVK	*Die Brotvermehrungskirche von et-tâbga am Genesarethsee und ihre Mosaiken*, 1934, A. M. Schneider
cm.	centimeters
Corpus	*Corpus of Palestinian Pottery*, 1930, J. G. Duncan
DAC	*Dictionnaire d'Archéologie Chrétienne et de Liturgie*
De Meester	See p. 254, note 6
Deut.	*Deuteronomy*
DHGE	*Dictionnaire d'Histoire et de Géographie Ecclésiastiques*
DP	*Denkmäler Palästinas* I & II, 1933-5, C. Watzinger
ECS	*Early Churches in Syria, Fourth to the Seventh Centuries*, 1929, H. C. Butler, edited and completed by E. B. Smith
Emmaüs	*Emmaüs, sa Basilique et son Histoire*, 1932, H. Vincent et F.-M. Abel, O. P.
EP	*Excavations in Palestine 1898-1900*, 1902, Bliss and Macalister
Euchologion	Εὐχολόγιον τὸ μέγα σὺν Θεῷ ἁγίῳ, 1873
Géog.	*Géographie de la Palestine* I-II, 1933, 1938, F.-M. Abel, O. P.
Gerar	*Gerar*, 1928, F. Petrie
Gerasa	*Gerasa, City of the Decapolis*, 1938, edited by C. H. Kraeling
Geyer	Geyer, P., *Itinera Hierosolymitana Saeculi IV-VIII*, 1898

Gezer	*The Excavation of Gezer 1902-5 and 1907-9,* I-III, 1912, R. A. S. Macalister
GIPT	*Die griechischen Inschriften der Palästina Tertia,* 1921, A. Alt
GT	*La Géographie du Talmud,* 1868, A. Neubauer
Guida	*Il museo della Flagellazione in Gerusalemme: Guida al Museo,* 1939, P. B. Bagatti, O. F. M.
h.	high
HAE	*Handbuch der altchristlichen Epigraphik,* 1917, C. M. Kaufmann
HCA	*Handbuch der christlichen Archäologie,* 1922, Id.
HGHL	*The Historical Geography of the Holy Land,* 25th revised edition, 1931, G. A. Smith
HL	*Das Heilige Land*
HPT	*The Handbook of Palestine and Transjordan,* 3rd edition, 1934, H. Luke and E. Keith-Roach
IGLP	*Introduction to Greek and Latin Palaeography,* 1912, E. M. Thompson
JAOS	*Journal of the American Oriental Society*
JEA	*Journal of Egyptian Archaeology*
Jericho	*Jericho, die Ergebnisse der Ausgrabungen,* 1913, Sellin und Watzinger
Jérusalem	*Jérusalem* I & II, 1912, 1914, Vincent et Abel, O. P.
JPOS	*Journal of the Palestine Oriental Society*
Kisa	Kisa, A., *Das Glas im Altertume* I-III, 1908
l.	long
Lopes	*Itinerario da Terra Santa e suas particularidades* composto por Frey Pantaleam d'Aveiro, edited by Simao Lopes, Lisboa, 1593
LS	*Loca Sancta,* 1907, P. Thomsen
m.	meters
MAA	*Mission Archéologique en Arabie,* 1909, PP. Jaussen et Savignac, O. P.
Mach.	*Machabees*
NBAC	*Nuovo Bullettino di Archeologia Cristiana*
Num.	*Numbers*
OC	*Oriens Christianus*
Onom.	*Eusebius, das Onomastikon der biblischen Ortsnamen mit der lateinischen Übersetzung des Hieronymus,* 1904, E. Klostermann
PA	*Die Provincia Arabia* I-III, 1904-9, R. E. Brünnow und A. von Domaszewski
PAAES	*Publications of the American Archaeological Expedition to Syria in 1899-1900*
PEF Ann.	*Palestine Exploration Fund Annual*
PEQ	*Palestine Exploration Quarterly*
PG	*Patrologia Graeca*
PJB	*Palästinajahrbuch*
PPUAES	*Publications of the Princeton University Archaeological Expedition to Syria in 1904-5*
Prentice	Prentice, W. K., *Greek and Latin Inscriptions* (Part III of *PAAES*), 1908
PS	*Pratum Spirituale Joannis Moschi*
QDAP	*Quarterly of the Department of Antiquities in Palestine*
QS	*Palestine Exploration Fund Quarterly Statement*
Raabe	Raabe, R., *Petrus der Iberer,* 1895
RAC	*Rivista di Archeologia Cristiana*
RB	*Revue Biblique*
RE	*Realenzyklopädie der klassischen Altertumswissenschaft,* Pauly-Wissowa
RLV	*Reallexikon der Vorgeschichte,* Max Ebert
RTSC	*Review of Terra Santa College*

Samaria	*Harvard Excavations at Samaria,* 1924, Reisner, Fisher, Lyon
SEG	*Supplementum Epigraphicum Graecum*
SEP	*The Survey of Eastern Palestine,* 1889, C. R. Conder
SGKA	*Studien zur Geschichte und Kultur des Altertums*
SWP	*Survey of Western Palestine: Memoirs* I-III, 1881-3
SWP Jer.	*Survey of Western Palestine: Jerusalem,* 1884, C. Warren & C. R. Conder
TOC	*The Thousand and One Churches,* 1909, W. M. Ramsay & G. L. Bell
TSF	*Terre Sainte,* French
TSI	*Terra Santa,* Italian
TSS	*Tierra Santa,* Spanish
Ugolinus	See p. 338
w.	wide
W.	Wroth, see p. 281
ZATW	*Zeitschrift für die alttestamentliche Wissenschaft*
ZDPV	*Zeitschrift des deutschen Palästinavereins*

CORRIGENDA

P. 49, l. 7 from below, instead of 7 read: 10
" 75, l. 9 " " , read: thimble
" 85, l. 2 " " , read: strengthening
" 149, note 4, read: Colonnettes
" 168, l. 9 from below, read: XXXVIII
" 169, l. 23 " above, " : extends
" 192, l. 4 " " , " : at Bethnambris
" 221, l. 10 " " , " : room 91
" 251, l. 22 " " , " : most pious
P. 254, l. 10 from below, read: the source
" ", note 6, l. 3, read: Stanbrook
" 255, l. 21 from above, read: Χ(ριστό)ς
" 259, heading, read: INSCRIPTIONS
" 274, note 1, l. 2, read: author's
" 285, ll. 4 & 18 from below, read: metallic
" 331, l. 8 from above, read: Leclercq
Pl. 31, top, is probably a capital or cap
" 69, 1, read: from the south

N. B. — A few inconsistencies in the use of the spiritus, the accent and in spelling, and the use of "1" instead of "l", are not noted here.

CHAPTER I

THE SITE AND ITS SURROUNDINGS

MOSES, the leader, lawgiver and prophet of the Hebrews, viewed the Promised Land, from which he was debarred by a special decree of God, from Mount Nebo, in the ancient Land of Moab; there he died and somewhere in the vicinity he was buried.[1] In honor of Moses a memorial was erected on the traditional site of those events; but in the course of time that monument was destroyed and forgotten. Modern explorers believe that the ruins which cover Siyâgha in Transjordan represent the memorial of Moses;[2] those ruins were systematically explored by the Franciscans of the Custody of the Holy Land and of the Biblical School of the same Order established at the monastery of the Flagellation, Jerusalem, in three expeditions in 1933, 1935 and 1937. Before going into detail regarding the discoveries which were made we will give a brief description of the site and its surroundings and review the explorations of the same from 1864 to 1939.

Siyâgha is located in that part of the Arab amirate of Transjordan which overlooks the northeastern part of the Dead Sea (Pl. 8). In ancient times this part of Transjordan was called Moab and today it is called el-Belqâ.[3] This region has been frequently visited and described;[4] its chief characteristic is the high plateau which rises over 1000 meters above the Dead Sea and the Jordan valley. The western edge of this plateau is cut by deep wadies alternating with high ridges. The western extremity of one of these ridges is called Siyâgha (Fig. 1). It projects from the table-land about midway between Madaba and Hesbân in the neighborhood of Kefeir Abu Bedd which stands on the watershed at a height of about 805 m. above sea level. Beyond Kefeir Abu ʿBedd the plateau begins to incline towards the west; here can be noticed the upper shallow ends of the wadies to the north and south of the Siyâgha ridge. The

1 *Deut.* 34, 1-6.

2 Abel, *Géog.* I, pp. 381 ff.

3 *HGHL* pp. 584 ff.; *HPT* p. 468.

4 See Chapter II and *HGHL* pp. 592 ff.

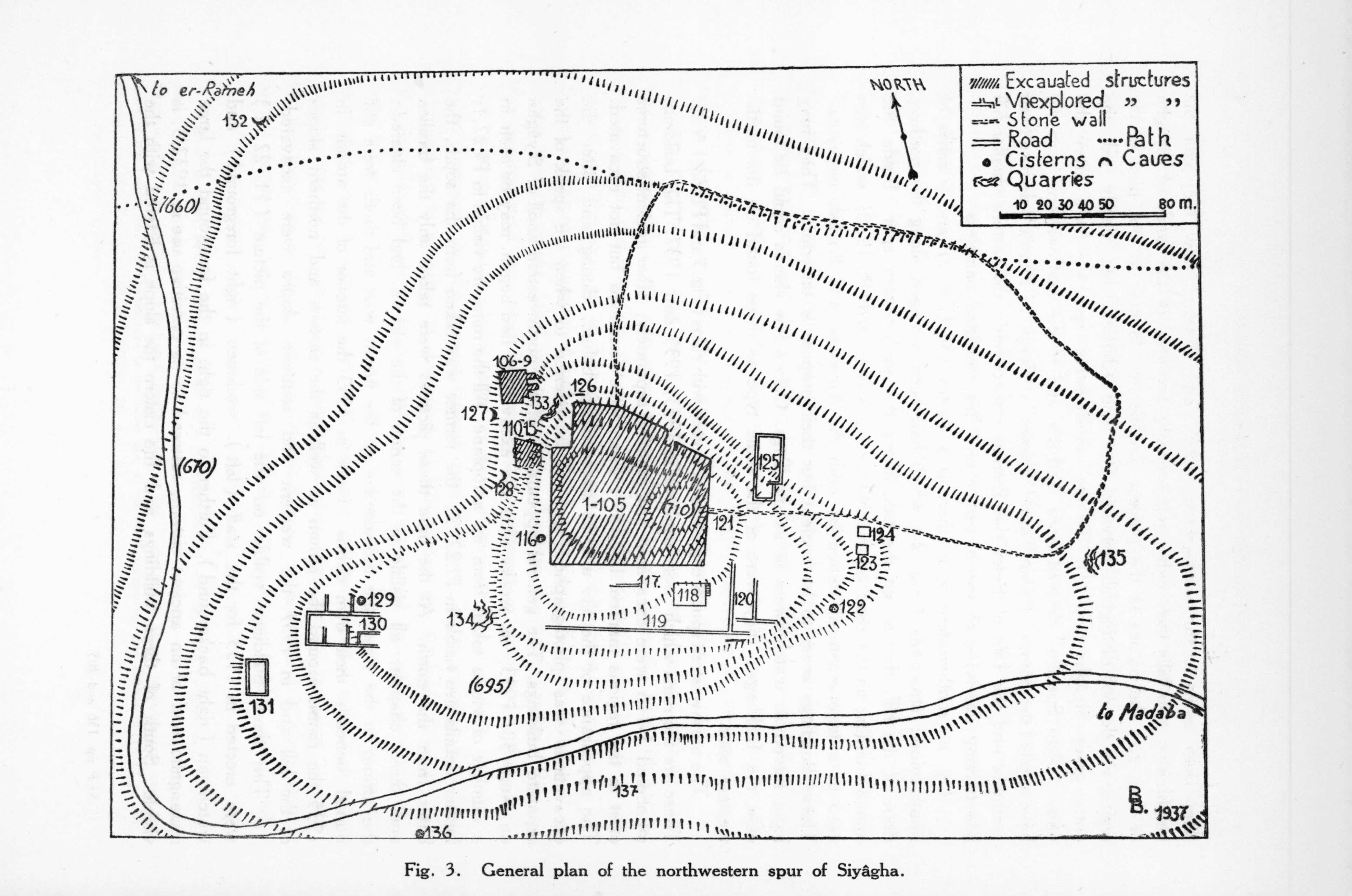

Fig. 3. General plan of the northwestern spur of Siyâgha.

remains of an ancient enclosure wall; these ruins extend to a path running east and west on the south side of the site. In 1935 a new road was built along the course of this path; this new road winds around the western side of the hill, where it meets another path coming from the east (Fig. 3). The road on the south and the west, the path on the north and the quarry 135 on the east indicate the approximate limits of the 19 dunams covered with ruins acquired by the Custody of the Holy Land for the purpose of instituting scientific investigations. This piece of land is oval in shape with the broader end towards the west and the narrower end towards the east. The highest point of this oval was crowned by the most important building of the group, the church. But the top of the hill was not large enough for the church, whose foundations were erected on the slopes and consequently a filling of earth was required on the interior of the walls in order to reach a common floor level; this was necessary already for the earliest church which was discovered beneath the eastern end of the basilica and also stands partially on the northern slope. All the other buildings around the church stand on the slopes of the hill, and, when shaken by an earthquake, their walls collapsed in the direction of the slope and some of the stones rolled far down the sides of the hill, in certain cases even beyond the limits of the property given above. A number of burials were made in these ruins, especially in the eastern part of the church, otherwise the ruins remained undisturbed since the day when the buildings collapsed; it was therefore possible to recover all the evidence that had a bearing on the history of that site.

* * *

The choice of this site for such extensive buildings may have been due to more than one reason; it is, however, not improbable that the marvelous view from this spot was one of the determining factors. The most magnificent view is that to the west, where it is entirely unobstructed down the western slopes of the plateau, across the plain through which the River Jordan flows to the Dead Sea and up the eastern slopes of the mountains of Judea and Samaria which shut off the view to the west (Pls. 8-10). On top of those mountains are the famous cities of Hebron, Bethlehem, Jerusalem, etc. Jerusalem is directly west of the northern end of the Dead Sea; its towers, especially those on the Mount of Olives, east of Jerusalem, can be made out by the naked eye. Patches of green trees both north and south of Jerusalem indicate the location of numerous smaller towns and villages. On dark nights the location of Jerusalem and Bethlehem is marked by their bright lights; early in the morning the rising sun is reflected from the windows of those two towns and produces a delightful play of colors for a few moments; towards evening when the sun drops behind the Judean ridge all the buildings which stand on its crest, especially the higher

to and from Siyâgha. The section of the road between Madaba and 'Ayûn Mûsa was constructed in 1931 for the purpose of transporting the materials required for the pumping-station at 'Ayûn Mûsa. In 1933 the Custody of the Holy Land built the branch road from Jebel en-Neba to Siyâgha ; in 1935 the Custody cooperated with the town of Madaba in extending the road from Siyâgha to the Ghor where it joins the 'Ammân - Jerusalem road at Shûneh. This last section of the road will shorten considerably the distance between Jerusalem and Siyâgha, but it is not yet (1940) fit for motor traffic, so all visitors to Siyâgha who come from Jerusalem are obliged to make the long detour over es-Salt, 'Ammân and Madaba. This may be the only way of reaching Siyâgha by car for a long time to come.

The distance between the Greek Orthodox church in Madaba with the famous mosaic map of Palestine (Pl. 20,1 left) and the church at Siyâgha is exactly 10 km. by road. Midway between the two places is Kefeir Abu Bedd (Figs. 1 and 2). Conder says that the place is called also Kefeir el-Gharby.[1] On the topographical map of Transjordan, scale : 250,000, 'Ammân sheet, compiled in 1937, the place is called Kefeir el-Wekhyan. The first name, meaning "the little village of the millstone", is derived from a large disc stone standing up in the midst of ancient ruins ; the second name, meaning "the western little village", indicates the relation of this place to several other ancient places in the neighborhood; the third name is derived from the tribe which has built its storehouses there.

The Wekhyan are a branch of the "'Arab el-Ghaneimât".[2] In summer the Wekhyan live in their tents in the region between Kefeir Abu Bedd and Jebel en-Neba (Pl. 20, 2), and cultivate the rich fields in that region ; but in winter they generally retire to the more sheltered valleys further west. Thirteen members of this tribe owned Siyâgha. This tribe always furnished the chief contingent of workmen during the excavations at Siyâgha. They informed us that in building their storehouses at Kefeir Abu Bedd (or simply "Qweir", as they call the place,) they found some plain mosaic pavements, a few fragments of marble, ancient cisterns, etc.

From Kefeir Abu Bedd to Siyâgha, a distance of 5 km., the road traverses the Nebo region. Before reaching Jebel en-Neba a road branches off to the left to el-Mekhayyat about 2 km. to the south, where there are extensive ruins of an ancient place identified with the town of Nebo ; that place will form the subject of a special study.[3] Further west the road passes between Jebel en-Neba

[1] *SEP* p. 134.

[2] *SEP* p. 293, 7.

[3] Accidental discoveries made there up to 1935 are summed up by P. B. Bagatti, O. F. M., in *RAC* 13 (1936), pp. 129-141 ; see *QDAP* 6 (1938), pp. 217 f. — In 1939 P. Bagatti cleared the so-called "Church I" and prepared a report which will appear in *QDAP* in 1940.

on the left and a ruin called el-Heisah on the right. El-Heisah is the "Kusr en-Neba" of Conder;[1] Musil thinks that the ruin represents a monastery.[2] On the northern slope of Jebel en-Neba can be seen a dolmen.[3] West of Jebel en-Neba in a depression of the ridge the road divides; the branch on the right continues down the northern slope of the ridge to 'Ayûn Mûsa, that on the left continues along the top of the ridge to Siyâgha (Pl. 1, 1). Up to the fork in the road the new track follows more or less the course of an ancient road (Fig. 2),[4] which also branched near the fork in the modern road; one branch of the ancient road went down to 'Ayûn Mûsa and the other crossed the el-Beidah ridge on the south to el-Mekhayyat; possibly a third arm extended to Siyâgha, but, if so, no evidence of it has been discovered. The depression in the ridge between Jebel en-Neba and Siyâgha is also the beginning of the Wady el-Hanîshiyeh which forms a natural division between the eastern and western parts of the ridge.

To the southeast and south of Siyâgha (Pl. 16, 1 and 2) there is a ridge which is nothing else than an extension of Jebel en-Neba to the southwest; it is called el-Beidah and Khashm el-Hanîshiyeh. On el-Beidah there are numerous ancient monuments; we already mentioned the ancient road which crosses el-Beidah to el-Mekhayyat. The road crossed the Wady el-Beidah over an ancient bridge; near this bridge another branch of the road crossed el-Beidah first in a westerly, then in a southerly direction (Pl. 17, 1). El-Beidah is divided into fields by ancient walls which serve no practical purpose at present; their origin is uncertain. On el-Beidah, as also on Jebel en-Neba and on the northern slopes between el-Heisah and 'Ayûn Mûsa, there are rock-cuttings (Pl. 18, 1), a cistern, small structures which may have served as watchtowers near the roads or fields (Pl. 17, 2), stone circles, dolmens (Pl. 18, 2), menhirs, etc., which were observed on our walks through the region. P. Bellarmino Bagatti, O. F. M., made special studies of all those monuments, the most important of which he photographed and entered on a plan of the region (Fig. 2).[5] One of the menhirs on the northwestern slope of Beidah (Pl. 19, 1) can be distinctly seen from Siyâgha. At the southwestern extremity of el-Beidah there are two ruins; near the upper one of the two glass mosaics and fragments of glass and clay vessels similar to those found at Siyâgha were collected. From these ruins the springs and wady in the neighborhood derived their name el-Keneiyiseh. From the southwestern spur of Siyâgha one obtains a fine view of Wady el-Keneiyiseh and its continuation towards the west as far as the Dead Sea. South of the Wady el-Keneiyiseh is

1 *SEP* p. 202.
2 *AP* I, p. 274.
3 *SEP* p. 203; Karge, *Rephaim*², p. 436; Schumacher, *ZDPV* 16 (1893), p. 163, Fig. 1.
4 *SEP* pp. 202 f.
5 See Karge, *Rephaim*², pp. 434-436.

the ridge called el-Maslûbîyeh which limits the view in that direction (Pl. 16, 2). The numerous dolmens on that ridge were studied in detail by the English surveyors.[1]

Of all the ancient monuments in the region those at Siyâgha are the most outstanding and they possess added interest from the fact that the event which they commemorate is known from literary sources which will be discussed in detail in a later chapter. The other monuments of the region and the scenery which we have been reviewing form a worthy setting for the monuments at Siyâgha, which, as we shall see, commemorate a touching tragedy impressing a sublime moral.

[1] *SEP* pp. 254-274.

CHAPTER II

THE EXPLORATION OF THE SITE (1864 - 1939)

1. In 1864 M. Le Duc de Luynes visited Siyâgha. It seems that he was the first scholar of modern times who explored the site and published an account of his discoveries.[1] His observations are interesting. In his time the place was called "Djebel Mousa" because, as he was informed, Moses had died there. The name was applied to both summits at the western end of the ridge; the northwestern oval shaped spur was covered with extensive ruins amid which he observed two cisterns in the atrium, the basilica with the fallen columns, the southern monastery and the southern cistern. He identifies these ruins with the monastery and church commemorating the death of Moses visited in 1217 by Thietmar, a crusader, who found Greek Christians living there, with whom he spent the night. He thinks that the buildings were destroyed by an earthquake possibly as late as 1759 or even 1837; but he could not ascertain anything definite on this point.

During the 70 years which elapsed between the visit of Luynes and the clearances begun in 1933 numerous other explorers visited Siyâgha.[2]

2. In 1872 H. B. Tristram studied the ruins at Siyâgha.[3] "The place", he says, "is known to the Arabs as Z'iara, and has been one of considerable importance. The pile of ruins is very large. The brow of the hill is flattened, apparently artificially, and its slopes are steeply scarped to the depth of about 20 feet, with traces of a wall of circumvallation below.

---

1 *Voyage d'exploration à la Mer Morte, à Pétra et sur la rive gauche du Jordain*, I, Paris, 1874, pp. 148 ff.

2 The following list of explorers who visited Siyâgha or passed nearby is not complete. Only those are listed who proved useful to the writer. — H. B. Tristram, *The Land of Israel*, London, 1865, pp. 535 ff., speaks of a visit to "Nebbah", but on that occasion he did not reach Siyâgha. — Warren visited Siyâgha in 1867; he calls the place "the town of Neba"; it took him 23 minutes to climb from ʿAyûn Mûsa to the "town of Neba", a climb of 710-30 feet, since he gives the heights of the springs at 1590 and 1570 feet respectively, whilst for "the town of Neba" he gives a height of 2300 feet; he assigns the same height to the neighboring hill to the southwest. See *QS* 1869-70, pp. 288 and 308. — The Rev. A. E. Northey has only a very short unimportant note regarding his visit to Siyâgha in April, 1871. See *QS* 1872, pp. 62 f.

3 *The Land of Moab*², London, 1874, pp. 328-335.

"In the hill itself, on the south side, about 30 feet down, has been excavated a magnificent cistern, with a finely vaulted roof, which is still quite perfect, with two square traps in the roof, through which the water was drawn up. We entered by the side where an entrance had been laboriously broken open for the purpose of sheltering flocks, for water had long since ceased to accumulate in the cavern. We could trace the method by which it was fed, throught cemented conduits, entering it near the top, and which brought down the drainage of the higher slopes to the cistern.

"The citadel of the place has stood at the east or projecting end of the platform. Next adjoining it is an old temple, with the bases of four columns in situ, and about a dozen columns lying prostrate, but unbroken, in a row in close order — overthrown, more probably by an earthquake than by man. There have been side aisles, running north and south, by the side of the columns, and from some indications at the east end, which is heaped with rubbish, I think the temple may have been utilized as a Christian Basilican church. To the south of the temple are the ruins of a Christian church, with its apse remaining; and eastwards, another fine deep tank, which has once been vaulted, like that below, but the roof is now broken in."

Then Tristram describes the view from Siyâgha and discusses the reasons why he considers "Z'iara" identical with "Zo'ar" of the Bible.[1]

3. In 1873 the first expedition of the American Palestine Exploration Society under the direction of Lieutenant Edgar Z. Steever spent approximately five months in Moab. *The Third Statement of the APES* published in Jan., 1875, contains a long article on pp. 3-90 by John A. Paine, the archæologist of the expedition, in which he treats of the identification of Mount Pisgah. That article has a direct bearing on our site.[2]

4. In 1875 the second expedition of the APES under the direction of Selah Merrill again visited the site. Merrill's remarks about the name of the place are worth noting. He calls attention to the fact that Pseudo-Jonathan in three places, *Numbers* 32,3 and 38; 33,47, has substituted for Nebo, "the place of the burial of Moses". The only substitution in Onkelos is *Numbers* 32,3, when we have "Seath, the place of the burial of Moses". On enquiry Merrill was informed that formerly all this ridge was called "Jebel Neba, or Jebel

[1] Numerous details in Tristram's description are inaccurate. Later explorers, familiar with the literary sources relating to this place, recognized the true character of the buildings; but many other details were brought to light by the excavations. This merely illustrates the well-known fact that surface explorations alone are not sufficient to unravel the history of a place; the investigation of literary sources and excavations play an important rôle in such research. The chief merit of surface explorations consists in this that they serve to arouse and stimulate interest in a site and its monuments. Regarding the name "Z'iara" and its identification with "Zo'ar" see the remarks of Conder in *QS* 1881, pp. 275-281.

[2] See Warren J. Moulton, *The American Palestine Exploration Society*, in *AASOR* 8 (1928), pp. 55-78. Unfortunately the present writer has not been able to consult the *Statements*.

Mûsa, and sometimes Jebel Siâghah". From him we also learn that "in De Saulcy's map there is a ruin marked Kh. Siara". "Duc de Luynes in 1864, Dr. Tristram in the same year, Captain Warren in 1867 and Mr. Northey in 1871, all made examinations of this locality, but none of them brought away the name "Siâghah", or any name corresponding to it. In 1872 Dr. Tristram made his second visit to this region, and found the name Ziara (which he writes زعاره) applied to the ruin on the summit just south of 'Ayûn Mûsa. In 1873, however, Rev. John A. Paine claims to have "discovered" the name "Siâghah", with the prefixes "Jebel" and "Râs", applied to the three western of what he calls "five flat summits which compose this group of hills"." According to Merrill "the name "Siâghah" is an Arabic word in common use on the west of the Jordan in connection with goldsmiths, and it is difficult to understand how, on the east of the Jordan, it should be, as Mr. Paine claims, a relic of the long-lost Pisgah".[1]

4. In 1881 the region in which Siyâgha is located was surveyed for the committee of the Palestine Exploration Fund by a party under the command of Captain C. R. Conder. The surveyors used the large cairn on the summit of the southwestern spur of Siyâgha, erected by the Americans, as a trigonometrical station,[2] and visited the northwestern spur of Siyâgha twice, on August 20, and September 7, 1881. This latter spur is called by them "Khurbet Siâghah", whilst the former is called "Râs Siâghah". They identify "Siâghah" with Pisgah and suggest that "this ruin probably takes its name from the Aramaic Seath (סיעת) which is called in the *Targum* of Onkelos (on *Num*. 32, 3), 'the house of the burial of Moses'." In their opinion the ruin "seems most probably to have been a Byzantine settlement, with a church towards the east of the site." "Six rude Ionic capitals", "a double column", "a moulding of a cornice", the well-cut masonry of the principal building —"whether church or temple"—, "the round arches of good masonry" of one vault and the ruder masonry of another vault are, according to these explorers, not very definite indications of date, but they "seem all to point to the early Christian period, or to that of the Antonines, as the time when this small town of Siâghah was built." Finally they observe that "as no crosses or inscriptions were found, it is not possible to say certainly whether the principal building is Christian or Pagan; but this ridge was known to Jerome (cf. Neba) as the site of Nebo, and also, apparently, of Peor. It seems, therefore, not improbable that a church may have been built on the

1 *East of the Jordan*, London, 1881, pp. 240 ff. Cf. *The Fourth Statement* published in 1877, regarding which see reference on p. 12, note 2.

2 *SEP* pp. 205 and 156. From "Râs Siâghah" the surveyors were able to obtain good views of several trigonometrical stations in Palestine. Of special interest is the following remark: "We were fortunate in obtaining clear weather in which to observe our old stations west of Jordan, and we were even able to obtain a good line from Siâghah to Nebi Samwîl, whence Jaffa — the original longitude station — can be seen." *QS* 1882, p. 7. Cf. ib. p. 111; *SEP* p. 287. This experience of the surveyors might be borne in mind in speaking of the final vision of Moses from Mt. Nebo.

supposed site of the spot whence Moses viewed the Promised Land, in or about the fourth century."[1]

5. In 1886 Dr. George E. Post came to Moab for the purpose of studying the flora and fauna of the region; among the ruins of Siyâgha he noted Ferula communis and Crambe Hispanica. "The ruins", he says, "consist of a deep vaulted chamber, surrounded by rubble walls now fallen and shapeless; also a well with a curb stone. It may have been one of the many high places of Baal, found all over the country. (Cf. *Num*. 22, 41.)" He thinks that "the two shoulders of Sîâghah suit well the narrative of Balaam. From the northern summit of Sîâghah... he would obtain a comprehensive view of the Israelites encamped in the plain. From the southern summit he would gain a still more comprehensive one. Both summits have ruins, which may be those of high places of Baal." He rejects the attempts to derive either "Pisgah" or "Zoar" from "Sîâghah."[2]

6. In 1891 G. Schumacher attempted to plan the ruined buildings. The Arabs hindered him from completing his study, but from what he saw he concluded that the ruins at Siyâgha represent early Christian buildings of the Byzantine period, and suggests that they are deserving of a more thorough investigation.[3]

7. In 1901 whilst exploring Moab A. Musil paid a number of visits to Siyâgha. He was familiar with the *Life of Peter the Iberian*, where mention is made of a large church and numerous monasteries in honor of Moses on a mountain half way between Livias and Madaba, so we need not be surprised to find that he confidently and correctly describes the ruins as a monastic complex with the large church on the north and habitations on the south and west.[4]

8. In 1907 R. Kittel found among the ruins of the church at "Sijâgha" a rectangular stone measuring about 50 cm. in length and about 30 cm. in width which had 9 cup marks of various sizes. He suggests that this stone may be a relic of an older pagan or Israelite (temple or) altar which once stood at this place and was incorporated into the Christian church in order to perpetuate the memory of the ancient sanctity of this place.[5]

9. Karge, however, asserts that this stone does not possess the extraordinary significance attached to it by Kittel. He maintains that it is a building stone like all the rest measuring 56×36×30 cm.; on the one surface it has a number of holes arranged, roughly speaking, in two rows. The holes vary in

[1] *SEP* pp. 154-156; *QS* 1881, pp. 275-281; 1882, pp. 7-15, 111; *Heth and Moab*, New Edition, London, 1885, pp. 132 ff.

[2] *QS* 1888, pp. 183-186.

[3] *ZDPV* 16 (1893), pp. 164-168.

[4] *AP* I, Wien, 1907, p. 273; cfr. pp. 265, 334-348, especially 341 ff.

[5] *Studien zur Hebräischen Archäologie und Religionsgeschichte*, in *Beiträge zur Wissenschaft vom Alten Testament*, I, Leipzig, 1908, pp. 144 ff.

size ; the largest is 11 cm. in d. and 4 cm. deep; others have a diameter of only 3 cm. Upon enquiry he was informed that the holes were made for a game called "mingale" (Conder: "Mankaleh"), for which 2 × 7 holes are needed. This number of holes could be made out though somewhat out of line. He adds that similar rows of small holes for games may be seen, for example, on flat horizontal stones at Petra which are frequently visited by shepherds.[1]

In this connection we may add that Conder observed that at Umm el-Hanâfîsh the top of a base and some of the shafts of columns were pitted with holes, which, he says, were 'evidently made by shepherds for playing the Mankaleh game ; and in one case the pebbles used in the game remained in the hole'.[2]

10. From 1907 to 1933 the site continued to be visited. There is apparently no longer any doubt in the minds of these later visitors that the ruins at Siyâgha are those of a church and monastery, though of course many details remained obscure. Père F.-M. Abel, for example, who visited the place both before the excavations and whilst the excavations were in progress, identifies the place and ruins with the sanctuary of Moses at Nabau visited by Aetheria in the 4th century A. D. and by Peter the Iberian in the 5th. He thinks that the buildings originated in the course of the 4th century A. D. and are a concrete expression of a more ancient tradition which associated that mountain with Moses.[3]

11. The Franciscans were always interested in Siyâgha and frequently visited the site.[4] The present writer was a member of the party which visited Siyâgha on Dec. 29, 1931. This party consisted of the faculty and students of the Franciscan Biblical School at the monastery of the Flagellation, Jerusalem. We were able to go only as far as Jebel en-Neba in the cars, the rest of the way we were obliged to make on foot. The day was very windy, and it was only with the greatest difficulty that we were able to reach Siyâgha and make our way about the ruins. In a sheltered spot we read the last chapter of Deuteronomy and the account of Aetheria's visit to the sanctuary of Moses at Nabau. Her description of the view corresponded perfectly with what we saw from the place where we were standing. On that occasion we saw nothing which might correspond to the small church visited by Aetheria, but we realized that the extensive ruins which covered the entire top of the hill might well represent

1 *Rephaim* ², Paderborn, 1925, pp. 435 f.; cfr. pp. 463, 465, 468.

2 *SEP* p. 247.

3 *RB* 40 (1931), 375 ff.; *Géog.* I, 1933, 379 ff.

4 See P. Barnabé Meistermann, O. F. M., *Guide du Nil au Jourdain par le Sinaï et Pétra*, Paris, 1909, pp. 298-305; Id., *Guide to the Holy Land*, London, 1923, pp. 384 f. — P. A. Arce, O. F. M., *Viaje al Nebo*, in *TSS* 19 (1939), pp. 193-196. A number of other unpublished records in the Jerusalem archives attest the same. Most interesting of all is the fact that a Franciscan who visited Siyâgha in the 16th century is the only link we have in the history of the site between the early pilgrims and the modern explorers ; (see the chapter on Literary Sources).

the large church and monasteries mentioned in the *Life of Peter the Iberian*. A clearance of the site would clear up a number of difficulties ; this would of course involve expense ; but the authorities of the school were convinced that the expense involved would be justified. It was agreed on that occasion that on the way back to Jerusalem we should call at the Department of Antiquities in ʿAmmân to propose our plan to the authorities. Upon our arrival in Ammân we learned that Mr. George Horsfield, Adviser to the Transjordan Department of Antiquities, was at the time ill in the Italian hospital of that town. There Father Leo Villuendas, O. F. M., the president of the school, called on him and made known our plans. Three days later, Jan. 1, 1932, Mr. Horsfield paid a visit to our school in Jerusalem and assured us that the authorities of the Transjordan Department of Antiquities favored the exploration of Siyâgha by our school and from that moment he promoted the undertaking in every way.

12. From Jan. 1, 1932 to July 13, 1933 all the preliminary steps were taken to make the exploration of the site possible. An understanding was reached between the authorities of the school and those of the Custody of the Holy Land to acquire the site and to cooperate in every possible way in the undertaking. The authorities of the Custody of the Holy Land entrusted the negotiations for the acquisition of the site to the experienced and energetic Brother Jerome Mikaic, stationed at the hospice in Jericho. He was successful; on Oct. 4, 1932, 13 members of the Wekhyan tribe signed the documents transferring their rights to the northwestern spur of Siyâgha to the representative of the Custody; and on the same day the Director of the Department of Antiquities and the Chief Minister of Transjordan approved the excavation permit issued by Mr. R. Head authorizing the writer, assisted by Brother Jerome Mikaic, to conduct excavations and soundings at Khirbet Siyâgha from April 1, 1933 to Sept. 30, 1933.

At the time the present writer was absent in Italy where he assisted at the third international congress of Christian Archæology at Ravenna from Sept. 25 to Sept. 30 and then participated in the excursions to Pola, Parenzo, Trieste, Aquilea, Grado and Venice from Sept. 30 to Oct. 3, during which numerous ancient monuments were visited and explained by competent authorities.[1] The experiences at the congress were a useful preparation for the expeditions to Siyâgha. On Oct. 17 the writer reached Palestine and was engaged in teaching at the Franciscan Biblical School from Oct. 1932 to July 1933. During the scholastic year he established contacts with the authorities of the school, the Custody and the Transjordan Department of Antiquities, and on three occasions visited Siyâgha in order to make himself thoroughly familiar with the work to be done.

[1] See *Studi di Antichità Cristiana pubblicata per cura del Pontificio Istituto di Archeologia Cristiana*, VIII: *Atti del III Congresso Internazionale di Archeologia Cristiana, Ravenna 25-30 Settembre 1932*, Roma, 1934.

13. On the first visit to Siyâgha on Febr. 28, 1933, the writer was accompanied by Father Antonio Berardi, O. F. M., and Brothers Jerome and Gervase. Father Antonio is the official photographer of the Custody; on that visit he photographed the ruins from all sides in order to have a record of their condition before the excavations began. Brother Jerome pointed out the cistern on the southern part of the site which he had cleaned and restored in order to provide water for the expedition; he had also discovered a stone decorated with a cross lying face downwards in front of the entrance to the basilica (Pl. 56, above). The writer was able to make a number of additions to the plan which Schumacher had published;[1] and registered a number of architectural fragments not mentioned by previous explorers.

On Mar. 13, 1933, suggestions for the first expedition to Siyâgha were submitted by the writer to the faculty of the school and later transmitted to the authorities of the Custody by Father Adolf Cadez, O. F. M., the president of the school.

14. On April 3, 1933, the writer paid a second visit to Siyâgha. On this occasion he was accompanied by Brother John Schoppen, O. F. M., the architect of the Custody, and by Brother Jerome and Mr. Head, the Chief Inspector of Antiquities. The chief purpose of this visit was to discuss on the spot the question of a camp. At the same time the writer obtained the views of the architect and Mr. Head on the proposed expedition. Our suggestions were submitted to the authorities of the Custody for approval. On May 5, 1933, the Most Rev. Father Nazzareno Jacopozzi, O. F. M., Custodian of the Holy Land, informed the president of the school that the plans for the expedition to Siyâgha were approved and that work could begin at our discretion.

15. On May 22, 1933, the writer visited Siyâgha a third time with the Very Rev. Father Francis Roch Martinez, O. F. M., the Procurator of the Custody of the Holy Land, for the purpose of settling definitely the question of a road to Siyâgha and of the camp. Father James Llull, O. F. M., drew up the plans and their execution was entrusted to Brother Jerome. He immediately set to work on the construction of the road from Jebel en-Neba to Siyâgha and on the camp at Siyâgha and by July 13, 1933, that work was sufficiently advanced to permit us to occupy the camp and begin excavations.

16. The first expedition to Siyâgha lasted from July 13, 1933 to Sept. 22, 1933.[2] Very early on July 13 the truck loaded with tools and supplies set out from Jerusalem for Siyâgha. The writer followed with the Procurator. At Jericho Brother Jerome loaded our car with fruit from his garden and then

1 *ZDPV* 16 (1893), p. 164.

2 A first attempt to make excavations at this site in 1927 by A. F. Futterer did not materialize. See *Palestine Speaks* by the Pioneer Golden Ark Explorer A. F. Futterer, Los Angeles, 1931, pp. 531-558, especially p. 556.

followed in a third car loaded with numerous other things required at Siyâgha. About noon the Procurator and the writer reached Siyâgha. For the first time it was not necessary to leave the car at Jebel en-Neba and walk to Siyâgha, since we were able to drive all the way to Siyâgha in our car over the new road which had just been finished by the Custody under the direction of Brother Jerome. Even the heavily loaded truck was able to travel safely over the same road and reached Siyâgha in the early part of the afternoon. The instruments were immediately unloaded and a number of men who were present were put to work near the apse under the supervision of the Procurator who wished to inaugurate the excavations personally. He had the pleasure of seeing the plastered apse of the baptistery preserved up to the cornice coming to light and further north the cornice of the diaconicon. A few small objects were also recovered from late Arab tombs above the presbytery of the basilica. Happy at the prospects of interesting discoveries he bade us farewell and returned to Jerusalem.

Brother Jerome arrived at Siyâgha that same evening and immediately took full charge of the camp. Doors and windows were inserted into the frames of two rooms that same evening and during the subsequent days the work on the building occupied by the staff was completed. A view of the building at this stage may be seen in Pl. 23, 2. During the following winter the gable roof was damaged by strong winds and was replaced by a flat roof. Another shelter of building stones laid dry and covered with a roof fastened to the walls was put up for the workmen ; this building was completely destroyed the following winter when the winds blew off the roof and dragged down the walls with it. These facts should be borne in mind, since they serve to show that the winds may have been a factor in the destruction of the buildings on this exposed promontory. Throughout the summer Brother Jerome continued to improve the camp and its surroundings ; he improved the roads on the site and the one leading to it; in short, he provided for everything that was necessary so that the writer was entirely free to devote himself to the work of clearing and studying the buildings on the mound.

On July 14, 1933, the systematic clearance of the site was begun with 25 workmen and this number was gradually increased to about 70 men ; no women or children were used, with the exception of the cook who was a Christian woman from Madaba, and a boy who went on errands. The men came partly from Madaba and partly from the immediate vicinity ; all were Arabs, but those from Madaba were Christians and those from the vicinity were Moslems. The Christians from Madaba provided the chief foreman, interpreters, stone-porters, etc. In this connection the writer wishes to acknowledge in a special way the faithful service rendered by the various members of the Shiwayhat family, which provided the procurator, the foremen, the cook and a number of other workmen. From Madaba came also the man named after the saint whose memorial we were exploring; Mûsa enjoyed a European training, spoke several languages perfectly, could read and write, was a mason, carpenter, cook and an enthusiastic archæologist, who had experience with other archæological expeditions and remained with us during all three expeditions; he became almost indispensable.

The local Arabs supplied the largest contingent of the workmen. They were under the immediate supervision of their mukhtar, who was informed of the number of men required, and he selected those who should work and those who should supply donkeys both for the transport of water, which had to be brought from ʿAyûn Mûsa during the greater part of the first expedition, and for the transport of the ground. Carts were used to remove small stones and porters for larger ones; only one or two of the local Arabs were able to carry stones on their backs, so this work was done mostly by experienced men from Madaba. In the selection of the workmen we followed the principle that the neediest should be given the first chance. The local Arabs were very jealous of others and sought in every way to exclude them; but since they could supply only 32 men they had to admit others. All in all, we were well satisfied with the men.[1]

During the first year we cleared the basilica, the baptistery, the Theotokos chapel, the north hall, the narthex, the interior of the atrium and a few rooms around the atrium. On the south and east sides of the basilica the ruins were removed to a level corresponding to that of the floor inside the basilica or a little lower.[2]

When required Father Antonio came from Jerusalem for the photographic work; Father James Llull, O. F. M., prepared the plans; Father Theophilus Antolin, O. F. M., made squeezes of some of the mosaic pavements and colored them on the spot; Father Raphael Fuster, O. F. M., spent much time on the site and assisted in supervising the work and studying the results. Brother Emil Dubois, O. F. M., with several of his workmen from the workshops at St. Savior's, Jerusalem, came to Siyâgha for several days to erect some sections of the shafts of the columns which had fallen. Mr. A. S. Kirkbride, Acting British Resident, cleaned and identified the coins found during the first expedition. The more detailed descriptions of the coins are due to Father Paulinus Lemaire, O. F. M.[3] Father Donatus Baldi, O. F. M., supplied us with the literature which we required and conducted a party of our students to Siyâgha on Sept. 11.

[1] To avoid all friction we took only the local Arabs as workmen in 1935; on an average they supplied between 20-30 men. In 1937 the local Arabs brought along many of their friends to work so we averaged between 60-70 men that year.

[2] See the ground plan (Pl. 161) nos. 1-13, 20, 22, 25, 26, 28-30, 79, 90-92; or consult the published preliminary reports indicated on p. 20, n. 3.

[3] In 1935 Mr. Kirkbride again cleaned and identified our coins; but in 1937 he was absent in Galilee so Father Lemaire cleaned and described all these coins.

Washington, D. C., and again at the Biblical School of the Franciscan Order at Jerusalem and was very anxious to see how an archæological expedition was organized and carried out. His interest was unflagging. To him was entrusted the study of all the pottery found on the site, most of which was recovered in 1937. At the Athenæum Antonianum in Rome in 1938 he submitted a thesis on the Siyâgha pottery for his licentiate and it was approved. He returned to Siyâgha in 1939 to restudy all the pottery on the site and after repeated consultations with Dr. C. Fisher at the American School of Oriental Research in Jerusalem arranged and prepared the illustrations and text on the Siyâgha pottery for the present publication.

Father Augustine Arce's interest in Siyâgha antedates the period of excavations as he himself pointed out elsewhere,[1] so at the end of the third expedition he readily responded to an invitation to come to Siyâgha for the purpose of photographing the material which came to light during this expedition. He preformed the long and trying task with patience and unwearying care. Other photographs of this expedition are due to Father Bellarmino and to Father Hilary.

Father Antonio was absent this year in Milano, Italy, where he made all the preparations for establishing his own photozincographic laboratory in Jerusalem. This laboratory was completed in 1939 and there Father Antonio prepared the clichés used for the majority of the illustrations in the present volume; this work was completed in April 1940.

The chief results of the 1937 expedition to Siyâgha were published in the form of short preliminary reports.[2]

The plans prepared by Fathers James and Bellarmino, the latter's designs, the photographs by Fathers Antonio, Bellarmino, Augustine, Hilary and James, as well as those by a number of visiting friends, the diary kept by the present writer, the registers of objects prepared by the writer and by Father Hilary form the basis of the present volume.

The great monastic complex brought to light by the excavations at Siyâgha (Pl. 161, 1-115) covers an area of about 6640 sq. meters. The center of the complex is occupied by a basilica (1-2), three chapels (3-5), a narthex (6) and an atrium surrounded by cells (7-30). Around this central group there are arranged three large monasteries on the north (31-52), west (53-63) and south (64-105). Beyond this complex there are a few other buildings of which only those on the northwest (106-109) and west (110-115) were cleared. Below the eastern end of the basilica were discovered the remains of an older building, very probably the oldest edifice on the site ; it will be described in the following chapter.

[1] *TSS* 19 (1939), pp. 193-196.

[2] *RTSC* 8 (1938), pp. 41-49; *Franciscan Herald*, 26 (1938), pp. 18-19, 93-98; cfr. *AJA* 42 (1938), pp. 171 f.

CHAPTER III

THE CELLA TRICHORA

The oldest monument in honor of Moses discovered during the excavations at Siyâgha is a type of structure known as a cella trichora (Fig.4, 3; Pls. 161, A-C; 25-30). The site chosen for this edifice was the summit of the northwestern spur. Originally this was probably the only building on the solitary hilltop. Later the cella trichora was converted into a basilica by the addition of a hall to its western side ; in this basilica the cella trichora formed the sanctuary. Later still the basilica and with it the cella trichora were destroyed; in reconstructing the basilica the plan of the cella trichora was ignored, but its remaining walls continued to serve as a foundation for the sanctuary and the sacristies. Some of the material was reused in the later edifice, but most of it remained where it had fallen on the east and north of the latest church. When the reconstructed basilica was overthrown by an earthquake its ruins completely buried the remains of the cella trichora (Pls. 25, 1 and 26, 1); only here and there a stone remained visible to betray the existence of that older monument. Those telltale stones were observed by some of the earlier explorers, such as Conder, but the true character of the building to which they belonged was revealed only by the excavations.

The cella trichora was completely excavated in 1933 and 1935. The walls still in situ below the eastern end of the basilica indicate the size, plan, material and methods of construction which were used in the primitive building ; whilst the parts which are no longer in situ enable us to form some conception of the superstructure of the building, its ornamentation and its furnishings. These latter elements represent the period in the history of the cella trichora which antedates the erection of the last basilica, the former represent all the periods in the history of the monuments of which they always formed an integral part.

A. THE PARTS IN SITU

The parts of the cella trichora still in situ occupy an area of about 280 sq. m. near the northeastern part of the hill. Its southern and western walls are on the crest of the hill but its eastern and northern walls are on the slope, the lowest point being at the northeast corner which is about 3 meters lower than the western wall. On the exterior the building is rectangular (Pl. 28) measuring 15.83 m. from south to north and probably 17.78 m. from east to west; but owing to the addition of later buildings on the western side of the cella trichora the plan on that side is somewhat obscured. On the interior the monument has three internal apses, from which it derives its name the cella trichora. The chord of each apse measures 5.80 m.

The northern apse of the cella trichora was discovered below the northern sacristy of the basilica (Pls. 161, A and 30,2). The outline of the apse can be recognized at floor level. One stone in the center of the apse rises above the level of the sacristy's floor and protrudes from the northern wall. A clearance in front of this stone revealed the fact that the apse is perfectly preserved down to its very base. The area inside the apse was filled up with ground to a height of 2.80 m. in order to establish a common floor level with the rest of the building. On the filling of earth flagstones inscribe an inner semicircle, which very probably marks the limits of a mosaic pavement, destroyed when the south wall of the sacristy was built. All the walls which rise above floor level are of later date than the cella trichora.

The southern apse of the cella trichora exists beneath the southern sacristy of the basilica (Pls. 161, B and 30,1). Here there was no pavement of any kind, so that the entire interior of the apse could be completely explored. The apse still has a maximum height of 2 m. The lower part of the apse, to a height of 1.10 m., is still perfectly preserved; it was constructed of rubble masonry and was concealed from view by a filling of earth below the level of the floor. Near the center of the apse two courses of dressed masonry were partially preserved to a height of 90 cm. above floor level in spite of the fact that they projected into the sacristy and thus destroyed its symmetry. The walls which rest on the apse are of later date.

The eastern apse of the cella trichora is no doubt also preserved below floor level, but it is now completely hidden from view by the apse of the basilica, around which there are 5 tiers of seats built of solid masonry (Pl. 39, 1).

The plan of the western side of the cella trichora is uncertain; here later additions were made and they no doubt caused some modifications in the original plan. The limits of the cella trichora on this side seem to be defined by a wall discovered beneath the floor at the eastern end of the basilica's nave (Pl. 161, C). All that remains of the wall is a course of rubble laid in a shallow trench in the rock. The masonry resembles that of the lowest courses of the apses of the cella trichora. The wall varies in thickness between 110-120 cm. and terminates both on the north and the south near the base of a column of the basilica. Its connection with the rest of the cella trichora could not be ascertained owing to the mosaic pavements which we did not wish to disturb; but this wall had no apparent function in the basilica, hence it seems reasonable to bring it in connection with the cella trichora, as is done in the plans (Fig. 4, 3 and Pl. 161, C).

Between the chancel rail and the door to the northern sacristy there is a buttress against the wall. The buttress rests on a wall 80 cm. wide and 160 cm. long from north to south. It could not be ascertained what relation this wall had to the cella trichora.

On the exterior the walls of the cella trichora are preserved up to the same height as on the interior. The southern and northern walls were partially reconstructed with older materials and hence present more or less the same appearance as in the original monument. The foundation courses are built of rubble, the upper courses consist of relatively large stones most of which have a margin and boss. Details of these walls are given in Fig. 4, 1, A - C.

The exterior of the southern wall of the cella trichora was completely buried beneath fallen stones when the excavations began (Pl. 25, 1). After removing the fallen stones (Pl. 25, 2 and Fig. 4,1, A) we found that the western end of the wall was partially concealed by the baptistery and a tower east of the baptistery; further east the base of the wall was covered by the mosaic pavement of room 91, whilst the eastern end of the wall immediately above the level of the mosaic pavement in room 91 is bonded into the eastern wall of the southern monastery (Fig. 4, 1, A & B, **a** and Pl. 27, 2, upper stone against which a measuring rod rests). This southeast corner of the cella trichora provides all the evidence required to prove that the southern wall is not preserved in its original state but is a reconstruction in which the older material was reused. The evidence goes to show that the southern wall of the cella trichora, which we see today, was erected after the original cella trichora had been destroyed; it is contemporaneous with the eastern wall of the southern monastery into which it is bonded; and it is anterior to the baptistery which was built against it. As an absolute date we suggest the last quarter of the sixth century A. D.

In reconstructing the southern wall with older stones the masons were obliged, by the very character of the material, to use the same coursing which had been used in the primitive structure; we may, therefore, feel reasonably secure that this wall is a good replica of the original southern wall of the cella trichora.

The eastern wall of the cella trichora (Fig. 4, 1, B and Pls. 26-28) was buried beneath 2 strata of building stones when the excavations began (Pl. 26,1). In 1933 the upper stratum of stones, which belonged to the latest church, was removed and we came upon the first vestiges of the cella trichora still in situ (Pl. 26, 2). The lower stratum consisted of the material which once formed the superstructure of the cella trichora; on removing that material in 1935 (Pl. 27,1) we exposed to view all that still remained in situ of the eastern wall of the cella trichora (Pls. 27,2 & 28). This wall has preserved its primitive appearance unaltered in the lower 4 to 7 courses (Fig. 4, 1, B).

The foundation course consisting of rubble masonry was laid in a shallow trench made in a layer of clay more solid than the native rock directly below it. Since the wall is built on the slope of the hill several more courses were required at the northern end than at the southern in order to overcome the difference in level, but this was not the deciding factor in the choice of the material used in the various courses. Rubble masonry occurs in from one to four courses. It may have been covered with plaster of which traces were observed on the wall.

Above the foundation courses most of the masonry was drafted. Both the margin and the boss are irregular and the stones vary in size and form. One stone south of the basilica's apse is 154 cm. long; three other stones represent a course 119-122 cm. high and their length varies between 74 to 95 cm.; they are stretchers; above them there is still a single stone in situ which represents a course of headers. The material used for all these stones was a heavy limestone known as "mizzi".

Of the northern wall of the cella trichora (Fig. 4, 1, C and Pls. 28 & 29) the upper part of two stones was visible before excavations began; the entire wall was brought to light in 1935. Since the foundations of this wall stand on the slope of the hill it was considered advisable to shore them up; this shoring of rubble masonry conceals the real foundation walls (Pl. 29, 1). Above the shoring several courses of drafted masonry are still in situ; one of the drafted stones is 178 cm. long. The upper part of the wall is reconstructed partly of old and partly of new material; this latter consists of smaller stones with a plain surface ; they are a soft and light limestone known as "nari".

The walls of the cella trichora still in situ are witnesses of the entire monumental history of Siyâgha.

B. THE PARTS NOT IN SITU

The remaining elements of the cella trichora which are no longer in situ were found principally on the eastern and northern sides of the original cella trichora. Some of the material was utilized again in the later buildings or was discovered in dumps above room 41 and in the area 53 ; only a few pieces were found elsewhere, as, for example, in the atrium and in the southern monastery. The criterion used in assigning such material to the cella trichora was first of all the position in which it was found. Thus, for example, none of the moldings were found in 1933 when we removed the upper layer of stones east of the basilica (Pl. 26, 2), but when we began to remove the large stones which evidently belonged to the earlier structure we also found the moldings; so it seems logical to associate these moldings with the primitive building even when the material differs from that which was generally used in the construction of the cella trichora.

The characteristic material of the cella trichora contrasts sharply with the material used for the later buildings. For the cella trichora a hard heavy limestone, called "mizzi", was used; for the later buildings a softer and lighter type of limestone, known as "nari" and "kakule", was preferred.[1] The building stones of the cella trichora were on an average larger than those of the later buildings; the former stones were generally drafted, the latter plain; in short, after handling nearly all the stones on the site and comparing them with the stones still in situ, it immediately became clear to what building they should be ascribed even if they were far removed from their original context. What was said regarding the stones holds also for other materials, such as marble, mosaics, etc.

Owing to the context or to the character of the material, we have assigned to the cella trichora all the large drafted stones and a few which are not drafted, the cornice, the gable, the jambs and moldings of a window, the iron bars of a window, bases, shafts and capitals of half columns and double columns, the wall mosaics, some marble, etc.

Of the drafted stones one attracted special attention owing to the Greek inscription carved in bold characters on its upper and lower margin (Fig. 4, 2, C). The stone represents a course which was 131 cm. high; it was found face downwards next to the ground about 4-5 m. northeast of the basilica's apse; this suggests that its original position was in the center of the wall about 4 or 5 m. above the ground level. The names carved on the stone are probably those of the architects; the first name is preceded by a cross, which would indicate that the individual who is named was a Christian. For further details see inscription XI.

Another large stone found near the wall directly behind the apse of the basilica has a perfectly smooth surface on which are scratched a number of graffiti; regarding these see inscription XII.

Near the edge of ruins east of the southeast corner a large stone was found which measures 190×60×46 cm. (Fig. 4, 2, A and Pl. 33, 9). The peculiarity of this stone is the vertical perforation through its splayed end. It may have served as a spout at the southeast corner of the cella trichora.

The eastern wall of the cella trichora was crowned by a cornice of which a dozen stones were found. These stones (Fig. 5, 12-16; Pls. 35, 13-17; 36, 1-6) represent a course averaging about 29 cm. in height; their molding consists of a simple splay with round or rectangular bosses which are decorated with carved ornaments consisting of triangles (Fig. 5, 12; Pls. 36, 1; 35, 15),

[1] See G. S. Blake, *The Stratigraphy of Palestine and its Building Stones*, Jerusalem, pp. 103 ff., for further information regarding these three varieties of building stones.

Greek crosses (Fig. 5, 13; Pl. 36, 2 & 5), St. Andrew's crosses (Fig. 5, 14 & 16; Pls. 35, 14; 36, 4), rosettes (Fig. 5, 15; Pls. 35, 16; 36, 3),

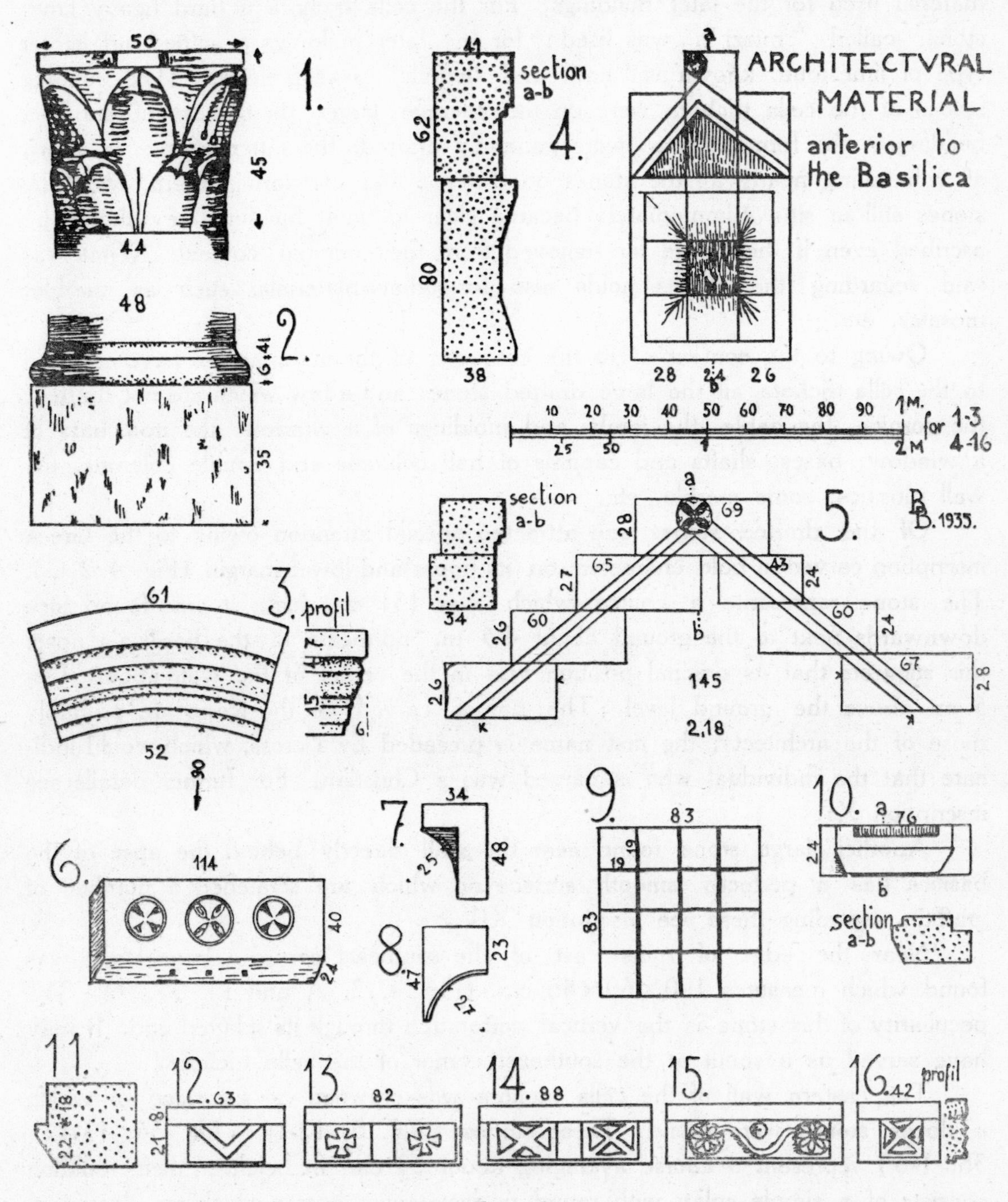

Fig. 5.

a circle surrounded by a zigzag line (Pl. 35, 13), rectangles (Pl. 36, 5) and festoons (Pl. 36, 6). On one stone the round bosses (Pl. 35, 17) seem to be plain ; in this case the fillet above the bosses has a zigzag line as an ornament (not visible in the picture). In every case an horizontal line is incised about 8 cm. below the top of the stone to mark the division between the fillet and the splay. All these stones were found east of the cella trichora in the lower stratum. A few similar stones come from other parts of the site.

The type of cornice described here was observed by the writer also in one of the churches at Umm er-Rasâs some 40 km. to the southeast of Siyâgha. There it is still in situ on the interior of the apse, where it was observed already by Tristram who writes: " In the central apse of one (of the churches) the Greek crosses on the bosses of the bead line along the architrave still remain very distinct, alternating with sculptured knots or figures." [1] The position of the Umm er-Rasâs molding on the interior of the apse would suggest a similar position for the cornice at Siyâgha ; but since none of the stones found at Siyâgha show any traces of curvature, which would be expected if they had served as the cornice of an apse, we suggest that this cornice adorned the exterior of the eastern wall of the cella trichora.

Crosses carved on bosses were found also in the neighborhood of Jericho, the Greek cross on an abacus supposed to come from Tell el-Matlab and the St. Andrew's cross on a corbel from the same place.[2]

Another group of 11 stones found in the lower stratum east of the cella trichora represents two pediments (Fig. 5, 4 & 5 ; Pl. 35, 1-3). The raking molding on all these stones consists of a double fillet ; the apex of each pediment is surmounted by a roundel with a carved cross. The larger group of stones (Fig. 5, 5 and Pl. 35, 1 & 3) very probably belongs to the gable of the roof, whilst the smaller group (Fig. 5, 4 and Pl. 36, 2) comes from a window, to which several other stones with splayed inner edges very probably belong (Pl. 35, 7 & 8). Father Bagatti suggests that the moldings may have belonged not to a real window but to a blind one.

A real window in the eastern wall of the cella trichora is represented by 5 or 6 other stones and by an iron grating, but not by glass. To this window we assign the stones of a frame with a rounded arch and spandrels (Fig. 5, 7 & 8; Pl. 35, 10-12), the jamb with 3 carved crosses on the face and three holes in the side for the bars of the iron grating (Fig. 5, 6; Pl. 57, 9), the sill (Fig. 5, 10; Pl. 35, 9), and a few other stones, of which one has holes for

[1] See *PA* 2, p. 69. — The church in question is the southern one in the southeastern part of the walled town; see the plan in *PA* 2, p. 65, Fig. 647. The writer noticed 3 Greek crosses carved on three bosses of the cornice. — All over Umm er-Rasâs there is abundant material which serves to illustrate the material found at Siyâgha; there are numerous lintels and other stones decorated with crosses, stars, plants and altars; the ornaments are found on plain surfaces, on bosses, in tabulae ansatae, etc.; Ionic capitals - three in one group - are decorated with crosses. A thorough study of all the monuments at Umm er-Rasâs is to be recommended. — See also the sculptured frieze with five medallions having a Greek cross and rosettes in circles over the door of a tomb at el-Kahf; *SEP* p. 119.

[2] *ARP* 2, p. 17, E and p. 18, A & B.

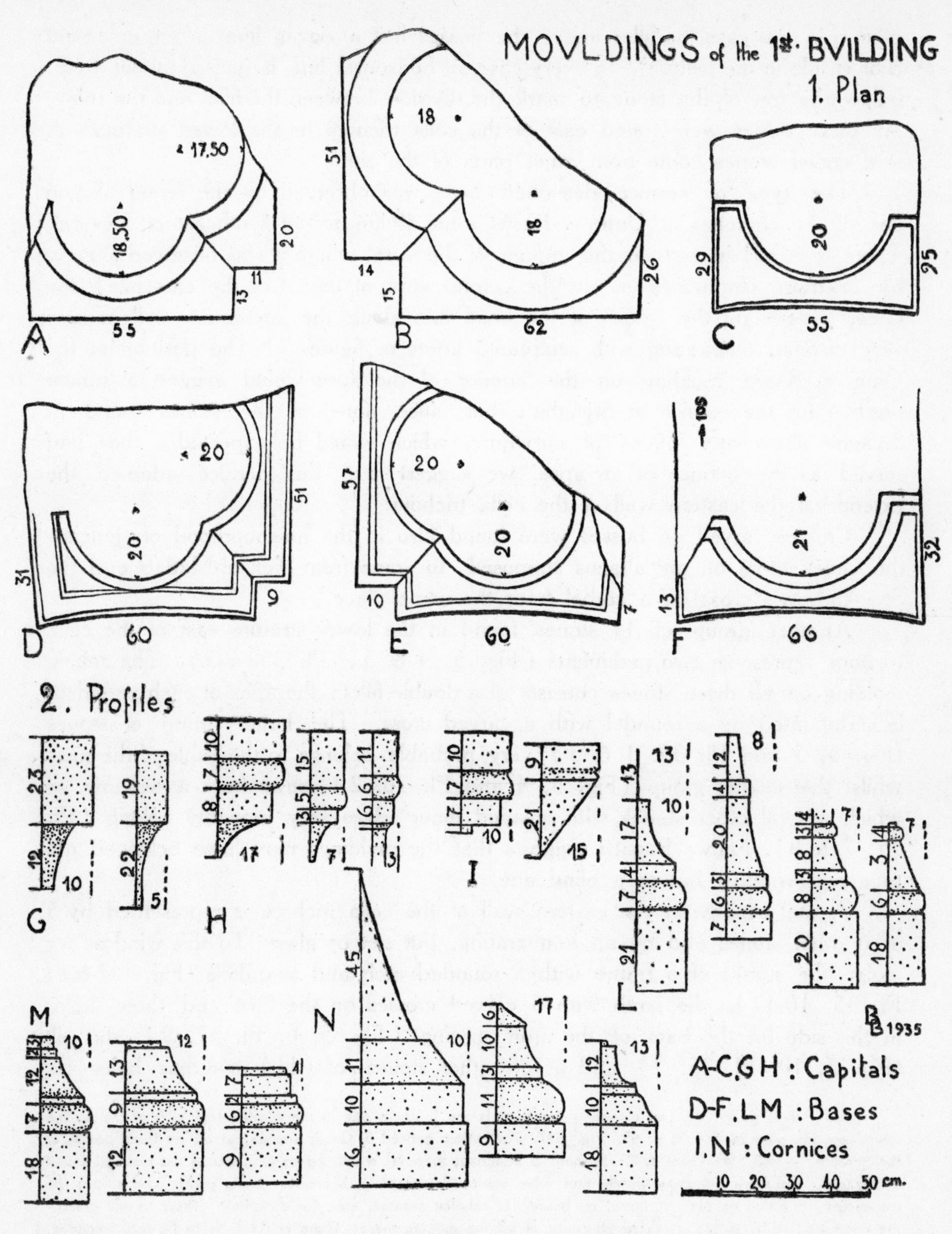
MOULDINGS of the 1st. BUILDING
1. Plan
A
B
C
D
E
F
2. Profiles
G
H
I
L
B 1935
M
N
A-C,G,H : Capitals
D-F,L,M : Bases
I,N : Cornices
10 20 30 40 50 cm.

Fig. 6.

the bars of a grating, and another, reused as a step in room 101, has three holes for bars and three sculptured crosses, as the jamb mentioned above.

The iron grating of the window will be treated in the chapter on metals.

Of the elements of the cella trichora no longer in situ some belonged in its interior; such are the engaged columns, some cornices, fragments of plaster, mosaics and marble.

The engaged columns are represented by about 70 stones, of which about 40 are shafts, 15 bases and 15 capitals. All are made of the hard and heavy limestone ("mizzi") characteristic of the earliest edifice. The ornamentation of the bases and capitals consists of simple flattish moldings.

The bases have a molding consisting as a rule of 5 members: the plinth, the torus and three flattish bands, of which the lower and upper ones are narrow fillets and the middle one a splay or a cavetto. The moldings do not conform to a uniform measure, but vary somewhat on the different stones (Fig. 6, L, M; Pls. 31, 2, 3; 32, 2, 5, 6; 33, 7).[1]

The capitals are mere caps consisting of an abacus and a cavetto. The abacus may be severely plain (Fig. 6, G; Pl. 32, 4 upside down) or, more commonly, divided into three members which are all very flat, but in certain cases it appears that an astragal was intended (Fig. 6, H; Pls. 31, 1 upside down; 32, 1, 3 upside down; 33, 1-3, 6 upside down).

Both the bases (Pls. 31, 2; 32, 5, 6) and the capitals (Pls. 31, 1; 32, 3; 33, 6) have, at times, a neck or part of a shaft attached to them; in one case (Pl. 32, 5) the shaft attached to a base is 73 cm. long.[2] In another case (Pl. 32, 6) both the base and shaft form one end of a large block, which serves to illustrate the appearance of the wall next to the column; from this example it appears that the molding of the column's base was extended along the wall in the form of a cornice; compare Pl. 32, 6 with Fig. 6, N (first in the group of three).[3]

The moldings of the bases and capitals of half columns are found on one, two or three of their sides; of double columns on 4 or 5 sides, but the side

[1] The bases designed in Fig. 6, D-F, L and M do not, as a rule, correspond to those illustrated in Pls. 31 ff.; they were chosen to illustrate variations in the typical base. The typical double base illustrated in Pl. 31, 2 is designed in Fig. 6, D and L (2nd place). It is 40 cm. h. and has a molding on 5 sides; the one side has a slight curvature which suggests that it was placed next to the apse. It possesses the 5 molded members characteristic of these bases; some of the bases lack one or the other molding; thus, for example, two bases designed in Fig. 6, L have only four members; the first in the group lacks the upper fillet directly below the shaft (see Pl. 32, 6), the last is without the fillet above the torus, but has an additional annulet on top.

[2] The total height of the base and shaft is 118 cm.; the base is 42-45 cm. h.; its one side is 68 cm. w., its other 45 cm. and the two small sides forming a right angle measure 8 and 9 cm. respectively.

[3] The block is 82-85 cm. h.; 112 cm. l., 65-89 cm. w.; the base at the one end of the block is 50 cm. h. and the shaft 35 cm. h.

which was concealed by the wall, to which the columns were attached, remained undressed and in certain cases very rough (see Pl. 32, 3).

The shafts of these engaged columns were severely plain ; only the part which was visible was dressed ; the part which was inserted into the wall remained rough. The shafts consist of one or more pieces or drums varying in length between 28 - 157 cm.; the longest drum possibly indicates the average length of the shafts. The columns with the bases and shafts may have averaged about 2-2½ m. in height.[1]

The engaged columns which stood at the corners were double (Fig. 6, A, B, D, E ; Pls. 31, 2, 3 ; 32, 5, 6 ; 33, 5). Those which stood against other parts of the walls were, as a rule, half (Pls. 32, 1-3 ; 33, 1-4, 6) or three-quarter columns (Pl. 31, 1). The plinths of some of the bases and capitals (Fig. 6, C-F) have a slight curvature, which proves that they could not have been an ornamentation of the exterior of the cella trichora, but stood on the interior around the apses. Some of these columns still had plaster, painted gray, adhering to them when they were found, but this has fallen off. On some of the detached pieces of this gray plaster graffiti were observed. (See the chapter on inscriptions.)

Since none of the columns were found in situ their disposition around the walls of the apses is a matter of conjecture. Some pieces of the columns are evidently missing; they were probably reused in the walls of the later buildings. In a number of cases it was also difficult to decide whether a certain molding had been used as a base, a capital or a cornice. In general the arrangement of the material proposed by Father Bagatti (Fig. 6) deserves close attention, in spite of some difficulties which one encounters in disposing the material. He thinks that of the 13 pieces which belonged to double columns 6 are drums (Pl. 33, 5), 5 bases (Pls. 31, 2, 3 ; 32, 5, 6) and 2 capitals (Pl. 32, 4); of the 57 pieces which belonged to half columns 34 are drums (Pls. 32, 3 ; 33, 1, 4, 6), 10 bases and 13 capitals; see Pls. 31, 1 ; 32, 1, 3; 33, 1-3, 6.[2]

One of the double columns was seen by Conder, regarding which he writes as follows : " A double column was also found, resembling those of the Galilean synagogues. Each of the two shafts was 1 foot 6 inches in diameter. These double columns are also found at Tyre (perhaps relics of the old Temple of

[1] Shafts of double columns vary between 35-99 cm.; those of half columns between 28-157 cm. In fact very few drums are of the same length; double drums, for example, are 35, 35½, 40, 69, 73, 97, 99 cm. l. ; half drums are 28, 35, 42, 45, 64, 66, 70, 78, 79, 100, 124, 134, 154, 157, etc. cm. l. ; if we allow for a few missing drums and suppose 16 columns, their shafts would average about 157 cm. in length as is suggested by the longest drum of a half column.

[2] Let us suppose that there were 16 columns, 4 double columns, placed at the 4 corners of the apses, and 12 half columns, of which 4 stood against the wall of each of the 3 apses. In this supposition only a few pieces would still be missing and one or the other piece considered a base would have to be considered a capital or vice versa. Everything considered, this seems to be the most satisfactory disposition of the material.

Melcarth), at Khurbet Belât ('Memoirs,' vol. i., p. 171), and at Jerâsh ; they were certainly, therefore, used by Jews and Romans in the second century of our era." [1]

Double columns were used in the Herodian peristyle at Askalon,[2] in the Herodian peristyle house at Samaria,[3] on the west tell at Tulûl edh-Dhahab in Transjordan,[4] in the odeum at ʿAmmân [5] and in the basilica at Bethlehem.[6]

Half columns, attached to the interior of the walls of buildings, are found in the Galilean synagogues,[7] in the temple at is-Sanamên,[8] in a rock-cut chamber at Petra,[9] in a chapel (?) at Elealeh [10] and in numerous other monuments,[11] all of which suggest an early date, possibly between the 2-5 centuries A. D.

The panels formed by the columns seem to have been framed by a cornice of which 19 stones with moldings were found. Some of the moldings resemble those of the bases of the columns (Pl. 33, 8), others resemble the moldings of the capitals (Pl. 34, 1, 2). These moldings suggest an upper and a lower cornice. If we suppose that one or the other stone is missing, which is the rule with all the material recovered, then we can allow about eight such stones for each apse, four for the upper and four for the lower parts of the panels between the half columns.

The lower part of the walls was plastered and painted gray as is evident from fragments of plaster found adhering to the stones and lying in small fragments east of the basilica. It is doubtful whether the fragments of plaster, painted with red, black and yellow ornaments, found on the north side of the cella trichora and on the northern slope, should be brought in connection with the cella trichora or with the north hall. No complete motifs were recovered.

Other plaster, painted red, found in great quantities east of the cella trichora and in smaller quantities on the northeastern slope, above room 41 and in area 53, represents the matrix of the mosaic which decorated the upper part of the

1 *SEP* p. 155. — For the double columns of the ancient synagogues of Galilee and a valuable discussion of that material see *ASG* pp. 165 f.

2 *QS* 1924, p. 28 and Pls. II & III.

3 *Harvard Excavations at Samaria 1908-1910* by Reisner, Fisher and Lyon, I, Cambridge, 1924, pp. 180 ff. and Fig. 97. Cf. Galling, *BRL* 272.

4 *RB* 47 (1938), p. 412 f. — See *BASOR* 35, p. 12; *PJB* 10 (1914), pp. 49 f.; *ZDPV* 48 (1925), p. 296.

5 *SEP* p. 36.

6 *Bethléem*, Pl. II.

7 *ASG* p. 28, Abb. 52; pp. 48 f., Abb. 96 ff. None of the half columns were found in situ, but it is presupposed that they decorated the inner wall of the upper story, as, for example, in the theater at Bosra, regarding which see *PA* 3, pp. 47 ff. and the illustrations 945/6, 948, 950/1, 959, 966.

8 *ECS* pp. 14 f. and Ill. 6, A. Here the columns engaged with the side walls carry extensions of the entablature. The temple is dated 191 A. D.

9 *PA* 1, p. 272, Fig. 302; p. 273, Fig. 303; see p. 159, Fig. 181.

10 *SEP* p. 17.

11 See for example the monuments at el-Kahf, *SEP* pp. 116 ff. The monuments are assigned to the early Christian period (5th century A. D.).

the first expedition in 1933 and explored them thoroughly in 1935. Wherever the mosaic pavement of the basilica was missing we made investigations below the level of the floor and discovered one tomb in the center of the sanctuary (**e**), a second in the southwestern part of the sanctuary (**d**) and three immediately outside the sanctuary in the eastern end of the nave (**a-c**).

In the methods of construction and in form the tombs are very similar. The walls are constructed of well-dressed masonry with a plain surface laid in regular courses (Fig. 8, 1). The two tombs in the sanctuary have a paved floor, and **e** has a pit in the center; they are plastered on the interior and are closed by a row of slabs placed on top of the walls. The three tombs outside the sanctuary have no floor besides the native clay or rock; they are not plastered and are closed by stone slabs which do not rest on top of the walls but on ledges inside the tombs about $\frac{2}{3}$ of the distance from the bottom.

Tomb **e** in the middle of the sanctuary (Pl. 40, 1) is 224 cm. l., 63 cm. w. and 82 cm. h. on the interior; the pit in the center, which is formed by the omission of one of the paving slabs, is 50 cm. wide and 40 cm. deep; its bottom is formed by the native rock. The tomb had been broken open in ancient times. The covering slabs at the western end were missing and part of the northern wall was broken down. After the contents of the tomb had been thrown into disorder it was filled up with stones and earth. Among the stones were parts of two marble slabs decorated with a cross and a piece of a chancel post made of black "Nebi Mûsa" stone. Mixed with the débris were a number of bones which represent at least one human burial. This tomb was restored by us and may be inspected by visitors by removing a lid which covers a small opening near the center of the top. This was the first tomb discovered in 1933.

Tomb **d** near the southwestern part of the sanctuary (Fig. 8, 1; Pl. 86, 1) is 204 cm. l., 62 cm. w. and 85 cm. h. on the interior. It differs from tomb **e** in this that it does not have a pit in its center; by removing one of the slabs of the floor it was ascertained that it rested on the native rock 25 cm. below the floor of the tomb. The stones which cover the tomb are 28 cm. thick; above them is a layer 18 cm. thick; this forms the bed of the mosaic pavement which at this point is 168 cm. above bedrock. The mosaic pavement still covers the greater part of the tomb; at the western end, where part of the mosaic pavement is missing, one of the stones covering the tomb was cracked; through this aperture soil had penetrated into the interior of the tomb, otherwise it was undisturbed. The bones of human skeletons inside the tomb are decayed and have to a great extent crumbled to dust; to judge from the fragments of skulls found at the western end of the tomb it seems that several burials had been made here.

Tomb **d** contained a number of small objects. An iron rod was found lying on top of the bones in the eastern half of the tomb; it is 30 cm. l. and 5-12 mm. in d.; at the upper end it has an open ring 28 mm. in d.; below the ring the shaft tapers to a point. Fragments of pale blue glass lamps had found their way into the tomb ; these lamps had a diameter of 77 mm. at the mouth ; the rims are thickened and rounded. A few other glass fragments belong to a different type of vessel.

About a dozen small Roman coins characteristic of the 4th and 5th centuries A. D. came from this tomb ; one has been ascribed to Constantius II (337-361 A. D.) and several others to Arcadius (395-408 A. D.).

The tombs **a-c** outside the sanctuary form one group (Pls. 41, 1 ; 42, 1), which occupies the greater part of the space between the pulpit and the northern colonnade, though there is enough space between the colonnade and the tombs for another tomb (Pl. 161, 2, a-c). A clearance on the west and north of the tombs revealed the fact that the native rock crops out directly beneath the floor of the basilica on the western side of the tombs, but drops away suddenly to the east and north, so that the easternmost column in the northern colonnade (Pl. 41, 1 and 2) stands on a pilaster constructed in a deep natural trench. From this we conclude that the three masonry tombs were constructed in a natural trench nearly three meters deep, in fact the eastern wall of the tombs is exactly 295 cm. high; on it rests the base of the chancel's screen; in other words, the bottom of the tombs is 295 cm. below the said base (Pls. 41, 2 and 42, 1). The northern, western and southern walls of the tombs are somewhat lower than the eastern one. The tombs are on an average between 204-210 cm. l., 80-82 cm. w. and are divided into a lower and upper section by a ledge, which projects 13-15 cm. and represents a course 27½-30 cm. h.; the section of the tomb below the ledge is 166-178 cm. deep; above the ledge the walls rise 82½-87 cm.

On the ledge of each tomb were placed 4 slabs 24 cm. thick; they closed the tomb tightly and it would have been difficult to remove them had it not been for a round hole in one slab of each tomb which facilitated the lifting of the same ; then all the other stones could easily be removed. The perforated slab was always either the first (Pl. 42, 1) or the second from the west. In tomb **c** the hole was closed by a large upright stone placed over it ; smaller stones closed the other holes.

Also the tombs found in room 21 on the western side of the atrium were closed by slabs of which one was perforated. The perforated stone is no doubt the one which is called "the pellaïkon (τὸ πελλαϊκόν) of the mouth of the tomb" in several inscriptions found over tombs in a chapel of a 6th century monastery at Beth-Shan. There it is expressly stated that the "pellaïkon" is perforated. The translation reads as follows : "Where the wreath-cross is, there lies the (pellaïkon) of the mouth of the tomb, having rings ; and he who wishes lifts up the wreath-cross and finds the (pellaïkon) and buries the dead."[1] The word πελλαϊκόν puzzled FitzGerald, who did not translate it; since the word designates

[1] *Beth-Shan* IV, pp. 14 f.

the door of the tomb, it may be translated into English by the word "door". Πέλλα means "stone"; πελλα-ικον signifies "something made of stone", hence a "stone door".[1]

The contents of the tombs **a-c** were found undisturbed. They contained 17 burials, 8 each in **a** and **c**, and 1 in **b**. The extended bodies had been placed one on top of the other, the heads at the west, the feet towards the east.

Besides the skeletons practically nothing else was found in these tombs. A tiny 4th or 5th century coin, otherwise not identifiable, was found in tomb **a**. In tomb **b** was found a quantity of lead; it was lying directly below the perforated slab and had probably served as a plug for the slab. One man saw some of the lead still adhering to the sides of the hole in the slab; all the pieces of lead were rounded in such a way as to suggest that they had covered a round object, say a rod, which had been inserted into the hole. The amount of lead does not suffice for a coffin, so that possibility is excluded.

Above the slabs, the shafts of the tombs were found filled up with ground to floor level. The floor itself had consisted of mosaics of which two levels can still be seen beneath the pulpit which extends somewhat over the southern side of tomb **c**. Also at Beth-Shan a mosaic pavement was placed over tombs in spite of the fact that they were intended for later burials, as the inscriptions there suggest.[2] The same inscriptions mention a "wreath-cross", which seems to have covered a part of the tomb. Actually a marble slab was found on which was carved a wreath enclosing a cross.[3] Similar marble slabs were found also at Siyâgha (see Pls. 124 f.); it is possible that one or the other of them was used for covering at least a part of these tombs.

Below the steps to the sanctuary were found several other interesting marble objects which will be mentioned in the chapter on marble.

Shaft tombs built of masonry were common during the Roman and Byzantine periods in Palestine.[4] The arrangement into groups of three seems to have a special significance. It is found both in the cella trichora and in the atrium room 21. In both cases there was space for a fourth tomb. At a monastery near Gaza, Peter the Iberian, who visited Siyâgha twice in the 5th century A. D., caused a similar group of three tombs to be constructed. He himself was buried in the central tomb, whilst two of his companions were buried in the lateral ones. Later the followers of Peter removed his remains to a tomb constructed especially for him under the altar.[5] From this narrative we may conclude that the tomb in the center of a group of three was reserved for a

1 *QS* 1931, p. 67, n. 6, FitzGerald himself states that "the context points to something like a stone door." Perhaps the word was derived from πύλαι (door, entrance) in order to designate a stone which served as a door.

2 *Beth-Shan* IV, pp. 4 and 14 f.

3 *Beth-Shan* IV, pp. 3 and 14 f.

4 See *QDAP* 4 (1935), pp. 70 ff.; 6 (1937), pp. 153 ff.

5 Raabe, p. 129, no. 142; p. 131, no. 145.

higher dignitary; as a matter of fact we find that at Siyâgha the lateral tombs contained 8 burials each, whereas the tomb in the middle contained only one. Peter enjoyed a great reputation for sanctity; for this reason his followers transferred his remains to a special tomb beneath the altar; a pari it seems probable that he who was buried beneath the altar of the church at Siyâgha was one who enjoyed a high reputation for holiness. In the monastery at Beth-Shan munificent benefactors of the monastery were buried in the church.[1] So at Siyâgha the tombs may have served for the burial not only of monks but also of benefactors. The inscriptions on the mosaic pavement mention benefactors, but it is not certain whether they were buried in these tombs.

The arrangement of the tombs in groups of three is a relic of an older tradition according to which burials were made on three sides of a chamber; that practice was still in vogue during the 4th century A. D., and it may have influenced the arrangement of the shaft tombs in groups of three; there is no other apparent reason for such a grouping.

The 5 tombs with their 20 or more burials within the limits of the cella trichora characterize that monument as a mortuary or memorial chapel.

D. THE DATE

After describing all the elements which at one time or other formed a part of the cella trichora we may attempt to fix the time when this monument was erected. There is no inscription which informs us of the exact date at which the monument was begun or finished; but a comparison with the other buildings on the site and in the region and a study of the literary sources dealing with the monuments at Siyâgha throws some light on this problem.

The literary sources will be studied more in detail in a later chapter; here it suffices to note that they indicate the existence of the basilica in the fifth century and of the cella trichora towards the end of the fourth.

The excavations brought to light one inscription which gives an absolute date. That inscription exists in the baptistery and states that the baptistery and the church were completed in the year 597 A. D. If the relation of the cella trichora to these two dated buildings is studied it becomes apparent that it must be an older structure. Here we wish to stress only two points: the position of the cella trichora and its characteristic building materials.

The primitive cella trichora is located beneath the eastern end of the basilica where its remains, still in situ, serve merely as a foundation; its original plan is ignored; some of its characteristic material can be seen in the walls of the

[1] *Beth-Shan* IV, p. 15.

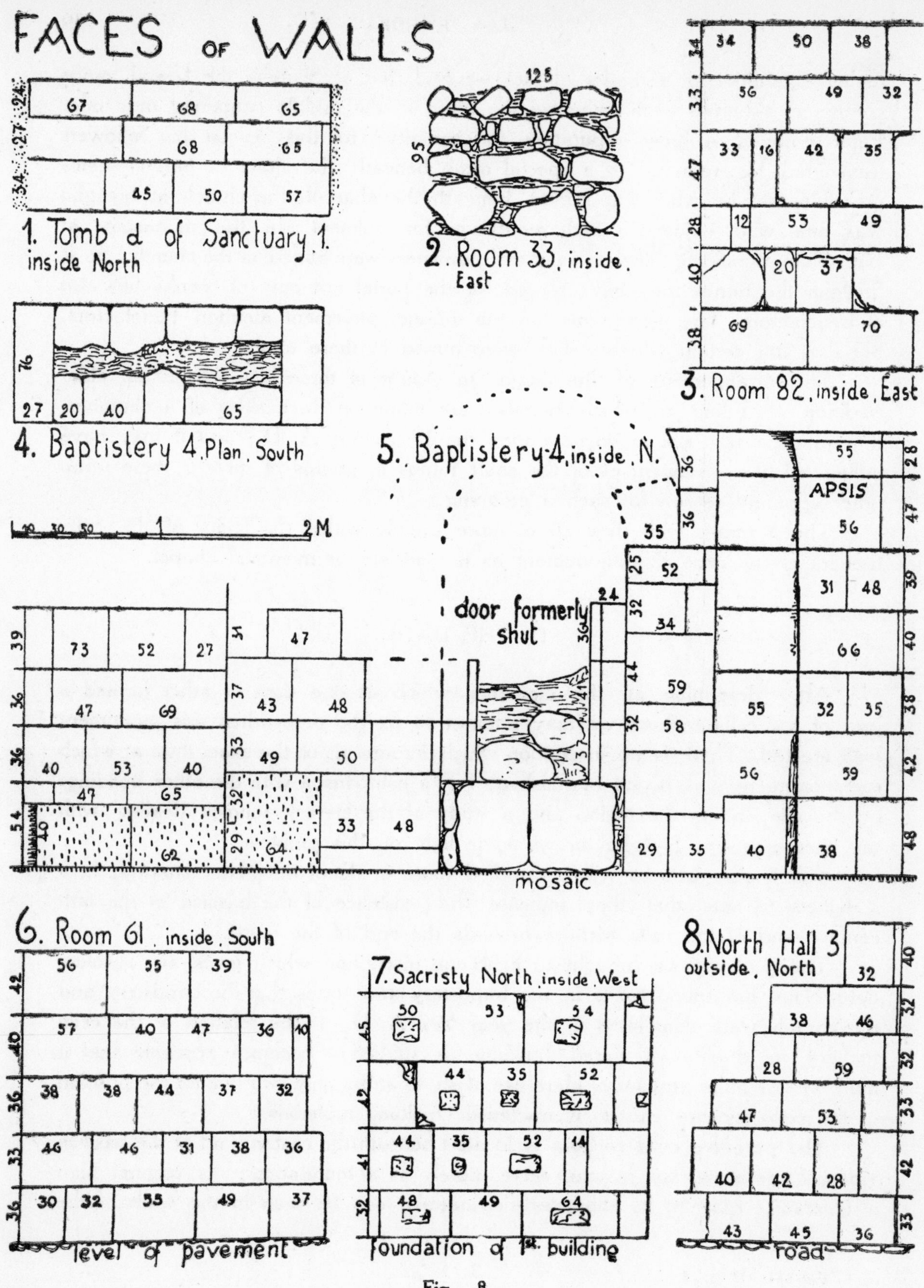
FACES OF WALLS
1. Tomb d of Sanctuary 1. inside North
2. Room 33. inside. East
3. Room 82. inside. East
4. Baptistery 4. Plan. South
5. Baptistery 4. inside. N.
APSIS
door formerly shut
mosaic
2M
6. Room 61. inside. South
level of pavement
7. Sacristy North. inside. West
foundation of 1st building
8. North Hall 3 outside. North
road

Fig. 8.

later buildings, but most of the material, no longer in situ, lies around the exterior. This goes to show that the cella trichora was already in ruins when the last basilica was erected, or, in other words, its position proves that it is older than the basilica and the buildings around the basilica.

The drafted masonry, the engaged columns and the trefoil plan are other elements which distinguish the cella trichora from the later buildings at Siyâgha and point to interesting relations with other monuments of the region. The drafted masonry and the engaged columns show points of similarity with second and third century monuments, whilst the trefoil plan suggests a relationship with monuments of the fifth century and later.

In the latest buildings at Siyâgha the masonry is not drafted, the stones are relatively small, carefully squared and dressed with a plain surface (Fig. 8, 3 ff.); mixed with the stones having a plain surface are others of medium size (Fig. 8, 7) which have, as a rule, a small flat boss and a wide margin; these very probably represent an intermediate period at Siyâgha. Vastly different from this material of the later buildings is that used for the cella trichora; it consists of rubble, stones with a plain surface and stones with a drafted surface. Rubble was used for the foundations and lower courses of the cella trichora, the plain and the drafted stones occur in the upper courses, where those with a margin and boss predominate (Fig. 4, 1, A-C).

It is this mixture of rubble, plain and drafted masonry which distinguishes the cella trichora from the Roman, Jewish and Nabatæan masonry of the second and third centuries of the Christian era. In those earlier monuments the masonry is generally more uniform ; thus, for instance, the northern tomb at Kh. es-Sûk is built entirely of stones with a plain surface,[1] whilst the Kusr es-Seb'ah is built entirely of stones with a drafted surface.[2]

In discussing the acropolis walls at ʿAmmân, Butler observes that "there can be no doubt that draughted masonry was employed by Greek builders in Syria in the second century B. C., and there is abundant proof that it was used by Roman builders as late as the second century of our era, especially in military constructions. In the later military architecture, of the Christian period in Syria, draughted masonry is generally of a different character, blocks with draughted edges being mixed with ordinary smooth quadrated blocks... There are many examples in the Haurân in which a castle or tower of the Antonine period, in draughted masonry, was renovated or rebuilt in the fourth century with an admixture of smooth blocks."[3]

Conder asserts that "drafted masonry is found in all the enumerable Byzantine buildings which have been planned during the course of the survey.

[1] *SEP* after p. 144; *PA* 2, pp. 179 ff.
[2] *SEP* after p. 176; *PA* 2, pp. 207 ff.
[3] *PPUAES* Div. II, Sec. A, Part 1, p. 38.

... It is impossible to suppose that in every case where a monastery was built, ancient foundations or old drafted stones were found and used up. The only natural explanation is that the masons in the fourth, fifth and sixth centuries were in the habit of dressing their masonry, and this is borne out by the fact that in a great many cases the stones have evidently been cut to fit the place in which they stand in the walls."[1]

How difficult it is to distinguish drafted masonry of the second and third centuries of our era from that of the Byzantine period may be seen from the description which Conder gives of the masonry of the Kusr es-Seb'ah. "The stones", he says, "in the outer walls of the building are drafted with a bold rustic boss. They are 2 feet to 4 feet long, and 1½ feet high; the bosses (?)[2] are 4 inches to 6 inches wide, and the projection is 2 inches to 4 inches. On the interior of the walls, the stones of the four lower courses are also drafted, but the bosses do not project so much. The dressing is very much like that in Byzantine masonry, the draft being dressed with an adze, and the face picked over roughly. This building... might be as early as the second century A. D. or possibly as late as the third, but is most probably of the Antonine age (second century A. D.)."[3]

Conder did not see any of the drafted masonry of the cella trichora, but on other grounds he suspected a date as early as that of the Antonines for the ruins at Siyâgha.[4] Had he seen the drafted masonry, which is so similar to that of the Kusr es-Seb'ah, he might have been confirmed in his view. Yet it should not be forgotten that the rubble used in the lower courses of the cella trichora distinguishes this monument from the so-called Kusr es-Seb'ah. We have less uniformity here; this may indicate a different period, say a fourth century date; but the evidence is too uncertain to be decisive; together with other evidence, however, it may acquire some force.

The chief reasons why Conder suspected "the early Christian period, or that of the Antonines" as the date of the ruins at Siyâgha seem to be "six rude Ionic capitals" and "a double column".[5] He compares the Ionic capitals with those at Tantûrah and elsewhere, and adds that "in the Christian buildings of the Hauran (second to fourth century) similar Ionic capitals are common". The context suggests that the so-called Ionic capitals seen by Conder are nothing else than the exposed and consumed surfaces of the capitals of the basilica, which are not earlier than the fifth century A. D.

1 *SWP* 3, p. 445.
2 More probably the margin or draft is meant.
3 *SEP* p. 175.
4 *SEP* p. 155.
5 *SEP* pp. 154 f.

The double column seen by Conder at Siyâgha reminded him of pagan temples and ancient Jewish synagogues generally assigned to the second or third century of our era. It is true that most of the examples of double columns which we know belonged to monuments of the Roman period, but this type of column was still in use in the Byzantine period, as the double columns in the basilica at Bethlehem prove. Hence this indication of date is also somewhat vague and uncertain. At the most we can say that the double columns and, for that matter, all the engaged columns found at Siyâgha point to a certain relationship of the cella trichora with second and third century monuments of Transjordan and Palestine.

On the other hand the trefoil plan indicates a connection between the cella trichora and a class of monuments which is supposed to have found its way to Palestine and Transjordan not before the fifth century of our era.[1] The earliest example of a cella trichora in Palestine is supposed to be the memorial church of St. John the Baptist in Jerusalem; this church is attributed to the fifth century. All the rest are ascribed to the sixth century; thus, for example, the church at the monastery of St. Theodosius, the church of St. George at et-Taiyibeh, that of the Parthenike at Madaba, the small church at ed-Junêne and the chapel over the tomb of Aaron on Mt. Hor. The same plan is found in the reconstructed basilica at Bethlehem and in the Anastasis at Jerusalem as reconstructed by Modestus after the Persian invasion. The principal room in the palace at el-Meshetta, to the east of Madaba, has the plan of a cella trichora. These parallels seem to suggest that the cella trichora at Siyâgha is of the same date or at least not much earlier than other monuments of the same type in these regions.

We should, however, not forget that the cella trichora is known along all the shores of the Mediterranean Sea before the 5th century of our era;[2] therefore we need not be surprised if in one or the other instance we come across a cella trichora in Palestine or Transjordan which must be dated before the 5th century. The monks at Siyâgha came, in part, from Egypt,[3] where the cella trichora was known, and they may have brought along this tradition from there. At the same time it seems worthy of note that while in most of the other examples of the cella trichora the apses protrude on the exterior, at Siyâgha the apses are inscribed inside a rectangular plan. This reminds one forcibly of the mausolea of the region with their rectangular exterior plan and rectangular inner chambers.[4] This compact arrangement of the apses serves to link up the

[1] Watzinger, *DP* 2, pp. 137-139; Vincent, *Bethléem*, pp. 21-32.

[2] Kaufmann, *HCA* pp. 160 ff. See *Atti del III Congresso Internazionale di Archeologia Cristiana*, pp. 295 ff.

[3] Raabe, pp. 83-85, nos. 85-87.

[4] Watzinger, *DP* 2, pp. 99 ff.; R. W. Hamilton, *The Domed Tomb at Sebastya*, in *QDAP* 8 (1938) pp. 64 ff. The base of the bust illustrated in Pl. XL, 1 has a molding resembling the moldings of the capitals (or bases?) of the cella trichora at Siyâgha; cf. our Pls. 31, 1; 32, 1 and 3; 33, 1-3, 4.

2. *Sixth century.* The restoration of the ruined basilica was undertaken immediately and completed in the year 597. This is the basilica which the excavations brought to light; it will be described in detail below. Here it suffices to note that the basilica continued to be used during the seventh century and was most probably not entirely abandoned before the eighth. Even after its abandonment the basilica continued for a time to serve as a place of refuge for a few squatters or passers-by. But neglect and a variety of natural causes, such as earthquakes, gradually led to the destruction of the church.[1] The hall was the first to cave in. The timbers of the roof were collected and used as fuel; not a single trace of them remains.

The sanctuary survived for some time after the collapse of the body of the church. This is evident from the fact that one of the capitals of the nave had been rolled into the center of the sanctuary where it served as a table. Vandals broke up the marble furnishings of the sanctuary and scattered them about; they broke into the tomb in the center of the sanctuary, destroyed a large part of the mosaic pavement around it and blackened the remaining mosaic pavements by their fires. Eventually also the roof of the sanctuary collapsed.

3. *Sixteenth century.* About the year 1564 a Portuguese Franciscan visited Mount Nebo. At his time the church was completely ruined.[2]

4. *Nineteenth century.* The ruined sanctuary was converted into a cemetery in the first half of the nineteenth century. The tombs were built with the neatly squared stones of the basilica. The heap of ruins was lowest in the center of the sanctuary; there, about one meter above the floor, the first interment was made. Above this grave others were placed until the entire sanctuary and the adjoining sacristies were occupied up to the level of the cornice. The sepulchers were concealed so well beneath a layer of stones that no one seems to have suspected their existence before the excavations began.

The date of this cemetery is fixed by the following considerations. The local Arabs declare that they never used these ruins as a burial place nor do they know who was laid to rest here. But they suggest that formerly the Beni Sakhr camped near Siyâgha and they may have entombed their dead in the ruins. From this it is evident that the cemetery antedates the memory of living men.

In the tombs a number of small objects were found, such as colored glass bracelets, bronze finger rings, a bronze spatula and coins. The coins belong to the second quarter of the nineteenth century; that is most probably the date of the majority of the interments.

As far as we can judge the ruins presented the same appearance to the first modern explorers who visited Siyâgha, as they did to us when we began excavations (Pl. 37, 1).

[1] See *Gerasa*, pp. 68 f., 172 f.

[2] Lopes, pp. 186 f.

5. *The clearance.* In 1933 the basilica was thoroughly cleared down to the level of the floor, and in 1935 soundings were made under the level of the floor wherever the mosaic pavement was missing. Work began at the eastern end of the basilica and proceeded systematically towards the west. The score or more of tombs at the eastern end was first removed and the bones in them were transferred to a common grave beyond the ruins. As the work progressed the basilica changed its appearance (Pl. 37, 2); buried walls, columns, mosaic pavements and a number of small objects came to light. Some of the drums of the fallen columns were replaced on the bases which were still in situ (Pls. 38, 39, 93, 94). Today we again see the basilica in which pilgrims venerated Moses during the sixth and following centuries.

B. THE SIXTH CENTURY BASILICA

1. *The ground plan.* Pl. 161, 1 & 2; Fig. 9. The ground plan of the sixth century basilica differs from that of the fifth century in this that the eastern end is completely changed; instead of three apses the remodelled basilica has a single apse and two lateral rectangular chambers. The chambers have doors connecting them directly with the sanctuary; there are no doors between the chambers and the side aisles. This is the feature which is peculiar to the sixth century basilica at Siyâgha, and distinguishes it from most other basilicas not only in the immediate vicinity but also in remoter regions. The same feature was observed in a few small chapels of Syria which are attributed to the sixth century. Otherwise the eastern end of the basilica resembles more closely another group of sixth century churches of Syria, whose lateral chambers communicate with both the sanctuary and the side aisles.[1]

The dimensions of the basilica were influenced by the cella trichora; roughly speaking the basilica is twice as large as the cella trichora; it has the same width, but is twice as long.

In common with many other basilicas the church has an apse, a threefold division of the eastern and western parts, side chapels, a narthex and an atrium. The chapels will be treated in the following chapter.

2. *The apse.* Pls. 26-28, 39, 41, 161. The entire apse of the basilica protrudes beyond the eastern wall. It stands on the eastern wall of the cella trichora and is built partly of old and partly of new material. The walls are still 2.34-2.94 m. h.; on the south they are preserved up to the level of the cornice in the southern sacristy; on the north the walls are one or two courses lower

[1] *ECS* p. 189, n. 338.

(Pl. 36, 1) ; there is nothing to show whether the apse had a cornice or not. It was probably roofed by a semidome built of stone. On the exterior and on the interior the apse is semicircular ; its chord measures 6.20 m. On the outside (Pls. 26,2; 27,2) the southern part of the apse is concealed by a part of the eastern wall of the cella trichora which remained standing. On the inside the ends of the apse are marked by columns inserted into the walls ; to these columns may have belonged two capitals found east of the basilica.

The one capital (Pl. 60, Fig. 1, 2) was lying directly east of the apse; it probably belonged to the southern column. This capital has no other ornamentation than an incised horizontal line on the abacus.

The other capital (Pl. 60, Fig. 2, 2) was found at the edge of the ruins on the northeastern slope; it could have rolled down there if it fell from the northern column. This capital has splayed edges beneath the corners of the abacus. Near the lower part of the splay there is a pellet. The leaves are blocked, but only the overlapping tips are worked out more in detail. Similar capitals (Pl. 59, 5-8; Fig. 5, 1) were found in the atrium. They show that the so-called splay beneath the corners of the abacus was intended for a leaf, which in one case (Pl. 59, 6) has three pellets arranged horizontally in a row. Similar pellets occur on the capitals of the basilica (Pl. 45) and on a small capital found in the southern monastery (Pl. 59, 2); they seem to establish a close connection between all these capitals, which very probably, originally, belonged to the fifth century basilica. These characteristic pellets are found in the flutings of a shell motif occurring in Egypt and assigned by Kaufmann[1] to the fifth or sixth century; they seem to indicate a certain relationship between the two places.

The columns in question supported the arch of the apse; this may have had a molding of the type illustrated in Fig. 5, 3 and Pl. 34, 13-15.

The walls of the apse were plastered; there is no evidence of other ornaments.

Around the interior of the apse there are five tiers of seats built of solid masonry and plastered. This synthronon is 1.80 m. wide at the base and 1.27 m. high; each tier averages about 25 cm. in height; the lowest course of the synthronon is laid on a bed 25 cm. below the level of the floor; these stones are 50 cm. high. The ends of the synthronon extend beyond the limits of the apse on both sides. This solid mass af masonry forms a firm support for the surrounding walls. Such seats for the clergy, arranged in the form of an amphitheater around the apse, are a common feature in ancient churches; generally the seat for the bishop is somewhat higher than the others.[2] Actually the stone in the center of the highest row of seats in the basilica at Siyâgha is a little

1 *HCA* p. 513, 7.
2 *HCA* p. 186, no. 82; *Gerasa*, pp. 183 f., e.

Fig. 9. Siyâgha from an aeroplane ; looking south (March 20, 1940).

higher than the others, but this is not very pronounced; it probably marks the place of the abbot of the monastery.

Basilicas with a single external apse are not uncommon in the Christian architecture of Transjordan and the neighboring countries; the type is not known in the towns of el-Mekhayyat [1] and Madaba,[2] but at Gerasa [3] 5 churches have an external apse and in three cases the apse is semicircular on the outside and on the inside, like the apse of the basilica at Siyâgha.[4]

3. *The choir.* Pls. 39,1; 41,1; 161,1. That part of the sanctuary which is between the apse and the nave of the basilica may be designated as the choir; it is a rectangular space measuring about 8 by 6.70 m. The walls on the north and south do not rest on older walls, but are constructed on a filling of earth a little below the level of the floor. The material used for the walls was, at least partly, derived from the older buildings. Thus, for instance, in the southern wall (Pl. 40,2) there is a large stone of the cella trichora cut so as to suggest the upper part of a conch; it probably comes from the semidome of the southern apse. Near the previous stone is another one with a boss; associated with them are stones with a plain surface; between the stones there are broken fragments of marble. The walls were plastered.

In each of the two walls there is a large cupboard and a door. The cupboard in the southern wall (Pl. 40,2) is 90 cm. wide and is still 190 cm. high; the top is missing; the one on the north has similar dimensions; both were plastered. The doors are near the western ends of the walls; they join the choir and the lateral chambers (Pl. 40,2). Above each door, but no longer in situ, was found its lintel; it is surprisingly rough and without any ornament. In the northern chamber, however, three stones decorated with crosses were discovered; two of these may be seen in Pl. 30, 2, leaning against its western wall and one lying on top of its northern wall; the former two are reproduced in Pl. 57,5 and 7; that on the wall resembles the one illustrated in Pl. 57,5. One or the other of these crosses may have been in the wall near the door.

The walls on the north and south of the choir do not continue in a straight line up to the chancel rail; the sections which we have described have the function of curtains between the choir and the lateral chambers; on the east they begin near the columns marking the ends of the apses, on the west they terminate against the western wall of the lateral chambers. Compare Pl. 39, 1

1 *RAC* 13 (1936), pp. 129 ff.

2 *NBAC* 1899, pp. 149 ff.

3 *Gerasa*, pp. 189 f.

4 An external apse, oriented towards Jerusalem, is found also in some of the later Byzantine synagogues; see E. L. Sukenik, *Ancient Synagogues in Palestine and Greece*, London, 1934, pp. 31 f. and Fig. 7; Id., *The Ancient Synagogue of Beth Alpha*, Jerusalem, 1932, p. 13 and Pls. III & XXVII; — D. C. Baramki, *An Early Byzantine Synagogue near Tell es-Sultân, Jericho*, in *QDAP* 6 (1938), p. 75 and Fig. 1.

with Pl. 40, 2. These curtain walls have the appearance of later additions, but they may be contemporaneous with the surrounding walls.

Two walls, distinct from the curtain walls and bonded in with the western walls of the lateral chambers (Pl. 43, 2), served to extend the choir into the first bay of the nave. At the same time they carried the arch of the chancel and performed the function of responds at the eastern end of the basilica's colonnades. In the core of the wall on the south was found a large fragment of a molded marble slab ; it can be seen in Pl. 43, 2.

Between the western ends of the last-mentioned walls there was a screen which separated the choir from the nave. Of this screen we have some interesting remains still in situ; they consist of the sockets and grooves for posts and panels, and of bases for columns. See Pls. 39, 41, 161.

The base of the chancel screen was the upper of the two stone steps between the choir and the nave. Those steps are supported in the center by the eastern wall of the three tombs a-c ; at the northern end (Pl. 41, 1 & 2) they rest on a mosaic pavement of plain large tesserae ; at the southern end their foundation was not examined, because the pulpit stands there (Pls. 41, 1; 43, 1 & 2). The mosaic pavement of the nave, on which the pulpit stands, is 7-8 cm. lower than the tread of the chancel's lower stair. Below this mosaic pavement there is an older one ; both terminate against the rise of the step and are more recent than the plain mosaic at the northern end on which the lower step rests. The stairs were plastered.

In the top step there are 5 sockets for chancel posts ; many such posts or fragments of the same were found scattered about the site, but especially in the basilica and the Theotokos chapel; the majority are made of marble (Pl. 132), a few are of black " Nebi Mûsa" stone.

Between the sockets there are grooves which indicate the position of the panels between the posts. A fragment of a marble panel was still in situ next to the pulpit; it had been cemented into the groove. Fragments of similar marble slabs were very numerous; hundreds of them were collected and studied ; one of the first discovered inside the sanctuary has a Greek inscription carved on the molded frame (Pl. 121, 1 ; see Pls. 124 & 125).[1] Three such marble slabs were required for the screen, two for the section north of the entrance to the sanctuary and one for the southern section. The entrance to the sanctuary was in the center of the parapet. At the southern end the parapet remained open to give access to the pulpit which stood outside the screen.

The most interesting discovery, which we made, regarding the chancel screen was its transformation from a low parapet to a high colonnade. The

[1] See inscription XVI.

evidence for this transformation is the following: four stone bases, a number of marble shafts and a stone capital.

Two of the four stone bases were found in situ to the right and left of the entrance to the sanctuary (Pls. 39 & 41). These stone bases partially cover the sockets for the posts of the screen and suggest that they were substituted for the posts at a later period. The plinths of these bases are 45-46 cm. square and 9 cm. high; the moldings consist of a torus, fillet and cyma recta somewhat more carefully worked than other moldings used at Siyâgha. The material used was a hard red limestone which was highly polished and produces a very pleasant impression. But larger fragments have been chipped off from the upper part of each base, and one base has been completely shattered. This may have been a deliberate act of vandalism or due to an attempt to extract the bronze dowels which had served to join the bases and the shafts. One of the two bases no longer in situ was found lying in the eastern end of the northern aisle; it fitted exactly into a cement impression at the northern end of the screen. Enough fragments of the fourth base were found to be certain of its existence; it must have stood at the southern end of the screen, though there is nothing to indicate the exact spot.

The two marble shafts illustrated in Pl. 129, 9 & 10, were found in the basilica, the one in the first bay at the east end of the north aisle and the other between the pulpit and the first column of the southern colonnade. These columns are made of grayish white marble with black veins; they are 2.20 m. l. and 25 cm. in d.; the filleted ends are 27½ cm. in d. Each of these two columns was broken into two pieces which could be fitted together so that we are able to form an estimate of the height of the colonnade to which they belonged. All other marble shafts which were found are incomplete, but there are enough fragments for many more such columns, of which four were required for the screen of the basilica and four others for the screen of the Theotokos chapel (see Pl. 131, Fig. 1).

Along with the red stone base and the marble shaft found in the eastern end of the north aisle, there was discovered the stone capital illustrated in Pl. 42,2. This basket-shaped capital is unique among the capitals recovered at Siyâgha. Its proportions correspond to those of the rest of the capitals used in the basilica, but its ornamentation differs from all the other capitals found at this great sanctuary. The abacus has an incised horizontal line; the sides are divided into an upper and a lower panel by a double fillet. In the upper panel 4 doves are represented between four crosses. The doves are placed below the corners of the abacus; they stand on the raised band and are arranged in two groups, each of which faces a cross and has a cross between its spreading tails. Three types of crosses are used: the floral, Greek and monogrammatic; the latter two are enclosed in rings, of which one is plain and flat and the other imitates a rope. Regarding the monogram see inscription X. The lower panel is decorated with a series of acanthus leaves; large serrated leaves arranged in pairs alternate with single three-lobed leaves. A tiny three-lobed leaf is inserted above each dove under the corners of the abacus.

This is a characteristic Byzantine capital which combines Christian motifs with the familiar acanthus motif of the classical Corinthian capitals. In general this capital resembles one found in Egypt assigned by Kaufmann [1] to the 7th-8th centuries; the details of ornamentation differ. For the dove ornament see the capital form Abu Menas attributed by Kaufmann [2] to the 4th-5th centuries.

This "dove-capital" was associated with material, which, we think, belongs to the chancel screen; it fits the marble shaft with which it was found ; so we feel justified in assuming that this was one of the capitals of the screen. The capital may date from the time when the high colonnade was substituted for the low parapet. This was not before the 7th century, for in the Theotokos chapel, which was finished at the beginning of the 7th century, the low rail was used first and then also replaced by a colonnade. The change may have occurred during the course of the 7th century. An interesting example of such a colonnade, dating from the 7th century of our era, may be seen in the church at Torcello, near Venice in Italy. The colonnade represents a transition from the low chancel screen to the high ikonostasis.[3] The church at Siyâgha was abandoned before the ikonostasis came into use.

If we assume that the columns of the chancel screen had capitals, we may ask whether any other capitals were found which would fit the shafts of those columns. In the basilica itself no such capitals were recovered. No other "dove-capital" or one similar to it was found anywhere on the site. Seven marble capitals were found; most of them, however, are too small for the columns of this screen. In Pl. 131, Fig. 2, three of the marble capitals are illustrated. The upper two represent the type of capital found in the Theotokos chapel ; their base has a diameter of 20-21 cm.; this is much too small for the shafts of the basilica's screen. The lowest of the three capitals was found in the atrium room 16, where it had no apparent function; its base measures 27 cm. in diameter; this is exactly the size required by the shafts, so we may tentatively assign this capital to the colonnade of the screen.

Two stone capitals, found respectively in room 24 and locus 101, were evidently brought there from elsewhere; they may also have been used for our colonnade. The one, illustrated in Pl. 59, 2, found in the area 101, is a small capital of the same type as those used in the body of the basilica; it is, there-

[1] *HCA* p. 513, Abb. 258, no. 8.
[2] *HCA* p. 464, Abb. 222, lowest row, 2nd from left.
[3] *HCA* p. 185, no. 81. See *Gerasa*, p. 250.

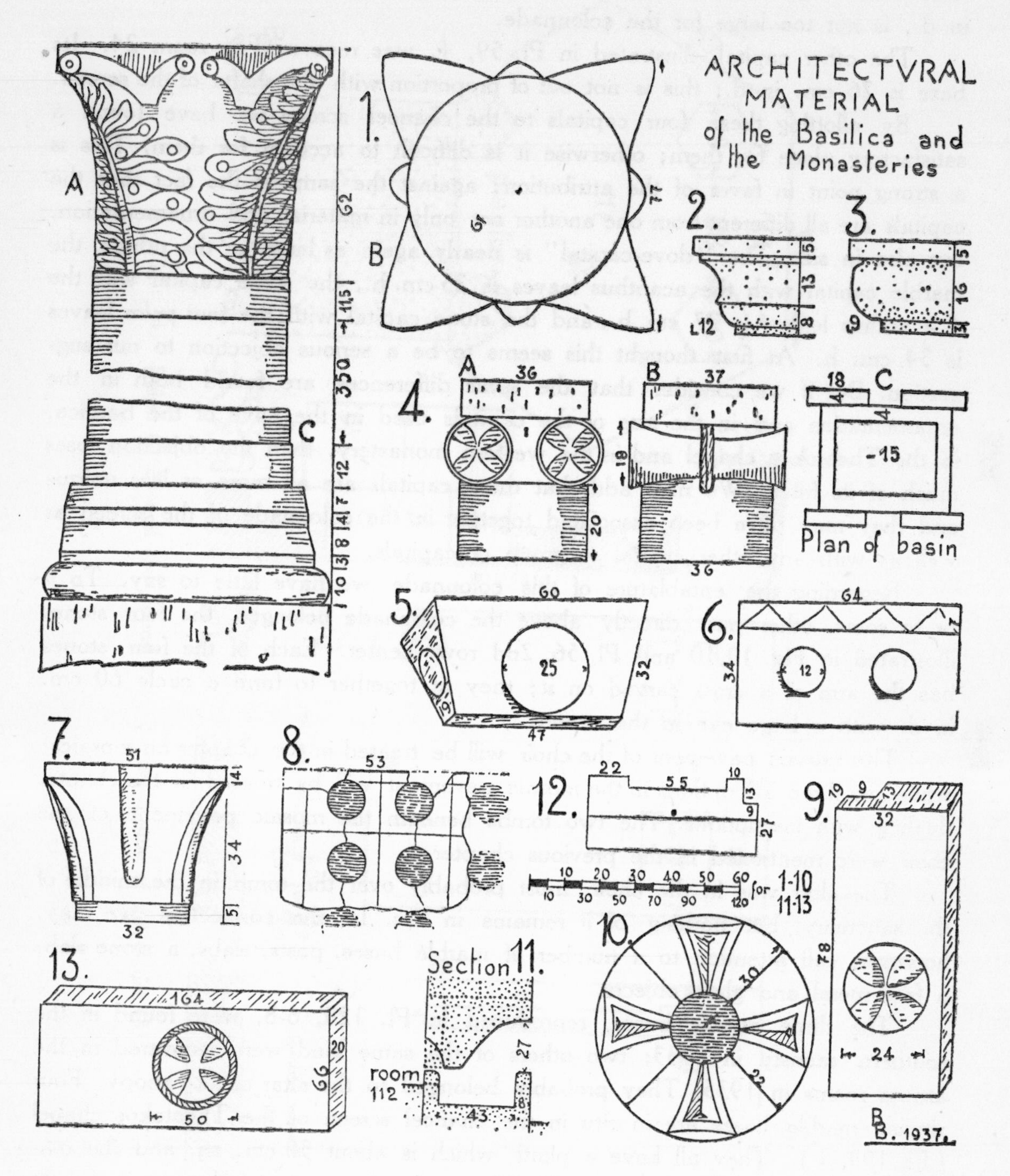
ARCHITECTVRAL
MATERIAL
of the Basilica and
the Monasteries
Plan of basin
Section 11.
room
112
for 1-10
11-13
B. 1937.

Fig. 10.

between the columns; these panels may have been the antipendia of the altar or they may have served as a screen between the columns of the canopy.[1] A large fragment of such a panel was found in the southern sacristy (Pl. 124, 3).

Regarding the marble posts and columns, which may have been used for the altar, see Pls. 128-130. Fragments of marble, representing several altar slabs, are illustrated in Pl. 126; some of them may have served for the altar of the basilica. A black stone slab of the same type is shown in Pl. 60, Fig. 3. Marble reliquaries found at Siyâgha can be seen in Pl. 127, Fig. 1. Other marble vases are represented by the few fragments illustrated in Pls. 126, 24-26; 129, 11; 121, 2. Since we are not certain of the original context of all that material, we will refrain from details here and speak of them when we treat the different kinds of materials not found in situ.

Here we wish to make special mention of the rather rough limestone slab found outside the sanctuary near the northern side of the pulpit (Fig. 11, 3, a & b; Pl. 46, 1 & 2). It measures 107 × 78 × 15 cm. On its lower surface there are mortises at the four corners to receive the tenons of posts on which the slab was placed; the prolongation of the mortises in the form of a groove may indicate that the posts were joined by a frame on which the slab rested. On the upper surface there are several other cavities (of which two are visible in the photograph, and a third is suggested in the drawing); of these one is round and still partially filled with plaster containing a fragment of glass, the others are rectangular. I think these cavities were for relics and that the slab was used for an altar.[2]

Pilgrims inform us that beneath the altar there was a "vessel of oil and of grace". The vessel in question was probably a lamp which was lighted over the spot which was considered most holy; from that lamp pilgrims may have obtained a small quantity of oil for themselves.[3] At Siyâgha we found a large number of broken glass lamps, some pottery lamps and a single tiny bronze lamp. Many of the large glass bowls used as lamps have bases sufficiently large and flat to enable them to stand (Pl. 140, 1-15); very many had three handles by means of which they could be suspended. For the triple suspension chain of such a lamp see Pl. 137, Fig. 1, no. 6. The three chains are attached to a disk; each chain consists of a long central bar, links at both ends of the bars, perforated disks between the links and hooks at the lower end. Other pieces of such chains may be seen in Pls. 135, Fig. 1, nos. 5-7, 19; 138, Fig. 2, nos. 6, 11, 14.[4]

1 See Kaufmann, *HCA* pp. 184 f.
2 See Kaufmann, *HCA* pp. 179 ff.; see also below the remarks on the pulpit.
3 See Kaufmann, *HCA* pp. 593 ff.
4 See the chapters on glass and metals.

The choir of the basilica at Siyâgha differs from that of the vast majority of ancient Christian basilicas in this, that it occupies a relatively large area between the apse and the nave, and, in spite of this, does not extend far into the nave of the basilica. In this respect it resembles the church of the Archangel in il-Anderîn, Syria, where the position of the choir between the two lateral chambers is considered an innovation.[1]

4. *The sacristies*. Pls. 30,1 & 2; 40,2; 161, A & B. In the sixth century basilica the northern and southern apses of the earlier structures were transformed into rectangular chambers which served as sacristies. Irregularities in the plan of these chambers, especially in that on the north, are due to their dependence on the earlier edifices. Under the floor level the walls of the cella trichora are preserved and serve as foundations; above that level the walls date from the sixth century reconstruction. The material used in building these rooms is a mixture from various periods. On the exterior the large drafted stones of the cella trichora served to give these rooms an antique appearance. Details were given when we described the cella trichora. On the interior most of the stones used have a plain surface; but those, of which the western wall of the northern sacristy is constructed, generally have a wide margin and a small boss (Fig. 8,7; Pl. 30,2); that might represent a characteristic of the masonry used for the interior of the original cella trichora or of the fifth century basilica. Similar stones are found in all the walls of the basilica and in the walls of the atrium and western monastery.

In the southern sacristy (Pls. 30,1; 40,2) the walls are unusually well preserved; this is true especially of the eastern and southern walls which are still crowned by a cornice, the only place in the entire basilica where the cornice is still in situ. The molding of this cornice is a cyma recta. One molding of this type was found east of the basilica (Fig. 10,2; Pl. 35,19), and a few stones of the same type were found in the northern sacristy, but no longer in situ (Pl. 30,2). The fate of many of these moldings may be judged from those still in situ (Pl. 40,2). There it will be seen that on some of the stones, which are made of a soft limestone, the molding has weathered away completely; this readily explains why many stones which are no longer in situ cannot be recognized for what they were originally.

The molding of the southern wall represents a course 26 cm. h.; the rest of the wall above the rubble foundations is 309 cm. h. In this wall there are three small cupboards.[2] Between the stones of this wall there are a number of broken marble fragments which were used as fillers. In the lower courses a number of bases of the cella trichora were utilized. One of the stones of the

[1] *ECS* p. 189 and Ill. 193, N, which should be compared with Ill. 193, M; the former is supposed to be a further development of the latter.

[2] See *ECS* p. 218.

wall has a number of graffiti scratched on its surface; they could not be deciphered. Some characters were carved on the interior of the northern wall of this sacristy; Roman numerals seem to have been intended. Other mason marks were observed on the exterior of the northern sacristy's eastern wall.

The lateral chambers at the eastern end of the basilica at Siyâgha are noteworthy for their position in relation to the apse and for the position of their doors. In most of the churches, not only in the immediate vicinity [1] but also in remoter regions,[2] the lateral chambers flank the apse; their doors almost invariably communicate with the side aisles, rarely with both the side aisles and the apse or space in front of the apse; [3] and even more rarely do they communicate exclusively with the apse or space in front of the apse.[4] At Siyâgha the sacristies do not flank the apse, but they are placed at the sides of the large choir in front of the apse; they do not communicate with the side aisles of the basilica, but exclusively with the choir. This is the chief peculiarity in the plan of the basilica and should be stressed accordingly.

We have already noted above that the same peculiarity was observed in a few chapels of Syria. There it was presupposed that the type was due to some liturgical necessity. What that necessity might have been is not specified.

At Siyâgha the arrangement seems to have been influenced by the earlier monuments. It is true that after the cella trichora had collapsed the architect was not bound to the original plan as strictly as he would have been had the cella trichora been standing. But we seen, for example, that he preferred not to remove the remnants of the cella trichora still rising above floor level at the southeast corner (Pls. 26, 2; 27, 2). This obliged him to erect the eastern wall of the southern sacristy further west; his determination to utilize the foundations of the cella trichora for his new edifice decided the position also of the southern and western walls; the curtain wall on the north completed the room. Similar considerations and the question of symmetry determined the position of the northern room.

Evidently the purpose, for which these lateral chambers were erected, was equally well attained whether their doors opened into the choir or into the side aisles. Usage favored the position of the doors on the west facing the side aisles; to deviate from an established custom required some reason; such a reason existed at Siyâgha; it was the presence of a monument of special significance at the eastern end of the southern aisle (Pl. 43, 2). We presume, for the present, that such a monument existed at that spot when the sixth century basilica was

1 Regarding el-Mekhayyat see *RAC* 13 (1936), pp. 129 ff.; regarding Madaba see *NBAC* 1899, pp. 149 ff.

2 See *Gerasa*, pp. 181 ff.; *ECS* pp. 187 ff. and passim; *ACB* passim.

3 At Gerasa the churches of St. John, St. George and St. Cosmas; see *Gerasa*, p. 181; in Syria half a dozen instances are known; see *ECS* p. 189, n. 338.

4 In Syria 3 examples were noted; see *ECS* p. 189, n. 338.

built; the architect was obliged to show consideration for that monument; hence he omitted the door between the southern sacristy and the southern aisle. No monument of the same type existed on the north side of the basilica; but there too the door of the sacristy opens only into the sanctuary, not into the side aisle. The arrangement on the south, no doubt, influenced the arrangement on the north side.

The two lateral chambers at Siyâgha, as elsewhere, had a special name and a special purpose. Kaufmann[1] informs us that they are known as prothesis and diaconicon, as sacristies, as pastophoreia and secretaria. The earliest Christian example of such sacristies dates from the year 372, but the Christian sacristies had their antecedents in pagan temples of the 2nd century A. D.[2]

In the prothesis the offerings for the sacrifice were prepared and from there they were brought to the altar. In the diaconicon the vestments, sacred vessels and the liturgical books were kept. The latter room is often directly connected with the apse.

Crowfoot[3] has made a careful study of the ancient literature dealing with the diaconicon and the prothesis in connection with the numerous churches cleared by him at Gerasa. He reached the conclusion that the chapels found in connection with many of the churches at Gerasa were fitted to serve as a sort of prothesis; where they are wanting other rooms were found which might have served the same purpose. At Siyâgha there are a number of chapels which might have served the same purpose, provided that such a place was required by the liturgy used there.[4] In this case neither of the rooms on either side of the sanctuary need be considered a prothesis, they may have served another purpose. Crowfoot suggests that these lateral chambers served as sacristies or vestries, in which lamps and other properties were kept. This was probably the use to which the lateral chambers at Siyâgha were put.

5. *The nave and the aisles*. Pls. 37-39; 43-45; 161,2. The body of the basilica consists of a hall divided into a central nave and two side aisles by two rows of columns. This hall measures 23.50 × 13.10 m. on the interior. The foundations of the walls were not explored owing to the mosaic pavements

1 *HCA* p. 170.

2 See *ECS* p. 14 and Ill. 6, A & B.

3 *Gerasa*, pp. 177 f., 181 ff.

4 See *ECS* p. 175; FitzGerald, *Beth-Shan* III, p. 20, observes: "In churches of the Byzantine rite the Diaconicon (or vestry) is on the south side of the altar, and on the north is the Prothesis, in which the bread and wine are placed before the Liturgy and whence they are carried in procession to the altar. We cannot, however, be certain that any of the rooms here (namely, in the Round Church at Beth-Shan,) served for this purpose, as in the Liturgy of St. James, which may have been in use at Beth-Shan, it would seem that the bread and wine were on the altar from the beginning and consequently there was no need for a Prothesis (A. Fortescue, *Lesser Eastern Churches*, p. 348); moreover, churches earlier than the reign of Justin II, even in Constantinople, were originally built without either Prothesis or Diaconicon (E. Freshfield, *Archæologia*, XLIV (1873), p. 383)."

on both sides; above the floor level 3-4 courses of the walls are preserved; these average about a meter in thickness. The eastern walls are identical with those of the lateral chambers; some characteristics of their masonry were noted above. The northern and southern walls are common with those of the adjoining chapels.

By referring to Fig. 8,5 and to Pls. 47,1; 48,1 & 2, a number of interesting points of the southern wall can be noted. First of all the apse wall of the baptistery does not bond in with the wall of the basilica but is built against it (Pl. 47,1). West of the apse there was formerly a door (Pl. 48,1) with a rounded arch of which a springer is still in situ on the east side of the door. This door was walled up when the baptistery was built, and another door was made further west (Pl. 48,2). Between the old and the new door the wall has a straight joint and there is a slight variation in the coursing. The straight joint indicates that an addition was made at this point. The stones are of medium size; some of the stones west of the joint have a low flat boss, others have a plain surface. The same characteristics may be noticed in the remaining walls, which still survive.

In the northern wall there was also an opening opposite to the walled up door in the southern wall (see Pl. 48, 1, in the background, left). If it was originally an opening through the wall, then it was only large enough for a man in a stooped position to squeeze through. It survived as a kind of niche at floor level.

Of the 4 doors, which were in use during the 6th and following centuries, one is in the northern wall, two in the southern and one in the western. The doors in the northern and southern walls give access to the adjacent chapels; the door in the western wall is the main and only entrance to the basilica (Pl. 39, 2). The main entrance to the basilica is 1. 47 m. wide on the exterior; the rebated interior is 1. 57 m. wide. One of the stones on the north side of the door has a recess for the insertion of the lock or bar by means of which the door could be closed from the interior. The height of the main door is uncertain. It had a large lintel which was found lying in the doorway; it is broken into two pieces which may be seen standing on end near the north and south sides of the door in Pls. 38, 2; 49, 2. Originally the lintel measured 242 × 66 × 35 cm.; it has a drafted margin 8-9 cm. wide on the one face; otherwise the surface is flat and without ornament.

One of the stones of the main door with a rebated side, which shows that it had been used as a stop, is decorated with a carved cross enclosed by two concentric circles (Pl. 56, above). This stone was discovered on the top step of the narthex on one of the preliminary trips to the site; it was of special interest to us, since it was the first case in which the symbol of Christianity was observed at Siyâgha. Both Conder and Schumacher expressly state that they could not find any trace of a cross at Siyâgha. In the course of the excavations we discovered at least 88 stones on which the cross is carved (see Pls. 56-58); and it is found on numerous other objects. The crosses all differ from one another in one or the other detail; the peculiarity of the cross in question is the zigzag line incised between the two concentric circles enclosing the cross. The stone measures 88 × 36 × 22 cm. and the circle enclosing the cross was 40 cm. in d.; it seems to have extended to the adjoining stones.

Near each of the other three doors, inside the basilica, the lintel was found; there is nothing noteworthy about the lintels of the two doors in the southern wall, but the lintel over the door of the northern wall (Pl. 55, 2) deserves special notice, since it is the only lintel found at Siyâgha which is decorated with a cross. The stone measures 164 × 63 × 24 cm.; the cross which decorates the lintel is enclosed by a double circle 50-52 cm. in d.; the space between the two incised circles has a series of incisions which suggest a rope design.

Conder states that "another peculiarity by which Byzantine buildings may be known, is that a large and heavy lintel, generally having the cross upon it, once existed above every door. The weight in many cases is really taken by a low relieving arch above, but the lintel seems to have been used invariably, and is often all that remains to show the site of a large building." [1]

None of the doors of Siyâgha have a molded frame or any other ornamentation besides the cross or crosses. The same holds good of the majority of early churches in which old classical material is not reused.[2]

The walls of the basilica were covered with a double coat of plaster without any trace of other ornaments. This plaster was still adhering to the walls when the excavations began, but when it was exposed to the air most of it fell off.

Each of the two colonnades, which divide the basilica, consists of 8 columns and responds at the ends of the colonnades. The colonnades are not continued beyond the chancel screen. There are two columns at the ends of the apse in line with the columns of the body of the church; the space between the colonnades of the nave and the columns near the apse is occupied by the walls of the sacristies.

The columns do not rest on a stylobate, but each column has its own foundation built of stones. We could not examine the foundations of all the columns; those which we examined generally have one course of stones as a foundation. The column at the eastern end of the northern colonnade stands on a foundation consisting of a number of courses; the excavations revealed at least three, which form a pier 1.40 m. h.; it is very probably higher than this, since we did not reach its base. Between this pier and the eastern respond

1 *SWP* 3, p. 445.
2 See *Gerasa*, p. 186; *ECS* p. 219.

there is a wall, but such a wall was not observed elsewhere between the columns.

The spacing between the columns is irregular; it varies between 1.70 – 1.84 m.; between the columns and the responds the space varies between 1.20 – 1.50 m.

None of the columns were standing when the excavations began (see Pl. 37). They had all been overthrown, very probably by an earthquake, and had fallen in a northerly direction; the columns of the northern colonnade fell against the northern wall and were heaped in the northern aisle; those of the southern colonnade fell into the nave, where they remained at full length. The surface of the columns, which was exposed to the weather, was badly consumed; but the part which was buried and protected was well preserved. We found that the entire column had been covered with a coat of plaster in its final period of use; this was probably done to conceal the defects of some of the columns.

The bases of all the columns were found in situ (see Pls. 37, 2; 43, 2; 93 & 94). Most of the bases have pieces chipped off; the one which is preserved almost perfectly is illustrated in Fig. 10, C and in Pl. 44, 2. Its plinth is partially buried beneath the mosaic pavement which encloses it. In general the plinths, which we were able to measure, were 80 cm. sq. and varied in height between 18-30 cm. The plinth in question preserves traces of the plaster which covered it. The molding consists of the torus and four flat fillets. This type of flattish moldings is very similar to that used for the bases of the half and double columns (see Fig. 6, 2, L & M; Pls. 31 & 32). They are probably closely related also in time; the one group belonging to the fourth, the other to the fifth century; this latter class continued in use in the sixth century basilica.

The shafts of the columns consist of two or three drums which average about 3.70 m. in length; and 60-55 cm. in d.; they have a fillet about 12 cm. wide at each end. Forty-one drums were found in the basilica; nine columns, therefore, had three drums each, and seven two each. One drum of each column was replaced on its base, the rest are near the side walls. The shaft of the easternmost column of the southern colonnade has a rectangular socket cut into the side to receive the end of a beam.

Sixteen capitals were found in the basilica; 15 are of one type and one of another; all were required for the 16 columns. Typical capitals of the basilica are illustrated in Fig. 10,1, A & B and in Pl. 45. They all vary somewhat in details; we may distinguish a low squatty variety, represented by the one illustrated in Pl. 45, below; and a taller variety, which is quite graceful in form (Pl. 45, above and center). These two varieties measure between 50-62 cm. in height, 55 cm. across the base and 77 cm. across the top at its greatest width. In general these capitals resemble those of the Corinthian order, but their ornamentation is peculiar; the leaves and caulicoles are present, but the former are not acanthus leaves and the latter have no real volutes.

The leaves of the taller capitals resemble those of the fern, whilst the leaves of the squatty capitals remind one of the familiar shell motif often used in conches. Each capital has four leaves, which have a broad and flat central vein and fluted leaflets with rounded tips; many of the leaflets contain a pellet, which reminds one of the sporangia or spore cases of ferns. Very probably the sculptor intended to represent fronds of ferns. Owing to these spore-bearing leaves, which are characteristic of these capitals, we may call them "sporophyl" capitals.

The caulicoles are represented by two pairs of flat bands on each side of the abacus; the bands end in a depression containing a pellet, like that in the leaflets of the fronds. These pellets, which look like the heads of nails by means of which the bands are affixed to the abacus, are supposed to suggest the volutes of the classical caulicoles.

The pellets, so characteristic of these capitals, are found also on other capitals at Siyâgha described above.

The "sporophyl" capitals were observed by a number of visitors to Siyâgha. Conder[1] makes mention of their "rude foliage" which, he thinks, resembles "the work of the Basilica of Justinian in the Aksa mosque". Schumacher[2] compares the leaves at the four corners of the capital with palm leaves or with a series of olive leaves; he noted the tiny round ornaments of the single leaves and of the volutes. He compares these capitals with those which he saw at Tell Umm el-ʿAmâd, in Transjordan.[3] They may also be compared with the capitals from Beersheba.[4]

A sixteenth capital of the same type as those used in the basilica was found in the southern monastery, but it is too small for the colonnade of the nave, so we suggested above that it was used for the colonnade of the chancel screen.

The sixteenth capital required for the colonnade of the nave may have been broken, when the fifth century basilica was destroyed or suffered damage, and in the restored basilica another type of capital was supplied for one of the columns. This capital (Pl. 44,1) is smaller than the average capital of the basilica; it is only 18 cm. high, 52 cm. across the base and 60 cm. across the top. Its ornamentation consists of a broad wavy incised line on the sides of the abacus and on the cavetto molding below it. This type of capital resembles those of the cella trichora, which also consist merely of an abacus and a cavetto.

1 *SEP* p. 155.
2 *ZDPV* 16 (1893), p. 165.
3 G. Schumacher, *Abila of the Decapolis*, London, 1889, pp. 25 ff., nos. 1-3.
4 *PEF Ann.* 3, Pl. XXVII, 2; see Watzinger, *DP* 2, Tafel 37, Abb. 93.

The dimensions of the various parts of the columns differ slightly, but they seem to have averaged about 4.85 m. in height above the floor level. This corresponds farely well with what we know regarding columns from other sites.[1]

We know very little about the upper part of the church. Probably the columns carried arches which supported a wooden roof covered with tiles; there were glazed windows whose frames and tracery were made, in part, of small tiles and plaster.

There were very few stones in the nave when excavations began (see Pl. 37, 1 & 2). From this we conclude that the superstructure was mostly of wood, which has completely disappeared; not a single piece of wood was found in the nave, but near the top of the stones which filled the northern sacristy a few beams were found in a decayed condition.

Among the stones and along the northern side of the basilica and north hall a number of broken roof tiles were found. The good tiles were perhaps taken away with the wood.

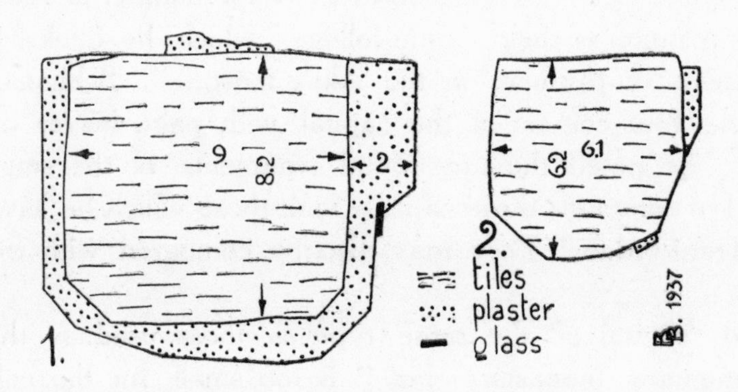

Fig. 12.

A large number of small tiles was found in the church and north hall. Their chief characteristics and use may be studied by referring to Fig. 12 and Pl. 157, 51-53. In Pl. 157, 51 the form and size of these tiles may be seen. The form may be compared with the heel of a shoe. They are not perfectly flat; at times one surface is slightly concave; there may be 6 straight sides or 3 straight and one curved side. The largest of these tiles measures $9.3 \times 9 \times 2\frac{1}{2}$ cm.; the smallest $5.8 \times 5.7 \times 2\frac{1}{2}$ cm.; there are various intermediate sizes.

The surface of these tiles is covered with plaster; frequently a number of these small tiles is plastered together so as to form a small post. The post is plastered on three sides, the fourth is unplastered. One such post has a piece of glass on one side held in place by a layer of plaster; see Fig. 12, 1 and

[1] Regarding Syria see *ECS* p. 235; regarding Southern Judea see *ACB* passim.

Pl. 157, 53. This piece of glass makes clear the purpose of the tiles and posts. They served as window frames and mullions. The unplastered side of the post was placed against the stone wall enclosing the window opening ; the three sides which were visible were coated with plaster ; a plate of glass covered the opening and it was held firmly in place by another layer of plaster placed over the edges of the glass plate.

Window frames made of tiles are mentioned by Kaufmann.[1] Such tiles were observed on the Ophel Hill of Jerusalem[2] and in the monastery at Beth-shan ;[3] in the latter place they were also plastered together to form a post.

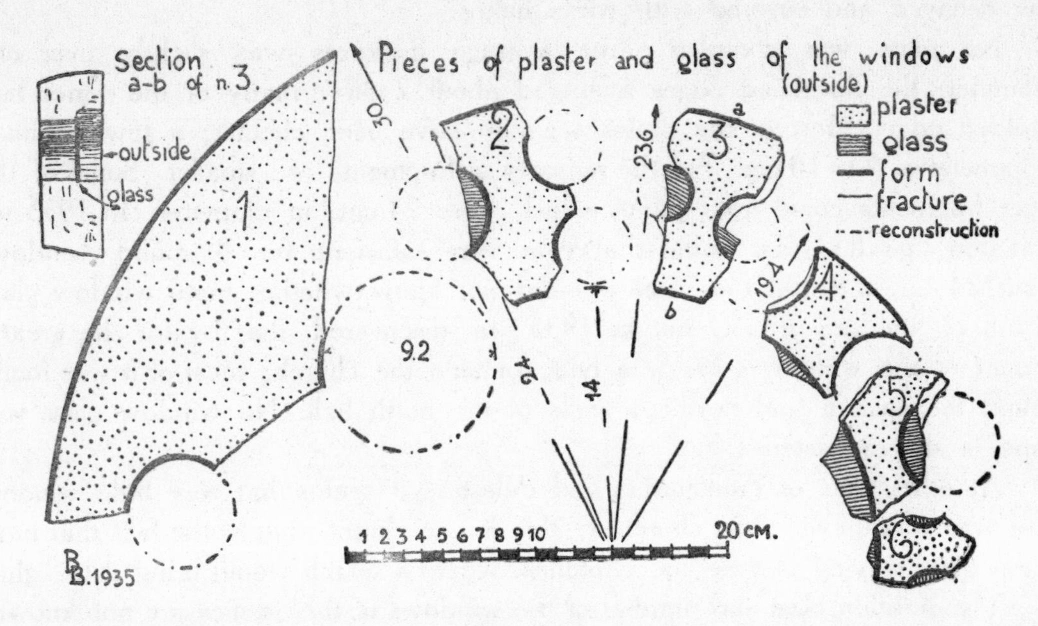

Fig. 13

Besides the tiles, plaster alone was used to form the tracery of windows. Some fragments of this plaster tracery are illustrated in Fig. 13 and Pl. 139, Figs. 1 and 2. Only 9 fragments were found in 1933 and one more in 1935, but there were undoubtedly more of them. In Pl. 139, Fig. 2, one can distinctly recognize the two layers of plaster and see between them fragments of the glass which closed the small openings in the window. The openings were generally round, but probably not always. The window to which this tracery belonged

1 *HCA* p. 171, Abb. 58 ff.

2 *PEF Ann.* 5, pp. 72, 84, 124.- Here FitzGerald calls them "floor-tiles".

3 *Beth-Shan* IV, p. 3. FitzGerald mentions the discovery "of a number of small tiles, 9 centimetres square, coated with plaster, some of which were laid one above the other so as to form small piers"; in this case he does not suggest the use to which they had been put, but since they were found near the chapel door, they may have come from a window which was above the door. — Father Bagatti saw similar tiles in the church at Kh. el-Merd.

was round. At Gerasa was found "one fragment of the stucco tracery in which two "bulls-eyes" were set side by side (Plate XXXV, b)".[1] Chitty reports similar tracery from St. Euthymius' monastery.[2] Stone tracery was also used at Siyâgha as is evident from the fragments found near the western monastery (Fig. 10, 8).

Broken glass panes were found inside the church and along the north side of the north hall; the fragments were most abundant immediately east of the north hall. Most of this glass is blue and transparent; inside the church some fragments of yellow, brown, red, green and black glass were recovered; all the glass is transparent except the black, which is opaque. Much of the glass is now decayed and covered with white flakes.

No pane was complete; the average thickness was slightly over one millimeter; the thickened edges averaged about 2 mm.; many of the panes had a folded edge. Most of the panes seem to have been circular; a few still have a diameter of 9 to 10 cm., but the majority of fragments are smaller. Some of the larger fragments come from panes which were 24 cm. in diameter. In 1933 we estimated that the glass found that year was sufficient for 8 round windows about 24 cm. in d.; at that time we did not know whether more window glass existed on the site or not, but in 1935 we discovered that by far the greater amount of the window glass was lying outside the church; most of it was found around the eastern and northern walls of the north hall. No window glass was found in the monasteries.

At other sites of Transjordan and Palestine it seems that very little window glass was found even near churches; this is, no doubt, due to the fact that most of the glass is lying outside the churches, where a search would bring it to light.[3]

The position, size and number of the windows of the basilica are not known. A few stones, which most probably belonged to windows, suggest small openings with a rounded arch and a splayed sill (Pls. 58,4; 35,4); but it is not certain whether these stones belonged to the church or to one of the other buildings.

The pavement of the nave and aisles consisted of mosaics; there are two levels; where they were worn out, they were repaired with plaster. Further details are given in the chapter on mosaics.

The tombs beneath the eastern end of the nave have been described above.[4]

The pulpit stands at the eastern end of the nave against the southern part of the chancel; it was placed partly on the mosaic pavement of the nave and partly on the steps between the nave and the chancel; one stone, at the east end, is on the mosaic pavement of the chancel. An opening in the

1 *Gerasa*, p. 187.
2 *QS* 1928, p. 177.
3 See *Gerasa*, pp. 186 f.
4 See pp. 37 f.

southern end of the chancel gives access to the pulpit. See Fig. 11,1 & 2; Pls. 39,1 & 2; 41,1; 43,1 & 2; 161,1. In its present condition the pulpit consists of a raised platform and an hexagonal stone base on the western side of the platform. This hexagon measures 117 × 92 × 17 cm. and has four hexagonal sockets for posts which supported the western extension of the pulpit's platform. This stone is not in its original position; two of the sockets filled with plaster are inserted partially beneath the western end of the platform, so that no posts could have stood in them in their present position.

A similar hexagonal stone, but without sockets, was found in the north hall in the same position as the pulpit of the basilica. The Dominicans found a stone of the same type with six sockets at Maʿin[1] and another at St. Stephen's Jerusalem.[2] At Gerasa, it seems, that no such stone was observed; but in the church of SS. Cosmas and Damian the ambo differed from all the rest in this that it rested on three little columns.[3]

Near the northern side of the pulpit was found a rectangular slab of hard limestone which measures 107 × 78 × 15 cm. (Fig. 11,3). This stone has the proportions which would be required by the western extension of the pulpit's platform; moreover, grooves in the lower surface prove that it rested on a frame of some kind, and the sockets in the upper surface could have served for the balusters of a railing enclosing the pulpit. Owing to all these details and to the position in which the slab was found, it is tempting to bring it in relation to the pulpit. But by referring to Pl. 46,1, it will be observed that one of the two rectangular sockets is scarcely visible and hence could not have been a real socket for a baluster; moreover, the round depression had a piece of glass plastered into place, as if to cover a relic of some kind; it is this fact which induces me to consider this stone as the slab of an altar. See p. 56. Other material will, no doubt, be found in the course of time to clear up this problem; here it suffices to call attention to it.

The eastern end of the southern aisle is occupied by the stone monument illustrated in Pl. 43,2. This monument is something which is peculiar to the basilica at Siyâgha and for this reason deserves special attention. It is 2.83 m. l., 1.22 m. w. and 1.50 m. h.; at the northwestern corner there are narrow stairs consisting of 6 steps. There is no access to these stairs from the south aisle; a narrow curtain wall between the monument and a pilaster, built against the southeastern side of the column at the eastern end of the southern colonnade, hinders this. The stairs can, however, be reached from the sanctuary by a narrow passage near the pulpit. The entire monument was plastered.

1 *RB* 47 (1938), p. 230, 7 and Fig. 1, e.
2 Ibid. n. 4.
3 *Gerasa*, p. 246.

The position and character of this monument are worthy of note. It stands at the very place where most basilicas have a door joining the southern aisle with the southern sacristy. Already above we noted that the presence of this monument induced the architect to depart from an accepted tradition ; primarily on its account he omitted the door between the southern aisle and the southern sacristy, and joined the latter exclusively with the sanctuary. The monument, to which such an important change in the plan of the basilica is due, is, no doubt, the cenotaph of Moses mentioned by pilgrims as early as the fourth century.

Aetheria informs us that, when she visited the memorial of Moses on Mount Nebo, she saw near the pulpit "a place a little, as it were, higher, occupying as much space as memorials are wont to occupy" ("Intra... ecclesiam, in eo loco ubi pulpitus est, vidi locum modice quasi altiorem, tantum hispatii habentem, quantum memoriæ solent habere"). A glance at Pl. 43, 2, will convince the reader that the description fits the monument in question ; it is near the pulpit, visible on the left ; and it is somewhat higher than the pulpit, which, in its present condition, is 79 cm. high (see Fig. 11, 2 A), whilst the cenotaph is 1.50 m. h., that is, 71 cm. higher. Furthermore, the monument occupies as much space as memorials or cenotaphs are wont to occupy.

Such cenotaphs are still to be seen all over Palestine and Transjordan ; they all represent an ancient tradition and some are very old. They are to be seen in Jewish,[1] Moslem[2] and Christian shrines ;[3] many of them were erected in honor of Old Testament personages, such as the patriarchs,[4] the prophets,[5] Aaron[6] and Moses.[7] Thus, for example, the shrine in honor of Aaron on Mount Hor, near Petra in Transjordan, contains a cenotaph in honor of Aaron in the mosque proper, whilst his tomb is supposed to be in the grotto below. The mosque stands on the site of an ancient trefoil church which resembled the cella trichora of Moses on Mount Nebo. From the reconstruction of Wulzinger[8] we see that in the trefoil church on Mount Hor the cenotaph of Aaron occupied the same place, on the south side of the chancel and at the eastern end of the southern aisle, as the cenotaph of Moses on Mount Nebo.[9]

1 For example at Meiron in Galilee, in honor of Rabbi Simeon Ben Jochai and his son Eleazar; see *SWP* I, p. 253; *QS* 1919, pp. 112-117; ibid. 1932, pp. 78-82, especially p. 79.

2 See T. Canaan, *Mohammedan Saints and Sanctuaries in Palestine*, in *JPOS* 4 (1924), pp. 22 ff.

3 For example, the monument of St. George at Lydda; see Meistermann, *Guide to the Holy Land*, London, 1923, p. 73.

4 At Hebron; see Vincent and Mackay, *Hébron*, Paris, 1923, passim.

5 At Jebel Osha in honor of Hosea; see Press, *Neues Palaestinahandbuch*, Wien, 1934, p. 413; Duncan, *QS* 1927, pp. 192 ff.; De Vaux, *RB* 47 (1938), pp. 407 f.

6 Wiegand, *Sinai*, pp. 136 ff.; Forder, *Petra, Perea and Phœnicia*, London, 1923, pp. 53-55; Savignac, *RB* 45 (1936), pp. 259 ff., Pl. XIII and Figs. 10-12.

7 See L. A. Mayer, *Two Inscriptions of Baybars*, in *QDAP* 2 (1933), pp. 27-32.

8 See in Wiegand, *Sinai*, p. 144, Abb. 140.

9 The place against the eastern wall of the south aisle seems to have been a favored position for tombs; see Wiegand, *Sinai*, pp. 136 ff.; FitzGerald, *Beth-Shan* IV, pp. 3 f. and Pl. XIV.

In the modern mosque in honor of Aaron a green pall is spread over the top and sides of his cenotaph and votive lights are kept burning near it; these immediately attract the attention of the visitor to that particular spot. No doubt, something similar attracted the attention of Aetheria to the cenotaph of Moses when she entered the church at Mount Nebo. Upon enquiring into the meaning of that place she learned from the monks that the monument had something to do with the sepulture of Moses.[1]

It is natural to expect that the cenotaph of Moses should have survived in some form or other in all the churches erected at Mount Nebo. Regarding the church of the 5th century we know that pilgrims saw there not only an altar, but also a second object, which is rendered by Raabe[2] by the term "table"; this, I presume, was the cenotaph of Moses. In the sixth century church we actually have a monument near the pulpit which corresponds remarkably well with the one described by Aetheria; we conclude that this is the cenotaph of Moses. We are, of course, aware of the fact that the pulpit, which stands on the mosaic pavement of the sixth century church, is not the identical pulpit which Aetheria saw, at least it need not be the identical one in every detail; the same holds good of the cenotaph; both, however, carry on the same tradition; were it not for Aetheria, we would not have known the true meaning of the monument at the eastern end of the southern aisle of the basilica.

At the eastern end of the northern aisle of the basilica there is no special monument. About 50 cm. above the level of the mosaic floor a thick layer of ashes overlies débris, which was not removed in order that at some future time its true meaning could be investigated. See Pl. 91, 1.

Other details regarding the interior of the basilica will become clearer when we describe the mosaic pavements. Besides the objects already mentioned, and a number of marble, iron and glass fragments nothing else was found inside the basilica. It is noteworthy that inside the basilica practically no pottery vessels were found; coins occurred only in two tombs.

6. *The narthex.* Pls. 49, 1 & 2; 161, 6, 10, 11, 30, 29; see 38, 1 & 2; 54, 2; 55, 1; Fig. 9. The basilica of Siyâgha has a narthex, which extended, originally, along the whole western side of the church and its adjoining chapels (Pl. 161, 11, 10, 6, 30), but later was limited to the breadth of the basilica alone (Pl. 161, 6).

The state of the narthex before excavations began may be seen in Pl. 49, 1; it was cleared in 1933 (Pl. 49, 2); in 1935 the platform at the north end (Pl. 161, 11) was removed and the well-preserved mosaic pavement (Pl. 96, 1) came to light.

[1] Geyer, p. 53, no. 12.
[2] P. 85, no. 87.

The original narthex was a platform about 26½ m. l., 4.60 m. w. and on an average about 1.50 m. higher than the atrium to the west of it. The platform was formed by constructing a wall parallel to the western side of the basilica and filling the interior to the required level; on this raised surface was laid a mosaic pavement, which is sufficiently well preserved to indicate that the narthex originally extended from the northern wall of 11 to the southern wall of 30 (Pl. 161, 11, 10, 6, 30).

The later narthex was an open porch in front of the western side of the basilica; it measures 14 × 4.60 m. (Pl. 161, 6). The condition in which we found the narthex may be seen in Pl. 49. Its mosaic pavement is worn out. In front of the main entrance to the basilica, the narthex was paved with fragments of marble and a stone slab; at both sides of the main entrance, there are stone benches against the wall of the church; at the northern and southern ends of the narthex, stone bases of columns are in situ; a flight of stairs joins the narthex with the atrium; in the atrium are drums and capitals of the narthex's colonnade. The colonnade probably supported a lean-to roof. Doors from the narthex lead into the basilica and into the rooms as its northern and southern ends. Regarding the mosaic pavement see the chapter on mosaics; the other finds will be treated briefly here.

The stone slab which was found directly in front of the main entrance to the basilica is illustrated in Pl. 61, 1. Only half of the slab was used here, the other half was found in the area 12. The decorated part of the stone was placed downwards, so that its ornaments have been preserved. The material of which this slab is made is a black stone which is called "Nebi Musa". This black bituminous limestone, according to Blake,[1] "was used by the architects in the early centuries for indoor work. Pavements made of this material exist in the ninth century convent north of Jericho where also it has been used for internal square columns." At Siyâgha this same material was used for several other ornamented slabs, a post and balusters.

In its present condition the slab consists of 7 fragments found in 1933, illustrated in Pl. 61,1, and another small fragment found in 1935, which is not illustrated. The slab measures 111 × 81 × 7½ cm.; when complete it was perhaps 145-150 cm. l. The frame of the slab is plain; its sunken panel is decorated with interlacing circles and half circles filled in with two types of floral crosses, whilst the curved and grooved bands of the circles are broken to form a third type of symbol known as the swastika.

This panel should be compared with the one found in the palace of the Umayyad Period (about A. D. 705-750) at Khirbet el-Mefjer, north of Jericho, and illustrated in *QDAP* 6 (1938), Plate LIX, 1. There the field is divided into

[1] *The Stratigraphy of Palestine and its Building Stones*, p. 45.

lozenges by a fret whose straight lines intersect to form swastikas; the lozenges contain four-petalled and elongated six-petalled rosettes alternating with one another. The latter are very similar to the floral crosses used along the border and in the central horizontal row of circles on the Siyâgha panel; here each arm of the cross has three petals; resulting in 12 petals in all; the lower pair of petals of each arm intersects the petals of the adjoining arms. The former rosettes with their four pod-shaped petals are similar to the other type of floral cross on the Siyâgha panel whose four arms consist of petals overlapping one another and terminating in double lobes. In spite of the close similarity of the two panels, it is obvious that the rosettes of the Siyâgha panel strive after the cruciform effect, whereas the rosettes of the el-Mefjer panel studiously avoid that effect. The latter is to be expected in a Moslem palace, the former in a Christian church. The similarities indicate a close proximity in date; the Christian panel may date from the 7th century A. D., the Moslem panel from the 8th century.[1]

That crosses were intended by the floral ornaments on the panel from Siyâgha, which we have described, becomes more apparent when we compare this panel with a second one also found at Siyâgha and illustrated in Pl. 61,2. This slab was found in the upper part of the ruins against the western wall of room 15. It is made of the same material as the other slab and is incomplete; its two fragments form a piece which measures $55 \times 50 \times 6\frac{1}{2}$ cm.; when complete the slab was probably as large as the other one and had the same type of ornamentation, though all the details differ slightly. The intersecting circles and half circles are formed by a simple flat band, not by a grooved band as in the other; the circles are not broken by straight lines to form swastikas; the diameter of the circles is only 18 cm., in the former it is 26 cm.; the other decorations have similar relative proportions; the crosses are of three types, of which one resembles the floral cross used on the other panel. Each arm of this floral cross is three-lobed, but the lobes are not grooved as in the former, nor do the adjacent lobes intersect. Of the other two types of crosses, the one is a typical Greek cross, whose arms have straight sides; the other is a floral cross with four rounded lobes as arms and a bud in the center, as in the case of one of the el-Mefjer types of rosettes.

In this connection we may note also the black stone post, illustrated in Pl. 61,5, which has a cross cut into one side; the arms spread and end in a quarter circle; the depression was probably intended to receive a metal cross. The other black stone slab, illustrated in Pl. 61,3, was decorated with a number of crosses. All this material belonged to the Christian shrines at Siyâgha.

[1] Other interesting parallels have been found at the Qasr el-Heir el-Gharbi in Syria; see *Syria* 20 (1939), p. 328 and Pls. XLIV, 1; XLVII, 2 & 4.

The fact that the first mentioned slab was broken up and placed in front of the main entrance to be walked over may possibly indicate a period when the Christians were no longer in charge of the shrine at Siyâgha; that, at least, was the writer's first impression. The miserable repair of the pavement in front of the main entrance by means of this stone slab and a number of broken marble slabs, while the rest of the pavement was not repaired at all, seems to point to a poverty-stricken community, which, very probably, used the church as a place of refuge, rather than a place of worship.

The stone benches on both sides of the entrance to the basilica were constructed after the narthex had been paved with mosaics; they stand on the mosaic pavement and helped to preserve at least a part of it. The bench on the south side of the door (Pl. 49, 2) rises in a series of steps towards the south, as if to give access to the roof of room 30. The bench on the north side of the door contained a drum of a medium-sized stone shaft and a marble capital of the same type as those used in the Theotokos chapel (Pl. 60, Fig. 2,1; compare with Pl. 131, Fig. 2, top and center).

Of the colonnade along the western side of the narthex two stone bases remain in situ, whilst other material of the same lies in the atrium below. All this material was derived from earlier structures on the site.

The base at the southern end of the narthex (Pls. 49, 2; 54, 2; 31, 2) was obtained from the cella trichora; it is a typical double base. Corresponding to this double base, there are three drums of a double shaft measuring 35½,40 and 97 cm. respectively, or 172½ cm. all together. No double capital was observed.

At the northern end of the narthex a base of a different type is still in situ; its characteristics may be seen in Fig. 5, 2. Drums of a shaft that might fit this base are lying in the atrium and one is in cistern 8; the 5 drums lying in the atrium measure 50, 66, 112, 118 and 121 cm. in length respectively; their total length, 467 cm., is more than twice that of the double column. The shaft in the cistern, which is partially buried, was not measured; it is longer than any of the other shafts. These shafts suffice for three columns; taken together with the double column at the southern end, we may assume that the colonnade of the narthex consisted of 4 columns. One of the shafts had two sockets for beams.

To this colonnade, no doubt, belong four capitals found in the atrium; one is without ornaments, like the one found east of the basilica (Pl. 60, Fig. 1, 2); the other three (Pl. 59, 5-8 [6=7] and Fig. 5, 1) resemble one found on the northeastern slope (Pl. 60, Fig. 2,2).[1] They are all in a very poor state of preservation. This type of capital with uncut leaves is very common in

[1] See p. 48.

all the surrounding regions.[1] The pellets in the leaves are somewhat more uncommon; recently a capital was seen at Maʿin which has pellets between the leaves.[2]

Like the shafts, so the capitals seem to indicate that the narthex was an open porch with four columns, which supported a lean-to roof.

The stairs between the narthex and the atrium consist of 5-6 steps, 5 on the south, 6 further north; they extend beyond the limits of the later narthex both on the south and on the north (Pls. 49,2; 161,6-7).

At the southern end the stairway as a whole is preserved quite well, though the individual steps have suffered greatly from use. The northern end of the staircase stood on the roof of a cistern and, when the latter collapsed, the entire flight of stairs at this end was thrown out of position. What remains of that broad stairway helps to convey some idea of the monumental character of this approach to the narthex and the church.

The northern and southern ends of the original narthex were converted into rooms, some of whose walls stand on the mosaic pavement of the narthex.

The room at the northern end of the narthex (Pls. 38,2, in the foreground; 161,10 & 11) occupies that part of the original narthex which is west of the north hall. The room has two doors; the one on the south connects it with the narthex. This southern door had a large lintel measuring 140 × 68 × 34 cm.; it is without ornaments; but near it was found a stone measuring 84 × 37 × 20 cm., which is decorated with a carved cross in a double circle 32 cm. in d. (Pl. 57,7). Another stone, measuring 95 × 38 × 16 cm., found in the atrium, is also decorated with a cross in a circle 19 cm. in d.; it may have belonged to a door of this or another room of the narthex. The western door joins this room with the area 12; between the two there is a stairway consisting of 5 steps; the top one is made of the round drum of a column.

On the interior the room is divided into two sections by responds which supported an arch that spanned the room transversely. North of the responds there is a platform (Pl. 161, 11), formed by a transverse wall 2 courses high, and behind it there is a packing of earth, stones and other materials on which

[1] See *ECS* p. 237, where we read: "The commonest type (namely, of Corinthian capital) has the general proportions and parts of a regular classic capital; but the details are left uncarved. The leaves have flat surfaces and straight edges; the volutes are often only indicated by incised lines (Ill. 257, A) or are omitted entirely. I have described this capital as the "uncut Corinthian" because it has the appearance of a capital of the Corinthian order blocked out, but with the finer details of carving left undone for lack of time or skill. The more one sees of the pre-Roman architecture of Syria, the more he is led to believe that this form of leaf, which the French call *feuille d'eau*, was not an unskilled attempt to imitate the acanthus leaf of the Corinthian capitals, but a representation of another kind of foliage, probably one of the arums. Leaves of this form were used at ʿArâk-il-Emîr early in the second century B. C." — The writer has observed the same type of capital at numerous sites in Palestine, for example, near both the Greek and Latin church at Jufna. — See some interesting varieties of this type of capital recently found at Maʿin and published in *RB* 48 (1939), Pl. I, 1-2.

[2] See *RB* 48 (1939), p. 81, Fig. 2.

a stone floor was laid. This platform at the northern end of room 10-11 reminds one of the so-called "mastabeh", which, according to Dr. Canaan,[1] is found in some Arab houses. "This plastered mastabeh", he says, "is covered with a carpet or bedding and serves as a seat in day time and as a bed at night."

Among the objects found in the room we may note a few stones, some marble and a pottery lamp. One stone (Pl. 36,10) has a large boss on which a circle is carved; another (Pl. 34,9; compare with no. 8 ibid.) has shallow moldings. A slab made of black "Nebi Mûsa" stone (Pl. 60, Fig. 3), which measures 78 × 74 × 4-8 cm., is incomplete. On the one surface there is a panel enclosed by a frame whose one side is divided into a series of bays. The same type of frame is found on a number of marble slabs illustrated in Pl. 126, 1-8, 13,20. These slabs belonged to altars. I noticed a similar slab at Antioch, Syria. Kaufmann[2] gives other examples.

One fragment of an inscribed marble slab (Pl. 121, 1) with the Greek letters : ΠΡΕ comes from here. A number of other marble fragments were found in the packing of the platform. From that packing comes a complete lamp of a type generally assigned to the 7th century (Pl. 143, 23). This lamp may serve to indicate the time when the platform was built. Another indication of time is the mosaic pavement; when the platform was made, the mosaic was still quite well preserved, as we discovered upon removing the filling below the floor of the platform. Elsewhere the floors continued in use long enough to permit the last vestiges of the mosaics to be worn away. I am of the opinion that this room need not be later than the end of the sixth or the beginning of the seventh century, and that it was used by the sacristan as his living quarters. The traces of fire in the southeast corner and the bones of animals, which had served as food, date from the final period of use.

The room at the southern end of the narthex (Pls. 54, 2; 161, 30) occupies that part of the original narthex which is west of the Theotokos chapel. It originated by inserting a wall on the west between the eastern wall of room 28 and the end column of the colonnade, and on the north across the mosaic floor of the narthex. This northern wall has a door; there is a second opening in the southern wall giving access to room 29 on the south. The mosaic pavement will be described in the chapter on mosaics.

In room 30 were found 3 stones decorated with crosses, fragments of marble, a clay brick, nails, glass, a fragment of a stone bowl, a pottery bowl, bones and a few coins.

The two coins are of the Umayyad period. The pottery bowl (Pl. 151, 37) is the first vessel of this material which came to light. The fragment of the stone bowl is of the same type as the class illustrated in Pl. 133, Fig. 1. The

[1] *JPOS* 13 (1933), p. 28; see ibid. pp. 35 ff.

[2] *HCA* pp. 180 f., where he suggests that this type of slab may have been used for a prothesis table.

material, "gneiss-schist", is soft and crumbles easily, so that it has at times been mistaken for clay; its color is dark gray; it contains sparkling particles. Among the Arabs it has a reputation of being able to cure women who suffer from fright; hence the men put some of the pieces into their pockets to take them away. The stone is pulverized and mixed with water; and in this form it is used by the patient.

The clay brick found in room 30 is of the same type as those used in room 22, the only place at Siyâgha where bricks were used, as far as we know.

Of the three stones decorated with crosses, the one illustrated in Pl. 56, center row, left, is to be noted on account of its peculiar shape, which reminded someone of a bust. The head is round; in a depression of the face is a cross in relief with 4 wedge-shaped arms hollowed out in the center. Below the head the bust has sloping shoulders and a hollow breast; the lower part is wedge-shaped. Another stone of the same type was found in the Theotokos chapel (Pl. 56, center row, right); the latter stone is a little larger and has a few additional incised lines as ornaments. Both those stones should be compared with the stones which belonged to the apexes of gables found east of the cella trichora (Pl. 35,1 & 2). There a small disk containing a cross reminds one of the head of the stones in question; there the disk crowns a gable molding, which suggests that the two stones from room 30 and from the Theotokos chapel probably were the keystones of arches above which the head with the cross was visible.

The other material from room 30 need not detain us here.

South of room 30 and the narthex there is room 29, which is on a level about 40 cm. lower than that of the narthex (Pls. 54, 2; 55, 1; 161, 29). The eastern wall shows a straight joint at the point where this room and room 30 meet; this is probably the southern limit of the original narthex, and, probably, also indicates the point where this room was added to the earlier buildings. This room is paved with large plain tesserae; the cubes are between 3-5 cm. sq. Along the northern and southern walls of this room there are stone benches.

From room 29 come fragments of marble, pottery, glass, a timble and a coin. This coin is a large Byzantine follis characteristic of the end of the sixth century; the thimble (Pl. 138, 8) is open at two ends; the glass represents lamps with hollow stems (Pl. 140, 16 ff.); the pottery sherds belong to jars with thick heavy walls, as those illustrated in Pl. 144. Among the marble fragments one, measuring 32 × 28 × 4 cm., is decorated with a six-armed star in relief enclosed by a branch with leaves; the star with its spike-shaped arms resembles one on a screen from Ascalon,[1] with this difference that the latter is without a knob or hub in the center.

[1] See Sukenik, *Ancient Synagogues in Palestine and Greece*, Pl. XIV, above, right.

Rooms 29 and 30 were probably both used by the sacristan for storing things required in the church and chapels.

The narthex in both its earlier and later form has numerous parallels in Transjordan, Palestine and Syria. The plans of churches "1" and "8" at Madaba published by Manfredi,[1] of the churches in Southern Judea published by Mader,[2] of numerous churches of Syria published by Butler,[3] show a narthex which occupies the entire western side of the church; in some cases rooms or towers are indicated at the ends of the narthex. Speaking of Northern Syria, Butler[4] says that "the churches with western portals were generally provided with a porch or narthex extending across the whole façade. The narthex, in its simplest form, consisted of six monolithic piers with architraves which carried a wooden roof. In other examples the ends of the narthex were closed with walls which were returned towards each other." The latter was the case in other parts of Syria and at Siyâgha.

The date of the narthex is not certain. Probably it was constructed as a part of the fifth century basilica; it was retained in the sixth century basilica and at this time or not much later the end rooms were added; the rooms remained in use up to the eighth century, as the Umayyad coins testify. More light will be thrown on this problem when we study the mosaic pavement.

7. *The atrium*. Pls. 49,1 & 2; 50,1; 161,7-9,12,13; see Fig. 9. The atrium, west of the basilica and narthex, is a rectangular area measuring 22 m. from east to west and 24½ m. from north to south; its level is on an average 1½ m. below that of the narthex. Only the eastern part of the atrium is paved; below the level of the pavement there are two cisterns; in the northern section of the area a number of walls exist and scattered about inside this courtyard a few other objects of interest were discovered. The condition of the atrium before excavations began may be seen in Pl. 49,1; in 1933 the stones which filled the atrium were all removed (Pl. 49,2) and in 1935 a more thorough clearance resulted in further discoveries, all of which will be treated here.

The pavement in the southeast corner of the atrium consists of large flags; directly in front of the main entrance to the basilica up to cistern 9, it consists of large tesserae, whose surface is 3-5 cm. sq.; the same type of tesserae was used in the northeast corner of the atrium, near loci 12 & 13. In the rest of the atrium no pavement was found.

Beneath the flags in the southeastern part of the atrium there is a drain which unites the catch-basin in room 28 with cistern 8 in the center of the atrium. The pavement in front of the basilica's stairway slopes towards the north and drains into cistern 9.

1 *NBAC* 1899, p. 151 and p. 163.
2 *ACB* passim.
3 *ECS* passim.
4 *ECS* p. 177; see pp. 178, 198 f.

The cistern in the center of the atrium (Pls. 49, 1 & 2; 161, 8) is about 5½ × 6 m. sq.; its sides are diagonal with the walls of the atrium. It was cut into the native rock and its sides covered with masonry which was probably plastered. The stones used for the walls are relatively small and roughly dressed; they are placed in regular courses between which there is a packing of smaller chips. The vaulted roof has fallen in and in the débris which fills the lower part of the cistern a long column shaft is partially buried. The cistern has not been cleared; it is in the same condition today as it was when the earliest explorers saw it.

Conder declares that this "vault of rudely squared stones, the joints of the masonry packed with smaller stones"... "is also a peculiarity of Byzantine work, as at Bidieh ('Memoirs,' vol. ii., p. 306), or in the Birket Isrâîl at Jerusalem."[1] According to Thomsen cisterns which are entirely lined with masonry are to be ascribed to the Roman-Byzantine period.[2]

The second cistern in the northeastern part of the atrium (Pl. 161, 9) is also cut into the natural rock; its walls are lined with masonry which is coated with plaster; against the walls are the pilasters which support round arches; the spandrels are filled with masonry; on the arches and spandrels are placed the stone slabs which form the flat roof of the cistern. The arches and roof of the southern end of the cistern have fallen and fill its interior, the northern end is in a better state of preservation. Amid the débris on the interior of the cistern one may see a number of human skulls, some bones and rags, which attracted the attention of Luynes and many who followed him. This cistern has not been cleared.

Regarding this cistern Conder writes as follows: "The roof is supported on ribs over round arches of good masonry, the voussoirs 2½ feet deep, the span 10 feet, the pier 2½ feet thick. Across these ribs a flat roofing of flags is placed – an arrangement found sometimes in Byzantine work (cf. Deir ʾArâby, 'Memoirs,' vol. ii., p. 313). A few fragments of a skeleton and rags of clothing were found in this vault, and there were traces of cement on the walls, showing that (as in other ruins) it was probably once used as a rain-water tank underground."[3]

Arches are preserved only here and in the western monastery at Siyâgha; in both cases they are semicircular[4] or flattish, so that some almost seem to be horizontal. They may be considered typical of the Byzantine period.

1 *SEP* p. 155.
2 *RLV* 2, p. 14.
3 *SEP* p. 155.
4 See *SWP* 3, p. 445, regarding this type of arch.

Cisterns are a characteristic of the atriums of many churches; [1] an interesting example was discovered recently by Gauer at et-Tâbghah.[2]

In the northern part of the atrium there are a number of walls indicated in the plan (Pl. 161) and visible in Pl. 50, 1. The one section begins near room 10 between two stairs and extends along the northern side of cistern 9 to a point somewhat west of the cistern where it comes to an abrupt end. Another section of a wall further north begins near the wall between rooms 18-19 and its eastern end overlaps the preceding wall or section of a wall. At the center these walls are preserved only at the average level of the courtyard, but at the two ends the walls rise above that level and suggest that they served some practical purpose even in the final period of the atrium's history; they probably served to form a partition by means of which the northern section of the atrium was screened off from the rest.

At the eastern end of this northern section of the atrium there is a staircase, an oven and two loci enclosed by low walls standing on the mosaic pavement (Pls. 161, 12 & 13; 49, 2; 50, 1). The staircase joins room 10 with the area 12. In the northeast corner of area 12 there was an oven built of various stones. One of the stones used for the oven formed part of the slab illustrated in Pl. 61, 1; the other part was found in front of the main entrance to the basilica and was described in that connection. Another stone, consisting of material known as "kakule", has preserved the marks of a toothed instrument and is decorated like the stone illustrated in Pl. 36, 7, but the lines of the design are simple, not double. Here was found also a fragment of a circular basalt millstone (Pl. 60, Fig. 1, 10).

West of the oven were discovered an iron knife, with a curved blade and a socket for a handle (Pl. 138, Fig. 2, 27), some eggshells and pottery sherds.

In the low stone enclosure 13, which suggests a kind of bin, were discovered a marble post (Pl. 128, below), a marble slab (Pl. 125, 29, right), decorated with a cross in a ring and enclosed by a shell motif, and a complete pottery lamp of the channel-nozzle type which still contained the blackened wick and green earth, suggestive of oil (Pl. 143, 19).

In the wall north of 13 and 12 three stones have incised ornaments on bosses; they consist of an X in a square, a rhomb and an X in a rhomb.

Further west was found another millstone (Pl. 60, Fig. 1, 8); north of the partition wall was found the fragment of the marble slab with the cross and the Greek letter Π which is the beginning of inscription XVI (Pl. 121, 1); south of the same partition wall the only funeral stela found at Siyâgha came to light

[1] See Kaufmann, *HCA* p. 175.

[2] Gauer hints at this discovery in *JPOS* 18 (1938), p. 245; the existence of such a cistern was known to the earlier explorers of the church at et-Tâbghah; see Schneider, *BVK* p. 21 and Plan I. For the existence of cisterns in the atriums of other churches see *QDAP* 3 (1934), p. 92: Suhmâtâ; ibid. 4 (1935), p. 118: Khirbet Kûfîn.

(Pl. 56, below, left);[1] near the cisterns in the atrium there are three stones hollowed out at one end so that they could serve as basins for water or as mortars; there were also a few coins and an inscribed sherd (Pl. 123, 3); [2] all this material will be referred to again later.

The atrium at Siyâgha served a twofold purpose ; it had the function of an open courtyard in front of the basilica and that of a central courtyard of a group of monastic buildings arranged on three sides of it, as in the houses of the courtyard type so familiar in all periods of Palestinian history.[3] The rooms grouped around this atrium will be treated in speaking of the monasteries.

The atrium on the western side was certainly a feature of the latest basilica at Siyâgha ; and it most probably existed already at the time of the fifth century basilica. That earlier basilica may have had a second atrium along its southern side before the two southern chapels were erected. We already mentioned the door in the southern wall of the basilica (Fig. 8, 5) which was found walled up; that door may have served to connect the basilica with a southern atrium around which there were also monastic buildings (see Pl. 161, 79-105) ; when the two southern chapels were built the plan was altered, and the basilica as well as all the chapels around the basilica could be reached only from the western atrium. This western atrium could be reached by two entrances : the one on the north through 16, the other on the south through 25 ; the latter seems to have been the main entrance; it, in turn, could only be reached by passing through the courtyard 68, on whose southern side, at 71, was the chief entrance to the entire complex.

The western atrium is a feature of a number of other churches in these regions ; the best parallels are to be found at Madaba[4] and Gerasa,[5] both in Transjordan, at id-Dêr[6] in Syria, at et-Tâbghah,[7] Beth-Shan,[8] Bethlehem[9] and Isbeita[10] in Palestine.[11]

1 See inscription XV.
2 See inscription XXXVI.
3 See Galling, *BRL* columns 267 ff.
4 *NBAC* 1899, p. 151 ; see *HCA* p. 198, Abb. 78.
5 *Gerasa*, pp. 187 f. and passim.
6 *ECS* pp. 85 ff. and Ill. 91.
7 *BVK* p. 21 and Plan I.
8 *Beth-Shan* IV, p. 4, A and Plate II, A.
9 *QDAP* 3 (1934), pp. 1-8 and passim; ibid. 5 (1936), pp. 80 f.; ibid. 6 (1938), pp. 63 ff.
10 *PEF Ann.* 3, p. 82, Fig. 14.
11 For other examples in the Negeb see *PEF Ann.* 3, Fig. 25: Abda; pp. 118 ff.: el-ʿAuja; pp. 123 ff.: Kurnub; — in Southern Palestine see *ACB* passim; — in other parts of Palestine see *QDAP* 3 (1934), p. 92: Suhmâtâ; p. 113: ʿEin Hanniya; ibid. 4 (1935), p. 118: Kh. Kûfîn.

CHAPTER V

THE CHAPELS

A. IN GENERAL

1. *Position.* Pl. 161, 3-5; see Fig. 9. In Fig. 9 one can see three chapels along the northern and southern sides of the basilica: that on the north is known as the north hall (Pl. 161, 3); of the two on the south, the one towards the east is the baptistery (Pl. 161, 4), the other towards the west is dedicated to the Theotokos (Pl. 161, 5).

2. *Purpose.* The ground plan (Pl. 161, 3-5) shows that all these chapels communicate exclusively with the basilica; from this it seems to follow that their purpose is intimately associated with that of the basilica; in other words, it seems that these chapels were destined for liturgical functions and for the administration of the sacraments. As a matter of fact, we know for certain that the southeastern chapel served for the administration of the sacrament of baptism; this presupposes a place for catechumens; the north hall may have been reserved for them. The later Byzantine liturgy required a prothesis; the southwestern chapel may have served that purpose. Other reasons for these views will be given when we speak of the chapels more in detail.

We may, however, note already here that the north hall and the southwestern chapel seem to have been used much more than the baptistery; for the mosaic pavement between the doors of those two chapels and the nave is completely worn out and had to be repaired in ancient times; the repair was made with plaster. The mosaic pavement in front of the baptistery is perfectly preserved.

3. *General condition.* The upper parts of the chapels had collapsed and those ruins concealed all that still remained in situ; see, for example, Pls. 25,1; 37, 1 & 2. The general outlines of these chapels could be made out before the excavations, but their true character was not recognized.

In 1933, whilst clearing the basilica, we discovered the doors leading into the side chapels; through these we penetrated first into the Theotokos chapel, then into the baptistery and finally into the north hall. In the same year we made clearances around the exterior of the two southern chapels (Pl. 38, 1), and in 1935 around the exterior of the north hall (Pls. 29, 2; 62, 1 & 2).

Viewed from the exterior the chapels present the appearance of two oblong rectangular halls, one on the north and the other on the south of the basilica. But on the interior there is a difference; the hall on the north is undivided and rectangular also on the interior; but that on the south is divided into two chapels each of which has an internal apse.

The walls of the north hall bond in with those of the basilica and seem to be contemporaneous with it; those of the southern chapels do not bond in with the walls of the basilica and make the impression of later additions.

These general observations may be illustrated by a detailed study of each chapel.

B. THE NORTH HALL

1. *The name.* The north hall derives its name from its position and form. The designation "north" indicates its relation to the basilica, along whose northern side it stands; the term "hall" determines its size and general appearance. Neither expression has anything to do with the purpose of the chapel.

The site chosen for the north hall is on the northern slope of the ridge parallel to the north aisle of the basilica. This site is on an average about two meters lower than the floor of the basilica's nave and aisles. An area measuring 25.40 m. from east to west and 6.90-7.90 m. from north to south was enclosed by walls; on the interior this area was raised to the level required for the floor; along the north and south wall were placed five pairs of piers which supported transverse arches carrying the roof. The roof, arches and upper parts of the walls have fallen; but the lower parts of the walls, the mosaic pavements and a few other objects serve to give us an idea of the original structure.

2. *The walls.* On an average 7-12 courses of the stone walls have been preserved (Pls. 29, 1 & 2; 62, 1; 97, 1). The foundation course is laid on a bed of hard clay; the stones used are roughly dressed. This foundation course projects somewhat beyond the rest of the wall; the corner-stone at the northeast corner projects sufficiently to impress one with the fact that it may become "a stone of stumbling and a rock of scandal".[1]

[1] It was such a stone which was the occasion for several interesting comparisons in the Bible; see *Job* 38, 6; *Psalms* 118, 22; 144, 12; *Isaias* 28, 16; 1 *Peter* 2, 6; *Ephesians* 2, 20.

The upper courses vary in height between 32-42 cm. (Fig. 8, 8); the stones used are generally carefully squared; some have a margin and boss; a few have a rough surface; but the majority are plain (Pl. 62, 1). The wall is highest at the southeast corner where it bonds in with the wall dividing the northern sacristy from the north aisle of the basilica; this shows that the north hall is contemporary with the basilica. The north wall extends beyond the western limits of the chapel.

In the uppermost surviving course of the north wall a shaft of the cella trichora was used; this shows that this part of the wall was constructed after the cella trichora had collapsed.

The western wall is identical with that of the narthex and continuous with the western wall of the basilica; the southern wall is identical with that of the basilica. The door to the north hall is in the western end of this southern wall; its lintel decorated with a carved cross was described above (p. 61).

3. *Superstructure.* Of the arches which supported the roof only the piers remain along the interior of the north and south walls (Pl. 97, 1). The arches must have resembled those used in cistern 9 and in hall 56; but very probably the roof did not consist of stone slabs, as is the case in cistern 9, since no slabs of sufficient length were found; wooden rafters were most probably used and they have disappeared. Tiles were found inside and outside the north hall, but it is not certain whether they were used to cover the roof of this hall or of the adjoining basilica. The same is to be said of the glass and small tiles which were found; we do not know whether they represent windows of the north hall or of the basilica.[1]

Along with a large amount of window glass discovered outside the eastern wall of the north hall, there was found an iron bar terminating in a pair of spirals at each end. Two other bars of the same type (Pl. 136, 118-120) were found along the outside of the atrium's western wall; there too the context suggests that the bars should be associated with windows.

4. *Ornamentation and furnishings.* On the interior the walls were plastered; probably they were also painted, at least in part, to judge from the numerous fragments of plaster with decorations in red, yellow, black and green, which were picked up outside the chapel, especially on the east and northeast. Red seems to have been the background on which designs in other colors (yellow, black and green) were executed. About 130 fragments of painted plaster were collected, but none of them preserved any designs; about 50 fragments were colored only red, and the remainder exhibited also other colors. In a few cases a coating of red over a yellow coat was observed.

[1] See pp. 64 ff.

We may recall here that the background of the wall mosaics of the cella trichora was red. In the western monastery red crosses were painted on the walls.

Similar tempora were found at el-Mekhayyat, Gerasa,[1] Umm el-Jemâl,[2] in various churches of Syria,[3] the Negeb[4] and Palestine.[5]

The chief ornamentation of the north hall is, of course, the mosaic pavement to be described more in detail in a later chapter.

Of the furnishings of the north hall practically nothing can be said with certainty. In the chapel were found fragments of balusters made of black stone, a post of the same material (Pl. 61, 5), also pieces of marble shafts and slabs. Here also were found four stones decorated with crosses (Pl. 57,16 one is illustrated) and a fragment of a basalt millstone (Pl. 60, Fig. 1, 9). What this material had to do with the north hall, we do not know.

Near the eastern end of the nave, in the same position as the pulpit in the basilica, was found lying on the mosaic pavement an hexagonal stone of the same type as that which is on the western side of the pulpit in the basilica, but it has no sockets for posts. It may be in situ and may have served as a pulpit.

5. *Purpose.* On the interior, as on the exterior, the north hall is rectangular, without an apse at the eastern end. The eastern end, however, served as a sanctuary and the western end as a nave; the former occupies two bays of the chapel, the latter four (Pl. 161, 3). The difference of purpose is indicated by the difference of level; the eastern end is higher than the western; the two parts are joined by two stone steps; in the top step one stone (Pl. 99, 1) has a shallow groove. This is the only indication we have that there may have been a screen here. The floor at the eastern end is on the same level as that of the basilica's nave and aisles, whilst that of the nave is about 50 cm. lower.

1 Crowfoot, *Churches at Jerash*, p. 38, writes: "It was with thin slabs of limestone that most of the walls were cased, though in the smaller churches they were plastered and painted; the only morsels of painting which have survived belong to the latest and poorest period and are without interest." See *Gerasa*, p. 185.

2 See *ECS* p. 181.

3 See *ECS* p. 218.

4 Regarding Isbeita see *PEF Ann.* 3, p. 89; *QS* 1935, p. 176; — 'Auja el-Hafîr, *QS* 1936, p. 217; — Abda, *PEF Ann.* 3, p. 106.

5 For example, at St. Euthymius'; see *QS* 1932, pp. 195 ff., 202. — Many churches and caves of the Judean desert contain paintings, but it is doubtful whether they go back to the Byzantine period; regarding the paintings in a cave at Kh. el-Merd see Mader, *HL* 72 (1928), pp. 33 ff.; id., *JPOS* 9 (1929), pp. 134 f.; regarding Deir el-Kelt see *SWP* 3, pp. 193 ff. and Schneider in *Römische Quartalschrift*, 1931, pp. 310 ff.; Deir el-Mukelik, *SWP* 3, p. 199; Jebel Kuruntul, *SWP* 3, pp. 201 ff.; Kusr Hajlah, *SWP* 3, pp. 214 ff., etc. — Paintings of an earlier date have come to light recently at Marwa in Transjordan; see C. C. McCown, *A Painted Tomb at Marwa*, in *QDAP* 9 (1939), pp. 1-30 and Pls. I-V; and near Ascalon in Palestine; see J. Ory, *A Painted Tomb near Ascalon*, in *QDAP* 8 (1938), pp. 38 ff., Figs. 1-2, Pls. XXV-XXIX. For the former a second or third century date is proposed, for the latter a fourth century date. — For painted tombs of the Hellenistic Period in Palestine the reader may be referred to *Painted Tombs in the Necropolis of Marissa* (*Marêshah*), by J. P. Peters and H. Thiersch edited by S. A. Cook, London, 1905.

Besides the twofold division of the north hall, in which respect it resembles the basilica and the other two chapels, there is nothing to indicate the purpose of this chapel. A liturgical purpose seems to be suggested by the twofold division of the chapel and by its close connection with the basilica. We already observed that the chapel seems to have been used very much, since the mosaic pavement between its door and the nave of the basilica was completely worn out and then repaired with plaster. What the precise liturgical purpose was, for which this hall was destined, remains a matter of conjecture.

Similar halls were found near three churches at Gerasa, where it is suggested that they were used for catechumens.[1] That sounds plausible, especially since those churches had baptisteries associated with them, where the catechumens could be baptized after their period of instruction had been completed. At Siyâgha there is a baptistery; this shows that the monks had the faculty to baptize; if they had the right to baptize, then they must have had the right to prepare candidates for that sacrament; in other words, they must have had catechumens and a place where the catechumens were instructed and permitted to assist at the liturgical functions. The north hall was an apt place for this.

Crowfoot[2] cites Chitty's references to *The Life of Cyril of Scythopolis* to show that at Mar Saba a hall in a similar position served as a diaconicon. Moreover, Chitty points out that a similar arrangement was observed in the cave of St. Theoctistus. From *The Life of St. Euthymius* it appears that the diaconicon at times served as a kind of chapter-house.

The north hall may have served one or more of these purposes simultaneously or successively.

According to Butler [3] this « hall type » of church or chapel is the simplest in form and "not only was derived from the narrow halls of Roman public buildings in this region, but also was undoubtedly used for Pagan sanctuaries."

C. THE BAPTISTERY

1. *Position*. Pls. 161, 4; 38, 1; Fig. 9. Against the southern wall of the basilica two chapels were erected which occupy an area measuring about 26.20 m. from east to west and 6.80 m. from north to south not including the western and northern walls; of these two chapels the one at the eastern end is the baptistery. It seems to occupy the site of some earlier structure; this is suggested by a closed door in the northern wall and by walls to the east of the baptistery and below its southern wall.

1 *Gerasa*, pp. 179 f., 246 f.
2 *Gerasa*, p. 178.
3 *ECS* p. 187.

The tower behind the east wall of the baptistery (Pl. 161,90) stands on the western wall of locus 90 a, which had evidently been abandoned when the tower and the baptistery were built ; I am presupposing here that the tower and the baptistery are contemporaneous. The western wall of locus 90 a, moreover, bonds in with a wall which extends towards the west beneath the southern wall of the baptistery. This can be seen best of all in Pl. 25, 2; there a man is standing in the gateway between 90a and 99. To the left of the man six courses of the southeast corner of the baptistery are visible ; the three lowest courses of the baptistery extend beyond the southeast corner up to the doorway in which the man is standing; there they bond in with the wall which runs north below the tower behind the baptistery and behind the man ; if the latter wall is earlier than the tower and baptistery it seems logical to affirm the same of the lowest courses in the southern wall of the baptistery, though the masonry in the lowest courses shows no marked difference from the masonry in the upper courses.

Regarding the character of the building which stood on the site now occupied by the baptistery nothing definite can be said. It was united with the basilica by means of a door which was walled up when the baptistery was built (Fig. 8, 5). If the door communicated with a room or building, then it probably served either as a sacristy or as a dwelling for the sacristan or some other official of the church; but it is also possible that the door opened into a portico or an atrium on the southern side of the fifth century basilica.

2. *The present condition in general.* Pls. 22, 1 ; 25, 1 & 2 ; 38, 1 ; 47-48 ; 72, 1, left; 103-108 ; 161, 4 & 90 ; Figs. 8, 4-5 ; 9. The baptistery was cleared in 1933 and proved to be one of the best preserved buildings on the site. It measures 11.20 × 6.80 m. on the exterior, not including the western and northern walls which it has in common with the Theotokos chapel and the basilica respectively ; on the interior it measures 10.50 × 6.10 m. Its walls average about 70 cm. in thickness (Fig. 8, 4); they have two faces with a filling of other materials in the core. The stones used have a plain surface, which seems to be a characteristic of the buildings of the end of the sixth century at Siyâgha ; the stones used for the earlier buildings generally have a boss. Seven to twelve courses of the walls are preserved; the walls are highest on the east.

The eastern wall does not bond in with the wall of the basilica, but is built against it; this seems to indicate that the baptistery is later than the basilica in its latest form. This eastern wall receives greater stability from a tower built behind it (Pls. 161, 90; 25, 2). The tower serves both as a brace for the eastern wall and as a bond between it and the basilica ; how efficacious this method of strenghtening the wall was, appears from the fact that this is one of the best preserved walls on the site.

The tower is built of mixed materials; some stones have a boss, others a plain surface. One stone in the eastern wall, facing the interior of the tower, is decorated with a carved cross; another stone near the top of the same wall has a small splayed opening which is plastered. There is no door in the tower, hence it does not seem to have served as a habitation, but as a brace. The interior of the tower was filled with stones, earth and other débris, such as fragments of marble, glass, etc. They throw no new light on the purpose of the tower.

The southern wall is continuous with that of the Theotokos chapel; there is no evidence of a difference in date between the two (Pl. 38, 1). The western wall is identical with that of the Theotokos chapel, and the northern one with that of the basilica (Pl. 48, 2). In the northern wall is the only door of the baptistery; it joins this chapel with the southern aisle of the basilica.

The chapel has an apse, a chancel and an undivided nave; the upper parts of the walls and the roof are no longer in situ; the floor is paved with mosaics; along the north and south walls there are stone benches; the font is still in situ; otherwise little of interest was observed.

3. *The apse.* Pl. 47, 1. The baptistery has an internal apse 2 m. deep and 3.80 m. wide along the chord. About a dozen courses of the apse are still in situ; on the interior 8-10 courses are visible; the lowest course on the interior is almost completely hidden by the mosaic pavement. The eighth course is a cornice, whose molding consists of a simple splay without any other ornament. The cornice is nearly complete, only at the southeast there is a break. In the northeast corner of the chapel the walls are preserved up to the level of the apse's cornice; there one sees that the cornice was not continued around the side walls; neither were other moldings found inside the chapel. A similar molding was used for the western wall of the atrium or the eastern wall of the western monastery, where very many such stones were found.

Butler [1] informs us that in the southern part of Syria such a splayed or "bevelled face was used almost exclusively, except in cases where old material from Pagan temples was introduced."

Above the apse's cornice two courses are partially preserved; they probably represent part of the half-dome with which the apse was roofed.

On the north and south sides of the apse there are cupboards; these openings are found in the third to the fifth courses from below; the one on the south is complete; the one on the north has a stone missing from the top. Like the rest of the walls the cupboards were plastered and in the plaster there are the marks of shelves, which have disappeared.

The walls were still covered with a coat of plaster when they were uncovered, but this has since mostly fallen off. In the plaster there are incisions, which were made for the purpose of keying on an outer coat.

[1] *ECS* p. 219.

The baptisteries at Gerasa,[1] 'Amwâs[2] and Isbeita[3] have internal apses.

4. *The chancel.* The space west of the apse is divided into two parts of unequal size by the stone base of a chancel screen (Pls. 161, 4; 47, 1; 103, 1 & 2). This stone base can be seen best in Pl. 103, 1. It has sockets for four balusters; between the sockets there are grooves for two slabs; at both ends and in the center there are openings in the screen.

The base of the chancel screen measures 6.10 m. from north to south and is 39-45 cm. wide. The rectangular holes for the balusters measure 22×25 cm.; the groove between the posts on the north is 1.22 m. l., that on the south 1.30 m.; the opening in the center is 74 cm. w., that on the north 92 cm. and that on the south 89 cm. No trace of the balusters or screens was found in the chapel, but the presence of the base with sockets and grooves shows that provision was made for a screen.[4]

The floor of the chancel and apse are on the same level as that of the nave. In the other chapels and in the basilica the floor of the chancel is higher than that of the nave.

5. *The nave.* Pl. 103, 2. The undivided nave of the baptistery is paved with mosaics like the rest of the chapel; they will be described in a later chapter. Next to the sill of the door a narrow strip was paved with marble. The lintel of the door was without ornament; near the door was found a stone decorated with a cross. The walls of the nave are not as well preserved as those of the apse; the character of the roof is not certain.

6. *Furnishings.* The chief characteristic of the baptistery is its font, which was found in situ and is almost perfectly intact. In front of the font a drum of a double column, 70 cm. long, was found standing on end; it seems to have served as a table. Along the northern and southern walls there are stone benches, 35 cm. wide, which were placed on the mosaic pavement (Pls. 47, 1; 48, 2; 103, 1 & 2; 161, 4).

The bench against the northern wall is entirely in the nave; it consists of a single layer of stones on the west and of a double layer on the east (Pl. 48, 2); corresponding to this eastern end there is on the south a solid base of masonry extending northwards (Pl. 47, 1); perhaps these two masses of masonry had nothing to do with the seats but carried an arch, like the responds in the north

[1] See *Gerasa*, Plate XLI, b and Plan XXXIII; Plate XLVIII, a and Plan XXXVII, B.

[2] See *Emmaüs*, Planche XXI.

[3] For the baptistery of the northern church see *PEF Ann.* 3, p. 82, Fig. 14; it is the chapel to the south-west of the church; for that of the southern church see *QS* 1935, Plate IV, after p. 180.

[4] Kaufmann, *HCA* pp. 227 f., thinks that pillars around a font at Abu Menas in Egypt served to suspend curtains by means of which the font could be screened off.— The screen in the baptistery between the apses of SS. John's and Cosmas' at Gerasa is supposed to date from a period when the room served some other purpose; it is supposed to have been removed when the room was transformed into a baptistery. See Crowfoot, *Gerasa*, p. 244. Whether the other baptistery at Gerasa, and those at other sites, such as 'Amwâs and Isbeita, had screens is not known.

hall. East of the southern pilaster the seats extended across the base of the chancel screen all along the wall as far as the apse.

Similar stone seats exist in the narthex, in the Theotokos chapel, at el-Mekhayyat and elsewhere. It was quite common in the Byzantine period to place such stone seats on the mosaic pavements even when they concealed interesting designs, as they did, for example, in the southeast corner of the baptistery, where one of the two birds was completely hidden by a stone which we removed.

The font is by far the most interesting object in the baptistery and deserves special notice (Pl. 47, 2). It stands on the chord of the apse (Pls. 103, 1; 161, 4), 1.05 m. from the east wall, 1.04 m. from the north and 1.30 m. from the south. The font is formed from a single yellowish brown stone, round on the outside and four-lobed on the inside down to the seats or steps, between which it is rectangular. Its lower half is inserted below the mosaic pavement, which surrounds it, so that its full height could not be ascertained; but since the basin inside the stone is 90 cm. deep, the stone itself must be somewhat over a meter high; its diameter is 1.33 m.; it rises 54 cm. above the surrounding pavement. The walls of the font are highly polished on the exterior, top and upper part of the interior; they are about 10 cm. thick; the chords of the lobes vary between 59-62 cm.; in each lobe there is a seat or step, 70 cm. below the top and 20 cm. above the floor of the font; the floor of the font is 90 cm. below the rim; it is rectangular, measuring 60 × 65 cm. In the floor there is a small hole by means of which the water was permitted to flow off.

The ornamentation of the font consists of two sunken panels with inscriptions, a cross and an anchor on the side facing the nave. The sunken panels are round and enclosed by incised lines which form circles; the latter are 37½ cm. in d., the former 28½ cm. For the Greek inscriptions carved on each panel see inscriptions II A & B (Pl. 115, 1 & 2). Between the two circles two other ornaments are carved on the rock: that on top is a cross (14 × 21 cm.), that below an anchor. The former is a symbol of faith, the latter a symbol of hope in the Christian religion. Both symbols are appropriate on a font at which baptism is administered.

The font has several cracks in the sides and one across the bottom. In order to preserve this interesting monument intact a metal hoop was placed around the rim in 1933.

A number of other fonts of this type are known in Transjordan and Palestine, but they are rarely found in situ.

In Transjordan such fonts are known to exist at Madaba and in two places near el-Kerak. The latter two will be published by Mrs. Canova in a volume on the Christian antiquities of the el-Kerak region which is ready for print; one of the two, found at ed-Deir, is illustrated in *La Terra Santa* 20 (1940), p. 3.

The font at Madaba is in a place used for storing straw; the proprietor informed the writer that it has the same form as the Siyâgha font, but is not so well preserved.

In Northern Transjordan [1] and in Northern Palestine such fonts do not seem to have come to light up to date; one is reported by Sepp [2] from Tyrus in Syria; but in Southern Palestine they are comparatively numerous; at least 13 are known; of these two exist at Isbeita [3] and one in each of the following places: Beit ʿAûwa, [4] Kh. Tekûa, [5] Kh. el-Merd, [6] Beersheba, [7] Kh. Zakarîyeh, [8] Malekatʿha, [9] Keratîya, [10] in a chapel south of the church of the Holy Sepulcher in

[1] Both fonts found in the baptisteries at Gerasa seem to have more or less the cruciform arrangement so common with the fonts in these regions, but neither seems to be a monolith. Regarding the one near St. Theodore's, see *Gerasa*, pp. 224 f., Plate XLI, b and Plan XXXIII; regarding the other near the churches of SS. John and Cosmas, see ibid. p. 244, Plate XLVIII, a and Plan XXXVII, B.

[2] *Meerfahrt nach Tyrus zur Ausgrabung der Kathedrale mit Barbarossas Grab*, Leipzig, 1879, pp. 210 ff. — See Kaufmann, *HCA* p. 227, note 1; Cabrol, *DAC* 2, col. 435, Fig. 1346.

[3] The one in the baptistery near the northern church was described by Mallon in *JPOS* 10 (1930), pp. 228 f. with a design. The basin is cut into a stone which is cruciform both on the interior and on the exterior; its depth is 90 cm. and its width 1.32 m.; each arm is about 51 cm. w. and two of the arms contain 3 steps each; the font is assigned to the sixth century. He thinks that the cruciform arrangement has a symbolical significance. The baptistery was completely cleared by the Colt expedition to Isbeita, which also discovered the baptistery and font near the southern church; see Baly, *QS* 1935, p. 177 and Pls. III, Fig. 2 & IV; this second font resembles the one in the northern baptistery; it is supposed to be of a somewhat earlier date in the sixth century than the other font.

[4] *SWP* 3, p. 321 with plan. The font is supposed to be fitted for immersion and is described as follows: "In the centre a square basin, 2 feet 3 inches side, 7 inches deep; four steps lead down, 5 inches high, 9 inches broad; the whole surrounded by four segmental recesses, the external form of the font being that of a rounded cross, the longest measurement either way being 5½ feet, and the total height outside 2 feet 4 inches." In other words, the font is four-lobed on the exterior and on the interior.

[5] *SWP* 3, pp. 368 f. with plan. It is an "octagonal font about 4 feet high and 4 feet 3 inches diameter of inscribed circle; on every other side is a design. Two of these designs represent crosses, a third is a wreath, the fourth is formed by two squares interlaced diagonally to one another. The font is of good reddish stone."

[6] *JPOS* 9 (1929), p. 126, where Mader describes it as follows: "A baptismal font worked from a single stone block, 65 cm. high and with a diameter of 1 m., in the centre of which there is a round basin of 32 cm. in depth with a diameter of 57 cm. and the frontispiece of which bears a cross in relief."

[7] *QS* 1902, p. 233 with photograph; see plan in *PEF Ann.* 3, p. 108, Fig. 43. Macalister informs us that this "large font, adapted for total immersion"... "is 5 feet in diameter, 2 feet 7 inches thick" and has a square hole in the bottom, which he thinks served "for a tenon or dowel to keep the font in position". The font is made of white limestone; it is round on the exterior, four-lobed on the interior and has steps in all the arms; one pair has two steps, the other one.

[8] *ARP* 2, pp. 356 ff. with sketches. Clermont-Ganneau calls the place also Kh. el-Kelkh. He says that "this font is made of a large cylinder of "*mizzeh*" stone, carefully polished, and about three feet high; the basin is hollowed out in the shape of a four-lobed cross, formed by four intersecting circles. At the bottom of the basin a hole has been made to let off the water. On the upper side has been carved a Greek inscription of one line." The Greek inscription is preceded by a cross and is rendered: "For the salvation of Sophronia, and (?) for the rest (?) of Baricha (?)... my (?)...". Séjourné, *RB* 1892, p. 123 and plan, gives the following measurements: height 90 cm., diameter 1.56 m.; the basin is 60 cm. deep and 1.20 m. in diameter. See *SWP* 2, pp. 336 f.

[9] *RB* 1896, pp. 272 ff. with plan. The font is four-lobed both on the interior and on the exterior; the rim has a Greek inscription. The monolith measures 1 m. in height, and seems to have a diameter of 1.18-1.35 m.; the basin to a depth of 35 cm. is 90 cm. in diameter, below that it is round and to a depth of 15 cm. it is 60 cm. in diameter. The rim is 14-18 cm. thick; the inscription on the rim reads: "For the salvation of Matheus and George."

[10] *SWP* 3, pp. 277 f. with plan; it seems to be square on the exterior, four-lobed on the interior and has a step in each arm; its diameter seems to be 37 inches (not "feet"), its height 2 feet.

Jerusalem,[1] at the Harem in Jerusalem,[2] in the basilica at Bethlehem[3] and at Jufna.[4]

All the fonts mentioned resemble one another in this that they are made of one stone; but in size, form and ornamentation they all differ slightly. The font at Siyâgha is one of the largest.

On the interior nearly all the fonts have the quatrefoil or cruciform arrangement; [5] but this form was not essential, as is evident from the fact that the fonts at Kh. Tekûa and Kh. el-Merd are round on the interior. The arms of the cross or the lobes may be rounded, as at Siyâgha and most other places; or rectangular, as at Isbeita. One or more of the arms or lobes may have seats or rather steps; these vary in number between 1-3.

On the exterior the fonts may be round, like the one at Siyâgha; or they may be rectangular, octagonal, or cruciform; in the latter case the arms may be rounded or rectangular. Inscriptions, crosses and a few other ornaments occur on the exterior.

Few of these fonts have been found in situ; they are all located in the apse, as at Siyâgha; thus, for example, in both baptisteries at Isbeita. [6]

One of the baptisteries at Isbeita is located near the southern side of the church, so also a baptistery at Gerasa. But both at Isbeita and at Gerasa and at numerous other places the baptisteries occupy a variety of other places, so that no fixed rule can be established regarding the position of baptisteries.

7. *Purpose.* If the purpose of the chapel would not have been revealed by the font,[7] which clearly indicates that it served as a baptistery, then it would have been indicated by one of the inscriptions in the mosaic pavement, where it is called in Greek "the photisterion"; this is a well-known Greek designation of a baptistery.[8] See inscription IA.

The presence of a baptistery in a monastery complex indicates that the monks also had the care of souls. This is not exceptional. Other monastic centers also have their baptisteries; thus, for example, Isbeita, Kh. el-Merd, etc.

1 *Jérusalem* II, pp. 137 f. with Fig. 92. It is rectangular on the exterior and four-lobed on the interior; it is 72 cm. high; its sides are 1.09 - 1.12 m. wide; the lobes measure 43½ - 44 cm. along the chord and are 23 cm. deep.

2 Meistermann, *Guide*, p. 197, mentions it without giving details.

3 *Bethléem*, pp. 92 ff. and Figs. 36 f.; it is octagonal on the exterior and four-lobed on the interior; its height is 94 cm., its diameter 1.75 m., each side is 67½ cm. wide, each lobe's chord is 68 cm. long. It is decorated with a cross and a tabula ansata containing a Greek inscription.

4 *SWP* 2, p. 323. Near the Greek church, south of the village, "is the ancient font, now not used; it is cylindrical, 4 feet 8 inches in diameter, with a central square well, 2 feet side, and four semicircular seats, forming a cross. (Compare Khurbet Zakarîya and many other Crusading and Byzantine sites, where fonts of the same kind exist.) The lower part of the font is rough, as if sunk below the church floor." — See Schneider, *OC* 1933, p. 158. — The font is 95 cm. high.

5 See *Emmaüs*, pp. 237 ff. regarding the significance to be attached to this form.

6 The fonts at Gerasa and at ʿAmwâs are in the same position.

7 The font is large enough to admit of immersion; this is supposed to be the manner in which baptism was administered in those earlier centuries. See, for example, *DAC* "*Baptême*" and "*Baptistère*".

8 See Kaufmann, *HCA* p. 225.

It is possible that the people of the surrounding regions preferred to be baptized at a great sanctuary; at el-Mekhayyat, for instance, four churches have been cleared, but in none of them has any trace of a baptistery or font been found.

The presence of the baptistery argues also for the existence of a place for catechumens; we already pointed out that the north hall may have served such a purpose.

The only other object of interest found in the baptistery was a stone with a grip on top and a carved cross below (Pl. 60, Fig. 1, 7).

8. *The date.* The baptistery was finished in the year 597 A. D. This date is given in one of the mosaic inscriptions which will be discussed more in detail later. See inscription I A & B. This is the only absolute date found at Siyâgha and is of the utmost importance for the history of the site. It enables us to arrange all the other monuments in a chronological order and to link them up with a number of monuments at Madaba, which were not only contemporaneous, but were constructed under the direction of the very men who had something to do with the construction and decoration of the buildings at Siyâgha; this will become more evident when we speak of the mosaic pavements.

The chapel in question, therefore, serves to illustrate a typical baptistery from the end of the sixth century of our era.

D. THE THEOTOKOS CHAPEL

1. *The name.* The second chapel on the southern side of the basilica was dedicated to the Theotokos, as we know from a long mosaic inscription at the eastern end of the nave (see inscription V). The name, therefore, does not indicate the purpose of the chapel, but merely informs us to whom it was dedicated. Thus, for example, at Mekhayyat there are churches dedicated to SS. Lot and Procopius and to St. George; at Madaba to St. Elias and to the Theometor; at Gerasa to numerous other saints; the same is the case in Syria and Palestine.

The Greek term "Theotokos" is equivalent to the English "Mother of God". Another term expressing the same idea occurs at Madaba; it is "Theometor". Churches dedicated to the Theotokos are found in all the surrounding regions;[1] they are a concrete expression of the doctrine defined at the Council of Ephesus in 431 A. D.[2]

1 Regarding Syria see *ECS* pp. 252 f. — A mosaic inscription found at Jericho mentions the church of Theotokos in Jerusalem, see *QDAP* 2 (1933), p. 161, no. 98. — At ʿAuja el-Hafîr; see *JPOS* 16 (1936), p. 282: "The *Theotokos* is invoked on an abacus from the South Church, and a graffito from N. 7 contains the phrase εὐχὴ τῆς θεωτόκου Μαρίας (prayer of the Mother of God, Mary)."

2 See Kaufmann, *HAE* pp. 223 ff.; id., *HCA* pp. 373 ff., 425 ff., 432, 589.

The same inscription, which informs us that this chapel was dedicated to the Theotokos, also contains an invocation, which is, however, addressed not to the Theotokos, but to Christ. This proves that the invocation does not always indicate to whom a church, chapel or other monument is dedicated.[1]

In this connection we may observe that all the other invocations which occur at Siyâgha are addressed to God or Christ; see inscriptions XII and XIII, possibly also X. Other texts, in which an allusion to the patron saint or saints might have been made, as, for example, in inscription IA, refer only to Christ. No inscription found at Siyâgha makes any direct mention of Moses to whom, according to our literary sources, the church was dedicated; but there may be an allusion to Moses in one of the fragments of the Samaritan inscriptions. See inscription XXVII.

2. *Position and general condition*. Pls. 161, 5; 22, 1-2; 38, 1; 109-111; Fig. 9. The Theotokos chapel is the western one of the two along the southern side of the basilica. It measures about 14.80 × 6.80 m., not including the western and northern walls. The western wall is identical with that of the narthex, the northern wall with that of the basilica, the eastern one with that of the baptistery and the southern wall is continuous with that of the baptistery and resembles it in every way. In the western part of the northern wall there is the door which connects this chapel with the southern aisle of the basilica. The upper part of the walls and the roof have collapsed.

When the ruins were cleared in 1933 it was discovered that 5-7 courses of the stone walls remained in situ; on the interior the walls were covered with three coats of plaster without any ornaments except incisions in the two lower coats which served to bind on the upper ones;[2] the mosaic pavement is quite well preserved; interesting remains of the chancel screen, the altar and stone benches, as well as a few other objects survived.

3. *The plan*. Pl. 161, 5. The plan of the Theotokos chapel is the same as that of the baptistery; it has an internal apse, a chancel and an undivided nave. The apse and chancel are on a higher level than the nave; they are joined with the latter by two stone steps; in this respect the chapel resembles the basilica and the north hall, but differs from the baptistery.

[1] Regarding this question see *ECS* pp. 252 ff. and note 465 ibid.

[2] Such incisions occur also in the plaster of the baptistery and of the southern wall of area 53. They seem to be a rather common feature of the Byzantine period. They have been observed at Gerasa on the famous fountain in the atrium of the cathedral, in buildings excavated on the Ophel Hill (Jerusalem, see *PEF Ann.* 5, p. 49), etc. — Three coats of plaster are not extraordinary; thus, for example, regarding Umm el-Jemâl Butler, *ECS* p. 181, writes: "I found that the walls, not only of the churches, but of all kinds of buildings, were covered with a thick stucco, two coats on the exterior and three on the interior. The first coat was of coarse mortar mixed with broken stone and pottery, filling up all the interstices; upon this was laid a somewhat finer coat which, on the exterior, was final. On the interior this coat was scratched to receive a third coating of exceeding fine plaster which was made smooth and waxed for the application of colour,"

4. *The chancel screen.* Pls. 161, 5; 109, 1 & 2; 110, 1. The sanctuary of the chapel was separated from the nave by a screen of which there is evidence on the top stone step and in the other parts of the chapel; this evidence consists of sockets, grooves, balusters, bases, shafts, capitals, pieces of marble and stone. These elements show that this screen underwent the same transformations as that of the basilica.

There are four square sockets for balusters in the upper stone step and between them are grooves for two panels; there was one opening in the center of the screen. Three nearly complete marble balusters (Pl. 132, 3, 4, 6 [=10, 9, 7 respectively]) and a number of fragments were found in the chapel. Their maximum length at present is about 1.12 m.; their sides vary in width between 17-20 cm.; two sides are plain, the third has a slot for a panel and the fourth is decorated. The heads in two cases are cylindrical, molded and have a flat top; in one case it is cone-shaped.

The finest baluster found in the Theotokos chapel is the one illustrated in Pl. 132, 3 (=no. 10 ibid.). It is 1.12 m. l. and 17×19 cm. square. Two sides are plain; one has a slot for a panel; the fourth has carved ornaments consisting of a vertical column of 8 laurel leaves, which resemble those used for the laurel wreaths represented on a number of the marble slabs found at Siyâgha (see Pls. 124, 3; 125, 22-24, 26-28, 30). This laurel motif should be distinguished from the vine motif found on two chancel posts of the basilica (Pl. 132, 1 & 2) and a number of marble and stone slabs (Pls. 121, 1; 125, 21; 61, 3). The head of the post is cylindrical; its ornamentation consists of a series of moldings; the top is flat. This type of head is found on only one other baluster at Siyâgha and this also comes from the Theotokos chapel (Pl. 132, 6 [= 7]). A few balusters at Gerasa have a flat head; there it is suggested that they may have carried colonnettes to which curtains could have been attached.[1]

The second baluster found in the Theotokos chapel (Pl. 132, 4 [= 9]) is somewhat chipped at the lower end, like most of these posts; its present length is 1.10 m.; its width is 19×20 cm.; its head is cone-shaped, like that of the majority of posts found at Siyâgha and other sites; its one side is panelled, a very common feature of chancel posts at Siyâgha and numerous other sites (see Pl. 132, 5-7).

The third almost complete post found in the Theotokos chapel (Pl. 132, 6 [= 7]) does not match perfectly with either of the others; it has a cylindrical molded head, like the first, but its ornamentation is different; in this latter respect it differs also from the second post, but closely resembles two other pieces of posts from this chapel of which the one is 55, the other 40 cm. l.

[1] *Gerasa*, p. 180.

See also Pl. 132, 5. All these posts have a line incised near the top of the rectangular part.

Between the balusters there were two panels; actually two panels were found in the chapel; the one of marble, the other of stone; both were broken into many pieces; we were able to piece together the marble slab, but the stone slab was too badly shattered to make a restoration possible.

The greater part of the marble slab was found between the entrance to the sanctuary and the remnants of the altar in the apse; a few of the fragments were lying in the southeastern part of the nave, near the chancel. The panel (Pl. 124, 1) is made of a slab of gray marble measuring $118 \times 95 \times 3\text{-}4\frac{1}{2}$ cm.; the one surface of the slab is plain, the other surface has a sunken panel enclosed on three sides by a molded border or frame; this type of molding is called a Lesbian cyma.

This marble slab has the size required by one of the screen's panels; this favors its use as such. The position, in which the greater part of the slab was found, seems to indicate that it was eventually used for the altar or table in the apse.

The fragments of the second slab made of black stone were found near the door of the Theotokos chapel. Its size is uncertain; a few of the larger fragments (Pl. 61, 3) show that it was decorated with vines terminating in leaves, with Maltese crosses, etc. It belongs to the Christian furnishings or ornamentation of the monuments at Siyâgha; its material is the same as that of several other stone slabs (Pl. 61, 1 & 2), chancel posts, etc. found in several places on the site, but we do not know where this material was used; the Theotokos chapel is not an unlikely place, yet the material does not seem to fit well with all the marble furnishings of this chapel.

As in the basilica, so in the Theotokos chapel the chancel screen was transformed from a low parapet to a high colonnade; this we know from marble bases, shafts and capitals found in the chapel. The colonnade consisted of four columns.

The four marble bases of the columns are all in situ (Pl. 109, 1). These bases do not stand on the base of the parapet as in the basilica, but are inserted below the level of the top step, so that the plinth is almost completely hidden from view. The torus and moldings (Fig. 14, 3) are visible; the tops of the bases are 24, 25, 26 and 27 cm. in diameter respectively. In the center of the top there was a metal tenon; a stump of one remains; it seems to be of bronze. From the hole for the tenon to the side facing the panels there is an incised line. The tops of the bases were covered with a layer of lead which served to bind the base and the shafts.

Of the marble shafts 7 pieces were found in the chapel (Pl. 131, Fig. 1); three of the pieces represent the filleted lower end, two the filleted upper end and two others intermediate pieces; the other parts of the shafts are missing.[1] They have the diameter required by the bases in situ. Their color is white and black.

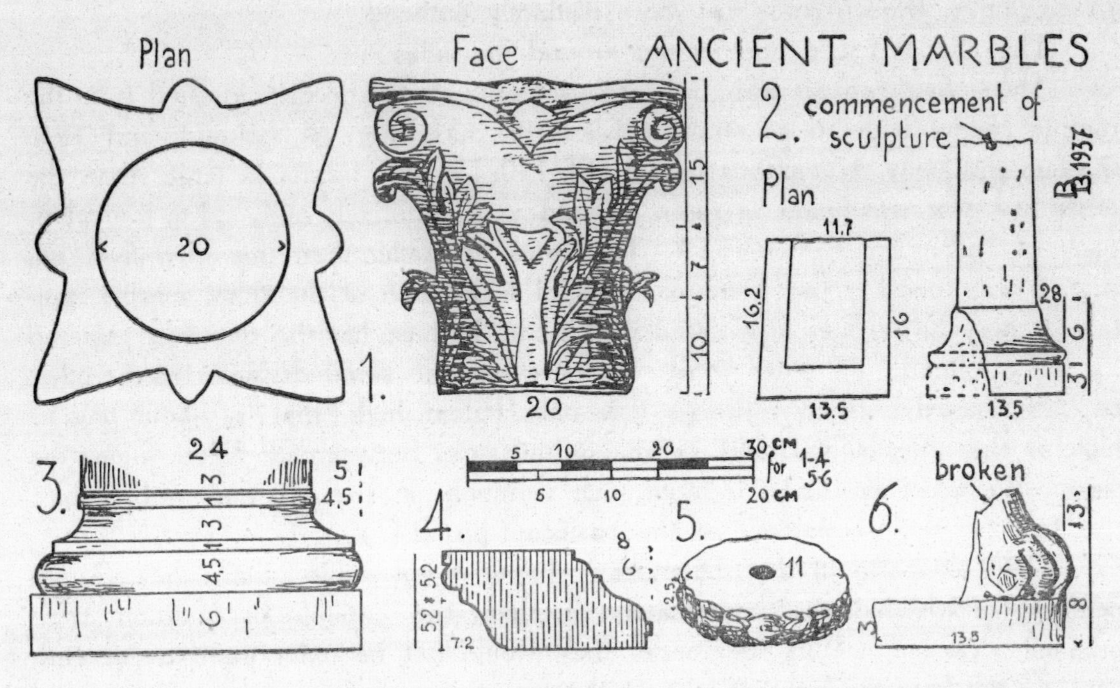

Fig. 14.

Four marble Corinthian capitals were found here. Three are of the type illustrated in Pl. 131, Fig. 2, top and center; see Pl. 60, Fig. 2,1 and Fig. 14,1. Two other capitals of this type were found; one had been reused in the stone bench in the north part of the narthex, the other was found in a room of the atrium. Their dimensions vary slightly; across the bases they measure between 20-21½ cm. in diameter; across the top the sides average between 34-35 cm.; in height they measure 25, 29, 29½, 32 and 33 cm. respectively.

Each one is decorated with 8 acanthus leaves arranged in two rows; those in the upper row are placed beneath the four corners of the abacus; or rather, beneath the volutes; those in the lower row alternate with the others. The central rib of each leaf is broad and flat; the lateral veins are indicated by pronounced grooves; the lower parts of blades are flattened out and the tips touch one another; the top of the blades droops.

[1] In other words, at least one of the lower ends, two of the upper ends and large parts of the intermediate sections were not found in the chapel. The pieces illustrated in Pl. 131, Fig. 1 have a total length of 311 cm. which allows an average of only about 78 cm. for each of the four shafts; the original columns must have had more than twice that length. The surviving fragments measure in length (beginning with the lower piece): 1) 71 & 23 cm.; 2) 47 & 38 cm.; 3) 33 & 32 cm.; 4) 67 cm.

The helices are present, but there are only 8 on each capital, namely, a pair beneath each of the four corners of the abacus, or, more accurately, there is only one volute beneath each angle and on the two sides of the volute spirals are indicated by incised lines. The cauliculi or stalks are at times merely indicated by a groove, though some are more distinctly outlined.

The abacus has a line incised around the sides.

These five capitals with 8 acanthus leaves should be distinguished from the marble capital with 16 acanthus leaves (Pl. 131, Fig. 2, below) and from the one with only 4 acanthus leaves (Pl. 130, 1). The former is larger than the other five ;[1] it was found in room 16 and was tentatively assigned to the colonnade of the basilica (see p. 52). The latter is smaller than the other five, but since it was found in the Theotokos chapel with three of the other marble capitals, it may have been associated with them. Its base has the diameter required by the colonnade; in other words, its base has the same diameter as the other capitals, namely, 20 cm.; though it is only 16 cm. high, that is, about half as high as the other capitals and its abacus measures between 28-30 cm. along the sides. We are accustomed to note such variations in size and form at Siyâgha ; see, for example, the capitals of the basilica (pp. 62 f.).

The colonnade of the Theotokos chapel is not earlier than the seventh century, as we shall see immediately; if, then, the capitals in question were originally destined for this colonnade, they would not be older than the seventh century. But from the fact that two of the first group of five capitals were found outside the chapel and one of a different type was associated with the other three, it seems logical to conclude that all those five capitals were originally destined for some other place and were later reused here ; they are most probably all earlier than the seventh century.[2] The smallest one may be later than the rest.

The presence in the chapel of both balusters and columns seems to indicate that they were used simultaneously ; yet in spite of this evidence it is not improbable that they were used successively, first the balusters with a low screen, then the colonnade forming a high screen. There is not room for both at the same time without useless crowding. The low railing was the older form and was still in vogue when this chapel was finished at the beginning of the seventh century, later the other form began to predominate and superseded the low screen also here.

[1] Its base is 27 cm. in diameter; it is 25 cm. high; and the sides of the abacus measure 37 cm.

[2] Similar capitals have been found on numerous other Christian sites; see, for example, the capitals from Abu Menas illustrated by Kaufmann, *HCA* p. 464, Abb. 222, where a 4th-5th century date is proposed for such capitals. Mader, *ACB* Tafel III B illustrates a capital of this type, which he assigns to the early Christian period (l. c. p. 118). The type should be compared with the Corinthian capitals of the Galilean synagogues discussed by Kohl and Watzinger in *ASG* pp. 168 ff. — See Watzinger, *DP* 2, pp. 111 f.; 122 f.; 128.

According to Shipman[1] the change in style was introduced by Justinian when he constructed St. Sophia at Constantinople. The Emperor made the barrier of 12 columns (in memory of the 12 apostles) and over the tops of the columns he placed an architrave which ran the entire width of the sanctuary. On this architrave or cross-beam large discs or shields were placed containing the pictures of the saints, and this arrangement was called τέμπλον (templum), either from the fancied resemblance to the front of the old temples or as expressing the Christian idea of the shrine where God was worshiped. Every church of the Byzantine rite eventually imitated the "great" church and so this open τέμπλον form of iconostasis began to be adopted among the churches of the East, and the name itself was used to designate what is now the iconostasis. Many centuries elapsed before there was an approach towards making the solid partition which we find in Greek churches of today.

The evidence at Siyâgha may serve to show that in these regions the transition from a low parapet to a high colonnade occurred some time after the beginning of the seventh century.

5. *Furnishings.* In the apse were found remnants of an altar ; at both ends of the chancel there are stone seats; near the southern side of the chancel a stump of a post has some special meaning; other pieces of the same kind of post were found in the nave; here also were recovered the fragments of a marble reliquary, which should be associated with the altar ; marble was used in the original pavement, for repairs of the mosaic pavement and in a pit in the southwest corner of the nave ; other damage done to the mosaic pavement was repaired with mortar. This mosaic pavement and the inscriptions in the same will be dealt with in other chapters; here the rest of the objects will be treated.

a. *The altar.* Pls. 109, 1 & 2 ; 161, 5. The Theotokos chapel has an internal apse 2.80 m. deep and 3.60 m. wide, which contains the most important piece of furniture in the chapel ; it is the altar, of which the four stone bases and a marble post were found in situ and near which other marble posts were lying. In front of the altar was found a marble slab. We may note also the sacrificial scene depicted on the mosaic pavement in front of the altar ; it throws some light on the meaning of the altar.

[1] *The Catholic Encyclopedia: "Iconostasis"*; see ibid. the article "*Altar*" by Hassett. The latter writer traces this type of barrier back to an ornamental feature in two fourth-century basilicas constructed by Constantine, the one at Rome (St. Peter's), the other at Jerusalem (the church of the Resurrection). — In this connection it may not be amiss to observe that in early basilicas the chancel frequently extended into one or more bays of the nave; the screen or rail, which enclosed the chancel, was then placed between the columns and unconsciously, so to say, balusters alternated with columns. For the columns of the screen special material was at times employed; thus, for instance, in the church of St. Stephen at Gaza, where according to Choricius: "The best of columns are the four that define the area forbidden to the laity; these nature has dyed with the colours of a king's raiment." See R. W. Hamilton, *QS* 1930, p. 188; Watzinger, *DP* 2, p. 142. Thus we have the beginnings of the colonnade simultaneously with the low balustrade.

The four stone bases of the altar are made of ordinary limestone roughly dressed; these bases are inserted into the pavement above which they project slightly. In the upper surface there are shallow holes which served as sockets for the posts. The bases are 24-28 cm. square. These four stone bases form a rectangle measuring 1.04 m. from north to south and 81 cm. from east to west.

The bases for altar posts found at a number of other places in recent years present the same characteristics as those of the Theotokos chapel; we call attention to those at el-Mekhayyat,[1] Gerasa[2] and et-Tâbghah.[3] They generally have four bases disposed so as to suggest an altar of the same size as that of the Theotokos chapel. The altars seem to average somewhat over a meter in length, and less than a meter in width. In the synagogue church at Gerasa the bases form a rectangle measuring 140 × 80 cm.; at et-Tâbghah 170 × 95 cm.; in these cases the bases represent the principal altar in the church, hence it is to be expected that it would be somewhat larger than the altar of a lateral chapel.

Lead was used to bind the bases and the legs of the altar. A layer of lead was found in each socket. The same material was used to join the bases and shafts of the chancel's colonnade. In the Aksa mosque, Jerusalem, 12 monolithic shafts were fastened to their bases by means of iron plugs and lead discs;[4] similar lead discs were found in the Umayyad palace at Khirbet el-Mefjer near Jericho.

The legs of the altar consisted of marble posts; of these one was in situ, three were found near their respective bases, and two others with a few marble shafts were discovered not far away.

The post in situ (Pl. 109, 1 & 2) is made of the same material and has more or less the same size as the other posts found in the chapel, but its moldings are quite different. In the latter respect it resembles a group of posts all of which were found outside the Theotokos chapel. All these posts (Pl. 128, below) consist of a pedestal and shaft in one piece. The pedestal is hexagonal and has flat moldings; those next to the die in the center are splays. The rounded shaft has reeding below and tapers towards the top. Another pedestal of the same type, as those described, was found; it is without a shaft (Pl. 128, below, right).

In an early Byzantine church at Tell Hassân near Jericho[5] a post was found which has the same kind of pedestal as the Siyâgha posts in question, but its shaft is like that of the marble columns illustrated in Pl. 130, 16-20. Another post of the pedestal and shaft type was found at Madaba.[6] The posts

1 *RAC* 13 (1936), p. 133, Fig. 20 and pp. 135 f., Figs. 23 f.
2 *Gerasa*, p. 183, b and passim.
3 *BVK* p. 16 and Abb. 2.
4 *ZDPV* 53 (1930), p. 212. — Regarding this use of lead see also *RE* 3, columns 563 f., lines 61 ff.
5 *QDAP* 5 (1936), Pl. LVI, 1.
6 See *MAA* p. 7, Fig. 5, fifth in the row.

of this group differ slightly in length; the shortest is 50 cm. long, the longest 60 cm., the others 53 and 57 cm. The bases are 20 cm. in diameter, the tops 11 cm. The base in generally hexagonal, but the shortest of these posts has a round one. Holes in the top and bottom of these posts were destined for tenons.

This group of 5 or 6 posts was most probably, originally, destined for one place; a trial proved that the bases fit perfectly into the sockets of the stone on the west side of the pulpit in the basilica (Fig. 11, 1); their height is sufficient to bring the western part of the pulpit to the same level as the eastern part. For this reason we suggest that these posts were originally destined and used for such a pulpit. In its present position the slab on the western side of the pulpit permits the use of only two posts, since two sockets are partially inserted beneath the eastern part of the pulpit; the other posts were free for different purposes; one of them was used for the altar of the Theotokos chapel.

The three other posts found near the altar's bases are also made of gray marble and, in general, have the same form as the posts of the previous group; but they are all shorter and have different moldings; in this respect they resemble three other posts found at Siyâgha. Five of the group were found in the Theotokos chapel (Pl. 128, middle group).

The height of these posts is 47, 45½ (two), 43½ and 35½ cm. respectively; this shows that they differ in height not only from the previous group, but also from one another. The sixth post of this type (Pl. 129,2) is represented only by the lower part.

In form the posts of this group differ slightly from one another and from those of the previous group. One has an astragal near the top, another is without the hexagonal base and the bead molding above it. All the posts of both groups have a cone-shaped upper half and nearly all have an hexagonal base, but in the lower half the latter group is cylindrical in form, whilst the former had the form of an hexagonal pedestal.

The chief difference in the two groups consists in the moldings; instead of the flat moldings of the former group, the latter has flutings between a bead and reed molding.

A fragment of this same type of post was found in the early Byzantine basilica at Tell Hassân near Jericho.[1]

The position in which three of these posts were found makes it certain that they were used as legs of the altar's table. Where the other two were used is not certain, but we would like to suggest that the two balusters with cylindrical heads (Pl. 132, 3 & 6) found in this chapel may have been crowned by two of these posts. The plugs in the ends of the posts show how they could have been fastened together.

[1] *QDAP* 5 (1936), Pl. LVI, 4.

Again one receives the impression that these posts were, originally, not destined for this altar but for some other place, and then were reused here. The posts give us a table that did not exceed 50 cm. in height.

West of the altar's bases was found the greater part of a marble slab (Pl. 124, 1); it measures 118 × 95 × 3-4½ cm.; this is more or less the size required by this altar. The dimensions of this slab also meet the requirements of a panel for the chancel's railing. It is possible that the slab served first as a panel of the chancel's screen, and later was used for the table of the altar. The position in which the slab was found makes the latter use quite certain.

In this connection we may call attention to other slabs which may have been used for altars. On p. 56 we expressed the view that a stone slab, measuring 107 × 78 × 15 cm., found near the pulpit of the basilica (Fig. 11, 3, a & b; Pl. 46, 1 & 2) served for an altar. It is a little too small for the altar of the Theotokos chapel, but its proportions in general correspond so well to those which we are led to expect of an altar's slab, in the light of recent discoveries, that the view expressed above seems to be confirmed. It also closely resembles an altar from Maden Dagh to be described below (p. 101).

Kaufmann's[1] description of altar slabs fits numerous fragments which were discovered at Siyâgha (see Pls. 60, Fig. 3; 126, 1-23); but since they were not found in the Theotokos chapel, they will not be discussed here.

Altars in the form of tables having four legs, like the one found in the Theotokos chapel, are known to have been in use in the Byzantine period;[2] excavations do not seem to have brought to light a complete altar of this type. Besides the bases for the legs little seems to have remained in situ; the legs themselves and the slabs are either missing or broken or scattered about in places far removed from the spot where they were originally used; in the one case in which a post was found in situ, namely, in the Theotokos chapel, it seems to be too short for an altar; in other words, the altar seems to be much too low. Other posts, which were much longer, were found at Siyâgha; see, for example, those illustrated in Pls. 129, 1 & 3-5; 130, 16-18 & passim. Similar posts found at Madaba,[3] Gerasa,[4] et-Tâbghah,[5] Jericho,[6] etc.[7] are considered to

1 *HCA* pp. 180 f.

2 See *HCA* pp. 179 f.

3 See *MAA* p. 7, Fig. 5, where 6 pieces are illustrated; 5 are Corinthian capitals with part of the shaft, 1 a base with part of the shaft.

4 *Gerasa*, Plate LI, c, third in the row; it looks complete with its base moldings and Corinthian capital; near it is a molded fragment.

5 *BVK* p. 28, no. 16 and Abb. 6: 2 fragments of the molded lower end and 2 of the upper part with Corinthian capitals. Schneider, l. c., affirms that this type was in use throughout the Mediterranean region. Ibid. p. 30, no. 17 and Abb. 7: 3 fragments with Corinthian capitals assigned by Schneider to the sixth century.

6 *QDAP* 5 (1936), Plate LVI, 1 & 4.

7 See *QS* 1932, p. 197, where Chitty writes regarding St. Euthymius' as follows: "We found the head of one leg of the Altar-table, an alabaster fragment from the table-edge on which was inscribed [ΦΙ]ΛΟCΟΦΙΑC,,, and fragments of a small spiral-fluted column which probably belonged to the Ciborium."

be the legs of altars and have the length required for a normal altar. Not all the posts or colonnettes of the longer type found at Siyâgha are required for the altar of the basilica; some of them could have been used for other altars or tables, yet not one of them was found in the Theotokos chapel.

The writer's first impression on seeing the low posts of the altar in the Theotokos chapel was that they either represent the altar's lower level, which was occupied by the reliquary, or that the posts represent a table, prepared in the final period in the history of the chapel for profane or non-liturgical purposes. But it is also possible that the posts represent the real level of the altar or table of a prothesis. As a matter of fact, an altar having about the same height and size was found at Maden Dagh. It is described as follows:[1] "Among the ruins I found the stone altar scarcely removed from its original position before the apse (it can be seen in Fig. 219). It was an oblong stone with two small outsets on three sides forming the base. It measured 1 meter by 0.70 across the top and was 0.56 high (Fig. 224). On the upper surface was cut a cross with splayed ends, and there were four oblong holes, one at each corner, presumably to hold lights, for they were blackened by fire. On the interior side (the side round which the base mouldings were not carried) was a small projection, something resembling in shape a terra-cotta lamp. The hole in this projection was not blackened, and I do not know what purpose it can have served."

At St. Euthymius' the stumps of a three-legged table of the Prothesis do not throw any new light on our problem. But the rectangular base of the altar with a square cement-filled gap at the back for relics at St. Euthymius',[2] the stones for relics beneath the altars at St. George's in el-Mekhayyat[3] and in several churches at Gerasa,[4] the stone beneath the altar at et-Tâbghah,[5] the reliquary beneath the altar at ʿEin Hanniya,[6] etc. should be borne in mind in explaining the altar in the Theotokos chapel. Actually a number of reliquaries was found at Siyâgha, and the fragments of one of them come from the nave of the Theotokos chapel.

b. *The reliquaries.* Fig. 15 and Pl. 127, Fig. 1, 1-3. At the rear of the Theotokos chapel were found the fragments of a small marble reliquary in the form of a sarcophagus. Originally it consisted of two parts: the casket and its lid. The material of the casket or lower part is gray marble, that of the lid or upper part is white marble; this might indicate two distinct reliquaries, but since in every other respect they fit together they will be treated here as one.

1 *TOC* p. 267.
2 *QS* 1932, p. 197.
3 *RAC* 13 (1936), p. 136, Fig. 24: A large rectangular stone has a quatrefoil cavity in the top.
4 *Gerasa*, pp. 183, d; 245 f.; 253; see Plate LI, a.
5 *BVK* pp. 16 f. and Abb. 2.
6 *QDAP* 3 (1934), p. 116; Plates XXXVII, 2; XXXIX, 2; XL, 2.

The lower part of the reliquary (Pl. 127, Fig. 1, 3; Fig. 15, 1) is a rectangular box measuring about 20.9 × 16.5 × 12.6 cm.; its walls are 2.5-3.6 cm. thick; on the interior it seems to have been subdivided into three narrow compartments; the partitions do not survive. The rim is rabbeted.

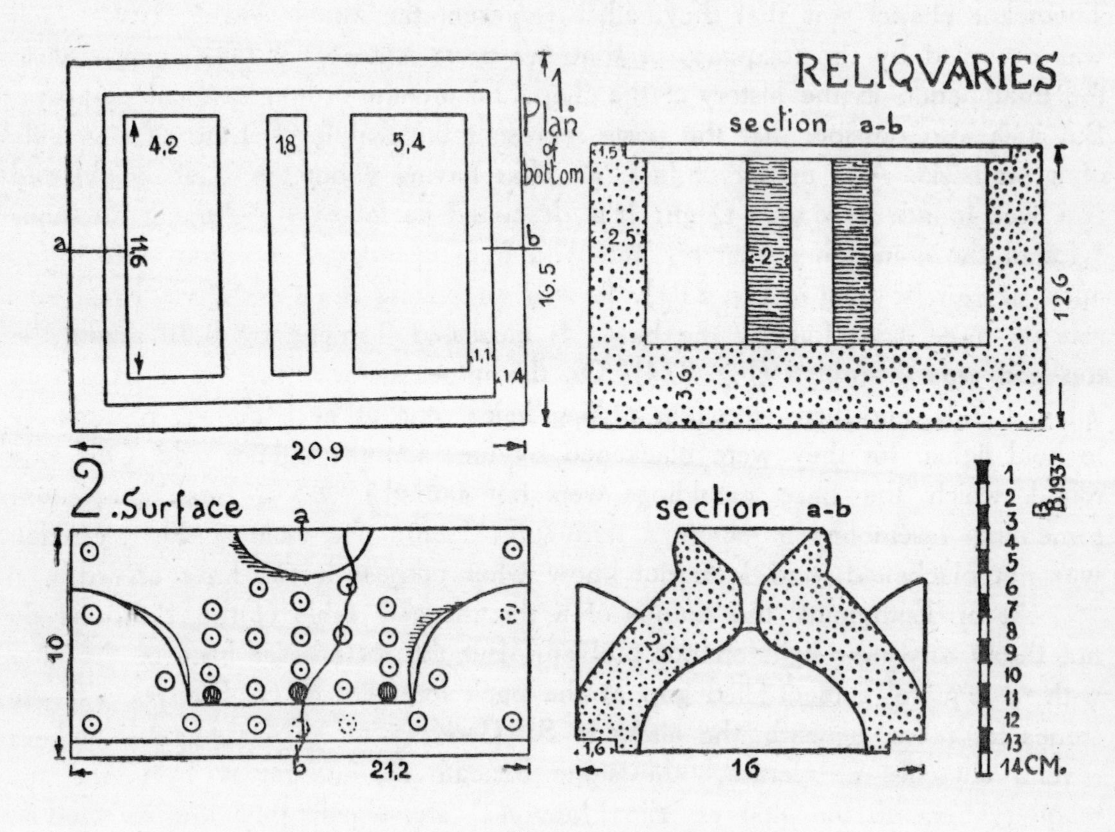

Fig. 15.

The cover of the reliquary (Pl. 127, Fig. 1, 2; Fig. 15, 2) is rabbeted around the rim to fit the casket. The interior is vaulted; the exterior has the form of a gable roof with acroteria at the four corners; in the center of the ridge there is a round opening enclosed by a raised rim. In each of the two long sides there are three small holes corresponding to similar holes in the casket. Traces of rust near these holes prove that metal clasps were used to fasten the lid to the box. The lid measures 21.2 × 16 × 10 cm.

The ornamentation of the reliquary consists of numerous tiny incised circlets with a hole punched into the center; the circlets and holes were colored red; faint traces of the red coloring matter have survived. The same type of ornamentation was used also on stone bowls (Pl. 133, Fig. 1, 1 & 2) objects of bone (Pl. 134, 1, first object in second row) and on a metal cross (Pl. 137,

Fig. 1, 1). This method of decoration is not peculiar to Siyâgha, nor even to the Byzantine period; it was used in all periods of Palestinian history.[1]

Several other pieces of reliquaries were found at various points at Siyâgha; they indicate that a number of reliquaries had been used there. The material, size and ornamentation of all is the same.

The original position of our reliquaries at Siyâgha is not certain. Most of the reliquaries found in situ in other places were located directly beneath the altar. Two such marble reliquaries were found at 'Ein Hanniya [2] in a rectangular cavity cut in the rock beneath the altar. The one "marble casket (Pl. XL, 2) containing bones, presumably relics, was found in a corner of the cavity encased by marble slabs (Pl. XXXVII, 2)," the other "rectangular marble block, hollowed out to form two receptacles (Pl. XL, 2)" stood in the middle of the cavity. Similar reliquaries have been found at Madaba,[3] Gerasa,[4] Khirbet el-Merd,[5] Jerusalem,[6] etc.

c. *The table*. Pl. 109, 1. On the southern side of the chancel not far from the center of the screen a stump of a marble post is still in situ. This post is flat on one side and molded on the others; the flat side faces the screen; the two adjoining sides have concave moldings; the fourth side is convex, but has a broad flat strip in relief extending vertically down the back.

In the chapel were found two more pieces of posts resembling the stump in situ; the one (Pl. 130, 10) fits the stump and no doubt belonged to it; the other piece (Pl. 130, 9) may have belonged to the same post or to another; it has two horizontal grooves across one end.

Whether there were other posts near the screen, like the one still in situ, is not certain, but there are some indications that there were. In Pl. 109, 1 some holes are visible in the mosaic pavement of the chancel. On the southern side, northwest of the stump in situ, there is a hole in the mosaic pavement which looks as if it were due to a post which stood there; in this case we would expect another hole corresponding to it further south for a third post, but near the spot where we would expect such a hole there is a large break in the mosaic pavement, so the evidence which may have existed there has been obliterated. We should, however, note that the base of the chancel screen has a groove running east and west on a line with the post in situ.

On the northern side of the chancel, in approximately the same position as the post on the southern side, only a little closer to the screen, there is a

1 See *Gezer* 2, p. 249, where this statement is illustrated by a useful table.
2 *QDAP* 3 (1934), p. 116.
3 See *Jérusalem* II, p. 798, note 1.
4 *Gerasa*, p. 183 and Plate L, b, left.
5 See Mader, *JPOS* 9 (1929), p. 126.
6 See *Jérusalem* II, pp. 797 ff.

hole in the mosaic pavement, which does not look as if it had been made accidentally, but intentionally; that may indicate the position of another post. The chancel base is so poorly preserved at this end that we are not able to see whether it had grooves like the base on the south.

But even if we abstract from all that is doubtful, there remains the stump in situ to be accounted for. Posts in similar positions have been found at el-Mekhayyat, Gerasa and et-Tâbghah. The one discovered in the church at el-Mekhayyat in 1939 is not yet published; Schneider does not know the meaning of the two posts found by him at et-Tâbghah, the one to the left the other to the right of the entrance.[1] At Gerasa traces of such posts were found in a number of chancels. The traces of the posts generally consisted merely of sockets. The sockets in the Synagogue church were in the northwest corner of the chancel;[2] in the church of SS. Peter and Paul they were in the northwest and southwest corners of the chancel;[3] in the southwest chapel of the cathedral three out of four sockets were still in position at the north end of the screen;[4] in the church of bishop Genesius there is a column drum in the middle of the screen of the north aisle, with the bottom of a corresponding one in the south aisle.[5]

These elements, whether sockets or column drums, are supposed to indicate the existence of tables. But the purpose of the tables is not certain. At first Crowfoot suggested that the tables served to receive the offerings of the faithful;[6] later he expressed the view that the table was "used perhaps in the Commemoration".[7]

The post in the chancel of the Theotokos chapel seems to indicate that a table existed there which had the same purpose as similar tables at other places.[8]

d. *The seats.* Pl. 109, 1 & 2. At the northern and southern ends of the chancel there are stone seats or benches, which stand on the mosaic pavement, where they conceal a part of the mosaic designs. On the southern side the bench consists of four stones which occupy the entire space between the apse and the screen. On the northern side there are now two stones which occupy

1 *BVK* p. 16 and Plan I. In the northwestern corner of the northern transept there are two rectangular stones with sockets, which, according to Schneider, l. c. p. 19, probably supported the posts or columns of small tables destined to receive offerings or the like.

2 *Gerasa*, p. 241 and Plan XXXVI.

3 Ibid. p. 253 and Plan XXXIX.

4 Ibid. p. 215 and Plan XXXI.

5 Ibid. p. 250 and Plan XXXVIII.

6 *Churches at Jerash*, pp. 20, 27 and 29.

7 *Gerasa*, p. 241.

8 In the church of St. Anne, Jerusalem, where both the Latin and Byzantine rites are used, the writer observed that during the liturgy according to the Byzantine rite two large pictures were placed on stands to the right and left of the entrance to the sanctuary. That practice suggested a possible use to which the tables or stands near the screens of ancient churches were put. But a small table or shelf near the railing could have served a number of other purposes, just as the railings in our churches serve a variety of purposes and for some of these purposes we find it at times advisable to place a small table near the railing.

the space next to the screen. There are no seats in the nave, as is the case in the baptistery (see pp. 87 f.); nor are there seats in or around the apse, as is the case in the basilica (see pp. 48 f.). In the church of St. George at el-Mekhayyat[1] there are stone benches on the north and south sides of the chancel, as in the Theotokos chapel; but that church has also a special seat in the apse.[2]

The seats were plastered at the same time as the walls of the chapel.

e. *No special furniture of the nave* came to light, but in this connection we may note the pit in the southwest corner of the nave and a stone decorated with a cross. The latter was discovered in the nave and was mentioned when we described a similar stone found in room 30 (p. 75). The pit in the southwest corner is rectangular and about 40 cm. deep; near the rim on the interior it is lined with marble; the bottom also consists of marble. There does not seem to be any outlet below or in the sides. If this pit served as a drain, then an outlet would be required. It is in a position in which we would expect a sump in which water could have been collected when the floor was washed; there is such a sump in the southwestern corner of the basilica's nave, which is round and shallow, as in most other places where such sumps were observed. It is surprising to find a sump lined with marble, but we have no other plausible explanation to offer for this pit.

6. *The date.* Various considerations have led us to the conclusion that the construction of the Theotokos chapel was begun during the last decade of the sixth century, that it was completed during the first decade of the seventh century and was still in use during the first quarter of the eighth century.

In studying the walls of the baptistery and the Theotokos chapel we reached the conclusion that they were built at the same time. After the walls had been completed the interior of the chapels was paved with mosaics and furnished; this took a number of years. The baptistery was finished first; there the work was completed in the year 597 A. D. From this we conclude that work on the two chapels had begun a year or two earlier, say, about 595 or 596 A. D. In that year the bishop Sergius completed the crypt of the church of St. Elias in Madaba and it seems that he then directed his thoughts to the embellishment of the church and chapels at Siyâgha. The baptistery at Siyâgha is the last monument dated within the episcopate of Sergius. Very probably this famous bishop of Madaba died soon afterwards and his undertakings were for a short time interrupted.

But Leontius, the energetic successor of Sergius as bishop of Madaba, soon continued and finished his predecessor's work both at Madaba and at Siyâgha. In Madaba he built the so-called cathedral in 604 A. D.; in 608 A. D. he

1 *RAC* 13 (1936), Fig. 23 and p. 136.
2 Ibid. Fig. 24 and p. 136.

finished the upper church of St. Elias which Sergius had begun. Perhaps he had obliged himself in a special way to complete the work begun at Siyâgha, for in a long inscription in the mosaic pavement at the eastern end of the nave of the Theotokos chapel (see inscription V) we read that the chapel owes its completion to a vow of the bishop Leontius. This statement enables us to date the completion of the Theotokos chapel within his episcopate. We do not know how long he was bishop, but since the dates 604 and 608 A. D. fall within his episcopate, we will not go far astray if we assign the completion of the Theotokos chapel to the first decade of the seventh century.

The same inscription which informs us that the completion of the Theotokos chapel was due to a vow of the bishop Leontius, also states that the abbots Martyrius and Theodore contributed towards the completion of the same by their diligence and exertion. The mention of these two abbots, especially of the former, is a valuable indication of time. The abbot Martyrius was a contemporary of bishop Sergius, as we know from the inscriptions in the baptistery (see inscriptions I and II). From the inscription in the Theotokos chapel we learn that he was also a contemporary of Leontius and helped to finish the chapel. The successor of Martyrius was the abbot Theodore; he too helped to finish the work on the Theotokos chapel.

The references to the bishop and the abbots in the Theotokos chapel prove that this chapel was finished somewhat later than the baptistery ; a date in the early part of the seventh century is certain.

The chapel existed long enough to undergo a number of changes ; its chancel rail was converted into a colonnade and the images of animals in the mosaic pavement were destroyed. We do not know the precise date at which the former change was made, but the iconoclastic visitation is supposed to have occurred in the eighth century during the reign of Yazid II (720-24 A. D.).[1] If this is true, then our chapel was still in use during the first quarter of the eighth century.

Furthermore, the damage caused by the iconoclasts was repaired ; this shows that the chapel continued to be used for some time afterwards. When the end came, we do not know. It seems that this chapel was in use for about 150 years, from the beginning of the seventh century to about the middle of the eighth.

7. *The purpose.* The inscriptions in the Theotokos chapel do not expressly state the purpose of this chapel; this must be deduced from its furnishings and its relation to the basilica. Had this chapel been found standing alone, its internal arrangement and furnishings would have suggested an independent chapel or church, fully equipped for all the liturgical functions. Even as it is, a priest

[1] *Gerasa*, pp. 172 f.

of the Greek rite insisted that this chapel served for the private performance of the liturgy by the bishop or abbot.[1]

But since this chapel is directly and exclusively connected with the basilica and was built at a time when the liturgy demanded a special place as a prothesis, it is not improbable that this chapel served as a prothesis.

In this connection we may call attention to the scene represented in the mosaic pavement directly in front of the altar (Pl. 109, 1). A temple with courtyards, an altar and an inner shrine is flanked by two young bulls whose sacrificial character is indicated by a Greek inscription above them.[2] The text, derived from *Psalm* 51 (Hebrew), 21,[3] proves that the scene is both symbolical and typical. The symbolism consists in this that two calves or bulls are represented as victims destined for sacrifice. The position of the scene in front of the altar of a Christian chapel, as well as the words of the *Psalm*, which the early Christian Fathers often explained typically, suggest that the calves were intended as types of the sacrifice of the New Law. But even if we admit the closest relation between this scene and the altar in front of which it is placed, it does not decide the question whether this was a prothesis table where the offerings were prepared or whether this was the altar on which the sacrifice was offered.

At a monastery near Gaza the followers of Peter the Iberian constructed a special chapel in the church; that chapel had its own altar beneath which a tomb was prepared to which the remains of Peter the Iberian were transferred a year after his death.[4] That was before the end of the fifth century. At that time the liturgy did not seem to require a special prothesis chapel, hence the chapel must have had a different purpose; as a matter of fact, it is called "a chapel for prayer". The altar in the chapel may have served for the performance of the liturgy on certain days, perhaps on the three days when the memory of Peter was commemorated in a special way. The same may have been the case in the Theotokos chapel at Siyâgha.

In many Byzantine churches such lateral chapels have been found, e. g., at Madaba, Isbeita, Gerasa, etc. Crowfoot[5] thinks that these chapels "in position and appointments"..."are fitted to serve as a kind of Prothesis". Unfortunately the chapel's furnishings were somewhat disturbed before its final abandonment. This adds to the difficulty of determining its purpose. But whatever may have been the purpose of this chapel, it is evident that it was much used, since the mosaic pavement between its door and the nave of the basilica was completely worn out and repaired with mortar.

1 According to Kaufmann, *HCA* p. 184, the oldest churches contained only one altar. If there were more altars, they were placed not in the church proper, but in distinct chapels.

2 Further details regarding this scene will be given in the chapter on mosaic pavements.

3 See inscription IV.

4 Raabe, pp. 131 f.

5 *Gerasa*, pp. 177 f., b.

CHAPTER VI

THE MONASTERIES

A. THEIR HISTORY

1. *Fourth century.* The earliest record of monks in the Nebo region is found in the account of Aetheria's visit to the memorial of Moses on Mount Nebo.[1] On the way from Livias to Mount Nebo her party visited the springs of Moses at the foot of Mount Nebo. Near the springs very many monks were living. At that place the monks were known as ascetics. The monks received the pilgrims very kindly; they offered gifts to their guests and explained to them the traditions associated with the springs. After that prayers were said, a text from the Bible was read and a psalm was recited. Then some of the monks accompanied the pilgrims to the top of the mountain where they again explained everything of Biblical interest.

The monks were evidently thoroughly conversant with all the events and traditions which rendered that region famous. Some of their remarks betray that they were not new arrivals in that region, but had been there already for some time.

That monks resided at ʿAyûn Mûsa in Aetheria's time is certain; she expressly states that very many monks were living there ("monachi autem plurimi commanent ibi") and incidentally refers also to their monasteries when she states that the rock from which the water flows is located between the church and the monasteries.[2] Whether monks lived near the church on the top of Mount Nebo or not is not certain; Aetheria makes no express mention either of monks or of their habitations there.

[1] Geyer, pp. 52 ff., lines 18 ff.

[2] Geyer, p. 366, observes that in Aetheria the word "monasterium" signifies "cellula"; therefore the plural form is generally used. — Bludau, *SGKA* 15 (1927), p. 263, indorses the view of Geyer. He adds that nowhere in Aetheria is there any mention of a laura or a cenobium, but only of monasteria, that is, independent cells, caves or huts inhabited by hermits or ascetics. From this he concludes that at the time of Aetheria the laura and cenobium were still unknown in Palestine.

From the fact that Aetheria speaks only of a small church on the top of Mount Nebo it does not necessarily follow that there were no habitations for monks there. Also in speaking of ʿAyûn Mûsa Aetheria at first mentions merely the church; later in speaking of the location of the springs she incidentally refers to the monasteries; had it not been for the springs near the monasteries, she might not have made any mention of them. The same may be the case regarding the top of Mount Nebo; there Aetheria was interested only in the church; even if she saw habitations for monks there, she had no special reason to mention them.

It is not improbable that at Aetheria's time most of the hermits lived near ʿAyûn Mûsa, where they had a chapel. Since the monks from ʿAyûn Mûsa accompanied Aetheria and her party to the church on the top of Mount Nebo and there explained everything to the pilgrims it seems reasonable to presume that they were in charge of the sanctuary on Mount Nebo, where they performed the necessary work and functions and acted as guides to pilgrims. Since pilgrims did not necessarily approach Mount Nebo via ʿAyûn Mûsa, we may presuppose that one or the other monk resided permanently near the church on Mount Nebo in order to receive pilgrims.

The same was the case in Sinai. There most of the monks lived in the valleys. From time to time one or the other visited the shrines on the hilltops, conducted pilgrims there, or resided there to take care of the place. And it is the same today in Sinai; most of the monks still live in the monasteries in the valleys; only occasionally one or the other visits the hilltop shrines.

At Mount Nebo, however, the development was different. After a time a large monastery was built on the hilltop and that became the principal center of monastic life in the region, though the monasteries and the church at ʿAyûn Mûsa were not completely abandoned. The reasons for this transfer become apparent when one has lived in the region for some time; the hilltop site is more easily reached than the valley, and above all it is a much healthier place; this last consideration may have been decisive.

Mount Nebo is not an isolated peak like Jebel Mûsa or Jebel Katherin in Sinai, but the western extremity of a ridge joined with the plateau to the east and easily accessible from that side; the approaches from all other directions are also much easier than the approaches to the solitary peaks in Sinai; hence a large monastery could be established at Mount Nebo without any difficulty.

The top of Mount Nebo is also healthier than the valley near the springs. Today no Arabs live in the valley, in spite of its abundant water supply and rich fields. They dread malaria. The same cause may have driven the monks from the valley to the healthier highlands.

2. *Fifth century.* Early in the fifth century monks had definitely established themselves near the memorial of Moses on the top of Mount Nebo. The anchoretic form of life still survived to some extent and was held in high esteem,

but the cenobitic mode of life had been definitely introduced and soon prevailed. All this we learn from Peter the Iberian who visited the monastery on Mount Nebo at least twice during the fifth century, the first time about the year 430 A. D. and the second time soon after the year 477 A. D.

Peter describes his first visit to Mount Nebo as follows:[1] "I recall that, when I was still a youth and had but recently come from the royal residence, I came to this hill in order to see it and in order to pray. And when I heard that one of the great Sketian monks was living here in peace, who had left Sketia with all the monks who were there, when a horde of Maziks attacked those monasteries, I asked the custodian of the church on the hill to favor me with his (the Sketian's) blessing and sight.

"This cell, however, which you see, is the one in which that holy man lived for 40 years without going out of the door and without crossing the threshold, an ascetic and prophet, and full of the grace of God.

"There were, however, three of us, I, my blessed John and furthermore another monk, a Cappadocian by birth, who travelled with us. Since he was a slave in his country, he fled on account of the severity of his service and came to Jerusalem, where he lived in peace. We, however, did not know one another, neither were we and our origin known to the inhabitants of that place.

"But when the aged man had given us permission to call on him and saw that we had entered, he said immediately: "It is good that you have come, Nabarnugios, son and grandson of a Bosmarios." Whilst I was filled with great astonishment at these words and was overcome with great fear and trembling, the aged man again said to us: "Recite the prayer." But when we, as laymen, remained silent, he continued to make the same demand. Then I, fool that I was, ventured to say: "Excuse us, venerable Father; we are sinners and laymen." But he, extending his hand towards the Cappadocian, said: "Slave, recite the prayer. Make no excuse."

"After the prayer had been recited — for how would that one have dared to refuse, seeing that such a holy man commanded it — he permitted us to sit down. And after he, in conformity with his goodness, had communicated many godly and wholesome words, narratives and consolations, he, in the end, after this spiritual meal, said to the one who shared his cell: "Take the brethren and give them refreshments, for they are from the world."

"On the following day when we came to him in order to obtain his blessing and take leave of him with prayer, he received us with joy. And after he had spoken a few words for our edification, he dismissed us with prayer. But as we were going out, he seized my mantle and held me fast. And when I turned to him, he gave me a sign with his hand to stay, whilst he permitted the others to go out.

[1] Raabe, pp. 83 ff.

"And when I had remained, he bade me to sit down on a small stool which was standing there, and said: "The fire of his love, which God has granted to you — no one in this generation has been privileged to possess it (in such a degree) — see to it that you do not extinguish it, but guard it carefully. And live with no one else than with this brother who came with you" — whereby he meant the blessed John, the eunuch. "God, however, will demand an account of you, if some one, be he a bishop or cleric, a monk or layman, comes to you, and you are silent and do not instruct him about God's judgments and precepts." This he said because in spirit he foresaw and foretold the gift of the priestly office with which I was to be privileged, who was entirely unworthy of it. But when I became confused at the word and wept bitterly (saying): "Who am I that your holiness commands me this, who have not even begun to be a disciple," he replied: "What you have heard, that you have heard." And thus he dismissed me, after he had grasped and kissed my head and recited a prayer."

In the last quarter of the fifth century Peter the Iberian came to Siyâgha a second time.[1] One of his associates on that occasion became his biographer. To the latter we owe the information that there were many monasteries around the church on the holy hill of Moses. Somewhere in that complex of buildings was the cell in which the famous Sketian ascetic lived whom Peter had visited about 40 years earlier. Peter led his followers to that cell and there related his experiences on his first visit to the monastery. The cell in which the Sketian had lived for 40 years was small, about 5 cubits square, and poorly lighted.

This narrative gives us an interesting glimpse of the monastery and life in the same. From the statement that many monasteries existed around the church we conclude that already in the fifth century monastic life was in a very flourishing condition at Siyâgha. The statement refers primarily to conditions in the last quarter of the century. In those monasteries there was a cell which Peter the Iberian pointed out to his followers in the last quarter of the century; that cell had existed already nearly half a century earlier when Peter came to Mount Nebo the first time. To visit that cell Peter obtained permission from an official whom he calls the paramonarius; the monk who lived in the cell had a companion who looked after the needs of Peter and his fellow-pilgrims. Furthermore, Peter and his companions spent at least one night at the monastery. These facts seem to indicate that there was an organized community living at Mount Nebo in the early part of the century, and that community was able to receive and entertain guests, in other words, there was also a hospice at Mount Nebo.

The narrative regarding the Sketian monk seems to carry the history of the monastery back to a period somewhat before the first visit of Peter the Iberian and also indicates some interesting connections between this monastery and ancient monasteries in Egypt.

[1] Raabe, pp. 82 f.

Peter the Iberian informs his followers that the Sketian monk spent 40 years in a cell at Mount Nebo. He was an old man when Peter called on him about the year 430 A. D. There is nothing to indicate that the monk was still living when Peter came to Mount Nebo the second time, so it seems certain that at least a part of that period of 40 years must be assigned to the time preceding Peter's first visit. If we assume that the ascetic had lived in the cell for 40 years when Peter called on him, then he would have been living on Mount Nebo already at the end of the fourth century; in other words, he would have come to Mount Nebo about the time Aetheria visited the memorial of Moses. But this assumption is not necessary. It suffices to note that monks were evidently residing at Mount Nebo for some time before Peter the Iberian came there the first time, and this carries us back to the earlier part of the fifth century.

The monk who was leading the life of a recluse at Mount Nebo in the early part of the fifth century is called a Sketian. The Sketian monks in general seem to have enjoyed a high reputation for sanctity and when Peter the Iberian heard that one of them was residing at Mount Nebo he expressly asked to see him. The Sketian desert is identical with the Wady Natrun, west of Cairo in Egypt. That desert was one of the earliest centers of monasticism in Egypt and some of those ancient monasteries have survived up to our own times.[1] It is interesting to note that the monastery on Mount Nebo offered hospitality to at least one monk from those Sketian monasteries. This suffices to establish a link between the two places and this connection should be borne in mind in studying the history of the monastery on Mount Nebo ; it was no doubt to a certain extent influenced by the traditions of monastic life in Egypt, in particular in Sketia.

3. *Sixth and seventh centuries.* The only literary evidence for the presence of monks at Mount Nebo in the sixth century is found in an itinerary assigned to the year 570 A. D.[2] There we read the following: "From the Jordan to the place where Moses passed away from the body, is eight miles, and thence it is not very far to Segor, in which places are many hermits."

That the so-called hermits were leading a community life under a common superior in the monastery on Mount Nebo is evident from the fact that three of the abbots are mentioned in the inscriptions found at Mount Nebo;[3] they are called Alex, Martyrius and Theodore. At the time of Alex the basilica was restored; at the time of Martyrius the basilica, baptistery and Theotokos chapel were finished; at the time of Theodore some work was completed in the chapel of the Theotokos.

[1] See, for example, W. Hatch, *A Visit to the Coptic Convents in Nitria,* in *AASOR* 6 (1926), pp. 93-103.— *Aegyptus* 18 (1938), p. 35.

[2] *Antonini Placentini Itinerarium* in Geyer, p. 200, lines 8 ff.

[3] See inscriptions VIII, I, II, V.

We do not know precisely when Alex was abbot nor the full extent of his work; his inscription is found in the mosaic pavement of the basilica's chancel; there he states that he renovated the holy place; this seems to refer primarily to the place where the inscription was found. But the same circumstances which demanded repairs in the basilica may have demanded repairs elsewhere. There is evidence of repairs in the monastery; these may have occurred at his time.

Martyrius was a contemporary of the two famous bishops Sergius and Leontius of Madaba; the former was bishop at Madaba at the end of the sixth century, the latter in the beginning of the seventh. Martyrius, therefore, represents the period of transition from the sixth to the seventh century. At his time the basilica and the baptistery were finished (597 A. D.); work on the Theotokos chapel was also carried out at his time, as is expressly stated in an inscription; but since his successor is also mentioned in that inscription, it is possible that he did not witness the completion of that work.

Theodore is mentioned in the Theotokos chapel together with Martyrius. His name is placed after that of Martyrius, so it seems that he was the successor of Martyrius. Together with Martyrius he was active in bringing the work in the Theotokos chapel to an end. He was a contemporary of bishop Leontius and his activity seems to fall entirely within the early part of the seventh century.

4. *Thirteenth century.* A Crusader, Thietmar[1] by name, claims to have visited Mount Abarim, where Moses died and was buried. He affirms that he found there a beautiful monastery inhabited by Greek Christians and there he spent the night. If this information is accurate then the monastery was still occupied as late as the thirteenth century; Thietmar is supposed to have made his trip in the year 1217 A. D.

Abel[2] accepts without reserve the statement of Thietmar that Greek Christians (probably monks) were living in a beautiful monastery on Mount Nebo as late as the year 1217, and suggests that the monastery was destroyed not long afterwards in the same century, if not by the Mongols in 1244, then by Baibars, who came to the throne of Egypt in 1260. This Sultan did much to promote the cult of Moses at the shrine of Nebi Mûsa west of the Jordan; in order to do away with competition, he is supposed to have destroyed the shrine at Mount Nebo. In spite of this, the cult of Moses at Mount Nebo survived at least up to the sixteenth century.

5. *Sixteenth century.* The Franciscan Pantaleon d'Aveiro[3] visited Mount Nebo about 1564 A. D. He found all the buildings in ruins and apparently they were completely deserted.

1 See Laurent, p. 35.

2 *Une Croisière autour de la Mer Morte*, pp. 177 f. — See G. R. Berry, *Old and New in Palestine*, Hamilton, New York, 1939, p. 64.

3 Lopes, pp. 186 ff.

6. *Ninteenth century.*[1] In 1864 Luynes visited Siyâgha. He thought that the extensive ruins which covered the site represented the monastery with its church which Thietmar visited in 1217; he concluded that it was destroyed by an earthquake in one of the following centuries. Tristram in 1872 thought that the ruins represented a citadel with a pagan temple later converted into a church. Wilson and Conder thought that the ruins represented a small Byzantine village with its church.

7. *Twentieth century.*[2] In 1901 Musil visited Siyâgha; he identified the ruins to the south and west of the church as those of a monastery. His view was quite generally adopted by later explorers.

8. *The excavations.* See Pl. 161, 7-116; Fig. 3, 117 ff.; Fig. 9. After the basilica, chapels, narthex and atrium had been cleared in 1933, a few of the rooms around the atrium (Pl. 161, 20, 26 & 28) and the passage between the atrium and the southern monastery (Pl. 161, 25) were likewise explored. In 1935 all the remaining rooms around the atrium (Pl. 161, 14-27) were completely cleared; in the same year the buildings on the northern slope (Pl. 161, 31-52) were brought to light. In 1937 the buildings on the western and southern slopes were excavated (Pl. 161, 53-115). By these clearances we have become thoroughly acquainted with the great central complex of buildings which covers about 6000 square m. (Pl. 161, 7-105) and with some of the outlying buildings and caves (Pl. 161, 106-115), cisterns (Fig. 3, 116, 118, 122, 136) and quarries (Fig. 3, 133-135). Other buildings and caves which have not been excavated completely (Fig. 3, 117 ff.) were explored as thoroughly as circumstances permitted. These excavations and explorations serve to fill in many details in the picture of the monasteries provided by the literary sources. The primary purpose of this chapter is to give all the details with which we have become familiar.

We think that a small group of cells on the northern slope (Pl. 161, 31-37) may be contemporary with the cella trichora; at the same time the caves on the northwestern slope (Pl. 161, 107, 108) may also have been inhabited. Early in the fifth century the monastery was planned and executed on a very grand scale (Pl. 161, 7-105); that monastery must have been contemporary with the basilica of the fifth century into which the cella trichora was incorporated. When the fifth-century basilica was destroyed or damaged, also the monastery suffered harm. The injury to most of the buildings was repaired; but the cells on the northern slope and possibly also those on the western slope were abandoned. The evidence of restorations and modifications is most apparent in the rooms around the atrium and in the southern monasteries. These last mentioned groups of buildings continued in use to the very end of the occupation of the site; in their final form they are contemporaneous with the basilica of the sixth century and with the chapels.

[1] See pp. 11 ff.
[2] See pp. 14 ff.

In the present chapter the monasteries will not be treated in the order in which they were built, nor strictly in the order in which they were discovered during the course of the excavations, but in a topographical order, beginning with the group of cells arranged around the atrium and then treating successively those in the central complex on the north, west and south of the basilica; and in the end a few words will be added regarding the outlying buildings, caves, cisterns, enclosure walls and quarries. In the central complex the cells are arranged along or around one or more sides of courtyards ; there are at least 5 such courtyards, and, accordingly, we may distinguish that many groups of cells.

9. *The name.* Before going into detail regarding the monastic buildings, it may be advisable to make a remark here about the present name of the site. If the site occupied by the monastery is Mount Nebo (Abarim, Fasga, Phasga or Pisgah), how is it that today it is called Siyâgha ? Conder suggests that Siyâgha (or Siâghah, as he and others write the word,) was derived from Seʿath, a word which is substituted by the *Targum* of Onkelos for Nebo in *Num.* 32,3. Granted that this is true, it still remains to be explained why the place was called Seʿath in the *Targum*. Conder does not solve this question, but he has pointed out the way for a solution.

In *Num.* 32,3 we read that "the sons of Ruben and Gad asked Moses and Eleazar for Ataroth and Dibon and Jazer and Nemra, Hesebon and Eleale and Saban and Nebo and Beon." The Aramaic versions or the so-called *Targums* have paraphrased some of these names; thus, for example, they do not say that the sons of Ruben and Gad asked for "Nebo", but that they asked for : וּקְבוּרְתָּא דְמשֶׁה, that is, literally, "the burial of Moses"; but from the context it is clear that they asked for the region in which Moses was buried; or for: וּבֵית קְבוּרְתֵּיהּ דְמשֶׁה , that is, "the house" or the "place of the burial of Moses", or simply "the tomb of Moses" ; or for : וְסִיעַת בֵּית קְבוּרְתָּא דְמשֶׁה, that is, "the society of the house of the burial of Moses".

The paraphrases are arranged as far as possible in a chronological order ; the oldest is the shortest, the most recent the longest ; both of these are to be found in the *Targum* of Onkelos ; the former [1] most probably represents the original version, which may go back to the second century of our era ; the latter [2] seems to represent a gloss which was added later. The third paraphrase represents an intermediate form both in date and in length ; it is found in three places of the *Targum* of Pseudo-Jonathan [3] whose redaction is generally supposed to be later than the sixth century, though it no doubt represents traditions which are older.

1 *BSP* I, p. 691.
2 *BSP* VI, p. 30.
3 *Num.* 32, 3 in *BSP* IV, p. 305; *Num.* 32, 38 in *BSP* IV, p. 307; *Num.* 33, 47 in *BSP* IV, p. 309.

These paraphrases represent the usage of the times in which they originated and at the same time they reflect historical situations. Thus, for example, at the time when the version of Onkelos was made, it must have been customary to speak of Nebo as the region in which "the burial of Moses" took place. At the time when the version of Pseudo-Jonathan was made, a memorial in honor of Moses had been erected at the traditional place of his tomb; this fact seems to be reflected in an addition to the original paraphrase; according to this addition the two tribes of Ruben and Gad are represented as asking not merely for "(the region of) the burial of Moses", but for "(the region with) the house of the burial of Moses"; this usage may have originated when the cella trichora was built on Mount Nebo. Finally, a community of monks established itself near the tomb of Moses; this community no doubt derived its name from the monument near which it was established and was called "the society of the house of the burial of Moses". The name of the community was used not only in speaking of its members, but also in speaking of the house and property of the community. We do the same today. According to this version the tribes of Ruben and Gad are represented as asking Moses and Eleazar for "(the property) of the society of the house of the burial of Moses". This rendering gives very good sense and explains adequately how Mount Nebo came to be called "Seᶜath" in the Aramaic version.

It remains to account for the origin and meaning of "Siyâgha". Was this name derived from "Seᶜath" or was it perhaps derived from some other word?

Conder thinks that Siyâgha (صياغه) is derived from Seᶜath (סיעת). "The Aramaic and the Arabic", he says, "are as close as possible, the important guttural being retained."[1] In this case Siyâgha is of Aramaic origin[2] and its meaning is the same as that of Seᶜath, namely, "the society" or possibly "the monastery" or "the property" (of the society or the monastery).

But there is another possibility; Siyâgha need not necessarily be derived from Seᶜath; it may represent a different tradition which also goes back to the time when Aramaic was still in use in these regions. As a matter of fact, there is an Aramaic word סְיָג or סְיָגָא which means "the enclosure"; from this meaning others are derived, such as "the place which is enclosed", "the monastery". This meaning fits so well that it immediately recommends itself. "Siyâgha",

[1] *SEP* p. 154; *QS* 1881, pp. 275 ff.

[2] Merrill, *East of the Jordan*, pp. 240 ff. discusses the name of the site; he maintains that "the name "Siâghah" is an Arabic word in common use west of the Jordan in connection with goldsmiths." Supposing that this derivation is correct, one naturally asks what connection there is between goldsmiths and our site. Merrill offers no explanation. The only possible explanation I could find was the following: on a dump above the northern monastery gold tesserae from the basilica could be picked up before the excavations; those gold tesserae were seen by the Arabs and were brought in connection with the activity of goldsmiths there. This explanation sounds somewhat plausible, but, in our opinion, it is not as good as the one which derives the name from the Aramaic. — For other discussions regarding the name the reader may consult G. E. Post in *QS* 1888, pp. 183 ff.

therefore, has the same meaning in Aramaic as "ed-Deir" in Arabic and as "the monastery" in English. When the monastery was in ruins, they called it "Khirbet Siyâgha", "the ruin of the monastery"; the hill they called either "Jebel Siyâgha" or "Râs Siyâgha", "the hill of the monastery" or "the head (that is, headland) of the monastery"; the surrounding region is called "Ard Siyâgha", that is, "the land of the monastery". The name Siyâgha, therefore, represents an ancient tradition which informs us that the ruins in question represent a monastery. The monastery was such a prominent feature in the region, that the region itself was better known by the name Siyâgha than by the name Nebo (Abarim, etc.).

Our conclusion, therefore, is that both Se^{c}ath and Siyâgha were names used in the times preceding the Arab invasion, to designate the monastery at Mount Nebo. The first name has been preserved by a written tradition, the second by an oral tradition. The first name refers directly to the community at Mount Nebo, and only indirectly to the building occupied by the community; the second name refers directly to the building occupied by the community. The building was called a monastery; the community living in the monastery derived its name from the sepulcher of Moses and was known as "the society of the tomb of Moses". Thus the names of Mount Nebo preserved in the Aramaic version of the Bible and by oral tradition contribute to our knowledge of the buildings on the site; the one name confirms the fact known from other sources that the buildings represent monasteries, the other name informs us of the very interesting new fact that the community of monks living at Mount Nebo was known as "the society of the tomb of Moses".

B. THE ATRIUM GROUP

1. *General condition.* The great complex of monastic buildings at Siyâgha consists of a series of courtyards with buildings grouped around them. One of the courtyards of the monastery is identical with the atrium on the western side of the basilica (Pl. 161, 7). The building around this courtyard consists of three wings which contain 15 rooms (Pl. 161, 14-28), most of which communicate directly with the atrium by means of doors. As all the other buildings on the site, so also this one was constructed of stone; the average stones were carefully dressed and have a plain surface; there are, however, some stones with a low flat boss; a liberal packing of small stones and chips was used. The upper parts of the walls and the roofs have all collapsed. The lower parts of the walls, parts of the doors, the pavements and some of the furnishings of the rooms have been preserved. In some of the rooms there is evidence of rebuilding,

remodelling and repairs. All in all, it seems that we have here a building which was constructed in the fifth century, remodelled in the sixth and used to the very end of the history of the site. In the reconstructed walls we find materials of the earlier periods ; but the contents of the rooms should represent the final period of their occupation, which very probably corresponds to the final occupation of the site.

Strictly speaking the rooms at the northern and southern ends of the narthex (Pl. 161, 10, 11, 29, 30) also belong to the atrium group, but they were described in speaking of the narthex (pp. 73-76); also the courtyard has already been described (pp. 76-79) ; here it suffices to make a few observations regarding the buildings around the atrium.

2. *The building* (Pl. 161, 14-28). The 15 rooms in the building around the atrium represent the apartments of an official (14 & 15), a refectory (16), a kitchen (17), a pantry (18), a number of small cells (19, 20, 23, 26-28), a burial vault (21), several larger halls (22 & 24) and a passage joining the atrium with the southern monastery (25).

Rooms 14 and 15 (Pl. 50, 2) are in the northern wing of the building, whose eastern end they occupy. In this part of the building the walls are still 3 - 5 courses high and on an average about 80 cm. thick. A door in the southern wall of room 14 joins this suite of rooms with the atrium. The wall between the two rooms stands on a mosaic pavement common to both rooms ; on this mosaic pavement stand also a pair of pilasters against the northern and southern walls of room 14, a stone bench along the eastern and northern walls of room 14 and another along the southern wall of room 15 ; at the level of the floor a number of pilaster bases are enclosed by the mosaic pavement. Stone, marble, clay, glass and metal objects were found in these rooms.

These discoveries indicate that originally there was only one large chamber here which was about 8.20 m. l. and 4.80 m. wide. It was paved with mosaics consisting of plain large tesserae whose surface measures on an average $3\frac{1}{2} \times 3\frac{1}{2}$ cm. The same type of tesserae was used in the atrium, in room 29 and to some extent in room 24.

Along the northern and southern walls the bases of responds enclosed by the mosaic pavement exist. There are three such bases along the northern wall and there are, no doubt, three such bases also along the southern wall, but only two are visible now; the third is concealed by a stone bench in room 15. The fact that these pilasters are enclosed by the mosaic pavement shows that they are either anterior to it or possibly contemporaneous with it. Most probably the building was so badly shaken by an earthquake that it had to be rebuilt completely. The walls were erected on the old foundations; the mosaic pavement was preserved ; the old pilasters were not utilized again ; their place was taken by a wall and a single pair of responds. Both the wall and the responds stand

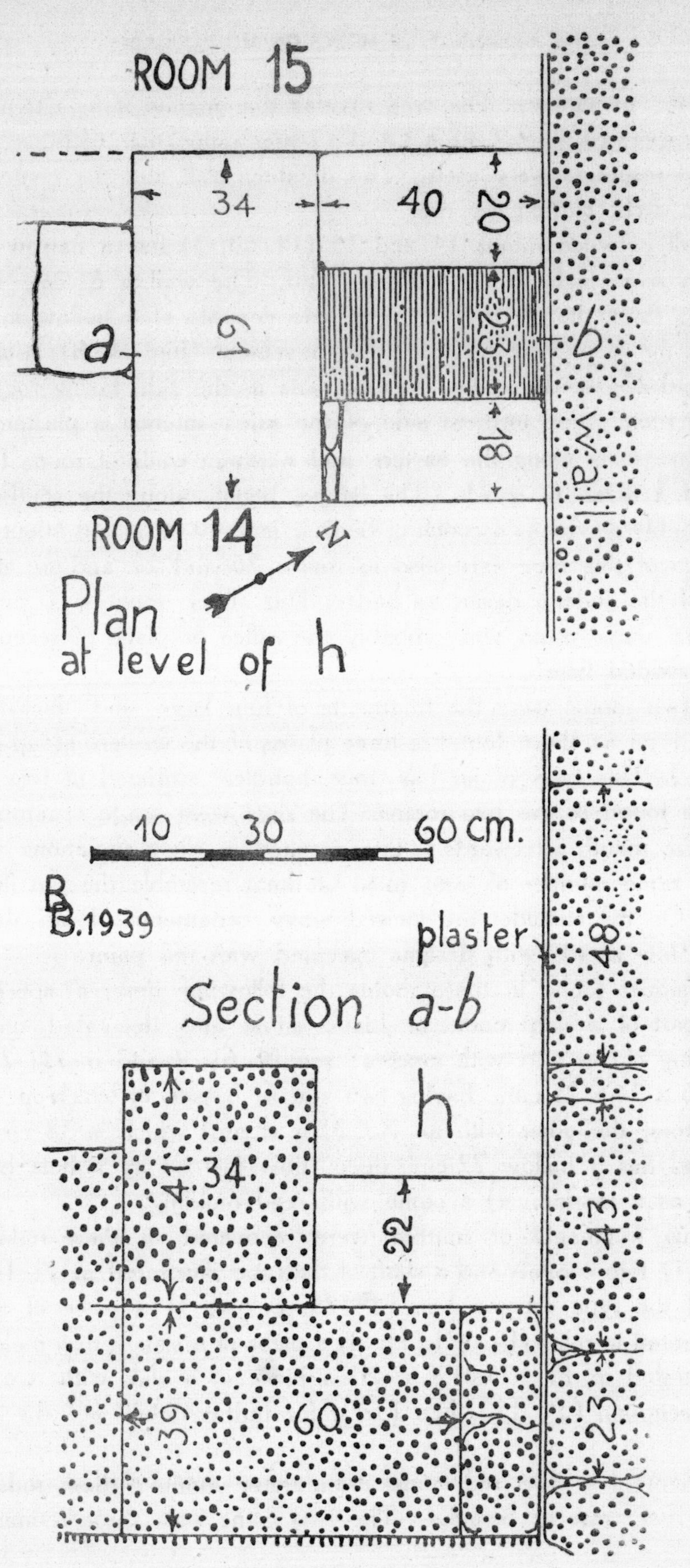

Fig. 16. The secret safe (h) in the northern end of the wall between rooms 14 and 15.

on the mosaic pavement. The wall divides the original large chamber into a smaller inner room (4.80 × 2.40 m.) and a larger outer room (4.80 × 5.20 m.); in the latter the responds were used. The dividing wall and the responds, which supported an arch, carried the roof.

The wall between rooms 14 and 15 (Pl. 50, 2) has a narrow door in the center and a secret safe at the northern end. The wall is 61 cm. thick. Near the door was found its plain lintel. The safe consists of a hollow in the center of the wall in the second course above the pavement (Fig. 16, **h**); it is 40 cm. l., 23 cm. w. and 22 cm. deep; the opening was in the side facing room 15, that is, the inner room ; the northern side of the safe's interior is plastered.

The stone seats along the eastern and northern walls of room 14 give the impression of a divan or couch. The stone bench along the southern wall of room 15 probably served as a couch or bed; it is 2.40 m. l. and about 60 cm.w.; stone benches of this type exist also in rooms 26 and 27 and are still used by the monks of the Judean desert as beds. This inner room was probably the bedroom, the outer room was probably the office or place of reception of the official who resided here.

In the two rooms were the fragments of four large and thick-walled jars of the same type as those found in three places of the western group of buildings (see Pl. 144). This type of jar has four handles arranged in two pairs ; 16 handles were found in the two rooms. The rims were made separately and inserted into the mouth afterwards ; this resulted in slight variations which also point to the same number of jars; most of them resemble the rim illustrated in Pl. 144, 3. On the shoulder are incised wavy ornaments. From these rooms come also a few sherds with designs executed with red paint.

Of the stones found in these rooms the following deserve special notice : 1) a large part of a slab made of black stone and decorated on one side with interlacing circles and with crosses ; see Pl. 61, 2 and p. 71; 2) a stone, measuring 66 × 34 × 25 cm., having two square bosses, of which one is decorated with a cross, the other with an X; 3) a stone, which is 38 cm. long, 33 cm. wide and has a hollow 22 cm. deep, now pierced by a hole below, may have served as a mortar; 4) a stone with reed molding.

Numerous fragments of marble were recovered in these rooms ; among these were : 1) two capitals and a shaft of the type illustrated in Pl. 129, 1, 3-5; 2) a post of the type illustrated in Pl. 128, below; 3) a piece of a slab with a fruit represented in relief (Pl. 121, 1); 4) a piece of a slab with a molding similar to that illustrated in Pl. 125, 4 & 5; 5) a piece of a slab with two lines of a Samaritan inscription (Pl. 122, Fig. 1, 4); for further details see the chapter on inscriptions.

A fragment of a glass rod comes from these rooms ; these rods (see Pl. 141, 17) are very rare at Siyâgha. The two coins from these rooms could not be identified.

As a rule a monk has only one small room for his living quarters. If the rooms are large or arranged in groups there must be a special reason, as, for instance, in this case. The small inner room was probably the private apartment of the monk who resided here. From the fact that there is also a large antechamber, we conclude that a high official of the monastery lived here; he needed this extra room for his official duties. In most monasteries only the highest superior has two rooms; this would seem to indicate that this was the suite of the abbot. The suite is conveniently located for an abbot; from room 14 he could reach the basilica by a private staircase leading to room 10 at the northern end of the narthex; the rooms are near the refectory; they are far enough removed from the main entrance to give a certain amount of privacy, especially if the wall in the northern part of the atrium served as a screen, as we suggested on p. 78.

But the presence of four large storage jars in these rooms seems to suggest that these were the quarters of the oikonómos of the monastery, especially since his secret safe has also been discovered. The presence of broken marble, etc. determines nothing about the purpose of these two rooms; those materials were probably used in restoring the walls, etc. Possibly the marble posts were used for a table or desk in the official's office.

Room 16 (Pls. 161, 16; 51, 1; Figs. 9 and 17) was the refectory. It measures 8 × 5 m. and is the largest chamber in the northern wing of the building. It has doors in the northern and southern walls, a cupboard in the eastern wall, a window in the western wall, a pair of responds against the northern and southern walls, a stone table against the western end of the northern wall and a mosaic pavement with geometrical and floral designs. In the room were found a marble base, two marble capitals, some decorated marble slabs, a piece of a millstone, fragments of stone and clay vessels.

The responds indicate that the room was spanned by a transverse arch to support the roof, as was the case in most of the larger rooms.

The doors in the northern and southern walls show that this room served also as a passage between the atrium and the region to the north; the floor is lower than the thresholds, inside which there are steps. For the jamb of the northern door a shaft of a column characteristic of the cella trichora was used; this seems to point to a reconstruction carried out after the cella trichora had collapsed.

The western wall of the chamber stands on the mosaic pavement which was common to rooms 16 and 17. From this it follows that rooms 16 and 17 resulted from the partition of a larger chamber. The wall which forms the partition has a window at its northern end in the third course above the floor (Pl. 51, 1; Fig. 17, f). This aperture is 40 cm. w. and 56 cm. h.; its sill corresponds to the thickness of the wall, 60 cm., and has, moreover, a projecting stone (Fig. 17, s) which serves as a shelf and joins the sill with the stone table against the northern wall (Fig. 17, g). The stone table is 2.35 m. l., 66 cm. w. and 74 cm. h. ; it is constructed of reused materials ; one of the stones (Fig. 17, m) has a splay. The stone in the top course to the left of the window is

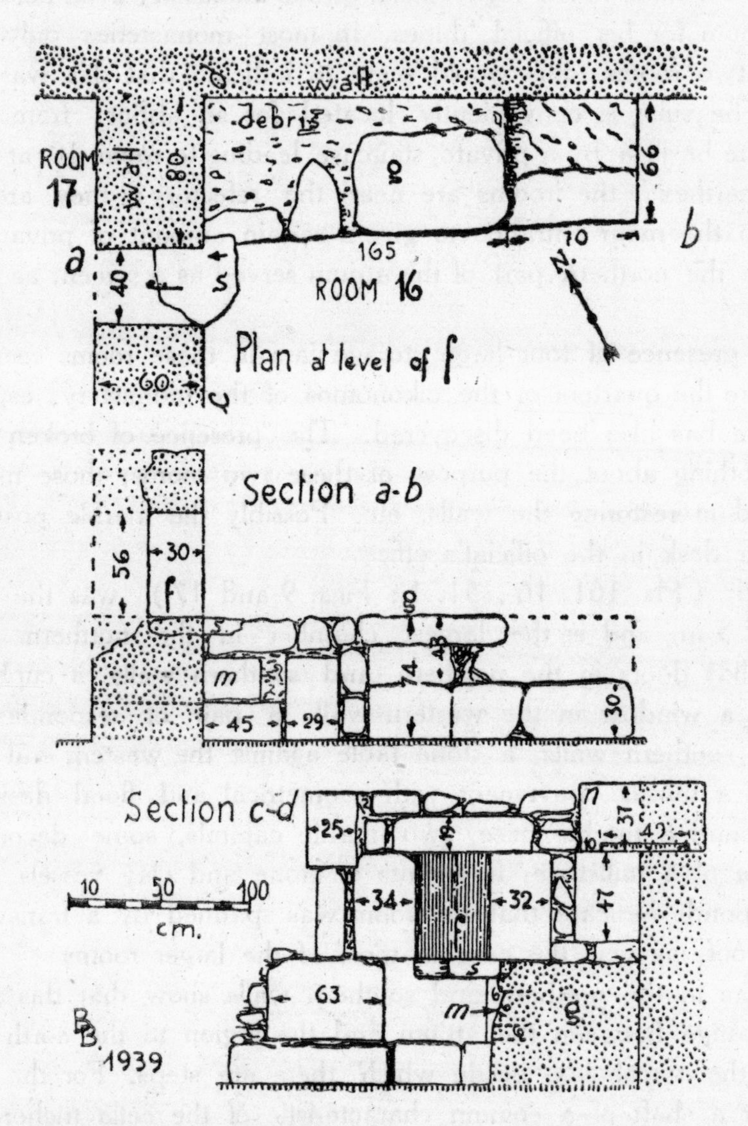

Fig. 17. The window (f) and table (g) in the northwest corner of room 16.

arched ; it occupies a position directly above the fireplace on the other side of the wall and looks like a flue.

The window in the wall with its shelf and nearby table characterize this chamber as the refectory and the room on the other side of the wall as the kitchen. Food from the kitchen was passed through the opening ; the table in the corner was used for the dishes; from there they were brought to the tables where the community was seated; after meals the dishes were brought back to the table in the corner and were returned to the kitchen through the opening which may have been closed by a wooden slide or shutter; hence we frequently speak of calling at the "shutter", or simply the "shut", for food. The area in front of the window was much used, as is evident from the fact that the mosaic pavement was entirely worn out here, just as it was between the two doors.

The cupboard in the eastern wall was used for tableware. The few fragments of stone and clay vessels found in or near the room give no idea of the kind of dishes used for table service. A stone mortar outside the northern door, a piece of a millstone inside the room and another millstone outside the southern door (Pl. 60, Fig. 1, 8 & 10) seem to indicate that grain was ground in this neighborhood.

East of the passage between the two doors a number of stones was arranged in a row from north to south; among these stones were a marble base and a marble capital. The base is of the same type as the three found in the room on the south side of the basilica's sanctuary (see Pl. 129, 6-8 and pp. 54 ff.) and no doubt belongs to that group. The capital is of the same type as the three found in the Theotokos chapel and the one in the stone bench of the narthex (see pp. 95 f.).

West of the passage between the two doors another marble capital was found which differs from all the other marble capitals in the number of acanthus leaves which decorate the calathus; it is the only one which has 16 leaves (see Pl. 131, Fig. 2, below and p. 96).

A fragment of a marble slab found here has preserved several arms of a cross in relief.

All this material seems to come from the basilica or chapels and represents a secondary and late use of the same.

The mosaic pavement will be described more in detail in the chapter on mosaics.

Room 17 (Pls. 161, 17; 51, 2; Fig. 9) was the kitchen. It occupies the northwest corner of the building and measures about 3.60 × 5.20 m.; it has a window in its eastern wall, a fireplace against the same wall, an entrance in the southern wall, a drain through the western wall, a number of low walls on the interior and a mosaic pavement. Some marble and a coin were found here.

The opening between rooms 17 and 18 is wide and without jambs. It served to join this room with the atrium via room 18.

There is a row of stones parallel to the southern half of the western wall. When the space between the wall and the row of stones was still filled with débris it looked like a bench or low table, like the benches in rooms 14, 15,

26 and 27. In all those cases the bench was formed by a row of stones parallel to the wall and by a packing of other materials. But after the packing had been removed we discovered that the western wall of the room was pierced by a drain. Perhaps we have here a sink, which would be required in a kitchen; the drain empties into the area 53, which we found enclosed by a low wall.

Another row of stones running east and west divided the floor-space into two sections. Its purpose is not clear; its top seems to represent a later level of the room; the floor is higher at the north and south and sags in the center.

Above the southern end of the row of stones just mentioned, against the eastern wall of the room, there was a fireplace built of stones and tiles. The stones of the wall are cracked by the heat of the fire; near the top of the wall is an arched stone, which probably served as a flue. North of the fireplace in the same wall is the window between this room and room 16. This window, the fireplace and the sink characterize this room as the kitchen.

The mosaic pavement in this room will be described in the chapter on mosaics. Here we wish to observe that it is the same pavement which we observed in room 16. The wall between the two rooms stands on the mosaic pavement and is of later date than the mosaic. Originally, therefore, there was one large hall here comprising rooms 16 and 17 and measuring 13 × 5.20 m. What the original purpose of this hall was, we do not know; it may originally also have served as a refectory.

In room 17 was found a marble post which bulges in the center (Pl. 128, top, sixth in row); also a small marble capital, of the type illustrated in Pl. 130, 3 ff., comes from here.

The only coin found in this room is a fels of Melek al-Kamil Nasir-ad-Din Mohammed who reigned from A. H. 615-635, that is, 1218-1238 A. D. This coin could have been lost by a passing traveller and no special significance would have to be attached to it, were it not for the fact that it seems to belong to the period shortly before the final abandonment of the monastery. In 1217, namely, Thietmar claims to have found Greek Christians still living here, and in 1244 or not long afterwards the monastery is supposed to have been destroyed (see p. 113, 4).

Room 18 (Pls. 161, 18; 51, 2; Fig. 9) has a door in the northeast corner. It is not certain whether the rough stones which fill the lower part of the room represent the pavement or a fallen wall; on removing some of the stones along the east side of the room we came upon a bed of lime. Owing to its close connection with the kitchen we suggest that this room was the pantry; nothing was found to confirm or contradict this view.

Room 19 (Pl. 161, 19; Fig. 9) has no door; its entire floor is covered with a thick layer of lime. Here were found some marble posts, a piece of a marble slab and a stone bowl. The one marble post consists of part of a shaft and a capital of the type illustrated in Pl. 129, 1, 3-5; the other is a piece of a shaft with a small square base. The largest of the four fragments illustrated in Pl. 126, 20 comes from here. The stone bowl (Pl. 133, Fig. 1, 1) is incomplete; it is made of a dark-gray stone called "gneiss-schist"; it has a flat bottom 12½ cm. in d., straight sides 3 cm. h. and is decorated with incised straight lines and small concentric circles with a punctured hole in the center. The straight lines are arranged in groups of two or three placed diagonally to suggest triangles; each so-called triangle contains three concentric circles.

Other more or less complete bowls of this type (see Pl. 133, Fig. 1, 1-5) and numerous fragments were found in the atrium and southern group of buildings; a few were recovered in other parts of the site. In general the context seems to indicate that this type of bowl was used at Siyâgha during the final occupation of the site.

Bowls of the same type were found in a tomb at Jericho[1] attributed to the fourth or fifth century; a similar dish found at Ophel (Jerusalem) is attributed to the end of the Byzantine period.[2]

Room 20 (Pl. 161, 20; Fig. 9) has a door in the northeast corner; there is no pavement. Here were found a stone decorated with a cross, three marble posts, fragments of two pottery lamps and a few other pottery sherds with designs executed in red, a few links of a chain and several coins.

One of the marble posts (Pl. 129, 5) has preserved a part of the shaft and the capital. The shaft consists of white marble with black stripes and is still 51 cm. long. The capital is of the Corinthian type with four acanthus leaves beneath the four corners of the abacus; it is 27 cm. high, 18 cm. wide along each side of the abacus and its base is 16 cm. in diameter. The second marble post is 55 cm. l.; the third, a fragment, is 44 cm. l.

The two fragments of lamps belong to varieties characteristic of the end of the Byzantine period. The one fragment, measuring 7 × 4 cm., represents about one half of the top of a lamp; it is made of light-red clay and its ornaments are executed in thin lines; they consist of a geometrical design on the spout and of clusters of fruits and rosettes enclosed by vines around the central opening. The other fragment represents that part of the base and top of a lamp which is opposite the spout; it is 4 cm. h. and 6 cm. in d.; it is made of gray clay. The ornamentation consists of a series of rounded arches with a vertical line in the center and at the place where one would look for the handle there is a cross, the tips of whose arms are bifurcated.

A bronze coin from here has been attributed to the Umayyad period.

1 *Jericho*, pp. 167 f., VI, 1 & 2.

2 *PEF Ann.* 5, p. 85 and Plate XVI, 5.

Room 21 (Pls. 161, 21; 52, 1 & 2; Fig. 9) is located in about the center of the western wing and directly opposite to the main entrance of the basilica. Its door is in the center of the eastern wall. In the room were found some pieces of marble and a wick-holder; below the floor there are three tombs which contained besides the burials some coins, a ring, tacks or rivets and buckles.

The three tombs occupy the greater part of the area below the floor of this room (Pl. 52, 2), though there was space both along the south and the west of the tombs which was not utilized. The tombs are built of masonry, plastered on the interior and paved with mosaics; there is a head-rest at the western end and a pit in the center.

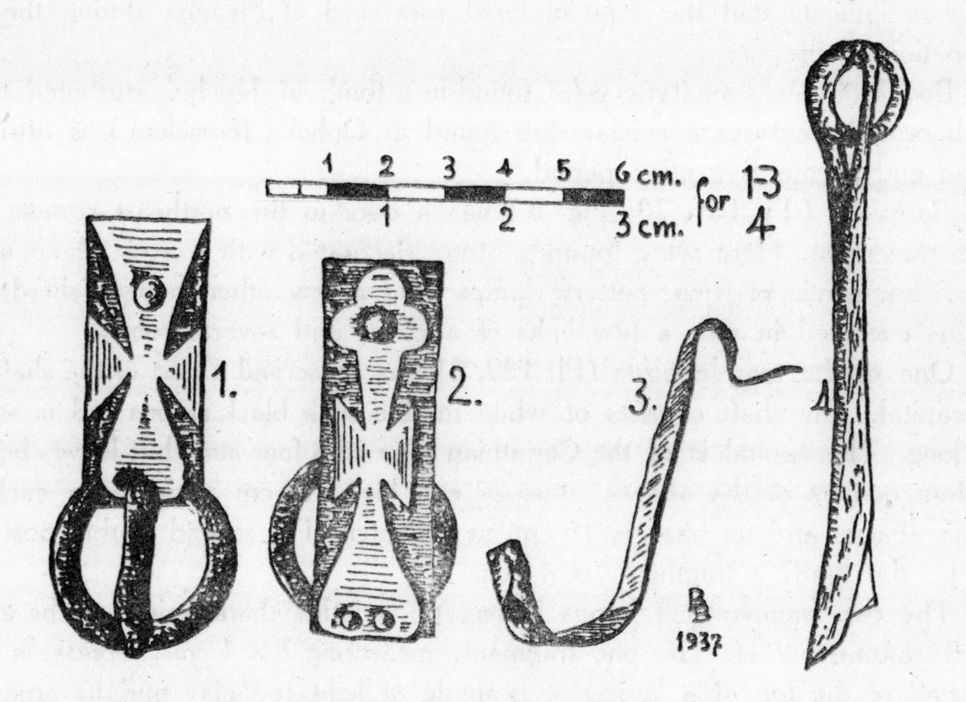

Fig. 18. Metal buckles (1 & 2), a wick-holder (3) and ring with two bars (4).

The tombs are 152-158 cm. l., 60-74 cm. w. and on an average about 2 m. deep. They are closed by slabs which rest on a ledge. The ledge is 21-23 cm. thick and projects 6-18 cm. Below the ledge the tomb is 124-130 cm. deep; above it the walls rise 44-48 cm.; the tops of the walls are on a level with the inner or lower of the two steps in the doorway. The slabs which close the mouth of the tombs are on a lower level than the walls at their sides, but higher than the pavement at the west. One slab of each of the two tombs, a and c, is pierced by a round hole.

This group of three tombs is very similar to the group of three tombs found at the eastern end of the basilica's nave (see pp. 37-39), but there are a number of differences. Thus, for instance, the tombs in room 21 have a head-rest and mosaic pavements, in which respect they resemble the early Christian tombs discovered by Clermont-Ganneau at el-Gherbâwy near el-Midieh in Palestine.[1]

Each of the three tombs was over half full of bones ; most of the bones were in a very decayed state ; the skeleton on top of the bones in the central tomb (Pl. 52, 2) was tolerably well preserved. The bones in the three tombs may represent well over 100 burials.

In the tombs were found about a dozen small bronze coins characteristic of the fourth and fifth centuries. Associated with the bones and coins were tacks or rivets and buckles which most probably belonged to belts. The buckles (Fig. 18, 1 & 2) consist of rings with a tongue and a metal plaque attached to a leather belt by means of small broad-headed rivets or tacks. The buckles are made of iron which is much corroded ; in spite of this, one is sufficiently well preserved to enable us to recognize all its parts (Fig. 18, 1); it was about 7 cm. long and nearly 3 cm. wide ; the plaque is cruciform. About a dozen small fragments enabled us to restore another buckle (Fig. 18, 2). About 14 tacks with broad heads suggest the existence of a number of other buckles. Other objects need not detain us here.

The tombs characterize this room as a burial chamber.

Room 22 (Pl. 161, 22; Fig. 9) is the largest in the western wing (8.40 × 3.40 m.). It has two doors in its eastern wall and one in its southern wall ; the western wall was strengthened by an addition against its interior; along the northern wall there is a platform with a cemented channel leading to an opening through the western wall. The southern part of the room is paved with plain mosaics. This is the only room in which clay bricks were used. A stone bowl (Pl. 133, Fig. 1, 4), an object made of bone (Pl. 134, 1, third row, last object), a metal link (Pl. 138, Fig. 2, 6), a glass bottle (Pl. 141, 2) and painted sherds (Pl. 145, 6) were recovered here.

The two doors in the eastern wall unite this room with the atrium ; these suggest that there may have been two rooms here originally; this seems to be confirmed by the mosaic pavement which exists only in the southern half of the room. The tesserae used for this pavement have a surface which is about 1½ cm. square. There are no designs.

Between the mosaic pavement and the platform along the northern side of the room there was a break in the pavement. In this break a number of loose clay bricks was found ; such bricks were used in the wall below the northeastern

[1] *ARP* 2, pp. 366 f.

door and for the platform with the channel. Nowhere else on the site were clay bricks used as a building material, as far as our experience goes. The bricks measure $21\frac{1}{2} \times 19\frac{1}{2} \times 6\frac{1}{2}$ cm. Bricks which are about 22 cm. square and about $7\frac{1}{2}$ cm. thick are attributed to the early Arab period ; in the Byzantine period the bricks are much thinner, about 3 cm. thick, and have a layer of mortar between them as thick as the bricks or tiles themselves. According to this principle we would have bricks whose dimensions correspond very closely to those attributed to the early Arab period.

The purpose of the channel on the platform was not to carry off an overflow from cistern 8 in the center of atrium, since there was no opening in the wall on the east. The channel drained through an opening in the western wall into the courtyard of the western monastery. The drainage could have flowed along the southern side of platform 57 as far as 58, where there is a small stone basin. There is no clear evidence to indicate the direction followed then; in area 59, however, the wall has an opening which seems to have had the purpose of collecting the drainage of the western courtyard, consequently also that from room 22, and conducting it to the channel in rooms 60 and 62.

This room may have been a lavatory or latrine. Other objects found in the room do not help to determine its purpose; they will be treated in speaking of the different kinds of materials of which they are made.

Room 23 (Pl. 161, 23 ; Fig. 9) occupies the southwestern corner of the building. It has two doors ; the one joins this room with room 22, the other with room 24. In the southern side of this latter door there is a stone with a shell ornament. On the exterior of the western wall a lintel, from which crosses seem to have been chiseled away, was utilized as a building stone. No pavement was found, but there is abundant evidence of fire in this room. The floor is covered thickly with ashes; the walls are blackened, reddened and cracked by heat especially in the southwest corner; along the western wall there is still a large quantity of cut straw which was used to feed the fire. In the northeastern corner there is a stone basin ; along the eastern end of the southern wall there is a stone bench. In the room were found a stone capital, a marble base, and a few fragments of marble slabs.

The stone capital is small ; the material of which it is made is black and brittle, but on three sides a three-lobed leaf can still be recognized.

The marble base is of the same type as the three found in the southern sacristy and the one recovered in room 16 (see Pl. 129, 6-8); five bases of this kind no longer in situ are known to us.

A fragment of a marble slab is decorated with three arms of a cross enclosed by a wreath in relief. On two fragments from this room there are graffiti; one is illustrated in Pl. 123, 1; see also inscription XXXIV.

The straw, ashes and other traces of fire seem to indicate that this room was used as an oven during the final occupation of the site. The Arabic graffiti suggest that this occupation must be dated in the early Arab period.

Room 24 (Pls. 161, 24; 53, 1-2; Fig. 9), on the southwestern side of the atrium, measures 9 × 5 m.; this is the largest room of the atrium group. Its walls are poorly preserved; a door exists in the western wall, uniting this room with room 23 ; there was no door in either the southern or eastern walls, but it is not certain whether there was a door in the northern wall joining this room with the atrium ; the walls there are very low and no jamb was found in situ or near the wall. In the southwest corner (Pl. 53, 1) the second stone from the top has a reed molding, similar to that of several other stones on the site. In the middle of the eastern wall one of the stones projecting into the room is pierced by a hole, through which a rope could be passed for fastening something.

The room has a mosaic pavement enclosing two stone bases. The mosaic consists of plain tesserae of four sizes : the largest have a surface measuring about 5 × 5 cm., another type measures about 3 × 3 cm., a third about 2 × 2 cm. and a fourth 1½ × 1½ cm. The largest and smallest types seem to have been used for the original pavement, which was repaired with tesserae of the intermediate sizes.

The stone bases enclosed by the mosaic pavements are about 90 cm. from the northern wall of the room ; one is about half way between the eastern and western walls, the other against the eastern wall; opposite the former base, near the southern side of the room, there are two large stone slabs in the pavement (Pl. 53, 2). Whether the stone bases served to support pilasters and arches, or possibly a table, is not certain.

In this room was found the stone capital of the Corinthian type, illustrated in Pl. 59, 1. Its ornamentation resembles the marble capitals which have four acanthus leaves. It is 27 cm. h., 26 cm. in d. across the base and 37 cm. along each side of the top. On pp. 52 ff. we suggested that it may have served for the colonnade which was substituted for the chancel rail of the basilica.

Fragments of a pottery jug with molded ornaments (Pl. 154, 4), a piece of a bowl with quatrefoil designs in squares executed with red paint (Pl. 151, 29), pieces of stone bowls with incised ornaments consisting of concentric circles, like those illustrated in Pl. 133, Fig. 1, 2, were collected in or near this room.

The purpose of this room is not certain. Its size indicates that it was destined not for the cell of a monk, but for the community. It may have been the library, a school, a reading room or a recreation room. The only foundation for these suggestions is the supposition that the stone bases along the northern side of the room served for a table or book-rack.

Room 25 (Pl. 161, 25; Fig. 9; see Pls. 53, 2 and 71, 2, background) has a door in the southern wall, steps on both sides of the northern wall, a stone bench in a recess in the southern end of the eastern wall and opposite it another small recess in the western wall. This is a mere passage, about 1.40-1.60 m. wide, which connects the atrium with the southern monastery. There is nothing to show that the northern end of the passage had ever been closed by a door. Near the southern end of the passage were found the jambs of the door. Inside the door the stone bench on the east served as a seat for the porter. Outside the door two steps lead down to the courtyard of the southern monastery (Pl. 72, 2, in background, left). Most of the pilgrims who visited the basilica must have passed through this narrow passage.

Room 26 (Pl. 161, 26; Fig. 9) is a typical monastic cell, about 4.80 m. l. and 2.20 - 2.50 m. w.; it has a door in the northern wall, a stone bench along the southern wall and no pavement. This stone bench, like the ones in rooms 15 and 27, served as a seat and a bed.

Room 27 (Pl. 161, 27; Fig. 9) is a small cell like room 26; no door was discovered; the floor is surfaced with mortar. The bench against the southern wall contained a number of marble fragments; among these were the shaft of a column, a small marble capital with four acanthus leaves and a piece of an altar's slab.

Room 28 (Pl. 161, 28; 54, 1-2; Figs. 9 and 19) occupies the southeastern corner of the building. In general it resembles the two preceding cells, but in the northern part of this cell there is a structure which distinguishes this cell from all the rest. It consists of a basin and conduit built of stone (Pl. 54, 1; Fig. 19). The platform containing the basin is on the same level as the threshold; in other rooms the floor is generally considerably lower than the threshold. The basin is 64 cm. deep and roughly rectangular, measuring 51 × 62 cm. Near the southwestern corner of the basin there is a conduit which passes beneath the northern wall of the room, west of the door, and can be traced beneath the stone pavement in the southeast corner of the atrium. The whole course of the conduit was not explored, since it would have required the removal of the flags of the pavement, but the conduit seems to empty into cistern 8 in the center of the atrium.

The presence of a basin and a conduit directly inside the doorway of a room seems somewhat surprising. A jar of water might have been kept here for pilgrims; such jars are porous and if they are kept in a place where there is a draft the water keeps fresh; lest any of the precious water which penetrated through the jar be lost it was collected in the basin and from there flowed off to the cistern in the center of the atrium.

But another explanation is even more probable. By referring to the ground plan (Pl. 161, 28 and 30) it can be seen that the basin is opposite the southern end of the original narthex. When it rained the water of the narthex and possibly also from nearby roofs was collected in this catch-basin and the overflow was carried to cistern 8 by the conduit. This latter explanation presupposes that the basin and conduit represent a period when rooms 30 and 28 did not exist. In the later reconstruction the basin and drain no longer served their purpose and were concealed beneath the floor of room 28. No pavement exists in this room.

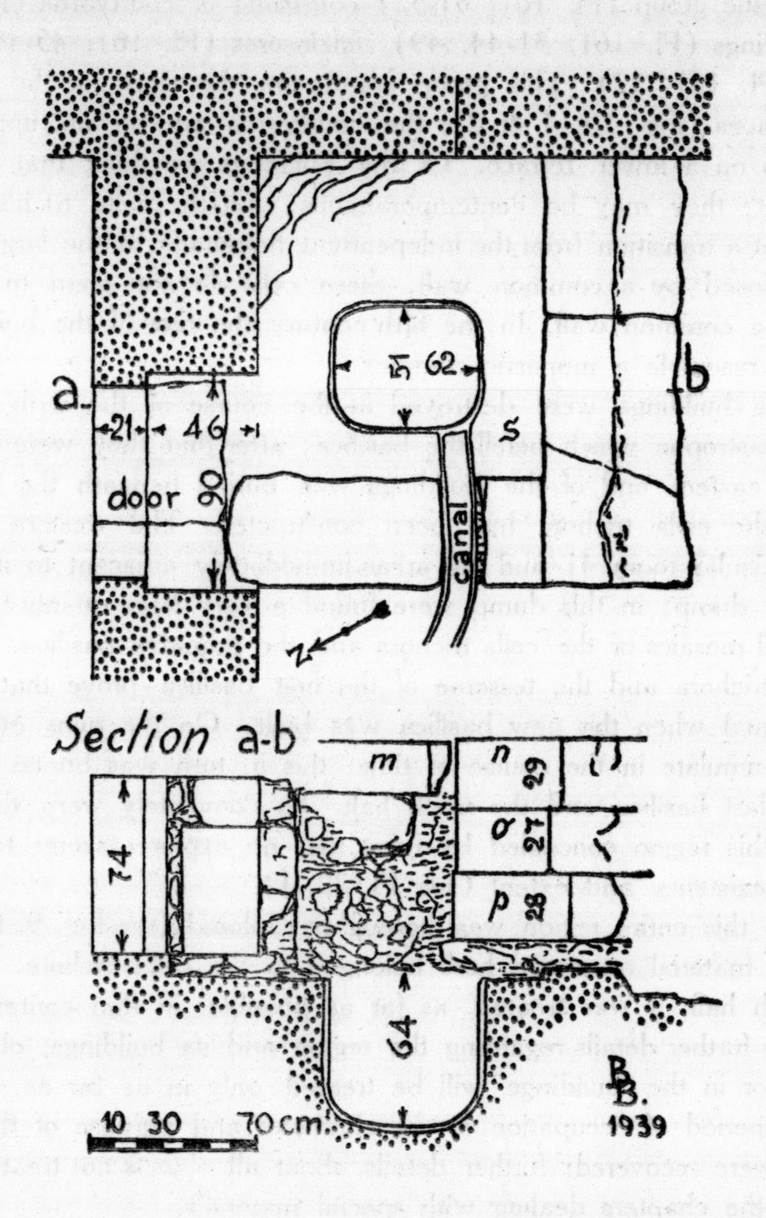

Fig. 19. The basin and conduit in the northern part of room 28.

C. THE NORTHERN GROUP

1. *General survey.* North of the basilica and the atrium group there is a second monastic group (Pl. 161, 31-52) consisting of courtyards (Pl. 161, 38 & 51), buildings (Pl. 161, 31-44, 49), enclosures (Pl. 161, 45-48, 50) and a passage (Pl. 161, 52). This group stands on the slope of the hill and is built on terraces (Fig. 20, 1 & 2); the courtyards are on an upper terrace, the buildings on a lower terrace. Of the buildings we think that cells 31-37 are the oldest; they may be contemporaneous with the cella trichora; perhaps they represent a transition from the independent hermitage to the large monastic complex enclosed by a common wall; these cells do not seem to have been enclosed by a common wall. In the fifth century the rest of the buildings were added; they resemble a monastic complex.

All these buildings were destroyed in the course of the sixth century, in the same catastrophe which befell the basilica; after that they were never again rebuilt. The eastern end of the buildings was buried beneath the huge stones from which the cella trichora had been constructed. The western end of the ruins, in particular room 41 and the areas immediately adjacent to it, was converted into a dump; in this dump were found a very large quantity of tesserae from the wall mosaics of the cella trichora and the primitive basilica. The stones of the cella trichora and the tesserae of the first basilica prove that this region was abandoned when the new basilica was built. On the ruins other rubbish began to accumulate in the course of time; this in turn was buried beneath the ruins of the last basilica and the north hall. So completely were the monastic buildings in this region concealed by ruins that no explorer seems to have suspected their existence and extent (see Pl. 22, 1).

In 1935 this entire region was thoroughly explored (see Fig. 9, foreground). Much of the material recovered here belonged to the cella trichora, the basilicas and the north hall; it was treated, as far as possible, in that context. Here we intend to give further details regarding the region and its buildings; objects found in this area or in the buildings will be treated only in as far as they throw light on the period of occupation or the character and purpose of the place in which they were recovered; further details about all objects not treated here will be found in the chapters dealing with special materials.

2. *The courtyards* (Pl. 161, 38 & 51). Along the northern side of the basilica and the north hall there are open spaces which served as courtyards; these are divided into two by a doorway, so that we may speak of an eastern and western section.

The eastern courtyard (Pl. 161, 38) is an irregular area enclosed on the south and southwest by the ancient walls of the cella trichora and by the north hall (Pls. 28; 29, 1 & 2; 62, 1), on the east by a retaining wall, on the north by a retaining wall and cells 31-35, on the west by room 39 and the large courtyard 51.

The relation of the western end of this courtyard to the north hall on the south and room 35 on the north may be studied in Fig. 20, 1. There it can

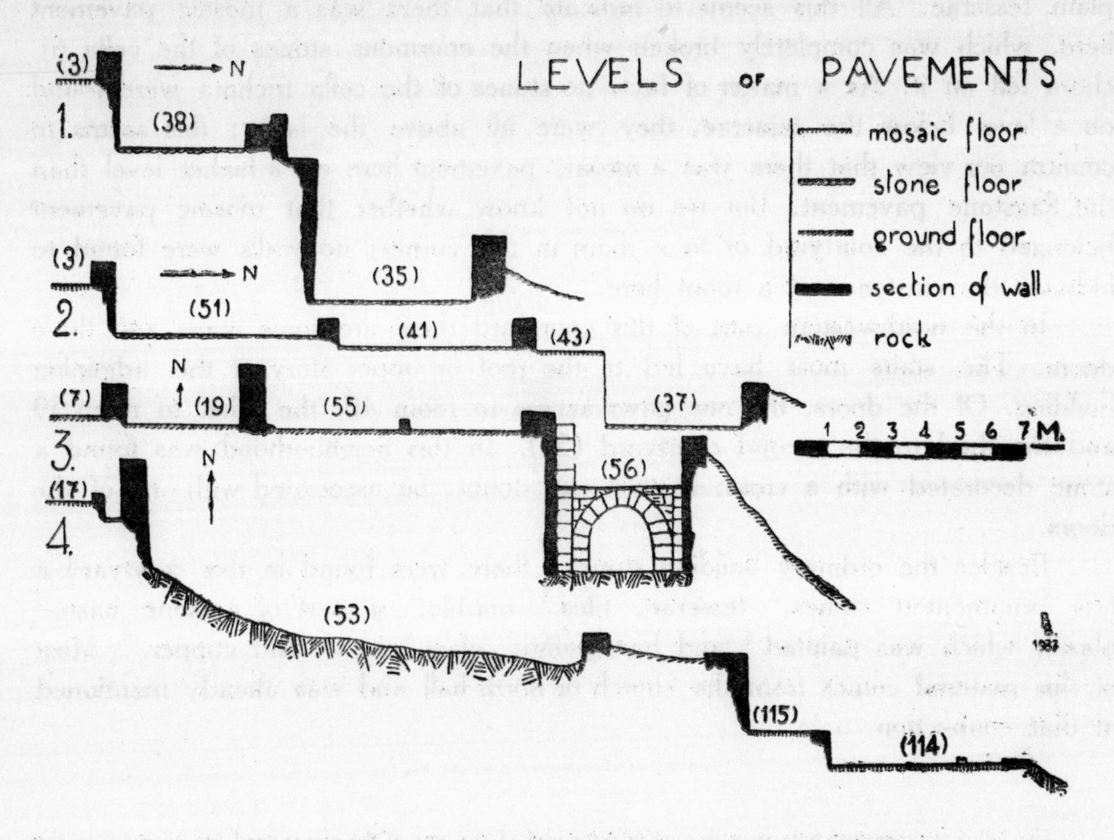

Fig. 20. Terraces on northern (1-2) and western (3-4) slopes.

be seen that the courtyard (38) is on a terrace about 2 m. below the level of the floor in the sanctuary of the north hall (3) and about 4 m. above the level of the floor in room 35.

This terrace was formed by a retaining wall along the east and north. On the east this retaining wall begins near the northeast corner of the cella trichora and extends northwards about 5 m.; a part of its face was uncovered, so that we are certain that it exists. Along the northern side of this courtyard there is also a retaining wall, distinct from the southern wall of rooms 32-35.

The greater part of the courtyard was paved with flagstones; the western end completely, the eastern end along the northern terrace wall; this latter strip of paving is 2-2½ m. wide and served both as a walk and as a protection to the terrace walls. In the corner formed by the basilica and north hall there is no pavement at present; this unpaved strip is 1.70-1.80 m. w. at the east and corresponds to the width of the north hall on the west. In this area, about 60 cm. above the level of the paved street, we came upon a layer of ashes and plaster about 15-20 cm. thick and in it were collected 13 baskets of large plain tesserae. All this seems to indicate that there was a mosaic pavement here, which was completely broken when the enormous stones of the cella trichora fell on it. As a matter of fact, no stones of the cella trichora were found on a level below the tesserae, they were all above the latter; this seems to confirm our view that there was a mosaic pavement here on a higher level than the flagstone pavement. But we do not know whether that mosaic pavement belonged to the courtyard or to a room in this corner; no walls were found to indicate the existence of a room here.

In the northwestern part of this courtyard there are some stairs and three doors. The stairs must have led to the roof or upper story of the adjoining building. Of the doors, the one gave access to room 40, the other to room 39 and the third to the second courtyard (51). In this neighborhood was found a stone decorated with a cross; it must, no doubt, be associated with one of the doors.

Besides the ordinary building stones [1] there were found in this courtyard a few ornamented stones,[2] tesserae, tiles,[3] marble,[4] a part of a stone basin,[5] plaster which was painted [6] and has graffiti,[7] glass,[8] iron [9] and copper.[10] Most of this material comes from the church or north hall and was already mentioned in that connection.

[1] The following measurements serve to convey some idea of the size of the stones used for constructing the cella trichora: 1) 89 × 75 × 54 cm.; 2) 110 × 49 × 52 cm.; 3) 125 × 70 × 62 cm.; 4) 125 × 89 × 40 cm.; 5) 160 × 74 × 56 cm. See Pls. 28 f.

[2] One is similar to the stone illustrated in Pl. 36, 7; there were several fragments of the plinth and torus of a small limestone base.

[3] The tiles are of two kinds: the one served to cover the roof, the other for window frames; both types were abundant.

[4] Marble fragments were very abundant; among them are pure white pieces of posts and slabs which belonged to altars; two fragments have Greek characters incised: CΦO and OΥ (see Pl. 121, 1); many of the pieces illustrated in Pl. 124, 2 come from here.

[5] Its sides are 3 cm. thick; at the mouth it is 35 cm. in d.

[6] These tempora were treated more in detail on p. 82, 4.

[7] See inscription XXXVII.

[8] Vases and panes of windows are represented; the largest quantity of window glass on the site was found near the pavement east of the north hall. See p. 82, 3.

[9] See p. 82, 3. A few nails come from here.

[10] A wick-holder.

The western courtyard (Pl. 161, 51) is larger than the eastern one; it is about 26.40 m. l. from east to west, 3.38 m. w. at the eastern end and 9.10 m. w. at the western end. It is enclosed on the south by the north hall, narthex and a part of the atrium; on the southwest by room 14; on the northwest by room 49; on the north by rooms 44, 41 and 39. The door between this courtyard and the eastern one was 1.38 m. wide. At the western end of the courtyard there is an opening between rooms 14 and 49 which is one meter wide; this gives access to a narrow passage which widens to 1.50 m. at the western end. On the northern side of the courtyard doors open into rooms 44 and 41. Built into the northern part of the western wall of this courtyard is a stone decorated with three crosses (Pl. 63, 1).

The entire courtyard, with the exception of a small section in the northwest corner, is paved with flags (Pls. 62, 2; 63, 2). The flags are placed at right angles with the walls of the building on the north, but not with the north hall; the base of the latter projects 17-20 cm.; between it and the pavement breaks are filled in with mortar. One flag has a circle, 50 cm. in d., another a cup, 14 cm. in d. and 5 cm. deep, cut into its surface. Both probably served for playing a game.

The level of the courtyard in relation to the adjoining buildings may be studied in Fig. 20, 2. There it will be seen that the floor of the north hall (3) is about 1½ m. higher than the pavement of the courtyard (51); rooms 41 and 43 are only slightly lower than the courtyard, but room 37 is over two meters lower.

The material which packed this courtyard to the height of the surrounding walls consisted principally of building stones, plaster, tiles, tesserae, glass and a few pottery sherds; none of these objects call for special notice here.

3. *The buildings* (Pls. 29, 2; 63, 2; 64, 1 & 2; 161, 31-37, 39-50; Fig. 9, foreground) in this northern region do not represent a compact and regular group arranged around the courtyard, as is the case elsewhere on the site. Thus, for example, the group of cells numbered 31-37 has no connection whatsoever with either of the two courtyards which we described; only a few of the remaining buildings have a direct connection with the courtyards. For this and other reasons it is better to distinguish several groups of buildings in this region; one comprises cells 31-37, the other loci 39-50.

a. *Cells 31-37* (Pl. 161, 31-37) are located on a terrace 2-4 m. lower than the courtyards (38 & 51) and the other rooms (see Fig. 20, 1 & 2). The cells are relatively large; their walls are comparatively well preserved; each cell has a door in its northern wall; several have cupboards; no traces of windows are preserved; the floors are paved with flags and are two or three steps lower than the sill of the door; of the roof nothing remains in situ; each room contained a number of small objects.

The masonry of these cells is, as a rule, of poorer quality than that of the other buildings on the site; rubble predominates, though there are some carefully dressed stones (see Fig. 8, 2 on p. 40; Pl. 64, 1 & 2).

Room 31 (Pl. 161, 31) was not excavated. The place where it is located was used as a path to the dump located beyond it to the northeast (Fig. 9, foreground, left end). A trench made outside its southern wall proves the existence of a room here. In the trench we found the coin of the first year of the reign of Justin II (565-6). It is difficult to imagine how this coin could have come there after the cella trichora had collapsed and covered this entire region with a thick layer of débris. This coin, therefore, possibly indicates a terminus post quem for the destruction of the cella trichora.

Room 32 (Pl. 161, 32; see Pl. 29, 2, foreground; Fig. 9, foreground, left) is located at the eastern end of the northern terrace. It measures about 4.35 × 4.67 m.; in other words, it is nearly square. Its walls are about 80 cm. thick and still stand to a height of 3.20 m. in the southeast corner; there is no trace of an upper story or of a roof in situ. In the western wall there is a cupboard 46 cm. wide; the upper part is missing, so its height is not certain. The door is in the center of the northern wall; its jambs are still in situ to a height of 60-80 cm.; in one of the jambs there is a hole to receive the bolt or bar by means of which the door was locked. The doorway is 90 cm. wide; two steps lead down into the room. The floor is paved with flags. In the southwest corner there was a fireplace built of tiles.

Among the objects found in this room we may note several stones, pieces of marble, a few metal objects, some glass, pottery and coins. Most of these objects will have special interest since they represent a sealed deposit. The room was, so to say, sealed by the collapse of the cella trichora; two large stones of that building were found lying above the ruins directly inside the door. The material found beneath these stones may be assigned to the period antedating the collapse of the cella trichora, the material found above the stones may be considered a later accumulation. This seems to explain satisfactorily the presence of early and late material in the same room.

Three stones found in the room have a perforation in the center; such stones did not occur elsewhere on the site; it has been suggested that they may have served for fastening horses. A fourth stone, measuring 44 × 25 × 17 cm., has 6 shallow holes in the one surface; the holes are $2\frac{1}{2}$-4 cm. deep and 8-10 cm. in d.; this stone was not found inside the room, but immediately outside and to the west of the door. A similar stone was found near the edge of the ruins on the east side of the basilica; it measures 55 × 38 × 32 cm. and has two rows of cup marks on one side; 7 holes can be recognized in one row and

5 in the other. This is the stone seen both by Kittel[1] and by Karge;[2] the former thinks that it may be a relic of an ancient altar, the latter says that the stone served for playing a game. The discovery of this second stone near the door of cell 32 with only six holes suggests another possibility. This last stone probably served to feed and water chickens or birds.

The thin slabs of marble found in this room may have been used as a slate, a palette or the like.

Iron nails were quite abundant. There was also a copper wick-holder. Most interesting of all the metal objects was the bronze arm of a small suspension lamp (Pl. 135, Fig. 1, 5); it is about 6½ cm. l.; at the lower end it has three branches terminating in eyes for the chains; at the upper end it has one eye.

The pieces of glass found in the room belong to window panes and to lamps.

Pottery sherds were abundant; most of them were collected in a layer of clay next to the pavement. The rim of a storage jar found here resembles those illustrated in Pl. 144, 5 & 6; the ware is thick and heavy; on the shoulder there is an incised wavy line; the rim is everted, grooved on the side and top; the diameter of the mouth is 15 cm. in the throat, 20 cm. at the edge of the everted lips. The everted lip distinguishes this jar from those found in the atrium and the upper part of the western monastery. The jar with an everted lip may be an earlier type than the jar with a straight neck. Two heavy handles with grooves (see Pl. 144, 2-4) and two disk-shaped bases (see Pl. 144, 7) belong to this same type of jar.

The majority of sherds from this room are ribbed; the surface of about one half of these ribbed sherds is black and of the other half is reddish or white. Many of the ribbed sherds have linear ornaments executed in white paint (see Pl. 149, 9 ff.). The sherds which are not ribbed frequently have incised lines as ornaments.

Jugs and cups are represented by a number of more or less complete specimens or larger fragments. Near the base of the western wall was found the jug illustrated in Pl. 154, 13; it is about 20 cm. h. and measures about 12 cm. in d. across the shoulders. The base of this jug, as well as that of another, is concave with a pellet in the center; this is the so-called "umbilicus" or "teat"[3] which is supposed to appear for the first time in the sixth century A. D.

One of the first objects found inside the door was a small clay cup, 13 cm. in d., with band combing consisting of 8 lines; another cup, 11.5 cm. in d. and 8 cm. h. with a white slip on the interior and exterior, has three incised horizontal lines as an ornament; the third cup, which also is decorated with band combing, is 10.5 cm. in d., 6 cm. h. and has a ring-base 4 cm. in d.; the ware is red and the white slip was used only for the exterior.

[1] See p. 14, 8.

[2] See pp. 14 f., 9.

[3] This latter term is used by Glueck in *AASOR* 18-19 (1939), p. 267; see Pl. 20, third and fourth rows.

One handle of a ribbed vessel has a seal impression (Pl. 158, 29 & 30). The impression is round, about 17 mm. in d., and contains a cross in relief with pellets between the arms of the cross. Handles were attached vertically or horizontally ; the majority are grooved down the back; only one, however, has a seal impression.

Four coins from this room were identified: one was attributed to Arcadius (395-408 A. D.), two to Justin II (565-578 A. D.) and one to Mauricius Tiberius (582-602) ; the last coin was minted in the eleventh year of the emperor's reign, that is, 592-3 A. D. The coins suggest that the cell was occupied during the fifth and sixth centuries; this may be approximately correct.

Room 33 (Pl. 161, 33; see Pl. 29, 2; Figs. 8, 2; 9) resembles the preceding one. Its walls rise 2.30 m. above the stone pavement on the south; in the eastern wall there is a cupboard which is 42 cm. wide and 48 cm. high. Of the roof a decayed beam was observed in situ extending from north to south across the room at a level about 1.10 m. above the pavement; the decomposed wood forms a layer 6-10 cm. thick. In the preceding room the stones of the cella trichora were also found on a level about 1.00-1.20 m. above the pavement. It may be well to stress that material found at the level of the beam and below it antedates the collapse of the cella trichora and that material found above it, that is, in the upper half of the room and above the walls, is most probably of later date.

Pottery from this room has the same general characteristics as that from room 32, but a few new types occur ; thus, for example, the lower half of a lamp with a cross in relief inside a ring-base (Pl. 143, 10) ; a bottle with incised ornaments on the neck and shoulders (Pl. 150, 9); a jug with ornaments consisting of cords and knots in relief, of punctured holes, incised grooves and shallow depressions (Pl. 154, 5); a jug with a strainer, consisting of five holes, inside the neck (Pl. 154, 28); and a tile in the form of a semitube 44 cm. l., 12-16 cm. in d. with walls 15 mm. thick.

Five coins were found in this room, but only one could be identified ; it belongs to the time of Arcadius (395-408 A. D.).

Room 34 (Pl. 161, 34 ; see Pl. 29, 2 ; Fig. 9) differs little from the preceding two in form and contents. Its western wall is sagging so much that it would fall if we removed the débris against it, so that part of the room was not completely cleared. In the southeast corner of the room was a small deposit of lime, in which was found the upper part of a thick-walled jar whose mouth is 26½ cm. in d. ; the everted lips of this jar resemble those of the jar found in room 32 and are 32.7 cm. in d. (see Pl. 144, 5). Other fragments of this jar were found in the northern part of this room, but neither here nor elsewhere in this region do they suffice to restore a complete jar or even the greater part of one.

The pottery mold for the lower half of a pottery lamp (Pl. 143, 12) from this room is the only one found on the entire site.

Six small coins come from this room; one, which could be identified, is a 20 nummia piece of Phocas (602-610 A. D.).

Room 35 (Pl. 161, 35; Figs. 9 & 20, 1) was not completely cleared owing to the condition of the walls, which are all in danger of collapsing. It is, however, certain that three steps lead from the door to the flagged floor. All objects which this room contains are still buried beneath a layer of earth. An Umayyad coin was found in the débris filling the upper part of the room. See room 40.

Between rooms 35 and 36 there is an area enclosed by the walls of the adjacent rooms; no wall was found on the north, so, as far as our knowledge goes, it seems that there was no room here. See room 40.

Room 36 (Pls. 64, 1-2; 161, 36; Fig. 9) is the largest in this group (6.60 × 4 m.); plaster was still adhering to the lower part of its southern wall. A bronze weight (20 × 12 mm.) is peculiar to this room. The character of the masonry and pavement can be seen in the illustrations; the pottery sherds, pieces of rusty nails, etc. filled two baskets, but exhibit no new features. See also rooms 40, 42 and 43.

Room 37 (Pls. 64, 1; 161, 37; Figs. 9 & 20, 2) is the westernmost of this group. Its walls with the two small cupboards in the southwest corner, its door and pavement can be studied in Pl. 64, 1. Also here several baskets of pottery and a few coins were recovered.

Area E (Pls. 161, E; 22, 2; Fig. 9). Rooms 31-37 are arranged around a depression in the northern slope of the ridge; the rooms face that depression and have a fine view in the direction of ʿAyûn Mûsa (see Pl. 12). In this position they were protected from the most violent winds which blow from the southwest and southeast. The large monastery, surrounded by a high enclosure wall, could afford to defy those winds; not so a few cells; these were obliged to seek shelter in a secluded spot, protected by nature and to some extent also by the church. But even this spot was not perfectly secure; an earthquake caused the walls of the cella trichora to fall and some of its large stones crashed through the roofs of these cells; after that they were abandoned. When the last basilica was destroyed, its ruins buried the cells beneath another layer of débris.

The convulsions of nature which brought about the ruin of the churches and the large monastery, not only caused the roofs and upper parts of the walls of these cells to fall but also distorted all the surviving walls, most of which incline in the direction of the slope. Had we removed the débris outside the rooms the walls would have fallen and there was danger of a general landslide which might have carried along the remnants of the churches. To avoid such a disaster we had to forego a thorough exploration of the area north of the rooms, at least for the present. Some light, however, was thrown on this area when we rolled back the stones on the surface. There was evidence of a wall, pottery and other remains.

The wall was encountered about 2-3 m. north of rooms 33-35; this was probably a retaining wall for the terrace on which the cells were built. In front of the cells on the same terrace there must have been place for a path along which the cells were reached.

A shallow trench dug north of the last-mentioned wall yielded abundant sherds; among them was the one with the two seals illustrated in Pl. 158, 4. Here too occurred fragments of a thick-walled jar of the type illustrated in Pl. 144, 5 ff.; its throat is 19 cm. in d. and its everted lips 27 cm. in d. The fragment of the upper part of a lamp has four parallel lines in relief on the spout and a ladder motif on the one surviving side. In short, four baskets were filled with sherds representing the various parts of many types of vessels.

Among the stones on the slope was one decorated with a cross formed by a series of punctured holes (Pl. 57, 14); three arms terminate in two prongs; the fourth arm rests on a semicircular mound by which Calvary or posssibly a globe was intended. Another stone, broken at one end but still 36 cm. h. and 34 cm. l., has a margin 2 cm. wide and a boss decorated with a large X, similar to that illustrated in Pl. 36, 7. Other stones found here were treated in speaking of the cella trichora and the basilica.

The entire slope from the walls of the church down to the edge of the ruins was littered with plaster, tiles, fragments of marble, tesserae, broken glass, pieces of metal, among which was a small bell, some coins, etc.

b. *Loci 39-50* (Pl. 161, 39-50). The term "locus" is used to designate all the places enclosed by walls whether they represent rooms or not. Loci 39-50 are on a higher level than rooms 31-37, but generally somewhat lower than the courtyards (38 & 51; see Fig. 20, 2).

Locus 39 (Pl. 161, 39; Fig. 9) is a small room 6 m. l. and 1.10-1.30 m. w. which occupies a narrow strip of the northeastern side of courtyard 51; its western and southern walls stand on the flags of the courtyard and its floor consists of the same flagging. The door is at the eastern end facing a staircase; it can be reached from courtyard 38.

A basket of pottery sherds was collected from this room; these sherds exhibit the same characteristics as those found in the rooms of the lower level. Thus, for example, the ribbed sherds frequently have painted white linear ornaments; the bases are disks or rings, flat or concave; the rims are all different from one another: some are plain, others molded; they may be straight, everted, flat, splayed or rounded; the handles are grooved.

One complete clay lamp was preserved in this room (Pl. 143, 5); its chief characteristic is the cross in relief on the nozzle; only a few of the lamps found at Siyâgha have the cross in this position; see the chapter on lamps.

A complete copper wick-holder from this room has a thin band 5 mm. w. and 7 cm. l. between the hook at the upper end and the clasp for the wick at the lower end; see Fig. 18, 3.

This may have been a porter's room.

Locus 40 (Pl. 161, 40; Fig. 9) is on the same level as courtyard 38; from this courtyard a narrow passage between room 39 and a staircase south of room 35 leads to the door of room 40. This door is in the southeastern corner of the room; only its sill is still in position and this is tilted towards the north; jambs and a stone decorated with a cross found in this neighborhood may belong to this door. The southern and western walls are preserved above the level of the floor, but the northern and eastern walls are not. The room has a mosaic floor made of plain tesserae whose surface is 2-2½ cm. square. Towards the east and north the floor has sunk. Some repairs were made by us to preserve it in the condition in which we found it.

This is the only room in the northern group of buildings which has a mosaic pavement in situ. Nothing else was found to indicate the purpose of this room; but its position near the entrance to the main courtyard (51) and the porter's room, as well as the fact that it is more carefully paved than the other rooms in the area, seems to indicate that it served as a parlor in which guests or pilgrims were received during the fifth and early sixth century.

Locus 41 (Pl. 161, 41; Fig. 9) is in many respects one of the most interesting places in the region; it marks the site of a dump and of a large room. At this spot mosaics were seen and collected by visitors to the site long before the excavations began. The presence of the mosaics gave the impression that an important building was located here; the excavations, indeed, brought to light a building, but it was buried beneath the débris in which the mosaics occur; this débris came from the church.

This room is roughly speaking about 8.60 m. l. and 4.20-5.20 m. w.; the eastern part is about one meter wider than the western part. In the former section the walls are built of rubble; they are about 65 cm. thick and still about one meter high. In the northern wall there is a door leading to room 42. The western half of the room is built of ashlar; it has a door in the southern wall, which joins the room with courtyard 51. The room has a stone floor, which is about 50 cm. lower than the courtyard (see Fig. 20, 2); inside the southern door is a stone step. A layer of clay covered the stone floor, above the clay ashes were abundant, especially in the northwestern corner. The rest of the room was filled with stones and earth to the top of the walls; mixed with this building material were fragments of pottery which filled two baskets, a little marble, some glass, a few pieces of copper and iron. Over the tops of the walls was a large deposit of plaster and mosaics.

No pottery vessel was complete. Among the sherds was the lower half of a lamp and two fragments of the upper half; spouts of jugs (see Pl. 154, 33 ff.) were observed first in this room; here too, pieces of large bowls without ornaments began to appear; sherds with white painted designs and others with incised straight and wavy lines occurred, but they were rare.

Among the pieces of broken glass there was the greater part of a wine glass whose stem has a knob in the center (Pl. 140, 38); bases, sides, rims and handles of various other vessels are represented.

The plaster found on the surface has the same characteristics as that found among the large stones of the cella trichora east of the basilica. Many of the fragments had one surface painted red; in this red surface were found tesserae, some of which were very small; in short, this material is exactly like that found east of the basilica (see pp. 33 ff.) and must come from the same source, namely, from the interior of the cella trichora and the basilica, where it served as a decoration of the wall or eastern apse. When that wall or apse was overthrown by an earthquake some of its decoration fell outside the church and remained buried there; some fell into the interior of the church. After the walls of the basilica had been rebuilt, the débris on the interior was removed; this could not be thrown outside the eastern wall, so it was carried out here and dumped into this region, which was not occupied again by new buildings. For the history of the northern group of buildings the dump is important; it is positive proof that they were abandoned during the period of the second basilica.

Locus 42 (Pls. 64, 2; 161, 42; Fig. 9) is north of room 41, with which it is united by a door. Only its southern and a part of its western and eastern walls are preserved; the rest of the walls have disappeared. Its stone pavement is tilted towards the north. To judge from the remnant of the western wall (Pl. 64, 2) it seems that the northern half of the room was built over room 36; the walls did not rest on those of room 36, but on the packing within the latter; when this gave way the walls and floor caved in. If this is true, then room 36 must have been abandoned when room 42 was built. Among the contents of the room there are fragments of large bowls; the rims are practically all different and call for individual study.

Locus 43 (Pls. 64, 2; 161, 43; Figs. 9; 20, 2) is north of room 41 and west of room 42; its northern part was built over rooms 36 and 37 and experienced the same fate as the northern part of room 42 (see Pl. 64, 2); it also had a floor paved with stones, now tilted towards the north. On the paved floor were the remnants of an oven which had been made of tiles. The door was not discovered. In the side of the eastern wall was found a 40 nummia piece of Anastasius (491-518 A. D.). The pottery sherds from here resemble those from room 42.

Locus 44 (Pls. 63, 2; 161, 44; Fig. 9) is one of the largest rooms on the site; it is 10.40 m. l. and 3.60-4.40 m. w.; the walls by which it is enclosed are highest around the eastern half of the room; the low walls of the western half are distinctly visible in Pl. 63, 2. The room has two doors; the one is in the center of the southern wall and the other in the northern wall. Steps in the southern doorway join courtyard 51 and room 44. The room was cleared to the level of a row of stone slabs placed across the center of the room from east to west. Above these slabs there was a layer of red earth; this kind of clay does not occur elsewhere at Siyâgha, but it is found at ᶜAyûn Mûsa; perhaps it was brought here for making pottery vessels. In the southeast corner there is an oven made of clay; it is on a higher level than the stone slabs used in the center of the room.

Metal, glass and pottery were quite abundant in this room. One copper wick-holder from here is complete. About 6 iron nails were collected; one (Pl. 136, 93) has a loop at one end and its shank tapers to a point; it is 9½ cm. l.

Among the glass fragments there were some which came from windows; others belonged to tumblers with concave bases, to lamps with hollow stems, to wine glasses, to bottles with thread ornaments in relief, etc.

Over three baskets of pottery sherds come from here. One fragment of the upper part of a lamp has a knob-handle with pellets on both sides and a linear ornament in a lower panel. Bowls, made of red clay with a molded ring-base and a great variety of rims, are well represented here. The first cover with a knob-handle was found in this room (see Pl. 157, 1-25). Sherds with ornaments in relief (Pl. 154, 7) also occurred.

Locus 45 (Pl. 161, 45; Fig. 9) may be reached from room 44 by a wide opening between two very thick walls; in this opening there are steps leading to a lower level. A trench along the eastern wall produced 6 baskets of pottery sherds; nearly all are ribbed and without painted or incised ornaments; among these sherds were fragments of lids with knob-handles; one of these lids has a perforation which served as an air hole. Fragments of red ware bowls occurred also here. The trench along the eastern wall established the fact that there are still very many other sherds further west. At the southern end the eastern wall is very thick; towards the north it becomes narrower; at the northeast it extends beyond the northwest corner of room 37. The trench was continued along the northern wall of 45; there very little masonry and absolutely no other finds came to light; the same is true of the entire northern area of locus 45. It seems that locus 45 is not a room, but an enclosure whose southeastern part was used as a pottery dump. In the dump further excavations could be made.

Locus 46 (Pl. 161, 46; Fig. 9) was visible before the excavations began; we thought that there was a cistern in the southern half of the area, but a clearance revealed that there exists here a relatively small pit whose upper part is lined with masonry, whilst its lower part is cut into the rock; it becomes very narrow in the southwest. This pit was not a cistern; its purpose is not certain.

Locus 47 (Pl. 161, 47; Fig. 9) has preserved a few low walls indicated in the plan; nothing else was found.

Locus 48 (Pl. 161, 48; Fig. 9) is a large enclosure which had relatively high walls to judge from the number of stones found on both sides of the low walls which are still standing. The enclosed area has an irregular surface sloping down from south to north. Since nothing of interest exists here the western half of the area was used for depositing stones; it is this heap of stones which appears in Fig. 9, in the western end of the area, between the atrium rooms and the large quarry (133) on the northwestern slope of the ridge.

Locus 49 (Pl. 161, 49; Fig. 9) looks like a room with a high rubble wall on the south, lower walls on the east and north and little of a wall on the west. There is a door in the southern wall; possibly there was an opening in the northern part of the western wall, but there is no clear evidence there. The floor was paved with stones. Near the southern wall there was a large deposit of lime. Some tesserae were found here. There was nothing else worthy of note.

Locus 50 (Pl. 161, 50; Fig. 9) comprises the entire area bounded on the east by room 49, on the south by rooms 16 and 17, on the north by the enclosure 48 and on the west by a low wall which is a continuation of the western wall of 48 as far as the northwestern corner of room 17. On the eastern side of this area there are some low walls between which there was a deposit of plain, comparatively large, tesserae which filled a dozen baskets. The entire surface of the area was as irregular as 48 and represents a mere enclosure. In this enclosure was found only one other object worth mentioning, namely, a stone mortar near the door to room 16.

The purpose of the individual loci in this region is not certain; but we think that the enclosures (45, 48 & 50) may have served as folds for sheep, goats and other animals. The tesserae in 50, the lime in 49, the clay in 44, the ovens in 44, 43 and possibly in 41 suggest workshops of the monastery; the rest of the rooms may have been used as habitations.

D. THE WESTERN GROUP

1. *General survey.* A third group of monastic buildings is arranged around a courtyard on the western slope of Siyâgha (Pl. 161, 53-63); the group forms a part of the great central complex, but is not connected with the rest of the buildings by any door. The eastern wall of the group is identical with the western

wall of the atrium and the southern monastery; the southern wall is a continuation of the southern monastery's southern wall; the northern wall of the group is the northern wall of room 54, which is on a line with the northern walls of the atrium and the north hall; the northern and western walls of area 53 are low enclosure walls and do not form a part of the building; the western wall of the group stands on the slope of the hill on a level over 4 meters below that of the eastern wall (Fig. 20, 3). In none of these walls did we discover a door; the walls on the north, east and south are so well preserved that we are certain that no door existed there; so the door must have existed in the western wall, but the exact point is not certain. The masonry consists of carefully squared stones with a plain surface.

The area occupied by the building and courtyard is about 14 m. w. from east to west and about 50-51 m. l. from north to south. The relation of this area to its surroundings may be studied in Fig. 20, 3 ; Pls. 22, 1 & 2 ; 67, 1 & 2; Fig. 9. In Fig. 20, 3 we see that the courtyard (55) is more or less on the same level as the atrium (7) and the rooms around the atrium (19), whereas the western wing of the building stands on a level over 4 meters below that of the courtyard. Débris covered all the walls, so that they were completely hidden from view (see Pls. 22, 1 & 2 and 67, 2); the existence of a building here was not suspected. In 1935 the upper part of the northern wall of 54 (see Pl. 65, 1) was discovered ; this was completely cleared in 1937 and as the work advanced it brought to light one of the largest and best-planned buildings on the site.

Before going into detail regarding the building (Pl. 161, 54, 56, 60-63), its courtyard (Pl. 161, 55, 57-59) and the objects found in them, a word must be said about area 53.

2. *Area 53* (Pls. 65, 1; 161, 53; Figs. 9 and 20, 4) is completely enclosed by walls ; those on the east and south are identical with the western wall of room 17 and the northern wall of room 54 respectively, those on the west and north are low enclosure walls. Of the eastern wall nine courses are preserved; in the sixth from below is the drain between room 17 and this area. Of the southern wall a dozen courses remain in situ ; they consist of neatly squared stones with a plain surface (Pl. 65, 1) ; the foundation course projects beyond the rest of the wall (Pl. 66, 1). The entire wall was covered with two coats of plaster. This plaster was still on the wall when it was excavated, but it has since mostly fallen off. The lower coat contains numerous incisions and a few rough pebbles (Pl. 66, 1-3) which served to key on the outer coat (Pl. 66, 3).

It was a rare thing at Siyâgha to find the outer wall plastered ; but the same was the case on the exterior of room 109 on the northwestern slope of the ridge and probably also on the exterior of the eastern wall of the cella trichora. In all three cases the walls stand on the slope of a hill, where the action of water might be harmful to the foundations, which were protected by two coats of plaster. In this case the plaster covered not only the foundation course (Pl. 66, 1-2) but also the upper parts of the wall (see Pls. 65, 1 & 66, 1-3). In the case of room 109 the plaster certainly covered and protected the foundation; whether it also covered the rest of the wall is uncertain. As regards the extent to which plaster was used on the exterior of the eastern wall of the cella trichora nothing certain can be said, since only a few traces were observed on the lower courses consisting of rubble masonry; probably the rubble masonry was concealed by the plaster.

Elsewhere also the exterior of walls was plastered; thus, for instance, at Umm el-Jemâl and at Olynthos; at the former place two coats were the rule;[1] at the latter place the excavators suppose that the plaster was used to protect the walls against humidity.[2]

The western wall of the area is built against the plastered southern wall; this indicates that it was built after the other wall had been finished and plastered. The western and northern walls are low enclosure walls; they were most probably never higher and the area which they enclose was most probably never covered with a roof; this seems to be confirmed by the irregular surface of the area enclosed by these walls. Within the area there is a drop of about 3 m. from east to west; no attempt was made to level off this area; in fact the top of its western wall is lower than the base of its eastern wall; see Fig. 20, 4, where the relation of this area (53) to the atrium rooms on the east (17) and the path as well as room 115 and courtyard 114 on the west is indicated. See also Pl. 66, 1.

The area enclosed by the walls was most probably used as a dump. It was not completely cleared; trenches were dug along the interior of the walls to their foundations and these revealed the stratification of the dump and the character of its contents. The upper part of the area was packed with the building stones of the neighboring walls; below these there were, and in part still are, layers of plaster with tesserae and pieces of marble, glass and pottery; a lower layer contained only ashes; throughout the dump bits of copper, iron and coins occurred.

One of the stones is decorated with a cross; it resembles two others found in the narthex and Theotokos chapel (see p. 75 and Pl. 56, second row, first and third stones); it can be seen on top of the wall in Pl. 65, 1, near the center.

[1] *ECS* p. 181; see above p. 92, note 2.

[2] *AJA* 43 (1939), p. 55. The excavators write that "during the fourth campaign at Olynthos it was noticed that the exterior north face of the "Villa of the Twin Erotes" — 4th century B. C. — had a cement or plaster coating. This is the first instance of exterior lime plaster found at Olynthos and its necessity is explained by the fact that the part of the villa in question is 55-75 cm. below the edge of the valley."

The plaster and tesserae resemble those found east of the cella trichora and in the dump above room 41; we may assume that they were brought here from the interior of the basilica at the time of its restoration. The same source of this material is indicated by the marble fragments.

One fragment of marble (Pl. 121, 2, second in row) comes from a plate with an everted rim on which a Greek inscription is carved; most of the other fragments of this plate were found east of the basilica. A fragment of a pierced screen (see Pl. 124, 2) resembles others found on the northeastern slope. Both fragments were parts of objects which were used in the earlier basilica and were later thrown here after the objects to which they belonged had been broken.

Bones were quite common; they probably represent refuse from the kitchen.

Metals are represented by bits of iron nails, copper wick-holders and a strip of copper $14\frac{1}{2}$ cm. l. and 3 cm. w. thickened along one edge and thin along the other (Pl. 135, Fig. 1, 4).

The glass fragments come from lamps and from bottles with a thread ornament in relief.

Pottery sherds collected here filled many baskets; among them were half a dozen fragments of lamps, two pan-handles, a large part of a bowl, etc. The bowl has a flat base over 11 cm. in d., straight sides 42 mm. h., a ledge-handle and ornaments consisting of series of incised circles bordered by punctured holes. It should be compared with the stone vessels in Pl. 133, Figs. 1 & 2.

In the dump were found 11 coins; 7 could be identified; of these 4 belong to the Byzantine period, 2 to the Umayyad period and one probably to the Abassid period. The earliest of the Byzantine coins belongs to the twelfth year of the reign of Justinian I (538-9 A. D.); the Abassid coin is not earlier than the second half of the eighth century; the interval is spanned by the remaining Byzantine and Umayyad coins. These coins, therefore, represent a period of over 200 years during which this dump may have been used.

3. *The courtyard* (Pls. 67, 1-2; 161, 55, 57-59; Figs. 9 & 20, 3) of the western group of buildings is enclosed on all sides by walls in which no doors are preserved; small sections of this open area are paved with stones; several masonry structures exist within its limits. Three stone capitals, moldings, lintels, basins, iron gratings, a leaden grille, a marble vase, a pottery seal, pottery vases with ornaments in relief, a large jar, a lid, painted sherds and Umayyad coins are some of the characteristic objects found here.

The entire eastern wall has preserved 4-5 courses of its masonry, yet nowhere in this wall is there a door to connect this courtyard with the atrium or the southern monastery; in other words, this western group of buildings has at present no direct communication with the atrium and the basilica, as might be expected if this building was inhabited by monks directly connected with the service of the sanctuary. This absence of a direct communication with the atrium and the basilica may be explained in several ways. At first we thought that this building was reserved for guests and pilgrims who were obliged to present themselves at the main entrances (71, 25, 16) controlled by the monks in order to gain access to the sanctuary. But it is also possible that the western group of buildings was no longer in use during the period of the second basilica; in this case the door which at one time may have served to join the western group with the atrium no longer served its purpose and was omitted when the atrium group was rebuilt.

There are a number of objects which lend support to the latter view; thus, for instance, several lintels, a drain and a conduit. Opposite rooms 23 and 64, in the courtyard, was found a large lintel, now broken into two pieces; originally it was 2.25 m. l., 64 cm. h. and 25 cm. thick ; there is no door in this neighborhood at present to which it could be assigned; so it seems not unreasonable to postulate the existence of a door here at some former period. The size of the stone seems to guarantee that it was not removed far from the place where it had fallen.

A second stone, from which crosses seem to have been chiseled away, exists in the wall of room 23 ; it seems to have been destined originally to serve as the lintel for a door and then was reused here. There is no clear evidence to show where that door was.

The drain in the wall between this courtyard and room 22 may also indicate that this region was abandoned in the final period of the site's occupation. It is difficult to imagine that the courtyard should have been converted into a place for sewage while it and the building surrounding it were still inhabited.

Finally, the abandonment of this region seems to be indicated by the conduit which traverses rooms 60 and 62, regarding which details will be given below.

Possibly, therefore, the abandonment of the western group of buildings during the final occupation of the site explains why this group does not communicate directly with the atrium and the basilica.

In the eastern wall of the courtyard there must have been a number of openings or windows closed by iron gratings. Bars of such gratings were found near the foot of the wall both north and south of 57; there were at least two, possibly three, such gratings. In all cases the iron bars have crumbled to pieces, but those recovered at the northern end are large enough to suggest a grating consisting of one bar in one direction and three crossbars. Several pieces represent a large bar about 7 cm. wide and 4½ cm. thick joined to and at right angles with a smaller bar about 3 cm. in d.; fragments of this smaller type of bar measure 26, 22, 18, 16 (4 pieces), 12, etc. cm. in length; these bars taper somewhat towards the ends which were inserted into the stone frame. An estimate based on this evidence gives a grating which was about half a meter square. South of 57, pieces of a grating were found in two places; the position in which the pieces were found may indicate two gratings; the pieces, however, are so poorly preserved that we cannot draw any definite conclusion from them regarding the number of gratings, or regarding their size and form. Another iron grating was found east of the basilica.[1]

The eastern wall of the courtyard was probably crowned by a cornice. In the courtyard and on the rest of the slope were found numerous stones with a molding consisting of a simple splay, like that used around the apse of the baptistery (see p. 86, 3). The stones represent a course varying between 29-41 cm. in height; the fillet above the splay averages about 7 cm. in width and is characterized by an incised horizontal line (see Pl. 35, 5 & 6).

Another stone (Pl. 36, 7) found in the northeastern part of the courtyard has as an ornament the X motif executed in double incised lines, crossed in the center by another pair of incised lines and bordered on two sides by single incised lines parallel to the central pair. The same motif with slight variations is met with a number of times on the site.

Here we may mention three capitals, which were found near the eastern wall of the courtyard. One of these capitals (Pl. 59, 3) was lying on the north side of 57. It has an abacus, ovolo and fillet. The type occurs in Syrian churches, where it is called a Doric capital by Butler;[2] the same type is found in the early synagogues of Galilee; it is called "a cyma-capital" by Kohl and Watzinger.[3] Only one such capital was found at Siyâgha.

The other two capitals (Pls. 60, 1 & 3; 59, 4; Fig. 10, 7) were found on the south side of 57. They have the outlines of a Corinthian capital, but their ornamentation is the simplest. The abacus has an incised line around the sides; below the four corners of the abacus there are plain, uncut leaves; on the sides between the leaves there are semicircular or engaged columns.[4] The leaves have straight edges and taper to a point near the top; some of the leaves (Pl. 60, 1) have a central vein in relief, others (Pl. 60, 3) lack that vein.

Two other capitals of the latter type were found at Siyâgha: one in the western end of 54, the other in the eastern part of the southern monastery. The former may be seen in Pl. 65, 1 on the western end of the wall, on the fifth course from the top. The latter is in a very poor state of conservation.

[1] See Fig. 5, 9 and pp. 29 ff.; see also the chapter on metals.

[2] *ECS* p. 236: "Capitals may be classed as Doric which have an ovolo or straight echinus."

[3] *ASG* p. 167. According to these writers the Doric capital is not represented in the synagogues; its place is taken by another order consisting of an abacus and an echinus which may be concave, convex, straight or some other molding. See, v. g., ibid. p. 133, Abb. 270; compare also with the capitals of the cella trichora described above p. 31.

[4] Colonettes or "candlesticks" in high relief were observed on several shafts at Umm Wilât. See *ECS* p. 239, Ill. 265. This latter element was observed also on a capital at el-ʿAl; see *SEP* p. 17.

In all there are four capitals of the uncut leaf type; since three of them were found in the western group of buildings, it seems probable that they were originally used there; later one of the group found its way into the southern monastery. As elsewhere on the site, so here there is associated with the three capitals of one type a fourth one of another type. The place where these capitals were originally used is uncertain; their presence seems to require other parts of columns, such as shafts and bases, but none were found on the western slope. They may have served for some portico in the western group. Similar capitals were seen at Mâᶜin,[1] el-ᶜAl[2] and at Muᶜallak.[3]

Platform 57 (Pl. 161, 57). Against the eastern wall of the courtyard there is a platform consisting of one course of masonry. This platform is opposite the room in the atrium which contains the tombs (Pl. 161, 21) and also directly opposite to the main entrance of the basilica. Standing on this platform one can look into the church on the east and at the same time one has an unobstructed view towards the west (see Pls. 8-10), north (see Pls. 11-15), south (see Pl. 16, 2) and southwest (Pl. 159).

The position of the platform and the view which one enjoys from this spot suggest this as a very likely spot from which the monks pointed out to pilgrims all the places seen by Moses, in his vision of the Promised Land, just before he died (*Deut.* 34, 1 ff.). This thought was suggested to us both by our own repeated experiences and by the experience of Aetheria recorded in her account of her visit to the memorial of Moses on Mount Nebo. Aetheria writes as follows:[4] "Then those who knew the place, the priests and holy monks, said to us: "If you wish to see the places written of in the book of Moses, go out of the door of the church, and from the very summit,[5] but on the side from which you can be seen from here, behold and see; we shall tell you all the places which are visible."

"At this we were delighted and went out (namely, from the church) at once. For from the door of the church we saw the place where the Jordan enters the Dead Sea, which place appeared below us as we stood.[6] We saw

[1] *RB* 47 (1938), p. 230, 2) and Fig. 1, b.
[2] *SEP* p. 17.
[3] *ECS* p. 239, Ill. 267.
[4] Geyer, pp. 53-55, no. 12, lines 29 ff. — The English translation is that of J. H. Bernard in *The Library of the Palestine Pilgrims' Text Society*, Vol. I, third place, pp. 27-29; the Latin text is given ibid. pp. 94-95 and the commentary by C. W. Wilson ibid. pp. 144-5.
[5] See Fig. 3; the place in front of, that is, west of the cella trichora is actually the very summit of the hill.
[6] See Pl. 8. The place where the Jordan enters the Dead Sea is easily recognized by the tongue of land which projects into the northern part of the Dead Sea. This point cannot be seen from Jebel en-Neba, hence that cannot be the place from which Aetheria viewed the scene; other places from which this point can be seen do not have ruins corresponding to those of a church visited by Aetheria. This passage is one of the most convincing proofs in favor of the identification of Siyâgha with the place visited by Aetheria. From this passage we also know that the door of the cella trichora was on the western side of the building, just as in the basilica; the excavations did not throw any light on this point, since only the foundation course of the cella trichora remains on the west; see pp. 24 f.

also opposite, not only Livias which was on the near side of the Jordan, but Jericho which was beyond Jordan, so prominent was the lofty place where we stood before the door of the church. The most part of Palestine, the land of Promise, was seen from thence, also the whole Jordan territory — that is as far as our eyes could reach.[1] On the left[2] we saw all the lands of the Sodomites, and also Segor, which Segor is the only one remaining today of the famous five. There is a memorial of it, but of those other cities nothing appears save the overturned ruins, just as they were turned into ashes.

"The place where was the inscription about Lot's wife was shown to us, which place we read of in the Scriptures. But, believe me, venerable ladies, the pillar itself is not visible, only the place is shown. The pillar is said to be covered up in the Dead Sea. We certainly saw the place, but we saw no pillar; I cannot deceive you about the matter. The bishop of the place, that is, of Segor, told us that it is now some years since the pillar was visible. It is about six miles from Segor to the place where the pillar stood, which the water now covers.

"Also we went out on the right side of the church,[3] and opposite were shown us two cities — Esebon, now called Exebon,[4] which belonged to Seon, King of the Amorites; and another, now called Sasdra, of Og the King of Basan. From the same place was shown opposite to us Fogor,[5] which was a city of the kingdom of Edom. All these cities which we saw were situated in the mountains. Underneath us the ground seemed to be somewhat flatter, and we were told that in the days when holy Moses and the children of Israel fought against these cities they encamped there; and the signs of a camp were there apparent.[6]

"On the side of the mountain that I have called the left, which is over the Dead Sea, a very sharp mountain was shown to us, which before was called Agrispecula.[7] This is the mountain where Balak the son of Beor placed Balaam the soothsayer to curse the children of Israel, and God would not allow him, as it is written.

"And so having seen all things which we desired, in the name of God returning through Jericho, we retraced to Jerusalem the whole route by which we had come."

From this narrative it is apparent that the cella trichora visited by Aetheria had a door on the west; from a spot in front of the door which is called

1 See Pls. 8-10.
2 That is, on the south or southwest; compare Pl. 159 with Pl. 8.
3 That is, on the north side of the church.
4 Today it is called Hesbân; see p. 7 and Pl. 12.
5 See Pl. 11, 1-3 and p. 6.
6 See Pl. 6, 2 and p. 7.
7 See Pl. 159 and p. 3.

"the very summit" (of the hill) Aetheria enjoyed the view which she describes. As a matter of fact, as we noted above on pp. 23 f., the cella trichora stands partly on the northeastern slope of the ridge; only its southern and western walls are on "the very summit" of the hill. The area in front of the door, to the west, is on the top of the hill (Pl. 161, C), so that when Aetheria stood in front of the church, she stood literally on "the very summit" of the hill.

Later when the basilica and the monasteries were added to the western side of the cella trichora the view from that particular point was obstructed, so that visitors had to take their stand further west in order to obtain an unhindered view of the Jordan valley and of all the other places mentioned by Aetheria. In looking for such a spot on our first visit to Siyâgha we unconsciously found ourselves in the neighborhood of platform 57. Later when visitors called, we observed that they also instinctively chose a spot in the neighborhood of the platform in order to take in the view to the west, or, if they did not go there of their own accord, we conducted them to the vicinity of the platform to explain to them the vision of Moses. This was done before the platform was discovered. Hence the reader may imagine that when we discovered the peculiar structure in the courtyard which we call the platform, we immediately associated it with the place from which pilgrims were shown the Promised Land and where the vision of Moses was explained to them. By this association of ideas the platform acquires special significance and interest, and we need not be surprised to find a place of this kind characterized by a special little memorial, with which we are strongly inclined to associate the capitals described above (pp. 149 f.). We know nothing about the form of that memorial, but a small portico seems highly probable.

Locus 58 (Pl. 161, 58) is opposite to platform 57, on the western side of the courtyard; it is enclosed by low walls, one course high on the east and south, and paved with stones. On this pavement near the eastern wall there is a stone basin. A fragment of marble and a piece of a pottery lamp were found here.

Between 58 and 57 there is a narrow strip which was also paved with stones. That pavement is somewhat irregular at present, but its level seems to be about half way between that of platform 57 and locus 58. This central paved area probably indicates the average level of the courtyard and unites the northern and southern sections of the same; no pavement was found in these latter parts.

The northern limit of the courtyard is marked by the southern wall of 54; the plan (Pl. 161, 54-55) indicates an opening in the eastern end of that wall; whether it was a door or a window is not certain. This northern end of the courtyard has two subdivisions; the one on the east (Pl. 161, 55) is partially enclosed by walls of sufficient height to suggest that there may have been a room there. In that place (55) was found half of a large jar lying on its side (Pl. 144, 3); it resembles several other jars found in 54 and 56. West of 55 there is another area enclosed by walls on three sides, but open on the south; that area is paved with stones and in its northwest corner there is a stone basin which has a drain through one of its sides (Pl. 33, 11). Stone basins are quite common in the western group of buildings.

The southern limit of the courtyard is marked by the northern wall of 60; near the center of this wall an opening is indicated in Pl. 161, 59-60; here too the writer doubts whether it represents a door or a window. West of this opening the wall is pierced by the rectangular opening of a drain, which is below the general level of the courtyard. A trench encountered other walls on the west and east, and in part also on the north, suggesting an enclosed area (Pl. 161, 59). The wall on the east is very thick; the precise purpose of this strong addition to the base of the existing wall has not been determined. The trench along the southern wall produced the pottery lamp illustrated in Pl. 143, 6, whose handle consists of the head of an animal with a cross on the throat; there are pellets between the arms of the cross. This was the only fragment of this variety of the Byzantine lamps found at Siyâgha. The variety seems to have been quite common during the Byzantine period in Palestine and good specimens may be found in most of the museums of Jerusalem.

Among the finds in the courtyard there were a few pieces of marble, metal and pottery, as well as coins which may be referred to very briefly here.

One of the marble slabs measuring 22 × 17 × 1.7 cm. has the one surface divided into 22 rectangles drawn with lead; they are arranged in two rows of eleven. Besides a piece of a marble column's shaft and a marble slab belonging to an altar, there was a piece of a marble bowl (Pl. 129, 11, top and 4th from top) whose exterior has vertical reeding and an everted wavy lip.

Besides the iron bars of gratings, nails and a knife we found here a small leaden grille measuring 43 × 49 mm. (Pl. 137, Fig. 1, 2), which consists of a rectangular frame joined to a central circle by means of 8 leaflets; at the four corners the frame has loops; at one side there seems to have been another circle with ornaments, but only a few traces of it remain. Two more pieces of such grilles were found on the site; they are also rectangular in form and each one encloses a circle fastened to the frame by a series of bars and having an ornamental motif also in its center.

Broken pieces of pottery were abundant in the courtyard. We already mentioned the large jar found in 55 and the lamp recovered in 59; a number of sherds are decorated with spirals and trees executed in red paint (see Pls. 146-148); others have ornaments in relief, like those illustrated in Pl. 154, 1 ff.; several others exhibit new elements. The sherd illustrated in Pl. 153,33; has an arched molding around the exterior below the rim; on the rim and on the exterior there are punctured holes which served as ornaments. This sherd resembles others illustrated in Pl. 153, 34-36. The object illustrated in Pl. 158, B, 31 was found in the southwestern part of the courtyard near the surface. It has a knob-handle like the lids illustrated in Pl. 157, 1 ff.; its lower part is ovate in shape with a flat surface on which there are groups of incisions which suggest that this object served as a seal; it would be the only original seal found at Siyâgha. The surface covered with incisions measures 40 by 55 mm.

Five coins from 59 have been assigned to the Umayyad period (A. H. 41-132 : 661-750 A. D.).

4. *The building* of this western group consists of three wings enclosing the courtyard on the north, west and south. The northern wing contains a single hall (Pl. 161, 54), the western wing a very long arched hall (Pl. 161, 56) and a room in the southwestern corner (Pl. 161, 61), the southern wing three rooms (Pl. 161, 60, 62, 63). The western wing most probably had a ground floor and an upper story. The ground floors of 56 and 61 are joined by a door; in the upper part of the eastern wall of room 61 there is a door which communicates with the rooms in the southern wing; this is the clearest evidence we have of an upper story in this building. Further details regarding walls, doors, windows, arches, plaster, mosaics, drains, inscriptions, stones, marble, bone, metals, glass and pottery will be given below.

Hall 54 (Pls. 65, 1-3; 66, 1-3; 144, 1 & 4; 161, 54; Fig. 9) measures 13. 60 × 5. 60 m. including the walls on the north, west and south which average about one meter in thickness. The northern wall presents a splendid appearance on the exterior (see Pl. 65, 1 and pp. 145 f.), but the masonry is not quite so good on the interior (Pl. 65, 2 & 3); the same holds, more or less, of the southern wall; the eastern wall is identical with the western wall of the atrium group (Pls. 65, 3; 161, 54-18); the western wall (Pls. 65, 2; 144, 1, right) is a part of the great western wall of the whole building which is poorly preserved at this northern end.

On the interior the hall is divided into three bays by two pairs of responds; the projecting bases of these half-pillars may be seen in Pl. 65, 2, left; the arches and roof supported by them have collapsed. Between two of the responds on the north, troughs are formed by means of a row of stones visible in Pl. 65, 2 (see Pl. 161, 54). The interior of these so-called troughs was filled with earth and ashes with which a few pottery sherds were mixed; this may be a packing to form benches. The tops of the stones forming the troughs or benches mark the level to which the northern part of a mosaic pavement, which existed in the hall at one time, had sunk; along the southern side of the hall the remnants of the mosaic pavement were on a somewhat higher level; the broken floor dips from south to north. The remnants of the mosaic floor are fairly continuous along the entire southern part of the hall, but little or no traces of it could be found on the northern side. At the eastern end of the hall the mosaic floor has the native clay as its foundation; further west we noticed beneath the tesserae, first a layer of plaster, then a thick layer of ashes,[1] lower still a layer of loose clay, below that a black layer from which lumps of charred wood could be picked.

To understand the evidence properly one must bear in mind that the hall stands on the side of the hill sloping from east to west; to establish a uniform level inside the hall the western end had to be raised somewhat; generally at Siyâgha the difference of level was overcome by a filling of earth and other débris. That may have been done also in this case; but the evidence seems to indicate that the western end was raised to the required level by a wooden substructure, which was destroyed and caused the mosaic pavement to break up and incline towards the north. We do not know the precise level of the floor, but it seems most probable that it corresponded more or less to the level of the courtyard on the south and the atrium rooms on the east (see Fig. 20, 3).

No clear evidence of a door was found. There is a break in the eastern end of the southern wall (Pl. 161, 54-55) which was filled with rubbish; when the débris was removed from that opening a piece of a pottery lamp, fragments of pottery cups with thin walls and a smooth outer surface and a bronze spatula were found, but at the time the writer failed to see clear signs of a door or window there; he is of the opinion that the door was in the western wall (Pl. 65, 2, rear), which seems to be destroyed below the level of the sill.

In the southwestern corner we found the remains of a large jar whose form was partially preserved by the adjoining walls (Pl. 144, 1); the rest was restored to a great extent (Pl. 144, 4).

One of the stone capitals with uncut leaves and colonnettes, mentioned on p. 149, was recovered in the western end of this hall.

Hall 56 (Pls. 67, 1 & 2; 68, 1 & 2; 69, 1; 144, 2; 161, 56; Figs. 9 & 20, 3) occupies almost the entire western part of the building, only the northwestern and southwestern corners are excepted; the former is a part of hall 54 and the latter is a separate room (61). This hall is the largest in the monastery; it measures 6 × 40.60 m., including all the walls except the northern one.

The walls average about 1.35 m. in thickness near their foundations. They are still 4-4½ m. high on the east, north and partially on the west; at the southern end of the western wall only a few courses remain in situ and these have been partially jolted out of place and are now inclining westwards in the direction of the slope of the hill, in spite of their great thickness. The stones used for the exterior of the walls seem to have been carefully squared and dressed with a plain surface (see Pl. 67, 1); those used for the interior seem to have been less carefully squared, hence they do not fit together perfectly; the interstices are

[1] See, v. g., *Beth-Shan* 3, p. 19; *PEF Ann.* 4, p. 111; ibid. 5, p. 48.

filled in with smaller stones (see Pl. 68, 2). Mortar used for the lower courses seems to have been pure lime; but in the upper courses, at least where the core is exposed, a strong mixture of ashes was observed in the lime.

Plaster covered the interior of all the walls; only one coat has been observed; numerous chips of stones are pressed into the surface of the plaster (see Pl. 68, 1 & 2). Such chips in the plaster were observed also in the lower coat of the southern wall of area 53 and in room 115; in area 53 they evidently served to key on the upper coat of plaster. Perhaps the walls of hall 56 were prepared to receive a second coat of plaster, but as far as we could see that coat was never applied. Small flat pebbles pressed into the surface of the plaster were observed during the excavations in the Tyropœon Valley, Jerusalem, in 1927, in a room registered no. 21; this room is assigned to the latter half of the sixth and the beginning of the seventh centuries A. D.[1]

Painted plaster was found in the neighborhood of cistern 116 and on the southern end of the hall's western wall. Only red was used. A large fragment of plaster found near the cistern has preserved three arms of a cross.

The only door on the ground floor which has been preserved is the one in the wall between the hall and room 61; there was probably another door in the neighborhood of the cistern. The great number of jambs and a few lintels decorated with crosses indicate that there were other doors in this part of the building. A few jambs in situ at the northern end of the western wall may indicate the position of doors or possibly windows of the upper story; near the fourth bay from the northern end of the hall was found a lintel decorated with a cross; it measures 110 × 39 × 24 cm.

Here we may mention a number of other stones found on the southwestern part of the slope. One, measuring 153 × 55 × 54 cm., is decorated with two crosses and part of a third. A second (Pl. 121, 5) has the right end broken off and missing; the piece is still 49 cm. l., 39 cm. h. and 30 cm. w.; it is decorated with a carved cross between whose arms there is a Greek inscription; both the cross and the letters of the inscription have preserved traces of red paint. See inscription XIII. A third, 63 × 34 × 26 cm., also has a cross carved on one side. A fourth one, 57 × 50 × 32 cm., has a boss decorated with a cross. A fifth stone, 75 × 46 × 34 cm., has three bosses: of the two on one side, one is square and the other is round; the latter is decorated with a cross; the third boss at one end of the stone is ornamented with a carved cross. A sixth stone, measuring 104 × 35 × 31 cm., is ornamented with two large incised triangles (Pl. 33, 10). A stone without ornaments, measuring 141 × 47 × 39 cm., serves to illustrate the larger type of stone used in the western wall (see Pl. 67, 1). Other stones of interest will be referred to later in the context in which they were found.

[1] See *PEF Ann.* 5, pp. 49 and 53.

A window seems to be represented by a number of pieces of stone which fit together and form a panel having four round openings (Fig. 10, 8); along two of the broken edges there are indications of other rounded openings. At present the panel measures 53 × 39 cm. Practically no window glass was found in this region, so that the windows do not seem to have been glazed. Stone slabs with small apertures for light were extensively used as window plates in Syria.[1]

On the interior the hall was spanned by 18 transverse arches which divided the hall into 19 bays; the arches seem to have supported a wooden floor of an upper story. Above the spandrels are the responds of another series of arches which carried the roof of the upper story. Little remains in situ of the arches in the upper story; of the arches on the ground floor, the four at the northern end of the hall are perfectly preserved, the rest are broken; but in every case enough remains in situ of each arch to establish its existence and position.

The arches were not all constructed in the same way. The two at the northern end of the hall (Pl. 68, 1 & 2; Fig. 20, 3), for instance, do not have a special pier and impost; the springer is placed on the floor and the curve begins immediately above the floor; their rise is a little less than two meters. The fourth arch (Pl. 69, 1), however, is carried by piers consisting of four courses; the arch itself is but slightly curved. Most of the arches which were exposed by the clearances were supported on piers. The arches are about 60 cm. wide. Above the fourth arch there are two courses of masonry (see Pls. 67, 1; 69, 1); they no doubt indicate the level of the floor above the arches. Elsewhere at Siyâgha transverse arches are preserved intact only in cistern 9 in the atrium (see p. 77), but they are a common feature of all the halls and larger rooms on the site, so, e. g., of nos. 3, 14, 16, 54, etc.

Of the 19 bays into which this hall is divided by the 18 arches only seven were completely cleared; the two at the northern end, the fourth to the seventh and one opposite cistern 116; the rest could not be cleared without endangering the eastern wall which is already very distorted at a number of places. Under the circumstances only about one third of the material contained in this hall has been brought to light, the rest still awaits the excavator. Though seven bays were cleared to the base of the foundations no pavement was found; the native clay or rock served as the floor. Its level is about $4\frac{1}{2}$ m. below that of the courtyard (see Fig. 20, 3).

In the northernmost bay (Pl. 68, 2, left) the lower part of the wall projects to form a shelf 113 cm. h. and 28-46 cm. w.; it is completely covered with a coat of plaster thickly studded with stone chips pressed into its surface. Similar

[1] *ECS* pp. 243 f.

plaster covers the wall above the shelf (Pl. 68, 1). There is no door in the northern wall communicating with hall 54. A few centimeters above the top of the arches, against the eastern end of the northern wall, was found a large, thick-walled jar (Pl. 144, 2), similar to the ones found in 54 (Pl. 144, 1 & 4) and 55 (Pl. 144, 3).

In the sixth bay from the north there is a large basin or tank (Pls. 69, 1, left, foreground; 161, 56) built against the western wall; it is one meter square, 56 cm. deep and its sides are 23 cm. thick. The plaster which completely covers the entire basin both on the interior and on the exterior has a smooth surface.

In the seventh bay the western wall becomes thicker towards the base by means of a series of narrow steps or projections on its interior. The exterior face of the wall was not exposed at this point, but further south, where both faces were exposed near the base, the wall is 1.35 m. thick; there, however, we could not ascertain whether the wall was constructed in the same way as in the seventh bay. North of the seventh bay the western wall does not have such a thickened base. The difference of construction between the northern and southern parts of the western wall is no doubt due to the fact that at the northern end the wall had more support from the exterior than at the southern end. We did not expose the exterior face of the wall at the northern end (see Pl. 67, 1), but a sounding, attempted several meters west of that part of the wall, reached the native rock 50-80 cm. below the present surface. From this we conclude that the northern end of the hall is cut into the native rock; the western wall is built against that rock and hence was able to resist the thrust from the east; this explains why this part of the western wall is well preserved in spite of the fact that it is not as thick as at the southern end, where there is no such natural abutment to receive the lateral pressure of the arches, with the result that at this end the western wall and the arches collapsed and caused the eastern wall to lose its stability; only the débris inside the hall hinders the eastern wall from collapsing.

At the northern end of the hall, where the arches of the ground floor are still intact, also the responds of the upper floor are still preserved; they consist of 3-4 courses (see Pl. 68, 2, right) forming piers which supported arches, but the arches and roof as well as the upper part of the walls of this upper story have collapsed. Also the floor of this upper story has completely disappeared. In bays 4 ff. the writer observed a layer of ashes about one meter above the level of the ground floor; above that layer there were also some pottery vessels and a few other objects. That layer probably represents a wooden floor of the upper story and the objects above it were in use in that story.

Of the objects found on or near the surface, we recall the large jar (Pl. 144, 2) and the spouted jug (Pl. 154, 15) found above the arches at the northern end of the hall. About a meter above the level of the ground floor, below the fourth arch from the north, was found the complete jug illustrated in Pl. 154, 12; more or less on the same level were found large pieces of the type of jar illustrated in Pl. 145, 17 ; here too were found four stone basins. The greatest number of objects, however, was recovered on or near the level of the ground floor. Among these were short horns of cattle, many of the bone objects illustrated in Pl. 134, 1, a small bronze head and antlers (Pl. 137, Fig. 2, 3!), a bronze, seated figurine (Pl. 139, Fig. 3, 1), pieces of glass bottles, fragments of pottery lamps, ribbed jars, painted bowls and basins, terra sigillata plates, sherds with incised ornaments and 15 coins. Most of these objects will be studied more in detail later; here we wish to signal out for special attention only a few.

One of the lamp-fragments has a cross on the spout and another belongs to the "candle-stick" type. Jars (Pl. 145, 17) made of red, ribbed ware with a plain band near the shoulder, a ribbon around the base of the neck and a straight neck are quite abundant in this hall. At Gezer,[1] Opel,[2] and Gerar[3] this type of jar is assigned to the sixth century. Associated with this jar was the rim of a thick-walled jar with everted, grooved lips characteristic of the northern group of buildings (see Pl. 144, 5 f.). Here too were found sherds of the black, ribbed jars with white painted ornaments (Pl. 149, 9 ff.). This seems to indicate that all three types were in use simultaneously. The large number of these storage jars seems to indicate that the hall was used as a place of storage.

In this hall were also recovered the bowls and basins with painted ornaments on the interior (Pls. 151, 1 ff. ; 153, 18 ff.) and several of the few terra sigillata sherds (Pl. 158, A, 7 & 8) found on the site. The presence of this painted and terra sigillata ware in this building was one of the reasons why we thought that it was used as a hospice for pilgrims. The monks were, no doubt, satisfied with the simplest table service, but for their guests, especially those of higher rank and dignity, they surely endeavored to have something better. This is the best ware which we found on the site ; furthermore, it is found only in this western building. While the ground floor was used for storage purposes, the upper floor could have been used for pilgrims; no place could have been more suitable or attractive for them ; from there they could constantly enjoy one of the most charming views. Our own camp was on the western side of the site, and we can testify to the fact that we never grew weary of the natural scenery which one beholds from there. That view has the added attraction of being the identical one enjoyed by Moses before he died. Today many visitors come to Siyâgha for the sole purpose of enjoying the view from there; it was, no doubt, so also

[1] *Gezer* I, p. 380 & Fig. 185; II, p. 226.
[2] *PEF Ann.* 5, pp. 72, 75 (7), 78 (XI), 81.
[3] *Gerar*, 48 h; *Corpus*, 48 X.

in ancient times ; from this western building they could take in every detail of the view to their heart's content.

The 15 coins found in this hall are very useful in determining the period during which it was in use. Two of the coins are not identifiable ; three are Roman types and 10 Byzantine types. The oldest coin is one of Constantius II (337-361 A. D.); the latest belongs to the reign of Maurice Tiberius (582-602 A. D.); the majority, however, were minted during the reigns of Justin I (518-527 A. D.) and Justinian I (527-565 A. D.). This evidence indicates that the hall was in use up to the latter part of the sixth century.

Room 61 (Pls. 161, 61 ; 67, 1 & 2; 69, 2; Figs. 8, 6; 9) is in the south-western corner of the building; actually there were two rooms in this corner : one on the ground floor and a second on the upper floor; but of the latter little remains except the wall on the east; on the south, west and north the wall is destroyed below the level of the upper floor.

The character of the masonry on the exterior may be seen in Pl. 67, 1 & 2; three to five courses are preserved on the south, only two on the west. The wall has two faces joined by mortar; often the outer face is broken away while the inner face and part of the mortar core are preserved and exposed to view. Details of the inner face of the southern wall are given in Fig. 8, 6. A part of the eastern and northern wall may be seen in Pl. 69, 2. The eastern wall is still over a dozen courses high; near its northern end it has a vertical crack, resembling a straight joint. Above its tenth course there is a door which joined the upper story of 61 with room 62 (see Pl. 69, 2, where the débris which fills the doorway has not yet been removed; a workman is visible beyond the door). The northern wall is preserved up to the ninth course of the eastern wall; its center is bulging into the room. At its western end this wall has a door communicating with the ground floor of hall 56. The jambs on both sides of the door have a groove which required a door that was drawn up and down, like a portcullis, instead of a swinging or lean-to door.

Against the southern and northern walls there are responds which carried an arch that served to support the floor of the upper room. The arch and floor have disappeared, but the door in the eastern wall indicates at what level the floor existed; it was perhaps 25 or 50 cm. lower than the door-sill, or, more or less, on the same level as the top of the northern wall. Whether there was a distinct room on the upper floor of 61, as on the ground floor, or whether the upper floor of 61 formed part of a large hall, we are unable to say at present.

Inside room 61, more or less on the level of the upper floor, was found a stone on whose one side there is a carving resembling the Greek letter Ψ (Pl. 121, 11); immediately outside the western wall of this room two more such stones were found. Since the carving resembles a letter, a further discussion of the same is reserved for the chapter on inscriptions (see inscription XIV).

Two other stones found outside the western wall of this room have bosses decorated with crosses and one is decorated with a six-armed star.

No plaster was observed on the walls of this room, though beyond the door, in hall 56, the plaster, with stone chips pressed into its surface and a red, painted cross, is still on the wall.

The room was filled from the top to the bottom not only with stones and earth, but also with pottery sherds and a few other objects. Near the level of the door-sill on the east two baskets of sherds were collected; among them was a fragment of a "channel-nozzle" lamp with which was associated an Umayyad coin. Lower down, say about a meter above the floor, were found fragments of inscribed pottery lamps[1] (Pls. 121, 6-8; 143, 2-4) and in their company the tiny, perfectly preserved juglet illustrated in Pl. 153, 39. At least half a dozen baskets were filled with sherds from this level, most of them came from vessels made of red, ribbed ware. Even more such sherds were found next to the floor, consisting of the native rock. The jars to which most of these sherds belong (see Pl. 145, 17) are of the same type as those found in hall 56; that is, they are made of red ware, having a rounded base with an omphalos, characteristic of the sixth century A. D., ribbed sides without other ornaments and a ridge at the base of the plain, straight neck. As in hall 56, so here a few sherds with a black, outer surface and white, painted ornaments occur. In both places sherds with incised lines and band-combing were observed. A coin found in the southwestern corner of this room, on the ground floor, belongs to the reign of Justin I (518-527).

The objects on the ground floor are undoubtedly in their original position; those somewhat higher in the room probably come from the upper floor; both these groups of objects seem to belong to the sixth century A. D. and suggest storage places. The objects on or near the surface seem to have accumulated there during the Umayyad period.

Room 60 (Pls. 69, 3; 70, 2; 161, 60; Fig. 9) is one of the three rooms in the southern wing of the building; it occupies the entire northern half of the wing along the southern side of the courtyard. The plan indicates an opening in the northern wall of the room, but it is doubtful whether it is a door or a window, possibly the latter. There is, however, a door in the southern wall communicating with room 62 (see Pls. 69, 3; 70, 1 & 2). Between this door and the northern wall there is a stone drain which is plastered on all sides. At the northern end this channel begins near a rectangular opening through the northern wall; it crosses the room on a steep slant; at the southern end it terminates against the sill of the door, which blocks the channel; a slit below the sill served to conduct the drainage to some receptacle below the door. This

[1] See inscriptions XXII-XXIV.

is remarkable, because on top of the sill a new drain begins which crosses room 62 (Pls. 69, 3; 70, 1 & 2) and terminates against its southern wall through which there is an aperture to permit the drainage to flow outside the building. Not only is the discontinuity of the channel surprising, but also its position in the doorway and the fact that it had no covering of any kind. A covering would have been required if a floor had been laid over it; no floor, however, was discovered in the western half of the room. In the eastern half of the room there is a stone pavement on a level high enough to cross the top of the channel, but too high for the doorway. All this makes one think that the channel was built after the room was no longer in use.

On the stone pavement in the eastern half of the room, against the northern wall, there was a quantity of ashes which seems to indicate a fireplace. In the ashes were two large coins of the twelfth year of Justinian I (538-9 A. D.); they were adhering to one another; each one is pierced by a hole and the surface is quite worn. They evidently served as ornaments for some time before they were lost here, hence some reserve must be used in using them as a means of dating this room and its contents.

The most interesting object found in this room is the stone basin cut into the top of an Ionic capital (see Pl. 60, Fig. 1, 6; Fig. 10, 4). The basin is nearly square (36 × 37 cm., including the walls which are about 4 cm. thick) and 15 cm. deep; through one side there is a drain. The base of the basin is formed by the necking of the capital which is 36 cm. in d. and 20 cm. long. Along two sides of the basin are the bundles resembling scrolls tied in the center; the extremities of the scrolls extend beyond the sides of the basin and terminate in flat disks, 18 cm. in d., decorated with carved crosses. The flat disks[1] with carved crosses instead of spiral volutes distinguish this Christian Byzantine variety of the Ionic capital from the classical capital of this order. This is the only capital of the Ionic order found at Siyâgha.[2]

[1] Watzinger, *DP* 2, p. 28, traces the use of flat disks for volutes back to the late Hellenistic period in Palestine. The usage was continued in the early synagogues of Galilee (see ibid. p. 111; *ASG* p. 67, Abb. 126; p. 68, Abb. 129; pp. 77 f., Abb. 149-154; p. 111, Abb. 215; p. 167) and in early Christian monuments (see below).

[2] Conder, *SEP* p. 154, claims that he saw at Siyâgha "six rude Ionic capitals, which resemble those found at Tanturah ('Memoirs of Western Palestine', vol. ii, p. 8) and elsewhere." He adds that "in the Christian buildings of the Hauran (second to fourth century), similar Ionic capitals are common." — The context seems to indicate that Conder is speaking of capitals seen by him in the basilica; these capitals were described above, on pp. 62 f.; not one of them is an Ionic capital, neither were Ionic capitals observed elsewhere on the site. The most probable explanation is that the capitals in the basilica made the impression of Ionic capitals after the ornamentation had been worn off from the exposed surface. With these so-called Ionic capitals at Siyâgha Conder compares the capitals seen by him at el-ʿAl (see *SEP* p. 18) and at Kh. Hamzeh, near Umm el-Hanafish (see *SEP* p. 247); for the former he proposes a date in the "fourth and fifth century." Those seen by him at Tanturah he assigns to the fifth century; "the capitals", he says in *SWP* 2, p. 8, "are of a rude Byzantine character, in imitation of the Ionic order, with large volutes resembling those in ruins east of Jordan and elsewhere, which are dated as of the fifth century."

This type of capital is quite common in Transjordan[1] and the neighboring countries.[2] Some of the closest parallels were seen by the writer in the courtyard of an abandoned building at Umm er-Rasâs.[3] Another very close parallel was seen by Clermont-Ganneau at Beit Thul[4] in Palestine.

Room 62 (Pls. 161, 62; 69, 3; 70, 1 & 2; Fig. 9) is in the southwestern part of the southern wing of the building. It has doors in the northern, eastern and western walls, which communicate with rooms 60, 63 and the upper story of 61 respectively. A stone, found here, measuring 72 × 37 × 34 cm., has a cross carved on one end. No pavement exists in this room; clay seems to have formed the floor. The room is crossed from north to south by a channel, mentioned in speaking of room 60; already there we stated that this channel is not continuous; in room 60 it terminates against the sill of the door and in room 62 it makes a new start on a higher level also near the door. The presence of this channel, in the doorway and above the level of the floor, seems to indicate that it was built when these rooms no longer served their original purpose. What that purpose was, we do not know; but if we are right in assuming that this building once served as a hospice, this suite may have been reserved for special visitors. The suite was reached from the second floor of 61; then from 62 both 60 and 63 could be reached.

From this room comes one of the very few complete glass bottles recovered on the site (Pl. 138, Fig. 1, 7); other glass fragments were also quite numerous here; see, v. g., Pl. 142, 36.

Several pottery lamps of the "candle-stick" variety were found in this room. Among the many sherds collected here there was one which attracted special attention by reason of the colors used in its decoration; they are both different from those found on the other vessels and also more numerous (Pl. 151, 5); the trellis is brown, the strip on the left yellow, the stems of the fruits brown, the fruits dark-brown and yellow; on other sherds and vessels we generally found only white on black, or red on white.

Room 63 (Pls. 161, 63; 70, 1 & 2; Fig. 9) is in the southeastern part of the southern wing of the building. Its door is in the western wall, where it communicates with room 62. South of the door the lower part of the western wall projects so as to form a shelf; the same is the case in the southern wall.

[1] Abel, *RB* 41 (1932), p. 239, reports such a capital from Wady Kharrâr; it is illustrated ibid. p. 242, Fig. 2.

[2] Regarding the Hauran Butler, *PAAES* Part II, p. 41, states: "In the dated buildings of the fifth century a crude imitation of the Ionic capital (see Fig. 18) is employed in private architecture." — The same authority in *ECS* p. 236 writes: "The Ionic capital in its debased form invariably lacks an echinus, but instead has a tall neck or bell above the astragal, where the capital is joined to the shaft, which makes its height equal to that of the Corinthian (Ill. 256)."

[3] See p. 29, note 1.

[4] *ARP* 2, p. 65; here too the disks are decorated with crosses.

On the shelves were found several copper vessels (Pl. 137, Fig. 3) and the only bronze cross discovered on the site (Pl. 137, Fig. 1, 1). Also a bronze lid (Pl. 137, Fig. 2, 2) comes from here. The eastern wall was partially exposed below the level of the floor (Pl. 70, 2, left), which was not paved; many of the stones used in the lower courses have a margin and boss. Several stone basins were found here.

E. THE SOUTHERN GROUP

1. *General survey.* A fourth group of monastic buildings, arranged around two courtyards, occupies the southern part of the great central complex (Pls. 161, 64-105; 22, 1 & 2; 23, 1; 25, 1 & 2; 38, 1; 71-76; 113, 1 & 2; 146, 29; 160; Fig. 9). It covers an area which is 69 m. l. from east to west and 19.60-33.40 m. w. from north to south; this area slopes gently from north to south. The group is divided into a western (Pl. 161, 64-78) and an eastern section (Pl. 161, 79-105). Each section has its own courtyard around which the rooms are disposed. The two courtyards are joined by a passage (Pl. 161, 74). The entrance to the entire group is in the southern wall of the western section (Pl. 161, 71).

Already before the excavations began the general outlines of extensive buildings could be recognized in this area (see Pl. 22, 1) and it was assumed that they represented a monastery. In 1933 the great mass of stones from the basilica, chapels and atrium buildings, heaped along the northern side of this region (Pl. 25, 1), was removed; rooms 91 and 90a (see Pl. 25, 2) and walls south of the baptistery and the Theotokos chapel (see Pl. 38, 1) came to light. In 1937 the clearance of the area was completed. The buildings which we see today were most probably constructed towards the end of the sixth century of our era and continued in use to the very end of the occupation of the site; but these buildings seem to have been preceded by earlier ones on practically the same lines; slight modifications were noted especially at the eastern end of the group in the vicinity of rooms 99-102. Certain classes of objects, represented in this group of buildings, did not occur elsewhere on the site, thus, for example, the large ovens in 93 and 105.

2. *The western section of the southern group of monastic buildings* (Pl. 161, 64-78) consists of a courtyard (68), rooms on its western (64-67), southern (69, 70, 72) and southeastern sides (75-78), a walled area (73) and a narrow paved strip (73a) on its northeastern side, and doorways or passages on the south (71), east (74) and north (25).

The courtyard (Pls. 161, 68; 71, 2; Fig. 9) has a stone pavement slanting from north to south, so that the water which fell during rains would flow out through the main gateway on the south (Pl. 161, 71). The courtyard was reached from the outside through the gateway on its southern side (Pl. 161, 71). From the courtyard one could reach the rooms on its southern and western sides. On the eastern side of the courtyard there is a passage which is the only means of reaching the block of rooms on the southeast (Pl. 161, 75-78) and the eastern section of the monastery (see Pl. 72, 2). On its northern side a doorway leads to the atrium (Pl. 161, 25). All the monks who lived in the southern monastery and all visitors to the basilica and chapels were obliged to pass through this courtyard, which must have witnessed a constant movement to and fro.

The southern wall of the atrium rooms 24-29 fell into courtyard 68 and into the adjoining parts of 73 and 74. Among the stones were the jambs of the door between the courtyard and passage 25; east of these jambs was found the stone illustrated in Pl. 36, 9; its peculiar molding and decoration with incised lines is not found elsewhere on the site, neither were other stones to match this one found at this spot.

In the courtyard was found a large piece of a boat-shaped stone vessel, similar to the one illustrated in Pl. 133, Fig. 1, 5. The wick-holder and the chains for suspending a lamp, illustrated in Pl. 137, Fig. 1, 3 and 6 respectively, come from here. The wick-holder is the only one of those discovered at Siyâgha which terminates in a cross at its upper end. The chains are the most complete specimens found on the entire site.

Rooms 64-67 (Pls. 161, 64-67; 71, 1), along the western side of the courtyard, were not completely excavated. A clearance along their eastern sides (see Pl. 71, 1) established the fact that the floors of these rooms are on an average about half a meter higher than the pavement of the courtyard. The whole group communicates with the courtyard by only one door in the northeastern corner of room 65. Room 64 is paved with stones; no clear evidence of a door was found. Room 65 is the largest in the group; three half-piers against its eastern wall suggest that there are corresponding piers against the western wall; they must have carried arches which supported the roof. This room has a mosaic floor consisting of plain tesserae. The mosaic continues beneath the southern wall of the room. In the eastern end of that wall there is a door connecting this room with room 66. The stone immediately west of the threshold has a cross enclosed by a circle carved on its northern side. Room 66 has a mosaic floor of the same character as that in room 65; since the wall dividing the two rooms stands on that mosaic floor, it may be that the two rooms were originally one and were later subdivided. The door to room 67 was not found, but most probably that cell was reached from room 66; its floor was flagged.

Rooms 69, 70 and 72, on the southern side of the courtyard, are on the same level as the pavement of the courtyard. Their mosaic floors consist of plain tesserae whose surface is about 2 cm. square; the same kind of tesserae were used in rooms 65 and 66; they are our so-called "medium-sized" cubes. In room 69 flags were used to repair the floor; the door is in the northwest corner. The door of room 70 was not found; that of 72 is in the northeast corner; near it was found a stone measuring 50 × 39 × 33 cm., which is decorated with a cross in relief (Pl. 58, 2); its arms are grooved and it is enclosed by a circle in relief, to which a triangular ear, also in relief, is attached. In the room is a stone measuring 40 × 36 × 32 cm., into which a basin is cut which is 24 cm. in d. and 11 cm. deep. A basalt millstone found here is 26 cm. h. and 36 cm. in d. at one end and 15 at the other. This was probably the porter's room.

Doorway 71 (Pl. 71, 2), between rooms 70 and 72, on the southern side of the courtyard, is paved with flagstones, like the courtyard. On its southern side was the large door of which only the stone threshold is still in position. The latter has sockets at its two ends in which the pivots of the door's wings turned. The jambs and lintel were found lying outside the entrance; one of the jambs, measuring 53 × 31 × 31 cm., is decorated with a carved cross; a second stone on which two crosses are carved is probably a piece of the lintel; a third stone is cut out like a section of a conduit, but it may have served as a small window-opening near the door. A fourth stone is hollowed out on one side in such a way as to leave a ridge across the hollow; this ridge served as a rod to which something could be fastened. At Umm el-Jemal, in the northern part of Transjordan, we noticed a number of such stones still in situ in the frame of the door at a point near the latch; there they evidently served to receive the latch which could be fastened to the bar so that it could not be drawn back from the exterior; or possibly the door itself was fastened to the bar by means of a cord or strap. Such a stone could likewise have served for fastening animals; this would of course depend upon its position. Outside the door a narrow strip is paved by a row of stones parallel to the sill.

This doorway is the entrance not only to the southern group of buildings but to the entire complex; there is only one other way of reaching the atrium, basilica and chapels from the outside, and that is through the refectory (Pl. 161, 16); that passage was surely not intended for the general public; the only way that remained, therefore, was this one. Here, then, a porter was necessary to receive the pilgrims; he must have occupied a room close to the main entrance; any of the three rooms on the southern side of the courtyard could have been the porter's room.[1] Here too there must have been room for the officials who

[1] The visitor who comes to Siyâgha today (1940) drives along the southern wall of the monastery as far as the ancient entrance 71 (see Fig. 9), where he is received by the Arab custodian of the site, who lives in a temporary structure erected in the courtyard in 1932 as a tool-house and a shelter for the workmen. He either accompanies the visitors personally or, if a Franciscan happens to be present, he summons the latter to guide the visitors.

looked after the needs of the pilgrims, guided them and distributed the so-called "eulogiae" or gifts which the monks were wont to give to pilgrims.[1] The rooms on the west and southeast of the courtyard could have served to meet all these requirements.

Area 73 (Pls. 161, 73; 72, 2) is in the northeastern part of this section. Only the foundation of the wall enclosing the area on the west and south has been preserved; this foundation course is of a uniform level (see Pl. 72, 2), which does not give the impression of a wall which has collapsed, but one which was reduced to this level by human agency; in other words, this wall no longer served any practical purpose when the monastery was rebuilt in its present form, and this entire area, along with passage 74, became a part of courtyard 68, which extended as far as the wall on the east dividing the western from the eastern section of the group. No pavement or partition was found inside this enclosed area. Along the northern side of the area, the lower courses of the atrium rooms extend beyond the southeastern corner of the atrium or room 29 as far as the eastern wall of this section. By this extension of the wall and by the southern wall of the Theotokos chapel a tiny, oblong recess or closet is formed (Pl. 161, 73a; see Pl. 72, 2) which is paved with plain, quite large tesserae; at the western end of this tiny apartment a number of pottery cups was found. They reminded us of the fact that the first thing travellers generally asked for when they reached Siyâgha was a cup of water; some who came from the Ghor were so parched that they could scarcely utter a word.

Passage 74 (Pls. 161, 74; 72, 2) connects the courtyards of the western and eastern sections. In its western half there are two stones placed opposite one another against the northern and southern walls; they may have been the bases of responds; or, possibly, they mark the posts of a gate or door by means of which the eastern section was closed off from the western section where the general public passed; such privacy was not only desirable but necessary in a monastery. Beyond this pair of stones, towards the east, there is a door on the right which leads into the block of rooms in the southeastern part of this section. At the eastern end of the passage there is a stone step, by means of which the wall between the two sections can be conveniently crossed. Near the northern end of this step, and west of it, there is a pit lined with tiles (Pl. 80, 4); its interior is 34.5 cm. l. from east to west and 25 cm. w. from north to south; its depth is not certain. The oblong, flat tiles which line the pit measure 30 ×

[1] See, e. g., Geyer, pp. 40, 10 & 19; 52, 25; 58, 15; 68, 22; in all these passages Aetheria states that she and her party received gifts from the monks; several times she explains that these gifts consisted of fruits obtained from the gardens cultivated by the monks. But the "eulogiae" (= "blessed mementoes") were also other objects, as, for instance, oil taken from lamps burning at the shrines of the saints. Some of the flasks in which oil was taken away from ancient sanctuaries have the word "eulogia" inscribed on them. See Kaufmann, *HCA* pp. 593 ff.

9 × 1.5 cm.; this type was not found elsewhere on the site. The walls built of these tiles are plastered and about 18 cm. thick.

Two drain-pipes were found near the northern side of the pit (Pls. 80, 4; 157, 50); both were broken; a restoration of the fragments resulted in one complete pipe and about half of another one. The complete pipe is 28 cm. l. and 9½-13 cm. in d.; its one end flares, the other contracts, so that it can be inserted into the flaring end of the adjoining tube, as illustrated in Pl. 157, 50. These tubes near the pit suggest that the latter was destined for drainage, but, though we seem to have reached the bottom of the pit, no outlet was found, as one would expect in a drain.

Rooms 75-78 (Pl. 161, 75-78; see Pls. 71, 2, right; 72, 2, right; Fig. 9) form a distinct block in the southeastern part of this section. This block can be reached by only one door in the northern wall communicating with passage 74. In the doorway there are steps leading down to the level of the stone floor in 75. East of the door in 75 there is a half-pier against the northern wall; it has not been ascertained whether there was a similar one against the southern wall, but most probably there was. At the eastern end there is an arrangement which we took to be a drain, but its beginning on the north and termination on the south have not been discovered. In the southeastern corner there is a door which gives access to room 77; the stone of the frame next to the threshold on the west is molded. West of the main entrance to the block there is a stone bench and a half-pier against the northern wall. Area 75 continues along the western wall of the block without encountering a partition; in its southern half there are responds at a point where there may have been a partition forming a distinct room. As it is, the plan indicates a kind of corridor around the northern and western sides of the block. From this so-called corridor rooms 76 and 78 must have been reached.

In the southwestern corner of 75 a woman had been buried; with the bones were found a few glass bracelets, some beads and a spatula. Scattered throughout the corridor were fragments of marble and pottery.

Room 76 is paved with stones; in its southwestern corner on the pavement was found a piece of a glass weight (Pl. 141, 18) with a Kufic inscription (see inscription XXXVI). One of the marble fragments with a part of a fruit and a knife in relief (see Pl. 121, 1) comes from here. Regarding room 77 there is nothing special to remark. In the western half of room 78 there is a stone pavement; in the eastern half of the room, where the pavement is missing, we dug below the level of the floor and reached a layer of ashes, in which we recovered the pieces of the colored glass vase illustrated in Pl. 139, Fig. 3, 2.

The center of this block was occupied by a wooden shed for the workmen at the time when the excavations were made; we did not remove that shed but dug all around it; in this way we recovered most of the plan of this block, but a few details remained doubtful, as indicated in the plan. Since then the shed has burned down (see Fig. 9) and the writer has been informed that there is a plain mosaic floor at the place where it stood, probably in the unnumbered locus north of room 76.

The eastern wall of 73a-75, 77 and 78 forms the partition between the western and eastern sections of this southern part of the monastery. At the northern end this wall has a straight joint; that is, it does not bond in with the wall of the Theotokos chapel; but on the south it seems to bond in with the southern wall of the monastery. A jamb was found on this wall at the eastern end of passage 74; it suggests that there was a door between the two sections of the southern monastery.

3. *The eastern section of the southern group of monastic buildings* (Pl. 161, 79-105) preserves evidence of two levels or periods; in the earlier period there were rooms along both the southern and the eastern sides of the courtyard; in the later period the rooms on the eastern side of the courtyard were eliminated and covered up; low walls on a higher level suggest a different subdivision of that part of the monastery.

The courtyard of the earlier period seems to have comprised the areas marked on the ground plan (Pl. 161) by numbers 79, 80, 83, 92-94; in the later period it seems to have included the areas numbered 99-102, and most probably also 90a and 91.

In the northwestern part of the courtyard (Pl. 161, 79) we discovered the beginning of a drain made of tiles (Pl. 76, 3) which entends as far as a cistern on the southern side of the courtyard in the area marked 83 on the plan. The drain is 2.82 m. l. and consists of 9 clay tubes, of which only one is complete and the others are semitubes; they average about 33 cm. in length and 30 cm. in diameter. In the drain was found a tiny clay lamp of the "candle-stick" variety. At the southern end the drain extends below a stone pavement around the mouth of the cistern (Pl. 76, 3; see Pl. 72, 1, right foreground).

Regarding the cistern (Pl. 161, 83) little can be said. Its top was once covered by a large stone in which there was not only a hole for drawing water but also a basin, cut into its surface. The natural rock or masonry on which the stone rested gave way and fell into the cistern and there the stone lies today. The mouth of this cistern was visible before the excavations were made (Pl. 38, 1); it is no doubt the one referred to by Post.[1]

In the southwestern corner of the courtyard there is a platform consisting of one layer of stones (Pl. 161, 80); it served as an approach to room 81.

East of area 83 there is a low wall running north and south, from the southern wall of the baptistery to the northern wall of room 88 (Pls. 72, 1;

[1] See p. 14, 5.

74, 1-3). It is generally only one or two courses high and at two points, at the north and in the center, no trace of it remains. It is laid on a bed of clay on a level somewhat below that of the thresholds of the doors in the wall on the southern side of the courtyard. The point may be made clearer by a reference to Pl. 74, 2; there three doors are visible; the one in the center (compare with Pl. 73, 1, nos. 94-95) is flanked on each side by a single course of masonry forming the top of the wall at present. Against this uppermost course and against the course below it, is built the wall in question which is visible on the right of the door. This wall rests on a layer of earth which covered the entire area west and east of it (see Pl. 72, 1, left foreground), and concealed from view not only the lower courses of the southern wall, namely, the third etc. from the top, but also all the lower walls to the east, none of which rise above the thresholds of the doors, as can be clearly seen in Pl. 73, 1, in the areas 94, 101 and 102. The layer of earth, therefore, represents the dividing line between a lower and an upper level in this entire area.

The evidence of a lower and an upper level is clearest in that part of the area which is east of 83. On the lower level the loci marked 92-94 belonged to the courtyard, whilst all the remaining loci (91a, 90, 99-102) belonged to the wing of the building east of the courtyard. After all these loci had been buried beneath a layer of earth, the upper level was divided into two parts by a wall running west and east. At the western end this partition crossed the southern part of the ovens in 93 (see Pl. 161, 93) and was removed during the excavations in order to study the ovens; at the eastern end it follows the line of an older wall and reaches the eastern wall at a point between rooms 100 and 102; this latter section of the partition can be seen in Pls. 72, 1; 73, 1; 74, 3; (a number of stones from this area are on top of it). The rooms in this area will be described in speaking of the building around the courtyard; here only locus 93 will be described more in detail and a few objects of special interest found in the courtyard will be mentioned.

Locus 93 (Pls. 161, 93; 73, 1; 74, 2 & 3; 75, 3; 76, 2; Figs. 9; 21, 2 & 3) is in the eastern part of the earlier courtyard; this was the bakery and very probably also the kitchen of the earlier monastery. From the condition of the walls which surround this locus at present we cannot be certain whether they represent a mere enclosure or a room; the latter seems more probable, especially since it is certain that the oven of the later period was in a room (see Pl. 161, 105). In this room there are two ovens (Pl. 74, 2); both are made in pits below the level of the floor; the one on the west is cylindrical, the other on the east is rectangular in form; the former is built of clay, the latter of tiles.

The cylindrical oven (Pl. 75, 3) in the western part of the room stands on the native clay or rock which forms its floor; the clay walls are about 4 cm. thick; the oven is 111 cm. deep and 130 cm. in diameter; it had a vaulted cover of the same material as the walls. On clearing the interior of the oven we found that the lower half was filled with ashes, the upper half with ground and between the two layers we recovered the fragments of the broken clay cover. It is evident that the fire was built inside the oven and when it was heated the bread was baked by slapping the dough against the heated sides. Such ovens were in use for about two millenia when this one was built and are still in use in Transjordan and the neighboring countries today; [1] this one is remarkable only for its size and good condition. Another one of this type, even larger, was found in room 105.

Since the fire was built inside the oven it gradually filled up with ashes; when the ashes were removed, it seems that they were deposited in the area east of the ovens which we found covered with a very thick layer of ashes. Also in room 104 we found a deposit of ashes nearly one meter deep covering the entire floor of the room. It seemed somewhat surprising to find ashes deposited in the rooms adjoining the bakeries. In looking for another explanation for the presence of ashes in such large quantities, we thought that wood for the fire in the ovens might have been stored in those rooms and it was possibly reduced to ashes by an accidental fire; yet it should be observed, that even if the rooms were stacked to their utmost capacity with wood, it would scarcely have produced such a large quantity of ashes as we found.

The rectangular oven (Pls. 74, 2, left foreground; 76, 2; Fig. 21, 2 & 3) in the eastern part of the room also seems to stand on the native clay or rock which forms its floor (Fig. 21, section c-d); on the interior it is about 170 cm. l., 78-89 cm. w. and 56-98 cm. deep ; at its southern end there is an opening in the wall which is 45 cm. w. ; the tops of the walls rise above the floor level of the room. The walls of this oven are built of tiles (Fig. 21, 3) which have become fused to a great extent by the heat, so that the tiles have formed great lumps of clay and it is difficult to recognize their original size and shape. They seem to have been less than 2 cm. thick and to resemble the tiles used for the pit in passage 74 (see pp. 167 f.). We do not know whether this oven was closed on top, and, if so, how. We have called this pit in the form of a trough an oven because a similar pit at Megiddo[2] has been called so. But such a pit could also have been used for boiling water, as is done today by the Samaritans at their place of sacrifice on Mount Garizim during their Paschal celebration,[3] or it could have been used for cooking food and the like. For this

[1] See, v. g., *EP* p. 21 ; *Gezer* 2, p. 41 ; *Jericho*, p. 88 and passim ; Thomsen, *RLV* I, pp. 318 f.; Galling, *BRL* cols. 75 ff.

[2] See Galling, *BRL* col. 76, 2.

[3] See J. Jeremias, *Die Passahfeier der Samaritaner*, in *Beih. ZATW* 59 (1932), passim.

reason we are strongly inclined to think that this trough-pit served as the stove; consequently this room was not only the bakery but also the kitchen of the fifth century monastery.

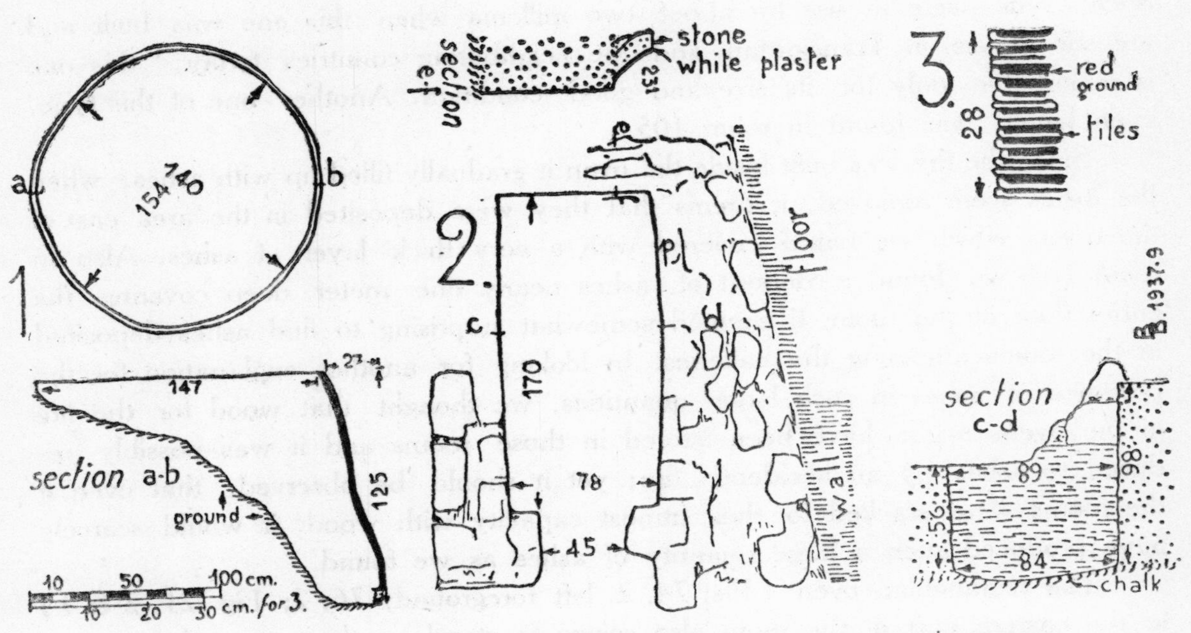

Fig. 21. The oven in room 105 (1) and the stove in room 93 (2 & 3).

The southern side of the oven and of the stove was covered by one course of the low wall on a higher level running west and east which served to partition off this area in the final period of the courtyard. We removed this wall. In doing so we observed that even at the point where it crossed the eastern wall of room 93 it did not rest directly on that wall; there were a few centimeters of earth between the two. The presence of that wall goes to show that the oven and stove were no longer in use during the last period of occupation. The relation of the upper wall to the oven, stove and lower wall is some of the clearest evidence we have of two levels and two periods in this area.

The stone illustrated in Pl. 76, 1 is in the outer face of the wall on the southern side of room 93; in other words, it can be seen only from area 94 (see Pl. 72, 1). It resembles the stones which cover basins placed below a wall in building 110-115 on the western slope; see Pls. 77, 2; 79, 2; in that case the purpose of the stones is clear, but not in this one. At Umm el-Jemal[1] a

1 See *ECS* pp. 216 f. and Ill. 218.

number of basins in various positions are covered with such stones; in the church of Gethsemane today one sees a similar stone over a shelf in the wall forming a niche in which the cruets for the water and wine used at mass are placed; again, these uses throw no light on the purpose of the stone in the southern wall of room 93; it was probably reused there.

A large jar and a marble slab found on the lowest level reached, west of the southwest corner of room 93, may have had something to do with the bakery. The clay jar (Pl. 147, 1 & 2) was thickly covered with a white coat of some material which was difficult to remove; possibly that material was flour and dough which was smeared onto the jar when handled by persons who were mixing water with flour in order to make dough; the jar contained the water required by the baker. The position of the jar and its white coating make it probable that it was used at the bakery.

The marble slab (Pl. 126, 1 & 3) found with the jar which we have just mentioned is the largest fragment of an altar which we found on the site, but also this fragment was broken into 10 smaller pieces before we discovered it. The upper surface of the slab with the cusped frame had been placed face downwards on the ground and in this way the original bright white color of the surface was somewhat disfigured and now it has large yellowish spots. The other surface of the slab, on which two monograms preceded by a cross are carved (see Pl. 121, 3 & 4; & inscription XVIII), has no molding; like the jar, it may have been used by the baker in his work.

In the area north of the bakery (Pl. 161, 92) a small channel was formed by a series of stones running parallel with the baptistery. The same area produced the only bronze lamp recovered on the site (Pl. 138, Fig. 1, 1); it is so small that it could have had but little practical value; perhaps it was intended merely as a votive offering to adorn the shrine of the saint. A coin found in the same place belongs to the reign of Justinian I, before the year 538 A. D.

A clearance on the floor level of room 93 brought to light the three hollow stems of glass lamps illustrated in Pl. 140, 22-24; these stems differ from the majority of others found at Siyâgha (see Pl. 140, 16-21; 25-29) in this that they bulge slightly above the center and are somewhat constricted above the bulge or directly below the cup.

Pieces of marble slabs with Samaritan inscriptions found in this region may be referred to here. Eight such fragments were found during the course of the excavations at Siyâgha (Pl. 122, Figs. 1 & 2); of these, four come from the area under consideration, two others from the immediate vicinity and only two more from other parts of the site. The first piece (Pl. 122, Fig. 1, 3) was found in 1933 whilst removing the stones along the southern side of the baptistery; the other three were recovered in 1937 whilst work was going on near the eastern wall of the monastery: two inside the wall, in the ash-layers of rooms 100 and 101, and one outside the same, opposite room 104. Of the other four fragments, one was found in 1933 directly behind the apse of the basilica at the lowest level reached that year; the second was found by the antiquities' guard in 1938 in the region east of the southern monastery; the third was found in 1935 in the upper part of the ruins in room 14 and the fourth in 1937 on the western slope near cistern 116.

The contents of these Samaritan inscriptions will be considered more in detail in the chapter on inscriptions (see inscriptions XXVI-XXXIII). Here it suffices to observe that they do not seem to contain any information of historical value. Thus, for instance, they do not inform us when they were inscribed or on what occasion they were placed here; neither can we deduce this with certainty from the character of the writing; hence the archæological context in which the fragments were found is of some importance in this question, and this is what we wish to stress here, though at the same time we must admit that this context is not very clear either; it does not enable us to fix the precise time when the Samaritans erected their tablets at Siyâgha. In spite of all this, the discovery of Samaritan inscriptions at Siyâgha is not without significance; they prove, for instance, that the Samaritans were interested in the site and exercised some influence there. Everything considered, it seems quite probable that the first quarter of the sixth century was the time when the Samaritans were at Siyâgha and erected their inscribed tablets there.

About 60-80 cm. of earth could still be removed from the northern half of the courtyard in the areas 83 and 79 (see Pl. 72, 1, left) and a number of other objects of interest might possibly be found there.

Buildings enclose the courtyard on practically every side; those on the north and west have no direct connection with this courtyard and do not concern us here; those on the south and east are connected with the courtyard and must be described more in detail. The rooms in these buildings are arranged differently from those around the atrium. There practically every room communicated directly with the courtyard, here the rooms are arranged in groups of two or more and, as a rule, only one of each group communicates with the courtyard. Thus, for instance, the building on the southern side of the courtyard contains 15 rooms or rather loci arranged in 4 groups having 5 doors connecting them with the courtyard.

Loci 81, 82, 84-87 (Pls. 161, 81-87; 73, 2; Figs. 8, 3; 9) form the first group in the western end of the southern building. The group is reached by a door in the northern wall of locus 81; from this other doors lead to the adjoining loci.

Locus 81 had a mosaic pavement consisting of plain tesserae, very like those used for the mosaic pavements in a number of rooms of the western section of the monastery (see pp. 165 f.). This mosaic pavement had been completely broken up, so that we found only loose tesserae and lumps of plaster in which they had been embedded. Below a layer of white plaster these lumps had a thick layer of gray ashes which together with the plaster served to form the bed of the mosaic.

The low wall on the southern side of room 81 does not at present have the character of a partition between two rooms, but merely marks the division of one room into two parts. The same is the case in the adjoining rooms 84-85, 88-89 and 95-96. Between 97 and 98, however, there is still a real wall containing a door; so also between 104 and 105. In the wall between 81 and 82 we likewise observed traces of a door in the same position as the door between 97 and 98; from this we conclude that there was at one time a real partition here which separated the space into two distinct rooms, but later the partition was removed and one large room resulted. The same probably holds good of the adjoining rooms.

Locus 82 was paved in the same manner as 81. The character of its masonry may be studied in Pl. 73,2, foreground and in Fig. 8,3, where details of the eastern wall are given. Most of the stones are squared and have a plain surface; but a few have a somewhat irregular surface and required a filling of smaller stones and mortar. The same holds good of the entire building, as may be seen in Pls. 73 and 74. This room was spanned by an arch from east to west, which has collapsed. A copper pan similar to the one found in room 63 (see Pl. 137, Fig. 3, right), the lower half of a bronze eagle on a stand of the same material (Pl. 137, Fig. 2,1), three copper wick-holders, iron nails, an iron knife with a socket for the insertion of a wooden handle, a fragment of a marble altar slab and a quantity of pottery come from here. Two of the pottery vessels were nearly complete; one was a pot (Pl. 150,27) and the other a lamp (Pl. 143,9); the latter was the only one of this type found at Siyâgha.

Locus 84 can be reached only by the door in its western wall communicating with 81 (see Pl. 73, left foreground). Its floor has preserved no pavement of any kind. A low wall, like that between 81 and 82, separates this place from locus 85, but in this case no evidence of a door was noted. A few pieces of marble, glass and pottery were collected here.

Locus 85 is the southern half of the room which resulted when the partition between it and 84 was removed; on its stone pavement were found a few bits of iron and two millstones. On its southern side there are two walled up *loci (86 & 87)* which resemble storage bins; they have no doors and can be entered only from the top. The one bin (86) was not completely cleared; near its top was found a fragment of a marble slab decorated with flutings of a shell motif and an arm of a cross in relief (Pl. 125,14); pottery sherds from here are characterized by interlacing wavy bands of combing (see, v. g., Pl. 152, 17 & 20). The other bin (87) was cleared to its earthen floor without finding anything.

This first group, therefore, consists of 6 loci, of which 4 were originally cells and 2 bins ; the four cells were later converted into two larger rooms.

Loci 88 and 89 (see Pl. 74,1 & 2, right background) form the second group in the southern building. The door in the northern wall of 88 joins this group with the courtyard. *Locus 88* has no pavement; here were found a piece of a column made of black stone and some pieces of marble and pottery. It is separated from locus 89 by a low wall, like that between 81 and 82, 84 and 85.

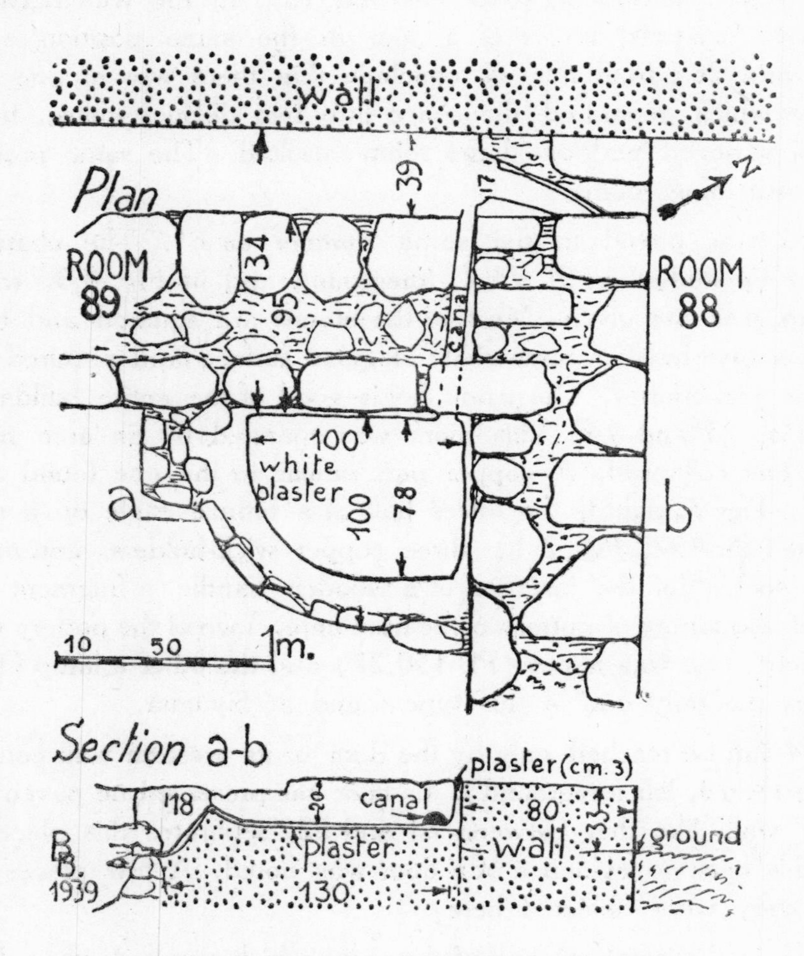

Fig. 22. The channel and basin in locus 89.

In *locus 89* there is a channel along the western wall and a basin in the corner formed by the channel and the northern wall (see Pls. 161, 89; 146, 29; Fig. 22). The channel (see Fig. 22) is formed by a wall 95 cm. thick running parallel to the western wall of the locus; it is 39 cm. w. and is joined by two drains at its northern end; one, which is plastered and about 17 cm. w., comes from a section of the northern wall and enters the channel on the northern side; the other served as a drain for the basin and joins the channel at the northeastern corner. The basin (Fig. 22; Pls. 75,1; 146,29) is built of rubble and plastered; the top of the same is on a level with the tops of the adjacent walls; on the interior it is about 20 cm. deep and measures 78 and 100 cm. along the northern and western sides respectively; the other side is rounded.

A small group of clay vessels was found near the southern side of the basin; they were crushed to pieces but it was possible to restore them almost completely; this was a rare thing at Siyâgha and adds to the interest of the group which consists of a large jar, a cooking pot, a dipper or a piece of a lantern and a tile, besides a few other fragments; after these objects had been restored they were photographed in practically the same place in which they were found (Pl. 146,29).

The jar (Pl. 146,3) serves to illustrate the form and decoration of this type of vessel and thus enables us to appreciate other fragments of the same ware which represent only a small part of a jar and its ornamentation. Near this jar was found a rather large fragment of the same type of vessel (Pl. 147,4). Jars of a different form but with a similar kind of decoration were found near both bakeries; that which was found near room 93 is illustrated in Pl. 147,1 & 2; the large fragment found near the oven in room 105 is illustrated in Pl. 148,2. In all cases the outer surface of the jars had a coating of some material which I take to be dough; hence also the jar in locus 89 seems to have been associated with the baker's work. Pls. 146-148 illustrate a number of other sherds of this type found at Siyâgha.

Complete jars of the same form and with the same decoration found in a Byzantine tomb at Jericho were ascribed to the 4th-5th centuries.[1] Sherds of the same type were observed by the writer at a number of sites in Palestine and Transjordan; they were most abundant at Umm er-Rasâs, the large Byzantine site to the southeast of Siyâgha. Glueck also noticed this type of ware at Umm er-Rasâs and at numerous other places during the course of his extensive explorations in Transjordan; he thinks that it may be dated to the 5th and 6th centuries A. D.[2] De Vaux[3] found similar sherds in a Byzantine context in the region around es-Salt. These observations may be useful in dating the Siyâgha material, or, vice versa, the Siyâgha material may serve to date other sherds coming from a less clear context.

[1] See *Jericho*, p. 162, B, 1 & 2 and Blatt 44, B, 1 & 2.
[2] See *AASOR* 18-19 (1939), p. 267; Pl. 21; see also pp. 77, 81, 116, 227; ibid. 14 (1934), p. 39.
[3] See *RB* 47 (1938), Pl. XXIII, 5, 6, 8, 10.

The pot (Pl. 150,30), made of the ribbed ware so familiar in the Byzantine period, is one of the very few recovered at Siyâgha that serves to convey some idea of the exact form of this type of vessel.

The object illustrated in Pl. 157,38 reminded the writer of a dipper, since it looks like one and was found near the basin. But its ware resembles that of the lanterns of which a number of fragments were found (Pl. 157, 26-37); it may have been the base of one of those lanterns.

The tile (Pl. 146,29) likewise is not without interest. It resembles the roof-tiles of the basilica; not one of those was complete, so we did not know their exact size or form. This one is 43 cm. l., 40½ cm. w. at one end and 33½ cm. at the other and on an average 2 cm. thick. The coating of plaster on the lower surface suggests that the tile had been used for covering the roof before it found its way into this room; in this case the tile indicates the normal size of those used for the roof. At the same time it serves to show that those tiles had a raised edge along the two long sides and that the other two sides were of different width. In this room the tile may have served as a tray or platter.

The basin and channel characterize this locus as a lavatory.

Loci 95-98 (Pls. 73, 1&2; 74, 1-3; 161, 95-98; Fig. 9) form the third large subdivision of the southern building. The door to the group is in the northern wall of *locus 95;* the stone pavement of this locus was observed only in the southeastern corner.

Locus 96 is separated from the preceding one by a low wall; below the floor level it is further subdivided by a wall running north and south. In the southeastern corner a structure of masonry reaches nearly to the top of the existing walls. A fragment of a stone bowl, pottery lamps and a coin serve to indicate when this room was used. The bowl belongs to a class of black stone vessels which are quite large and have flat bases, straight sides and ledge-handles. No complete vessel of this type was found at Siyâgha, but sherds are quite numerous (see Pl. 133, Fig. 2). Three of the pottery lamps found here are complete and several others are represented by sherds; two of the complete ones and several of the sherds belong to the "candle-stick" variety, the other complete one belongs to the "channel-nozzle" variety. The coin is a 40 nummia piece of the fourth year of Justin II (568-9 A. D.).

Locus 97 is a small room with two doors, one in the western and another in the southern wall. The southern half of the room was cleared to the level marked by the base of a step in front of the southern door; at that level there appeared a layer of ashes which contained a bead, some pottery sherds and a coin from the end of the sixth or the beginning of the seventh century A. D. The northern half of the room was not cleared to the same depth; there we recovered a tiny glass bottle with a brown ruffle at the base of the neck (Pl. 141, 1).

Locus 98 is separated from 97 by a wall with a door near which was found a stone measuring 66 × 32 × 18 cm. which is decorated with two carved crosses; this stone served either as a jamb or as the lintel. A wall running north and south exists below the supposed level of the unpaved floor in the cell; west of this wall was recovered a small collection of pottery vessels consisting of a "channel-nozzle" lamp, 2 jars (Pl. 145,2 & 3), cooking pots of which only a lid is complete (see Pl. 157,8) and a flat bowl with straight sides and incised ornaments (Pl. 153,1). The pottery seems to characterize this room as a pantry, but it may have been the cell of a monk who used these vessels either for his own needs or to provide for the needs of others.

Locus 98 is one of the smallest cells in the entire monastery; it is not quite 3 m. wide and about 3.70 m. long. These measurements correspond almost perfectly to those given by the biographer of Peter the Iberian for the cell of the great Sketian monk who lived in the monastery of Mount Nebo in the first half of the fifth century of our era. The biographer writes: [1] "And whilst we were there... the old man caused us to enter a small cell, which was about five cubits wide and long and not very bright." According to Butler [2] a cubit of 555 mm. was in use up to about 500 A. D.; five such cubits give us approximately three meters; in other words, the measurements of this cell and those given by the fifth century visitors to the cell of the Sketian monk agree remarkably well, especially if we bear in mind that those visitors did not measure it with a rod, but merely formed a rough estimate of its dimensions, a fact clearly indicated by the word "about" 5 cubits. Furthermore, we are told that the cell was not very bright. We found no window in the room; there may have been a small aperture for light and air near the roof; but if all the light came through the door alone, then there must have been very little light indeed, for the door opened into an adjoining cell and that one too seems to have been lighted only indirectly from locus 95.

We are, of course, not certain that this particular cell was the very one in which the Sketian monk lived. All that we wish to stress here is the fact that in proportions and in lighting, it answers so perfectly to what we know about the Sketian's cell that it may at least serve to illustrate that place.

As for the rest, it seems to follow from all that we read about this cell in the life of the Iberian [3] that it had acquired a certain interest and was, so to say, invested with an air of sanctity by the long and saintly life of the great Sketian monk in the same. Nay, it even seems that the cell was later set aside from common use and was readily accessible to visitors who might be expected

[1] Raabe, p. 83.
[2] *ECS* pp. 182 f.
[3] See pp. 110-112; Raabe, pp. 83-85.

to derive inspiration and benefit from the story of that monk's holy life. At any rate, on the second visit Peter was able to lead his followers into that cell without further ado and there explain his experiences to them. In short, one receives the impression from the Iberian's account that the cell of the Sketian was different from the others; that precisely is true of cell 98. It is the only one in the southern building (excepting 105) which has preserved its original form; its northern wall was not removed in order to enlarge it and provide it with more air and light, as was done in all the other rooms of the building; moreover, it is the only room in this building whose door was decorated with a cross, in fact, two crosses are carved on one stone found near the door. All this is calculated to attract attention to the place and gives rise to speculation regarding its meaning and purpose. The best explanation that suggests itself to us is that here we have the cell of the Sketian preserved in its original state. This supposition possibly throws some light on the significance of the other cells in this group; they may have been used by the so-called "deuteros" (δεύτερος) or the "synkelloi" (σύγκελλοι) of the Sketian.

The "deuteros" of the Sketian is mentioned by Peter the Iberian when he gives an account of his first visit to that recluse. Peter states that at the end of his visit the Sketian recommended his visitors to the "deuteros" and directed the latter to give them refreshments.[1]

Raabe has translated two Greek words of the biography of Peter by the German word "Zellengenosse", that is, "cell-mate": one is "deuteros" (δεύτερος),[2] the other "synkellos" (σύγκελλος).[3] This would seem to imply that the two Greek words are synonymous and from this it would follow that the so-called "deuteros", "assistant" or "associate" of the Sketian was also his "synkellos" or "cell-mate". This may have been true, but probably not in the strictest

[1] See p. 110, where we rendered the Greek word "deuteros" by the English phrase "the one who shared his cell", which is, strictly speaking, the equivalent of the Greek word "synkellos"; but in doing so, we followed Raabe, p. 84, who in German has "Zellengenosse", that is, "cell-mate". The archæological context, however, as we shall see, would seem to favor another rendering, such as, "associate".

[2] See the preceding note and Raabe, p. 97, where mention is made of another "deuteros", "Zellengenosse", called Peter. The latter lived in a monastery near Gaza, not far from the monastery of Peter the Iberian. In that same monastery there lived the monk Isaias, the Egyptian, who enjoyed a great reputation as an ascetic and prophet, so that many came to consult him. But he kept strictly to his cell and never admitted anyone to his presence. He communicated with the outside world only through his "deuteros" Peter, who was a priest and a man of great virtue; after the death of Isaias, Peter became his heir and the head of the monastery (see Raabe, pp. 116 f.). These observations throw some light on the character and functions of a "deuteros"; he was really a companion and an intimate associate of another monk.

[3] See Raabe, p. 123. When Peter the Iberian was on the point of death he appointed four heirs: John, Zachary, Andrew and Theodore. Zachary and Andrew are called the "synkelloi" of John. — St. Pakhomius introduced the practice of building larger cells in which a number (3) of monks lived together. See *DAC* 2,2, col. 2873, III. Even abbots and bishops had their "synkelloi", "concellanei", "cell-mates" or "domestics", whose purpose was not merely to assist those dignitaries in their work but also to watch over their conduct.

sense of the word. A wider meaning for the word "synkellos" seems to be suggested and demanded by our group of four cells reached from the exterior by a single door. The group may have been inhabited by a number of "synkelloi", "cell-mates", and still each one could have had his own cell and enjoyed a certain amount of privacy. Thus, for example, if the recluse, who never left his cell for 40 years, lived in cell 98, he would never have intruded on the privacy of his cell-mate in 97; the so-called "deuteros" could have lived in cell 97 where he would have been promptly at hand to hearken to the beck and call of the recluse in cell 98; he would indeed have had his own private cell, but nevertheless he could have been considered and called a "cell-mate" of the former without stretching the meaning of the word. The same holds good of the monk who lived in cell 96 before the partition separating it from 95 was removed; he too would have enjoyed privacy and at the same time could have been considered a "cell-mate" of the two living in 97 and 98. Whether 95 was also occupied by a monk or served merely as an adit to the other cells does not affect the present question in any way. The same holds good of the monks who lived in cells 81, 82, 84 and 85; they were no doubt considered and called "cell-mates"; but they were not cell-mates of the monks who lived in cells 95-98. The discovery of these two groups of cells throws new light on the internal arrangement of an ancient monastery, though it should be borne in mind that this arrangement differs from that in all the other buildings on the site considered so far and later was somewhat modified even here.

Loci 103-105 (Pls. 73,1; 74, 2 & 3; 75,2; 161, 103-105; Figs. 9; 21,1) form the fourth and last subdivision of the southern building, in which they occupy the eastern part. This group of three loci served as the bakery of the monastery in the sixth and seventh centuries. The one locus is a narrow passage along the western side of the group (103), the second contains the large oven (105) and the third served as a repository for ashes (104). The group is joined with the courtyard by means of two doors, and each locus has two doors.

Locus 103 (Pl. 73,1) served as a passageway through which the oven could be reached from the courtyard. In the northern doorway there are several steps by means of which one descends to the passage paved with rough stones; near its southern end there is a wide opening in the eastern wall (Pl. 75,2) formerly spanned by an arch which has collapsed, but a few voussoirs of the same can still be recognized on the half-pier on the southern side of the opening. Several stones with reed-molding found below the arch may have belonged to it. Through this arched opening the room with the oven could be reached.

Locus 105 (Pl. 75,2) occupies the southeastern corner of this group; it contains a large oven, which characterizes this room as the bakery. The interior of the oven is full of stones from the roof or the walls of the room; they were not removed, but a clearance around its top and along its western side established the fact that it is a cylindrical one built of clay, like the one in the western part of room 93, but somewhat larger; its walls are about 125 cm. high and 3-4 cm. thick; its diameter near the mouth is between 140-154 cm. (see Fig. 21,1); there is a round draft-hole, large enough to insert a man's fist, through the wall near the base of the western side; such a draft-hole did not exist in the cylindrical oven of room 93, but the opening in the southern side of the rectangular stove in that same room may have served such a purpose.

In the clearance around the oven we recovered some pottery sherds, a stone vessel and an iron disk. Among the sherds was the large fragment of a jar illustrated in Pl. 148,2; it resembles jars found in 89 and near 93 (see pp. 173 & 177). The stone vessel from here (Pl. 133, Fig. 1,5) resembles a boat with a flat bottom; its sides have incised ornaments. A fragment of a similar vessel was found in courtyard 68. The large iron disk, which is about 34 cm. in d. and has a perforation in the center 5 cm. in d., was found in digging the hole along the western side of the oven.

Locus 104 (Pl. 73,1) is north of the room with the oven. It has two doors; the one in the southern wall connects it with the oven-room, the other in the northern wall with the courtyard; this latter door is in the eastern half of the northern wall, whereas in other rooms (81, 88, 95) the door is in the western half of their northern wall. Several steps lead down from the northern door to the floor of the room which seems to have been paved with mortar. Along the western side of the room there is a row of stones placed parallel to the wall to form either a trough, a bench or a bed, as in many other rooms (see 14, 26, 27, 54). But the chief characteristic of this room was the deep layer of ashes which covered the entire floor and buried the stone curb on the west and the steps in the doorway. This large amount of ashes makes the impression that this room was used for depositing the ashes from the oven of the adjoining room. A similar deposit of ashes was found in the area north of 104; in speaking of that deposit we suggested on p. 171 that it came from the oven in room 93; as a possible alternative we indicated that a quantity of burning material stacked in those areas might have been destroyed by fire.

The few pieces of marble, of a black stone vase, of lamps and tiles recovered in room 104 were not very characteristic.

Loci 90a, 91, 99-102 are subdivisions of the eastern wing of the building (Pls. 22,1; 25, 1 & 2; 27,2; 38,1; 72,1; 73,1; 74,3; 113, 1 & 2; 161, 90a, 91, 99-102; Fig. 9). Only the eastern wall of this wing has preserved more than two courses of its masonry in situ; all other walls consist at present of only one or two courses; the former, in its upper part at least, is later than the latter. The date of the eastern wall is fixed by the fact that it bonds in with the southern wall of the second basilica and is contemporaneous with it, as it is also with the walls of the southern building in their present state. At the same time this eastern wall served as part of the enclosure surrounding the monastery on the east (see Pls. 72,1; 161, east side of 91, 100, 102, 104, 105).

The western wall of the group (Pls. 72,1; 73,1; 74,3; 161, west side of 90a, 99, 101) has preserved only one or two courses of its masonry and does not seem to bond in with the walls at its two extremities. Its date is determined by the fact that at its northern end a tower has been built over it (Pls. 25,2; 161, 90) and near its center, between 93 and 99, it is crossed by a wall on a slightly higher level running east and west. We think that the tower at the northern end is contemporaneous with the baptistery which was finished at the end of the sixth century (597 A. D.), hence the wall below it is earlier; it was probably constructed in the fifth century and belongs to the same period as the first basilica. The same seems to be indicated by the wall to which we referred; it served to divide this area at a later period into a northern and southern section.

The northern boundary of the group at present is the southern wall of the second basilica (see Pl. 25,2); the southern limit is the northern wall of loci 103 and 104.

On the interior this wing of the building is divided into 6 loci, all of which are to be assigned to the period antedating the second basilica on the evidence indicated when speaking of the walls enclosing the group. The 6 loci form two groups, each of which communicates with the courtyard on the west; the group on the south consists of 2 (101 & 102), that on the north of 4 (99, 100, 90a & 91). Five are practically on the same level and their pavement, wherever it is preserved, consists of flags; the sixth (91) is on a higher level and is paved with colored mosaics forming designs.

Room 91 with its mosaic pavement was discovered in 1933 (see Pls. 25,2; 113, 1 & 2); the relation of tower 90 to the western wall of 90a was ascertained by further clearances both inside and outside the tower in 1935 (see Pl. 161,90 & 90a); the rest of the area was cleared in 1937 (compare Pl. 25,2 with Pls. 73 ff.).

Loci 101 and 102, in the southern part of the eastern wing, could be reached from the courtyard by means of steps which crossed the western wall of *locus 101* (Pl. 161, 101). No traces of steps were found on the western side of the wall, but on its eastern side there are two; the upper one has preserved on the tread faint traces of two carved crosses enclosed by circles, and in the rise there are two small round cavities, like those we observed in the stone frames of windows, where they served to receive the ends of bars of an iron grating; this suggests that the stone once served as a part of a window's framework and was later used here; when this happened we are unable to say.

The wall on the south side of locus 101 has a door which gives access to corridor 103 (Pl. 73,1). The doorstone is higher than the top of the western wall, yet there are no stairs in front of it, as there are at the point where the western wall was crossed; this would seem to imply that at the time when the door was made the area north of it was filled up to a sufficient height to make access to the same easy without stairs; in this case the floor level of room 101 would have been raised so much that its western, northern and eastern walls would have been buried. That this was actually the case seems to be confirmed by the fact that none of the doors either to the east (102-104) or to the west of this one (94-95, 83-88) have steps leading up to them, although these would have been necessary if the original floor level of the areas north of them had been preserved.

At the northern end of the eastern wall there is an opening (see Pl. 72,1) through which locus 102 may be reached. The precise position and condition of the northern wall is somewhat obscured by a layer of earth which covers it and supports a later wall on a higher level. We wished to preserve this evidence of two levels, at least until our studies of the same were finished. See Pls. 72,1; 73,1; 74,3.

The room had a stone pavement which is still preserved. Above the layer of earth and ashes which covered this area, in fact, above the level of the walls on the east and west, we found a stone capital and a piece of a Samaritan inscription. The capital (Pl. 59,2) resembles those used in the body of the basilica, but it is much smaller and poorly preserved; one of its sides is completely missing and two others are damaged. It is 34 cm. h.; its base is 29 cm. in d. and the abacus measures about 53 cm. along each side. Below the 4 corners of the abacus are 4 large leaves with a broad and flat central vein and small grooved leaflets containing pellets, peculiar to the capitals of the basilica. The caulicoles are similar to those of the larger capitals. See pp. 62 f. On pp. 52 ff. we suggested that this capital was originally destined for one of the columns of the chancel screen and later was brought here, where it has no apparent function. The marble fragment with a Samaritan inscription was the sixth one found during the course of the excavation (see inscription XXXIII & Pl. 122, Fig. 1,5).

Locus 102 (see Pls. 72,1; 73,1; 161, 102), as far as we know at present, could only be reached from locus 101; it was the inner room of the group and and its history was the same as that of the outer room (101).

Loci 99 and 100 (Pls. 72,1; 73,1; 74,3; 161,99 & 100), in the center of the building's eastern wing, were reached from the courtyard through an opening in the western wall of locus 99; from there other openings gave access to loci 100 and 90a on the east and north respectively. The flagstone pavement of *locus 99* (Pl. 73,1) is tolerably well preserved; on it were found two fragments of pottery lamps; one has a crisscross design in its ring-base, the other belonged to the top of a "channel-nozzle" lamp.

Locus 100 (Pls. 73,1; 74,3) has preserved only a small portion of its stone pavement on its southern side. A row of stones rises above the southern edge of the pavement; above it is a layer of earth and a wall of a later period which we did not remove, hence it is not quite certain whether the row of stones represents a bench or the wall dividing loci 100 and 102; the latter is probable. Along the northern side of this room the native rock crops up above the floor level and immediately north of it that outcrop forms the highest point of this spur of the ridge. In the ashes which covered the floor of this room, there was a mere sliver of a marble slab blackened by fire, which has preserved a few Samaritan letters (Pl. 122, Fig. 1,7). See inscription XXXI.

Loci 90a and 91 occupy the northern end of the building's eastern wing (Pls. 25,2; 161,90a & 91); they seem to belong to the same group as loci 99 and 100.

Locus 90a was entered from the south by a wide opening in its southern wall (Pl. 25,2; the man is standing in the doorway; a glimpse of the same may be obtained in Pls. 72,1; 73,1, right foreground; 74,3). This opening is remarkable for its width and for the solidity of the masonry flanking it. In the gateway the rock slopes upwards from south to north, but no trace of a step was observed. The eastern and western walls terminate on the north against the foundation of the cella trichora which is in all probability still in situ there. The western wall is interesting for several reasons; firstly, it has a tower built over its northern end (see Pls. 161,90; 25,2); secondly, the lower courses of the baptistery's southern wall bond in with it near the gateway (Pl. 25,2). The relation of the wall to the tower proves that it is anterior to the latter; if the tower was built at the same time as the baptistery to serve as a brace and as a bond with the basilica, then the wall could be as old as the fifth century; and, if this is the case, then the wall which bonds in with it near the gateway could also be of that date.

The purpose of this locus is unknown. It is so narrow that it makes the impression of a passage, like the one in the southern part of the building directly opposite to it (Pl. 161, 103); that one led to the room with the oven (105); perhaps this one led to room 91; unfortunately we could not discover whether or how 90a and 91 communicated with one another. It is also possible that 90a gave access to an older building on the west which is now concealed by the baptistery. The existence of such an older structure below the baptistery was discussed in speaking of that chapel on pp. 84 f. There is a third possibility, namely, that this assumed passage led to a door in the southern apse of the cella trichora or the first basilica (see Pl. 161, B), but there is not the least evidence of this.

The tower (Pl. 161,90) was described in speaking of the baptistery and there too its purpose was mentioned. See pp. 85 f.

Locus 91 (Pls. 25,2; 74,3, foreground; 113, 1 & 2; Fig. 9), in the north-eastern corner of the building's eastern wing, marks the highest point of this hill. Its southern and western walls encase the native rock and rise only a few centimeters above the mosaic pavement which covers it. On the north there is the wall of the second basilica and on the east the wall enclosing the eastern side of the monastery. These two walls bond into one another at the north-eastern corner of the room; on the exterior (Pl. 27,2) one can see that the two walls were erected after the eastern wall of the cella trichora had collapsed, for the corner projects so far northward that it prevented the replacing of one of the large stones of the cella trichora which had fallen outwards. These two walls may have been erected in the sixth century, whilst the room may be from an earlier period, say the fifth century.

The colored mosaic pavement, regarding which details will be given in the chapter on mosaics, distinguishes this room from all others in the southern monastery. We already observed that this room occupies the highest point on the hill; this fact and the mosaic pavement made us think that we had discovered the spot at which the vision of Moses was commemorated. If this was the hill from which Moses viewed the Promised Land, then it would have been quite natural for him to look for the highest spot from which to take in the view; furthermore, if that fact was at all marked by a monument, it would also have been natural to choose the highest point for it. If the cella trichora had been destined to commemorate the vision of Moses it should have been placed four-square on the crest of the hill; but neither the one nor the other is the case; it is only in part on top of the hill and was erected over the tomb of Moses; it had no direct connection with his vision. But unfortunately for our theory, the literary sources do not associate the vision of Moses with any monument on the site, and the only spot favored in any way by those sources is one on the western side of the church, as we pointed out in speaking of platform 57 on pp. 150 ff. Another alternative is that this room was the sacristy of the first basilica; that monument had a door in its southern wall by means of which this room could have been reached; this is the explanation which appeals most of all to the writer at present.

With these observations on room 91 we complete our description not only of the southern group of buildings, but of the entire central complex, comprising loci 1-105 on the ground plan (Pl. 161). The outer wall of the monastery formed a large enclosure which must have been very impressive when it was still standing and from it the site has acquired its name: "Siyâgha", "the enclosure", "the enclosed site", "the monastery".

F. OUTLYING BUILDINGS, CAVES, CISTERNS, ENCLOSURES AND QUARRIES

1. *General survey.* Beyond the central complex of buildings there are other loci which belonged to the monastery and should be briefly noticed here. Those loci are all indicated in Fig. 3, 106-137; of these 106, 109, 110-115,

117, 120, 121, 123-125, 126 (?), 130 and 131 are buildings; 107, 108, 127 and 132 are caves; 116, 118, 122, 129 and 136 are cisterns; 119 and 137 are walls which served as an enclosure and as a dam respectively; also the wall around the northeastern part of the site may have been an enclosure or at least a boundary mark; 128, 133-135 are quarries. Stones marking tombs and encampments are not indicated. Some loci served several purposes and could be treated under several heads; thus, for example, locus 107 is a cave which very probably, originally, served as a habitation and was later converted into a cistern; the adjoining cave (108) may have served originally as a dwelling and later as a place of burial. In fact, the caves of Mt. Nebo have become invested with an air of mystery since they are supposed to contain the tomb of Moses and the ark of the covenant. We shall describe these loci in a topographical order, first those on the west, then those on the south, east and north.

2. *Loci 106-109* are located on the northwestern slope of the hill; their position on the site and their relation to the other buildings can be seen by comparing Fig. 3, 106-109 with Fig. 9; a general plan of the group is found in Pl. 161, 106-109; a general view of the greater part of the same may be found in Pl. 77, 1. In Fig. 9, right foreground, one obtains an excellent view of the spur of the hill into whose side this group of loci has been built. The top of the spur is crowned by the central complex of buildings; beyond the buildings on the northwestern slope there is a vast quarry (Fig. 3, 133) whose high southeastern escarpment casts a deep shadow over the flat area below it from which building stones have been taken, so that from the air it looks like a deep crater. Below the western edge of the quarry, further down the slope, there are two caves (Pl. 161, 107 & 108) and in front of them the rock has been cut perpendicularly to form a large flat area transformed into two rooms (Pl. 161, 106 & 109).

Before excavations were made here the two rooms and the southern cave (108) were completely buried beneath earth, which had been washed down from above, and that same earth completely buried the masonry in front of the northern cave (107). Above the masonry at the entrance to cave 107 (Pl. 77,1) there was a small opening through which one could crawl into the interior filled with soil washed in from above. At the northeastern corner of the cave some masonry could be recognized.

On one of the first visits to Siyâgha the writer was conducted to this cave and invited to enter; there all that was visible was pointed out and he was asked to take special note of the masonry in the rear of the cave. On that occasion he was reminded that a clearance of this cave might throw some light on the famous passage in *2 Machabees* 2, 4-8, where we read: "how the prophet Jeremias, being warned by God, commanded that the tabernacle and the ark should accompany him, till he came forth to the mountain where Moses went up, and saw the inheritance of God. And when Jeremias came thither he found a hollow cave: and he carried in thither the tabernacle, and the ark, and the altar of incense, and so stopped the door. Then some of them that followed him, came up to mark the place: but they could not find it. And when Jeremias perceived it, he blamed them saying: The place shall be unknown, till God gather together the congregation of the people, and receive them to mercy. And then the Lord will show these things, and the majesty of the Lord shall appear..." [1]

According to this tradition the ark, etc. are in one of the caves of Mount Nebo.[2] Influenced by these passages several ark explorers were attracted to Siyâgha, where they examined a number of caves, but did not carry out any excavations. Our own program called for a systematic exploration of the entire site; accordingly, when we came to caves in the course of our work they were also explored; only in this way could we hope to discover all that was to be known about this site; haphazard digging would only result in confusion.

At the end of the first expedition to Siyâgha in 1933 a sounding was made near cave 107; it brought to light certain details of the cave's interior, the wall closing its entrance and part of the mosaic pavement in front of the same. In 1935 the clearance in front of the cave was continued. The mosaic pavement there was completely uncovered and the entrance to cave 108 was discovered. The masonry closing the entrance to the latter was removed and the interior was explored. In 1937 the clearance was continued along the declivity southwards; in this way we came across locus 109 and established the fact that beyond its southern wall there are no other caves or buildings.

Cave 107 was not completely excavated on the interior, but the soundings which were made have established the fact that it is about 3.95 m. l., 2.95-3.10 m. w. and 2.90-3.75 m. high (see Fig. 23). Large crevices in the rock were closed with masonry and possibly the entire cave was lined with

[1] The text is cited according to Challoner's revision of the *Douay Version of the Old Testament*. — See Charles C. Torrey, *The Letters Prefixed To Second Maccabees*, in *JAOS* 60 (1940), pp. 149 f., for a recent English version of this passage.

[2] A similar tradition is recorded in the *Vitae Prophetarum* (see D. Theodor Schermann, *Propheten- und Apostellegenden nebst Jüngerkatalogen des Dorotheus und verwandter Texte*, Leipzig, 1907, pp. 31 ff., 81-89, 118-120, 197). According to this source Jeremias is supposed to have concealed the ark in a "rock" which is "between the two mountains in which lie Moses and Aaron"; "a fiery cloud" is said to mark the region. This indication of place is much more vague than in *2 Mach.* 2,4 ff. The same vagueness characterizes Thietmar's reference to the place of the ark's concealment; on leaving the monastery at Mount Nebo he declares that he "came to the rock where the prophet Jeremias buried the ark of the covenant; above that place a fiery cloud is still frequently seen at nights". The mention of a "rock" and "a fiery cloud" suggest that Thietmar was influenced by the *Vitae Prophetarum* rather than by *2 Mach.* Thietmar is the only pilgrim who associates the ark with the Nebo region. (See Laurent, p. 35 and supra p. 113, 4). An old Arab woman also claims to see a fiery cloud or "lights" in this region from time to time. She cannot specify the exact spot where lights appear nor does she know their meaning. But it is interesting to note that this fact corresponds to a detail referring to the ark in Thietmar and in the *Vitae Prophetarum*. It cannot be readily assumed that the woman is familiar with those sources.

masonry before it was plastered. A thick layer of plaster covers the walls. The entrance to the cave was on the west; it was walled up and in the center of the wall there was an opening which originally seems to have been a door but later was closed. The masonry and plaster suggest that this cave was used as a

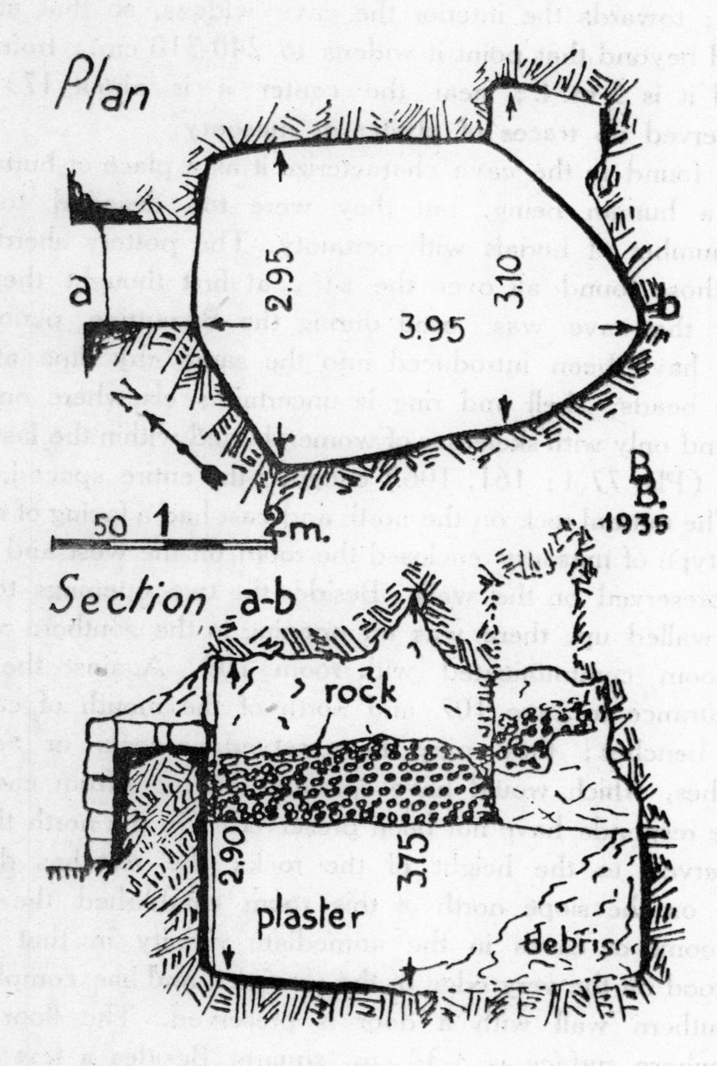

Fig. 23. Cave 107.

cistern, like so many other caves in Transjordan. But the door in the western wall seems to indicate that this cave was used as a dwelling before it was converted into a cistern. Originally it may have served as a refuge for a hermit.

Cave 108 (Pls. 77,1; 161, 108) was closed by means of 5 stones, one of which has a triangular section cut out of its surface. On removing these stones it was observed that fine black soil had penetrated into the cave and partially filled the interior; this ground was removed and in doing so some bones, 5 beads, a shell, a ring and a few clay sherds were found. On the interior the outlines of the cave are quite irregular; in general it is lower and narrower, but longer than the preceding cave. The entrance to the cave is about 90 cm. w. and 110 cm. h.; towards the interior the cave widens, so that after 2 m. it is 130 cm. w. and beyond that point it widens to 240-310 cm.; from the entrance to the rear wall it is 5 m. l.; near the center it is about 175 cm. high. Its walls have preserved no traces of plaster or masonry.

The bones found in the cave characterize it as a place of burial. The bones were those of a human being, but they were too decayed to enable us to determine the number of burials with certainty. The pottery sherds found in this cave resemble those found all over the site; at first thought they would seem to suggest that the cave was used during the Byzantine period; but these fragments could have been introduced into the same any time afterwards; the evidence of the beads, shell and ring is uncertain; elsewhere on the site such objects were found only with skeletons of women buried within the last century or so.

Room 106 (Pls. 77,1; 161, 106) occupies the entire space in front of caves 107 and 108. The natural rock on the north and east had a facing of rubble masonry and the same type of masonry enclosed the room on the west and south. Traces of plaster are preserved on the walls. Besides the two openings to the caves on the east, later walled up, there was an opening in the southern wall by means of which this room communicated with room 109. Against the eastern wall, south of the entrance to cave 107 and north of the mouth of cave 108, there are two stone benches; they may have served as seats or as the bases of pilasters or arches, which would have spanned this room from east to west, but on the west the responds have not been preserved. On the north the stone facing has been preserved to the height of the rock; the rest has disappeared. A sounding made on the slope north of this room established the fact that there are no other rooms or caves in the immediate vicinity in that direction. The western wall stood on the very edge of the precipice and has completely vanished. Part of the southern wall with a door is preserved. The floor is paved with plain tesserae whose surface is 3-3½ cm. square. Besides a few pottery sherds, there was found here a 40 nummia piece of the fourteenth year of Maurice Tiberius (595-6 A. D.).

Room 109 (Pl. 161, 109) occupies the southern part of the group under consideration. On the east and northeast the natural rock was cut down vertically to form the wall of the room; the other sides were enclosed by masonry of which only the lowest courses remain. The floor is the native rock brought to a level surface. At the eastern end of the northern wall there is a small opening in the rock through which one can look into cave 108. In the northeastern corner of the room there was a deposit of ashes near which most of the other small objects were recovered. Pottery sherds from here filled a basket; there were some iron nails, a leaden plaque, pieces of glass and 7 coins; the largest coin was a 20 nummia piece of Anastasius I (491-518 A. D.); the smaller coins resemble those in use during the fourth and fifth centuries A. D.

Outside the southern wall of room 109 the excavations were extended southwards for a short distance. No door was found in this wall, though this was probably the side from which the group was reached. The base of the wall on the exterior was protected against humidity by a thick layer of plaster. Regarding the use of plaster on the exterior of walls see pp. 145 ff. The declivity was strewn with chips from the quarry above; judging from the position of the chips, it would seem to follow that rooms 106 and 109 existed and were occupied at the time when the chips were deposited; for, as far as we could see, the chips extended up to the southern wall of 109, but not over the top of the rooms. Below the chips no other structures or caves were found.

We do not know when this group was first occupied and how long it remained in use; neither do we know with certainty who it was that lived here. But the evidence, taken as a whole, points to an occupation during the Byzantine period and on general principles we assume that the place belonged to monks, who arranged the group in its present form and also lived there; we know of no others who were permanently settled at Mount Nebo in Byzantine times. In number and general arrangement this group of four loci resembles very closely other groups of cells in the central complex, as, for example, the unit 95-98 (see pp. 178-181); but it differs from them in this important fact that it is outside the enclosure and at some distance from it on the northwestern slope, where it is practically hidden from view. This group, therefore, could not have been destined for and inhabited by the regular cenobites, but by hermits. If that is true, then this unit possesses a special interest, for it would serve to illustrate a comparatively well preserved hermitage of the Byzantine period.

We know from Aetheria that there were numerous hermits in this region in the fourth century; she mentions their "monasteries", that is, groups of cells or hermitages (see pp. 108 f.), but she does not give any details regarding the same. It has been assumed that the majority of the hermits lived in the caves near ʿAyûn Mûsa (see Pl. 13); there are traces of ancient masonry in front of those caves, but they have been so frequently occupied since the Byzantine times, that their original form has become obscured. This group near the top of Siyâgha, however, has preserved its original form and for this reason deserves close attention by those who are interested in these matters.

Originally the two caves may have afforded a refuge for two hermits; later, when one of the caves was converted into a place of burial and the other into a cistern, two hermits would still have found ample space in the two rooms in front of the caves. The one room may have been inhabited by a master in the spiritual life, the other by one of his disciples. That this was the case at times may be illustrated by a number of stories in the *Pratum Spirituale*. Thus, for example, in chapter 93 we read of a hermitage a Bethnambris, near Tell Nimrin, to the northwest of Siyâgha, which was inhabited by Sisinnios who had been a bishop but resigned his office and retired to that spot to lead a solitary life. His death occurred during the reign of Tiberius II (574-582 A. D.). At the moment of his death he was visited by the archimandrite Gregory, who found with Sisinnios his disciple; the latter also died before Sisinnios had been interred and was placed in the same grave with his master.[1]

Other facts regarding hermitages and solitaries in Transjordan have been collected by a number of explorers. Conder mentions those at ed-Deir [2] and in Wady Hesbân; [3] Abel those at Bethnambris,[4] at Sapsaphas,[5] in the desert east of the Jordan,[6] on the eastern shore of the Dead Sea,[7] in the Arnon valley,[8] at Ghoueir; [9] Frank [10] and Alt [11] the one in Wady el-Hesa; Glueck the one at Kilwa; [12] there are no doubt many others.

Our group of caves and rooms has enough in common with the hermitages which existed in other places to make it very plausible that it was also a hermitage. On this account the group claims our interest, and not because we have succeeded in establishing any connection between it and the ark referred to in the beginning of this section.

There are a few other caves on the northwestern slope of Siyâgha; one (Fig. 3,127), to the southwest of the preceding group, we cleared; it is very small, about the size of an ordinary coffin, and contained nothing besides a little soil and tiny bits of pottery washed in with the soil. A second cave, further down the slope, is quite large, but it has not yet been cleared. When one considers that this entire hill was occupied for hundreds of years by numerous monks, who used every inch of space for their dwellings, cisterns, burial places,

1 See *PG* 87, col. 2952; *RB* 19 (1910), p. 545.
2 *SEP* pp. 94-96.
3 *SEP* p. 249.
4 *RB* 19 (1910), p. 545; see *PS* 93 in *PG* 87, col. 2952: Sisinnios.
5 *RB* 41 (1932), pp. 248-255; see *PS* 1 and 2 in *PG* 87, cols. 2852 f.: the hermit John, etc.
6 *RB* 41 (1932), pp. 253-255; see *S. Sophronii Patriarchae Hierosol. Vita S. Mariae Aegyptiae* in *PG* 87, cols. 3697-3725.
7 *RB* 41 (1932), p. 255; see *PS* 21 in *PG* 87, col. 2868: an anchorite was killed by a Saracen; in the seventh century such solitaries were no longer sure of their lives in those regions, so this form of life gradually disappeared.
8 *RB* 41 (1932), pp. 252 f.; see *PS* 101 in *PG* 87, col. 2960: Pardus.
9 *Croisière autour de la Mer Morte*, p. 15: an abandoned hermitage.
10 *ZDPV* 57 (1934), pp. 207 f., Plan 9 B, Taf. 25 A: hermitage.
11 *ZDPV* 58 (1935), pp. 72 f.: Greek inscription of a late period.
12 *JPOS* 16 (1936), pp. 9-16: a hermitage with Arabic inscriptions dating from the end of the first millennium.

gardens, etc., it would be a most remarkable discovery, indeed, if the ark would be found there today.

3. *Loci 110-115* (see Pls. 161; 77,2; 78,1-3; 79,1-3; Figs. 3; 9; 20,4) belong to the most important outlying building cleared until now. The building is located on the western slope, to the southeast of the preceding group; a large quarry separates the two (see Figs. 3,133 & 128; 9); the first group is west of the quarry and below it; this one is east of the quarry and above it; in fact, the western wall of the building is on the very edge of the quarry. The area on the declivity destined for the structure was leveled by quarrying away the rock, leaving a natural wall on the north, east and south. The natural rock was faced with masonry; this facing has been preserved; on the north it cropped forth above the rock surface and betrayed the existence of the building which was partially cleared in 1937. Its southeastern and southern parts were crossed by a path to our dump in the quarry, so they could not be explored conveniently. The building is of the courtyard type with loci on the north and northeast, probably also on the southeast and south; the entrance to the building was very probably on the south. All the walls were plastered and the floors paved with plain mosaics.

Courtyard 114 (Pls. 161, 114; 77,2, foreground) is a rectangle measuring about 7 m. from east to west and about 6.20 m. from north to south. Its floor, paved with plain mosaics, is on a lower level than that of the loci around it (see Fig. 20,4). A large rectangular stone with a rectangular cavity has been let into the pavement in the center of the courtyard. In the northwestern part of the courtyard a low enclosure was formed by a single row of stones (see Pls. 77,2; 79,1); south of this one a few more stones in a similar position suggest a second enclosure of the same type. No doors were found; in the northern wall there are low arched openings over stone basins (Pls. 77,2; 79,2); they made it possible to reach into the basins and remove their contents. In the northeastern corner there was a narrow opening through which locus 113 was reached at one time, but later this opening was closed with masonry. On the east locus 115 is completely open on the side facing the courtyard (Pl. 79,3). On the southeast and south we were able to reach the lowest course of masonry next to the pavement of the courtyard, but all other details are concealed by a mass of earth. In the courtyard a 40 nummia piece of the fourth year of Heraclius (613-4 A. D.) was found.

Loci 110-113, 115 (Pls. 161, 110-113,115; 78,1-3; 79,3), on the northern and northeastern sides of the courtyard, were not rooms or cells which served as habitations, but had a different purpose, as will appear in studying the individual loci.

Loci 110-112, on the northern side of the courtyard, form a distinct group, in which the loci are separated from one another by low walls; there are no openings or doors in any of the walls, which are covered with as many as 5 coats of plaster; apparently these loci could be reached only from the top. Their floors are paved with plain tesserae. The chief peculiarity of each of these three loci is the stone basin in its southern wall; in locus 110 it is at the western end (see Pl. 78,1), in 111 in the eastern end (see Pl. 78,2, right) and in 112 in the center (see Pl. 78,2, left). In each case the basin is so placed that its edge rises a few centimeters above the floor of the locus, but in each case there is also a notch in the margin so that a liquid could drain slowly from the floors into the basins. On the side of the courtyard the basins — only two at present — are covered with arched stones (see Pls. 77,2; 79,2) so that one can conveniently reach into them and remove their contents. In the basin of locus 111 a few iron nails were found and in the débris above the three loci we collected a basket of sherds.

In the opinion of the writer these three loci are wine-presses. They served for treading grapes;[1] the juice flowed into the basins which served as receiving-vats and from there it was dipped into other vessels. Often such presses were paved with mosaics.[2]

Locus 113 (Pl. 78,3) is in the northeastern corner of the building; it differs from the preceding loci in this that high walls separate it from the adjoining loci on the west and south; it has a narrow opening in the southwestern corner communicating with the courtyard and had no stone basin of any kind. The walls were covered with at least two coats of plaster; the outer coat on the east had triangular indentations, on the north it had punctured holes, but on the west and south it was smooth. The plaster also covered the walls on both sides of the narrow entrance. Later the entrance was closed with masonry, behind which the plaster on the wall can be seen. The mosaic pavement consists of plain tesserae. In the débris which filled this locus a basket of pottery sherds, some glass and a piece of marble were recovered.

The purpose of this locus is not so clear as that of the three preceding ones, but it most probably had something to do with the work at the wine-press both before and after its entrance was walled up. Originally it probably served as a place of storage; later, when walled up, it could have served as a tank or reservoir, accessible from the top; its roof was easily reached by the passage on the eastern side of the building.

1 How this was done is illustrated in a number of mosaic pavements representing vintage scenes. One of these representations is in the church of SS. Procopius and Lot in the neighboring town el-Mekhayyat; see Lemaire, *RB* 43 (1934), pp. 390 f.; Pls. XXIV, 2; XXV, 1. For other examples at Beisan and Qabr Hiram, see Avi-Yonah, *QDAP* 5 (1936), pp. 20 f.; Pl. 16, 2; also FitzGerald, *Beth-Shan* IV (1939), p. 9, (8); Pls. XVI & XVII, Figure 3.

2 See Avi-Yonah, *QDAP* 3 (1934), p. 61, note 6. Also at Seilûn west of the "Pilgrims' Church" a press with mosaics exists.

Locus 115 (Pl. 79,3) is the only one on the eastern side of the courtyard which was cleared. The relation of this locus to the courtyard on the west and the area above it on the east may be seen in Fig. 20,4. Its western side, facing the courtyard, is completely open; the other three sides are constructed of masonry consisting of a mixture of rubble and dressed stones hidden from view by two coats of plaster; the lower coat has small flat stones pressed into its surface, which served to key on the outer coat; [1] in this respect it resembles the lower layers of the plaster on the walls of 53 and 56 (see p. 156). The floor is paved with plain tesserae. Half a dozen baskets were filled with pottery sherds from here, about half of them were on the floor level, the rest in the débris which filled the upper half of the room. The pottery characterizes this locus as a storeroom.

There are most probably other loci in the southeastern and southern parts of this building; if they could be cleared more would no doubt be learned about the purpose of this building. As it is, it seems that we have here an establishment for making wine.[2]

4. *Area 116*, south of building 110-115 and west of loci 54, 56 and 61 (see Pl. 161), was explored in 1937. West of the ruins visible on the surface (see Pl. 22,1, left) we dug a trench which extended from the large northwestern quarry to the one on the southwest (see Fig. 3,128 & 134). The trench served a number of useful purposes. It revealed the fact that the surface soil along that line differed in depth from practically nothing to about 80 cm.; at one point, opposite the southern end of hall 56, the soil was mixed with ashes, some tesserae, bits of pottery, glass, marble, bones and four coins. Two of the coins belonged to the reign of Justinian I, before the year 538 A. D.; two others to Justin II, the one to the first year of his reign (565-6 A. D.), the other to the tenth year (574-5 A. D.). Since no buildings, walls or stones were encountered along the line of the trench, we presume that the objects mixed with the earth belonged to a dump; they were deposited there during the sixth century. In the course of centuries the greater part of the rubbish in the dump was washed down the steep declivity on the west (see Pl. 4,2), which is sprinkled with numerous tiny bits of materials noted above; nothing of special interest was observed on the surface.

[1] A piece of plaster detached from this wall is about 4 cm. thick; the lower layer averages about 3 cm. in thickness, the outer 6-7 mm.; the lower layer consists almost entirely of ashes mixed with some crushed stones and lime; it easily disintegrates; the outer coat consists of pure lime and is much stronger; it is whitewashed; on the surface there are scratches and punctures, such as the sharp end of a straw might make. — At times crushed stones and tiny particles of pottery sherds are mixed with the lime.

[2] The Nebo region must have been rich in vines and olives to judge from the large number of presses still existing there. One, near the road between Siyâgha and el-Mekhayyat, is illustrated in Pl. 18,1; on the right is the round catch-basin and on the left the fan-shaped shallow press. If one compares the arrangement of this press and others found, v. g., at Ain Shems (see E. Grant and G. E. Wright, *Ain Shems Excavations*, V (1939), pp. 75 ff.) with that of loci 110-112 one receives the impression that these loci also served as presses. — See Galling, *BRL* cols. 538 f.

In the above-mentioned trench we constructed a retaining wall for a terrace (see Fig. 9, right), both of which helped to dispose of much of the material that cluttered the area in question. Other stones were piled up along the western edge of the terrace and the ground was dumped over the retaining wall. After all the stones had been removed from the surface (Pl. 67,2), a thorough clearance down to bedrock was begun; it brought to light a level terrace with a cistern and a number of other interesting objects.

The cistern (Pls. 67,1; 80,1; 161, 116; Figs. 3,116; 9; 24), cut into the native rock and plastered on the interior, is pear-shaped; it is about 7.80 m. deep and its bottom, which is roughly round and covered with silt, is 7.30-7.50 m. in diameter (see Fig. 24). Its mouth is closed by a large round stone (see Pl. 80,1) about ½ m. h. and 1½ m. in d., pierced by a round opening 45-65 cm. in d.; near the upper surface this opening is rebated to receive a cover and on two sides there are cavities into which a bar, that held the lid in place, was inserted. The top of the stone has a narrow and shallow groove cut into the surface all around the mouth; it was probably not intended as a mere ornament, but as a means of conducting back into the cistern water which was accidentally spilled. Rain-water was conducted into the cistern by means of a channel cut into the native rock on the southwest (see Pls. 67,1; 161,116). The channel was covered with stones. A careful clearance of the native rock next to the channel revealed a flat surface on which the rain-water could collect and flow slowly towards the channel and then into the cistern. Against the northern side of the stone which

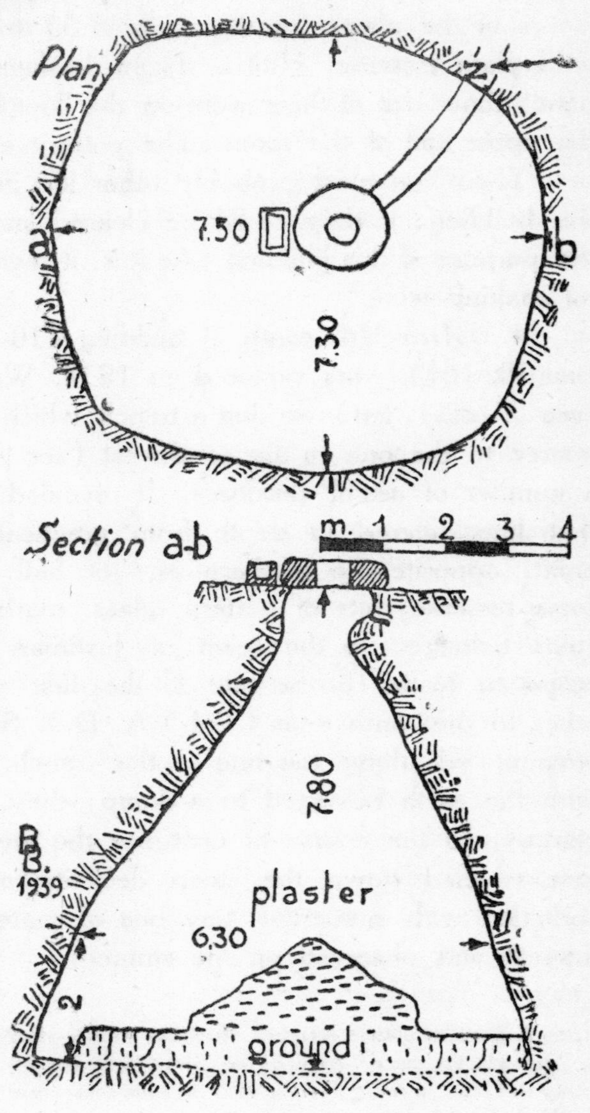

Fig. 24. Cistern 116.

covers the cistern there is a stone basin (Pl. 80,1; Fig. 24) which probably served for watering animals, though such basins are at times also used for washing clothes, etc. North of the basin a low wall, consisting of one course of stones running east and west (see Pls 67,1; 161,116), fixes a boundary in that direction; it determined the limit of our clearances towards the north. Beyond that line the ruins are still as we found them and serve to illustrate the condition of the western wall of hall 56 when work began.

The full extent of the terrace around cistern 116 is not known precisely. A sounding made a few meters further north reached the natural rock after 50-80 cm.; this indicates that the terrane is higher there than around the cistern; this same fact can be clearly seen at quarry 128. On the west the new retaining wall is near the edge of the terrace at a point where the slope begins to be abrupt and precipitous (see Pls. 3,1&2; 4,2; Fig. 9, right). On the south the terrace extends up to the edge of the southwestern quarry (Fig. 3,134). This southern part of the area seemed to be entirely free of ruins, so it was chosen as the site for our camp. As a matter of record we repeat here that all the buildings which are there, as well as the terrace wall and the cistern on the west, were constructed between 1933 and 1935 (compare Pls. 22,1&2; 23,2; and Pls. 3,1&2; 4,2; Fig. 9). The writer was informed that in digging the foundations for the buildings the native rock was reached everywhere in less than a meter of ground; nothing of archæological interest was discovered there. Further north, however, in the neighborhood of cistern 116, a number of objects were found which deserve to be noted. The painted plaster and the building stones on the terrace all come from the building on the east and were mentioned in speaking of hall 56 and room 61 (see pp. 156 f.; 160 f.).

On the terrace south of the cistern were found a fragment of a marble slab with a Samaritan inscription and 4 baskets of pottery sherds. The marble slab inscribed with Samaritan characters (Pl. 122, Fig. 1,1) was the largest fragment of this class recovered during the excavations. See inscription XXVII. Of the pottery sherds we wish to single out for special notice only two: the one (Pl. 154,43) is a spout in the form of an animal's head, the other (Pl. 157,48) has incised decorations consisting of a bird inside a rounded arch. The spout may be compared with the handle of a lamp, also in the form of an animal's head, found in locus 59 (see p. 153) and with similar spouts found in the early Byzantine churches at ʿEin Hanniya [1] and Kh. ʿAsida.[2] D. C. Baramki [3] informs us that "these animal figurines occur quite frequently in Early Christian churches."

1 *QDAP* 3 (1934), p. 116 and Pl. XL, 1.
2 *QDAP* 3 (1934), p. 19 and Pl. XII, 2, left.
3 *QDAP* 3 (1934), p. 116, note 1.

5. *Area 117-121* (Fig. 3; Pl. 22,1; Fig. 9), along the southern and eastern sides of the southern monastery, was not excavated; a number of walls and a large cistern were visible here before the excavations began and in the course of our work a few other facts were learned; systematic excavations are necessary to determine the plan of the area in detail; as it is, we know that it was enclosed by a wall on the south, east and northeast and that there are other walls on the western side of the large cistern, which is the most prominent feature of this area. There is also evidence of floors which were paved with mosaics and flagstones. Pottery, glass and other small objects seem to be quite abundant here; in general they resemble objects familiar from other parts of the site.

Wall 119 (Fig. 3) marks the southern limit of the area under consideration. At the western end it begins on the brink of quarry 134 (Fig. 3; Pl. 3,2) and extends eastwards to a point about midway between cisterns 118 and 122. It is parallel to the southern wall of the monastery and on an average about 40 meters distant from it. The contour-line which it follows has the same elevation as the terrace on which the camp-buildings stand. Only its foundation is still in situ, but we think that practically all the stones scattered over the southern slope of the hill (see Pls. 3,1&2; 22,1) come from this wall. This is, no doubt, the "wall of circumvallation" mentioned by Tristram, whilst the quarries are the scarps which he saw (see p. 11,2).

Wall 120 (Fig. 3) encloses the area in question on the east; it runs parallel to the eastern wall of the southern monastery at a distance of about 20 m. Its course was determined in 1937 when the private road which crossed the southern monastery from east to west (see Pl. 22,1) was transferred further south so as to pass along the southern side of the monastery (see Pl. 160 & Fig. 9). In preparing this road a wall was encountered exactly 19.76 m. east of the monastery (Pl. 80,2); it is 60 cm. thick and constructed of dressed stones; 2-3 courses were exposed at that point; on its western side a floor paved with flags came to light, whilst on its eastern side pottery sherds were abundant; among these was the large fragment of the amphora illustrated in Pl. 145,18; this type of jar had not been observed elsewhere on the site and made us realize that a clearance of this area would undoubtedly enrich our knowledge of the site as a whole. The contour-lines of the terrane suggest that this eastern wall was continued in a straight line south and north. At the southern end, where it should meet wall 119, there is a maze of other walls partly visible and partly concealed from view; their relation to one another must be determined by a clearance. At the northern end the wall is likewise hidden from view, but it very probably extends as far as wall 121.

Wall 121 (Fig. 3) determines the northern limit of the eastern section of our area. It was discovered in 1935 when we cleared the area behind the basilica and cella trichora to bedrock (see Pl. 161, D); along its northern face pottery sherds were abundant, though in the rest of the area behind the basilica practically no sherds were found. The sherds point to an inhabited area south of the wall. Only the foundations of the wall seem to be preserved, but since its top and southern face were not exposed its details are unclear (see Pl. 27,2, left foreground). At its western extremity it joins the eastern wall of room 91 at oblique angles; from there it follows a course slightly south of east (Pl. 161, south of D) and eventually — probably 20 m. east of room 91 — meets wall 120; and then seems to continue eastwards to the neighborhood of quarry 135 (see Fig. 3).

Wall 117 (Fig. 3) is 5.56 m. south of room 72 (compare Fig. 3,117 with Pl. 161,72); opposite to the wall between 72 and 75 (see Pl. 161) it forms a right angle with another wall extending southwards; unfortunately the course of this latter wall could not be thoroughly explored; other walls running north and south, further down the slope, west of cistern 118, may have some connection with this one. These latter sections of the walls were visible before the excavations were made, but the former were discovered in 1937 when the road was built along the southern side of the monastery; after their existence had been ascertained they were covered up again.

Cistern 118 (Fig. 3; Pl. 22,1&2) occupies practically the center of the area enclosed by walls 119, 120, 121 and 117. It was constructed in a depression on the southern side of the hill, at the head of a small wady (see Pl. 22,2 where the wady, further south, is plainly visible). In 1932-3 the cistern was cleared, repaired and restored to its original use. Its condition and use before that date are described by Tristram (see p. 12). On the interior this cistern is 6 m. w. from north to south, about 12½ m. l. from east to west and about 8½ m. deep. On its western and eastern sides catch-basins were built and trenches were dug to collect the water and conduct it to the cistern. In 1933, after the cistern had been restored, it rained so little that the water did not suffice for the needs of the expedition, and much of the water had to be brought from ʿAyûn Mûsa on donkeys. But in 1935 and 1937, after the water-supply had been augmented by the construction of a new cistern on the western side of our camp, the supply of water was not exhausted, though of course we could not be extravagant in its use; thus, for instance, we could not permit shepherds to water their flocks here regularly, neither could we allow this cistern to become a watering-station for long lines of camels, horses or donkeys; they would have used up the water in a short time. This possibly explains one purpose of the walls around the cistern; they, no doubt, served to protect the principal water-supply of the monastery from too aggressive travelers.

At the northeastern corner of the cistern a stone conduit (Pl. 80,3) was discovered which brought water to the catch-basin from the eastern side of the monastery. Its entire course was not investigated.

Trenches, dug both on the west and on the east of the cistern, brought to light numerous medium-sized tesserae of the same type as those used in 110-115 and elsewhere on the site; they point to the existence of mosaic floors and rooms in this area. In the trenches pottery, glass and stone vessels are abundant; in general, these objects resemble those found elsewhere on the site and point to the same period of occupation.

South of the cistern nothing worthy of note was observed. The entrance to the cistern mentioned by Tristram was in the southern wall; that opening was used for removing the silt which had accumulated inside; this deposit is to be seen southwest of the cistern (Pl. 22,1); it perhaps still contains all the objects found inside the cistern; at any rate, no such objects were brought to the notice of the present writer. After the opening had been closed, stones were heaped up against the cistern's southern wall; they served to reënforce it and to enlarge the roof-surface for collecting rain-water.

On the slope west of wall 117 down to the camp a road was built (see Fig. 9 & Pl. 22,1) which encountered many building stones, but nothing else which calls for special mention.

North of the cistern, between it and the southern monastery, there were very many building stones; among these were the three illustrated in Pl. 58,8-10, which are decorated with simple crosses; the tips of the crosses are generally bifurcated and in two cases the crosses are enclosed by circles.

East of the cistern the two trenches for collecting water (see Pl. 22,1) encountered walls and loose tesserae; both make it quite certain that there are rooms in this area. Further north, beyond the new road (see Fig. 9), stone circles were visible on the surface before excavations began; the appearance of the area has been somewhat modified by the fact that heavy stones were rolled over it when they were transported further east or south; but beneath the surface everything is still as it was before. The stone circles may indicate either tombs or camping places. The writer found tents pitched nearby on one of his preliminary visits to the site; but the rectangular stone emplacements used in tents for beds and the smaller circular arrangements of stones for other objects in the tents or for fireplaces, all seem to differ from the stone circles in question; hence it is probable that they represent comparatively late tombs, as elsewhere on the site. In arranging a path along the eastern wall of the monastery a fragment of a marble slab with Samaritan characters was found a few centimeters beneath the surface outside the eastern wall of room 104 (see Pl. 122, Fig. 1,6 and inscription XXIX). Near the eastern wall of this area we found the stone pavement (see Pl. 80,2) and several baskets of pottery referred to in speaking of that wall. Outside the northern wall of the area pottery was quite abundant. These observations give us a clew to what may be found in this area if it is thoroughly investigated.

The area around cistern 118 was most probably occupied in one way or other almost constantly from early Byzantine times down to our own days. The monastery depended upon the cistern for its largest supply of water; during its existence the cistern was no doubt carefully guarded and kept clean. After the destruction of the monastery the cistern remained almost perfectly intact down to our own time and seems to have served some useful purpose at all times. How long it continued to collect water and on that account attract settlers we do not know. In the course of time its interior, its catch-basins and its conduits were so silted up that not a drop of water entered any longer. Then an opening was made in its southern wall and it was converted into a place for storing things and into a shelter for men and beasts. This is the condition in which Tristram found it nearly 70 years ago; in 1932-3 it was once more converted into a cistern; its abundant waters were a great blessing during the excavations in 1933, 1935 and 1937 for all the members of those expeditions and for many thirsty travelers.

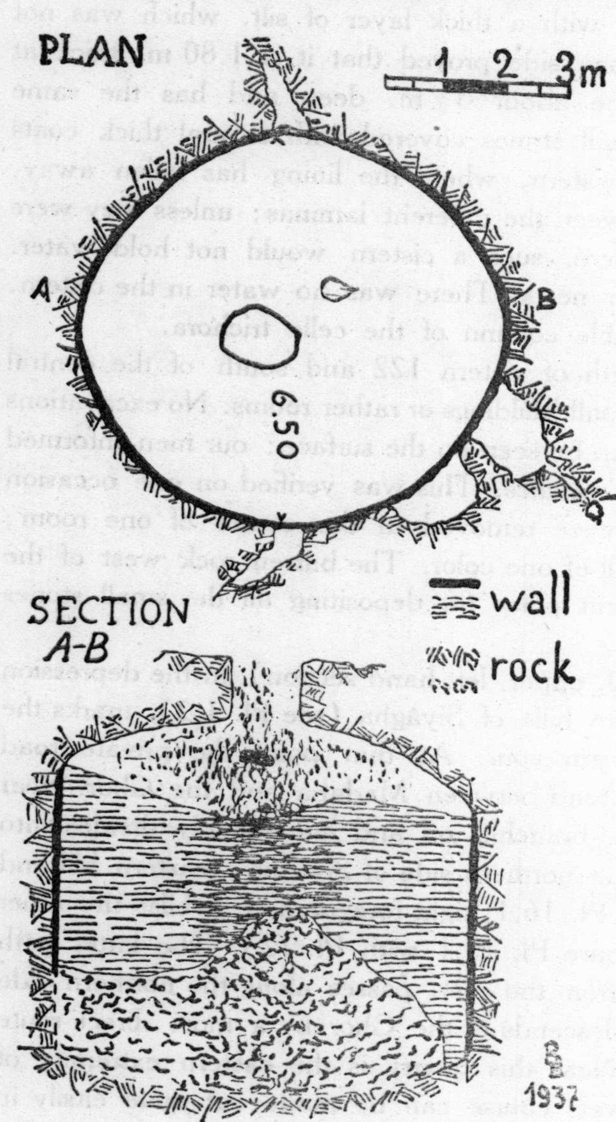

Fig. 25. Cistern 122.

6. *Area 122-124 and 135* (Fig. 3,122-124 & 135; Pls. 22,1; 160) is bounded by walls 120 and 121, quarry 135 and the new road (built in 1935) on the west, north, east and south respectively. Here the hill slopes gently down from west to east and along this declivity, where the native rock is visible almost everywhere, runs the private road to the ruins and the camp. The only reason for treating this area as a special unit is the existence here of a cistern (122) south of the road and of two small buildings (123 & 124) north of the same.

Cistern 122 (Fig. 25) can be seen in Pl. 22,1, east of the trenches which conduct water to cistern 118 and south of the road which crosses the site from east to west. It served to collect the water of the hill's southeastern slope. At the spot where it is located the barren rock appears on the surface; a layer of the natural rock-formations forms the roof of the cistern and in this layer are the openings through which the water reached the interior and was drawn out again. The bottom of the cistern is covered with a thick layer of silt, which was not removed; but a sounding made on one side proved that it is 1.80 m. thick at that point. The cistern seems to be about 6½ m. deep and has the same diameter. The walls are lined with small stones covered with several thick coats of plaster. In the upper part of the cistern, where the lining has fallen away, one sees wide and deep crevices between the different laminas; unless they were closed or covered by masonry, as here, such a cistern would not hold water. In the crevices pigeons had built their nests. There was no water in the cistern. In the silt there is a drum of a double column of the cella trichora.

Loci 123 and 124 (Fig. 3), north of cistern 122 and south of the central section of wall 121, seem to be two small buildings or rather rooms. No excavations were made in them, but their walls can be seen on the surface; our men informed us that these rooms are paved with mosaics. This was verified on one occasion when about 20 cm. of loose earth were removed in the center of one room; the tesserae are medium-sized and all of one color. The barren rock west of the two rooms was chosen as a convenient place for depositing all the small stones from the ruins (see Pl. 22,1).

Quarry 135 (Fig. 3,135; Pl. 160, upper, left hand section), in the depression between the northwestern and eastern hills of Siyâgha (see Pl. 1,2), marks the eastern limit of Siyâgha's northwestern spur. At that point the private road which crosses the hill joins the main road between Madaba and the Ghor. Near the same place (see Pl. 160) a path branches off and immediately divides into two, of which the one runs along the northern side of Siyâgha's eastern hill and joins the main road further east (see Pl. 16,1, right foreground), whilst the other leads down to ʿAyûn Mûsa (compare Pl. 16,1 with Pl. 12). The latter path also joins another one which comes from the east, passes along the northern side of Siyâgha (see Pl. 160, left) and descends to the Ghor by a more direct route than the new road built in 1935. Near this quarry is the eastern extremity of wall 121, whose straight east and west course can be made out quite easily in Pl. 160, to the north of the private road (see Fig. 3,121 & 135).

7. *Ruins 125 and their surroundings* (Fig. 3,125; Pls. 16,1; 22, 1 & 2; 159; 160). The location, extent and character of the ruins in question can be seen in Pl. 22,2. They occupy a long, comparatively narrow strip extending from south to north on the east and northeast of the cella trichora and the basilica; these ruins begin along the very fringe of the most distant stray stones of the cella trichora and the basilica and evidently constitute a unit by themselves. Whilst the full extent of this group is clear, still its details are very uncertain; no clearances have been made. At places the ruins seem to be mere heaps of

rubble mixed with squared stones (see Pl. 16,1, left foreground), but at many points it is evident that at least the foundations of well-defined walls are still in situ. Whether those walls represent buildings or mere enclosures or combinations of the two, can only be determined by a thorough clearance; their date and purpose also remain in doubt.

East of the ruins a level field (see Pls. 16,1; 22,1; 160) is sprinkled with a few tiny bits of pottery which resemble those found everywhere else on the site. A trench was dug in this field for the purpose of interring the bones of more than a score of persons whose graves had been made in the ruins. In the trench, which was over a meter deep and apparently had not reached bedrock, no antiquities of any kind were observed. To all appearances this field had served as a garden; here we deposited the ground from the excavations. This so-called garden had its own enclosure, consisting on the south of wall 121 (see Fig. 3), which extended from room 91 in the southern monastery eastwards to the neighborhood of quarry 135; there it turned northwards and continued down to a path along the northern side of the hill (see Pl. 160); this path it followed westwards and finally turned southwards to reach the northern monastery in the vicinity of loci 45 and 48. The general appearance of this area may be seen in Pls. 22, 1&2; 159; 160; Fig. 9.

8. *Loci 132, 129-131, 134, 136, 137* (Figs. 3 & 9; Pls. 1,2; 3, 1&2; 4, 1&2; 160) are not far distant from the paths and road around the northwestern and southwestern sides of the hill.

Cave 132 (Fig. 3) is north of the path along the northern side of the hill; in front of it there are remnants of masonry. In recent years it served as a fold for goats and sheep. Formerly it may have served other purposes, which escape our knowledge at present. Not far to the west of the cave is the new road to the Ghor (see Pl. 160); if one follows this road southwards, uphill, he has the steep western slopes of Siyâgha on his left (see Pl. 4,2), where other crevices of various sizes can be made out; some are so large that they suggest the existence of small caves there, but none of them have been entered on our plans. Between the foot of the hill and the road there is a level piece of ground which is used at times by the Arabs for pitching their tents; the rectangular and circular disposition of the stones seen there testify to this fact and we know it from the Arabs themselves.

Loci 129-131 (Fig. 3), on the southwestern slope of Siyâgha, represent a cistern and several buildings. *Cistern 129* was shown to the writer in 1933 soon after his arrival on Siyâgha. The Arab who guided him to the spot pointed out a mosaic border around the mouth of the cistern; [1] its interior was completely filled with earth; inside its mouth some one had made a small hole into the ground, but then had abandoned the task as too difficult or useless; the Arab

[1] See Avi-Yonah, *QDAP* 3 (1934), p. 61, note 7, for half a dozen other examples.

stated that in 1927 an explorer had made that hole in the course of his searches for the ark. No further investigations were instituted by us at that spot.

Loci 130 and 131 were no doubt buildings, but so little of them still remains in situ that it is difficult to make out their full extent and plan (see Fig. 3); hence it is also somewhat hazardous to speak of their purpose, yet in this case a definite purpose was suggested to us by a modern practice of which we were frequently witnesses. We noticed that the buildings were a focal point for travelers. Near them three paths meet (see Pl. 160): one comes from the plateau, the second from the Ghor and the third from the southwest. The one which comes from the plateau on the east is now to a great extent identical with the new road along the southern side of our site. The second path from the Ghor follows the same general course as the new road, but at many points it eliminates the windings of the new road and takes a more direct course; hence it is still extensively used; on the northwestern side of Siyâgha the old path reaches the new road and divides into two branches; the one continues straight east along the northern side of Siyâgha, the other runs along the western side of our hill straight for the buildings in question. The third path from the southwest unites this place with the springs, gardens, camps and ruins in Wady el-Keneiyiseh, Wady el-Herî, Wady el-ʿAdeimeh and other places beyond them. At the point where the three paths meet, there are not only the ruins under consideration but also *quarry 134;* at the quarry travelers frequently stopped to rest for a few hours of the night; they never disturbed us in any way; at the most, they now and then asked for a little water. These facts may throw some light on the purpose of loci 129-131. The buildings may have served as a kind of khan or caravansary where travelers found shelter and water; there they enjoyed more liberty than they could have enjoyed inside the monastery and were free to come and go when they liked. The caravansary may have belonged to the monks who looked after the needs of such travelers.

Cistern 136 (Figs. 3 & 26) is not on the northwestern but on the southwestern spur of Siyâgha, a short distance south of the point where the road crosses the saddle between the two hills (see Pl. 160, right). It is about 5.80 m. deep and 8.15-10.00 m. in diameter; its walls are vertical and made water-tight by means of masonry covered with plaster; the roof is formed by a layer of the native rock; in the same is the opening through which water was at one time conducted into the cistern and drawn out again; today it contains no water, but it harbors a sturdy fig-tree which has struck root in the earth that covers the floor of the cistern and rears its head to the mouth of the same, now almost completely closed by its thick foliage. Wild pigeons find a refuge there. The cistern supplied water to those who lived in the small buildings standing at intervals along the ridge to the southwest (see Fig. 2 and p. 3). To the southeast of the building on the crest of the hill (see Pl. 19,2) there is an unexplored cave. From the top of the hill one enjoys a most magnificent view. It was there that Aetheria located the events related in *Numbers* 23, 11-24. The following are her words: "On the side of the mountain that I have called the left, which is over the Dead Sea, a very sharp mountain was shown to us, which before was called Agri Specula. This is the mountain where Balak the son of Beor placed Balaam the soothsayer to curse the children of Israel, and God would not allow him, as it is written" (see pp. 150 f.).

When Aetheria stood in front of the church at Mt. Nebo she had at her left the region to the south of Siyâgha. In that direction the most distant "mountain" which she could have seen was the el-Maslûbîyeh ridge (see Pl. 16,2), but the western extremity of that mountain, which is over the Dead Sea, is not visible from the church at Siyâgha; it is hidden from view by the southwestern spur of Siyâgha (see Pl. 74,3, background); this southwestern spur, however, "is over the Dead Sea" (see Pls. 8 & 159) and, when seen from the church, looks "very sharp" or precipitous indeed.[1]

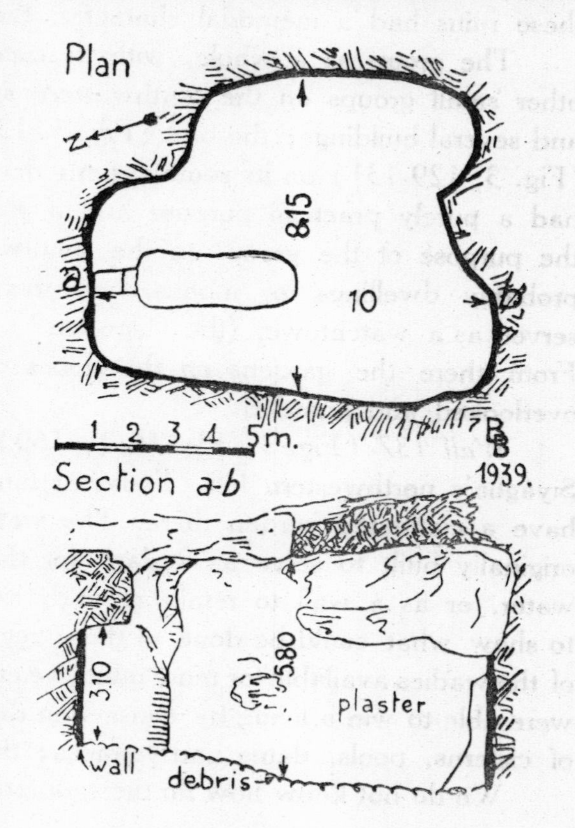

Fig. 26. Cistern 136.

According to Aetheria, therefore, the southwestern spur of Siyâgha is the mountain "which before was called Agri Specula" (see Fig. 2); [2] and since, according to *Numbers* 23,14, Balaam built seven altars there for the purpose of offering sacrifice, one is tempted to associate the ruins on that hill with the altars of Balaam. This does not imply that the ruins are those of the altars, but they could be memorials of the altars or at least of the Biblical event commemorated there. In Sinai, for example, and along the route of the Exodus, Aetheria found

[1] See Pl. 65,1, background; or Pl. 6,2; the air view in Pl. 159 flattens out the steep descent too much; after all, it is not the angle from which Aetheria viewed the mountain.

[2] See *Onom.* 13,16. "Agri Specula" (the Lookout of the Field) is Jerome's rendition of Eusebius' ἀγροῦ σκοπιά; the latter derived the term from the *LXX*; it is the equivalent of שדה צפים (Field of Zophim) in the Hebrew text and of "locus sublimis" (high place) in the Latin *Vulgate*. According to the *Onom.* l. c. the name designates a mountain overlooking the Dead Sea not far from the Arnon. According to Aetheria Agri Specula is a mountain between Mount Nebo and the Dead Sea. Thomsen, *LS* p. 14 and Bludau, *SGKA* 15, p. 25 agree that Eusebius, Jerome and Aetheria refer to the same mountain. If we accept this tradition which fixes Agri Specula to the south of Siyâgha's northwestern spur, then, at first thought, it would seem that we must reject

numerous memorials of Biblical events; they were generally small hermitages or chapels, many of which are still existing today, though the majority are in ruins. In the light of those monuments, therefore, it is not improbable that also these ruins had a memorial character, though this is is by no means certain.

The group as a whole, with its cistern and small buildings, resembles two other small groups on the northwestern spur, each of which consists of a cistern and several buildings; the one (Fig. 3, 122-124) is on its eastern slope, the other (Fig. 3, 129-131) on its southwestern declivity. These two groups seem to have had a purely practical purpose and it seems more probable that such was also the purpose of the group on the southwestern hill. Most of the buildings were probably dwellings for monks, workmen or passing travelers; one may have served as a watchtower (the "specula"), perhaps the one on the crest of the hill. From there the gardens on the slopes of the hill and in the wadies could be overlooked and guarded.

Wall 137 (Fig. 3; Pls. 16,2; 160) was built across the wady south of Siyâgha's northwestern hill. Today it hinders erosion and makes it possible to have a cultivated garden there. The wall seems to be ancient. Whether it was originally built to serve as a dam for the purpose of collecting and conserving water, or as a wall to retain ground, it is difficult to say today; but it serves to show what could be done in these regions to prevent erosion and make some of the wadies available for more intensive cultivation; in other desolate regions monks were able to win a living by conserving the water and soil through the construction of cisterns, pools, dams and terraces; the same was no doubt the case here.

We do not know how far the property of the monks at Mount Nebo extended.

the identification of Agri Specula or the Field of Zophim with a field near Tal'at es-Safa; for Tal'at es-Safa is not south of Siyâgha, but east of it (see Fig. 2); in other words, Aetheria would not have seen it to her "left", but would have had it directly behind her when she was standing in front of the church at Siyâgha. The identification of a field near Tal'at es-Safa with the Field of Zophim was proposed by Conder owing to the similarity of the names. In *QS* 1882, p. 9, he writes: "The Field of Zophim (שדה צפים, *Num.* 23,14) was at or identical with Pisgah or Nebo. The word signifying "views" comes from a root identical with the Arabic Safi, "clear" or "shining". My Arab guide volunteered the information that the ascent leading up from 'Ayûn Mousa to the top of Jebel Neba is called Tal'at es Safa. Thus on the side of Nebo we still find the name Zophim preserved unchanged, and this discovery, which I believe is entirely new, serves to confirm the ordinary identification of Nebo with Jebel Neba. We can have little hesitation in identifying the "Field of Zophim" with the plateau of arable land, a rich red field on the top of Tal'at Safa, from which the knoll of limestone called Râs Neba rises some 50 feet on the west..." See also *SEP* pp. 198 ff.; *Heth and Moab*, New Edition, p. 133. Others hold practically the same view; see, v. g., Musil, *AP* I, pp. 181, 272, 334, 345; Karge, *Rephaim* [2], p. 468; Thomsen, *LS* p. 14 and Bludau, *SGKA* 15, p. 25. The two last-mentioned writers identify the mountain mentioned by Aetheria with Tal'at es-Safa; this, as we stated above, does not seem to be absolutely accurate, for the mountain referred to by Aetheria is 3 km. west of Tal'at es-Safa; but it is true in so far as both places form part of the same ridge, which begins on the east in the neighborhood of Tal'at es-Safa and terminates on the west at the southwestern spur of Siyâgha ("Agri Specula", see Fig. 2 & Pl. 16,1); in this wider sense the discovery of this name on the same ridge is a most welcome confirmation of the tradition represented by Aetheria, Jerome and Eusebius; nor do I think that it is necessary to assume that the name has shifted somewhat; on the contrary, it may serve as a warning to us not to restrict the application of those names to too narrow limits; in other words, if we assume that the mountain referred to by Aetheria is not merely a knoll, but a ridge extending eastwards as far as Tal'at es-Safa, then all difficulties vanish.

If one considers, for instance, that the monks in Sinai have extensive possessions in widely separated valleys where they have houses and gardens in the neighborhood of springs and look after chapels and shrines on numerous hilltops, then it is not improbable that the large community of the tomb of Moses on Mount Nebo also had possessions at some distance from the central monastery. Those possessions may have consisted not only of lands but also of dwellings and chapels. In the light of statements made by Aetheria (see pp. 108 f.), we have every reason to think that the monks owned property at ʿAyûn Mûsa; and the biographer of Peter the Iberian clearly indicates close connections between Mount Nebo and the town of Nebo to the southeast (that is, el-Mekhayyat). [1]

* * *

The monastery at Mount Nebo, which we have just described in detail, is somewhat larger than the famous monastery of St. Catherine in Sinai with which memories from the life of Moses are also associated. According to Meistermann [2] the enclosure of St. Catherine's monastery is 72 m. long, 63 m. wide and 12-15 m. high; that of Mount Nebo is 83 m. l. from east to west and varies in width from north to south; if we exclude the northern group, then its minimum width at the eastern end (Pl. 161,1, 91, 100-105) is over 48 m.; in the center (Pl. 161,12, 7,27, 73-75) 53 m. and at the west (Pl. 161, 17-23, 64-67) 57 m.; if we include the northern group then its width varies from 60-80 m. We should not forget that there is a large walled area on the east and southeast which has not been excavated and hence was not included in the above calculations. Actually we should add 20 m. to the length of the monastery; that gives us an enclosure which is over 100 m. long; how much should be added to the width remains uncertain. Also the height of the enclosure wall at Mount Nebo is uncertain; on the western side it was surely two stories, say at least 6 m., high; whereas on the other sides it evidently varied; thus, for example, along the northern side of the basilica, north hall and narthex the wall may have been well over 6 m. h., whereas around certain other parts of

[1] The shepherd who had the vision of the tomb of Moses in a cave at Mount Nebo came "from the village of Nebo which is on the south side of the mountain." The inhabitants of this village were the first to hear of the vision and their faith led to the construction of the sanctuary at Mount Nebo, though it seems that others from the surrounding regions also helped along. Under the circumstances it would not be surprising if those pious people had endowed the sanctuary with property by means of which those who served the sanctuary could gain a livelihood. Thus, for example, el-Heisah, north of Jebel en-Neba may have belonged to the monks (see Musil's view on p. 9). At el-Mekhayyat itself the monk Julian is mentioned in an unpublished inscription found in the mosaic pavement of a church on the eastern slope of the town; several other churches exist at el-Mekhayyat and a lintel decorated with a cross found in the vicinity of ʿAin Jideid suggests the existence of a chapel there. At ʿAyûn el-Keneiyiseh there are other ruins (see p. 9) which may at one time have been occupied by monks. Further west in the same wady there are a number of other ideal places for monks and near some of them there are also ruins. But without further investigations or without documents it is impossible to determine precisely what property belonged to the monks.

[2] *Guide du Nil au Jourdain par le Sinaï et Pétra*, Paris, 1909, p. 122.

the monastery it may have been lower. In every case, the position of the monastery on the crest of the hill must have caused it to stand out very prominently even if its walls were not very high.

Inside the enclosure both at Sinai and at Nebo there are a church, chapels, courtyards with cisterns, cells and workshops. Outside the enclosures at both places there are a number of other buildings. The comparison could be extended to further details; [1] here, however, it suffices to emphasize that it is the memory of Moses which has rendered both Sinai and Nebo forever famous; his memory first attracted monks to those regions; from his example they derived inspiration and by their activity they have added greatly to the interest and attraction which those places have for us today.

Between Sinai and Nebo and in the nearby regions there were numerous other monasteries; [2] many are known only from literary sources; [3] relatively few are still occupied today; [4] the majority are in a ruined state and of these only a few have been cleared and studied in detail. [5] The monastery of Mount Nebo is the only one in Transjordan which has been excavated. [6]

[1] See Meistermann, *Guide du Nil* etc., pp. 115-141. Many visitors to the monastery at Mount Sinai have published their impressions; so, for example, H. V. Morton, *Through Lands of the Bible*, London, 1938, pp. 299-332. The present writer visited the monastery at Sinai in April, 1938; he is convinced that it is an excellent counterpart of the monastery of Moses on Mount Nebo.

[2] See Watzinger, *DP* 2, pp. 156 f. for a very brief but useful survey.

[3] Thus, for example, many monasteries of the fourth century are known to us from Aetheria; many of the fifth from *The Life of Peter the Iberian*; etc. — From these and other sources lists of monasteries have been prepared; so, for instance, R. P. S. Vailhé, *Répertoire Alphabétique des monastères de Palestine*, in *Revue de l'Orient Chrétien*, 4 (1899), pp. 512-542; 5 (1900), pp. 19-48; 272-292 enumerates 137 (comprising hermitages, lauras and cenobia).

[4] See, v. g., Meistermann, *Guide to the Holy Land*, London, 1923, pp. 365 f. (Convent of Couziba in the Wady el-Qelt; see Schneider in *Römische Quartalschrift*, 1931, pp. 297-332); pp. 371 f. (Mount of Quarantine); 375 f. (Convent of St. John the Baptist); 376 (Convent of St. Gerasimus); 410 ff. (Convent of St. Sabas); 413 (Convent of St. Theodosius); 298 (Convent of St. Elias). For Kh. el-Merd see Mader, *JPOS* 9 (1929), pp. 122-135; *OC* 34 (1937), pp. 27-58. Recently a church was cleared there.

[5] In the monasteries of the southern part of Palestine (see C. L. Woolley and T. E. Lawrence, *The Wilderness of Zin*, in *PEF Ann.* 3 (1914-1915), pp. 31 f., 84, 115,120) excavations have been made by the Colt expedition. Regarding Isbeita see *QDAP* 4 (1935), pp. 201 f.; 5 (1936), pp. 198 f.; C. Baly, *S'baita*, in *QS* 1935, pp. 171 ff.; G. E. Kirk, *Era-Problems in the Greek Inscriptions of the Southern Desert*, in *JPOS* 17 (1937), pp. 209-217; id., *The Era of Diocletian in Palestinian Inscriptions*, in *JPOS* 18 (1938), pp. 161-166; regarding ʿAuja Hafîr see G. E. Kirk, *Excavations at ʿAuja Hafîr: The Greek Inscriptions*, in *JPOS* 16 (1936), pp. 279-285. — In the central part of Palestine monasteries have been excavated at Rumeileh (see E. Grant and G. E. Wright, *Ain Shems Excavations*, Haverford, 1939, pp. 86 ff.) and at Khan el-Ahmar (see D. J. Chitty, in *QS* 1928, pp. 175 ff.; 1930, pp. 43 ff., 150 ff.; 1932, 188-203). — In the northern part of Palestine at Beisan; see G. M. FitzGerald, *A Sixth Century Monastery at Beth-Shan*, Philadelphia, 1939. — A number of other buildings near churches may have been monasteries.

[6] A number of others are known to have existed; thus, for instance, besides the hermitages referred to on p. 192, we know something about the laura of Kopratha, probably near Tell Kefrein (see *PS* 101 in *PG* 87, cols. 2943 f.; *RB* 41 (1932), p. 255); the laura of Sapsaphas, not far from the Jordan (see *PS* 1&2 in *PG* 87, cols. 2852 f.; *RB* 41 (1932), pp. 248-252); the convent of nuns rendered famous by Mary of Elusa (see Antoninus Martyr in Geyer, pp. 181 f.), perhaps at ed-Deir near Kh. Sûeimeh (see *RB* 41 (1932), pp. 254 f.). The region in which practically all of these are located is clearly visible from Mount Nebo. Other ruins which may represent monasteries are reported from Feinân (see Frank in *ZDPV* 57 (1934), pp. 223 f.; Alt in *ZDPV* 58 (1935), pp. 64 f.) and from a few other sites (see Glueck in *AASOR* 14 (1934), pp. 59, 60, 90; *AJA* 37 (1933), p. 381, Pl. XXXIX, 3; *AASOR* 18-19 (1939), p. 60. — Regarding the monasteries of the northern part of Transjordan and of Syria, see *ECS* pp. 83-112; Alt, in *PJB* 1939, pp. 93-104.

CHAPTER VII

THE MOSAICS

A. GENERAL SURVEY

1. *Wall mosaics* (Fig. 7 on p. 34). At Siyâgha mosaics were used to cover walls and floors. None of the wall mosaics were any longer in their original position, but their existence is certain. Most of them were found in a crushed condition among the large stones of the cella trichora east of the basilica. This context proves beyond doubt that the mosaics had decorated the walls of the cella trichora. They were described when we treated of that building. See pp. 33-35, 141 f., 147.

2. *One-colored mosaic pavements.* The floors of 75 loci indicated in the ground plan (Pl. 161, 1-116; Fig. 3, 117-137) were paved; for 45 or $\frac{3}{5}$ of them mosaics were used; of these 33 or nearly $\frac{3}{4}$ were made of cubes having the same color, which is generally dull-white, gray or light-black; these hues may of course mingle and cause a slight variation in the general tone of the floor, but that seems to be accidental. The cubes are, as a rule, larger than those used in the multi-colored pavements; in the latter case they are generally not over a centimeter square, whereas in the former they average between 2-5 cm. It was the rule to use only tesserae of the same size for the same floor, but there was always some variety. The largest tesserae occurred in the atrium and in a few loci around it; the smaller tesserae were used everywhere else. In such pavements the surround, border and field were indicated by different dispositions of the cubes; those of the border were arranged in rows parallel with the walls, whilst those of the surround and field were set in diagonal rows. Other details regarding these pavements were indicated in describing the loci in which they exist.[1]

[1] See loci 7, 12-15, tombs a-c in 21, 22, 24, 29, 40, 54, 65, 66, 69, 70, 72, 73a, between 75-76, 81,82, 106, 110-115, between 117-119, west of 120, 123 (or 124), 129.

3. *Multi-colored mosaic pavements* exist in 12 loci (namely, in those of the ground plan, Pl. 161, which are numbered 1-6, 10, 11, 16, 17, 30, 91). The following 8 colors occur: white, black, red, yellow, blue, gray, pink and brown. All 8 colors are found only in the Theotokos chapel; 7 are found in the north hall; 6 in the baptistery, in the nave of the basilica and in room 16; 5 in the presbytery of the basilica; 4 in most of the panels of each locus; 2 in a lower pavement of the basilica's nave. The 2-colored pavement is white and black; the 4-colored pavements are white, black, red and yellow; the four other colors are at times substituted for one of these or added to give greater variety. The color effect is heightened by various shades of the same color. Cubes of the wall mosaics were used in repairing the pavement of the basilica's sanctuary; the bright green, blue, purple, black and golden hues of these glass cubes contrast sharply with the duller shades of the stone cubes characteristic of the pavements; though it is a well-known fact that the colors of these stone tesserae also become quite vivid when oiled or waxed.

The subjects represented on these pavements are nearly all the same as those found on the mosaic pavements of numerous other ancient churches still existing in Transjordan and the adjacent countries. We find here human figures, animals, plants, fruits, instruments, vessels, a building with an altar, numerous geometrical patterns and inscriptions. Most of the motifs were designed and executed by skilled artists and workmen. The most interesting scenes are the ones represented in the chancels of the basilica and the three chapels, where there is evidently a close inner connection between the subjects represented and the place where they are represented. This connection is most apparent in the Theotokos chapel, where the artist depicted a sacrificial scene in front of the altar (see Pl. 109,1). The text above the scene clearly manifests the artist's intention and the position emphasizes the connection between the scene and the altar. This and other relations will become clearer when we study the scenes more in detail below.

Fig. 27 indicates the position and condition of all the multi-colored mosaic pavements, except the two in rooms 16 and 17. It appears that this type of pavement was reserved almost exclusively for the house of God; it was found in only three rooms of the monastery. In general these pavements were tolerably well preserved; some were worn out; others were damaged either deliberately or accidentally. Most of the harm done was repaired either with other cubes or with mortar.

The pavements of the basilica and the chapels are divided into two parts by the base of the chancel. Each part has its own surround, border and field; the fields are divided into panels or smaller compartments; and these, as a rule, contain other ornaments. In some cases the same ornament is repeated in each subdivision of a panel or field (see Pls. 110,1; 113,1); in other cases two

different ornaments alternate with one another (see Pl. 97); or we find that many different ornaments fill the compartments (see Pl. 99,1). What was said of the pavements in the basilica and chapels holds good also of the other pavements.

All the multi-colored mosaic pavements which were found and still exist at Siyâgha are illustrated in Pls. 81 ff.; we will describe firstly those of the basilica and its narthex, then those of the chapels and finally those of the three rooms in the monastery. The inscriptions will be treated in the next chapter.

B. THE MOSAIC PAVEMENT OF THE BASILICA

1. *The chancel or sanctuary* (see Fig. 27) was decorated with a large quatrefoil with a "rainbow" border; in its field there were representations of vases and vines which form medallions containing animals and birds; the surround contained a number of panels and a few free compositions. A great part of this mosaic has been destroyed. The ends of the northern and southern lobes of the quatrefoil were removed when the walls separating the two sacristies from the sanctuary were built; nothing remains of those lobes in the sacristies, but in the sanctuary a few traces of the same have survived. The fractured edges of the pavement next to the northern and southern walls in the sanctuary were repaired with large plain cubes, some of which can be seen in Pl. 84,1, right. In the center of the sanctuary the mosaic was completely destroyed; this act of vandalism seems to have been perpetrated by individuals in search of treasure; the vandals first broke into the tomb beneath the altar; then they extended their operations in all directions around the tomb; apparently the undertaking was not very remunerative, for it was abandoned before the entire pavement had been ruined. This could only have happened after the church had been abandoned, but before the walls and roof of the sanctuary had collapsed. The vandals may have been squaters or passers-by who had found a refuge in the sanctuary. The mosaics which they did not destroy they damaged by the fires which they built on them, thus not only blackening the tesserae, but also causing a number to crack and crumble. The few surviving sections of the pavement have a special interest for us; they represent the oldest decorated mosaic pavement discovered at Siyâgha. In these sections there are various patches representing repairs and one of the inscriptions which speaks of repairs was itself rendered partially illegible by a still later repair. This mosaic antedates the second basilica; it surely existed in the first basilica; whether it existed already in the cella trichora, it is more difficult to say; this much, however, is certain, that the quatrefoil design was determined by the trefoil plan of the cella trichora; but since the trefoil plan was preserved

in the sanctuary of the first basilica, the mosaic pavement could have been planned and finished at that time; that is, during the fifth century A. D.

a. *The surround* (Fig. 27) has preserved nearly a dozen different designs. In its northeastern section there are the triangular ear of a tabula ansata and the palm illustrated in Pl. 87. In the southeastern section only a faint trace of some unknown ornament has survived. In the southwestern section there are three panels and two free compositions. The panels are arranged in a row from east to west, next to the border of the quatrefoil's western lobe. The first panel, on the east (see Pl. 85,2), is an oblong rectangle divided into two parts; the one on the east contains a circle with a "rainbow" design; the other on the west contains a square with inscribed concentric circles; in the corners of both parts there are triangles. The second panel, in the center, contains a Greek inscription (see Fig. 27, c; Pl. 118,1 & inscription VIII). The third panel, on the west, extends up to the chancel rail. It also seems to have been rectangular and divided into two parts; the eastern half (see Pl. 86,1) contains a circle around whose inner edge there is a series of 7 (originally 10) half circles whose colors vary; one is black, the next is red, the third yellow, the fourth gray, etc.; in the center of the circle there is a square divided into smaller rectangles, each of which contains one or two colored blocks. The western half of the panel is not preserved. Between these three panels and the wall there is a space of varying width, which is mostly without ornaments, but in the wider strip in front of the door of the southern sacristy a square, divided into 8 triangles by four intersecting lines, and a palm are represented; see Pl. 86,2. For the palm the artist used not only ordinary black, red and yellow limestone cubes, but also green, pink and golden ones of glass; this latter type of material is known to have served for the wall mosaics; it was probably utilized here for repairs.

Between the western lobe of the quatrefoil and the gateway in the chancel screen there was a large panel with a Greek inscription; only the northern part of the same still exists; see Fig. 27, b; Pl. 117,2 & inscription VII.

In the northwestern section of the surround there were probably also three panels and possibly a few other ornaments, as in the southwestern section, but only fragments of two panels next to the border are preserved; the one on the east was probably rectangular and seems to have contained some other geometrical motifs (see Fig. 27 & Pl. 117,1, above); the other contains a Greek inscription; see Fig. 27,a; Pl. 117,1 & inscription VI. The rest of the pavement was either destroyed or without ornaments.

b. *The border,* illustrated in Pl. 85,1 & 2, is a band 16 cm. wide with black edges and red, yellow, gray and white stripes, producing a "rainbow" effect;[1] this effect is heightened by the diagonal arrangement of the cubes in

[1] See *Gerasa,* pp. 205 f.

the center. Each of the four lobes has preserved small sections of the border; they sufficed to determine the limits of the quatrefoil as indicated in Fig. 27.

c. *The four-lobed field* is about 9 m. long from east to west and probably had the same dimensions from north to south. Its decoration consisted of amphorae from which issued vines forming circular medallions containing representations of birds, animals and possibly other objects.[1] Only one amphora is preserved, namely, that in the eastern lobe. The parallel arrangement of two branches in the southern lobe (see Pl. 84,1) seems to suggest that they have issued from the mouth of an amphora at that point; this is the reason why I think that there may have been an amphora there; if this is true, then one would expect amphorae also in the lobes on the west and north; there is no other evidence for their existence. Traces of vines have been observed in all four lobes; they are, however, very scant in the northern and in the western lobes (see Pl. 85,2, below). The medallions of the eastern lobe contain only birds; those of the southern lobe only four-footed animals; the rest have disappeared.

In the eastern lobe enough remains of the vase, vine and birds to enable us to reconstruct the missing parts (see Fig. 27 & Pl. 81). The amphora stands in the center of the lobe with its base towards the west and its mouth towards the east; above it are two medallions each of which contained a pair of birds; on each side of the vase there was a very large bird and below these there were medallions filled in with other birds.

The amphora (Pl. 82)[2] has an ovate body with the wide part below joined by a spherical knob to a rectangular base; the neck is missing;[3] the mouth has everted lips to which are attached the upper ends of two handles terminating in spirals; their lower ends are attached to the upper part of the shoulder. A band of trellis-work decorates the shoulder below the attachments of the handles; below the shoulders the amphora was fluted.

Two vines issue from the mouth of the amphora; each one sends forth branches, of which the majority terminate in buds, flowers, fruits or leaves; some of the branches form medallions. So, for example, the first two branches above the amphora are plain and form circular medallions (Pls. 81 & 83,1); the second branch on the left (Pl. 81) terminates in two twigs with buds or flowers which fill in an empty space; the third branch on the left (Pl. 81) again describes the

[1] See *QDAP* 3 (1934), pp. 62 f.; *Gerasa*, pp. 302 ff.; *RB* 47 (1938), p. 233 & Pl. XI, 1.

[2] According to Biebel, *Gerasa*, pp. 302 ff., when there is only one amphora, it is placed "at the bottom of the field"; when there are more, they are placed in its corners. Here the amphora occupies the center of one of the field's lobes and is surrounded on all sides by the vine-trellis. The apparent difference is due to the peculiar form of the field, which is not rectangular but four-lobed. The amphora in each lobe of the quatrefoil corresponds to the amphora in each corner of a rectangular field.

[3] It was of the "round-necked type", which, according to Avi-Yonah, *QDAP* 3 (1934), p. 62, is more common than "the type with the sunken neck".

greater part of a circle and ends in a large digitate leaf; part of this branch is concealed by the shoulders of a very large bird (Pl. 81), whose thick neck and long beak fill the medallion; several other branches are destroyed; a fourth one, however, still exists near the base of the amphora (Pls. 81 & 83,2); it forms a loop open at the bottom and interrupted near the top by three pointed objects which are probably feathers of the wings of the large bird flanking the vase; this branch terminates in an irregular cluster which no doubt represents some kind of fruit; the medallion formed in this way contains a good representation of a rooster. The second vine no doubt divided the space on the southern side of the amphora in a similar way. We do not know where the vine terminated on the west. The type of vine intended by the artist is not certain; usually a grape-vine is depicted; [1] this may be a stylized rendering of one.

Of the birds [2] among the rambling vines 5 have escaped destruction; a pair existed in each of the medallions above the amphora (Pls. 81 & 83,1); [3] only one is in the medallion below the same (Pls. 81 & 83,2); whilst the large bird on the side occupies several medallions (Pl. 81). The bird below the amphora is certainly a cock; [4] those above it may be doves; the one at the side looks like a swan.[5]

Diamonds with indented edges are sprinkled among the other designs (see Pls. 82 & 83,1).

In the southern lobe of the quatrefoil a piece of the mosaic, measuring 1.40 m. from east to west and 1.00 m. from north to south (see Fig. 27 & Pls. 84, 1&2; 85,1), exhibits not only decorations but also repairs which throw light on the history of this pavement. Of the amphora nothing remains; its existence and position are suggested by two vines (Pl. 84,1) having the same parallel arrangement as the two vines in the eastern lobe at the point where they issue from the amphora (see Pls. 82 & 83,1). The vines terminate abruptly on the south (Pl. 84,1, right), where the pavement was destroyed at the time when the wall between the sanctuary and the southern sacristy was built; their branches end in large palmate leaves (Pl. 84, 1 & 2) of the same type as those which occur in the eastern lobe and form medallions filled in with four-footed animals facing the center of the sanctuary. [6] Traces of two such animals survive; the one on the western side of the lobe has claws and a spotted body; it is

[1] See the references given by Biebel in *Gerasa*, pp. 302 ff.

[2] *QDAP* 3 (1934), p. 65, 11; *Gerasa*, p. 301.

[3] For this arrangement see *QDAP* 3 (1934), p. 62,7.

[4] For other examples see *QDAP* 3 (1934), p. 65,11. Cocks were also painted on the walls of tombs at Beit Jibrin; for this motif in a Christian tomb of the Byzantine period, see *AASOR* 2-3, p. 100; for the same motif in pre-Christian tombs see Peters and Thiersch, *Painted Tombs in the Necropolis of Marissa*, pp. 6, 18, 88.

[5] According to Avi-Yonah, *QDAP* 3 (1934), p. 62,7 the amphora "is commonly flanked by two peacocks facing each other in an 'heraldic' pose;" perhaps the artist intended to depict peacocks also here.

[6] Regarding representations of quadrupeds see *QDAP* 3 (1934), p. 65,10; *Gerasa*, p. 301.

perhaps a panther (Pl. 84,2); the other on the eastern side of the lobe had small hoofs divided into two parts; nothing but the hoofs remain. The other ornaments which occur may be seen in Pls. 84,1 and 85,1. A tessellarius, who repaired the patch illustrated in Pl. 85,1, converted the inner straight edge of the border into a wavy one and filled in its sinuses with 4 other designs; on the side of the field a slanting rod with two curved crossbars looks like a patriarchal or archiepiscopal cross, but the knobs at the ends of the bars seem to indicate that a plant was intended; the next design reminds one of an anchor, though here too a plant may have been intended; on the other side of the wave are two rings with bars resembling an "anch" without the crossbar (see *HCA* p. 271). These designs were executed with small black, golden, green, blue and purple tesserae obtained from the wall mosaics. More to the right another design suggests a face with two eyes.

In the western and northern lobes of the quatrefoil only a few vestiges of the vine-trellis and other ornaments survive (see Fig. 27). The branches of the vine in the eastern and southern lobes consist of three parallel rows of black, yellow and gray tesserae; similar strips in the other two lobes point to the existence of the vine and its branches also there. Of other ornaments we were able to recognize some geometrical motif in the western lobe and a few circlets in the northern one.

The rectangular central section of the field (see Fig. 27) was so completely destroyed that not a single trace of it could be found intact. Loose tesserae were mixed with the earth around the tomb in the center of the sanctuary and some large fragments of marble slabs were found in the broken end of the tomb. It is not improbable that some marble was used in the vicinity of the altar for the pavement.

Biebel [1] informs us that at Gerasa "until the middle of the sixth century the chancels, except in the church of Procopius, were paved with stone, but after that date mosaic was common here also." The church of Procopius was paved in 526 or 527 A. D.; it "is therefore the earliest of the dated group built in the sixth century." [2] The mosaic pavement in the chancel of the basilica at Siyâgha is probably even older than that of Procopius' church at Gerasa.

Many of the motifs used for decorating the mosaic pavement of the sanctuary had a symbolical character in early Christian art; [3] on this account they are highly appropriate for that place and it is this fact no doubt which accounts for

[1] *Gerasa*, p. 297; see pp. 340 & 260 ff.

[2] Avi-Yonah, *QDAP* 3 (1934), p. 63, note 18, indicates a number of early churches in Palestine whose chancels are paved with mosaics.

[3] See *HCA* pp. 266 ff. passim.

their presence there. This seems to be true especially of the quatrefoil,[1] amphora,[2] vine [3] and birds.[4]

2. *The body of the basilica,* comprising the central nave, the side aisles and the intercolumniations, was completely paved with mosaics (see Fig. 27). Two pavements on different levels exist here; only the upper one has decorations; these will be described first; then a few words will be added regarding the lower one.

a. *The surround of the upper pavement* (see Fig. 27 & Pls. 90, 91, 93, 94) is tolerably well preserved on all sides except at the two ends of the nave. The best-preserved section is that along the southern wall (Pl. 93, right). The section along the northern wall (Pl. 90, left) has sustained a crack along its entire length from east to west; this was due to the fact that it had been placed over a projection of the wall; inside the wall the bed of the pavement settled and in this way a crack resulted; small sections of the surround disappeared completely; a strip along the western end next to the wall was repaired with larger tesserae (see Pl. 91,2, right). At the eastern end of the northern aisle the surround was not completely cleared, in order to preserve the evidence of fire existing there; it consists of a thick black layer of ashes above about 60 cm. of other débris (see Pl. 91,1, upper left corner).

The surround is a broad strip between the walls and the border averaging 53 cm. in width; its inner limit is marked by a single row of black tesserae. This strip is decorated with a vine and a few other designs. The vine has leaves and tendrils but no fruits. The stem of the vine, consisting of a double row of black and red cubes, follows a winding course around three sides of each aisle and terminates near the responds; in each of its bends there are a leaf and a tendril. The stem of the leaf and tendril is black; the leaf is heart-shaped and shaded half red and half yellow; the tendril ends in a single spiral beyond which curved lines suggest other coils.

Between the responds and the border there are other designs. The pair in front of the northeastern respond (Pl. 91,1, upper right corner) consists of indented squares with a pair of florets at each of the four corners; the two in front of the northwestern respond (Pl. 91,2, upper left corner) consist of a crisscross arrangement of florets; those in front of the southwestern respond have disappeared

1 Already above we noted that the quatrefoil was chosen because it fits the architectural form of the building; but it seems most probable that the deeper religious significance of this design did not escape the notice of those who chose it, especially when we consider that the same form was deliberately chosen for the font in the baptistery (see pp. 88 ff.).

2 The amphora has the same form as the chalice represented standing on an altar in one of the mosaics of St. Vitalis at Ravenna; see *HCA* p. 433, Abb. 207; for other chalices of this type see ibid. p. 572, Abb. 285; p. 557, Abb. 279; pp. 541 ff., Abb. 271; for its symbolical character, especially when associated with doves and other birds, see ibid. pp. 284 ff.

3 See *HCA* p. 293.

4 See *HCA* pp. 284 ff.

and those in front of the southeastern respond have either been destroyed or exist below walls built over them. Of the surround at both ends of the nave nothing is visible; most of it is destroyed; a small fragment may still exist beneath the pulpit in the southeastern corner.

The vine is found as an ornament of the surround also in the churches at et-Tâbgha [1] and at Suhmâtâ.[2]

b. *The border of the upper pavement* (Fig. 27 & Pls. 90-94) is a strip of the same width as the surround; from its outermost edge, consisting of a row of black tesserae next to the surround, to its innermost edge, next to the borders of the panels in the field, it is 53 cm. wide. Between narrow white, black and red stripes near the edges there is a broad central band of interlocking black and red dodecagons on a white background extending around the entire body of the church. The scheme looks like the ground plan of a screen consisting of posts and panels; the posts are represented by the larger dodecagons, the panels by the smaller ones; the posts are close together and grooved on the sides adjacent to each other; the panels are inserted into the grooves, where they are firmly fastened; this last fact is indicated by the interlinking of the dodecagons. The artist possibly wished to represent a fence which supported the vine represented in the surround. This type of border has not been reported from other sites.

Another peculiarity of this border is the fact that it extends around the entire body of the basilica, which must therefore, be considered as a single field; generally the nave and side aisles are treated as separate fields.[3] Unfortunately the border is destroyed or concealed at the western and eastern ends of the nave. In the side aisles, however, it is well-preserved. In Pl. 91,1, it can be seen that the border extends beyond the northern aisle into the space between the respond and the first column and comes abruptly to an end along the line near the nave where the mosaic pavement was completely destroyed; this proves that the border extended further; in other words, it enclosed also the eastern end of the nave and most probably still exists beneath the pulpit in the southeastern part of the nave. The same was observed at the western end of the basilica (see Pl. 91,2 upper left corner); it is, therefore, reasonably sure that the artist intended to treat the pavement in the body of the basilica as one large field.

c. *The field of the upper pavement* (Fig. 27) was divided into a number of sections by the colonnades and the columns; the larger sections in the side

[1] See Schneider, *BVK* p. 58, Abb. 11 (before p. 57). This vine also consists of a winding stem with a leaf and a tendril in each curve; the tendril is executed in the same way as the one at Siyâgha, but the leaf has deeper sinuses; from the form of the leaf Schneider concluded that the artist did not intend to represent the grape-vine, but a native plant which he calls the "Zaunrübe (Bryonia)." For other reference see l. c.

[2] Avi-Yonah in *QDAP* 3 (1934), p. 94, Pls. XXVIII, 1; XXX, 2. This is a grape-vine, as is evident from the clusters of fruits; the tendrils are like those of Siyâgha and et-Tâbgha; but the leaves are palmate, like those of the vine represented in the sanctuary of the basilica at Siyâgha.

[3] Regarding this point see *Gerasa*, pp. 297 f.

aisles were subdivided into smaller ones. In all there were originally at least 22 sections or panels: 1 in the nave, 3 in the north aisle, 4 in the south aisle and 14 in the intercolumniations; of these 20 are preserved completely or in part.

In the nave (Fig. 27; Pls. 88 & 89) the mosaic pavement was almost completely worn out by long and constant use; its bed is preserved in the western half and a few decorated fragments still exist near the northern and southern colonnades and beneath the pulpit.

The bed of the pavement consists of a layer of stones and earth and two layers of mortar. The stones mixed with the earth in the lowest layer are about the size of a fist; ashes are mixed with lime in the lower layer of mortar; pure lime was used for the upper layer of mortar which served as the matrix in which the tesserae were fixed. This technique was followed in all the later mosaic pavements of the Byzantine period observed in Transjordan and Palestine.[1]

Mortar was used to repair the pavement from the western wall to a line slightly east of columns 13 and 14.[2] Beyond that line towards the east, wherever the tesserae had disappeared, the bed of the pavement served as a floor.

The ornamented fragments preserved on the northern side of the nave are to be found near columns 7-11; the piece near the 7th and 9th columns (see Pl. 88, 1 & 2) measures roughly 2.00 × 1.20 m.; that near the 11th column about 55 × 29 cm. Those which still exist on the southern side of the nave are near columns 6-12; one piece near columns 6-10 (see Pl. 89, 1, 3, 4) is about 3.90 m. long and about 80 cm. wide; the other near the 12th column is very small, but serves to indicate that the same style of decoration extended at least that far westwards.

From these fragments we learn that the panel had a very simple border, but a very elaborate and complicated field-design. The border, next to the colonnade, is rectilinear; it consists of a narrow band having red, yellow, gray and white stripes. The field was divided by broad richly colored bands, forming interlacing hexagons, into semicircular, circular, triangular, quadrilateral and octagonal compartments filled in with a great variety of designs. The tesserae used for these designs are among the smallest observed in the pavements at Siyâgha; all are less than a centimeter square. Their colors are also more varied than those of the other panels of the basilica. Nine of these smaller compartments are preserved: three near the northern and six near the southern border.

Of the three compartments near the northern border, one is a triangle, the second a semicircle and the third a diamond. The triangle near the 7th column (Pl. 88, 1) is formed by the intersecting cable and rainbow borders of two hexagons and it is filled in with a rainbow motif. The semicircle near the 9th column

[1] See B. Gauer, in *JPOS* 18 (1938), pp. 233-253; for SS. Cosmas and Damian at Jerash, pp. 235 f. For Palestine, see Avi-Yonah in *QDAP* 3 (1934), pp. 71 f., 22.

[2] The same was done also elsewhere; for Palestine, see Avi-Yonah, *QDAP* 3 (1934), p. 73, 25; for Jerash, see Biebel in *Gerasa*, p. 306, 4.

(Pl. 88,2) has a series of crow-steps next to the curved border and, in the center, a fan-shaped design colored white, red, yellow, brown, pink and gray-black. Around its exterior are parts of two hexagons having rainbow and cable borders respectively; in the corners of the hexagons there are triangles; between the hexagons there is a part of a diamond-shaped compartment containing a design which looks like the metal container of a suspension lamp with an oval pendant below. Near the 11th column enough of a semicircular compartment exists to make it certain that the same panel extended westwards beyond the 11th column.

Near the southern border two complete triangles, three semicircles — one complete and the others fragmentary — and a part of an octagon still exist from the 6th to the 10th columns (see Fig. 27). The triangles (Pl. 89,1 & 4) and one of the semicircles (Pl. 89,4) are treated in the same way as those on the northern side of the nave; a second semicircle (Pl. 89,3) contains a shell-design; of the third semicircle (Pl. 89,1, right) only faint traces survive. Near the 12th column a small fragment of the design characteristic of the field was noted.

These fragments demonstrate that the greater part of the nave was certainly occupied by one large panel; whether this panel extended up to the border of the field on the west can no longer be ascertained; but on the east this fact could be established by removing the pulpit, beneath which a piece of the mosaic in the nave is still preserved.

The same method of dividing and decorating fields and panels is reported from at least 10 other places of Palestine and Transjordan. In Palestine [1] it was used in Jerusalem,[2] in Seilûn [3] and Suhmâtâ [4] north of Jerusalem, in Beit Jibrîn [5] and Beersheba [6] south of Jerusalem, and in Tell Hassân (Jericho)[7] and ʿEin Dûk [8] east of Jerusalem. In Transjordan it occurs at Mâʿin,[9] Madaba and Jerash. In the last two places the mosaics are dated; an inscription in the church of Procopius at Jerash [10] informs us that the work there was carried out in the year 526 A. D.; and from the inscription in the crypt of St. Elias at Madaba [11] we

1 See Avi-Yonah, *QDAP* 3 (1934), p. 59, pattern *H5*; add *QDAP* 5 (1936), Pl. LI, 1, above.

2 In the central aisle of the church in the convent of the Holy Cross; see the references given in *QDAP* 2 (1933), p. 163, no. 106; or, v. g., Vincent-Abel, *Jérusalem nouvelle*, p. 943, n. 1, Pl. LXXXV, 2-4.

3 In the central aisle of the basilica on the spot called el-Habs; see references in *QDAP* 3 (1934), p. 41, no. 302, especially *JPOS* 10 (1930), p. 161, Fig. 39; *QS* 1931, p. 85, Fig. 14.

4 In the narthex of the church; see *QDAP* 3 (1934), p. 94, Pl. XXVII, 1; about 555 A. D.

5 Only a link occurs as a repeating pattern of a border; see *QDAP* 2 (1933), p. 146.

6 *QDAP* 3 (1934), p. 49, no. 335, (3), Pl. XIV, 2.

7 In the north aisle of an early Byzantine church; see *QDAP* 5 (1936), Pl. LI, 1, above.

8 In the central nave of a synagogue; see *QDAP* 2 (1933), pp. 155 ff., (2), (B); or, v. g., *RB* 1919, p. 535, Fig. 1.

9 De Vaux, *RB* 47 (1938), pp. 235 ff., Fig. 3, Pl. X.

10 *Gerasa*, p. 338, 1 and Pl. LXXX, D: intercolumnar panel; p. 340, 4 and Pl. LXXXIII, d: nave of chapel. — Interlocking hexagons are used as fillers in a compartment of a field in the Synagogue church; see l. c. Pl. LXVI, 1.

11 See Sejourné, *RB* 1897, p. 652.

learn that the work there was completed in the year 595-6 A. D., when Sergius was bishop (see Pl. 89,2). A year or two later, namely, in 597 A. D., under the same bishop Sergius, the work in the basilica of Siyâgha was finished (see inscription I). All three dated mosaics of this type, therefore, belong to the sixth century A. D.; the one at Jerash is the earliest, that at Siyâgha the latest of the three.

In the northern aisle (Fig. 27) the field was divided into three panels, of which two (see Pl. 90) are still in a relatively good condition, but the third has almost completely disappeared (see Pl. 91,2).

The panel at the eastern end of the northern aisle (Pls. 90; 91,1; 92,1) extends from the eastern border to the third column in the northern colonnade (see Fig. 27,5); it measures 156 by 608 cm. A single row of black tesserae encloses a field with a yellow background on which are represented white designs, each of which is quartered by intersecting diagonal rows of black foils and in each quarter there are three florets. The white designs are arranged in two parallel rows each of which contains seven; these do not touch the border or each other. Avi-Yonah [1] considers these designs "petalled flowers". In this case each flower would have a corolla divided into 12 lobes or petals, 8 in the outer row and 4 in the inner one; those in the outer row have a red edge; the florets in each lobe or petal could represent the stamens and pistils. Biebel,[2] however, treats these designs as "scalloped squares... filled with scale pattern containing florets." The diagonal rows of foils intersecting one another divide the panel into squares.

The panel in the center of the northern aisle (Pls. 90 & 92,2) extends from the third column in the northern colonnade (Fig. 27,5) to a line west of the fifth column (Fig. 27,9); its western end no longer exists. A narrow rectilinear border surrounds the field divided into smaller compartments by intersecting squares and circles; each square contains a duplex sign and each circle other concentric circles filled in with an indented square. White, black, red and yellow tesserae were used for these designs. The panel in the southern aisle, directly opposite this one, was treated in the same way. Comparatively few examples of this method of dividing the field have been reported from Palestine [3] and Transjordan.[4]

The panel at the western end of the northern aisle was almost completely destroyed (Fig. 27); but the small fragment on its western side which has survived (Pl. 91,2) shows that the border consisted of a single row of tesserae and the field of square compartments containing floral crosses. The division of the field was effected by means of sprigs or florets arranged in diagonal rows intersecting

[1] *QDAP* 3 (1934), p. 95. It is his so-called type *J5* of which he gives 8 examples in Palestine; l. c. p. 59. Ibid. p. 66, Avi-Yonah states that this pattern belongs to a group of geometric ornaments, which "has its origin in Late Roman and Byzantine decoration, influenced by the Orient (especially Syria)."

[2] *Gerasa*, p. 335, b; see also p. 322, c.

[3] Avi-Yonah, *QDAP* 3 (1934), p. 59, *J2*, lists 4 examples; the pattern is one of those which he thinks have their origin in Late Roman and Byzantine decoration; see l. c. p. 66.

[4] See *Gerasa*, p. 338, 2 and Pl. LXXXII, a; p. 336, 2 and Pl. LXXVII, c.

one another. This method of dividing and decorating the field was very popular. At Siyâgha we meet with it four more times: in one of the intercolumniations (Pl. 95,9), in the narthex (Pl. 96, 1 & 2), in the Theotokos chapel (Pl. 110,1) and in room 91 (Pl. 113,1). It was used also at Madaba,[1] Jerash[2] and numerous places of Palestine.[3] The floral motifs used as space-fillers have four lobes bisected by lines extending from a central core to a point beyond the lobe; the lines emphasize the cruciform effect of the four-lobed corolla. These so-called flowered crosses are all alike in this panel. They closely resemble those of the north hall (Pl. 97,1 & 3); but they differ in a number of details, such as the margin and the core, from those in the Theotokos chapel (Pl. 111,4) and room 90 (Pl. 113,2). A similar floral design has been observed at Mekhayyat,[4] Madaba,[5] Jerash,[6] Jericho [7] and et-Tâbgha.[8]

A line consisting of a single row of tesserae marks the limit between the panels of the north aisle and the intercolumnar spaces.

In the southern aisle the field was divided in four panels (Fig. 27); three are complete (Pl. 93) and one is fragmentary (Pl. 118,2, below). As in the northern aisle, all these panels are separated from those in the intercolumniations by a simple line consisting of a single row of tesserae and around each panel there is a plain white surround. The frame of each panel consists merely of a straight line. The field in each case is treated differently.

The first panel on the east (Pl. 94) is 152½ cm. wide and 640 cm. long. It extends from the border at the eastern end of the aisle to the 3rd column in the southern colonnade (see Fig. 27, 6 & Pl. 93). Its field is divided into squares measuring 36 cm. along each side; each of these contains a much smaller square measuring 9 cm. on each side; the larger figures result from narrow indented red and yellow diagonal bands intersecting one another; the smaller ones are formed of white, red, black and yellow tesserae and have serrated edges. This method of dividing the field was used several times at Jerash [9] and at least 21 times in various places of Palestine.[10]

1 See *Nea Sion*, 1904, Eik. VI; 1905, Eik. XVIII; the former is in church "I" or "A", the latter in the church of the Theotokos.

2 See *Gerasa*, Pls. LX, a; LXI, a; LXXVI, b; LXXXII, b. Biebel, l. c. p. 314, calls this method of dividing the field "a diaper pattern of diamonds formed by... florets." Ibid. p. 298, n. 2, he explains that a ""diamond" indicates a square placed on its point or with its sides at a 45-degree angle to the main sides of the field.". Ibid. p. 301, n. 20, he observes that "the term "sprig" used by Avi-Yonah seems not to connote its floral origin."

3 Avi-Yonah, *QDAP* 3 (1934), p. 59, *H7*, has listed 14 examples of these "garlands enclosing lozenge spaces" (l. c. p. 68); add to these the ones found more recently at Tell Hassân, near Jericho (see *QDAP* 5 (1936), Pls. XLIX, 4; LII, 3); in Jerusalem (see *QDAP* 6 (1937), Pl. X, 2); in a synagogue northeast of ancient Jericho (see *QDAP* 6 (1937), Pl. XIX).

4 See *RAC* 13 (1936), p. 136, Fig. 24 (in St. George's).

5 See *Nea Sion*, 1905, Eik. X (upper church of St. Elias); Eik. XIX (in church Δ).

6 See *Gerasa*, Pl. LXXVI, b; Pl. LXXXII, b.

7 *QDAP* 3 (1934), Pl. XVII, 2-3.

8 *BVK* Tafel 25.

9 See *Gerasa*, Pls. LVIII, c; LX, c; LXI, c.

10 See *QDAP* 3 (1934), p. 59, *H1*.

The second panel from the east extends from the 3rd to the 6th column (see Fig. 27, 6-12 & Pl. 93); it is 148½ cm. wide and 765 cm. long; that is, it is somewhat narrower and longer than the preceding panel. The field is divided into 88 square and round compartments linked to one another and to the border; around each circle there are 4 spandrels; in each square there are straight-sided duplex signs; in each circle, disks divided into sectors of different colors. It is this last-mentioned element which distinguishes the circles in this panel from those in the panel directly opposite to it in the northern aisle (see Pl. 92,2); in fact, it is the only element which distinguishes the two panels from one another.

The third panel from the east, near the sixth column (see Fig. 27, d & Pls. 93, below; 118,2) contains a Greek inscription; see inscription IX.

The fourth panel, which occupied the entire western end of the southern aisle, was almost completely destroyed. As in the nave and in the northern aisle this damage was repaired with mortar. The small fragment which remains near the panel with the inscription (Fig. 27; Pl. 118,2, below) shows that it was decorated with 6 vertical rows of duplex signs having curved sides.[1] The same four colors (white, black, red and yellow) were used here as everywhere else in the southern aisle.

In the intercolumniations there were originally 14 distinct panels; 11 are complete; the other three are completely or almost completely destroyed. The panels differ slightly in size and nearly all contain different designs executed in the four customary colors: white, black, red and yellow.

Between the columns of the northern colonnade 5 panels still exist (see Pl. 90, right). The panel in the first intercolumniation from the east (Fig. 27, 1-3; Pl. 95, 1) measures 153 × 75 cm.; it is decorated with three circles; that in the second (111½ × 77 cm.) is decorated with a diamond on a yellow background (Fig. 27, 3-5; Pl. 95, 3); that in the third (143½ × 82½ cm.), with circles and squares (Fig. 27, 5-7; Pl. 95,5); that in the fourth (144½ × 80 cm.), with foils formed by intersecting circles (Fig. 27, 7-9; Pl. 95, 7); that in the fifth (122 × 60 cm.), with squares formed by diagonal rows of sprigs intersecting one another; they are filled in with squares having a serrated edge, but in one case a floral cross was used (Fig. 27, 9-11; Pl. 95, 9); this decoration is the same as that used for the westernmost panel in the northern aisle. The panel in the sixth intercolumniation (Fig. 27, 11-13) was 131 cm. long, but its width and ornamentation can no longer be ascertained; a few remnants suggest florets. In the seventh intercolumniation (Fig. 27, 13-15) nothing whatsoever remains of the mosaic; there the floor was repaired with mortar.

[1] The duplex sign is a foil with two lateral coils or hooks, which could have served to link the foils together; see, v. g., *Gerasa*, Pl. LXXIII, where 4 such designs serve to fill a square; or ibid. Pl. LXXX, E & F; *QDAP* 5 (1936), Pl. LII, 1 & 4.

Between the columns of the southern colonnade 6 panels still remain (see Pl. 94, right). The one in the first intercolumniation from the east (Fig. 27, 2-4; Pl. 95, 2) measures $107\frac{1}{2} \times 90$ cm.; it contains a rectangle with an inscribed circle enclosing a disk. The base of the 2nd column (Fig. 27, 4) is enclosed by a border consisting of a single row of tesserae. The panel in the second intercolumniation is the widest of all; its decoration represents a slight variation of that in the preceding one (see Fig. 27, 4-6; Pl. 95, 4). A simple border enclosing the bases of the 3rd-5th columns and the two panels between them (Fig. 27, 6-10) shows a tendency on the part of the artist to unite the panels into groups. That in the third intercolumniation (Fig. 27, 6-8; Pl. 95,6) measures 138×87 cm.; the 8 circles which occupy the field contain indented squares, of which 4 are parallel with the borders and 4 have their corners pointed towards the borders. That in the fourth intercolumniation (Fig. 27, 8-10) is the only panel which repeats a design found in another one; it is exactly like the panel directly opposite to it in the northern colonnade between the columns numbered 7-9 (see Pl. 95,7); on a yellow background intersecting circles form foils [1] among which there are a number of indented squares. That in the fifth intercolumniation (Fig. 27,10-12; Pl. 95,8) measuring $142\frac{1}{2} \times 89$ cm. is divided into 73 rectangular compartments of which 36 are white; the others red, black and yellow. The one in the sixth intercolumniation (Fig. 27,12-14; Pl. 95,10) resembles the two easternmost panels; but the circle inscribed inside the rectangle is treated differently in each case; here it is divided into 24 small parts by cycloids and hypocycloids. The panel in the seventh intercolumniation has disappeared; in its place we found a pavement made of mortar.

d. *An older mosaic pavement* existed in the body of the basilica about 15 cm. below the one which we have just described; traces of it have been found in several parts of the nave and in the northern aisle. The fragment beneath the northern end of the chancel screen and the one beneath the pulpit were mentioned on p. 50. A third fragment measuring about 130×20-40 cm. exists some 70 cm. south of the fourth column in the northern colonnade (see Fig. 27,7; Pl. 88,1, left). It has strips consisting of three rows of black cubes along its northern and eastern sides; they probably represent the border of a field which extended westwards from here and had no other decorations. Along the northern side of this field there is a stone in situ which seems to mark the original limits of the mosaic in that direction. This is the only piece of evidence which we have to show that this older pavement was at least 2-colored. The fourth fragment in the northwestern part of the nave between the respond (Fig. 27,17) and the door (240×85 cm.) consists of one-colored cubes; the cubes in the row next to the wall are twice as large as the rest; these in turn are about twice as large as those used for the upper mosaic pavement. The mosaic basin in the

[1] See *QDAP* 3 (1934), p. 59, *J4*, where other examples are given.

southwestern corner of the nave (Fig. 27,18) is 38-40 cm. in diameter and 15 cm. deep; its bottom is on the same level as the lower mosaic pavement, but its rim is on a level with the upper mosaic pavement; this indicates that it served as a sump for the latter. In the western end of the northern aisle the lower mosaic pavement came to light wherever we removed the mortar with which the upper pavement had been repaired after it had been worn out (see Fig. 27 and Pl. 91,2). Other pieces of this older pavement no doubt still exist beneath the upper one. To judge from the pieces which we have found, it seems reasonably safe to assume that the entire body of the basilica at one time had a 2-colored mosaic pavement. Since the upper mosaic pavement belongs to the end of the sixth century A. D. (597 A. D.), the lower one must be assigned to some earlier period; it most probably represents the floor of the fifth-century basilica.

This lower mosaic pavement seems to have been laid in a layer of mortar next to the native rock without any other foundation. The same was observed at et-Tâbgha by Gauer,[1] who thinks that it represents the technique used in the earlier part of the Byzantine period in Palestine and Transjordan.

3. *The narthex of the basilica,* which originally comprised not only the area west of the basilica (Pl. 161, 6) but also the areas west of the north hall Pl. 161, 10 & 11) and the Theotokos chapel (Pl. 161, 30), had a multi-colored mosaic pavement. Most of it has been worn out, but some parts of it have been preserved in the rooms at its two extremities, beneath their walls and beneath the stone benches along the eastern wall (see Fig. 27 & pp. 69 ff.). From these we learn that the narthex was decorated with three panels: a small one at each end and a large one between the two. In the surround there are indented squares and florets arranged crosswise; each panel has its own peculiar field-ornament (see Pl. 96, 1 & 2). The tesserae are less than a centimeter square, like those used for the upper pavement in the basilica; four colors are used: white, black, red and yellow.

a. *The small panel at the northern end of the narthex* (Fig. 27,11; Pl. 96,1) has a plain band as a border. Its field is divided into square, hexagonal and triangular compartments filled in with dentated squares and lozenges. The four squares are formed by plain bands; they are linked to one another and to the borders by serrated bands which intersect to form the rest of the field's subdivisions. This treatment of the field is found frequently in various places of Palestine [2] and at Jerash.[3]

b. *The small panel at the southern end of the narthex* (Fig. 27, 30; Pl. 96, 2, left) has a fret border and its field is sprinkled with florets A similar fret

1 See *JPOS* 18 (1938), pp. 233 ff.
2 Avi-Yonah, *QDAP* 3 (1934), p. 59, *H3*, enumerates a dozen examples.
3 See *Gerasa*, Pls. LXXX, a; LXXXI, c; both in Procopius' church.

Fig. 28. Detail of the mosaic pavement of the baptistery (see pp. 230 f.).

was used in the baptistery (see Pl. 106, 2) and in the Theotokos chapel (see Pl. 109, 2); it occurs at times also in other places.[1] Florets were used as an "all-over" pattern of the field also in the Theotokos chapel (Pl. 109,1) and in room 16 (Pl. 112, 1).[2]

c. *The large panel in the center of the narthex between the two small ones* (Fig. 27, 11-30; Pl. 96, 1 & 2) has a plain band as a border and its field is divided into squares by diagonal rows of sprigs intersecting one another; each square contains a cruciform arrangement of sprigs. The same method of dividing the field was used in four other panels (see p. 221), but the space-fillers here are different.

The date of the pavement is not indicated; it resembles the upper pavement in the basilica and those in the lateral chapels so closely that it would be natural to assign it to the same period; that is, to the end of the sixth or the beginning of the seventh century A. D.

C. THE MOSAIC PAVEMENT OF THE NORTH HALL

1. *The chancel of the north hall* (Fig. 27; Pls. 97,1; 99 ff.) is rectangular and its mosaic pavement closely follows that outline. It measures 606 × 708 cm. The greater part of the pavement is in a good state of preservation; a few patches seem to have been destroyed accidentally.

a. *The surround* next to the walls and the chancel screen is 57-70 cm. wide; it is decorated with two series of repeating ornaments; those in the outer series are indented squares; those in the inner, florets; in the center of the inner series on the western side there is a larger design consisting of a circle with projecting rounded links on four sides (see Pl. 99,1).

b. *The border* (see Pls. 99,1; 102,1) is a band 57 cm. wide. The edges are straight; next to the outer one there is a broad plaited strip;[3] next to the inner one there is an uninterrupted series of wave-crests;[4] between the two there is a rectilinear strip.

[1] See *Gerasa*, Pl. LXX, d; but the type used in the Theotokos chapel seems to be more common; see *Gerasa*, Pls. LXXIII; LXXIV, a & b; LXXVI, a & b; LXXXIV, b; Pl. LXXVII, a; *QDAP* 3 (1934), p. 58, *A19*: 4 examples.

[2] See *Gerasa*, LXI, b; *QDAP* 1 (1932), Pl. LVII; 6 (1937), Pl. X.

[3] Avi-Yonah, *QDAP* 3 (1934), p. 58, *B4*, gives 4 examples of this type of plait in Palestine; see also *Gerasa*, Pls. LXXII, a-c; LXXXIV, a.

[4] Wave-crest borders seem to be quite common in Palestine; Avi-Yonah, *QDAP* 3 (1934), p. 58, *B7* & *8*, enumerates 20 examples; in Transjordan they seem to be much more rare; see *Gerasa*, Pl. LIX, b; LXVI, b; LXVII, a.

c. *The field* (Fig. 27; Pls. 99 ff.) is decorated with 30 quatrefoils linked to the border and to one another; they divide it into 72 compartments filled in with a variety of motifs. The interior of the quatrefoils is decorated only with florets (see Pls. 99,1; 102,2); there are 12 such ornaments in each figure; one in each of the four lobes, one at the tip of each of the four cusps and four in the center. Quatrefoils were used to divide and decorate a field in the upper church of St. Elias at Madaba, finished in 608 A. D. (see Pl. 102, 4)[1] and in an early Byzantine church at Tell Hassân, near Jericho;[2] otherwise it seems to be rare.[3]

Around and between the quatrefoils there are 42 other compartments; 22 are along the borders and 20 among the quatrefoils. Of the compartments along the borders 18 are filled in with plant motifs and 4 with geometrical designs; the latter group, consisting of two rectangles with zigzag bases and two diamonds, is along the western side of the field; the former along the other three sides. The following plant motifs were used: single foils in each of the four corners of the field (see Pl. 102,2); two foils in the 2nd and 3rd compartments along the eastern side; plants represented by two spirals, a stem and one or three leaves in the first, third and fifth compartments along both the northern and the southern sides (see Pls. 99,1; 102,2); a floral design with five petals in the second and fourth compartments along both the northern and the southern sides (see Pl. 102,3).

The 20 compartments among the quatrefoils are arranged in five rows (see Fig. 27 & Pl. 99,1); the four in the first row on the east are filled in with four large fruits with vines, leaves and buds. All the fruits look familiar, but in attempting to specify the fruit intended by the artist there is some divergence of opinion;[4] this should be borne in mind when we suggest that the first may be a pomegranate (Pl. 101,1),[5] the second a melon (Pl. 101,2), the third a cucumber (Pl. 101,3) and the fourth a beet (Pl. 101,4). Those in the second row contain clusters of grapes and shaded disks; the cluster at the southern end of the row is illustrated in Pl. 100,1; the disks in Pl. 101,5 & 6. Of the four compartments in the third row the two end ones contain representations of fish,[6]

1 See *RB* 1897, pp. 652 ff.; ibid. 1911, p. 439; *Nea Sion*, 1905, Eik. X.

2 *QDAP* 5 (1936), Pl. LI, 2, above; here the motif was used for the south aisle.

3 It is reported to have been used in the chambers of Eutropius and Ulpiane at the Karm esh-Sheikh, Sebastya; a 5th-6th century date is suggested. See *QDAP* 3 (1934), p. 39, no. 290. — We call attention also to the large quatrefoil of the basilica's chancel; see above pp. 211 ff.

4 Regarding this point see also Avi-Yonah, *QDAP* 3 (1934), pp. 65 f., no. 12; Biebel, *Gerasa*, p. 302.

5 It should, however, be noted that it has a somewhat different appearance in the baptistery where it is represented hanging on a tree (see Pls. 103,1; 106,1).

6 Fishes are one of the types of decoration especially favored by the Christian communities of Palestine and Transjordan; regarding the former see Avi-Yonah, *QDAP* 3 (1934), pp. 62 f., no. 7; he gives 8 examples; regarding Mekhayyat, see *RAC* 13 (1936), p. 131, Fig. 19; p. 134, Figs. 21 & 22; there are other examples in the same town, which have not yet been published; for Madaba, see *Nea Sion*, 1905, Eik. XVI; for Jerash, see *Gerasa*, Pls. LXVIII, b; LXXIV, b. See also the next note.

the second from the north a quatrefoil and the third a rectangle with inscribed concentric circles. For the fish at the southern end of the row see Pl. 99,2. In the fourth row a basket[1] filled with bread occupies the first compartment at the northern end (Pl. 100,2) and a floral cross the second ; the other two compartments and their ornaments have been destroyed. In the fifth row each compartment seems to have been filled in with a bird, with a plant having a flower and buds and with a twig. The pair of birds at the northern end (see Pl. 101, 7 & 8) is well preserved and enough remains of the bird in the third compartment to suggest a similar group at the southern end (see Pl. 99,1); partridges were probably intended.

Most of the ornaments of the chancel seem to have a neutral character ; but it does not seem to be purely fortuitous that grapes, fish and baskets filled with bread were represented in the center of the chancel, where an altar would normally stand. These objects are the well-known symbols of the sacrifice offered on the altars of Christian churches and their presence at that particular spot is therefore significant.[2] Already in speaking of the chancel of the basilica we noted that the artists chose objects which served to emphasize the character and purpose of that place ; here we notice the same careful selection of ornaments.

2. *The nave of the north hall* (Fig. 27; Pls. 97 & 98) is decorated with one large panel. Several large cracks in the pavement are due to the fact that its foundations have settled; fires also disfigured a few parts; but the greater part of the pavement is still in a tolerably good state.

a. *The surround* is decorated with two or three series of repeating ornaments; those in the outer series are indented squares, those in the inner florets (Pl. 98,1 & 2). On the east and west there are special designs ; that on the

[1] This basket has a concave base, concave sides and an everted rim ; handles ending in spirals are attached loosely to the rim and the sides ; the interwoven splints are indicated by zigzag bands. The contents of the baskets are indicated by circlets, which we presume represent loaves of bread. Baskets are especially common in vintage scenes where they serve for collecting and transporting grapes ; for such representations in Palestine, see Avi-Yonah, *QDAP* 3 (1934), p. 62, no. 7 and note 15 ; p. 66, nos. 12 & 13 and note 7, where 5 examples are listed ; add *QDAP* 3 (1934), p. 115, Pl. XXXVI. For Mekhayyat, see *RB* 43 (1934), Pl. XXIV, 2 ; for Jerash, see *Gerasa*, Pl. LXXIX, c ; other baskets are either empty or their contents are uncertain, but when placed among vines they show that they were destined for grapes ; see ibid. Pl. LXXXIII, c. The basket illustrated in Pl. 100, 2, does not contain grapes ; its contents resemble those of the basket represented behind the altar at et-Tâbgha ; see *BVK* p. 57, Tafel 1 ; there the round objects are marked with crosses and Schneider, l. c., has definitely shown that the objects represent loaves of bread ; the same may be assumed here ; there the basket with loaves and the fish flanking it refer to a definite historical fact ; here the symbolical meaning of the basket with loaves seems to have been intended ; regarding this last point, see not only Schneider, l. c., but also *HCA* pp. 268 f., Abb. 124. — Since in the two preceding rows the object represented at the northern end is repeated at the southern end, it is highly probable that a second basket was represented at the southern end of this row.

[2] See *HCA* pp. 266 ff. ; 274 ff. and passim.

east (Pl. 98,1) is a large disk, whose center contains several concentric circles, from which rays of varying colors shoot forth in all directions; that on the west (Pl. 98,2) is a large circle with a concentric arrangement of squares and circles, linked to one another and to the border. A parallel to the former was discovered in an early Byzantine basilica at Tell Hassân, near Jericho;[1] to the latter in Jerash[2] and el-Kanetra;[3] but in the latter case the ornaments are sculptured.

b. *The border* consists of rectilinear stripes, a guilloche and wave-crests, like the one of the chancel (see Pls. 97,1; 98,2). But the wave-crests are treated differently in each case; in the chancel the waves follow one direction all around the field; in the nave they change their direction near the center of each side. The guilloche is also different in each case; the type used for the nave seems to be rare in these regions. No other example has been reported from Transjordan and from Palestine we have only one.[4]

c. *The field* (Pls. 97,1-3; 98,2) is divided into squares containing circles, which in turn are filled in alternately with floral crosses and leaves. The circles are linked with the four sides of the squares; in the four corners of each square small triangular segments are cut off by indented lines. The floral cross as a space-filler occurs repeatedly at Siyâgha; it was treated on pp. 220 f. The leaf as a space-filler is met with for the first time here; we will meet with this ornament again in the chancel and nave of the baptistery, in the chancel of the Theotokos chapel, in rooms 16 and 91 of the monastery; in three of these cases the leaf serves as a very effective element of the border. The same motif has been reported from Madaba,[5] Jerash,[6] Jericho,[7] Jerusalem,[8] el-Hammâm near Beisan[9] and a few other places of Palestine.[10] Here alone it is enclosed by a circle.

The tesserae used for this pavement are on an average a centimeter square; seven colors occur: white, black, red, yellow, brown, gray and pink.

1 See *QDAP* 5 (1936), Pl. LII, 2.

2 See *Gerasa*, Pls. LXII, b; LXXXI, a & b; LXXXIII, a.

3 See *ZDPV* 9 (1886), p. 306, Fig. 63.

4 See *QDAP* 3 (1934), p. 58, *B13*.

5 See *RB* 43 (1934), p. 261, Fig. 3, where leaves cover the whole field in diaper pattern.

6 See *Gerasa*, Pls. LXI, a; LXII, a; LXXVI, b. In all these cases the leaves serve as fillers for lozenge-shaped spaces; in the second example the leaves point down, in the third to the left; in both these cases they are arranged in diagonal rows and alternate with other motifs; in the last case the motifs are floral crosses, as in the north hall; this close parallel occurs in the eastern end of the southern aisle in the church of SS. Peter and Paul.

7 See *QDAP* 6 (1937), Pl. XIX: In a synagogue heart-shaped leaves alternate with diamonds in lozenge-shaped spaces over an entire field.

8 See *QDAP* 6 (1937), Pl. X, 2: In a chapel the leaves are arranged as in the last-mentioned place.

9 See *QDAP* 5 (1936), Pl. XV: Heart-shaped leaves fill the interstices between the waves of the plastic ribbon.

10 See Avi-Yonah, *QDAP* 2 (1933), p. 148, note 2; 3 (1934), p. 59, *J6;* ibid. p. 66, no. 12. — See Vincent-Abel, Jér. nouv., II, Pl. XLIII, 2.

D. THE MOSAIC PAVEMENT OF THE BAPTISTERY

1. *The chancel.* As in the basilica and in the other two chapels, a stone base for a screen divides the floor into two parts ; that which is east of the screen is here designated as the chancel ; in this case the floor is not on a higher level as in the other three chancels, but it is on the same level as that of the nave. The font which stands on the chord of the apse (see Pl. 103,1) serves to divide the floor-space of the chancel into a number of sections, each with its peculiar ornamentation ; the first section is in the apse, behind the font; the second, directly in front of the apse to the north and south of the font; the third, between the font and the base of the screen. The presence of the font evidently had some influence on the choice of the ornaments, just as the altars in the other chancels influenced the choice of the ornaments for those places.

a. *The apse* (Fig. 27 ; Pls. 103,1 ; 104,1) is partially occupied by the font. The space between the font and the walls of the apse varies in width between 104-130 cm.; it was paved with mosaics and decorated with a semi-circular panel. The greater part of the pavement behind the font was destroyed, but at both sides of the same sections of the panel remain ; they indicate the kind of ornamentation which was used and at the same time betray traces of vandalism.

The narrow surround next to the wall and the font is without ornaments. The border consists of crow-steps between curved lines. This same type of border was used for the semicircles in the nave of the basilica (see Pls. 88 & 89). Avi-Yonah has listed half a dozen examples of this type of crow-step.[1] The field was decorated with a series of white disks containing a variety of ornaments; also the small segments between the disks were decorated. Of the disks only three still exist ; two on the northern side of the font and one on its southern side.

The object represented in the first disk on the north (Pl. 104,1, left) was intentionally destroyed; it is the first evidence of iconoclasm at Siyâgha; we shall discover more evidence both in the baptistery and in the Theotokos chapel ; it is significant that no evidence of that movement was observed in the basilica

[1] *QDAP* 3 (1934), p. 58, *A4*.

and the north hall. Today it is quite generally assumed that the iconoclastic movement responsible for this destruction took place in the first quarter of the 8th century of our era, during the reign of either Omar II (717-720) [1] or Yazid II (720-724).[2] This would indicate that the chapel was still in use at that time and continued in use for some time afterwards, for the damage done was repaired.[3]

In the second disk on the northern side of the font a vine with tendrils, leaves and a bunch of grapes is represented (Pl. 104,1, right). Bunches of grapes were represented also in the chancel of the north hall (see Pl. 100,1) and in the rear of the Theotokos chapel (see Pl. 109,2).

On the southern side of the font only a small piece of a disk remains (see Pl. 103,1); in it a bird was represented, as is indicated by claws still preserved there.

Between the disks (see Pl. 104,1) there are circlets with foils on one side and possibly fruits on the other; crosslets fill the smaller spaces.

b. *The space immediately in front of the apse on the north and south of the font* (Pl. 103,1) is filled in with two pairs of birds facing plants, two circles with Greek inscriptions and two leaves. The birds at the northern end may be herons (Pl. 105,1), those at the southern end geese (Pl. 105,2). Regarding the Greek inscriptions, see inscription I; regarding leaves as space-fillers (Pl. 104,2), see the observations made in speaking of the nave of the north hall.

c. *The space between the baptismal font and the base of the chancel screen* (Pl. 103,1) is occupied by one large panel. In the surround on the north there is a series of florets; very probably there are similar florets beneath the stone bench on the southern side. The border consists of rectilinear edges and a fret similar to the one around the panel at the southern end of the narthex. The field was decorated with 5 trees and 6 animals; most of the latter were deliberately destroyed by iconoclasts and the damage done was repaired with plain tesserae, which are larger than those used for the pavement originally.

The five trees look very much alike; their lower branches are cut back to the trunks; their spreading upper branches are covered with leaves and fruits. The trunk of the central tree has four shoots near its bottom, two on each side; the two end trees have each three shoots near the side next to the center of the panel. The trunks, branches and leaves are all alike, but their fruits differ in size and form. The fruits of the first, third and fifth trees are large and round (Pl. 106,1); they are pomegranates, a fruit which is still very common in those regions today. Those on the second tree from the north are small

1 De Vaux, *RB* 47 (1938), pp. 256-258, presents the evidence for this view.

2 Crowfoot, *Gerasa*, pp. 172 f., adopts this later date.

3 Baramki and Avi-Yonah, *QDAP* 3 (1934), pp. 19 & 115, also adopt a date in the beginning of the eighth century for the iconoclastic movement.

and pear-shaped (Pl. 106,2); they probably represent pears, though figs are not impossible; figs are very common in the Nebo region today, but the writer cannot recall having seen any pears there. Those on the fourth tree from the north are medium-sized and ovate (Pl. 107,1; Fig. 28); they may represent apples; though apricots or citrus fruits are also possible. By reason of the fruits, it is evident that the artist intended to represent at least three kinds of trees. The same was noted by De Vaux at Mâ'in [1] and already in ancient times by Choricius at Gaza.[2] When the trees have no fruits it is difficult to say what species was intended by the artist; so, for example, in the Theotokos chapel, where only a part of a tree of this type without fruits is preserved (see Pl. 110,2, upper right corner). Trees of this type are very common in Transjordan; so, for instance, at Mekhayyat,[3] Madaba [4] and Jerash;[5] but in Palestine they seem to be rare; one is reported from Seilûn.[6]

Six animals arranged in two groups facing the center at one time filled in those parts in the lower half of the panel which were not occupied by the trees. In the corners at the two ends of the panel there were fowls; the one at the northern end was deliberately destroyed and only its legs remain; the other at the southern end was spared by the iconoclasts, but was nearly destroyed by a stone from the roof which knocked a deep hole into the pavement where the fowl is represented (see Pls. 103,1 & 107,2); the bird is probably a guinea-fowl; we may assume that the one at the northern end was of the same species. The second tree from each end was faced by gazelles, which were deliberately mutilated; but their outlines and parts of their bodies can easily be made out (see Pls. 103,1; 106,1 & 2; 107,1); in the Theotokos chapel a representation of a gazelle has survived (see Pl. 109,1). Nothing remains of the two animals — probably birds — which flanked the central tree (Pl. 103,1).

A similar arrangement of plants and animals will be found in the panel west of the altar in the Theotokos chapel; as the altar influenced the choice of the objects represented there, so, we think, the font influenced the choice of the objects represented here. Such representations caused Kjaer at Seilûn [7] and De Vaux at Mâ'in [8] to think that certain rooms at those places served as baptisteries in spite of the fact that no fonts were found in them. If then we

[1] *RB* 47 (1938), p. 235, Fig. 2 and Pls. XI-XVI; on p. 240 he expressly notes that the foliage on all the trees is identical, but the fruits are different; he distinguishes three species: apricots, quinces and pomegranates.

[2] See *Gerasa*, p. 304; in the sixth-century churches of St. Stephen and St. Sergius he saw among the decorations "pears and pomegranate and bright fruited apple trees." See also R. H. Hamilton, *QS* 1930, pp. 178-191.

[3] See *RB* 43 (1934), Pls. XXIV, 1; XXV, 2.

[4] See *Nea Sion*, 1906, Eik. XXVI; *RB* 47 (1938), Pl. XI, 2; ibid. 1897, p. 652.

[5] See *Gerasa*, Pls. LXVIII, a & b; LXXV, a.

[6] See *JPOS* 10 (1930), pp. 139-145 and Fig. 30.

[7] See *JPOS* 10 (1930), pp. 139-145.

[8] See *RB* 47 (1938), pp. 232-4.

actually find such a scene placed directly in front of a font a close connection between the two is obvious and should be stressed.[1]

2. *The nave* (Fig. 27; Pl. 103,2; see Pls. 47,1; 48,2) is decorated with one large panel almost completely preserved; the mosaic pavement extends into the doorway, where a narrow strip next to the threshold is paved with marble.

a. *The surround* is divided into two strips by an uninterrupted series of round and elliptical figures alternating with one another; florets decorate both strips; those in the outer one are half way between the wall and the belt of circles and ellipses; those in the inner one are arranged in a series around the border (see Pl. 108,1).

In the doorway there is a Greek inscription; see inscription III.

b. *The border* (Pl. 108,1) consists of a band which is decorated with white leaves alternating with squares and circles; crosslets fill in all the interstices. The stem of each leaf rests on the corner of a square and its trifid blade points towards a circle; the stipules are very small. Such a leaf-border was used also in the apse of the Theotokos chapel (see Pl. 109,1); in Fig. 29 it is rendered in colors, which bring out all the details more clearly. The differences in the two borders consist in such minor details as the stipules and the space-fillers. In the Theotokos chapel the stipules are relatively large and the space-fillers consist of single white cubes; in the baptistery, where the stipules are very small, the space-fillers are larger and consist of 5 cubes having a quincuncial arrangement. The same kind of border occurs at Mekhayyat,[2] Mâᶜin[3] and Jerash[4] in Transjordan; the writer knows of no examples from Palestine.

c. *The field* (Pls. 47,1; 48,2; 103,2; 108,1 & 2) is decorated with rectangular figures and florets. Around the sides of the field near the border are 64 oblong figures; in the four corners there are squares; in the rest of the field 64 large squares and 81 small ones are united to one another and to the figures around the sides by florets, which in turn form triangular compartments next to the borders and 6-sided figures in the rest of the field. Only the larger squares are filled in with other designs; each one contains a smaller square with a quincunx. The general division of the field resembles that of the panel at the northern end of the narthex.

The tesserae used in this chapel are generally a little over a centimeter square; at least six colors occur; white, black, red, yellow, orange and blue (see Fig. 28). This pavement was finished in the year 597 A. D.

1 See *HCA* pp. 283 ff. for the symbolism of animals in early Christian art and pp. 292 ff. for the symbolism of plants. — Plants are symbols of Paradise; Adam and Eve forfeited their right to the earthly Paradise by eating of the forbidden fruit; the trees laden with beautiful fruits serve to remind us of that; the right to the heavenly Paradise was restored through the waters of baptism; the font at which baptism was administered reminds us of this.

2 See *RB* 43 (1934), Pls. XXIV, 2; XXVII, 1. Very similar to the one in the baptistery.

3 See *RB* 47 (1938), Pls. XII; XVI, 2. The stipules and space-fillers are not used.

4 See *Gerasa*, Pl. LXXXIV, b. Here, as at Mâᶜin, the stipules and space-fillers are wanting.

Fig. 29. Details of the mosaic borders of the Theotokos chapel.

E. THE MOSAIC PAVEMENT OF THE THEOTOKOS CHAPEL

1. *The chancel* comprises the apse and the space in front of the same up to the base of the chancel screen (Fig. 27; Pl. 109,1).

a. *The apse* (Pl. 109,1) is decorated with a semicircular panel which is well preserved, though it received a few dents from stones when the roof collapsed. In the surround there is a series of indented squares connected with one another by a serrated line. The border (Pls. 109,1; 111,1; Fig. 29, above) is divided into strips, of which two are relatively wide; that near the exterior is a black and yellow fret; that near the interior is a broad red band decorated with white leaves alternating with white, black and yellow squares and circles. The fret occurs again in the nave, west of the first large panel from the east (see Pl. 110,1, below); the so-called leaf-border occurred in the nave of the baptistery; there a few differences between the two were noted and other examples were indicated. The field is decorated with a diaper pattern of florets. See p. 225, 3, b, for other examples.

b. *The space between the apse and the base of the chancel screen* (Pl. 109,1) is decorated with a large rectangular panel. Between the mosaic pavement and the stone base of the screen there is a narrow strip of marble. In the surround on the north there are florets; probably also on the south beneath the stone bench. The panel has a cable border which is quite common both in Transjordan and in Palestine. The field is decorated with four animals, two plants and a building; above the animals flanking the building there is a Greek inscription.

The animals were the objects of iconoclastic attention; the pair next to the building was almost completely destroyed and the pavement was repaired with mortar; the animal at the northern end was spared; what the iconoclasts did with the one at the southern end we do not know; that part of the mosaic was ruined by falling stones. All the animals face the center, as in the large panel in front of the font in the baptistery. There the trees are the principal feature and the animals occupy subordinate positions; here, however, the animals are more important than the plants.

The animal at the northern end of the panel is a gazelle; it has a bell attached to its neck by means of a ribbon, which suggests that it was domesticated. It is very probable that a gazelle was represented also at the southern end of the panel. The fact that the gazelle was spared seems to indicate that it touched a soft spot in the heart of the iconoclast. These graceful creatures are at home in Transjordan where they are still quite numerous; they were quite frequently represented on mosaic pavements; we already noted those which were represented in the baptistery; they are also found on the mosaic pavements of Mekhayyat,[1] Madaba,[2] Jerash[3] and several places of Palestine.[4]

The animals which flank the building are bulls; they were both deliberately destroyed, but their outlines and parts of their bodies remain; their tails and feet were treated in the same way; the one on the right has short horns, such as we found in the western monastery, and in its nose there is a ring. The inscription above these two animals proves that the artist intended to represent bulls (see inscription IV); the same representations and the same inscriptions occur at Mekhayyat[5] and Mâ^{c}in;[6] bulls are represented also without this inscription at Mekhayyat,[7] Mâ^{c}in,[8] Madaba,[9] Jerash[10] and in a number of places in Palestine.[11]

The bulls represented at Siyâgha and Mekhayyat (and very probably at Mâ^{c}in, but now destroyed) face altars with blazing fires; the artist leaves no doubt regarding his inten-

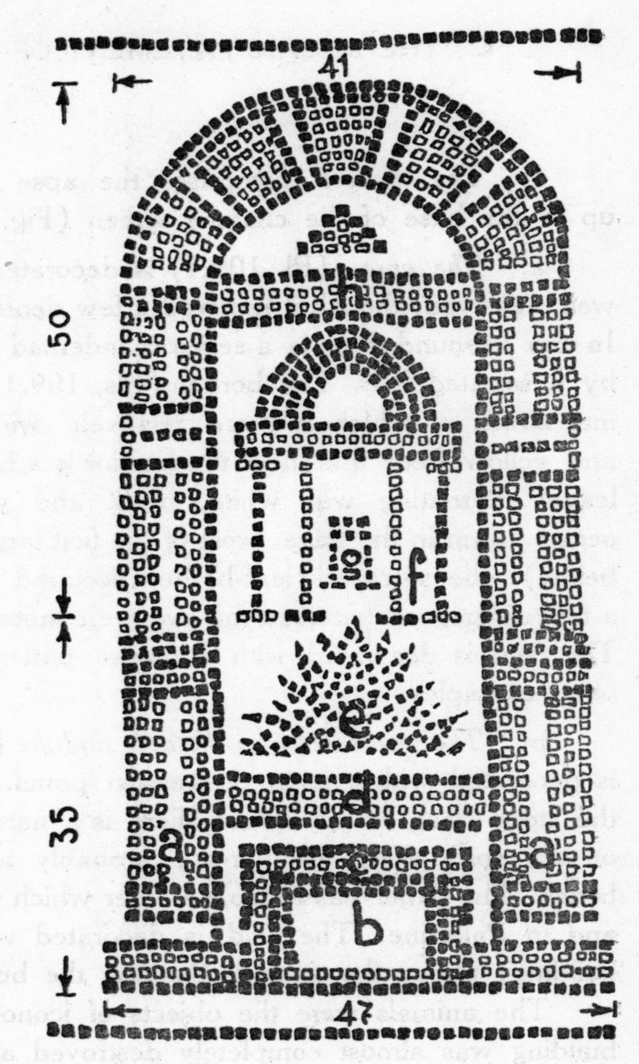

Fig. 30. The temple of Yahweh at Mount Nebo.

1 Not yet published.
2 See *Nea Sion*, 1905, Eik. XVIII.
3 See *Gerasa*, Pls. LXIII; LXXII, d; LXXIII.
4 See *QDAP* 3 (1934), p. 65, no. 10, where Avi-Yonah refers to 5 examples.
5 See *RB* 43 (1934), Pl. XXV, 2; p. 397.
6 See *RB* 47 (1938), p. 230 (*Ps.* 50 [51], 21); Pl. X, above.
7 In the church of St. George; not yet published.
8 See *RB* 47 (1938), Pl. XI, 1; pp. 233 f.; this representation is accompanied by a text from *Is.* 11, 7; the symbolism implied is discussed by De Vaux, l. c.
9 See *RB* 1892, p. 636; *RB* 47 (1938), pp. 233 f. & Pl. XI, 2; *Nea Sion*, 1906, Eik. XXVI; in the house of Joseph Saleh Alamat two large bulls are represented eating from a tree.
10 See *Gerasa*, Pl. LXXIII.
11 See *QDAP* 3 (1934), p. 65, no. 10, where Avi-Yonah indicates 4 places.

tions; by means of an inscription, taken from *Ps.* 50 (51), 21, he makes it clear that he intended to represent victims destined to be offered on an altar as a sacrifice.

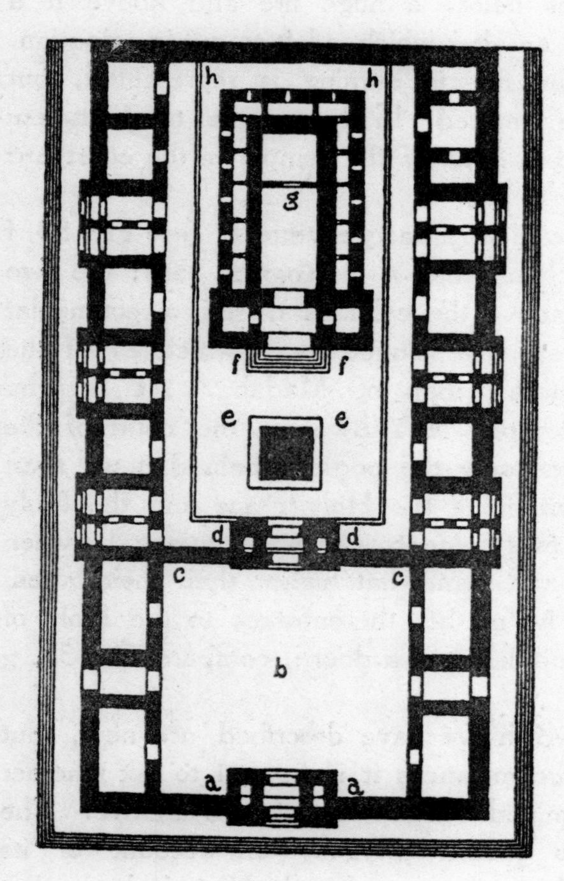

Fig. 31.
The temple of Yahweh in Jerusalem.

The two plants represented in this panel were probably mere spacers, which served to divide the panel into sections and to separate the animals from one another.

The so-called building in the center of the group is really a large complex consisting of an enclosure, courtyards, an altar and a temple. The details may be studied by referring to Pl. 109, to the colored frontispiece and to Figs. 30 and 31; the latter figure is a ground plan of the temple of Yahweh in Jerusalem, taken from Kortleitner's textbook of archæology; the juxtaposition of the two figures brings out at a glance that the artist who planned the design for the pavement at Siyâgha intended to represent the well-known temple of Yahweh, which existed in Jerusalem up to the year 70 A. D. Inside a rounded arch one sees two courtyards; the inner one contains the altar and the temple.

The rounded arch is 85 cm. high and 41 cm. wide; it rests on a rectangular base which adds 6 cm. to the total width (= 47 cm.) (Fig. 30, a). On the mosaic map of Madaba[1] and in the churches of St. John the Baptist and SS. Peter and Paul at Jerash[2] the gates of walled cities are quite generally represented with rounded arches. Here the gateway corresponds to the large gate leading into the court of the women in the temple in Jerusalem (see Fig. 31, a); we must imagine the walls enclosing the court.

Looking through the large gateway one sees first of all a small court enclosed by walls (Fig. 30, b); this corresponds to the court of the women in the temple of Jerusalem (Fig. 31, b).

[1] See Palmer and Guthe, *Die Mosaikkarte von Madeba*, I. Tafeln, Leipzig, 1906, especially Taf. III, VII ff.
[2] See *Gerasa*, Pls. LXVII, b & c; LXVIII, a & b; LXIX, a; LXXV, a; LXXXVI — XCIII, passim.

Above and beyond the small court one sees a much larger one, whose limits are marked by the horizontal strips "d" and "h" in Fig. 30; the entrance to this court is left to our imagination. It corresponds to the court of the priests in the temple of Jerusalem (see Fig. 31, d-h).

In the court of the priests one sees below a huge fire and above it a temple. The fire (see Fig. 30, e) suggests an altar which is left to our imagination. At Mekhayyat[1] the altar on which the fire is burning is represented, but the gateway, courtyards and temple are omitted. In the temple of Jerusalem the great altar for bloody sacrifices stood in front of the temple in the courtyard of the priests (see Fig. 31, e).

Above and behind the altar there is a tetrastyle temple (see Fig. 30, f and frontispiece). Each of the four columns has a rectangular base; the two end columns have rectangular capitals; above the columns there is a rectangular architrave or entablature and above it there is a vaulted roof. Structures of the same form are represented on the mosaic map of Madaba.[2] At Siyâgha the tetrastyle building represents the temple of Yahweh in the court of the priests (see Fig. 31, f).[3] Actually we see only the portico; behind it we must imagine the main part of the building containing the Holy Place and the Holy of Holies. But the artist did not leave everything to our imagination; between the two central columns of the portico and somewhat higher than their bases, in order to indicate a place further back, he marked the entrance to the Holy of Holies by means of the bases, jambs and lintel of a door; compare Fig. 30, g with Fig. 31, g.

Practically none of the elements which we have described are new, but their combination is new;[4] under the circumstances it is natural to ask whether there is any special reason which determined the choice of this motive. The writer is convinced that the scene was chosen primarily on account of its typical relation to the altar before which it was placed. Historical reasons, such as the altars and sacrifices of Balaam or the temple of Yahweh at Nebo destroyed by Mesa, may have influenced this choice in some way.

It is indeed a remarkable coincidence that sacrificial scenes should have been represented on the mosaic pavements of churches in the very section of the country where Balaam offered his sacrifices and nowhere else in those regions, so far as we know. The coincidence becomes even more remarkable when we consider that Balaam offered sacrifices at three places, and such rep-

1 See *RB* 43 (1934), Pl. XXV.

2 See Palmer and Guthe, *Die Mosaikkarte von Madeba*, Taf. VI & VIII.

3 See Helen Rosenau, *Some aspects of the pictorial influence of the Jewish temple*, in *QS* 1936, pp. 157-162 and Pls. IV-IX.

4 De Vaux, *RB* 47 (1938), p. 242, gives a summary of the mosaic representations of buildings discovered in these regions up to date; they are especially numerous in Transjordan where the influence of Antioch, Syria, was strong. They show a strong tendency to represent historic monuments.

resentations were found only in three places.[1] Most remarkable of all is the fact that the scenes have been found at such places as have come into consideration when there was question of identifying the sites at which Balaam offered sacrifice. Experience has proven that Byzantine artists were familiar with the Bible and were influenced by it in the choice of their motifs; hence, when we find sacrificial scenes at Mâᶜin, Mekhayyat and Siyâgha, it is not at all improbable that the artists wished to perpetuate interesting historic events intimately associated with those sites or at least with their immediate surroundings.

In the story of Balaam only altars are mentioned, hence we need not be surprised if, for example, at Mekhayyat only an altar was represented — regarding Mâᶜin we cannot speak with certainty, since too little remains there. The only place in that entire region in which Yahweh had a temple was at Nebo; this we know from the famous stela of Mesa.[2] It is not certain whether the temple was in the town of Nebo or on Mount Nebo outside and at some distance from the town. Some scholars have suspected that the temple of Yahweh destroyed by Mesa was outside the town on Mount Nebo and they think that the Christian church on Mount Nebo served merely to perpetuate the ancient sanctity of the place.[3] At any rate, it is very remarkable that at the only place in the region where Yahweh is supposed to have had a temple, a representation of a temple with its sacrifices should be found. Under the circumstances it does seem highly probable that the artist knew that fact and on that account decided to represent a temple in the mosaic pavement at Siyâgha. There is no reason why the inhabitants of the region should not have been familiar with the stela of Mesa and its contents. It was found near the surface at Dhibân and may have been standing yet at the time when the mosaic pavement was executed at Siyâgha. The language of the stela was also familiar to those people, who spoke a dialect similar to it.

From the famous mosaic map at Madaba[4] and from the representations of churches found recently in a church at Mâᶜin,[5] we know that the artists of the region loved to represent places and monuments of historic interest. Owing to this general tendency it seems highly probable that historic monuments are also commemorated by the altar and temple represented on Mount Nebo. Be that as it may, the writer is convinced that, if the artist had in mind the altars and sacrifices of Balaam and the temple of Yahweh at Nebo, he did not represent

[1] The places are mentioned in *Num.* 22,41; 23,14; 23,28. See the commentaries on those texts for identifications which have been proposed; already on pp. 205 f. we pointed out that a Byzantine tradition fixed the scene of the second sacrifice near Siyâgha.

[2] See G. A. Cooke, *A Text-book of North-Semitic Inscriptions*, Oxford, 1903, pp. 1-14; lines 14-18 refer to Nebo; G. A. Barton, *Archæology and the Bible*, 6th edition, Philadelphia, 1933, p. 460. Mesa took away from Nebo "the altar-hearths of Yahweh."

[3] See Alt, *PJB* 30 (1934), pp. 29 ff. — For Kittel's view see above p. 14, no. 8.

[4] See Palmer and Guthe, *Die Mosaikkarte von Madeba*, Tafeln I-X.

[5] See De Vaux, *RB* 47 (1938), pp. 240-255; Pls. XII-XVI.

them for their own sake, but on account of the connection which he saw between them and the altar and church of the New Dispensation. But even if we abstract from any association with those monuments, we find a sufficient reason for such a scene here. It is, namely, a well-known fact that the Early Fathers of the Church considered the temple in Jerusalem with its sacrifices and ritual as symbols and types of the Christian place of worship with its altar and sacrifice. This then would explain adequately why the artist represented the temple of Yahweh in front of the altar in the Theotokos chapel.

The clew to the correct understanding and interpretation of this whole scene was given by the text placed above it by the artist. The words are taken from *Ps.* 50 (51), 21 (see inscription IV); they mention an altar and the victims to be placed on the altar. According to the Fathers those words in their literal sense refer to the sacrifices in the temple in Jerusalem, but in a typical sense they refer to the sacrifice of the New Law. The position of this scene in front of the altar of the chapel indicates that the artist was conscious of this typical meaning. This scene with its inscription prompted us to look for a deeper meaning in the principal representations found in the other chancels at Siyâgha and in each case we have endeavored to indicate what that meaning is. That we were justified in doing so was confirmed by a very interesting discovery made recently at Mâᶜin. There the words of *Is.* 11,7: "And the lion as the ox shall eat straw," above a representation of these two animals, indicate that the scene was intended as a symbol of peace and as a type of the conditions that will prevail in the Messianic kingdom when the souls of men have been regenerated through grace. See De Vaux, *RB* 47 (1938), pp. 233 f.

2. *The nave* of the Theotokos chapel was originally completely paved with mosaics, but some were destroyed and the pavement was repaired with mortar or fragments of marble (Fig. 27; Pl. 109,2).

a. *The surround* is decorated with a series of square and elliptical figures alternating with one another and united by a serrated line (see Pls. 109, 1 & 2; 110,1; 111,2).

b. *The border* (Figs. 27 & 29; Pls. 109,2 ; 110,1 ; 111,2) consists of a broad black band decorated with a plastic ribbon whose folds are shaded white, light blue (overlooked in the colored reproduction in Fig. 29), yellow and orange; between the folds there are pellets and plant motifs ; the latter consist either of three lanceolate leaves, or of two such leaves and a flower ; the edges are formed by narrow white, red and black stripes. Parallels were found at Madaba,[1] Jerash[2] and Beisan.[3]

1 See *RB* 1897, p. 652; *Nea Sion*, 1905, Eik. XIV: in the crypt of St. Elias finished in 595-6 A. D.

2 See *Gerasa*, Pls. LXVIII, b ; LXIX, a & b; LXX, c : in the church of St. John the Baptist finished in 531 A. D.

3 See *QDAP* 5 (1936), Pls. XIII, XV, XVI.

c. *The field* is divided into 4 panels. The narrow one on the east contains a long Greek inscription from which we learn that this chapel was paved during the first decennary of the 7th century of our era (see inscription V).

The second panel from the east (Pl. 110,1) has a rectilinear border on the north, east and south; on the west it has a fret similar to the one used for the outer strip of the border in the apse (see Fig. 29, above). The field is divided into squares by diagonal rows of florets intersecting one another; each square contains a flowered cross. Regarding this method of dividing and decorating the field see the observations made on pp. 220 f. in speaking of the panel at the western end of the northern aisle of the basilica. If the flowered crosses (Pl. 111,4) are compared with those in the north hall (Pl.97,3) it will appear that there are slight differences in the color of the core and the form of the margin of each lobe.

The third panel from the east (Pls. 109,2; 110,2) was almost completely destroyed and then repaired with plaster; but, as usual, here and there a fragment of the original pavement escaped the hands of the iconoclasts and from these we learn that the panel was decorated with a hunting scene. On the left there is a bowman on foot; in the center a mounted spearman; on the right we must imagine that being which is attacked; in the rest of the landscape there are trees. Of the bowman only the left hand holding the bow and arrow still remains. Of the rearing horse one can see the hoofs of his hind legs and the greater part of his forefeet; of the horseman only the outline of an arm or a cloak has survived; of the spear which he held the two ends were spared; the pointed end of the spear, between the forefeet of the horse, is directed towards the object — probably some wild animal — which is being attacked, but of this nothing at all remains, or at least nothing can be made out. Of the trees which seem to have filled in the ends of the panel only a few branches and leaves still exist; they resemble those represented in the baptistery in front of the font.

Human beings were represented only in this panel at Siyâgha; there were two and both were so thoroughly destroyed that only the fingers of one hand of the bowman remain. In the neighboring town of Mekhayyat representations of human beings were very common in all the churches and none of them were mutilated in any way;[1] among them there are also hunters on foot[2] and on

[1] At least 34 such representations are known to us: 17 in St. George's, 12 in SS. Procopius and Lot and 5 in the church of the priest John; the people represented are engaged in many different ways, especially in vineyards; some are engaged in fishing, others in hunting, etc. See *RB* 43 (1934), Pl. XXIV, 2; *RAC* 13 (1936), p. 134, Figs. 21 & 22; p. 137, Fig. 25; *QDAP* 6 (1937), p. 218.

[2] See *RB* 43 (1934), Pl. XXIV, 2.

horseback.[1] Also at Madaba,[2] Jerash[3] and in a number of places in Palestine[4] persons were quite frequently represented; the hunting scenes depicted in a mosaic pavement[5] and in a tomb[6] at Beit Jibrîn may serve to illustrate our scene.[7]

The fourth panel at the western end of the field (Pl. 109,2, foreground) was badly disfigured by the iconoclasts who destroyed some of the representations and repaired the damage haphazardly with broken fragments of marble.

The border of the panel is a fret formed of rainbow bands. The fret resembles the one used for the panel at the southern end of the narthex and for the large panel in front of the font in the baptistery, but there are a number of differences. In the last two cases the fret is formed of narrow fillets (see Pls. 96,2; 106,2), which are much more simple than the broad rainbow band used here; there the swastika-shaped fretwork is continuous, here it alternates with square openwork (see Pl. 111, 3 & 5). There were originally 24 such sections in the border: 12 of the swastika type and 12 of the other; the latter contained a variety of ornaments; most of these seem to have been birds or possibly other animals; they were excised by the iconoclasts, though here and there the outline of a bird can still be made out. The three surviving compartments contain fruits; the one in the northeastern corner (Pl. 111,5), 4 pears or a similar fruit; the one in the southwestern corner, pomegranates (Pl. 111,8) which look like the one represented in the chancel of the north hall (see Pl. 101,1); the one in the center of the western border, a cluster of grapes (see Pl. 109,2); other compartments, for example, those in the other two corners, may have contained fruits. For this type of fret see the references given on p. 225, note 1.

The same kind of a fret-border served to divide the panel into two parts; the ornament in the square compartment in its center has disappeared. Each of the resulting parts (see Pl. 109,2) is subdivided into 9 smaller compartments by a large circle and 4 half-circles; the former is in the center, the latter along the 4 sides; they are linked to one another and the border;[8] the same type of

1 See *RAC* 13 (1936), p. 137, Fig. 25. — Avi-Yonah, *QDAP* 3 (1934), p. 64, observes that "the nobility of the Roman and Byzantine empires is represented by the hunter galloping on his steed..."

2 See *Nea Sion*, 1904, Eik. VIII; ibid. 1905, Eik. XVIII; ibid. 1906, Eik. XXV & XXVI. Regarding the bust in the last picture referred to, see also De Vaux in *RB* 47 (1938), p. 234.

3 See *Gerasa*, pp. 299 f.

4 See *QDAP* 3 (1934), pp. 63 f., nos. 7-9.

5 See *RB* 31 (1922), p. 267, Fig. 2 & Pl. X, 4.

6 See J. P. Peters and H. Thiersch, *Painted Tombs in the Necropolis of Marissa*, London, 1905, pp. 23 f. and Pl. VI. Here the horseman is followed by a man blowing a long straight trumpet (2nd century B. C.).

7 Biebel, *Gerasa*, p. 304, makes some interesting observations which deserve to be recalled in this connection; he writes as follows: "Any discussion of the subject-matter of East Christian art must take into account the combination of religious and non-religious elements which existed during this period. St. Nilus protested against this practice at the beginning of the fifth century when he wrote to Olympiodorus the Eparch begging him to abandon his plan of decorating his church with "the hunting of all kinds of animals... and the eager hunters spiritedly pursuing them..""

8 A similar division of the field was used for the mosaic pavement existing in the hall of the Russian museum, Jerusalem; see Vincent-Abel, *Jér. nouv.* II, Pl. XLIII, 1.

rainbow band which was used for the border was used also here. All the small compartments were filled in with other designs; 5 of the 9 compartments in each section still contain ornaments; again the birds (and possibly other animals) were deliberately chiseled away; only the plants, leaves and fruits remain.

The plants and leaves fill in the 8 half-circles; there are 4 plants and 4 leaves; the former serve as space-fillers for the northern and southern semicircles, the latter for the eastern and western ones. For plants and leaves as space-fillers see pp. 226 & 228.

The fruits are preserved in the northwestern and southwestern corners of the field; that in the northwestern corner (Pls. 109,2; 111,6) looks like a melon, from which a few slices have been cut out; near it is a knife with a straight blade tapering towards its point; that in the southwestern corner (Pls. 109,2; 111,7) may be a cluster of grapes; near it is a knife with a curved blade. This is the only panel of the mosaic pavements at Siyâgha in which representations of knives occur; these knives should be compared with the two represented on a marble slab (see Pl. 121,1), where both have curved blades and ribbed handles terminating in circular or triangular knobs, and also with the iron knives which were actually found at Siyâgha (see Pls. 136, Fig. 2,105-112, 114-117, 122; 138, Fig. 2,27). Representations of knives and sickles have been found at Mekhayyat,[1] Jerash,[2] Beit Jibrîn,[3] Beisan,[4] etc.

The cubes used for the mosaic pavement of this chapel have the same size as those in the baptistery; that is, their surface is on an average somewhat over a centimeter square. The colors used are: white, black, several shades of red, yellow, blue, gray, pink, orange and brown; in other words, more colors were used here than in any other original pavement at Siyâgha. It is also the only place in which the field of the nave was divided into a number of larger panels, each with its own peculiar decoration. A tendency to use more colors and a greater variety of ornaments seems to be asserting itself in the last floor to be paved with mosaics at Siyâgha in the beginning of the 7th century A. D.

F. THE MOSAIC PAVEMENT OF ROOMS 16, 17 & 91

Rooms 16 and 17 (see Pl. 161) conserve traces of a decorated mosaic pavement which was planned and executed when they formed one room; the wall which now separates the two stands on the mosaic pavement. Most of the pavement has been worn out, especially between the doors and in the

[1] In the church of St. George a vintager and a reaper hold such blades; see *TSI* 15 (1935), pp. 259 & 261.
[2] See *Gerasa*, Pl. LXXXV, a: a sickle.
[3] See *RB* 32 (1922), Pl. X, 1.
[4] See *QDAP* 5 (1936), p. 21 and Pl. XVII, 4; *Beth-Shan* IV, Pls. XVI & XVII, 1.

center, but 10 pieces still exist, 7 in room 16 and 3 in room 17, and from these we must judge the original appearance of the floor. The tesserae are not all of the same size; the majority average somewhat over a centimeter square, but others are about 2 centimeters square, and a few even larger; the patches in which the larger tesserae occur are not decorated; they probably represent later repairs. For the decorated patches white, black, red, yellow, gray and pink tesserae were used; of the ornaments very few are preserved.

a. *The surround* is represented better than any other part of the pavement; to judge from a rather large fragment in the southwestern corner of room 16, it was decorated quite elaborately. This fragment measures 160 × 85 cm. and continues beneath the western wall into room 17. The surviving ornaments consist of a panel and some florets (Pl. 112,3). The rectangular panel measures 102 × 63 cm.; its frame, consisting of a narrow fillet, encloses a field decorated with leaves and a diamond containing fretwork which in turn surrounds a small diamond in the center. Fretwork as a space-filler is quite common at Jerash.[1] Leaves, consisting of a heart-shaped blade, a stem and a stipule, filled the 4 corners of the panel, where they served as space-fillers, as in the north hall, Theotokos chapel, etc.; one has been destroyed. Florets can be seen to the east and west of the panel; those on the west are partially covered by the wall dividing room 16 and 17; other florets were observed near the southern wall of room 17. Florets were a favorite decoration of the surrounds at Siyâgha; they are found in front of the responds in the basilica, in the narthex, in the chancel and nave of the north hall and the baptistery, in the chancel of the Theotokos chapel and in room 91. Very probably such ornaments were also in the other three parts of the surround; but this fact is now obscured by later repairs (see Pl. 112,2 & 4) or by the complete disappearance of certain sections of the surround. West of the doorways along the southern and northern walls the surround averaged about 80 cm. in width; east of the doorways along the northern wall the surround seems to have been in the neighborhood of 126 cm. in width and along the eastern wall 98 cm.; this indicates a difference in the eastern and western sections of the pavement, which will be noticed also in the case of the borders and the field.

b. *The border* consists of a narrow band between the surround and the field. Small sections of it have been discovered on the eastern, southern, northwestern and northern sides of the pavement. The section of the border on the east can be recognized by the position of its tesserae (see Pl. 112,1, above); here they form rows parallel to the wall, whereas in the surround and field they form diagonal rows. On the south the band consists of parallel stripes of black, white, red and yellow tesserae (see Pl. 112,3, below). This multi-colored band is exactly like the one on the northern side of the field (see Pl. 112, 2),

1 See *Gerasa*, Pls. LXVI, a, top, right; LXXVIII; LXXX, A; LXXXI, c; LXXXII, a; LXXXIV, a.

but differs from the one-colored band observed on the eastern side of the pavement. In the northwestern part of the pavement a tiny part of the border forming a corner was executed with medium-sized one-colored tesserae (see Pl. 112,4); it is probably part of a later repair. Along the northern side of the pavement, near the southeastern corner of the table in room 16, there are two patches with the traces of a border (Pl. 112,2); the patch on the east has a border exactly like the one on the south; since the one on the south continued westwards into room 17, we may presume that the one on the north did likewise; but here, a little further west and apparently on a somewhat higher level (see Pl. 112,2), there is a tiny piece of a design, consisting of a mixture of white, black, red, yellow, gray and pink tesserae, which at first sight looks like the corner of a border, but it is very probably a part of a later patch represented by very large tesserae to the north and west of it. The surviving fragments of the border seem to point to two panels or possibly two fields and to later repairs; the one seems to have existed east of the passage between the doors in room 16 and the other west of it; this latter was repaired at least once; the same was suggested by the surround and seems to follow from a study of the field.

c. *The field* seems to have been divided into at least two panels or possibly there were two fields. The one east of the passage between the two doors in room 16 was decorated with florets (see Pl. 112,1), like the panels at the southern end of the narthex and elsewhere (see p. 225). The other panel west of the passage seems to have occupied the rest of the field; this we deduce from three tiny fragments of the same which still exist: the one near the southern border in room 16 (Pl. 112,3, right foreground), the other near the northwestern part of room 17 (Pl. 112,4, left foreground), the third near the northern border of room 16 (Pl. 112,2, right). This last mentioned fragment is the largest of the three; the surviving part of a design reminds one of the flutings of the shell motif used to fill a semicircle in the nave of the basilica (see Pl. 89,3 and compare with Pl. 88,2); it should, however, be noted that the position of this design in relation to the border is somewhat different here than in the basilica. The tesserae used here are also larger than those used for the upper pavement in the basilica, but smaller than those used for the lower pavement; they are on an average about 1½ cm. square; white, black, gray, red and yellow cubes were used.

In the middle of room 17, on a lower level than the pavement which we have described, there is a narrow strip of pavement consisting of a mixture of cubes and pebbles colored white, black, red, yellow and pink. Such colored pebbles were not observed elsewhere at Siyâgha; they may be mere chips of the slabs from which the cubes were derived, nevertheless they serve to recall the oldest mosaic pavements known to exist; those were made entirely of pebbles.[1]

[1] See F. v. Lorentz, *RE* 16, cols. 328 ff.; V. Müller, *The Origin of Mosaic*, *JAOS* 59 (1939), pp. 247-250.

In these regions no pebble mosaics have been found; here mosaic pavements are supposed to have been introduced during the Roman period,[1] when rectangular or square cubes were the fashion.

The division of the pavement into two distinct panels, or possibly into two distinct fields, reminds one of the division of the pavements in the basilica and the chapels; here as there the smaller panel or field is on the east, the larger on the west. The similarity of arrangement suggests similarity of purpose; that is, the hall may have served as a chapel before it was converted into a refectory and kitchen.

2. *Room 91* (Fig. 27; Pl. 113,1 & 2) measures 7.40 × 2.02 m.; its decorated mosaic pavement suffered harm on the southern side of the room, otherwise it is in an excellent state.

a. *The surround* is 29-37 cm. wide; in the wider strip next to the basilica on the north it is decorated with florets.

b. *The border* is 35 cm. wide; between narrow stripes along the edges there is a broad black band decorated with a wavy ribbon shaded white, gray, black, red and pink; the curves are filled in with white leaves having a heart-shaped blade, a stem and a stipule. The ribbon is not quite as elaborate as the one used in the Theotokos chapel; this type occurs at Mâʿin,[2] Beisan[3] and several other places in Palestine.[4]

c. *The field* is divided into squares by intersecting diagonal rows of florets; each square contains a flowered cross. Regarding this method of dividing and decorating the field see pp. 220 f.[5]

The tesserae used for this pavement have the same size as those used for the chapels; the colors are: white, black, red, yellow, gray and pink.

At Beisan a small sixth-century monastery was found in which not only the chapel, but also the courtyard and a number of rooms around the courtyard and south of the chapel were paved with figured mosaics.[6]

* * *

In describing the multi-colored or decorated mosaics discovered at Siyâgha we have endeavored to indicate their relation to other known mosaics of Trans-

1 See Avi-Yonah, *QDAP* 3 (1934), pp. 71 f., nos. 21 & 22; Watzinger, *DP* 2 (1935), pp. 149 ff.
2 See *RB* 47 (1938), p. 236, Fig. 3.
3 See *QDAP* 5 (1936), Pl. XV; here also leaves are used as space-fillers.
4 See *QDAP* 3 (1934), p. 58, *B1*: 3 examples. — It is also very common in the mosaic pavements at Antioch, Syria; see *Antioch* I & II, passim.
5 See also *Beth-Shan* IV, Pl. XIII.
6 See *Beth-Shan* IV, Pls. VI-XXII; a number of the ornaments are very similar to those used at Siyâgha.

jordan[1] and Palestine;[2] this relationship extends also to mosaics in more distant regions;[3] not a single decorative element has been found at Siyâgha which cannot be duplicated elsewhere, but one or the other combination of those elements seems to be peculiar to Siyâgha; this seems to be true especially of the representation of the temple of Yahweh before the altar of the Theotokos chapel; for this reason it is reproduced in colors in the frontispiece of this volume.

[1] In Transjordan there are still very many mosaic pavements which have not yet been cleared and studied. We ourselves have seen cubes at many sites (see, v. g., pp. 8 & 9); so also Conder, *SEP*, passim; Glueck, *Explorations in Eastern Palestine*, *AASOR* 14,15, 18-19, passim; and others. — R. Horning, *Verzeichnis von Mosaiken aus Mesopotamien, Syrien, Palästina und dem Sinai*, *ZDPV* 32 (1909), pp. 113-150, indicates the literature dealing with the mosaics known up to his time in Transjordan on pp. 134 ff. To that list, which only mentions: el-Hosn, Khirbet Safût, es-Salt, el-Yadûde and Madaba, add:

(1) Madaba and its surroundings, namely, Mekhayyat and el-Yadûde: H. Leclercq, *DAC* X, 1, cols. 878 ff.; — Savignac, *RB* 20 (1911), pp. 437 ff.; — Abel, *RB* 43 (1934), pp. 260-262.

(2) El-Yadûde: Savignac, *RB* 12 (1903), pp. 434 ff.; Alt, *ZDPV* 55 (1932), pp. 132 ff.

(3) Mekhayyat: Lemaire, *RB* 43 (1934), pp. 385-401; *TSF* 15 (1935), pp. 194-197; — Bagatti, *RAC* 13 (1936), pp. 129-141; *TSI* 15 (1935), pp. 257-263; — *QDAP* 6 (1937), pp. 217 f.

(4) Mâ'in: De Vaux, *RB* 47 (1938), pp. 227-258; — *QDAP* 8 (1938), pp. 161 f.

(5) Jerash: J. W. Crowfoot, *Churches at Jerash*, passim; F. M. Biebel, *Gerasa*, pp. 297-351; C. H. Kraeling, ibid. pp. 351 f.; Gauer, *JPOS* 18 (1938), pp. 233-253, passim.

(6) El-Quweisme, near 'Ammân. The church in that village was restored and paved with mosaics in 717-8 A.D. The inscription which informs us of this fact was copied by Ibrahim Effendi Abu Jaber, Inspector of the Department of Antiquities, and brought to the notice of the present writer who pointed out its significance in an article prepared for *JPOS* (not yet published); a summary of that article may be found in *TSS* 19 (1939), pp. 324 f. In 1939 Father Bagatti was able to pay a visit to the village; he ascertained that the mosaic is well preserved and now exists in the courtyard and several rooms of a modern building.

(7) Officials of the Department of Antiquities in 'Ammân and other individuals informed the writer of a number of other interesting pavements which have not yet been published. A record of them no doubt exists at the office of the Department of Antiquities.

[2] See Avi-Yonah, *Mosaic Pavements in Palestine*, *QDAP* 2 (1933), pp. 136-181; 3 (1934), pp. 26-73; etc., passim.

[3] See H. Leclercq, art. *Mosaique* in *DAC* XII, 1, cols. 57-332. — During the recent excavations at Antioch, Syria, hundreds of mosaic pavements were discovered; on a visit to the expedition's buildings on the 8th and 9th of February, 1937, the writer was able to ascertain for himself that those of the Byzantine period have many points in common with the mosaics discovered at Mount Nebo; see *Antioch* I & II, passim; for the *Catalogue of Mosaics* see ibid. II, pp. 180-204 and Pls. 23-80; in the church at Kaoussie, Antioch, Room 5 (= southern nave of the cruciform church [387 A. D.]), for example, the same type of decoration was used as for the nave of the basilica at Mount Nebo; see l. c. II, pp. 16 f.; Figs. 4 & 14; Pl. 49, no. 67; — for hunters, see *Antioch* I, Figs. 1, 2, 4-8; II, Pls. 28, 64-66; 71-73; — for trees, see l. c. II, Pls. 72 & 73, etc.

CHAPTER VIII

THE INSCRIPTIONS

A. GENERAL SURVEY

1. *Number, languages and materials*. About 40 inscriptions were found at Siyâgha: some 25 are Greek; 8 fragments have Samaritan characters; 5 objects have Kufic inscriptions and a few others have signs which may be inscriptions or masons' marks. Only 9 of the inscriptions were still in their original position; they exist in the mosaic pavements and on the baptismal font. The rest were found on objects scattered about the site. Those on large stones are probably not far from the place where they had been placed originally and are generally quite complete; but others which were on marble slabs, plaster, pottery and glass are in a fragmentary condition; scarcely ever has it been possible to recover all the pieces of these inscriptions and since the connection between the different pieces is missing the number of inscriptions is also somewhat doubtful and can be indicated only approximately.

2. *Order*. In the following list the inscription with an absolute date is placed first and all the other inscriptions are considered and ordered in relation to it, no matter whether they are earlier or later. The dated inscription is in the baptistery, so the inscriptions in the baptistery are treated first. The abbot mentioned in the inscriptions of the baptistery is mentioned also in one inscription of the Theotokos chapel; he serves to link up these two groups, so those in the Theotokos chapel are treated in the second place. The dated inscription in the baptistery refers also to the basilica, but the inscriptions in the basilica contain no reference to those in the baptistery, so they are treated in the third place. Next come the inscriptions on building stones, marble, plaster and pottery. All these are Greek inscriptions. The Samaritan inscriptions probably belong to an intermediate period and are listed here after the Greek inscriptions. The Kufic inscriptions are the most recent; they are treated last.

3. *Distribution and significance.* Of the 25 Greek inscriptions 3 are in the baptistery (I-III), 2 in the Theotokos chapel (IV-V), 4 (possibly 5) in the basilica (VI-IX), 6 on stones (X-XV), 5 on marble (XVI-XX), a few on plaster (XXI) and 4 on pottery lamps (XXII-XXV). The fragments of marble slabs with Samaritan inscriptions (XXVI-XXXIII) were recovered from various parts of the site, but the majority come from the eastern part of the southern monastery (see pp. 173 f.). The Kufic inscriptions on marble, pottery, plaster and glass (XXXIV-XXXVIII) were found east of the north hall, in the atrium and the southern monasteries.

These inscriptions throw light on a period in the history of the site regarding which other literary sources are silent; they indicate interesting relations with the town of Madaba, with the Samaritans and the early Arabs; since some are accurately dated they give us fixed points for the study of numerous other questions.

B. THE GREEK INSCRIPTIONS

I. Pl. 114,1 & 2. In two circles in the baptistery to the north and south of the baptismal font[1] (see Pl. 103,1); the circle on the north is 57, the one on the south 53 cm. in d.; the former was somewhat damaged near the upper left side where the inscription begins, the latter is complete.

Transcription: A: [×Σὺ]ν βοη×|[θείᾳ] τοῦ Κυ(ρίου) ἡμ|[ῶν Ἰ(ησο)ῦ] Χ(ριστο)ῦ ἐτελει|ώθη τὸ ἔργον τοῦ| ἁγίου ναοῦ σὺν | τῷ φωτιστη| +ρίῳ+|

B: × ἐπὶ τοῦ| ὁσιωτ(άτου) Σεργίου| ἐπισκ(όπου) καὶ Μαρτυ|ρίου θεοφιλ(εστάτου) πρεσ|β(υτέρου) καὶ ἡγουμέ(νου), ἐπὶ | τῆς ιε' ἰνδ(ικτιῶνος), ἔτους| υϙβ'. ×

Translation: A: With the help of our Lord Jesus Christ the construction of the holy church and the baptistery was finished,

B: under the most pious bishop Sergius and the most God-beloved priest and hegumen Martyrius in the 15th indiction of the year 492.

Observations: 1. "With the help of our Lord Jesus Christ." — The help of God is frequently invoked in ancient Christian inscriptions;[2] it was therefore only natural that the divine assistance should also be acknowledged when an undertaking had been finished successfully; this is actually done, not only here, but in a number of other inscriptions; so, for example, at Madaba in the churches of St. Elias[3] and the Theotokos;[4] at Beisan in the sixth-century monastery,[5] etc.

1 Regarding the form of inscriptions and their usual position, see *QDAP* 3 (1934), p. 71, no. 20.
2 See, v. g., Avi-Yonah, *QDAP* 3 (1934), pp. 68, no. 17; 97 & 99.
3 See *DAC* 10, 1, col. 873; in fact, here the entire work is ascribed to Christ: "Christ, God, erected this house" etc.
4 See *DAC* 10, 1, col. 864.
5 *Beth-Shan* IV, p. 16, VI, 1.

2. "The construction... was finished." — The inscriptions frequently distinguish between different kinds of work or different stages of the work; they speak of a building being erected, finished, restored, paved, decorated, etc. Here we are informed that certain buildings were finished; who began the work is not stated; neither is it stated what part of the buildings was finished; but since the inscription exists in the mosaic pavement it seems probable that it refers to the pavement.

3. "The holy church and the baptistery." — The inscription mentions the completion of two buildings: the one is called ὁ ἅγιος ναός, the other τὸ φωτιστήριον; the former is a common designation for a church,[1] the latter for a baptistery.[2] The church referred to is evidently the basilica adjoining the baptistery.

4. The bishop of the diocese at the time when the work in question was finished was called Sergius. His see was at Madaba, where he is mentioned in a number of churches; he is mentioned the first time in the church of the Apostles finished in 578-9 A. D.;[3] his name occurs for the last time in the upper church of St. Elias finished in 607-8 A. D.;[4] the lower church of St. Elias was finished during his episcopacy (595-6 A.D.) and the upper church was begun whilst he was still the incumbent of the see, but apparently he did not live to see its completion, for it was completed under his successor; in fact, he must have died before the year 603-4 A. D. when his successor is already mentioned.[5] As far as we know, the church and baptistery at Siyâgha were the last works completed during the episcopacy of Sergius.

In our inscription the epithet "most pious" is applied to Sergius; this does not necessarily express a personal quality; the title was due to him by virtue of his office. It expresses what a bishop should be and what the people have a right to expect of him. The same epithet is applied to the abbot in the next inscription, and to a priest who is an economos in el-Quweisme (not yet published).

The mention of Sergius indicates intimate relations between the monastery at Mount Nebo and the ecclesiastical authorities in Madaba. The energetic bishop, who did so much to provide worthy places of worship in the center of his diocese at Madaba, made his influence felt also in the chief sanctuary within the limits of his diocese; this influence is especially noticeable in the character of the mosaic pavements at both places. Thus, for example, the same scheme was used to decorate the nave of the basilica at Siyâgha as was used for the crypt of St. Elias at Madaba, as we pointed out on pp. 219 f. In the baptistery we find the same kind of trees in the large panel of the chancel as we see in the apse of St. Elias' crypt at Madaba; the beautiful ribbon border of the Theotokos chapel at Siyâgha is the same as that around the field in the crypt of St. Elias; the quatrefoils in the sanctuary of the north hall of Siyâgha have a close parallel in the quatrefoils of the upper church of St. Elias at Madaba; the comparison may be extended to the character and contents of the inscriptions. The work begun at both places by Sergius was completed by his successor Leontios.[6]

Once the intimate relation between Siyâgha and Madaba has been established, it is easy to discover numerous other bonds of unity between the two places; one is suggested

1 See *Gerasa*, p. 603, 1, for references; note especially inscriptions 309 & 331. — *ECS* p. 249: "The old Greek word for a Pagan temple, ναός, is apparently employed to designate a whole church..." — *PJB* 29 (1933), p. 95.

2 See *RB* 1921, p. 479; *Syria*, 1920, pp. 302 f.: Djiyeh in Syria; *HCA* p. 225.

3 See *DAC* 10, 1, col. 878.

4 See *DAC* 10, 1, cols. 871 f., 880.

5 See *DAC* 10, 1, cols. 879 f.

6 See *DAC* 10, 1, cols. 867-874 & Fig. 7427.

by the names of the saints, namely, Moses and Elias, to whom the monuments at Mount Nebo and at Madaba were dedicated. From the Bible we know that both Moses and Elias were great wonder-workers; in Madaba, a town located between deserts on the east and the west and constantly in danger of drought, the two saints were admired and venerated on account of their ability to provide their people with water; this we know from an interesting anecdote in the life of Peter the Iberian and from an inscription in the upper church of St. Elias at Madaba.

It was in the latter part of the fifth century A. D., shortly before Pentecost, that Peter the Iberian visited these regions for the last time. The country was suffering from a great drought. But when Peter was on his way from Mount Nebo to Madaba clouds suddenly gathered and a most beneficial rain fell; the people ascribed this to the powerful intercession of Peter whom they acclaimed as a second Elias and Moses, seeing that the former procured rain for his country after it had suffered from drought for 3 years[1] and the latter caused water to gush forth from a rock to save the people who were dying from thirst.[2] This acclamation betrays a conviction that was uppermost in the minds of the people, namely, that Moses and Elias could help them in times of drought.[3] That conviction finds expression also in an inscription discovered in the upper church of St. Elias at Madaba, where the Saint is invoked as "the bringer of clouds which produce rain" and is asked to remember the donors and their poor town.[4]

This simple invocation and petition in the church of St. Elias at Madaba and the story from the life of Peter the Iberian reveal the practical character of the devotion to Elias and Moses; they were venerated as the patrons of rain and of fountains; to enlist their help the people made offerings, by means of which the two great shrines in honor of the saints could be erected, decorated with mosaics, repaired, etc., as the circumstances required. The faith of the people in the power of Moses to help them in times of drought was evidently a strong link between the sanctuary of Moses at Mount Nebo and the people of the town of Madaba. In this connection it is interesting to note that the name of Moses is still applied to the springs in the wady immediately north of Siyâgha; and those very springs are the source from which the people of Madaba secure their water today (see p. 7); it is not at all improbable that the water-problem was after all the chief link between the Nebo region and Madaba in ancient times as it is today.

The preceding considerations serve to show why the bishops of Madaba should have manifested some interest in the sanctuary of Moses on Mount Nebo. Whether they actually did or not is answered by inscriptions II and V; the present inscription merely informs us that work on the basilica and the baptistery was finished at the time when Sergius was bishop. It was customary to indicate the time when an important ecclesiastical work was carried on or completed by a reference to the ecclesiastical authorities concerned with the undertaking in some way. In this case both the local and the diocesan authorities are indicated and from this it follows that the monastery at Mount Nebo was subject to the bishops of Madaba, for both bishops mentioned at Siyâgha governed the diocese of Madaba. Incidentally these inscriptions at Siyâgha are also useful for determining the territorial limits of Madaba, as Beyer has pointed out.[5]

1 See I (III) *Kings* 18.
2 See *Exodus* 17.
3 See Raabe, pp. 86 f.
4 See *DAC* 10, 1, col. 872.
5 *ZDPV* 58 (1935), pp. 153 f.

5. The abbot of the monastery at Siyâgha at the time when the basilica and the baptistery were finished was Martyrius. He is mentioned again on the baptismal font and in the Theotokos chapel; he was the contemporary of bishop Sergius and his successor Leontios; from this it follows that he was the head of the monastery at Siyâgha during the last years of the sixth century and the first years of the seventh century A. D. As in the case of the bishop so also in the case of the abbot the present inscription makes no mention of his personal contribution towards the completion of the work in the basilica and the baptistery. His name serves merely to indicate the time when the work was accomplished. For his contribution towards the completion of the Theotokos chapel see inscription V.

The official title of Martyrius was hegumen; this title is added to his name here, on the baptismal font and in the Theotokos chapel. Two other hegumens are mentioned in the inscriptions at Siyâgha; the one is called Theodore (see inscription V), the other Alex (see inscription VIII). The same title is given to the heads of monasteries at Jericho (566 A.D.),[1] Beisan (between 553-4 and 568-9 A. D.),[2] ʿAuja el-Hafîr (592 and 628 A. D.),[3] etc. It was evidently the common designation of an abbot at that time.[4]

Martyrius was also a priest; comparatively few monks were priests in the ancient monasteries; the abbot or hegumen was one of the few and this fact is generally stated in the inscriptions.

"The most God-beloved" is one of several honorific epithets given to members of the clergy.[5] Bishop Sergius has this same epithet in an inscription existing in the upper church of St. Elias at Madaba;[6] at Beisan it is given to a priest who is a recluse (or monk: ἐγκλειστός);[7] at Shellâl to a priest who is a sacristan (παραμονάριος);[8] Alt observes that it is given as a rule only to bishops and to priests who rank immediately after the bishops in dignity.[9]

6. The date: "in the 15th indiction of the year 492." The indiction[10] is useful for discovering the era used. As early as the fourth century of the Christian era this mode of computing time was in use in the regions known today as Palestine and Transjordan. In this case the indiction indicates that the era of Bostra or of the Roman province of Arabia

1 See *QDAP* 2 (1933), p. 161, no. 98.

2 See *Beth-Shan* IV, p. 16.

3 See *JPOS* 16 (1936), pp. 282 ff.

4 See A. Fortescue, *Eastern Monasticism* in *The Catholic Encyclopedia*, X, pp. 467 ff.; Kaufmann, *HAE* p. 280; Avi-Yonah, *QDAP* 3 (1934), p. 69: *The hierarchy*.

5 See Kaufmann, *HAE* p. 63.

6 See *ZDPV* 32 (1909), p. 138; *DAC* 10,1, col. 871.

7 See *Beth-Shan* IV, p. 16; here the Greek word is rendered: "the most religious."

8 See *QDAP* 3 (1934), p. 42.

9 See *ZDPV* 52 (1929), p. 101.

10 *Webster's Imperial Dictionary*, Chicago, 1907-8, p. 860, explains the word as follows: "In chronology, a cycle of fifteen years, instituted by Constantine the Great; originally a period of taxation. Constantine, having reduced the time which the Romans were obliged to serve in the army to fifteen years, imposed a tax or tribute at the end of that term, to pay the troops discharged. This practice introduced the keeping of accounts by this period. But, as it is said, in honor of the great victory of Constantine over Mezentius, September 24, A. D. 312, by which Christianity was more effectually established, the council of Nice ordained that accounts of years should no longer be kept by Olympiads, but that the indiction should be used as the point from which to reckon and date years. This was begun January 1, A. D. 313." See, however, Kaufmann, *HAE* p. 460, who declares that the method of reckoning by indictions was not introduced in 312, as the Chronicon Paschale indicates, but under Diocletian in 297, as can be seen from the dates on papyrus discoveries.

was used;[1] that era, according to Brünnow-Domaszewski,[2] began on the 22nd of March, 106 A. D.; the 492nd year of that era corresponds to the year 597-8 A. D.; the 15th indiction, to the year 596-7; so the work at Siyâgha must have been finished between 22.3 and 1.9.597 A. D.[3]

The use of the era of Bostra for dating the monuments at Mount Nebo reminds us of the fact that the sanctuary of Moses was within the limits of the Roman province of Arabia, which existed from the 2nd to the 7th century of our era. The *Onom.* of Eusebius and Jerome mentions many Biblical sites which at their time were in Arabia; when Aetheria set out from Jerusalem to visit the memorial of Moses at Mount Nebo she spoke of going to Arabia; likewise Peter the Iberian found the sanctuary of Moses in Arabia; in all these cases the Roman province of that name is meant. Mount Nebo was near the western limits of that province.

7. For epigraphics this inscription is important, since it is dated. Crosslets are used as ornaments; some of the letters have ornamental details; the spelling of the words is correct; contractions and abbreviations are used;[4] punctuation occurs. If we compare the other inscriptions found on the site with this dated one, we find in general that the inscriptions which seem to be earlier than this one, are less ornate; those which are later, are more ornate; but the same differences exist already in the two panels of this first inscription; this can readily be observed if the vowels (A, E, Ω) and the consonants (K, N, Φ) are compared; those in the northern panel are more ornate than those in the southern panel, though both were executed at the same time, perhaps by different workmen.[5] The divine names (Lord, Jesus [?], Christ) are contracted;[6] all the titles of Sergius (bishop, must pious) and of Martyrius (hegumen, priest, most God-beloved) and the word "indiction" are abbreviated;[7] contractions are indicated by horizontal lines above the letters; abbreviations, as a rule, by a short diagonal stroke — once by a small ʾ, once by inscribing a small T in an ω, once by a small ε and once by the common S-shaped sign.[8] The ligature for OY is not used in the first panel, but occurs frequently in the second one, though not always. Punctuation is used only once, namely, in the second panel between the phrase referring to the bishop and that referring to the abbot; it consists of three points in a vertical row. The point after the first letter in Sergius' name in the second line is a slip of the workman.[9] Compare these two panels with one from Madaba finished two years earlier (Pl. 89,2); there the ends of most letters have additional ornamental strokes; this is a characteristic of the inscriptions in the Theotokos chapel at Siyâgha (see Pl. 116, 1-3) which was finished later than the baptistery. On the basis of these inscriptions we may predicate a slight variety in form in the same period, but no evolution or development of forms. We shall have occasion to call attention to a few other characteristics later in connection with the other inscriptions.

1 The table indicating the indictions according to the era of Bostra is given in *PA* 3, p. 307. — A brief formula for discovering the era is given by Clermont-Ganneau in *ARP* 2, p. 424, note; see also E. Vogt, *Zeitrechnung* in *Die Religion in Geschichte und Gegenwart*, 5, pp. 2193 f.

2 *PA* 3, pp. 303 ff.

3 See *SEG* 8, p. 49, no. 318.

4 See M. Avi-Yonah, *Abbreviations in Greek Inscriptions (The Near East, 200 B. C. — A. D. 1100)*, in *QDAP* 9 (Suppl. 1940), pp. 1-125.

5 See C. B. Welles, *Gerasa*, pp. 365 ff.; our letters resemble his so-called oval alphabet, Fig. 16. — For the cursive δ in the second last line of the second panel, see *QDAP* 3 (1934), p. 100.

6 See *QDAP* 9 (Suppl. 1940), pp. 25 ff.

7 *Ibid.* p. 21: *Suspension.*

8 See *IGLP* pp. 76 ff.; Welles, *Gerasa*, p. 365; *QDAP* 9 (Suppl. 1940), pp. 29 ff.

9 See Welles, *Gerasa*, p. 365.

II. Pl. 115,1 & 2. In two sunken panels on the baptismal font described on p. 88. In the lower half of the panel on the south an erasure is indicated by the rough surface. This inscription serves to illustrate the forms of letters on stone at the end of the sixth century. In general they resemble those on the mosaic pavements of the baptistery and the Theotokos chapel; the expanding tips of the letters closely resemble those of the Theotokos chapel. O and ω are interchanged; this did not occur in the first inscription. For OY the ligature is used each time they occur. The Greek word for God is contracted and this is indicated by an horizontal line. As in the preceding inscription all the titles of Sergius and Martyrius are abbreviated; here the abbreviation is never indicated by a diagonal stroke, but in 3 cases by smaller letters written above (T in ω) or after (o after K) others; in only one case, namely, at the end of the third line in the second panel, the ordinary S-shaped sign is used.[1] (Whether the dot above the preceding letter was intentional or accidental is difficult to see; there are other small holes nearby, so that the dot or hole might be due to accidental pitting.) Crosslets occur in the first panel near the top and below at the end of the inscription; in the second panel near the top and originally there may have been one also near the end of the inscription.

Transcription: A: +|Σέργιος ὁ| ἁγιώτ(ατος) ἐπίσκο(πος)| τ[ῷ] Θ(ε)ῷ. Τὰ σὰ| σοὶ προσφ|έρ[ω]+|
B: +|Ἐπὶ τοῦ ὁ|σιωτ(άτου) Μαρτυ|ρίου ἡγουμ(ένου)|....

Translation: A: Sergius the most holy bishop to God: Thine I bring to Thee.
B: Under the most pious abbot Martyrius....

Observations: The same bishop and the same abbot are mentioned here as in the first inscription; but the epithets given to them here differ from those used in the former inscription. Here the bishop is called "most holy" and the abbot "most pious;" in other words, the abbot receives the same epithet here as the bishop received in the preceding inscription, whilst the bishop receives a new one, also frequently applied to members of the clergy; it is the third such term with which we have become familiar so far. It shows that these terms were used indiscriminately for the clergy of higher rank and the epigraphist believed in variety.

Martyrius is called merely hegumen; in the first inscription and again in the fifth one he is also called priest. The absence of this title may be accounted for in several ways; it may have been omitted originally or effaced later; there is clear evidence of an erasure in the lower part of the second panel (Pl. 115,2); so it looks as if the title had been removed; in either case we do not know why it was done.

The new element in the inscription consists in this that the bishop addresses himself to God with the words: "Thine I bring to Thee." These words are taken from the liturgy[2] and imply that the bishop has made some contribution or offering to the church; the character of the offering is not stated expressly, but since the inscription is on the baptismal font it seems highly probable that this font was the gift of the bishop. If the bishop conferred on the monks at Siyâgha the faculty to baptize, then it was very appropriate on his part to advertise, so to say, this fact by donating a font to the baptistery and inscribing it as he did. For us this gift is a new argument that the monastery of Mount Nebo was under the jurisdiction of the bishop of Madaba, for it would be difficult to imagine that a bishop should venture to make such an offering to a monastery of another diocese. At the same time this inscription answers the question whether Sergius was really interested in the monastery at Mount Nebo and how he manifested his interest practically.

[1] See *Gerasa*, p. 365; *QDAP* 9 (Suppl. 1940), p. 37. Here it is called a typical sixth-century sign.

[2] See the references given in *Antonianum* 9 (1934), p. 353; W. K. Prentice, *Greek and Latin Inscriptions in Syria*, p. 51, no. 920.

We stated above that the words: "Thine I bring to Thee," are derived from the liturgy; the exact expression occurs at the mass immediately after the consecration, where the Greek liturgy has the words: τὰ σὰ ἐκ τῶν σῶν σοὶ προσφέρομεν κατὰ πάντα, καὶ διὰ πάντα; [1] but it is very probable that the choice of the phrase was influenced by the prayer recited on the occasion when the foundations of a new church were blessed. The prayer begins with the words: Κύριε ὁ Θεὸς ἡμῶν, i. e., "O Lord, our God;" this invocation, with which the prayer begins, may have been the reason why the epigraphist represents Sergius as addressing himself to God: "Sergius to God." Then the prayer continues: ὁ ἀρεσθεὶς καὶ ἐπὶ ταύτῃ τῇ πέτρᾳ οἰκοδομηθῆναί σοι Ἐκκλησίαν· αὐτὸς τοὺς τὰ σὰ ἐκ τῶν σῶν σοὶ προσκομίζοντας ἔπιδε,[2] etc.

The time when Sergius made this offering is indicated by a reference to the abbot; from the previous inscription we know precisely when this was. The font was probably inscribed and installed a short time before the pavement was laid which contains the dated inscription and still encloses the font.

III. Pl. 115,3. In the mosaic pavement of the doorway between the baptistery and the basilica (see Fig. 27, f; Pl. 48,2). About half of the inscription still exists, the rest was destroyed; the surviving part begins with a crosslet (X); in general the letters resemble those used in the first panel of the first inscription, but the letter A resembles the form used in inscription IX, though the apex is treated differently. The inscription is placed in such a way that it can be read by one leaving the baptistery, but not by one who is about to enter it.

Transcription: X Εἰρήνη πᾶ[σι...X].

Translation: X Peace to all [... X].

Explanation: In explaining the inscription on the baptismal font we pointed out that the principal phrase there was derived from the liturgy; also this greeting occurs very frequently in the liturgy and we think that it was derived from there,[3] especially from the liturgy used for baptism, where the greeting occurs twice.[4] In each case there follows: Τὰς κεφαλὰς ὑμῶν τῷ Κυρίῳ κλίνατε; but this phrase is too long to be supplied here. Hence one must supply a shorter phrase[5] or presume that the remaining space was filled in only as we have indicated above.[6] To understand the full import of the expression one must study the prayers

[1] *Euchologion*, p. 64; ibid. p. 92 (where instead of προσφέρομεν the participial form προσφέροντες is used). In English: "In all and for all we offer Thee Thine own of what is Thine own." De Meester, p. 65 (see below p. 254, note 6). — The same idea is expressed in the same way in the Latin liturgy.

[2] See *Euchologion*, p. 316. — English: "O Lord, our God, Who wast pleased that a church was erected to Thee also on this rock, have regard for those who offer to Thee Thine own of what is Thine own," etc. But here the verb (προσκομίζοντας) differs from the one used in the inscription.

[3] See *Euchologion*, pp. 4, 5, 10, 70, 86, 101, 113, 126, 143, 329 and passim. — A. Fortescue, *The Uniate Eastern Churches*, London, 1923, p. 232, observes that this Greek phrase is one of the few expressions in Greek still heard and used in the Byzantine liturgy of the Melkites; otherwise they use Arabic. — In the mass the choir answers the priest: Καὶ τῷ πνεύματί σου; that is: "And with thy spirit."

[4] See *Euchologion*, pp. 156 & 161.

[5] Such as: "Ἀμήν," as in the synagogue at Jerash; see *QDAP* 3 (1934), p. 129; or τοῖς ἐν Χ(ριστ)ῷ, as in *I Peter* 5, 14: "Peace to all who are in Christ."

[6] The phrase: Εἰρήνη ☧ πᾶσιν," without any addition, was used above the door of a tower at Umm el-Jimal in northern Transjordan; see *ZDPV* 20 (1897), p. 161, Abb. 71. — For similar phrases see Prentice, nos. 196, 197a, 198, 259; Kaufmann, *HAE* p. 62: "Paxformel." — Regarding a similar formula in synagogues ("Peace upon Israel" or "Peace upon all Israel," derived from *Ps.* 125 [124 in *LXX*], 5) see Avi-Yonah, *QDAP* 3 (1934), pp. 128 f.; E. L. Sukenik, *The Ancient Synagogue of Beth Alpha*, Jerusalem, 1932, p. 27, Fig. 28. Commentators of the text from the *Psalm* consider it a liturgical formula. See *ZATW* 1896, p. 153.

accompanying this greeting, especially those used in administering baptism;[1] they throw light also on the use of the word photisterion which is used in the first inscription instead of the word baptisterion.

IV. Pl. 116, 1 & 2. In the mosaic pavement in the chancel of the Theotokos chapel (see Fig. 27, g; Pl. 109,1). The inscription is divided into two parts by the representation of a temple; that on the north is 90 cm. l., that on the south 116 cm. A few letters in the northern section have been damaged; otherwise the inscription is complete. The letters resemble those used in the first panel of the first inscription (see Pl. 114,1), but here the tips of many more letters have an additional tiny stroke as an ornament; at Siyâgha — not necessarily elsewhere — this form of the letters represents a later development.

Transcription: Τότε ἀνοίσουσιν ἐπὶ τὸ|θυσιαστήριόν σου μόσχους.

Translation: Then they shall lay calves upon thy altar. *Ps.* 50 (51), 21.

Observations: This text is taken over word for word from *Ps.* 50 (51), 21. It occurs again at Mekhayyat and at Mâʿin, as we pointed out on p. 234. To appreciate the spirit which influenced the choice of this text, one must not only consider the immediate context in which this verse was used but also other texts of Holy Scripture used in mosaic pavements, etc., for example, at Mâʿin,[2] at Jerash,[3] in Palestine[4] and in Syria.[5] The texts are generally taken from the *Psalms*, as here, but at Mâʿin also a text from *Isaias* was found. The use of these texts indicates that the epigraphist saw a close connection between them and the place at which or the scene near which he put them. This relation should be investigated in each individual case and it would serve to throw light on the meaning attached to those texts in the early Christian church. We already used the text in question here to explain the scene it accompanies (see pp. 234-8); there we expressed our conviction that the artist represented the calves, altar, etc. not merely for their own sake nor even to recall an historical fact, but primarily on account of their symbolical and typical meaning. To prove this we appealed to the position of the scene in front of the Christian altar and to the interpretation given to this text by the Fathers. Here the process must be modified somewhat; we must consider the position of the text in relation to the scene in the mosaic pavement and to the Christian altar in order to discover what meaning the artist put into the words of the *Psalm*. This process results in a modest contribution to Biblical exegesis.

Ps. 50 (51), 21, was thes ource of the text under consideration; this is certain; but it is not so certain whether it was the direct and immediate source of the epigraphist's inspiration. The doubt arose in the writer's mind when he observed that certain words and phrases in the inscriptions at Mount Nebo which could be derived from the Bible have a form which resembles much more closely that which is found in the liturgical prayers; if those other texts were derived from the liturgical prayers, it was only natural to expect the same in this case. This text was actually used in the Greek liturgy; and the context was such that it convinced the writer of its liturgical origin.

That conviction was strengthened when the writer was privileged to witness the Greek liturgy in Jerusalem. That, according to St. John Chrysostom,[6] is divided into two parts: the

1 *Euchologion*, pp. 152-161.
2 *RB* 47 (1938), pp. 230 (*Ps.* 50 [51], 21), 239 (*Ps.* 86 [87], 2; *Ps.* 117 [118], 20), 233 (*Is.* 11,7).
3 See *Gerasa*, pp. 485 f., no. 331: *Ps.* 85 (86), 1-3.
4 See *QDAP* 3 (1934), p. 69.
5 See Prentice, pp. 16 ff.
6 *Euchologion*, pp. 42-78; see especially p. 58. — *The Divine Liturgy of our Father among the Saints John Chrysostom;* Greek text with introduction and notes by Dom Placid De Meester, O. S. B.; English Translation by the Benedictines of Stanbrock; London, 1926; see especially pp. 52-53.

first of the catechumens and the second of the faithful; in the second part of the liturgy there is a procession during which the offerings are brought from the prothesis to the altar; after they have been placed on the altar, the rubrics instruct the priest to incense them thrice, saying: Τότε ἀνοίσουσιν ἐπὶ τὸ θυσιαστήριόν σου μόσχους, that is, "Then shall they lay young calves upon thy altar." The epigraphist at Mount Nebo was no doubt thoroughly familiar with this practice; it caused him to place the text in front of the altar and it also influenced the representation of the temple complex with its altar and the young calves.

This liturgical use of the text suggests that the altar before which it was placed was not the altar of a prothesis, where the offerings were prepared, but the altar on which the sacrifice was offered.

V. Pl. 116,3. In a rectangular panel, 425 × 20 cm., in the mosaic pavement at the eastern end of the nave of the Theotokos chapel (see Fig. 27,h; Pl. 110,1). Only one letter is missing and this can easily be supplied. The letters have the oval form and the ornamental details which we noted in speaking of the first and fourth inscriptions; A differs in this that it has an angular central bar; O and Ω are interchanged 4 times; once H is written instead of E; once I instead of P (the circlet on the upper right side was accidentally overlooked by the workman); these interchanges are quite common in the Byzantine period; we met with some in inscription II.[1] The ligature for OY is not used.

Abbreviations (both contractions and suspensions) are used somewhat more sparingly in this than in the first inscription; not all the expressions relating to the deity are abbreviated, only Κ(ριστ)ός and Θ(εό)ς; of the ecclesiastical titles only one is abbreviated, namely, πρεσβ(υτέρων); in this case the last letter of the suspension is doubled and after each there is a wavy vertical sign of abbreviation, that is, the sign of abbreviation is also doubled.[2] Here for the first time we meet the abbreviated form of Καί; it occurs 5 times and each time it consists of a K with a small half-moon (spiritus asper shape) attached to the lower diagonal bar of the letter.[3]

Transcription: Ὁ κτίστης κ(αὶ) δημιουργὸς τῶν ἁπάντων Χ(ριστὸ)ς ὁ Θ(εὸ)ς ἡμῶν κ(αὶ) εὐχῇ τοῦ ἁγίου πατρὸς ἡμῶν Λεοντίου ἐπισκόπου | ἐτελ[ε]ιώθη τὸ πᾶν ἔργον τῆς Θε[ο]τ[ό]κου σπουδῇ κ(αὶ) ἀγ[ῶ]νι Μαρτυρίου κ(αὶ) Θεοδώρου π[ρ]εσβ(υτέρων) κ(αὶ) ἡγου[μ][έ]ν[ω]ν.

Translation: O Creator and Maker of all things, Christ our God, the entire work of the Theotokos was finished with the permission of our holy Father, bishop Leontios, by the exertion and anxiety of Martyrius and Theodore, priests and abbots.

Observations: 1. "O Creator and Maker of all things, Christ our God." — This inscription begins with an acclamation of Christ as "our God," "the Creator" and "the Maker" "of all things." The elements of this acclamation may be found in Holy Scripture,[4] in ancient liturgical prayers[5] and in other ancient inscriptions;[6] but the combination of all these elements is found elsewhere only in liturgical prayers,[7] which must, therefore, be considered the most

1 See *QDAP* 3 (1934), p. 98.

2 Avi-Yonah, *QDAP* 9 (Suppl. 1940), p. 11, no. 5, observes that there are "46 different abbreviations of the word πρεσβύτερος;" see ibid. pp. 96 ff.; our form is the first on p. 118 l. c.

3 See *QDAP* 9 (Suppl. 1940), p. 39, B, (i); p. 74; *Gerasa*, p. 365.

4 Regarding ὁ κτίστης see, v. g., *1 Peter* 4, 19; *Ecclesiasticus* 24, 12 (8); *2 Mach.* 1, 24; 7,23; 13,14; etc. For ὁ δημιουργός see *Hebr.* 11,10.

5 Very many prayers in the Greek liturgy begin with the words: Κύριε ὁ Θεὸς ἡμῶν; see *Euchologion*, passim. Χριστὸς ὁ Θεός, however, is rarer; see, v. g., *Euchologion*, p. 163.

6 See, v. g., *Beth-Shan* IV, p. 14, II & III, where Χριστὲ ὁ Θεός occurs twice: once with ἡμῶν and once without that word.

7 See *Euchologion*, pp. 120, 315, etc.

likely sources of this acclamation, especially since we have repeatedly seen in the preceding inscriptions that the epigraphists at Siyâgha showed a marked preference for liturgical language. The thought implied by this invocation seems to be the same as that expressed in the beginning of the first inscription; there it is stated that the basilica and the baptistery were finished with the help of God; this is not expressly stated in the present inscription, but by calling Christ the "Creator" and "Maker" "of all things" it seems that the epigraphist wished to indicate, at least indirectly, that He contributed in some way towards the successful completion of the work on the Theotokos chapel. Christ is called both ὁ κτίστης and ὁ δημιουργός; these terms seem to be synonymous here; both express the same thing; namely, that He is the "Creator." The dogmatic content of this formula must be investigated in the light of the liturgical prayers from which it is derived; but the fact that the formula is used in a chapel dedicated to the Theotokos may explain why the epigraphist insists on the fact that "Christ" is "God" and that "He" is "the Creator and Maker of all things," whereas the prayer used, for example, at the blessing of the foundations of a house does not insist so much on the identity of Christ and God, but insists even more on the universal character of God's creative power, which is expected to extend even to the most insignificant house.[1]

The fact that Christ is acclaimed in this inscription does not imply that the chapel was dedicated to Him; actually it was dedicated to His Mother Mary, the Theotokos; this dedication accounts sufficiently for the fact that He is acclaimed. At the same time this inscription may serve to show that the acclamation need not necessarily indicate to whom the chapel is dedicated.

2. "The entire work of the Theotokos was finished." — After the acclamation there comes an historical notice which was evidently the main object of this inscription and is of special interest to us; it informs us of the character of the work which was completed and of the persons responsible for it; incidentally we also learn to whom the chapel was dedicated and the approximate date at which the work was finished.

"Work" (ἔργον) here signifies "the chapel" of the Theotokos. The same Greek word occurred in the first inscription; there we translated it "the construction" of the holy church, etc. It is a very common expression used in numerous inscriptions of Transjordan,[2] Palestine,[3] etc.[4] and designates both the acts and the results of those acts; here then we could translate either "all the work on the Theotokos chapel" or "the entire Theotokos chapel" was completed.

The words "entire" and "finished" should be taken strictly; for it seems that the Theotokos chapel was built at the same time as the baptistery; but the indications of date in the mosaic pavements show that a number of years elapsed between the completion of the mosaic pavement in the baptistery and that in the Theotokos chapel; the inscription refers to the time when this chapel was entirely finished.

"Theotokos." — This word indicates that the chapel was dedicated to the Theotokos; hence the name Theotokos chapel; see pp. 91 f.

1 See *Euchologion*, p. 315. The prayer begins as follows: Ὁ Θεὸς ὁ παντοκράτωρ, ὁ ποιήσας τὸν οὐρανὸν ἐν συνέσει, καὶ θεμελιώσας τὴν γῆν ἐπὶ τὴν ἀσφάλειαν αὐτῆς, ὁ κτίστης καὶ δημιουργὸς τῶν ἁπάντων, etc. This prayer most probably inspired the acclamation in our inscription.

2 See *SEG* 8 (1937), pp. 53, no. 339; 54, no. 346; *Gerasa:* inscriptions nos. (6), 72, 189, 277, (278), 280, (281), 306, 330.

3 See *QDAP* 2 (1933), pp. 142, no. 13; 145, no. 22; 149, nos. 26 & 77; ibid. 3 (1934), p. 53, no. 346; p. 69, no. 17; see *SEG* 8 (1937), pp. 2 ff. passim; *Beth-Shan* IV, p. 16, VI & VII.

4 See *Antioch* II, p. 42. — For other expressions used in Syria see *ECS* pp. 249 ff

3. "With the permission of our holy Father, bishop Leontios." — The word εὐχή, according to Sophocles,[1] was used to signify not only "prayer," "vow," "a mere wish or aspiration (as opposed to reality)," but also "permission of a superior." — The church laws prescribe that the permission of the higher ecclesiastical superiors must be obtained for any undertaking which involves extraordinary expenses. It is possible that after the authorities of the monastery at Mount Nebo had decided to finish the work in the Theotokos chapel they informed the bishop, who approved of the project; in this case the initiative would belong to the authorities of the monastery. — Much more commonly the word indicates that a certain work was undertaken or finished in fulfillment of a vow;[2] that may of course be the meaning also here and in this case it would indicate that the bishop took the initiative.

The bishop in question was called "Leontios." In Madaba a man by this name completed the undertakings begun by Sergius; thus, for example, he finished the upper church of St. Elias in the year 608 A. D.;[3] even earlier than that, namely, in the year 604 A. D.,[4] he built another church in that town. So it seems that he succeeded Sergius as bishop of Madaba some time before the year 604 A. D. That agrees remarkably well with what we know regarding Leontios from the Siyâgha inscriptions. Under him work at Siyâgha, which had already been begun under Sergius, was continued and finished. In Madaba Leontios was called "ἱερεύς;"[5] at Mount Nebo he was called "ἐπίσκοπος;" ἱερεύς and ἐπίσκοπος indicate the same office,[6] so there is no difficulty on this score.

The bishop is called "ὁ ἅγιος πατὴρ ἡμῶν;" father is a common title given to members of the clergy, especially to bishops; the appellative ἅγιος is generally in the superlative; here, however, the positive form is used.

All in all, the reference to the bishop is instructive; as in the first and second inscriptions it indicates that the monastery at Mount Nebo was dependent upon the bishop of Madaba; at the same time reference to the bishop serves to fix the time when the Theotokos chapel was finished; this must have been during the first decade of the 7th century of our era. If the statement regarding the bishop in this inscription is compared with the statement made in the first inscription we find it much more satisfactory; there we were informed that the basilica and the baptistery were finished at the time of bishop Sergius; but if we ask what he had to do with the work, there is no reply; all is left to our imagination; here, however, we are informed what the bishop had to do with the work; one word, εὐχή, says it; that suffices for us; the time when the work was completed can be deduced from that statement.

4. "By the zeal (pains, exertion, trouble) and anxiety of Martyrius and Theodore, priests and abbots." — As in the baptistery so here not only the bishop but also the abbots are indicated at whose time the work in the Theotokos chapel was finished. But this inscription mentions the bishop and abbots not only for the sake of indicating the time when the work was finished, but also for the purpose of indicating how each one contributed towards that end. The bishop did so by his εὐχῇ (permission), the abbots by their σπουδῇ (exertions) and ἀγῶνι (anxiety); a few such words lend a little personal touch to the inscriptions. The

1 *Greek Lexicon of the Roman and Byzantine Periods (from B. C. 146 to A. D. 1100)*, Boston, 1870.

2 But in these cases one generally finds: κατ' εὐχήν (see the references given in *Gerasa*, p. 602, H; Prentice, nos. 358, 369, 380 and passim) or ὑπὲρ εὐχῆς (see *QDAP* 3 [1934], p. 68, no. 17; *AJA* 39 [1935], p. 583; Reinach, *Traité d'Épigraphie Grecque*, p. 383); see also *ECS* pp. 257 f.

3 See *RB* 1897, pp. 652 ff.; 1911, p. 439; *DAC* 10, 1, cols. 871 f.

4 See *RB* 1911, pp. 437 ff.; *DAC* 10, 1, cols. 879 f.

5 See the preceding note.

6 See *RB* 1924, p. 598; ibid. 1930, p. 476.

effect of this statement is not necessarily lessened by the fact that we find the same words elsewhere; all great undertakings cause work and worry for those who are directly responsible for them; therefore we need not be surprised if this thought is repeatedly expressed in the inscriptions. In the lower church of St. Elias at Madaba the priest Sergius was directly responsible for the execution of the work and he did it with zeal (σπουδῇ);[1] at el-Yadûde the floor was paved with mosaics by the exertions (διὰ σπουδῆς) of the deacon Silanos;[2] at el-Quweisme a church was restored from the foundations and paved with mosaics by the zeal (σπουδῇ) and diligence (ἐπιμελείᾳ) of the priest and economos Obeos;[3] etc.[4] The word ἀγών, anxiety, seems to be peculiar to this inscription and very probably indicates real difficulties encountered by the abbots in carrying out their project.

In the baptistery only one abbot was mentioned; his name was Martyrius; here two are mentioned: one is called Martyrius and the other Theodore. Martyrius may be presumed to be the same one who was mentioned in the baptistery and Theodore was no doubt his successor. The official title of each one is hegumen and each one is a priest. The mention of Martyrius in this chapel shows that he was the contemporary of two bishops: Sergius and Leontios. The mention of Theodore seems to indicate that the Theotokos chapel was finished a few years later than the baptistery; this corresponds to the time suggested already by the mention of bishop Leontios, who was the successor of bishop Sergius at Madaba. The abbot Theodore is mentioned only here; he must have entered upon his office during the first years of the 7th century A. D. It may be emphasized once more that the mention of the abbots serves to establish the fact that at Siyâgha we have a monastic center.

Note. — In the northeastern corner of the sanctuary of the basilica a broken fragment of the mosaic pavement has preserved the triangular ear characteristic of a tabula ansata, which generally contains an inscription (see Fig. 27); it probably indicates that an inscription existed there at one time; but since not a single letter of the inscription remains, we have not registered it as an inscription.

VI. Pl. 117,1. In the mosaic pavement near the northwestern part of the chancel of the basilica (Fig. 27,a; see p. 212,a). A rectangular panel, measuring 120 × 110 cm., is divided into 4 sections by horizontal lines; each section contains two lines of writing; generally the second line is not completely occupied. A large part of the panel was completely destroyed and over half of the surviving part has been blackened by fire; as a result the beginning of several lines and the central parts of all the lines are missing, but nevertheless the general import of the inscription is clear. Contrary to the practice in the chapels the letters of this inscription are without any ornamental details; the lines, whether straight or curved, are severely plain. The letter A in this inscription differs in form from that used in the mosaic inscriptions of the chapels; the A on the baptismal font is an intermediate form; the A in the other inscriptions of the sanctuary of the basilica has the same form as in this inscription. At Jerash[5] this form occurs in all periods; at Beisan[6] we find this same form in the sixth-century monastery, etc. One word which occurs three times is abbreviated each time; it is λαμπρότατος; the first time the abbreviation consists of 4 letters: ΛΜΠΡ, the second time of 5

1 See *DAC* 10,1, col. 873.
2 See *DAC* 10,1, col. 883.
3 The Greek text is not yet published; see above p. 245, note 1, (6).
4 See *QDAP* 3 (1934), pp. 68 f., no. 17; *ECS* pp. 254-258.
5 See *Gerasa*, pp. 358-367, Figs. 8-16.
6 See *Beth-Shan* IV, Pls. XX-XXII.

letters: ΛΑΜΠΡ, the third and last time the original abbreviation is uncertain since only three letters:.. ΜΠΡ remain. The sign of abbreviation in each case is a short diagonal stroke through the last letter, which is always Ρ.[1] — In the transcription double lines (||) indicate the end of each section (except the last).

Transcription: Πρ[οσφορὰ........τ]οῦ λ(α)μπρ(οτάτου) | [κόμητος.........]υ, || [.............τοῦ] λαμπρ(οτάτου) | [.....], || [ὑπὲ]ρ σωτ[ηρίας...τοῦ λα]μπρ(οτάτου) | καὶ τ[οῦ.......]. || Μνή[σθητι Κύριε τῷ]δε | κλη[ρικῷ καὶ μο]ναχῷ.

Translation: An offering of [N. N.] the most illustrious [count], [on behalf of the memory of N. N.] the most illustrious [count], for the welfare of [N. N.] the most illustrious and... [........]. Remember, [O Lord,] this cleric [and] monk.

Observations: 1. This inscription commemorates benefactors who have made offerings to the church for someone's welfare and ends with an invocation. All the proper names are missing, but the general tenor of the inscription is clear and a number of details can be supplied by comparing the various sections of the panel with one another and the whole inscription with panels at other sites in which benefactors are mentioned.

2. Προσφορά signifies an offering made by someone for a certain purpose. One of the inscribed marble slabs found at Siyâgha begins with the same word (see Pl. 121,1). At Mekhayyat, in the church of St. George, this word is followed by the names of a number of donors and then the purpose of the benefactions is indicated as here (not published). Another good example exists in the monastery at Beisan.[2]

3. Λαμπροτάτου. — In the first line there is room for about 22 letters; this would permit us to insert a proper name of about 8 letters after προσφορά; the proper name was followed by the honorific epithet: λαμπρότατος. According to Prentice "this title is applied commonly to persons of high rank."[3] In the Roman province of Arabia the epithet is given so frequently to a count ("comes"), that we have ventured to supply that word in the beginning of the second line of the first section. Another name or title followed in this line, but of it only the letter Υ remains to indicate where this sentence ended and to suggest that in the second section a new sentence begins.

4. In the second section of the panel only the abbreviation of "most illustrious" remains.

5. In the third section the purpose of the offering is indicated; it is "for the welfare"[4] of another "most illustrious" individual and possibly also for his family.

6. The inscription in the fourth section begins with three letters which suggest the familiar invocation, addressed either to God (ὁ Θεός) or to our Lord (Κύριε) or to Christ (Χριστέ), to be remembered.[5] The verb μνήσθητι is followed either by the genitive or the dative

[1] See *QDAP* 9 (Suppl. 1940), pp. 36 f. — For the different ways in which this word is abbreviated in inscriptions see l.c. pp. 80 f., 116.

[2] See *Beth-Shan* IV, pp. 13 f., I; see ibid. p. 19.

[3] Prentice, no. 332; see ibid. nos. 75, 380a, 400; — *PA* 3, p. 282; — Seeck, *RE* 5, col. 1870; *Gerasa*, inscriptions nos. 273, 277, 278, 279; Sukenik, *The Ancient Synagogue of el-Hammeh*, Jerusalem, 1935, pp. 43 ff.; Avi-Yonah, *QDAP* 3 (1934), p. 99, observes that this "honorific prefix is the equivalent of the Latin *clarissimorum*, denoting in the sixth century counts of the lowest, purely titular, class. More fortunate individuals indicate carefully in their inscriptions that they are Κόμης πρώτου τάγματος."...

[4] See also inscription IX; at Mekhayyat the same purpose is expressed by the same word in the majority of the inscriptions (6 times). It was a very common practice to make offerings to the church to secure the welfare of some one; see, v. g., *QDAP* 3 (1934), p. 68. This Christian practice is derived from an older non-Christian practice; see, v. g., *Gerasa*, p. 601, *H*.

[5] See *QDAP* 3 (1934), p. 68, no. 17; Kaufmann, *HAE* p. 144; Mader, *JPOS* 9 (1929), p. 127; — the formula is very common in the Greek liturgies from where it may have been derived in inscriptions. (— For the abbreviation MNH see *QDAP* 9 [Suppl. 1940], p. 86.)

or the accusative; the dative, used here, must perhaps be ascribed to the influence of (or confusion resulting from) the much employed βοηθεῖν.

The person who asks to be remembered is indicated by parts of three words. The first word, at the end of the first line of this section, ends in ..δε; hence we assumed that the pronoun τῷδε (this) had been used; there is a free space after this word, so the three letters at the beginning of the second line most probably represent the beginning of another word. We take them to stand for "cleric" [1] which combines quite well with "monk" [2] at the end of the line. At Mekhayyat a monk called Julian is mentioned at the end of an inscription (not yet published).

VII. Pl. 117,2. In a rectangular tabula ansata of the mosaic pavement of the basilica's chancel, near the opening in the chancel screen (see Fig. 27, b). The southern part of the panel has disappeared; but a calculation based on its relation to the door of the chancel screen suggests that the panel measured 65 × 180 cm.; the inscription consists of 5 lines with an average of about 30 letters to the line; if this calculation is correct over half of the inscription is missing; thus, for example, in the first line about 13 letters, in the second about 18, etc. should be supplied. The letters resemble those in the preceding inscription.

Transcription: Ἱκετεύω σε τὸν εἰσιό[ντα ἐν ταύτῃ τῇ πύλῃ αἶτ] | ήσασθαι ὑπὲρ Ζ[...............]| καὶ ἐλεεινο[ῦ................]. | Δωρόθεος Χ[ριστῷ τῷ Κυρίῳ ἡμῶν εὐχα] |ριστῶν ἐψ[ήφωσα τὸν ἅγιον τόπον.]

Translation: I humbly implore you, who are about to enter [this gate] to pray for Z [.... N. N. ....] and for the pitiable [N. N. ....]. (I) Dorotheos returning thanks to Christ [our Lord] have paved [the holy place] with mosaics.

Observations: 1. In spite of the fact that over half of the inscription is missing, its general import seems to be quite clear, though of course a number of details remain uncertain. It seems that the chancel was paved with mosaics by a benefactor of the church called Dorotheos; he is represented supplicating the priest, about to enter the sanctuary to offer the sacrifice, to pray for those whom he has in mind.

2. "I humbly implore you who are about to enter." — We suggest that the one speaking in the first person is Dorotheos mentioned at the beginning of the fourth line. The person addressed is indicated by the second person singular: "you;" he is further described as one "who is about to enter" a certain place. The name of the place mentioned in the original inscription is not preserved, but it can be supplied from the context. One could have supplied: εἰς τὸν ἅγιον τόπον, a phrase which occurs in the next inscription and gives very good sense; or εἰς τὸν οἶκον Θ(εο)ῦ or εἰς τὸν ἅγιον ναόν, as in the prayer used by the priest (and deacon, if one is present,) when about to enter the sanctuary (εἰς τὸ ἱερόν).[3] Actually we supplied: ἐν ταύτῃ τῇ πύλῃ, because these words are found in the verses from *Ps.* 117 (118), 19 & 20, placed near the doors of churches in Transjordan,[4] Palestine[5] and Syria.[6] The inscription can only be read by one standing in the doorway or by one on the point of passing through the doorway of the chancel in order to enter the sanctuary; under the circumstances the words supplied seem to be peculiarly appropriate. But no matter what words stood in the text originally, the position of the inscription makes it clear that the words

1 According to Kaufmann, *HAE* p. 271, clerics are mentioned as early as the 4th century A. D.

2 See *QDAP* 3 (1934), p. 69: *The hierarchy.*

3 See *Euchologion*, p. 31; De Meester, pp. 6 f.

4 See *RB* 47 (1934), p. 239: Mâʿin.

5 *QDAP* 3 (1934), p. 69.

6 See Prentice, p. 44, inscription 911.

were addressed to one who was about to enter the sanctuary. That person may have been either the priest or the deacon.

3. "To pray for." — At the end of the first line of the inscription the root of some verb must be supplied; the verb αἰτέομαι fits into the grammatical and logical context; it is followed by ὑπέρ and means: "to pray for." The purpose for which prayers were requested was originally expressed in the greater part of the second and the third lines of the inscription; now only one letter remains after ὑπέρ in the second line and two words in the third line.

The surviving letter in the second line is Z; it could stand for such words as ζωῆς (life) or ζώντων (living), but it is more probable that a proper name must be supplied; there are quite many names beginning with this letter;[1] so, for example, Zosius, the name of a bishop in the nearby town of Esbous.[2] Zosius attended the Council of Ephesus in 431 A. D. and that of Chalcedon in 451 A. D. Formerly scholars were of the opinion that Mount Nebo belonged to the diocese of Esbous; today, after the discovery of the inscriptions in the baptistery and the Theotokos chapel at Mount Nebo, one or the other still holds that view; others distinguish and suggest that Mount Nebo belonged to Esbous during the fourth and fifth centuries and later was transferred to the diocese of Madaba. If we suppose that the monastery at Mount Nebo belonged to the diocese of Esbous during the fifth century, it would not be surprising to find the diocesan bishop mentioned in one of the inscriptions, as was the case in the chapels at the end of the sixth and the beginning of the seventh century A. D. In both the baptistery and the Theotokos chapel the bishop is mentioned first and then the abbot; moreover, in the baptistery the bishop is mentioned twice and in each case in a panel distinct from that in which the abbot is mentioned. In the sanctuary of the basilica an abbot is also mentioned, namely, in the inscription in front of the pulpit; if the bishop was mentioned, we would expect his name in the panel under consideration; if it did not exist here, then we must assume that the bishop was not mentioned in any inscription of the basilica. See also inscription X, where there seems to be a reference to Esbous. If the bishop of Esbous was mentioned, then his name was most probably followed by titles similar to those used for the bishops in the chapels. See no. 4 below: "Dorotheos."

In the third line we have the two words: "and pitiable." This term is used by a monk speaking of himself;[3] inscriptions and liturgical prayers contain other expressions which would suggest this adjective; so the constant repetition of Kyrie eleison (ἐλέησον) would readily suggest the adjective ἐλεεινός, pitiable, deserving or in need of pity or mercy. After such an adjective one would naturally expect a noun which is also an expression of humility, such as ὁ δοῦλος, the servant or slave, namely, of God or Christ. Regarding the proper name which probably existed in the same line, we can only suggest that the person (or persons) mentioned was a member of the family of Dorotheos.

In this connection it may be useful to observe that in the Greek liturgy, the deacon stands in front of the entrance to the chancel when he recites the petitions in which the objects or intentions for which prayers should be offered up are enumerated.[4] At Mount Nebo, therefore, he would have been facing the inscription under consideration in which a benefactor asks for prayers.

[1] See, v. g., *Gerasa*, p. 595, for a list of such names occurring at Jerash; other very popular names beginning with this letter are indicated in *ZDPV* 46 (1923), p. 60, no. 11.

[2] See *PA* 3, pp. 344, 346; *DHGE* 3 (1924), cols. 1178 f.

[3] *Aegyptus*, 18 (1938), p. 100, 4°, 6, b.

[4] See De Meester, pp. 24 & 25; 40 & 41; p. 103, note 25, where he observes: "The deacon acts as an interpreter between the priest and the people. This is why he stands between the sanctuary and the body of the faithful."

4. "Dorotheos." — Only one proper name is preserved in the entire inscription; it is in the nominative case. We may assume that this Dorotheos is the same person who addressed himself to the priest or the deacon in the first three lines of the inscription with a request for prayers. Analogous cases would suggest that he requested those prayers primarily for himself and the immediate members of his family. Probably the inscription also stated who Dorotheos was and what he did.

The two letters εψ in the last line of the inscription suggest the verb ἐψήφωσα, that is, "(I, Dorotheos,) paved with mosaics." In this case Dorotheos would be represented as indicating the reason why he considers himself entitled to special prayers. Avi-Yonah[1] observes that the verb ψηφόω, according to the usage of the time, refers to the donors and not to the makers of the mosaic pavement; in this case Dorotheos would be the donor, or at least one of the donors, for other benefactors of the church were mentioned in the preceding inscription.

The place which was paved with mosaics was probably mentioned in the original inscription; the position of the inscription suggests that it was the sanctuary.

The letter X in the fourth line may indicate the word Χριστῷ and the letters PICTΩN at the beginning of the fifth line may be the end of the word εὐχαριστῶν. In this case the motive which prompted Dorotheos would be indicated, namely, gratitude to Christ for some favor received. The same thought is expressed in inscriptions from the vicinity of Ascalon and Gaza.[2]

VIII. Pl. 118,1. In a rectangular tabula ansata, measuring 50 × 100 cm., in the mosaic pavement at the southwestern part of the chancel of the basilica (Fig. 27, c). The panel contains 4 lines of writing; in each line there were originally about 18 letters, but a few have been destroyed by a repair in the upper right hand corner and others have been blackened by fire. The letters have the same form as those in the other two panels in the sanctuary. Originally several abbreviations were used, but only one still exists, namely, one of the abbot's epithets; the sign of abbreviation is an inverted S, which occurs also at the end of the second line, thus indicating the existence of a second abbreviation there at one time.

Transcription: Ἐπὶ τοῦ εὐλ[αβεσ(τάτου) καὶ θεο]|σεβ(εστάτου) Ἀλεξ[άνδρου πρεσβ(υτέρου)]| καὶ ἡγουμέν[ου ἀ]νενεώ|θη ὁ ἅγιος τόπος.

Translation: Under the most reverend and most pious priest and abbot Alex...... the holy place was renovated.

Observations: 1. "The holy place." — This phrase was used in a number of places as a designation for churches or synagogues; churches are meant at Mekhayyat,[3] Madaba,[4] el-Yadûde,[5] Wady el-Hesa[6] and et-Tâbgha;[7] a synagogue at Jerash,[8] etc.[9] Here it very probably means the basilica.

[1] *QDAP* 3 (1934), p. 73, no. 24.

[2] See Sukenik, *The Ancient Synagogue of el-Hammeh*, Jerusalem, 1935, pp. 62 f., 64, 65, 68, 69; *SEG* 8 (1937), p. 39, no. 267; p. 42, no. 277.

[3] See *SEG* 8 (1937), p. 52, no. 336.

[4] See *DAC* 10,1, col. 878; *SEG* 8 (1937), p. 51, no. 331.

[5] See *DAC* 10,1, col. 883.

[6] See *SEG* 8 (1937), p. 53, no. 344.

[7] See *SEG* 8 (1937), p. 2, no. 6; Schneider, *BVK* p. 55, note 1.

[8] See *Gerasa*, p. 473, no. 285; it is noteworthy that the phrase was apparently reserved for the synagogue at Jerash and not used for any of the numerous churches in that town, though elsewhere in Transjordan the phrase seems to be quite common.

[9] See *SEG* 8 (1937), p. 39, no. 267.

2. "Was renovated (ἀνενεώθη)." — The same verb is used in speaking of work carried out at other places. So, for example, at el-Quweisme,[1] Jerash,[2] Jerusalem[3] and Gaza;[4] often we are informed that the building in question was restored from the foundations. The verb presupposes the previous existence of the building which was repaired, restored or renovated. At Siyâgha the verb could refer to the transformation of the cella trichora into the basilica in the fifth century; or it could refer to the restoration of the basilica at the end of the sixth century. This latter undertaking was finished at the time of bishop Sergius and the abbot Martyrius (see inscription I).

3. "Under the most reverend and most pious priest and abbot Alex......." — The time when the holy place was renovated is indicated more precisely by a reference to the abbot. The first 4 letters of the abbot's name are certain; they indicate that the first part of his name was Alex. There is exactly sufficient space in the second line for the name Ἀλεξάνδρου followed by the abbreviated form of πρεσβ(υτέρου); at the end of the line there is a sign of abbreviation, which requires an abbreviated form before it. The Y after Ξ in the name Alex may have been the work of him who repaired the destroyed section of the panel.

Hegumen is the official title of Alex; that he was also a priest and that this fact was stated in the inscription may be inferred not only from the space and sign of abbreviation at the end of the second line but also from the conjunction καί at the beginning of the third line. The other two abbots were also priests, as we learned from the first and fifth inscriptions. The honorific epithets given to Alex differ from those given to the other abbots and also from those given to the bishops. The epithet εὐλαβέστατος, most reverend, is given to the deacon Saola at Jerash;[5] it is used also in inscriptions reported from neighboring countries, such as Palestine,[6] Egypt[7] and Syria.[8] Prentice observes that this title "was applied to officials of lesser dignity, e. g., to presbyters (nos. 70, 73), to deacons (*C. I. G.* 8647), or even to the clergy collectively (*C. I. G.* 8619)."[9] — The second epithet θεοσεβέστατος, "the most devout" or "the most pious," is given to bishop Theodosius at el-Yadûde,[10] to the presbyter Zacharias at Kabr Hiram[11] and to monks speaking of themselves in Egyptian papyri.[12]

We do not know when Alex was abbot of the monastery at Mount Nebo and consequently we do not know when the repairs referred to were carried out; neither do we know precisely to what repairs the inscription refers. But since the inscription exists in the basilica, it evidently refers to repairs made on or in the basilica; the character of the inscription suggests that this work antedates that which was carried out in the chapels. The inscription is of the same date as the other two in the sanctuary; it existed long enough to stand in need of repairs, which effaced a part of it. Moreover, in the judgement of the writer, the inscription belongs to the same period as the original pavement of the sanctuary; this, as we stated above pp. 211 f., antedates the second basilica and may possibly date from the fifth century A. D. It should, however, be stated that a date in the first half of the 6th century or even in the

1 See above p. 245, note 1, (6).
2 See *Gerasa*, inscriptions 274 and 293.
3 See *SEG* 8 (1937), p. 26, no. 172.
4 See *SEG* 8 (1937), p. 39, no. 268; p. 42, no. 277.
5 See *Gerasa*, p. 479, no. 304.
6 See *ARP* 2, p. 404, no. 5.
7 See *Aegyptus*, 18 (1938), p. 46.
8 See Prentice, nos. 70, 73, 85, 276.
9 See Prentice, no. 85.
10 See *DAC* 10, 1, col. 883.
11 See *DAC* 10, 1, col. 864.
12 See *Aegyptus*, 18 (1938), p. 46.

middle of that century would satisfy all the archæological evidence in as far as we are capable of interpreting it at present.

The inscriptions studied so far mention three periods of construction: — (1) the restoration of the basilica at the time of the abbot Alex; (2) the completion of the basilica and the baptistery at the time of the abbot Martyrius and bishop Sergius (597 A. D.); (3) the completion of the Theotokos chapel at the time of the abbots Martyrius and Theodore and bishop Leontios. The very expressions used in speaking of these operations clearly indicate other periods of construction.

IX. Pl. 118,2. In a rectangular panel, measuring 43×145 cm., in the mosaic pavement in the southern aisle of the basilica (see Fig. 27, d). The panel contains 4 lines of writing; in each line there were originally 14-21 letters; the 21 letters were used in the last line which is crowded. At two places the panel was damaged and as a result one or the other letter is missing in each line. Some of the letters differ in form from that used in the other inscriptions considered so far; so, for example, the letter A; it could be compared with the A used in inscription III, but its closest parallel is to be found in inscription XI (see Pl. 119,2); E and Σ have the square form also characteristic of inscription XI; the ligature for OY is never used; O is peculiarly small; the tips of the letters are without ornaments.[1] Other peculiarities will be noted below.

Transcription: Ὑπὲρ εἰρήνης [καὶ] σω|τηρίας τοῦ δ[ού(λου)] σου | Ἀνώσα [κ(αὶ) π]αντὸς τοῦ | εὐλογημ[έ]νου αὐτοῦ οἴκου.

Translation: For the peace and welfare of your servant Anosas and all his blessed house.

Observations: 1. "For the peace and welfare." — It was a common practice in Byzantine times to make offerings to the church for a definite purpose; this purpose is frequently expressed by the phrase: ὑπὲρ σωτηρίας, either alone or with a variety of other words,[2] but the present writer could not discover any other inscription in which the purpose is expressed by the phrase ὑπὲρ εἰρήνης. In the liturgy this phrase occurs very frequently in the so-called eirenika[3] and there the words have the same order as here; we must assume, therefore, that liturgical usage influenced the choice of this phrase, as it did in a number of other cases at Siyâgha. In the liturgy there are a number of additions which are instructive; the petition reads as follows: Ὑπὲρ τῆς ἄνωθεν εἰρήνης, καὶ τῆς σωτηρίας τῶν ψυχῶν ἡμῶν, τοῦ Κυρίου δεηθῶμεν; that is: "For the peace from on high, and for the salvation of our souls, let us pray the Lord." — In the inscription there is neither a subject nor a verb; if we supply: "Let us pray to the Lord for...," the sentence becomes complete; the character of the peace and salvation asked for is also determined more precisely: "Peace from on high," "salvation of souls."[4]

1 See *Gerasa*, p. 366, Fig. 14.

2 See inscription VI; *SEG* 8 (1937), passim; *Beth-Shan* IV, pp. 13 f.: ὑπὲρ μνήμης, τελείας ἐν Χριστῷ ἀναπαύσεως, σωτηρίας, ἀντιλήμψεως: "on behalf of the memory, the perfect rest in Christ, the preservation, the succour," etc.

3 "A litanic form of prayer, so-called because the first petitions allude to peace (εἰρήνη)." De Meester, p. 104, note 26; see ibid. pp. 24 f.; — see *Euchologion*, pp. 13, 42, 115, 138, 152, 162, etc.

4 See also the so-called ektenes, where a similar formula occurs, which also contains the two words in question (εἰρήνη, σωτηρία) along with numerous others. According to De Meester, pp. 113 f., note 39, "the *ektenes* (ἐκτενής) is another form of the δέησις or impetratory prayer.... There are many variants in the commemorations which are made in this prayer...." The petition to which we would call attention may be found ibid., pp. 40 ff.; it begins as follows: Ἔτι δεόμεθα ὑπὲρ ἐλέους, ζωῆς, εἰρήνης, ὑγιείας, σωτηρίας, ἐπισκέψεως, συγχωρήσεως καὶ ἀφέσεως τῶν ἁμαρτιῶν τῶν δούλων τοῦ Θεοῦ, etc.; that is: "Again let us pray for mercy, life, peace, health, salvation, protection, forgiveness and remission of sins of the servants of God...." See also *Euchologion*, pp. 51, 189 ff. Such petitions were repeated so frequently in the liturgy that we need not be surprised to find them also in inscriptions.

2. "Of your servant." — This phrase is very common in inscriptions.[1] Christians call themselves the servants of God or of Christ. This usage is derived from Holy Scripture and from there it found its way into the liturgy and into Christian inscriptions. In this case only the first letter of the word is preserved; originally there could have been only two or three more letters; this would imply either that the word was abbreviated[2] or that a syllable was accidentally omitted, as happened, for example, in an inscription at Khirbet el-Merd, where τουλον σου was written instead of τὸν δοῦλόν σου.[3] The pronoun indicates that the words are addressed to God or to Christ.

3. "Anosas." — The person for whose peace and welfare an offering was made or for whom prayers were asked was named immediately after the phrase: "of your servant;" in the transcription and the translation we indicated the name "Anosas," which does not seem to be known from other sources and hence doubts regarding its correctness have arisen.[4] Another reason for doubting the correctness of this name is the form of the letter Σ, which would be round here, whereas elsewhere in the inscription it is invariably square; hence some have considered the round Σ an abbreviation sign either for the previous proper name ("Ano") or for καί which is required by the context (see, v. g., Wroth, p. CVIII, Abbreviations). Finally this name would either not leave room for the conjunction καί or would at the most admit an abbreviated form of it. But to these difficulties we may reply that new names are found from time to time; the square and round Σ were at times used in the same inscription;[5] the abbreviated form of καί was suggested in the transcription. All other suggestions are also open to difficulties, so we may continue to call the person in question "Anosas."

4. "And all his blessed house." — The same phrase was used in two inscriptions of the sixth-century monastery at Beisan.[6] There in both cases the phrase begins with the abbreviated form of the conjunction "and" [κ(αί)], which we supplied in the transcription of our text. There the Greek word for "all" is παντός, as transcribed here. There the word "blessed" refers to the families of men with illustrious titles, here to "a servant" of God. In the *New Testament* εὐλογημένος is used of men, εὐλογητός of God; in the *LXX* there are some exceptions to this rule.[7] The *New Testament* usage is followed here.

X. Pl. 42,2, below. On a stone capital described on pp. 51 f. This capital is decorated with crosses one of which has letters attached to the extremities of its arms. The horizontal bar of the cross has a square E at its one end and a square Σ at its other end; the vertical bar has the letter B at its lower end and the ligature for OY at its upper end. All the letters are perfectly preserved except the first. If the letters are read in the order described a proper name of a place results.

Transcription: Ἐσβοῦ[ς]: Esbous.

Observations: To the northeast of Siyâgha there is a large ruined site which today is called Hesbân (see pp. 6 f.); it corresponds to the Biblical Hesebon and to the Roman-Byzantine

[1] See inscriptions XII & XIII; *SEG* 8 (1937), nos. 149, 150, 212, 241, 272, 275, 316, 337, 344; *QDAP* 3 (1934), p. 68, no. 17; *Gerasa*, inscriptions 331, 336, 344.
[2] See *QDAP* 9 (Suppl. 1940), p. 60, for different ways in which this word was abbreviated.
[3] See *JPOS* 9 (1929), p. 127.
[4] See *Antonianum* 9 (1934), pp. 358 f., note 2; *SEG* 8 (1937), p. 50, no. 326.
[5] See *QDAP* 3 (1934), p. 100; *Beth-Shan* IV, Pls. XX ff. passim; *Gerasa*, p. 366, Fig. 14.
[6] See *Beth-Shan* IV, pp. 13 f. & Pl. XX.
[7] See, v. g., Plummer, *St. Luke*, on chapter 1, verses 42 & 68.

Esbous.[1] In the Byzantine period it was the seat of a bishopric.[2] It is not improbable that the people of Esbous presented this capital to the sanctuary of Moses on Mount Nebo.

XI. Pl. 119, 1&2; Fig. 4,2, C. On a large stone of the cella trichora, measuring 131 × 131 × 40 cm., found on the eastern side of the basilica (see p. 27). The margin around the boss averages about 9½ cm. in width; on the upper one a cross and seven letters are carved, on the lower one 9 letters. A few of the letters are damaged owing to the fact that small pieces of the stone have been broken away. In general the letters resemble those used in inscription IX; compare especially the letters A, E and Σ. Owing to the position in which the stone was found the inscriptions on it must be assigned to a period antedating the last basilica.

Transcription: On the upper margin: + Σαλαμᾶς: Salamas.

On the lower margin: Ἐπιφάνιος: Epiphanios.

Observations: The two words are proper names; the former is Semitic, the latter Greek. Nothing is known about the men who were called Salamas and Epiphanios, but very probably they were the masons or architects who built the cella trichora or transformed it into the first basilica. The stone was originally too high in the eastern wall to be easily reached by casual visitors to the site (see p. 27); the inscriptions must be the work of the original builders.

XII. Pl. 120. On the flat and smooth face of a stone measuring 59 × 60 × 68 cm., which was found next to the ground directly behind the apse of the basilica (see p. 27). The position in which the stone was found suggests that it occupied a place in the eastern wall of the cella trichora and the first basilica at such a distance from the ground that it could be easily reached and its unusually smooth surface tempted people to scratch their petitions on the same. The entire face of the stone is covered with graffiti. In the majority of cases the letters cannot be made out easily, but the inscription in the lower right corner may be considered typical of the rest. It is preceded by a monogrammatic cross and consists of three lines of writing; the letters resemble those used in the sanctuary of the basilica; so, v. g., the letter A. — H is written for E, I for H, Ω for O, Ω for A. The word Κύ(ϱιε) is abbreviated by the method known as suspension, though elsewhere at Siyâgha contraction is more commonly used in abbreviating the divine names.[3] The sign of abbreviation is an horizontal bar.

Transcription: ☧ Κύ(ϱιε) ἐλ[έη]σ[όν] μ[ε] τὸν | δοῦλ[ό]ν σου Ἰωάνν[η]ν | τ[ὸ]ν γϱάψ[α]ντα.

Translation: ☧ O Lord, have mercy on me your servant John, the writer.

Observations: 1. ☧: Χϱ(ιστός); see *QDAP* 9 (Suppl. 1940), pp. 112, 121; *HCA* p. 270. This crux monogrammatica occurs only on this stone at Siyâgha.

2. "O Lord, have mercy on me." — This same petition was repeated frequently on this stone, as is evident from some of the letters which can still be made out. The same invocation occurs hundreds of times in Christian inscriptions, where it is but a faint echo of the endless repetitions of the same in the Greek liturgies.

3. "John." — This invocation was addressed to God by an individual who calls himself John. No other proper name could be recognized among the other graffiti on this stone.

1 See Meistermann, *Guide du Nil au Jourdain* etc., pp. 278-281; *Onom.* p. 84, line 4; p. 85, line 4; Abel, *Géog.* II, pp. 186 & 348 f.; Glueck, *AASOR* 14 (1934), pp. 6, 75 f.; *AASOR* 18-19 (1939), pp. 242-251. De Vaux, *RB* 47 (1938), pp. 249 f., no. 10.

2 Bishop Gennadios was present at the Council of Nice in the year 325 A. D. and bishop Zosius at the Councils of Ephesus in the year 431 and of Chalcedon in the year 451 (see p. 261,3); see *DHGE* 3 (1924), cols. 1172 and 1178 f. respectively. — See Abel, *Géog.* II, p. 186, note 4, regarding bishop Theodore about 650 A. D.

3 See *QDAP* 9 (Suppl. 1940), pp. 25 ff., 79, 123.

John calls himself the servant of the Lord, like Anosas in inscription IX. He also informs us that he was the one "who wrote" this invocation. The letter Ψ of the root of the word suggests the aorist form, whilst the Ω following it in the original would suggest a present form. At Seilûn[1] and in Syria[2] the aorist form was used in a similar case and this is suggested in the transcription.

4. Other marks on the stone. — To the left and above the inscription a cross is carved in bolder lines than the other graffiti (see Pl. 120). It was this cross which first caught our attention and led to a closer examination of the stone and to the discovery of the graffiti on the same. — Above and somewhat to the right of the cross a rectangle, partially visible in Pl. 120, was carved. — On the rest of the stone at least 4 rectangles seem to have been outlined to contain inscriptions; one of them has the handles of a tabula ansata. — In these rectangles and elsewhere on the stone the letters: KY can be recognised quite easily; they suggest the same petition as the one we considered. Other letters certainly exist, but their relation to one another is not so clear.

XIII. Pl. 121,5. On a stone which most probably served as a lintel for some door in the southern part of the western monastery; one end of the stone is broken off and has not been discovered; the other end measures 49×39×30 cm.; it is decorated with a carved cross between whose arms there is a Greek inscription; both the cross and the letters of the inscription have preserved traces of red paint. At the right end of the stone a few letters are missing. Unfortunately none of the letters can be made out in Pl. 121,5.

Text:

$\overline{\text{KE}}$ BOH	ΘΙ......
Λ Ο Υ	ΣΟ......

Transcription: Κ(ύρι)ε βοή|θ[ε]ι [τοῦ δού]||λου | σο[υ......].

Translation: O Lord, help thy servant N.

Observations: $\overline{\text{KE}}$. — In the preceding inscription the divine name was abbreviated by the method called suspension; here contraction is used. — Such invocations in which the Christian describes himself as a slave and asks for help are very common in Christian inscriptions. See inscriptions IX and XII.

XIV. Pl. 121,11. — Ψ. — Three stones found near room 61 (see p. 160) have a carving on one side which looks like the Greek letter Ψ and this is the reason why they are treated here. One of these stones is certainly a voussoir and most probably the other two were also; two measure 61×40×36 cm. and one 69×34×31 cm. The stone that was certainly a voussoir has the Ψ-shaped carving on that side which faced the adjoining stone; the carving was, therefore, not intended to be seen, but served to bind together two voussoirs or to hold the three-pronged end of a bar from whose other extremity something could have been suspended. The writer has seen similar stones at the Herodian site of Jericho, at Khirbet el-Mefjer[3] and in the garden of the archæological museum in Jerusalem; in all cases the stones seem to have been voussoirs; we may, therefore, dismiss the impression that the carving is a Greek letter; for the same reason other suggestions, namely, that it may represent a candelabrum, a Bedouin symbol, a Himyaritic cheth or the like, may be dismissed.

[1] See *SEG* 8 (1937), p. 21, no. 148.
[2] See Prentice, inscription no. 207.
[3] D. C. Baramki, *QDAP* 5 (1936), p. 132, writes: "It is of interest to note the manner in which the stone voussoirs were keyed firmly together by crosses grooved in some and cut in relief in others and then fitted into each other (Pl. LXXVI, 2-3)." — The stones with the Ψ-shaped grooves are not illustrated. — At Siyâgha the writer did not notice any stones with the Ψ in relief so that it could have been joined to the grooved Ψ after the manner of a tenon with a mortise; hence an alternative explanation was proposed above.

XV. Pl. 56, lowest row, left. On a tombstone, measuring 71 × 31 × 8 cm., found in the northern part of the atrium, west of cistern 9 (see pp. 78 f.). On one of the two flat sides, near the top, there are an arch, a cross and three letters of an inscription. In all these respects it resembles another tombstone from el-Kerak, now in the museum at ʿAmmân, illustrated in Pl. 56, lowest row, right, opposite the one from Siyâgha. The arch is merely a rounded carved line. The cross's arms end in three prongs; only the ends of two arms remain; the rest of the cross was deliberately effaced. Above the arch is an inscription consisting of three letters; that near the upper left corner of the stone is the letter A, whose form resembles that used in inscriptions III, IX, XI; those near the upper right corner of the same are the letters ON. The three letters most probably stand for an abbreviated word.

Transcription: Ἀ(νάπαυσ)ον.

Translation: Rest or (Lord) grant rest.

Observations: The phrase: Κύριε or Χριστὲ ἀνάπαυσον, meaning "Lord" or "Christ grant rest," occurs in a number of inscriptions;[1] it is, therefore, not improbable here. Other forms of the same verb[2] and the noun[3] expressing the same idea are so common in inscriptions that it becomes virtually certain that the same idea was expressed here in an abbreviated form which was readily understood.[4]

XVI. Pl. 121,1. On the molded border of a marble slab, which had been broken to pieces and scattered over the site. Six of the fragments with 15 letters (not all complete), a cross and a sign of abbreviation were recovered,[5] but the slab and the inscription are still incomplete. The letters resemble those used in the sanctuary of the basilica; the word πρεσβύτερος was abbreviated; the sign of abbreviation resembles an S, used also in the chapels and the sanctuary of the basilica.

Transcription: + Προσφο[ρὰ .....]ου πρε[σβ](υτέρου) καὶ Μ[.........].

Translation: + The gift of the priest N. and ....

Observations: A cross marks the beginning of the inscription. The first word of the inscription is the Greek equivalent for "gift;" the second word was probably the name of the donor, which has not been recovered; the donor was a priest; this title is followed by the sign of abbreviation, the word καί and the Greek letter M, which may be the beginning of the name of a second benefactor. — Sukenik[6] has called attention to a number of inscribed slabs which served as screens and ventured the view that it was the rule to inscribe such

1 See *SEG* 8 (1937), nos. 1, 275, 316.

2 See *SEG* 8 (1937), nos. 275, 299-305, 334.

3 See *SEG* 8 (1937), nos. 5, 148, 175-177, 336.

4 See *PEQ* 71 (1939), pp. 183 ff., where, among other interesting observations, we find the following: "The sense is "rest from troubles," and the group of formulæ was probably Egyptian in origin; it is found in Jerusalem, but is rare in Syria (*ARP* 2 [1896], pp. 408 f., no. 10; *PJB* 28 [1932], p. 100; *ZDPV* 44 [1921], p. 150). It is common at Gaza, Beersheba, and the towns in the south, with the striking exception of Auja Hafir; absent at Kerak and Kh. Ader. There are 41 dated examples, which fall between A. D. 450 and 679. All but six of these fall between A. D. 510 and 613." — Ibid. p. 186, there are tabulated 172 inscriptions from 11 places; of these 86 use the formula under consideration. — Of the 20 inscriptions known until a few years ago from the el-Kerak region none contained this formula; since then Mrs. Canova (see above p. 88) has discovered hundreds of inscribed tombstones in the el-Kerak region; it will be interesting to learn how her discoveries will affect the results indicated above. — For abbreviated forms of the formula see *QDAP* 9 (Suppl. 1940), p. 48.

5 The fragment with the cross and Π comes from the atrium (see p. 78), that with O from the southern slope, those with ΣΦΟ and ΟΥ from the northeastern slope (see p. 134, note 4), that with ΠΡΕ from rooms 10 & 11 (see p. 74); that with SKAIM from the sanctuary of the basilica (see p. 50). Another fragment (not illustrated) from the northeastern slope has faint traces of 2 more letters.

6 See *The Ancient Synagogue of el-Hammeh*, pp. 58 ff.

slabs; at Siyâgha, where many such slabs were used and came to light, only this one was inscribed; it is, of course, possible that one or the other of these inscribed fragments belonged to another slab, but even this assumption is not very probable.

XVII. Pl. 121,2. On the border of a broken marble plate. Five inscribed fragments of this plate were found: 4 among the large stones east of the basilica (see p. 35) and 1 in the dump in area 53 (see p. 147). This context suggests a date before the second basilica. Of this inscription we possess only 8 complete letters, averaging between 13-15 mm. in height, and parts of 3 others; the letters resemble those of inscription XI, but the tips are more ornate and they were filled in with a black paste. Two of the inscribed fragments represent corners of the plate and they may represent the beginning and the end of the inscription, provided it did not continue around two or more sides of the vase. The import of this inscription is uncertain.

Transcription: Αδ υτ ωνος βα κ.

Observation: No word is complete. The vase belonged to the furnishings of the sanctuary; that gives us a clew to the possible meaning of the text; but since all the words are incomplete and uncertain other suggestions would only be misleading.

XVIII. Pl. 121, 3 & 4. On the lower side of a slab which was used as a table. The letters are arranged in two groups to form monograms. The first group is preceded by a cross. In this first group the letters Ν Α Ξ Ο Υ are the most prominent whilst T, Σ and I can also be made out;[1] in the second group Π is clear; above Π there is the letter T; the three strokes on the right may be read as P, E, Σ; the lowest letter as Ω or, if the left curve alone is considered, as O.[2]

Transcription: + Νάξου πέτρος.

Translation: + Stone of Naxos.

Observations: The monograms, as we noted above, exist on the lower side of a slab, where they would not readily be seen by anyone. It is not very probable that a donor who wished to be remembered would have had his name put in a place where it would not have been seen, but we could imagine a workman, a firm or a place supplying the material putting his or its mark in some unobtrusive part of the slab. Naxos, the largest island of the Cyclades, possessed marble quarries in ancient times;[3] possibly this marble slab came from those quarries.

[1] A very similar block of letters was used on coins for the name of the emperor Anastasius I (491-518 A.D.); see Wroth, I, p. 7, nos. 59 f.; Pl. II, 2. But there the O and Υ are distributed over the two upper ends of N; whilst here they form a ligature above the right vertical stroke of N and Ξ remains to be explained. — Very similar is also the block used on coins for the name of Justinian I (527-565 A.D.); see Wroth, I, pp. 72 f., nos. 414 ff.; Pl. X, 15 & 16. — See ibid. p. CIX regarding monograms on Byzantine coins in general. — In the transcription we propose to ignore the last three letters; in this way we obtain a tolerably satisfactory reading.

[2] The most obvious reading seems to be some form of Πέτρος, taken either as a common noun, as here, or as a proper name; in this second case we could read: "Peter of Naxos;" or we could presuppose that both in this and in the preceding monogram we have the names of workmen, say in the genitive case, and we could supply some word like: ἔργον, on which the genitive depends; so, v.g.: "(the work) of X. Anastasius and Peter." — Instead of the proper name "Peter" one could read Πρῶ(τος) or Πρώ(του). — In fact, the writer hesitated between the transcription given in the text and the one suggested here. If the readers do not find the text acceptable, the writer would urge as the best alternative reading: "(the work) of X. Anastasius and Protus."

[3] See *DAC* 12, 1, col. 1019; *RE* Zweite Reihe 3 (1929), "*Steinbruch*," cols. 2263 f.

XIX. Pl. 121, 9. — A. — On the plinth of a marble column's base, found in area 75. Only a part of the base's plinth is preserved and on it is carved the letter A. Since this letter exists near the left end of one of the plinth's sides and since the plinth was originally about twice as large as it is now, we think that there may have been one more letter and that it was Ω. A & Ω are apocalyptic letters[1] frequently used in inscriptions.[2]

XX. A fragment of a marble slab, measuring 17 × 13½ × 6 cm., polished on one side and rough on the other, has plaster adhering to the rough side and beneath it a number of incised letters, among which ANN can be recognized; there are other letters before and after these three. Very probably a workman scratched his name here; he was probably called: IΩANNHΣ.

Transcription: [Ἰω]άνν[ης].

Translation: John. — See inscription XII for this name; the person is not necessarily the same in both inscriptions.

XXI. Pl. 121,10. — B. — Graffiti on plaster. Fragments of plaster with graffiti were found east and northeast of the basilica; the plaster has a gray color and the graffiti are black; none of the graffiti represent a complete word or even a group of letters; in all cases the plaster is broken to such tiny bits that, as a rule, only parts of letters survive; but in a few cases complete letters were found, such as B,N, etc. They go to show that scribbling on walls was practiced also here.

XXII. Pls. 121,6; 143, 3. On the upper part of a pottery lamp, found in room 61 (see p. 161). The inscription begins to the right of the so-called "candlestick" on the spout and must be read from left to right around the edge of the lamp, though in this case a number of letters are inverted; so, e. g., A, N & Ω; but this is due to a defect in the mold; a few letters have degenerated into mere strokes or circlets. Abbreviations were also used for the divine name and for the last word. The very same characteristics were noted on a lamp discovered during the excavations at Ophel, Jerusalem,[3] and on a lamp in the Flagellation museum; they suggest that the lamps were all formed in the same mold or, at least, that the same model was used for all.

Transcription: Φῶς Χ(ριστο)ῦ φ[αί]ν[ει] πᾶσι[ν] ἡ(μῖν).

Translation: The light of Christ shines for us all.

Observations: The same text is found on numerous lamps discovered in Palestine, so, v. g., at Beisan,[4] Gezer,[5] Jerusalem,[6] etc.[7] This lamp and the one to be mentioned next are the first ones with this inscription reported from Transjordan. The text seems to be derived from the liturgy,[8] though ultimately it may be traced back to Holy Scripture.[9] The type of lamp in question was in use throughout the Byzantine period,[10] but the inscription

1 See *Apocalypse* 1, 8; 21, 6.
2 See *HCA* p. 270; *QDAP* 9 (Suppl. 1940), p. 53.
3 *PEF Ann.* 4, p. 195, Fig. 209.
4 See *SEG* 8 (1937), p. 14, no. 56.
5 See *Gezer* 2, pp. 227 f.
6 See *SEG* 8 (1937), p. 32, no. 216; *PEF Ann.* 4, p. 195, Fig. 209 (11 or 12 examples), etc.
7 See *HCA* p. 588, where mention is made of a text on a lamp from Jerusalem which ends in the word: ἡμῖν like our text. — See *DAC* 8,1, cols. 1108-1111, nos. 54, 55, 59. — Galling, *ZDPV* 46 (1923), p. 18, no. 1. — There are dozens of such lamps in the museums of Jerusalem, mostly of unknown origin; thus, for example, the Flagellation museum possesses more than two dozens of them.
8 See *Euchologion*, pp. 113, 119; *DAC* 8, 1, col. 1111; *HCA* p. 588.
9 See, v.g., *John* 1, 4, 5, 9; 8, 12.
10 See *QDAP* 4 (1935), pp. 177 f.

on the lamp is probably a somewhat later feature, dating possibly from the sixth century of our era.[1] The inscription has assumed a great variety of forms;[2] in the case of the lamp under consideration the text is tolerably well preserved.

XXIII. Pls. 121, 8; 143, 4. On a fragment of the upper part of a pottery lamp from room 61 (see p. 161). Only 6 letters are preserved; they resemble those on the previous lamp in every respect; they are: ΕΝΗΠΑΣ.

Transcription: [Φῶς Χ(ριστο)ῦ φαί]ν[ει] πᾶσ[ιν ἡ(μῖν)].

Observation: The text on the complete lamp to which this fragment belonged was no doubt substantially the same as on the preceding lamp.

XXIV. Pls. 121, 7; 143, 2. On a pottery lamp whose spout is missing; it was found in room 61 (see p. 161). The ornamentation of the top of the lamp consists of a number of letters; it is doubtful how we should read them; if read as if arranged around the central opening we have: N (inverted), P, Y or A, ornament, P or A, Y, K (inverted), Λ, A. In every case the inscription is distorted.

Transcription: [Λυχ]ν[ά]ρ[ι]α κ[α]λά.

Translation: Beautiful little lamps.

Observations: The letters which can be made out on the lamp do not correspond to those used on the two preceding lamps. A number of lamps with the inscription suggested in the transcription are known;[3] it seems that it gave rise to the letters decorating the lamp under consideration; more than this we do not wish to affirm. From this and similar inscriptions we know that these small lamps were called lychnaria (in the singular: lychnarion).

XXV. Another small fragment of a pottery lamp (not illustrated) has a type of decoration resembling that on the preceding lamp. One or the other letter may be recognized.

C. THE SAMARITAN INSCRIPTIONS

XXVI. Pl. 122, Fig. 1, 2. On a piece of a marble slab, measuring 16 × 13 × 3.1 cm., found in 1933 behind the apse of the basilica (see p. 174). The fragment is broken on three sides, but the fourth seems to be intact and very probably represents the upper edge of the original slab. On the one side six fine horizontal lines, 17-19 mm. distant from each other, are ruled. Below the first line there are 6 complete letters and part of a 7th one, below the third 2 and below the fifth 4. Dots were used to separate the words; two can be seen in the first line: one after the first (incomplete) letter and another after the fifth; no other fragment has evidence of such a division of words.

Transcription: *1* .˙בלבך˙ נט | *2* חן | *3* וחכם

Translation: *1* in your heart . . *2* . . *3* . . . .

1 See *PEF Ann.* 5, p. 92.

2 See especially *Gezer* 2, pp. 227 f.; *PEF Ann.* 4, pp. 194 f.

3 See *PEF Ann.* 4, p. 194, Fig. 10: 3 examples; ibid. 5, p. 92, Pl. XVII, 28; *SEG* 8 (1937), p. 32, no. 215; *SWP Jer.* p. 540, 1; *RAO* 1, p. 171, note 2. A number of lamps with this inscription are known, though they are perhaps not so numerous as those of the previous class.

Observations : 1. No connection could be established between the 8 pieces of marble with Samaritan inscriptions which have been discovered so far, hence also the text on the fragments is disconnected and we must content ourselves with a few observations regarding each fragment, especially since we are not certain whether they originally formed part of only one or of more slabs. The material used is the same in all cases; it is gray marble with a smooth finish on each side, but more highly polished on the inscribed side. The fragments differ in thickness between 31-35 mm., but such variations in thickness do not necessarily indicate different slabs; the same variations in thickness were frequently noted on various parts of the same slab at Siyâgha. The space between the ruled lines on the different fragments is not always the same in width; it varies between 13-14 and 17½-20 mm.; but here too it will be observed that even on the same fragment the spacing is not strictly uniform.

2. No complete sentence has been recovered; a few words and phrases give us some clew to the character of the text inscribed on the slabs and the 16 different letters used are interesting epigraphically. The majority of the Samaritan inscriptions which have come to light consist of texts derived from the *Pentateuch;*[1] if this was the case elsewhere, it would seem to be true a fortiori at the sanctuary dedicated to the author of the *Pentateuch*.

3. בלבך, meaning "in your heart," is the only complete phrase on this fragment of the slab. It is separated from the preceding and following words by dots.[2] The phrase in question occurs frequently in the *Pentateuch,*[3] but the writer was unable to discover a context in which the letters (preceding and) following it occur.

XXVII. Pl. 122, Fig. 1, 1. On a fragment of a marble slab, measuring 19.5 × 18 × 3.2 cm., found in 1937 south of cistern 116 (see pp. 174, 197). The fragment is broken on all sides except one, which represents the left edge of the original slab. On the one side there are 9 horizontal and 2 vertical ruled lines; the latter are near the left end of the slab; the former are 18-19 mm. apart. The letters on this slab belong to 5 lines of writing. Between the first and second ruled lines there are 4 letters, between the third and fourth 3, between the fifth and sixth 3, between the seventh and eighth 7 and below the ninth 2. Noteworthy is the fact that the last letter of each line — it still exists in 3 of the 5 lines — is separated by a relatively wide space from the rest of the word and placed near the edge of the slab between two vertical lines. The 19 letters represent a few complete words or phrases in the second, third and fourth lines and on these disconnected words and phrases must be based our conclusions regarding the original text.

Transcription : *1* מנתן | *2* מוך | *3* הכל | *4* אך הנביא | *5* מ..ו

Translation : *1* . . . . *2* like unto thee *3* all *4* but the prophet *5* . - .

Observations : 1. The meaning of the 4 letters in the first line is uncertain.

2. [כ]מוך, "like unto thee." — This phrase occurs in *Deut.* 18, 18, and is of special interest, since it refers to Moses and, according to Gaster, forms the basis of the Messianic hope of the Samaritans. Regarding these two points Gaster writes as follows : "The Samaritans

[1] See J. A. Montgomery, *The Samaritans*, Philadelphia, 1907, passim; S. Raffaeli, *A Recently Discovered Samaritan Charm, JPOS* 1 (1920), pp. 143 f.; W. R. Taylor, *Recent Epigraphic Discoveries in Palestine, JPOS* 10 (1930), pp. 18 ff.; id., *Samaritan Inscription from Gaza, JPOS* 16 (1936), pp. 131 ff.; L. A. Mayer and A. Reifenberg, *A Samaritan Lamp, JPOS* 16 (1936), pp. 44 f.; A. Alt, *Zwei Samaritanische Inschriften, ZDPV* 48 (1925), pp. 398 ff., etc.

[2] Regarding this method of dividing words in Samaritan inscriptions see, v. g., Taylor, *JPOS* 10 (1930), pp. 18 ff.; Alt, *ZDPV* 48 (1925), pp. 398 ff.; C. Warren, *Underground Jerusalem*, London, 1876, pp. 232 ff.

[3] See the concordance of Mandelkern, pp. 629 ff.; so, v. g., *Lev.* 19, 17; Deut. 6, 6; 7, 17; 8, 2 & 17; 9,4; 18, 21; etc.

rest their expectation of the advent of the Restorer on the promise given in their tenth commandment and on *Deut.* XVIII, 15 and 18: 'The Lord thy God will raise up unto thee a prophet from the midst of thee, of thy brethren, like unto me: unto him ye shall hearken,' and 'I will raise them up a prophet from among their brethren l i k e u n t o t h e e; and I will put my words in his mouth, and he shall speak unto them all that I shall command him.' They therefore interpret this promise to mean that out of the tribe of Levi, i. e. Moses's brethren, a prophet will rise like unto Moses; and as no one can be like unto Moses in all his perfection, they hold that perhaps Moses himself will come to life again and bring them the promised happiness. He will carry the rod of Moses in his hand, and perform all those signs aforementioned, and as further proof that he is the true Restorer, he will discover the hidden vessels of the Temple..." [1] In view of this doctrine this fragment of the Samaritan inscription becomes vested with more than passing interest and deserves special attention.

3. כל, "all." — This word also occurs in *Deut.* 18, 18; but if the letter preceding this word in the third line is ה a different context must be looked for.

4. אך הנביא, "but the prophet." — This phrase is found in *Deut.* 18, 20, from where it seems to be derived.

5. In the fifth line the two existing letters are separated by a space in which one or the other letter was chipped away and in this way the connection between the two has been destroyed.

The words of *Deut.* 18, 18-20, would be a very appropriate text for the sanctuary of Moses on Mount Nebo, whether accepted in the Samaritan sense indicated above in no. 2 or in the Christian sense (see the Commentaries).

XXVIII. Pl. 122, Fig. 1,3. On a fragment of a marble slab, measuring $12\frac{1}{2} \times 8\frac{1}{2} \times$ 3.1 cm., found in 1933 in area 92 (see p. 173). The fragment is broken on all sides. On the one side there are 6 horizontal ruled lines 17.5-18.5 mm. apart. There are traces of 4 lines of writing; of the first line only an indistinct sign remains, of the second we still have 4 letters (2 incomplete), of the third 4 and of the fourth 5 (4 incomplete).

Transcription: *1* . | *2* ה אתך | *3* [ע]יניך | *4* . כם . .

Translation: *1* . *2* . . . . *3* your eyes *4* . . . . .

Observation: Only in the third line do we have a phrase which is more or less complete; it occurs at least 15 times in the *Pentateuch* [2] and a number of times in Samaritan inscriptions; [3] it is often associated with the phrase which we considered in inscription XXVI,3; a Biblical text in which both phrases occur is very probably the source of this phrase. [4]

XXIX. Pl. 122, Fig. 1,6. On a fragment of a marble slab, measuring $10.5 \times 8 \times$ 3.5 cm., found in 1937 in area 121, immediately east of room 104 (see p. 174). The fragment is broken on all sides. On the one side there are 6 horizontal ruled lines 18 mm. apart. There are traces of 4 lines of writing; of the first line only a few indistinct signs remain; of the second we have 4 letters, one incomplete; of the third 4 letters, one incomplete; of the fourth traces of several letters, but none complete.

Transcription: *1* . . | *2* [ה]במה | *3* .דכא | *4* . . ל

Translation: *1* . . *2* the sanctuary *3* . . . . *4* . . .

[1] M. Gaster, *The Samaritans*, London, 1925, p. 91.

[2] *Gen.* 13,14; 31,12; 46,4; *Ex.* 13,9; 13,16; *Deut.* 3,21; 3,27; 4,9; 4,19; 6,8; 7,19; 10,21; 28,34; 28,67; 29,2.

[3] See, v.g., *JPOS* 16 (1936), p. 132, no. 33.2542: *Deut.* 6,8. It is part of the text used for phylacteries and for mesusas on the doorposts of houses; see *Ex.* 13,2-16; *Deut.* 6,4-9; 11,13-21.

[4] See, v.g., the texts referred to in the previous note.

Observation: [ה]במה, in the second line, was rendered in the translation by: "the sanctuary." — According to Gesenius [1] the word may mean: (1) *A high place, a height,* a general word including mountains and hills. (2) *Fortress, castle,* built upon a mountain. (3) *Sanctuary* or *chapel.* (4) It very often has the same meaning as בית הבמה "a sanctuary built on a mountain" to God or idols (compare No. 3), . . . and it is even applied to *any sanctuary* or fane, *Jer.* 7,31, compare Aethiop. . . . : a mountain, also a convent, Germ. Hag, pr. a grove, hence a church or temple there built. (5) It rarely signifies a *sepulchral mound,* Greek βωμός.

XXX. Pl. 122, Fig. 2. On a fragment of a marble slab, measuring 16.8 × 8.7 × 3.3 cm., found in 1938 probably in area 121 (see p. 174). The fragment is broken on all sides. On the one side there are 9 horizontal ruled lines 18-18½ mm. apart. There are traces of 4 lines of writing; in the first line 4 letters remain, in the second 3, in the third 3 and in the fourth 2; several are incomplete.

Transcription: *1* יסרת | *2* [ל]הי | *3* [ע]יפ | *4* [כ]ע

Translation: *1* you founded *2* . . . *3* . . . *4* . .

Observation: No satisfactory context could be discovered for the word and letters preserved on this fragment.

XXXI. Pl. 122, Fig. 1,7. On a mere sliver of a marble slab, measuring 17 × 4.5 × 3.3 cm., found in 1937 in room 100 (see p. 174). Its surface is blackened by fire. On the one side there are 7 horizontal ruled lines and a vertical one; the former are 17½-20 mm. apart. There are traces of 4 lines of writing, but only one letter is complete. In the first line there are traces of 2 letters (ח|[כ]), in the second 2 (ב, this is the complete letter, |[מ]), in the third one ([ג]|) and in the fourth one (|[ל]). The vertical line is between the two letters in the first two lines, before the letter in the third line and after the letter in the fourth line. Vertical lines existed also on the fragment treated under no. XXVII; there it represented the left edge of an inscription; possibly this fragment also represents the left end either of that or another inscription.

XXXII. Pl. 122, Fig. 1,4. On a fragment of a marble slab, measuring 10 × 9 × 3.3 cm., found in 1935 near the top of the ruins filling room 14; it had probably been used as part of the filling between the layers of masonry when the walls of the room were built (see pp. 120 & 174). On the one side there are at least 3 horizontal ruled lines 13-14 mm. apart. The spacing distinguishes this and the next fragment from the 6 preceding ones; this might indicate an inscription different from the one represented by the preceding pieces, but the point should not be stressed too much, for the same difference in spacing occurs at times on one and the same slab. [2] There are remains of two lines of writing; in the first line there are 5 letters and in the second 3; the letters are smaller than those on the preceding fragments; this is evidently due to the smaller space between the lines and may possibly point to a different inscription, though not necessarily, as we pointed out above.

Transcription: *1* לעריך | *2* [ל]א י

Observation: With the 5 letters in the first line a variety of words can be formed; the immediate context would have to determine what the original combination was, but of

[1] *Hebrew and Chaldee Lexicon to the Old Testament Scriptures,* translated with additions and corrections from the autor's *Thesaurus* and other works by Samuel Prideaux Tregelles, pp. CXXIV f.

[2] See, v. g., *SWP* 2, plate after p. 204.

that context nothing has been discovered. — In the second line the first two letters probably represent the negative particle לא, not.

XXXIII. Pl. 122, Fig. 1,5. On a fragment of a marble slab, measuring 9.7 × 9.5 × 3.2 cm., found in 1937 in room 101 (see pp. 184 & 174). The fragment is broken on all sides and blackened by fire. On the one side there are 8 horizontal ruled lines 14 mm. apart, as on the preceding slab. There are remains of 4 lines of writing; in the first, one letter is complete and there are traces of two others; in the second, there are 3 letters; in the third, 3; in the fourth, traces of 2. There is a rather wide vacant space in each line; this may indicate the end of the lines or possibly there was one more letter near the edge of the slab between vertical lines, as in no. XXVII, now broken away.

Transcription: . . *4* | למר *3* | אמר *2* | [ל]ע[ו] *1*

Observation: Again none of the words are certain.

D. THE ARABIC INSCRIPTIONS

XXXIV. Pl. 123,1. On 2 fragments of a marble slab found in 1935 in room 23 (see pp. 128 & 247). On one side of the slab, which has a rougher finish than the other, near the upper right hand corner, there was a line of writing, of which a few characters have survived. The fragment of the slab illustrated in Pl. 123,1, represents the beginning of the inscription; several letters on this piece of marble have been almost completely effaced, whilst on the next piece, adjoining the former on the left, all the characters are so faint that it is useless to reproduce it. Photographs or copies of this and the following 4 inscriptions were submitted to Mr. St. H. Stephan, who was kind enough to attempt a reading, transcription and translation, which he transmitted to the writer on February 20, 1940. [1]

Transcription: [ومن شكّ] بالله كفر: wa man shakka bi-llâhi kafar.

Translation: [And he who doubts] in God blasphemes (or is an unbeliever or an infidel).

Observation: Mr. Stephan considers the above reading purely "tentative;" he bases it on a "current Islamic sentence." Owing to the character of the writing Mr. Stephan suggests a date "at the end of the 9th century." The suggested date is over a century later than the writer would have expected in the light of the other material; if correct it would fill in a lacuna in the history of the site and as such the fragment would have a very definite value which should be emphasized.

XXXV. Pl. 123,2. On a fragment of a tile picked up somewhere at Siyâgha. Below an horizontal line there are traces of 4 or 5 signs scratched into the clay when it was still soft. At first the writer classified these signs as "potter's marks." When the time arrived for arranging the plates it was suggested to the writer that this was a Kufic inscription and this led to

[1] The writer is not in a position to form an independent judgement regarding this and the following inscriptions; but he believes that the reader should not be deprived of the views of a competent authority who has been able to see and study the original photographs and discuss the subject with others. After discussing these inscriptions with Professor L. A. Mayer, Mr. St. H. Stephan, in a letter addressed to the writer on December 23, 1940, once more emphasized the fact that the reading cannot be established beyond doubt. The suggested reading expresses religious sentiments similar to those expressed by the Greek and Samaritan inscriptions; this is a point in favor of the proposed reading. — The writer takes this opportunity to thank Mr. Stephan and Mr. Mayer for their help.

the inclusion of the sherd in Pl. 123,2.[1] The chief interest of the fragment consists in this that it was the only tile found at Siyâgha with signs which may represent an inscription.

XXXVI. Pl. 123,3. On a fragment of a clay sherd of a vessel found in the atrium in 1933 (see pp. 79 & 247). The sherd, broken on all sides, measures 16.8 × 11.5 × 1.2 cm.; the ware is red; the inner surface has marks of fingers; the outer surface is black and has an inscription which was traced while the clay was still soft. Originally there may have been several lines of writing; clear marks in the clay to the right and left of the chipped upper part of the sherd suggest one line there; a second line exists in the lower half of the sherd; it seems that the beginning of this second line is lost, but the end of the same has been preserved.

Transcription: [يؤ]من بالله تعالى: yu'minu bi-llâhi taᶜâla.

Translation: He who believes in Allah, exalted be He.

Observation: The inscription has been read in a variety of ways by different persons; the only word on which all agreed was the word "Allah" which seems to point to its religious character; in this respect it resembles the majority of inscriptions found at Siyâgha. What precedes and follows is doubtful. — The writer has adopted the transcription and translation suggested by Mr. Stephan, who was careful to point out that the reading is open to question; the suggestion of that scholar that this text "is a curious form of a Moslem formula, blessing the person who believes in Allah" etc., deserves to be noted. He suggests a "10th century" date for this text. — The context in which this sherd was found would permit almost any date; if the date suggested is correct another century in the history of Siyâgha would be represented; we have no other clear evidence for the 10th century A. D.

XXXVII. No illustration. Graffiti on a small piece of plaster found in area 38 in 1935 (see pp. 134 & 247). There are traces of 2 lines of writing too faint to be reproduced well, but a photograph and a copy made from the original were submitted to Mr. Stephan, who informed the writer that the text "seems to be an incomplete dating. I read: ᶜishrûn | dhi-l-qiᶜda: عشرون | ذيلقعده." [Dhi-l-qiᶜda or Zilkaᶜada is the 11th month of the Mohammedan year; hence the date would be the 20th of the month Zilkaᶜada.]

XXXVIII. Pl. 141,18. On a piece of a glass weight found in room 76 in 1937 (see pp. 168[2] & 247). About half of the weight is preserved. Originally it was round and about 29 mm. in diameter; its one side was flat; its other side had a raised edge about 4 mm. thick forming a border for a sunken section about 2 mm. thick, which had six or seven horizontal lines of writing in relief; the right end of each line is preserved.

Transcription: *1* — | *2* بسم | *3* الله | *4* مام[ون] | *5* ع[ط] | *6* و | *7* ف

Translation: *1* — *2* in the name *3* of God *4* (the) Trustworthy, *5-6-7* (the) Propitious (One).

Observation: The Arabic glass weights in possession of the Department of Antiquities in Palestine were classified recently; the writer was informed that the specialist engaged in that work saw the copy of the inscription on this fragment from Siyâgha and declared that nothing could be made out of this fragmentary inscription.[3] — Such glass weights were also used in the Byzantine period.

[1] The final suggestion made to the writer before going to print is that the signs are Greek letters; they do not look like uncial letters, which were the rule in all the Greek inscriptions found at Siyâgha.

[2] On p. 168, line 9 from below, read inscription XXXVIII instead of XXXVI.

[3] The transcription given here is that of Mr. Stephan, who suggests a 10th century date for the weight; the words were translated by Mr. J. A. Calis, to whom the writer hereby expresses his gratitude. — For good published specimens of this type of weight see S. Lane-Poole, *Catalogue of Arabic Glass Weights*, 1891.

E. MISCELLANEA

XXXIX. Graffiti scratched on a stone near the upper part of the southern wall of the southern sacristy; they could not be deciphered (see p. 58).

XL. Roman numbers: IV & VI, carved on stones near the lower part of the northern wall of the southern sacristy (see p. 58).

XLI. Various signs on stones near the lower part of the northern sacristy's eastern wall — on the exterior; probably masons' marks.

XLII. An oval surmounted by a tau (ȸ) on the lower side of the fragment of a marble slab found in area 80 in 1937 and illustrated in Pl. 126, 15. It may be a mason's mark or a monogram. See *QDAP* IX (Suppl. 1940), p. 105 for abbreviations of this type. Another fragment of a marble slab had two monograms in a similar position (see inscription XVIII).

XLIII. On small fragments of a marble slab found in hall 56 in 1937 there are faint traces of graffiti (registered no. 1990 a & b).

N. B. — The coins also have inscriptions; they will be treated in the following chapter. Only on coins was Latin used.

CHAPTER IX

THE COINS

A. GENERAL SURVEY

During the 3 expeditions to Siyâgha 188 coins were found. Mr. A. S. Kirkbride, Curator of coins in the museum at Ammân, cleaned and identified the coins found in 1933 and 1935; [1] Father P. Lemaire, O. F. M., cleaned and identified the coins found in 1937; the latter also prepared the detailed description of all these coins. We hereby acknowledge this help with pleasure and gratitude.

Only bronze coins came to light; all are in a very poor condition; the coins which could be identified with certainty represent Roman, Byzantine, Early Arabic and Ottoman coinages. Nothing of special value or interest for the history of coinage was noted. These coins are, however, important for the history of Siyâgha; they indicate, more precisely than any other source taken alone, the period during which the site was occupied in one way or other; they serve to supplement the other sources and help to fix an accurate chronological framework for the history of the site.

B. THE TABLES

I. ROMAN

Commodus,	180-192	1
Constantine I,	306-337	1
Constantius II,	337-361	2
Theodosius I,	378-395	3
Arcadius,	395-408	11
Honorius,	395-423	2
Fourth-Fifth cent. types,		13
Total		33

II. BYZANTINE

Anastasius I,	491-518	3
Justin I,	518-527	8
Justinian I,	527-565	7
Justin II,	565-578	7
Tiberius II,	578-582	1
Maurice Tiberius,	582-602	4
Phocas,	602-610	3
Heraclius,	610-641	1
Early Byzantine types,		9
Total		43

[1] At the end of the expedition in 1937 Mr. Kirkbride was absent in Galilee; in 1939 he returned to Transjordan as British Resident. — For a general classification of approximately 5000 ancient coins found in various parts of Transjordan between the years 1928 and 1937, see A. S. Kirkbride, *Currencies in Transjordan*, *PEQ* 71 (1939), pp. 152-161.

III. EARLY ARABIC

Umayyad,	A.H. 41-132:	661- 750 A.D.	19
Abbasid,	A.H. 132-650:	750-1258 A.D.	1
Melek al-Kâmil Nasir-ad-Din,	A.H. 615-635:	1218-1238 A.D.	1
Total			21

IV. OTTOMAN

Mahmûd II,	A.H. 1223-1255:	1808-1839 A.D.	8

V. SUMMARY

Roman	33
Byzantine	43
Early Arabic	21
Ottoman	8
Identified	105
Not identified	83
Total	188

C. THE CATALOGUE [1]

I. THE ROMAN COINS

Commodus, 180-192.

1. From 7; 4.8 grms.; 16-17 mm.; *obv.:* bust to r., youthful, bareheaded; inscr.: AV K IN; *rev.:* bust of Zeus-Ammon to r.; inscr. partly obliterated, partly off die, but on l.: A BO. [2]

Constantine I, 306-337.

2. From 2-6; 2.5 grms.; 18-21 mm.; *obv.:* head of Constantine to r., laureate; inscr.: CONSTAN TINVZAVG; border of dots; *rev.:* camp-gate surrounded by three little watch-towers; inscr. begins on r. below and is struck backwards: PROVIDEN TIAE AVGG; in exergue (also struck backwards): SMANTE. Struck at Antioch by the fifth officina after 324 A.D. [3]

Constantius II, 337-361.

3. From tomb 1 d; 1.5 grms.; 12.5 mm.; *obv.:* bust of Constantius II to r., diademed and draped; inscr. worn out; *rev.:* common type of a legionary (or emperor) fixing a prostrate foeman (or monster). (Type: Felicium temporum reparatio.)

4. From 56; 2.5 grms.; 16.5 mm.; *obv.:* bust of Constantius II wearing diadem, paludamentum and cuirass; inscr.: D . . . ONSTAN IVS; *rev.:* the emperor standing to l. fixing with a spear a foe crouching to l. with his head turning to r. upwards; inscr.: FEL . . MP REP . . . .

[1] The descriptions indicate: 1) the place where each coin was found; 2) the approximate weight in grammes after the final cleaning; 3) the maximum diameter; 4) details of the obverse and reverse which could be made out; and 5) at times some source where a good parallel or further information may be found.

[2] See G. F. Hill, *Catalogue of the Greek Coins of Arabia,* London, 1922, p. 18, no. 12 (?). Local coinages gradually disappeared during the course of the third century A. D.; see H. Mattingly, *Roman Coins from the Earliest Times to the Fall of the Western Empire,* London, 1928, pp. 212-214; this is the only specimen of local coinage discovered at Siyâgha.

[3] For further information regarding the details given in the description of this and the following Roman coins the reader may consult Mattingly (see previous note) or M. Bernhart, *Handbuch zur Muenzkunde der roemischen Kaiserzeit,* Halle, 1926.

Theodosius I, 378-395.

5. From 7; 1 grm.; 11 mm.; *obv.:* bust of Theodosius to r., diademed and draped; inscr.: DN . . . . VS P . . .; border of dots; *rev.:* a cross on a line; inscr.: .ON AVGGG (Concordia Augustorum); in exergue: ANT .; border of dots. — Struck at Antioch by the third officina.

6. From 117-119; 1.5 grms.; 11 mm.; *obv.:* bust to r., diademed; inscr.: N ODO ; *rev.:* cross; around: CONCORDIA AVGGG; in exergue very probably: SMKA. — Struck at Cyzicus by the first officina.

7. From 7; 1.8 grms.; 10 mm.; *obv.:* bust to r., diademed and draped; inscr. out of die; *rev.:* cross in wreath tied at the bottom with a medallion on top; inscr. in exergue, but almost entirely out of die, perhaps: SMK?

Arcadius, 395-408.

8. From 33; 2.8 grms.; 13.5 mm.; *obv.:* bust of Arcadius to r., diademed and draped; inscr. on l.: ARCAD; *rev.:* a Victory walking l. holds a trophy on her r. shoulder and trains a captive by her l. hand behind; inscr. around: SALVS REIPVBLICAE; in field on l. crux monogr.; in exergue: CONSA. — Struck at Constantinople by the first officina about 400 A. D.

9. From tomb 1 d; 1.5 grms.; 10 mm.; *obv.:* bust of Arcadius to r., diademed; rest oblit.; *rev.:* common type of SALVS REIPVBLICAE as 8, but oblit.; in exergue: CON.

10. From 1-125; 2.5 grms.; 12 mm.; *obv.:* bust of Arcadius to r., diademed and draped; inscr.: DN ARCADIVS; *rev.:* common type of SALVS REIPVBLICAE (see 8).

11. From tomb 1 d; 1.5 grms.; 11-12 mm.; *obv.:* bust of Arcadius to r., traces of inscr.; *rev.:* common type of SALVS REIPVBLICAE (see 8); in exergue: MK (Cyzicus)?

12. From 68; 1.5 grms.; 11-12 mm.; *obv.:* bust of Arcadius to r., diademed; inscr.: . . . . DIVS; *rev.:* Victory walking to l.; inscr.: SALVS REIP ; in exergue: ALEA (Alexandria first officina).

13. From tombs in 21; broken; 11.5-13 mm.; *obv.:* bust of Arcadius to r., diademed; inscr.: DNA FAVG; *rev.:* Victory walking to l. with a captive behind; common type of SALVS REIPVBLICAE.

14. From 68; 1.5 grms.; 12 mm.; *obv.:* bust of Arcadius to r., diademed; inscr. oblit.; *rev.:* worn out; prob. SALVS REIPVBLICAE type.

15. From 68; ½ grm.; 9-10 mm.; *obv.:* bust of Arcadius to r., diademed; inscr.: ARCAD; *rev.:* as 14.

16. From 32; 1.7 grms.; 13-13½ mm.; *obv.:* bust of Arcadius to r., diademed and draped; inscr.: ARCAD IVS P P ; *rev.:* three legionaries facing; inscr.: IAEX R ITV (Gloria exercitus type); reel border.

17. From tombs in 21; 1.5 grms.; 12.5 mm.; *obv.:* bust of Arcadius to r., diademed; inscr.: AR IVS P F AVG; *rev.:* within wreath: VOT X MVLT XX.

18. From tombs in 21; 1.5 grms.; 12.5 mm.; *obv.:* bust of Arcadius to r., diademed; inscr.: DN A; rest oblit.; reel border; *rev.:* within a double circle: VOT X MVLT XX.

19. From tombs in 21; 1 grm.; 10 mm.; *obv.:* bust of Arcadius to r., diademed; inscr.: AR . A ; *rev.:* type of VOT X MVLT XX.

Honorius, 395-423.

20. From 5; 2 grms.; 10-11 mm.; *obv.:* bust of Honorius to r., diademed, draped and cuirassed; inscr.: DN HONORI VS P ; *rev.:* partly obliterated, but type of GLORIA AVGVSTI; emperor standing to r., receives a crown from a Victory standing to l.; in exergue, name of mint, prob. Constantinople.

21. From 41; 1.5 grms.; 11 mm.; *obv.:* bust of Honorius to r., diademed and draped; inscr.: DN HONOR VG; *rev.:* cross; in exergue: CON.

Fourth-Fifth century types, whose attribution is somewhat doubtful.

22. From Siyâgha; broken; about 13-14 mm.; *obv.:* bust, possibly of Theodosius, to r.; *rev.:* Gloria exercitus type.

23. From tomb 1 d; 1.2 grms.; 10.5-11 mm.; *obv.:* bust of Arcadius (or Theodosius) near the left side of the die to r., diademed; inscr.: VS PP AVG; *rev.:* Victory walking to l. training a captive; in field on l., crux monogr. (⳩); inscr.: PVBL.

24. From tombs in 21; 1 grm.; 10 mm.; *obv.:* bust of Arcadius or Theodosius II (408-450) to r., diademed; rest unclear; *rev.:* possibly a Salus reipublicae type.

25. From 68; 1.5 grms.; 11-12 mm.; *obv.:* bust; rest unclear.

26. From 56; 2 grms.; 13 mm.; details unclear.

27. From tomb 1 d; 1 grm.; 11-12 mm.; *obv.:* bust to r., diademed; *rev.:* A with P intersecting the lower end of the r. bar and S between the lower ends of the two bars; within reel border.

28. From tomb 1 a; 1 grm.; 12-13 mm.; *obv.:* bust to right; rest effaced.

29. From 56; 4 grms.; 21 mm.; *obv.:* worn out; *rev.:* figure standing to l.

30. From 108; 1 grm.; 9 mm.; details obliterated.

31. From tomb 1 d; 1.5 grms.; 12-13 mm.; rest as 30.

32. From 7; 1 grm.; 10 mm.; rest as 30.

33. From 38; 1 grm.; 12 mm.; rest as 30.

II. THE BYZANTINE COINS [1]

Anastasius I, 491-518.

34. From 43; 16.5 grms.; 33 mm.; *obv.:* bust of Anastasius r. beardless, wearing diadem, cuirass and paludamentum; inscr.: D N ANASTASIVS PP AVG; *rev.:* M on r., star; on l., star; above, cross; in ex., CON; beneath, E. — See W. I, p. 4, nos. 28 & 29.

35. From 11; 11.5 grms.; 31 mm.; *obv.:* bust badly preserved; inscr.: VS PP AVG; *rev.:* as 34, but the officina is obliterated.

36. From 109; 4.5 grms.; 21 mm.; *obv.:* bust as 34; inscr.: . NANA; *rev.:* K on l., long cross; on r., perhaps Γ. — See W. I, p. 5, no. 31.

Justin I, 518-527.

37. From 21; 14.5 grms.; 32 mm.; *obv.:* bust of Justin r.; rest as 34; inscr.: DN IV . . INVS PP A . .; *rev.:* as 34; except in ex., . ON; beneath, A.

38. From 12; 16 grms.; 29-30 mm.; *obv.:* as 37; inscr.: . . IVSTINVS PP AVG; *rev.:* M on r., cross; on l., star; above, cross; in ex., CON; beneath, Γ. — See W. I, p. 14, no. 31.

39. From 56; 15 grms.; 29-34 mm.; *obv.:* as 37, but nearly worn away; inscr.: NVS PP; *rev.:* M on r., star; in ex., ON; rest worn out.

40. From 56; 12 grms.; 29-32 mm.; *obv.:* as 37, but faint; *rev.:* M on r., star or cross; on l., doubtful; above, cross; in ex., O; beneath, Γ.

41. From 56; 15 grms.; 29-31 mm.; *obv.:* as 37; inscr.: D STI; *rev.:* M on r., cross (?); on l., star; above, cross; in ex., NIKM; rest obliterated.

[1] See Warwick Wroth, *Catalogue of the Imperial Byzantine Coins in the British Museum*, in two volumes, London, 1908. — Abbreviated: W.

42. From 56; 16 grms.; 31-32 mm.; *obv.:* as 37; inscr.: D N IVSTINVS PP AVG; *rev.:* M; rest obliterated.

43. From 61; 15 grms.; 30-32 mm.; *obv.:* as 37; inscr.: D N T; *rev.:* M on r., star; above, cross; beneath, Γ; rest obliterated.

44. From 4; 13 grms.; 31-32 mm.; *obv.:* as 37 (details doubtful); inscr.: VS P; *rev.:* M; rest obliterated or uncertain.

Justinian I, 527-565.

45. From 116; 11 grms.; 29-31 mm.; *obv.:* bust of Justinian r.; rest as 34; inscr.: D N IV IANVS PP AVG; *rev.:* M on r., star; on l., star; above, cross; in ex., O; beneath, A. — See W. I, p. 30, no. 33.[1]

46. From 56; 13.5 grms.; 29-30 mm.; *obv.:* as 45; inscr.: TINI; *rev.:* M on r., star; above, cross; in ex., CON; beneath, B (?); rest uncertain.

47. From 116; 16.5 grms.; 31-32 mm.; *obv.:* as 45; the paludamentum is fastened by a brooch ornamented with a star; inscr.: D N IVST; *rev.:* M on l., star; on r., cross; above, cross; in ex., C; beneath, Γ. — See W. I, p. 29, no. 30.

48. From 60; pierced and used as ornament; 20.5 grms.; 43 mm.; *obv.:* bust of Justinian, beardless, facing; wears helmet with plume and armour; r. hand holds globus cruciger; l. hand (not represented) supports shield decorated with the group of a horseman r. attacking a prostrate enemy, rudely represented by a thick line beneath the horse; in field r., cross; inscr.: D N IVSTINIANVS PP AVI (the final letter stands for G; see W. I, p. 30, note 1); *rev.:* M on l., ANNO; above, cross; in ex., CON; on r., XI [I] (538-9 A.D.);[2] beneath, Γ. — See W. I, p. 31, no. 42.

49. From 92; 14 grms.; 27-29 mm.; *obv.:* as 45; inscr.: S NVS P AV; *rev.:* M on l., cross; on r., cross; above, cross; in ex., NIKM; beneath, B; — before 538 A.D.

50. From 60; pierced and used together with no. 48 as an ornament; 17 grms.; 41 mm.; *obv.:* as 48, but almost completely effaced; inscr.: ANV; *rev.:* M on l., ANNO; above, cross; in ex., NIK; on r., XII (538-9 A. D.); beneath, B. — See W. I, p. 45, no. 189.

51. From 53; broken; 5.5 grms.; 21 mm.; *obv.:* obliterated; *rev.:* K on l., ANNO; above, cross; r., XII (538-9 A. D.); beneath, uncertain.

Justin II, 565-578.

52. From 116; 13.5 grms.; 29-30 mm.; *obv.:* Justin II (on l.) and Sophia (on r.) nimbate, and wearing tall headdresses and long robes, seated facing on double throne; Justin holds in r. globus cruciger; Sophia holds in r. cruciform sceptre; inscr.: D N IVSTINVS PP AVG; reel border; *rev.:* M on l., ANNO; above, cross; in ex., CON; on r., I (565-6 A. D.);[3] beneath, B.

53. From 96; 13.5 grms.; 26-27 mm.; *obv.:* as 52, but mostly obliterated; *rev.:* M on l., ANNO; above, cross; in ex., CON; on r., IIII (568-9 A. D.); beneath, Γ. — See W. I, p. 79, no. 39.

54. From 116; 12 grms.; 28.5 mm.; *obv.:* as 52; *rev.:* M on l., ANNO; above, cross; in ex., . ON; on r., X (574-5 A. D.); beneath, Γ (or possibly B).

55. From 53; broken; 13 grms.; 31 mm.; *obv.:* as 52; *rev.:* as 52, but on r., XI (575-6 A. D.); beneath, A. — See W. I, p. 82, no. 77.

[1] These undated coins of Justinian I were struck before April A. D. 538; see W. I, p. XVI & pp. 29 f.

[2] "The years of Justinian's reign are reckoned from his accession as joint-ruler with Justin I, i. e. from April 1, 527 A. D. His twelfth year therefore corresponds to A. D. 538-9, beginning April 1." W. I, p. 30, note 3; see ibid. pp. XIV & XVI.

[3] Justin's accession took place Nov. 15, 565; see W. I, p. 78, note 4; ibid. p. XVIII.

56. From 32; 9 grms.; 29-30 mm.; *obv.:* as 52; *rev.:* M on l., ANNO; above, cross; in ex., NIKO; on r., VII (571-2 A. D.); beneath, A. — See W. I, p. 87, no. 137.

57. From 31-38; 13 grms.; 29 mm.; *obv.:* as 52; *rev.:* as 56, but on r., XII (576-7 A. D.); beneath, B. — See W. I, p. 88, no. 156.

58. From 32; 3 grms.; 15-16 mm.; *obv.:* bust of Justin II r., wearing diadem, cuirass and paludamentum (partly worn out); inscr.: D N IV NVS PP; *rev.:* I + B in ex., ΑΛΕΞ.— See W. I, p. 97, nos. 241 ff.

Tiberius II, 578-582. [1]

59. From 29; 12 grms.; 30 mm.; *obv.:* bust facing, but nearly entirely obliterated, so also inscr.; *rev.:* M on l., ANNO; above, ?; on r., VII (580-1 A. D., if the attribution to Tiberius II is correct); [1] in ex., CONB (or Γ). — See W. I, p. 109, nos. 29 f. or 31.

Maurice Tiberius, 582-602.

60. From 56; 10.5 grms.; 26 mm.; *obv.:* bust of Maurice Tiberius facing; badly preserved; inscr.: N MAV; *rev.:* M on l., ANN(O); above, cross; in ex., (C)ON; on r., VIIII (590-1 A. D.); beneath, E. — See W. I, p. 132, no. 52.

61. From 32; 10 grms.; 27 mm.; *obv.:* bust of Maurice Tiberius facing (as Consul); wears consular robes and crown surmounted by trefoil device (mostly chipped away); in upraised r., mappa; in l., sceptre (chipped away); inscr.: D N MAURI; reel border; *rev.:* M above, cross; on l., ANNO; in ex., THEUP /; [2] on r., XI (592-3 A. D.); beneath, Γ; reel border. — See W. I, pp. 144 f., nos. 173-6.

62. From 106; 11 grms.; 27-30 mm.; *obv.:* as 61, but mostly effaced; *rev.:* as 61, but on r., XIIII (595-6); beneath, E. — See W. I, p. 145, no. 184.

63. From 56; 7 grms.; 30 mm.; *obv.:* details unclear; *rev.:* M above, cross (?); on l., (AN)NO; in ex., TES; on r., XX (601-2 A. D., provided the attribution is correct); [3] beneath, B.

Phocas, 602-610.

64. From 56; 28-30 mm.; *obv.:* bust of Phocas facing, bearded, wearing crown and consular robes; in l. (not visible), cross; *rev.:* (XX)XX on r., sign for 5 (606-7 A. D.); in ex., CO. — See W. I, p. 166, no. 44.

65. From Siyâgha, but at first not recognized as a coin, hence not registered more accurately; clipped and pierced; 11 grms.; 30-34 mm.; *obv.:* bust of Phocas facing, wearing crown; rest unclear; inscr.: D N FOCAS PERP AVG; *rev.:* XXXX above, ANNO; on r., sign for 6 (607-8 A. D.); in ex., CO. — See W. I, p. 166, no. 45.

66. From 34; 6 grms.; 20-24 mm.; *obv.:* bust of Phocas facing (details indistinct); inscr.: . N FOCAS; *rev.:* XX above, cross; in ex., CONA. — See W. I, p. 167, no. 49.

Heraclius, 610-641.

67. From 114; 12 grms.; 27-31 mm.; *obv.:* Heraclius (on l.) and Heraclius Constantine (on r.), a shorter figure, standing facing; each wears long robes and crown with cross, and holds in r. globus cruciger; rest uncertain; inscr.: ddN h VST (?) PP AVG; *rev.:* M on l.,

[1] W. I, p. XX: "In the dates on his coins he usually reckons his 'reign' as beginning with his Caesarship (Dec. 574), but there is no evidence that decisively proves that he struck money till he became sole ruler and Augustus."

[2] Antioch; see W. I, p. C: "After A. D. 528 (see p. 53, n.), the name of the city having been changed to Θεούπολις, 'Antioch' disappears from the coins, and we find the new name . . . commonly in the Latin form THEUPO; THEUP/."

[3] In this case it would be a coin not represented in the British Museum Catalogue; — see W. I, pp. 138 f.

ANNO; above, cross; in ex., NIK ; on r., IIII (613-4 A. D.); all the details of rev. are in a small inner circle 20 mm. in diameter. — See W.I, p. 217, nos. 240 ff.

Early Byzantine types, whose precise classification is somewhat doubtful.

68. From area E; half of coin; 8 grms.; 32 mm.; *obv.:* bust, prob. of Justin I (518-527), r.; inscr.: . VSTI; *rev.:* M on r., cross; rest worn away.

69. From 61; 15 grms.; 28-30 mm.; *obv.:* bust, prob. of Justin I (518-527), r.; *rev.:* M; rest obliterated.

70. From area E; 8 grms.; 17-18 mm.; *rev.:* K; rest obliterated.

71. From 53; 13.5 grms.; 30-32 mm.; *obv.:* faint traces of 2 figures, prob. Justin II and Sophia (565-578); *rev.:* M on l., ANNO; above, cross; in ex., CON; on r., X (574-5 A. D.) [?]; all this is very faint and the rest is obliterated.

72. From 53; corroded; 19-21 mm.; *obv.:* 2 figures, prob. as 71; *rev.:* K on l., ANNO; above, cross; beneath, TES. — See W. I, pp. 84 ff., nos. 105 ff.

73. From 53-63; 2.5 grms.; 15-17 mm.; *rev.:* faint traces of M; possibly of the time of Constans II, 641-668 A. D.; see, v. g., W. I, Pl. XXXI, below.

74. From 56; clipped; 3 grms.; 8-16 mm.; *rev.:* small M surmounted by cross; see 73.

75. From 60; 28-29 mm.; M type; details uncertain.

76. From 97; 11 grms.; 28-30 mm.; M type; details uncertain.

NB. A large proportion of the unidentifiable coins certainly must be assigned to the Byzantine period, though they are too poorly preserved to be classified more accurately.

III. THE EARLY ARABIC COINS

Umayyad, A. H. 41-132: 661-750 A. D.

77. From 7; this coin was retained by the Transjordan government for its collection; regarding the same, Mr. Kirkbride writes as follows: "A no mint, no date type of the early Umayyad coins bearing the usual profession of faith in curiously attenuated letters with the dots of the circles spaced out abnormally."

78. From 59; 3 grms.; 19-22 mm.; with formula of faith only. [1]

79. From 53; 3 grms.; 16-18 mm.; as 78; in a circle, disposed in 3 lines.

80. From 59; 5 grms.; 18 mm.; as 78.

81. From 59; 1.5 grms.; 14-15 mm.; probably as 78.

82. From 61; 2 grms.; 16-18 mm.; as 78.

83. From 59; 2 grms.; 14 mm.; as 78.

84. From 1 B; broken; 5 grms.; 11 mm.; thick; prob. as 78.

85. From 30; 3 grms.; 9 mm.; prob. as 78.

86. From 35; 2 grms.; 13 mm.; prob. as 78.

87. From 7; 2 grms.; 19 mm.; as 78, but *obv.:* has double circle between which lines form tiny compartments; *rev.:* obliterated.

88. From 59; 4 grms.; 19 mm.; as 78; traces of marginal inscriptions around the central ones.

[1] See, v. g., Stanley Lane-Poole, *Catalogue of the Collection of Arabic Coins Preserved in the Khedival Library at Cairo,* London, 1897, pp. 111 ff.

89. From 53; 2.5 grms.; 17-18 mm.; *obv.:* a circle encloses the usual formula of faith in 3 lines; see 78; *rev.:* in centre a trefoil; inscr. around margin: محمد رسول الله عمّان : Mohammed, apostle of God, ʿAmmân.[1]

90. From 7; 2.5 grms.; 16 mm.; with formula of faith in one line and around the margin (?) on each side.

91. From 30; 4 grms.; 18-21 mm.; prob. as 78.

92. From 59; 2 grms.; 17-18 mm.; with name of mint, prob. Damascus.

93. From 20; 3.5 grms.; 17 mm.; details uncertain.

94. From 43; 11×11 mm.; very thin with straight edges and faint traces of inscription.

95. From 1 A; 12-14 mm.; very thin; faint remains of letters.,

Abbasid, A. H. 132-650: 750-1258 A. D.

96. From 53; 4 grms.; 19-21 mm.; inscr. arranged in 3 lines on each side.

Melek al-Kamil Nasir-ad-Din, A. H. 615-635: 1218-1238 A. D.

97. From 17; 4 grms.; 22-24 mm.; fels.

IV. THE OTTOMAN COINS

Mahmûd II, A. H. 1223-1255: 1808-1839 A. D.

98. From late tomb above the sanctuary of the basilica; pierced; 1.5 grms.; 20.5 mm.; mettalic or 10 paras; *obv.:* floral wreath enclosing 2 horns tied at bottom by a fillet; within, Tughra (that is the name applied to the form in which the Sultan's titles are arranged); on r., عدلى: (the) righteous; *rev.:* floral wreath and horns as obv.; within, the inscr. is arranged in 4 lines: ١٢٢٣ ضرب في قسطنطينيه ٢٨ : 28 struck at Constantinople 1223. — The 28th year of the reign of Mahmûd is A. H. 1250, that is, 1835 A. D.

99. From late tomb above 1 B; 1.8 grms.; 20.5 mm.; like 98, but the date on rev. is the 31st year of Mahmûd, that is, A. H. 1253: 1838 A. D.

100. From late tomb above 1 B; 1.5 grms.; 21.5 mm.; like 98, but part of the date is worn away, so it cannot be fixed accurately.

101. From late tomb above 1 A; 2 grms.; 20.5 mm.; as 98, but note on *obv.:* a stem with leaves to r. of Tughra; on *rev.:* the date is year 3 of a reign whose terminus a quo is worn away; prob. the same Sultan as 98.

102. From late tomb above sanctuary of basilica; pierced; 1 grm.; 20 mm.; like 98, but only traces of wreath remain; rest obliterated.

103. From late tomb above 1 B; pierced; 14.5 mm.; half mettalic or 5 paras; *obv.:* within a circle, Tughra; *rev.:* faint traces of inscr.; date prob. approximately the same as 98 ff.

104. From late tomb above sanctuary of basilica; pierced and broken; 13 mm.; like 103.

105. As 104, but not broken; 13-14 mm.

[1] See R. S. Poole, *Catalogue of Oriental Coins in the British Museum, I: The Coins of the Eastern Khaleefehs in the British Museum,* London, 1875, p. 184, no. 54.

CHAPTER X

STONE

A. GENERAL SURVEY

Stone was the principal material used for the buildings and their furnishings. Limestone was used for the buildings; marble, Nebi Mûsa stone, basalt, gneiss-schist and steatite for their furnishings. Limestone was obtained from the local quarries; the other varieties of stone were brought from more distant places.

The chief characteristics of the building stones were mentioned in the preceding chapters. There we spoke not only of the stones still in situ, but also of those no longer in their original position; among the latter we noted over 300 parts of columns, cornices, doors, windows and arches; their decoration, consisting of sculptured designs, moldings, incised lines, crosses (at least 67) and bosses with or without other ornaments (at least 26), distinguishes many of these stones from the ordinary building stones; they were all treated in the context in which they were found.

Marble was used for chancel screens, altars, tables, some vessels, parts of floors and probably also of walls. In a dozen cases marble was found in its original position or in a place where it had been reused, [1] but most of the marble was found in a broken condition, scattered about the site, far from its original

[1] Namely: 1) between the courses of masonry in the northern and southern walls of the southern sacristy; 2) in the core of the wall south of the pulpit; 3) in a groove at the southern end of the basilica's chancel base; 4) inside the door of the baptistery a strip of the pavement; 5) in the sanctuary of the Theotokos chapel an altar post; 6) ibid. 4 bases of the colonnade; 7) ibid., inside the colonnade, a stump of a post; 8) ibid., inside the colonnade, a narrow strip of the pavement between the chancel base and the mosaics; 9) in the nave of the Theotokos mutilated sections of the pavement were repaired in a makeshift fashion with fragments of marble slabs; 10) ibid., in the southwest corner, the upper part of a small pit has a revetment of marble slabs; 11) in front of the entrance to the basilica the narthex was carelessly paved with fragments of slabs of different colors; 12) in a stone bench north of the entrance to the basilica a marble capital was embodied. — The broken fragments incorporated in the walls (see nos. 1 & 2) are clear evidence that at least some of the marble had been used in the earlier basilica or cella trichora; they also explain why we were unable to recover all the marble which had been used at one time.

context. All the fragments were collected and an attempt was made to restore the objects to which they belonged; but, although fragments were found from the first day to the last during each expedition and many fitted together, the majority of objects remain incomplete; in other words, we have recovered only a fraction of the marble which was originally used. Gray marble was most abundant; some fragments were pure white; others white or gray with black, red, green or yellow stripes. Practically all these varieties of marble are known to exist in Transjordan and Palestine, [1] but we do not know whether the marble used at Siyâgha was procured here or imported from more distant places; [2] in every case, the marble had to be brought from some distance and if we consider the relatively large quantity found at Siyâgha, the size and weight of some of the pieces, the difficulties of transport, etc., we gain the impression that we are dealing with a monument of some importance.

The marble fragments represent slabs, balusters, posts, columns, reliquaries, vases, moldings, a piece of sculpture, etc. The slabs were used as panels for screens, as parts of altars and tables, for paving floors and as revetments of walls. Some of the slabs are perfectly plain, with the surface polished on one or two sides; others have a frame around a sunken panel; the frame may be plain, molded, cusped, inscribed, etc.; the panel may be plain, perforated or decorated with a laurel wreath, a vine, plants, leaves, fruits, knives, crosses, stars, shells, spirals, etc. Balusters were used for the screens; columns and posts for screens, altars and tables, etc. Practically all the other marble objects served some practical purpose in the sanctuaries of the basilica and the chapels.

A black bituminous limestone, known as Nebi Mûsa stone, was also used for slabs, balusters and posts, some of which exhibit quite elaborate carvings; the objects made from this material were evidently destined for one of the sanctuaries at Siyâgha.

Basalt was used for millstones, pestles and a vase.

Gneiss-schist was used for a group of small bowls with flat bottoms, straight sides and incised ornaments.

Steatite was used for relatively large bowls having the same form as the preceding group but no ornaments. A peculiarity of these bowls is the fact that they are frequently formed of several pieces held together by copper bands.

[1] See G. S. Blake, *The Stratigraphy of Palestine and its Building Stones*, Jerusalem, pp. 116-119. — In Transjordan green marble exists east of el-Meshetta; large blocks of that marble may be seen in the courtyard of the unfinished palace at el-Meshetta; it had evidently been brought there from the quarry in question; the green marble used at Siyâgha could have been procured from the same quarry, but this is not certain; at any rate, very little green marble was found at Siyâgha.

[2] Quarries from which marble was procured in ancient times are listed in *RE*, zweite Reihe, 3, 1929, cols. 2256-2269. — Monograms on one slab found at Siyâgha (see inscription XVIII on p. 268), if correctly solved, would seem to indicate that at least some of the marble used at Siyâgha was imported from the Greek islands; the island of Naxos seems to be named; on that island there are quarries which in ancient times produced both gray and white marble (see l. c. cols. 2263 f.).

A few other types of stone and some petrified objects were found on the site.

Most of the stone objects were mentioned in the context in which they were found; there some of them were also described in detail. The following catalogue aims merely at completing the register of these objects. [1]

B. THE CATALOGUE

I. MARBLE

Slabs: plain, pierced and decorated.

1. Pl. 124,1. Plain slab; 37 fragments; incomplete; gray; served originally as panel of screen, later probably as altar or table; see pp. 94 & 100.

The threefold division of the frame's molding is typical of nearly 200 registered fragments; the plain surface of the sunken panel serves to illustrate hundreds of unregistered fragments found on the site. Similar slabs have been reported from other sites, so, v. g., from ʿEin Hanniya. [2]

2. Pl. 124,2. Pierced slab; 29 fragments, found in widely separated places; incomplete; gray; frame resembles that of no. 1, that is, it is divided into three strips, but the width of the strips is different and the inner strip of the two upper fragments is not flat but rounded — concave; the sunken panel is pierced and on one side carved in bas-relief to imitate interlacing vines terminating in leaves, similar to the vines on unpierced slabs. This panel with openwork is older than the others which are not pierced. [3] Similar panels or transennae have been reported from Jerash, [4] Gallicantu in Jerusalem, [5] Ascalon, [6] etc.

3. Pl. 124,3. Slab decorated with laurel wreath; 4 fragments, found against the apse of the cella trichora in the southern sacristy (see p. 56); incomplete; its original height was 90 cm.; its thickness below 4.5 cm., above 10 cm.; its original length is uncertain, at present it varies between 13-45.5 cm.; gray. The sunken panel is surrounded by a frame whose molding consists of three strips below and four above. The sunken panel is decorated in low relief with a laurel wreath enclosing a cross and fleurs-de-lis and fastened below by a fillet or vine which most probably terminated in leaves, as illustrated, v. g., Pl. 125,2. Such a wreathed cross was known in Greek as a stephanostaurion (στεφανοσταυρίον). [7]

The wreath consists of 12 bundles of laurel (or olive) leaves divided into two groups of six; the bases of the lowest pair are tied by the fillet or vine; their tips and those of

[1] The original general register of objects found at Siyâgha contained over 1200 entries of stone objects; this number represents 3/8 of all the entries. Over 300 entries represent building stones; over 800, marble; less than 200, other types of stone. After classifying the material and eliminating from the register all those objects described in speaking of the buildings, their mosaics, decorations and furnishings, the catalogue becomes much less bulky.

[2] *QDAP* 3 (1934), p. 115 & Pl. XXXVII,1.

[3] For this view, see Kaufmann, *HCA* p. 185.

[4] *Gerasa*, p. 254, Pl. L, b: stone; found near ambo and probably used there.

[5] *RB* 1914, Pl. VI,2.

[6] *ZDPV* 37 (1914), p. 72 & Tafel XVI,2.

[7] See *Beth-Shan* IV, pp. 3, 14 f.; Pl. III, Figure 5.

the following four pairs overlap the bases of bundles above them; the tips of the sixth pair touch an ovolo in the upper part of the wreath. Traces of similar wreaths were observed on 18 other fragments found at Siyâgha; they represent a number of other panels of this type (see Pl. 125, 22-24, 26-28, 30). Similar stephanostauria or wreathed crosses have been found at Madaba,[1] Jerusalem,[2] Beersheba,[3] Beisan,[4] etc.[5] There are differences in minor details, such as the number of bundles (10, 12, 14, 20), the form of the ovolo and ribbon. The wreath was used extensively not only in the Christian but also in the Jewish and the pagan art of Palestine.[6] The object represented inside the wreath generally determines the character of the monument in which it was used; thus, for instance, the candelabrum points to a Jewish monument,[7] whilst the cross suggests a Christian one.

Inside the wreath a cross is carved; this symbol of Christianity was noted at least 29 times on the marble fragments collected at Siyâgha.

Fleurs-de-lis are carved between the arms of the cross; this seems to be a favorite ornament both at Siyâgha, where it occurs on at least 10 fragments (see Pl. 125, 10, 24, 27, 28), and elsewhere, though at Siyâgha we also find different arrangements, so, v. g., a fluted background (see Pl. 125, 14, 22, 29 to right), etc. (see Pl. 125, 23).

The vine (or fillet) attached to the lower part of the wreath extends in a wavy line along the lower part of the panel and terminates in each corner in a heart-shaped leaf; the ends of the vines with the leaves are missing, but parallels from other sites and fragments with such leaves found at Siyâgha (see Pl. 125, 2 and compare with 7-9) suggest the same arrangement here. The manner in which this vine is attached to the wreath seems to be the more common in these regions, but a different mode of attachment was also used (see Pl. 125, 30).

4. Pl. 125,2. Gray frag., 36 × 23 × 5 cm., serves to illustrate the heart-shaped leaf terminating a vine, as on no. 3.

5. Pl. 125,22. Gray frag., 29 × 27 × 5 ½ cm., as no. 3, but the wreath encloses a fluted shield on which 2 arms of a cross are preserved; on the other side of the slab another cross was carved; of this 2 arms remain.

6. Pl. 125,23. Gray frag., 27 × 25 × 4 ½ cm., as no. 3, but inside the wreath a 3-striped band encloses another design, prob. a cross.

7-10. Pl. 125,24, 26-28. Seven frags. forming 4 connected but incomplete pieces, as no. 3.

11. Pl. 125,30. Two gray frags. forming one incomplete piece, 47×32×5 cm., as no. 3; the knot, however, is different.

12. Pl. 121,1. Gray fragments (25) of a slab or slabs decorated with a vine or vines forming medallions enclosing other motifs; 66 such fragments were registered. The frame resembles that of no. 2; below, it has a narrow fillet between 2 flat bands; above, it has a flat band above the fillet and a concave one below it; on the uppermost strip is carved a Greek inscription preceded by a cross (see inscription XVI, pp. 268 f.). The vine decorating the sunken panel has 3-pointed leaves along its sides; in the medallions formed by it, there

[1] See *DAC* 10, 1, col. 875, Fig. 7431; *NBAC* 1899, p. 162; *ZDPV* 19 (1895), p. 120, Figs. 7 & 8; *ZDPV* 53 (1930), Tafel 11, A.

[2] See *ZDPV* 53 (1930), pp. 215 ff., Taf. 10, B; *RB* 1914, Pl. VI, 5; *PEF Ann.* 5, Pl. XVIII, 13.

[3] See *PEF Ann.* 3, p. 107, Fig. 42.

[4] See *Beth-Shan* IV, Pl. III, Fig. 5.

[5] Mader gives a list of such panels in *ZDPV* 53 (1930), pp. 215 ff. — Regarding Carmel, see C. Kopp, *Elias und Christentum auf dem Karmel*, Paderborn, 1929, Bild 4.

[6] See *ASG* pp. 188-191.

[7] See *ASG* p. 160, Abb. 291.

are leaves (see also Pl. 125, 7-9), fleurs-de-lis, 3 large fruits and a small one, 2 knives near two of the fruits, a knot formed by interlacing 3-striped bands, a star (see Pl. 125,21), crosses (see also Pl. 125,7), etc. A slab from Ascalon, dated 604 A. D., has a similar type of vine-decoration; its medallions enclose rosettes and stars. [1] Vines, fruits, knives, etc. were used also for the ornamentation of the mosaic pavements (see Pls. 83,1 & 2; 111,6 & 7, etc.).

13. Pl. 125,21. Gray frag., 31 × 28 × 4 cm., decorated with vine and 6-armed star, like one found at Ascalon; see no. 12.

14. Pl. 125,1. Gray frag. of border divided into only 2 strips.

15. Pl. 125,3. Gray frag. illustrating the frame and an arm of a cross.

16-17. Pl. 125,4-5. Two gray frags. illustrating the molding occurring on 9 others. Along the upper edge are holes for joining this slab with another object by means of nails or pins.

18. Pl. 125,6. Gray frag., 34 × 19 ½ × 7 ½ cm., from tomb 1 e, illustrates a type of slab whose frame consists of only one band; only 9 fragments with this kind of border were found. The sunken panel is decorated with a cross.

19. Pl. 125,7. Gray frag. with 2 arms of a cross and a leaf on a stem.

20. Pl. 125,8. Gray frag. with a leaf.

21. Pl. 125,9. Gray frag. with a leaf and traces of vines.

22. Pl. 125,10. Gray frag. with a cross on each side; on one side fleurs-de-lis between the arms of the cross. Found in blocked opening at the eastern end of the basilica's northern wall.

23. Pl. 125,11. White and black frag. with an arm of a cross.

24. Pl. 125,12. Gray frag. with a plant, 4 of whose branches are complete and terminate in knobs, probably representing buds. See Pl. 125,18 for another plant motif.

25. Pl. 125,13. White frag., 51 × 37 × 7 cm., with an arm of a cross; from tomb 1 e.

26. Pl. 125,14. Gray frag., 35 × 35 × 5 cm., with flutings and an arm of a cross; back rough; from 86. Only 4 pieces with flutings were found; [2] 2 others are illustrated on Pl. 125,22 & 29 to right; the fourth (*reg.* 1968) is a small white frag., 11 × 10 × 4 ½ cm., on whose fluted side 2 arms of a cross remain; on the other side there is also an arm of a cross.

27. Pl. 125,15. White frag. with an ornament occurring only once.

28. Pl. 125,16. Gray frag. on which concentric circles and an indistinct angular design are carved. — On a frag. *reg.* 2682 a simple circle is carved.

29. Pl. 125,17. Gray frag. with a spiral; traces of red paint exist in the incision. See nos. 30 & 31.

30. Pl. 125,18. Complete gray slab, 41 × 17 ½ - 23 ½ × 3 ½ - 4 cm.; back, rough; edges, splayed; in the upper edge, a hole for a nail or a pin; the upper surface has a plain fillet along the top end and is decorated in low relief with a plant and spirals. The plant may be the lotus with large pinnate leaves and umbellate flowers. Between the 2 spirals there is a fleur-de-lis. The surface of the ornaments is smooth; the rest is rough and was colored red; few traces of color remain; marble does not as a rule retain colors well.

31. Pl. 125,20. Gray frag. with part of stem, leaf and spiral. — Only 4 slabs found at Siyâgha used the spiral as an ornament; see nos. 29 & 30; the fourth fragment (*reg.* 2686) is not illustrated.

32. Pl. 125,19. Gray frag. of an openwork panel; see no. 2.

33. Pl. 125,25. Flat disk with incised lines radiating from a point near the center of one edge after the manner of a sundial.

1 *JPOS* 15 (1935), pp. 152 ff. & Pl. XV. — See also the panels from Hammath-by-Tiberias, ibid. Pl. XIV.

2 Regarding this design see *ASG* p. 190; *JPOS* 15 (1935), Pl. XII, b.

34. Pl. 125,29, left. Gray frag., 36×24×2 cm.; the frame is a narrow fillet; the panel is decorated with double interlacing bands whose interstices are filled in with 3-pointed buds, around which the surface is rough and betrays faint traces of some color (see no. 30).

35. Pl. 125,29, right. Gray frag., 27 × 23 × 3 cm.; in the center of a fluted shell motif there is a circle, 7 ½ cm. d., containing a cross. See no. 26.

Altar slabs: white fragments with molded frames from every part of the site.

36. Pl. 126,1. Frag. of the rounded section of a sigma-shaped (ᗝ) slab found west of 93 (see p. 173), 88 × 44 × 4.2 - 1.6 cm., is noteworthy for its cross, monogram, cusped

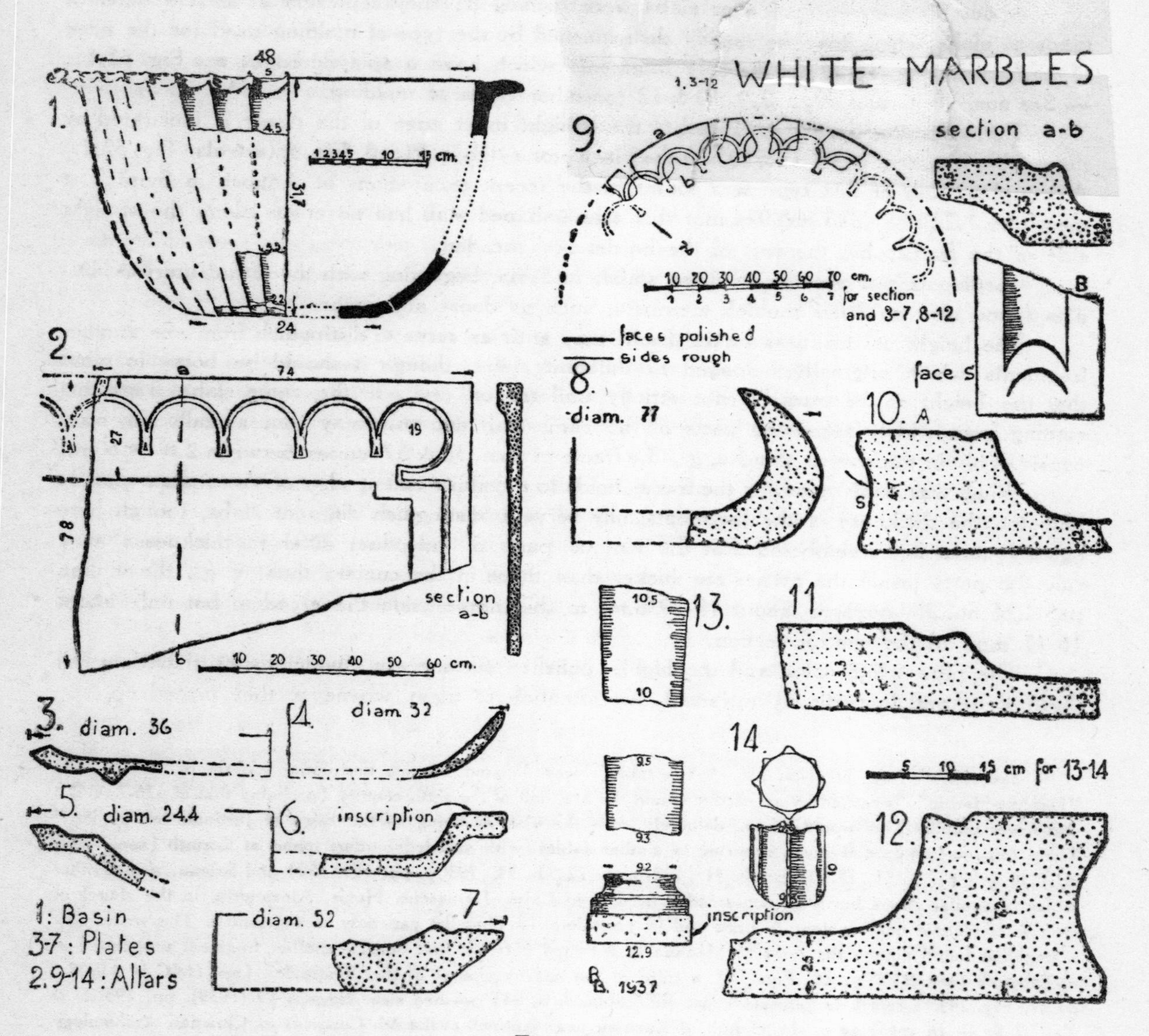

Fig. 32.

frame and straight edge. The cross and monogram are on the lower surface of the piece at the extreme right (see Pl. 121,4 & inscr. XVIII). The cusps form horseshoe arches along the inner edge of the frame. The arches are 15½ cm. deep, 19½ cm. wide near the tips and 22 cm. wide near the center. The edge of the frame is straight and slightly splayed, as indicated in Fig. 32,11; this serves to distinguish it from several others used at Siyâgha. See after no. 39.

37. Pl. 126,3. Frag. of the straight section of the same slab as no. 36 and found with it, 31½ × 21½ × 4.6 cm.; it also has a monogram on its lower surface (see Pl. 121,3 & inscr. XVIII), but its frame is not cusped. See after no. 39.

38. Pl. 126,2. Frag. like no. 36, but thicker (34-36 mm.) than either end of no. 36; moreover, it was found in a different place on the site. See after no. 39.

39. Pl. 126,4. Frag. like no. 36, but from a different part of the site.

About 90 fragments of altar slabs were registered; they represent at least 4 different kinds of slabs which may be readily distinguished by the type of molding used for the edge of the frame. Nos. 36-39 are the only fragments which have a splayed edge; see Fig. 32,11. — See nos. 40 ff. and Fig. 32,9, 10 & 12 for other types of molding.

The transition from the cusped to the straight inner edge of the frame is illustrated by the marble fragment in Pl. 126,20 and the black stone slab in Pl. 60, Fig. 3 (see also Fig. 32,2). A complete slab of this type was found in the recent excavations at Antioch in Syria;[1] it measures 1.225 × 1.225 × 0.044 m.; this sigma-shaped slab has no cusps along the straight side of the frame, but the rest of the border is "arcaded."

Cusping is not peculiar to these slabs; in Syria, beginning with the fifth century A. D., it is found also on other molded members, such as doors and arches.[2]

The height or thickness of the frame may at times serve to distinguish from one another fragments which originally belonged to different slabs, though it should be borne in mind that the height of the frame is not strictly uniform on one and the same slab; fragments coming from widely separated parts of the same slab not only may, but actually do, vary considerably in thickness; thus, v. g., the frame of nos. 36 & 37 varies between 2.8 - 4.6 cm.

What was said regarding the frame holds to a certain extent also of the sunken panel; here too the thickness of the fragments may serve to distinguish different slabs, though here again it must be remembered that the various parts of the panel differ in thickness; as a rule the parts inside the arches are thicker than those in the center; thus, v. g., the sunken panel of no. 36 averages about 18-19 mm. in thickness inside the arcades, but only about 16-17 mm. in the central section.

The pure white color and the highly polished surface are characteristics shared by all these slabs and immediately attracted our attention to them whenever they turned up.

[1] See *Antioch* II, p. 178, no. 226. "The table" was "found among destruction debris of a villa" at "Daphne-Harbie" "wrecked by an earthquake in the first half of the sixth century (probably that of 526-7 A. D.) and never rebuilt. This would, then, definitely date the slab as being of the reign of Justinian or earlier." There too the literature is given referring to similar tables with arcaded borders found at Corinth (see, v. g., *AJA* 30 [1926], p. 51, Pl. II, E; ib. 31 [1927], p. 72; ib. 34 [1930], pp. 444, 450) and Salona, and to other tables of similar shape but with non-arcaded borders in Cairo, Damascus, Homs, Alexandria, in the church of Deir Abu Hennis near ancient Antinoë and in Jerusalem. — That list can now be augmented. The writer saw a fragment found among the ruins of Madaba (mentioned here the first time); another fragment was found at et-Tâbghah (see *BVK* p. 28, Fig. 15), a third at the nearby chapel of the Beatitudes (see *RAC* 14 [1937], p. 27, Fig. 24), a fourth in Jerusalem (see *PEF Ann.* 5, p. 94). — See also *Aegyptus* 19 (1939), pp. 195 ff. & Taf. II ff. — In speaking of the church of Kaoussu near Antioch at the 4th Congress of Christian Archæology in Rome, Lassus, according to Ferrua in *L'Osservatore Romano* for 20th of Oct. 1938, no. 244 (23,828), p. 4, declared that in Syria the altar in many cases and for a long time preserved the shape of a semicircular table characteristic of private dining rooms. — See *HCA* pp. 180 f., where Kaufmann suggests that the slabs with cusped frames may have been used for the table of the Prothesis.

[2] See *ECS* pp. 48, 61, 62, 72, 136, 137*, 149, 185*, 220, 221*, 225*, 230*. — The star (*) denotes an illustration.

40. Pl. 126,5-8,18,21. Five fragments (18 is the lower side of 6 somewhat enlarged) of a sigma-shaped slab like nos. 36-39 (see Fig. 32,9), but differing from it in this that its edge has a molding as indicated in Fig. 32,9, section a-b. One more fragment (*reg.* 1485, not illustrated) has the same type of molding. The frame of these fragments varies in thickness between 33-48 mm.

41-44. Pl. 126,9-12. Four disconnected fragments of frames 65 mm. thick with the type of molding illustrated in Fig. 32,12; they represent a third type of slab used at Siyâgha; they are so similar to one another that originally they may have belonged to one and the same slab.

45-52. *Reg.* 74, 78-80, 1375-6, 1487, 2258, 2621. Eight disconnected fragments of frames, having the same type of molding as nos. 41-44, but varying in thickness between 63-68 mm., belonged to the same type of slab as nos. 41-44, possibly even to the very same slab.

53-54. Pl. 126,17. Fragment of frame as nos. 41-52, but 58 mm. thick. Another fragment (*reg.* 2694) is like this one.

55. Pl. 126,16. Fragment of a frame with a molding very similar to nos. 41-54, but slightly modified, as illustrated in Fig. 32,10; moreover, its thickness, 48 mm., is less. — See nos. 56-61.

56. Pl. 126,15. Fragment like no. 55, 47 mm. thick; near the end of the molding it has two semicircular incisions, as indicated in Fig. 32, 10, B; on its lower side is the sign discussed on p. 277, inscr. XLII. — See nos. 57-61.

57-61. Five other fragments are like nos. 55 & 56; in thickness they vary between 47-42 mm. (*reg.* 2690: 47 mm.; *reg.* 2691: 47 mm.; *reg.* 2693: 47 mm.; *reg.* 157: 44 mm.; *reg.* 2692: 42 mm.; this last fragment represents the corner of a frame and has notches, like those of no. 56 [see Fig. 32, 10, B], at the end of the molding on each of the two sides). — Nos. 55-61 represent a fourth slab or at least a fourth type of slab.

62. Pl. 126, 20 & 14 (the latter is a slightly different view of the fragment at the left end of no. 20). Four fragments of a slab fitting together to form a piece 44 × 26½ × 4-3.1 cm.; its cusped frame is similar to that of nos. 36-39 & 40; the molding of its edge resembles that of nos. 55-61; its thickness, 31-40 mm., is less than that of fragments 55-61. The frame-molding suggests that this piece belongs to the same slab as fragments 55-61; if not, a fifth slab would be represented. Whether the slab was originally sigma-shaped (as nos. 36-39 & 40) or rectangular (as the slab illustrated in Pl. 60, Fig. 3; Fig. 32,2) is uncertain, but the latter seems more probable.

63. Pl. 126,13. A cusped fragment, which has no direct connection with any of the others mentioned above.

64. Plain fragments representing the sunken panels of slabs are relatively less numerous than the fragments representing the frames; some were reused in constructing the walls of the second basilica; this accounts for the disappearance of many of them.

N. B. — For other material which belonged to altars, see nos. 65 ff., reliquaries, posts and columns.

Other objects of the same white and highly polished material as the altar slabs.

65. Pl. 126,23. A fragment resembling those described as parts of altar slabs; it differs from them by its sharply splayed edge and its low frame or rim. It may have been part of a shallow plate; see Fig. 32,7.

66. Pl. 126,22. Three fragments form one incomplete piece 26 × 10 × 5 cm.; it has the same flat lower part as the altar slabs mentioned above and as some of the plates to

be mentioned below; but its rounded incurved side is peculiar; see Fig. 32,8. It may have been part of a shallow basin.

67. Pl. 126,19. A fragment, $8\frac{1}{2} \times 6 \times 6$ cm., like no. 66; see Fig. 32,8.

68. Pl. 129,11. Three fragments of a deep basin reconstructed in Fig. 32,1; its inner surface is plain; its outer surface has a series of semicircular vertical ridges (reeding) which form an everted wavy lip around the mouth of the vessel. These few fragments represent some of the best work found at Siyâgha.

69. Pl. 121,2. Ten fragments (9 found among the large stones east of the cella trichora and 1 in the dump of area 53) of an incomplete plate with a flat base, splayed sides about 24 mm. high and an everted flat lip about 20 mm. wide on which a Greek inscription is carved; see p. 269, inscr. XVII & Fig. 32,6.

70-72. Pl. 126, 24-26. Three fragments of vessels; perhaps they belonged to plates; see Fig. 32, 3-5. — A few other such fragments came to light.

73. Fig. 32,13. Base (see Pl. 121,9 & p. 270, inscr. XIX) and 2 fragments of a shaft.

74. Pl. 128, 1st in 1st vertical row; Fig. 32,14. Fragment of a fluted shaft.

N. B. — The reliquaries were described on pp. 101-103.

A pedestal and posts.

75. Pl. 127, Fig. 2,1. Pedestal; its base measures $13.5 \times 16.2 \times 9$ cm. (see Fig. 14, 2, where the type of molding used is indicated); its shaft, $7.6 \times 14.5 \times 16$ cm.; cream color with darker stripes.

76. Pl. 128, top panel, 1st. Gray post 33 cm. h.; base $10 \times 10 \times 10$ cm.

77. Ib. 4th. Frag. of gray post like 76.

78. Ib. 2nd. Part of post still 30 cm. h.; top missing.

79. Ib. 3rd. Gray piece of a post.

80. Ib. 5th. Gray piece of a post or small column.

81. Ib. 6th. Gray post or roller bulging in center, tapering towards the ends.

82-84. Three other posts resemble no. 81; *reg.* 1114, 1181-2.

85-90. Pl. 128, central panel, 1st-5th & Pl. 129,2. Six posts; see pp. 99 f.

91-97. Pl. 128, lowest panel, 1st-4th; ib. 6th in 2nd vertical row. Four posts and an hexagonal base like that of the posts; another post of this type is in situ in the sanctuary of the Theotokos chapel. See pp. 97-99. *Reg.* 1143 belongs to this group.

98-100. Pl. 130, 9 & 10. Two pieces of posts similar to a stump in situ in the Theotokos chapel; see p. 103, c.

101. Pl. 130,8. Gray fragment like nos. 98-100.

102. Pl. 130, 11. Fragment of post.

103. *Reg.* 2230. Gray frag. of post still 48 cm. long; flat on 2 sides, each 14 cm. wide; the rest rounded.

104-109. Pl. 128, 2nd in 1st vertical row, 2nd-5th in 2nd vertical row and *reg.* 2231. Fragments representing bases of 6 posts or small columns.

Colonnettes: monolithic, but none complete; from various parts of the site.

110. Pl. 129,1. Corinthian capital of colonnette 27 cm. high, 16 cm. diameter at base, 18 cm. along each side of abacus. From north aisle of basilica.

111. Pl. 129,3. Corinthian capital as no. 110 and part of a colonnette's shaft — 2 pieces — 43 cm. long and 14 cm. in diameter; gray with black stripes.

112. Pl. 129,4. As no. 111; total length 60. cm.

113. Pl. 129,5. As no. 111; total length 51 cm.; from room 20.

114. *Reg.* 1133. As no. 111, but somewhat smaller type; from room 20.
115. *Reg.* 1166 a. As no. 111; from room 14.
116. *Reg.* 1166 b. As no. 111; from 14.
117-122. Pl. 130, 2-7. Pieces of capitals or heads of colonnettes.
123-126. Pl. 130, 12-15. Four pieces of shafts. About 70 other pieces of shafts were registered.

127. Pl. 130,16. Two connected pieces of an incomplete gray colonnette 80 cm. long with an hexagonal base; both the base and lower end of the shaft have moldings. From 5.

128. Pl. 130,17. As no. 127, but somewhat longer, whilst the base is square and the moldings are slightly different. From 5.

129. Pl. 130,18. Lower end of a colonnette 56 cm. long like no. 128. From 5.
130. Pl. 130,19. Molded lower end of colonnette like no. 128.
131. Pl. 130,20. Like no. 130.

No direct connection was established between fragments representing the lower and upper ends of monolithic colonnettes; it is very probable that the bases described in nos. 127-131 belonged to colonnettes with capitals of the type described in nos. 110-116, but some of these colonnettes may have had bases like those illustrated on Pl. 128, in the 2 vertical rows on the right (except the 2 pieces on top), especially the last one in the 2nd row (= pedestal base). As a matter of fact, such pedestal bases were used for colonnettes found at Madaba and Tell Hassân near Jericho, whereas the type of base described in nos. 127-131 was used for colonnettes found at Jerash and et-Tâbghah (see pp. 100 f. & notes 3-6 ib.); very probably both types of bases were used for the monolithic columns at Siyâgha.

Columns whose bases, shafts and capitals are separate pieces.

132-140. Pl. 129, 6-8; Fig. 14,3 on p. 95. Nine marble bases of the same type: 3 were found in the southern sacristy of the basilica (see pp. 54 ff.); 4 are in situ in the Theotokos chapel (see p. 94); one comes from room 16 (see p. 123); another was found in room 23 (see p. 128).

141-146. Pl. 129, 9 & 10; Pl. 131, Fig. 1, 1-4. Two complete shafts (broken) were found in the basilica (see p. 51); 7 fragments of possibly 4 different shafts come from the Theotokos chapel (see pp. 94 f.).

147-153. The 7 marble capitals found on the site are described and discussed on pp. 52 & 95 f.

Balusters or chancel posts.

154. Pl. 132,1. A nearly complete baluster from the basilica, 1.20 m. long and about 20 cm. wide on each side. Two sides are plain, the third is grooved to receive the end of one of the screen's panels and the fourth, opposite the grooved side, is decorated with a vine enclosed by a frame. The vine is wavy with a serrated leaf in each curve; it is very similar to the vine represented on the slab illustrated in Pl. 121, 1; originally the baluster and that slab may have been associated with one another. Vines were also represented on balusters from Khirbet el-Merd and Beit Jibrin.[1] In the cone-shaped head 5 small holes are arranged crosswise; probably a metal cross was affixed there. The post was destined for one of the sides of the entrance to the sanctuary, as is evident from the position of the groove and the decoration.

155. Pl. 132,2. Like no. 154.

[1] See *JPOS* 9 (1929), p. 126, Fig. 6.

156. Pl. 132,3. A baluster from the Theotokos chapel described on p. 93; its grooved side is to the left of the decorated one; this suggests that the baluster was destined either for the southern extremity of the screen or for the left side of the entrance to the sanctuary, provided the ornament was viewed from the nave.

157. Pl. 132,4. A baluster from the Theotokos chapel described on p. 93; its panelled side is opposite the grooved one; this suggests that it was destined for either the one or the other side of the entrance through the screen.

158. Pl. 132,6. A baluster from the Theotokos chapel described on p. 93; two sides are panelled; the grooved side is opposite the plain one; it was destined for one of the ends of the screen.

159. Pl. 132,5. A baluster broken into two large pieces (smaller fragments are missing); it is panelled on two opposite sides and grooved on the other two; this fact indicates that it was destined for the central section of a screen, probably in the basilica.

160. Pl. 132,8. A small fragment of a baluster.

Nearly 20 other small pieces of balusters were registered; they illustrate the same features as those described in nos. 154-160.

Miscellanea.

161. Pl. 127, Fig. 2,2. A yellowish block with moldings on two opposite sides, of which details are given on p. 95, Fig. 14,4. The material used is exceptional. It was found beneath the steps leading from the nave of the basilica to the sanctuary.

162. Pl. 127, Fig. 2,3. See also p. 95, Fig. 14,6. A piece of a slab with a sculptured foot. The slab measures 13.5 × 6 × 3 cm. The division between the 6 toes of the foot is marked by bored holes. [1] The material has white, black and brown stripes. One more fragment of a slab of the same material (*reg.* 662), 11½ × 6½ × 3½ cm., was found with the preceding one in the same place as no. 161.

163. Pl. 128, 2nd vertical row, top. A truncated cone (frustrum) 7.8 cm. high, 7½ cm. in diameter across the one end and 6½ cm. across the other. A round arch is incised on the side.

164. *Reg.* 1489. A gray slab, 22 × 17 × 1.7 cm., on whose one side 22 rectangles are ruled with lead. The rectangles are arranged in 2 rows, 11 in each row; perhaps a gameboard.

165. *Reg.* 1983. A small object, 85 mm. high and 40 mm. in diameter, is flat at one end, pointed at the other and grooved around the sides.

Hundreds of slabs, some interesting for their green, red, white-black, yellow and brown colors or stripes, not to mention the much more common gray ones, were collected, but not registered unless they formed part of an object registered for some other reason. Further clearances will undoubtedly bring to light still more marble at Siyâgha. — Comparative material may be found in most reports on excavated churches, but both in amount and in variety the material found at Siyâgha is noteworthy.

II. NEBI MÛSA STONE

The objects made from this material were adequately treated in the context in which they were found: the decorated slabs on pp. 70 ff. & 94; the post on pp. 71 & 83; the

[1] Regarding this technique, see *HCA* p. 475.

balusters on pp. 36,50 & 83. The balusters were panelled in the same way as the marble ones; they are so badly shattered that it is difficult to form an estimate of their number, but there seem to have been only a few.

III. BASALT [1]

Millstones.

166. Pl. 60, Fig. 1,8. The round upper stone of a rotating mill found in room 16. The hollow projections on two sides served to insert beams by means of which the stone could be turned. The interior is shaped like two hollow cones with the contracted part in the center; the grain to be ground was poured into the one hollow end, the other was placed over a conical tenon in the middle of the face of the nether stone around which it was rotated. The nether stone was not found with this one. See no. 167. Galling [2] considers this type of millstone a Roman importation.

167. Pl. 60, Fig. 1,9. A fragment of a millstone found in the western end of the north hall. It probably represents the conical tenon in the middle of the face of the lower stone, over which the upper stone (see no. 166) was placed and around which it was rotated whilst the grain was being ground.

168. Pl. 60, Fig. 1,10. An upper millstone found in room 22. The perforation in the center is enclosed by a raised rim; near the edge there are two small holes for handles by means of which the stone was rotated. No lower stone was found with this one, but see no. 169. — At Gezer similar hand-querns with the complete perforation of the upper stone were found; according to Macalister, [3] such hand-querns do not appear before the early Arab period. At Gezer, according to the same authority, "there is never a second hole for the insertion of a turning handle; this seems not to have been introduced in Palestine till after the early Arab period." Thomsen adopted the views of Macalister regarding the Arabic origin of rotating hand-querns, but Dalman [4] on literary evidence maintains that such mills were in use already in the first century A. D. and that their use became general during the second century of our era.

169. *Reg.* 347. A lower millstone found in the eastern part of the southern monastery is 35 cm. in diameter and 7½ cm. thick; the knob in the middle of the face is 7 cm. high and 5 cm. in diameter near the top; it probably served as the tenon over which the perforated upper millstone (see no. 168) was placed and around which it rotated when the grain was ground.

170-2. *Reg.* 164. Two millstones found in the southern monastery; each one is 30-34 cm. in diameter and 7 cm. thick; each one is perforated in the center; one has a hole for the handle near the edge (see no. 168). — *Reg.* 85. Millstone, probably like nos. 170-1, 31 cm. in diameter, has a hole for a handle near the edge.

173. *Reg.* 346. Millstone, probably like no. 166, is 32 cm. high, 48 cm. in diameter at one end and 24 cm. at the other.

174-5. *Reg.* 72 & 73. Small fragments of millstones.

[1] For the sources of this material, see Blake, *The Stratigraphy of Palestine and its Building Stones*, pp. 88 ff., 120.
[2] *BRL* cols. 387 f.; see G. Dalman, *Arbeit und Sitte in Palästina*, III, Gütersloh, 1933, pp. 230 ff.
[3] *Gezer* II, pp. 36 f. & Fig. 229.
[4] *Arbeit und Sitte in Palästina*, III, pp. 227 ff.

Mortars, pestles, a rubber.

176. *Reg.* 355. A basalt stone, which is 26 cm. high, 15 cm. in diameter at one end and 36 cm. at the other, is hollowed out somewhat at the larger end; this suggests its use as a mortar. Most of the mortars found at Siyâgha were made of limestone (see below).

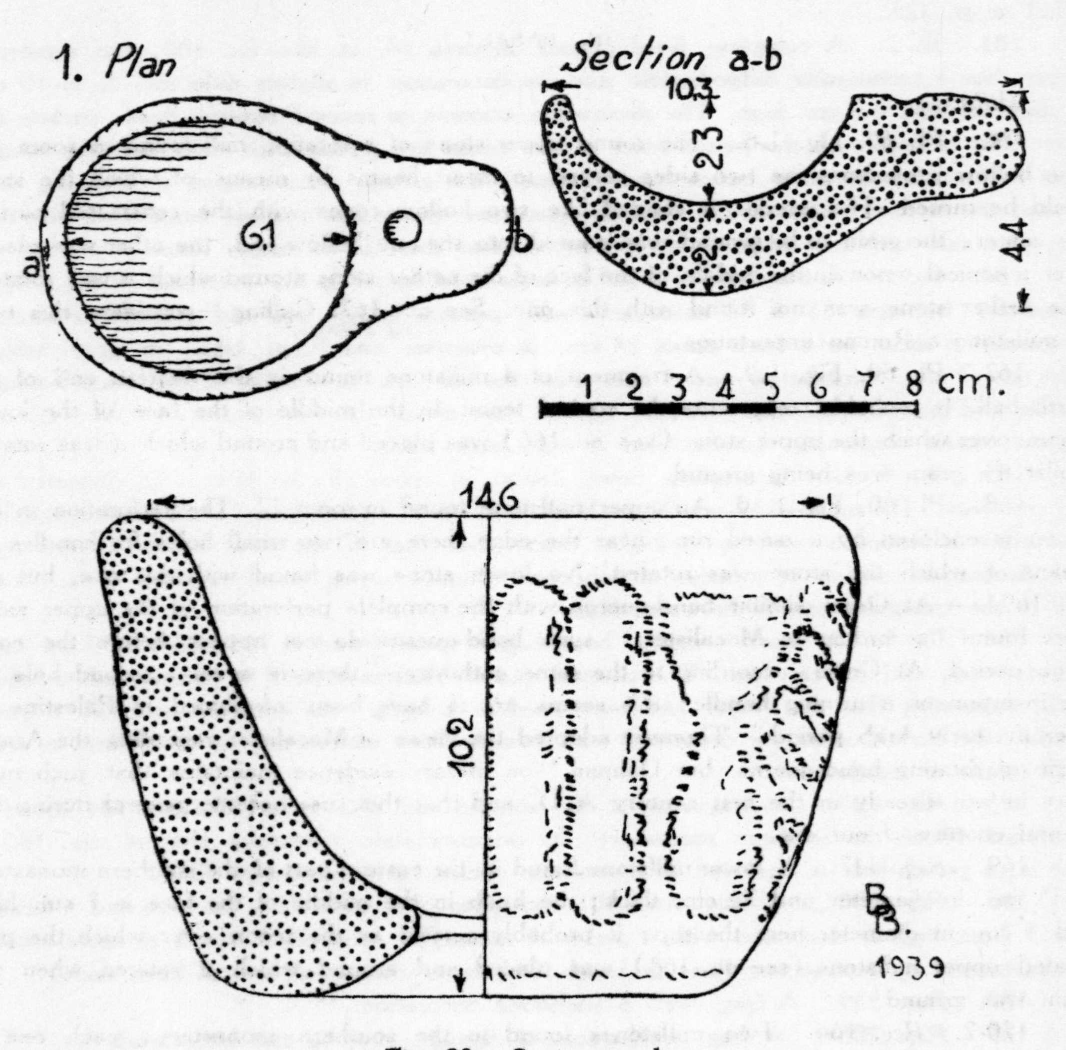

Fig. 33. Stone vessels.

177. Fig. 33, below. Two fragments suggesting a vase at least 10.2 cm. high with walls 44 mm. thick near the base. The interesting feature is the vertical reeding around the exterior, like that of the marble vessel no. 68. This small bowl may have served as a mortar.

178. Pl. 60, Fig. 1,5. A cone-shaped pestle.

At least two dozen other stones of about the same size as no. 178, but exhibiting a great variety of forms, may have served as pestles.

179. Not registered. An oblong rounded piece of basalt picked up directly above a wall of the western monastery may have served as a rubber, that is, as the upper stone of the older type of mill used in Palestine, as illustrated, v. g., in *BRL* col. 387,1.

IV. GNEISS-SCHIST

180. Pl. 133, Fig. 1,1. A small incomplete bowl with a flat base, straight sides and incised linear ornaments around the exterior, found in room 19, was described more in detail on p. 125.

181. Ib. 2. A complete bowl, found in area 59, is like no. 180, but somewhat larger, has a rectangular ledge-handle and its decoration is slightly different. It is 10 cm. in diameter and 4.7 cm. high. The decoration consists of incised straight lines, circlets and dots. The circlets with the punch-holes in the center are arranged in rows between straight lines to form bands; three bands form a group; the groups are arranged in a zigzag order around the exterior; each of the resulting triangular spaces has a single band of circlets near the open side and one circlet in the center, so that there is no empty space.

182. Ib. 3. A fragment of a rather large bowl found in the courtyard of the western monastery between 55 & 57 associated with pottery which has red painted ornaments. Originally it must have been about 24 cm. in diameter and 9 cm. high; its grayish-black sides are 7 mm. thick below and 4 mm. near the rim; on the exterior it has a knob-shaped handle and incised ornaments. Double vertical lines divide the outer surface of the vase into narrow panels containing rhombs filled in with latticework.

183. Ib. 4. An incomplete bowl, found in room 22, is 10 cm. in diameter and 3.9 cm. high. The material of which the bowl is made is reddish green and semi-transparent; its surface is smoother and has a higher polish than that of the other bowls of this type. The decoration consists of a series of concentric rhombs having small incisions in each angle and in the triangular spaces between them.

184. Ib. 5. A nearly complete boat-shaped vessel found in 105 which is 13 cm. long, 6.8 cm. wide and 3.7 cm. high. The pointed end is blackened as if it had served to hold a wick, suggesting that the vessel had been used as a lamp; the opposite end has a knob-handle; the curved sides are decorated with straight lines intersecting so as to form a series of X-motifs or trestlework.

185. *Reg.* 2001. A fragment of the pointed end of a vessel like no. 184 found in courtyard 68 of the southern monastery. Its ornamentation resembles that of nos. 180-1, that is, a punch-hole is enclosed by concentric circles between straight lines.

186. *Reg.* 2002. A frag. from 101 consisting of a piece of a flat base and a straight side 3.7 cm. high is decorated with a series of rectangles subdivided into 6 or more smaller compartments by intersecting lines or bands (the latter consist of several lines each).

187. *Reg.* 539. A frag. with a wishbone decoration.

188. *Reg.* 2064. A frag. with traces of zigzags, rhombs and latticework.

189. *Reg.* 1228, 2061, 2632 & 2633. Four fragments decorated with concentric circles and incised lines.

190. *Reg.* 1884. Frag. with a crisscross arrangement of lines.

191. *Reg.* 1885-7, 2059 (about 74 mm. d.), 2635-6. Six fragments with traces of incised lines only.

192. *Reg.* 2062-3, 2065, 2339, 2429, 2634. Six fragments with concentric circles only. See pp. 102 f. regarding this type of decoration.

193. Other fragments which were not decorated were not registered; they were neither large nor numerous.

The use to which some of this material was put by people of the Nebo region was mentioned on pp. 74 f.

Bowls of the same type as those described in nos. 180-193 were found at Madaba, Jerash, Jericho, Jerusalem and Beisan. Regarding the material from Madaba and Jerash we have only oral communications. The bowls from Jericho were found in a Byzantine tomb assigned to the 4th-5th centuries; they are made of green stone, have flat bases, straight sides and ledge-handles, but no ornamentation; the one is 15 cm. in d. and 6.5 cm. h.,[1] the other is 7.5 cm. in d. and 4.5 cm. h.[2] — The bowl from Jerusalem was recovered in a "Late Byzantine Level" or "under the Arab Level;" it is made of the same dark-gray friable material and has the same form and decoration as the Siyâgha bowls.[3] — A similar bowl found at Beisan has incised decoration. FitzGerald compares it, on the one hand with the stone bowl from Jerusalem mentioned above, on the other hand with pottery bowls which have the same form and decoration and are attributed to the Arab period.[4] — The context in which the Siyâgha bowls were found seems to favor a date at the end of the Byzantine period or at the beginning of the early Arab period (see p. 125).

As regards the purpose of these vessels, it has been suggested to the writer by a competent authority that they may have been used as offering boxes, that is, as receptacles for the offerings made by visitors to the shrine. We ourselves expressed the view above that the boat-shaped vessel may have served as a lamp (see no. 184).

V. STEATITE

194. Fig. 34,1; Pl. 133, Fig. 2,3. Incomplete bowl with a flat base, slightly convex sides, a ledge-handle, but without ornamentation. The dark-green friable material is similar to that used for the smaller decorated bowls treated above (nos. 180-193). It is 15½ cm. in d. near the base, 14½ cm. near the mouth and 8 cm. high; its sides are 7-10 mm. thick. The crescent-shaped ledge-handle near the center of the side is about 8 mm. thick, projects about 10 mm. and extends along the side of the vessel about 8 cm. Vertical marks on the sides were produced by a chisel or knife in trimming the vessel.

195. Fig. 34,2; Pl. 133, Fig. 2,8. A piece of a bowl like no. 194, originally about 18 cm. in d. and about 10 cm. h.; the bowl consisted of several pieces with straight edges held together by means of metal clamps. Along a straight edge of both the side and the base there are still three small holes each, for the insertion of the binding material; this consisted of a narrow strip of copper, as is evident from pieces still in the holes; see also Pl. 133, Fig. 2, 1 & 4; in the latter case a somewhat wider band of metal is folded over the rim to cover the joint between two pieces. — *Reg.* 1874-5 are fragments which may have belonged to no. 195. — Such vessels could not have served to contain liquids neither could they have been used as cooking pots, though this is suggested by their blackened surface; but they could have served as containers for grain, floor and the like.

196. Fig. 34,6; Pl. 133, Fig. 2,6. A piece of a bowl like no. 194, originally about 25 cm. in d. and about 9 cm. h.; its nearly triangular ledge-handle is 5 mm. thick, projects 18 mm. and extends along the side of the bowl 8½ cm. On the rim and at the juncture of the base

[1] *Jericho*, p. 167, VI, 1 & Abb. 214.
[2] Ib. 2 & Abb. 213.
[3] *PEF Ann.* 5, p. 85 & Pl. XVI, 5; see ib. Pl. XVI, 29.
[4] *Beth-Shan* III, p. (43) & Pl. XL, 4. — Compare with ib. Pls. XXVI, 3; XXVII, 1; XXXIII, 20 & 31. — A similar incised flat-bottomed and straight-walled pottery bowl was found at Siyâgha; see Pl. 153,1.

and side there are traces of the use of a toothed instrument in dressing the surface; on the sides there is evidence of paring; part of the surface was blackened by fire. See no. 195.

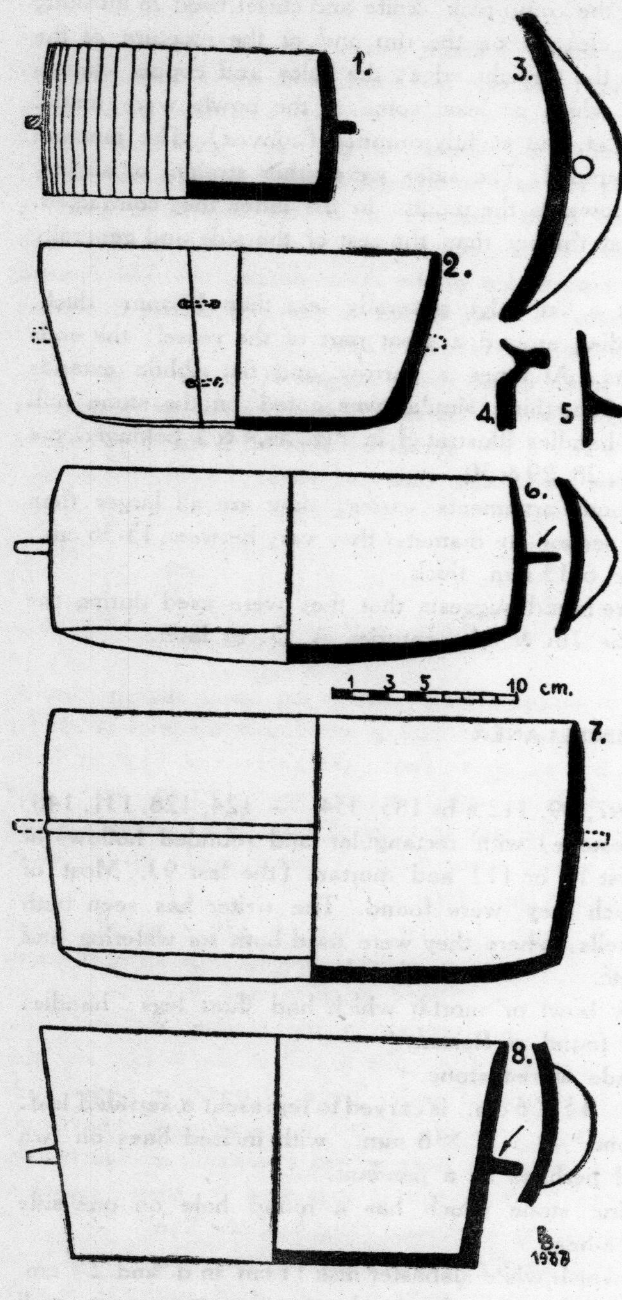

Fig. 34. Stone bowls.

197. Fig. 34,7; Pl. 133, Fig. 2,2. A part of a bowl like the preceding three, about 26 cm. in d. and 13 cm. h.; instead of a ledge-handle it has a narrow belt around its center; the belt is 6-9 mm. wide and projects 10-20 mm.; as the preceding bowl so also this one was finished off with a comb-pick and a knife.[1] Both the interior and the exterior were blackened by fire.

198. Fig. 34,8; Pl. 133, Fig. 2,5. A part of a bowl like the preceding ones, about 23 cm. in d. and about 13 cm. h.; its semicircular ledge-handle projects about 2 cm. and extends along the side of the vessel about 6 ½ cm. The base serves to illustrate how these bowls were pieced together (see no. 195); along the straight edge of the piece there are three small holes, two of which still contain the copper wire which served to fasten this piece to another one.

199. Fig. 34,3; Pl. 133, Fig. 2,7. About half of a crescent-shaped ledge-handle, like that on no. 194, attached to a piece of the vessel's side; originally the handle extended about 20 cm. along the side of the vessel. This fragment is noteworthy for the perforation through the handle and the side of the wall adjoining it.

200. *Reg.* 1911. A part of a bowl from 96 which was originally about 31 cm. in d. and 14 cm. h.; its sides are 7-8 mm. thick; on the surface marks of the chisel are visible. The ledge-handle is 9 mm. thick, projects 28 mm. and is 14 cm. long; the sides are not blackened.

201-234. *Reg.* 1865, 1867, 1872-5, 1877-82, 1888, 1890, 2365-71, 2391,

[1] See *PEF Ann.* 4, p. 148,3 for another instance of the use of the comb-pick in dressing the surface of a stone vessel. Ib. pp. 147 f. mention is made of vessels made of soft stone found with Arab pottery; one such vessel is illustrated in Pl. XVI,4; it is a flat-bottomed mug with sides slightly expanding like the sides of a barrel and was trimmed down with a chisel or knife but not smoothed off. It reminds one forcibly of the bowls from Siyâgha which we are now considering.

2430, 2549-51, 2737-41, 2834-5. Fragments — 34 — collected from the western and southern parts of the site serve to illustrate how these bowls were made, their form and size.

On many fragments there are marks of the comb-pick, knife and chisel used in finishing off the surface; the marks of the comb are clearest on the rim and at the juncture of the base and side. A number of pieces illustrate the straight edge, the holes and copper clamps used to join together the different pieces of which at least some of the bowls were made.

The base was generally not perfectly flat, but slightly rounded (convex). The juncture of the base and side was either angular or rounded. The sides were either straight or slightly convex; in the former case they expanded towards the mouth, in the latter they contracted. The rim was always severely plain, somewhat thinner than the rest of the side and generally rounded.

The handles always have the form of a flat ledge generally less than 10 mm. thick, projecting less than 30 mm. and often extending around a great part of the vessel; the ends generally taper down to narrow flat ribbons. At times a narrow and flat ribbon extends around the entire vessel like a small belt. Something similar was noted on the stone mill illustrated in Pl. 60, Fig. 1,8. — The ledge-handles illustrated in Fig. 34,4 & 5 belonged not to stone but to pottery vessels; see Pl. 153, 28, 29 & 30.

The size of this group of bowls without ornaments varies; they are all larger than the ornamented bowls treated in the previous section. In diameter they vary between 15-36 cm.; in height, between 7-14 cm.; the walls are 6-13 mm. thick.

The context in which these bowls were found suggests that they were used during the latest period of the site's occupation, say the 7th & 8th centuries A. D. or later.

VI. MISCELLANEA

235-254. *Reg.* 71, 74 a-b, 90, 94-5, 97, 99, 112 a-b, 183, 354, — 124, 128, 131, 140, 267-8, 280, 286-7. About 20 stones (limestone) with rectangular and rounded hollows of varying size were probably basins (the first 10 or 11) and mortars (the last 9). Most of them were mentioned in the context in which they were found. The writer has seen both types of stones near modern cisterns and wells, where they were used both for watering and feeding animals and for washing clothes, etc.

255. Pl. 61,4. A part of a shallow bowl or mortar which had short legs; handles project from the rim, as on similar vessels found at Beisan. [1]

256. Fig. 33, above. A dipper made of red stone.

257. *Reg.* 1986. A small stone, $4\frac{1}{2} \times 4\frac{1}{2} \times 6$ cm., is carved to represent a serrated leaf.

258. *Reg.* 2069. A small green stone, $40 \times 17 \times 8$ mm., with incised lines on two sides and perforated at one end, was used perhaps as a pendant.

259. *Reg.* 2077. Half of a crystalline stone which has a round hole on one side suggesting that it had been used as a mace-head.

260. Pl. 126,27; Fig. 14,5. A brownish white alabaster disk 11 cm. in d. and $2\frac{1}{2}$ cm. thick is perforated in the center and has the edge carved in such a way as to suggest small heads arranged in groups of three; the groups are arranged in two pairs facing each other.

N. B. — A few stone beads come from late tombs; various small stones interesting on account of their color and form were collected; their purpose is uncertain; perhaps some were used as weights or for games.

1 See *Beth-Shan* III, p. (43) & Pl. XL,3 & 6.

CHAPTER XI

BONE

Bone artifacts were not numerous at Siyâgha; the majority of them come from the western monastery or from the dump immediately west of it and are illustrated in Pl. 134,1. They represent rings, tubes, whorls, a disc, inlays, rods, pins, spoons and possibly personal ornaments. Their decoration consists of moldings, incised lines, circlets and punch-holes. In general they resemble objects found on other sites occupied during the Byzantine and early Arabic periods, as, for example, at Gezer, Beisan, Jerusalem, etc. In the following list further details are given.

THE CATALOGUE

1. Pl. 134,1, top row. Three pieces representing a ring and 2 tubes which fit together. The ring is molded and flanged to connect two tubes like the one at its right; its diameter is about 36 mm. A similar object was found in Jerusalem.[1] The first tube to the right of the ring fits neatly into the latter's flanged end; on its outer surface double lines are incised to form an obtuse angle. The second tube fits into the first one; a tiny hole evidently served to insert a pin for fastening the parts together; its exterior surface has fine ribbing; at Beisan[2] two objects resembling this last piece were found. All three pieces combined have a strong resemblance to the mouth-piece of the flute in the hands of a musician represented on the mosaic pavement of the church of SS. Procopius and Lot at el-Mekhayyat.[3]

2. Pl. 134,1, 2nd row, 1st. Whorl, plano-convex in form, perforated in the center and decorated on the convex side with incised concentric rings, inside which there are 6 tiny circlets with punch-holes in their center. From 56.

The plano-convex form is common to both spindle-whorls and buttons; the latter are distinguished from the former by being usually smaller and by having two perforations.

Linear ornaments are a common feature of these objects; the circlets occur also on other objects found at Siyâgha, as we pointed out on pp. 102 f.

[1] See *PEF Ann.* 5, Pl. XXI, 37.
[2] See *Beth-Shan* III, Pl. XL, 23.
[3] See *RB* 43 (1934), Pl. XXV, right.

Similar material has been reported from Gezer,[1] Jerusalem[2] and Beisan.[3]

3. Ib. 2nd. Whorl, like no. 2, but without any ornamentation.

4. Ib. 3rd. Flat disc; in place of the perforation there is a faint mark on one side as if an attempt had been made to pierce the disc; on the same side 4 double faint curved lines serve to cut off 4 arcs around the border; a somewhat similar ornamentation was used for an object found at Beisan.[4] The disc may represent an unfinished whorl or a playing-piece.[5]

5. Pl. 134,1, right end of 1st & 2nd rows. Inlay; the 2 fragments consist of numerous slivers found in 56 and rearranged; originally they may have belonged to one and the same piece. The 2 fragments are perforated by 6 tiny round holes, which seem to indicate that this thin strip was affixed to the surface of another object by means of rivets made, say, of bone or wood. The visible surface was decorated with linear ornaments which suggest large leaves. Such decorated inlays were used in Palestine since the days of the Hyksos.[6]

6. Pl. 134,1, 3rd row, 3rd object. A piece of a ring found in a trench west of the pulpit in the basilica. Originally it was about 33 mm. in d.; its band is 1 mm. thick and 5 mm. wide; on the outer surface a zigzag line is incised; opposite each angle in that line there is a short straight line extending from the edge in the direction of the angle.

7. *Reg.* 2655. Ring which seems to have been used in its natural form. From 93.

8. Pl. 134,1, 3rd row, 1st. Piece of a rod, which has a molded end and 2 pairs of incised lines around the bulging central part.

9. Ib. 4th row, 1st. Small rod with both ends molded; the upper molded end is completely pierced by two perforations.

10. Ib. 2nd. A frag. of a rod 5 mm. in d. with one molded end (lower).

11. Ib. 5th. A rod consisting of 2 pieces mortised in the center. The rounded heads and the bulging central parts are each encircled by a pair of grooved lines; next to the tenons each piece has small circlets with punch-holes, like those of no. 2.

12. Ib. 6th. A rod with plain axle-like ends; the rest is molded.

13. Ib. 6th row. A complete rod 16.4 cm. l. and 5 mm. in diameter. The head is molded; the opposite end is threaded.

These rods (nos. 8-13) were used for the framework of small articles of furniture.[7]

14. Ib. 4th row, 3rd. Pointed end of a pin 53 mm. l. and 4-1½ mm. in diameter.

15. Ib. 4th. Pointed end of a pin 40 mm. l. and 8 mm. in diameter.

16. *Reg.* 2665. Upper end of a pin with molded head and tapering shank. See no. 17.

17. Pl. 138, Fig. 2,20. Complete pin with molded head and shank tapering to a point.

Pins resembling nos. 14-17 were found also at other sites, so, v. g., at Gezer.[8] They are supposed to have served the same purpose as bronze pins, namely, to fasten cloaks.[9]

18. Pl. 134,1, 4th row, 7th. Spoon; the end of the shallow bowl is broken away and missing; the flat, relatively short and broad handle is molded and has 2 perforations.

19. Ib. 3rd row, 2nd. A flat rounded object resembling a small ovate leaf.

20. Ib. 4th. A flat piece of bone with a perforation at each end; from room 22.

1 See *Gezer* II, pp. 72 ff., 90.

2 *PEF Ann.* 4, p. 173; ib. 5, Pl. XXI, 36 & 40.

3 *Beth-Shan* III, Pl. XL, 24 & 32.

4 See *Beth-Shan* III, Pl. XL, 22.

5 See *Gezer* II, pp. 302 f.

6 See, v. g., *Gezer* II, pp. 247 ff.; *BRL* cols. 145 ff., nos. 4 & 6.

7 For other material of this type see *BRL* cols. 143 f., no. 2; there suggestions regarding their use are made; see *Beth-Shan* III, Pl. XL, 30 & possibly 25, 27, 31.

8 See *Gezer* II, p. 88 & Fig. 278,3.

9 See *BRL* col. 143, no. 2.

CHAPTER XII

METAL

A. GENERAL SURVEY

The excavations at Siyâgha brought to light objects made of the following 5 metals: gold, copper, bronze, iron and lead.

Gold occurred only in the form of thin sheets on cubes of the wall mosaics described on pp. 34 f.

Copper and bronze were used for a number of articles, such as the suspension chains of lamps, for at least one lamp, for wick-holders, for a cross, a weight, some vessels, clamps, bells, coins, figurines, plaques, rings, spatulae, articles of dress, etc. To the suspension chains belong hooks, links, bars, discs, etc. All this material is covered with a green coating produced by corrosion; on removing the coating we found simple ornaments on a number of pieces.

Iron was used for the gratings of windows, nails, rivets, staples, hooks, bolts, pins, ornamental pieces, knives, rings, discs, buckles, etc. Iron objects exceed those made of other metals both numerically and quantitively. The greater number is due especially to the presence of many nails; the greater quantity, to the window gratings and a large disc. In general iron objects are much more poorly preserved than others; all are very rusty and many have crumbled to tiny bits.

Lead was used as a binding material between the bases and shafts of the altar posts and of the columns of the screen in the Theotokos chapel (see pp. 98 & 94 respectively). Lumps of lead were found in tomb 1 b; their purpose was discussed on p. 38. A few interesting pieces of openwork found in the western monastery were made of this same material; they were described on p. 153.[1] Lead ranks next to iron in quantity, though relatively few objects are represented.

[1] This openwork may be compared to that of a thuribulum illustrated by Kaufmann in *HCA* p. 579, Abb. 289,2 (see the base of no. 1 ib.). — See also *QDAP* 3 (1934), p. 12, no. 18 & Pl. VIII, 15, for such openwork.

The metal objects found in 1933 are illustrated in Pl. 138, Fig. 2; those found in 1935 and 1937, in Pls. 134,2; 135-137; see also Pl. 138, Fig. 1, 1-5; Pl. 139, Fig. 3,1.

We have seen that a rather limited use was made of gold and lead at Siyâgha; that use has been indicated sufficiently and need not detain us any longer here. Copper, bronze and iron were used much more extensively; the objects made of these materials are listed and described in the catalogue.

B. THE CATALOGUE

I. IRON

Gratings.

1. Pl. 134,2. A grating, found embedded in the soil about 5-6 m. northeast of the apse of the basilica, was buried beneath the large stones of the cella trichora and beneath the smaller stones of the later basilica; from this we conclude that the grating belonged to a window in the upper part of the eastern wall of the cella trichora or of the first basilica or of both. It consists of 6 bars: 3 horizontal and 3 vertical ones, averaging about 83 cm. in length and 3-4 cm. in diameter; they intersect one another so as to form 16 openings (see p. 28, Fig. 5,9); they taper somewhat towards the ends, which were inserted in sockets in the jamb stones of the window. Stones with precisely 3 sockets were found east of the basilica and elsewhere; see pp. 29 ff. and Fig. 5,6. The bars are corroded and have crumbled to pieces. Such gratings were common since the early Roman period, so, v. g., at Pompeii.[1]

2-3. Fragments of 2 or 3 gratings like no. 1; see pp. 148 f.

Nails.

4-31. Pl. 135, Fig. 2,33-60. More or less complete nails (28) found in 1935 and 1937 in the monasteries; they serve to illustrate both the size and the form of typical nails used on the site. The largest nail, or rather spike, is 11½ cm. l. and its dome-shaped head is 3-3½ cm. in d.; the smallest is 47 mm. l. and its head is 14 mm. in d. The heads seem to have been hemispherical in shape, but this fact is generally obscured by their poor condition. The shanks are round in section and taper gradually to a point. All the nails are rusted and somewhat disfigured.

32-38. Ib. 61-67. Seven fragments of nails representing heads and the upper part of shanks; see nos. 4 ff.

39-43. Ib. 68-72. Five large nails with lower ends bent to form hooks.

44-45. Ib. 73-74. Two heads of nails.

46-62. Pl. 138, Fig. 2,29 (6th & 8th-14th) & 30. Nails (17) found in the regions explored in 1933 (see p. 19); about 13 are practically complete.

[1] See *RE* 6, col. 2184, ll. 18-28.

63-76. Some 14 small nails with broad heads and thin shanks, found in the atrium tombs 21, a-c, may have served to fasten metal strips to leather belts, as illustrated on p. 126, Fig. 18,1 & 2; see p. 127.

Besides the 73 nails mentioned in nos. 4-76 more than 200 others are represented by smaller pieces, such as heads or heads and a part of the shanks (about 80), by the lower pointed end of the shank (about 160) or by intermediate sections of the shank. Granted that about 300 nails are represented by the pieces which we recovered, we must no doubt assume that the original number used was much greater; a few may have crumbled to pieces, but the majority were probably carried away with the wood which was collected for other purposes. According to Macalister[1] nails in iron appear as soon as the metal itself is introduced.[2]

Rivets.

77-80. Pl. 136, Fig. 1,78-81. Four rivets. The heads are hemispherical like those of the nails; the shanks are angular and straight, not round and tapering like those of the nails; it is the form of the shaft which distinguishes these rivets from the nails. The largest is 4½ cm. l. and its head is 16 mm. in diameter.

81-83. Ib. 84-86. Three rivets like nos. 77-80. Each of the 3 bolts has two pieces of metal attached to it; this serves to indicate their use as rivets.

Staples.

84-86. Ib. 75-77. Three incomplete angular staples.

87-91. Five staples resemble nos. 84-86, but they are even more poorly preserved.

92. Pl. 138, Fig. 2,29, 7th. A more or less complete rounded staple.

Hooks, pins and bolts.

93. Pl. 136, Fig. 1,82. A flat strip of metal, 97 mm. l. and 28 mm. wide, is hook-shaped at one end; the opposite end is broken away and missing.

94. Ib. 83. A flat incomplete strip with a hooked end like no. 93.

95. Ib. 87. A flat strip, 55 mm. l., is hooked at one end and pierced by an eye at the opposite wider end; this is the only complete object of this kind found on the site.

96. Ib. 88. A round bar curved at one end to form a hook and broken at the opposite end.

97. Ib. 89. As no. 96, but originally the curved end may have been closed to form an eye of a pin.

98. Ib. 90. A T-shaped piece.

99-103. Ib. (91?), 92, 100-2, 104. Five (or 6) bars, round in section as nos. 96-8, terminating at one end in a hook and at the other generally in an eye formed as a rule by a loop.

104-110. Ib. 94-99, 103. Seven pieces with an eye at one end, but broken at the other; at the latter end there was probably a hook; but one or the other may have been straight and pointed, so that it could have served as a pin or a bolt. See no. 137.

111. Pl. 138, Fig. 2,29, 3rd. A round bar pointed at one end and hooked at the other.

112. Ib. 4th. As no. 111, but hooked at both ends.

113-136. About 2 dozen other hooks are round in section like nos. 96-112; the largest is about 20 mm. in diameter. Those with an eye opposite the hooked end could be fastened

[1] See *Gezer* II, p. 246; cfr. *RLV* 8, cols. 421 f.

[2] See G. E. Wright, *Iron: The Date of its Introduction into Palestine*, in *AJA* 43 (1939), pp. 458-463 (the 12th century B. C.). — For wrought iron Macalister, *Gezer* II, pp. 269 ff., seems to prefer a date closer to the year 1000 B. C. — See also Richardson, *Iron: Prehistoric and Ancient*, in *AJA* 38 (1934), pp. 555-583; ib. 41 (1937), pp. 441 ff., Madame Hertz replies to Richardson; for the latter's answer see ib. pp. 447-451.

to another object by means of a nail; those which were pointed could themselves be driven into another object.

137. Pl. 136, Fig. 1,93. A bar, 98 mm. l., with an eye at one end and tapering to a point at the opposite end, may have served as a pin or a bolt. See nos. 104-110.

Plaques.

138. Pl. 136, Fig. 2,120. Plaque found in 38, 18 cm. l., 35 mm. w. in the center and 65 mm. at the ends. This flat bar is perforated in the center, where it is widest; the spirals at each end suggest that the bar had some ornamental purpose. See p. 82,3.

139-140. Ib. 118-9. Two plaques like no. 138 found in the courtyard of the western monastery.

Knives.

141. Ib. 105. A knife, about 14.5 cm. l., has a round socket, 2.5 cm. in d., for a wooden handle, of which decayed traces exist inside the socket; the blade, now broken into two pieces, is 3.4 cm. w. and slightly rounded along the edges.

142. Ib. 107. A knife with a round socket for the insertion of a handle; the blade diminishes in width towards the rounded tip.

143. Ib. 109. A knife with a round socket for a wooden handle and a straight-sided blade ending in a point near the thin cutting side (upper side in illustration). The socket is threaded around the exterior near the end, but neither this nor any other socket or tang has such pronounced ribbing as that of the grips of the knives represented on the marble slab illustrated in Pl. 121,1.

144-147. Ib. 110-2,115. Four pieces representing rounded sockets of knives like those of nos. 141-3. — In 5 sockets traces of decayed wood were noticed. — Some 20 flat pieces of iron found with the sockets may be fragments of the broken blades.

148. Pl. 138, Fig. 2,27. A knife with a socket for a handle and a curved blade whose sides gradually converge to a point. From 12.

149. Pl. 136, Fig. 2,106. A knife with a tang for a handle and a straight-sided blade narrowing towards the point which is broken off and missing.

150. Ib. 108. A knife with a tang and blade whose straight sides diminish in width towards the point which is missing.

151. Ib. 114. A dagger-shaped blade whose tang, similar to that of no. 149, is broken off and missing.

152. Ib. 116. A dagger-shaped blade whose point and hilt are missing.

153. Ib. 117. A tang and part of a blade like nos. 150-2.

154. Ib. 122. Two pieces; the one consists of a blade and tang; the other is a flat piece of metal whose edges are folded at one end to form a socket into which the tang of the knife fits; the broad end of this second piece is perforated; the latter may have served as a grip for the knife.

Rod, rings, buckles, links, vessel, disc, etc.

155. Ib. 121. Pieces of an iron rod found in tomb 1 d (see pp. 36 f.) remind one of the metal part of a crosier. Abbots received a crosier from the emperor after their election by the monks and after the approval of the bishop or patriarch; this rod was found in a tomb below the inscription mentioning the abbot Alex. (see pp. 262 ff., inscr. VIII).

156-161. Pl. 138, Fig. 2,21-26. Six rings 48-70 mm. in d. from the late tombs among the ruins; they probably served as bracelets and date from the beginning of the 19th century A. D.

162-169. Eight small rings 24-54 mm. in d. from the tombs and elsewhere may have been used as ornaments or as parts of belts and the like (see nos. 170-172).

170-171. Fig. 18,1 & 2. Two buckles described on p. 127. — There were most probably many more, but all are corroded.

172. Pl. 136, Fig. 2,113 & p. 126, Fig. 18,4. An object consisting of two blades riveted together near their center and terminating at one end in rings; one of the two pieces has lost both the ring and the point at the opposite end. This object reminds one of a pair of scissors; but it could also represent a piece of a harness.

173. Pl. 138, Fig. 2,28. A strong ring with another piece, possibly of a chain, attached.

174. *Reg.* 2281. Two links of a chain.

175. *Reg.* 2289. Fragments of a plate with a low rim; details uncertain.

176. *Reg.* 2290. A large broken disc found in 105, west of the oven, was originally 34 cm. in d.; in the center it has a perforation 5 cm. in diameter; it may have had something to do with the work at the bakery.

N. B. — A small quantity of scrap-iron no doubt represents a number of other objects whose original form and purpose can no longer be made out.

II. BRONZE AND COPPER

Lighting apparatus: lamps, suspension chains and wick-holders.

177. Pl. 138, Fig. 1,1. Lamp, found in area 92, is only 8 cm. l. and 2 cm. high. See p. 173.

178. Pl. 137, Fig. 2,2. A cover (upside down) of some vessel, possibly of a lamp; from 63. It is almost exactly like the cover of the lamp from Saloniki illustrated by Kaufmann, *HCA* p. 591, Abb. 295,2. In both cases the lid was attached to the lamp by a hinge. Similar lids for lamps were used at Beisan. [1]

179. Pl. 137, Fig. 1,6. Chains for suspending a lamp found in 68 (see p. 165). The chains consist of discs, links, rods or bars, hooks and a ring. At the upper end there is a dome-shaped cap or disc; its upper surface has 6 ridges; its apex has a perforation through which two ends of a wire, which forms a ring above the cap, were inserted and held fast by bending the ends below the cap; the ring served to attach the chain to a hook or the like. Near the edge of the cap the pointed ends of 3 ridges are perforated to permit the attachment of 3 chains. Two of the chains are still attached; the third was detached and partly lost. The surviving parts of the chains differ slightly; the one on the right consists of 8 parts: 4 links, 2 discs, 1 bar and 1 hook; they are disposed in the following order from top to bottom: links, disc, links, bar, links, disc, links and hook. The second chain, namely, the one in the center, resembles the first, but at the lower end a disc and some links are omitted or missing. Of the third chain we found only a hook and some links along with the other 2 chains; the hook is larger than the other 2. — The piece of a chain on the left was not found with the other 2, but it closely resembles them; it comes from 102. The disc is pierced in such a way that a cross results in the center. As to the use of this and similar chains see p. 56.

[1] See *Beth-Shan* III, Pl. XXXVII, 9; Pl. XXXVIII, 1.

This suspension chain for a lamp is not complete, but it is the best specimen found at Siyâgha and serves to explain the purpose of a number of other metal pieces found on the site; see nos. 180 ff. Such chains were in common use during the Byzantine and early Arabic periods as is evident from similar chains found at several sites, such as Jericho[1] and Jerusalem,[2] and from representations of such chains on the mosaic pavements of Jerash[3] and Naᶜaran near Jericho.[4] In fact such triple suspension chains for lamps are still in common use today; in details there are of course differences.

180. Pl. 135, Fig. 1,5. Several parts of a triple suspension chain somewhat similar to no. 179. Instead of the domed piece of no. 179 to which the 3 chains were attached, we have here a 3-pronged support for the chains; this was found in room 32 (see p. 137). The links which are illustrated vary in size. The rod is slendor, like those used for the chains found both in the 9th century Nestorian hermitage near Jericho and like 3 of the rods found in the 8th century synagogue near the same place; see no. 179.

181-182. Ib. 6 & 7. Two slendor rods, like the one mentioned in no. 180.

183. Pl. 138, Fig. 2,6. A flat band, 13 cm. l. and 8-14 mm. w., has three disc-shaped sections, one in the center and one at each of the 2 ends; the latter are pierced. This band has the same function in a suspension chain as the much narrower rods used in no. 179. The holes at the 2 ends serve to attach other parts of the chain. Similar flat bars were found in the 8th century synagogue at Jericho and in Jerusalem; in the former case, 9 such pieces were found; 2 are complete and the rest fragmentary; in the latter case, the 3 strips are complete and a few links join them to hooks. See references under no. 179.

184. Pl. 135, Fig. 1,19. Two fragments of a bar like no. 183.

185. Pl. 138, Fig. 2, 13 & 14. Links of chains.

186. Ib. 11. A hook of a chain.

187. Ib. 12. A ring which may have served for suspending lamps.

188-222. Ib. 1-5; Pl. 135, Fig. 1, 8-10; Pl. 137, Fig. 1, 3 & 5; see p. 126, Fig. 18,3. About 35 wick-holders and a few fragments of the same kind; of these approximately a dozen are practically complete. They consist of a narrow and thin strip of metal of varying length, whose one end is folded to form a clasp for a wick, whilst the other (upper) end is bent into a loop by means of which the wick-holder was attached to the rim of the vessel which served as a lamp. In one case the upper end of the wick-holder has the form of a cross (see Pl. 137, Fig. 1,3). Such wick-holders were found also at Jerash.[5]

Ornamented and ornamental objects.

223. Pl. 137, Fig. 1,1. A small Maltese cross with a perforation on top for suspension is decorated on one side with 5 incised circlets each of which encloses a punch-hole; there is one on each arm and one in the center. It was found in 63 with other metal objects; see p. 164. For other occurrences of this ornament at Siyâgha see pp. 102 f. Similar crosses

1 See *QDAP* 4 (1935), p. 82 & Pl. LIV, 1, for a specimen from a Nestorian hermitage dated to the 9th century A. D.; *QDAP* 6 (1937), p. 75, Pl. XXII, for other good examples found in a synagogue assigned to the 8th century A. D. — Chains of the same type were used also for censers; good specimens are preserved in the Flagellation Museum, Jerusalem; see *Guida*, pp. 53 ff., no. 61 and Fig. 24 (from Jericho).

2 See Bliss, *Excavations at Jerusalem, 1894-1897*, London, 1898, Pl. XXVIII, no. 61. — See also *Beth-Shan* III, Pl. XXXVII, 1-4.

3 See *Gerasa*, Pl. LXIX, a & b, where birds are represented holding such chains in their beaks.

4 See Sukenik, *Beth Alpha*, p. 26, Fig. 27, where two lamps hanging from a menorah are represented suspended by such triple chains.

5 See *JEA* 17 (1931), p. 207.

have been reported from a vaulted tomb at Askalon dated to the 3rd-4th centuries A. D.,[1] from a rock-cut tomb at Tarshîhâ dated to the 4th-5th centuries,[2] from Gethsemane,[3] etc.[4]

224. Pl. 135, Fig. 1,17 (see Pl. 138, Fig. 1,4). A thin flat strip decorated on one side with incised lines, circlets and punch-holes. A straight line divides the surface into 2 parts; at each end of this line there are 2 pairs of diagonal lines drawn from it to the edge; 2 corners have a pair of diagonal lines drawn from one edge to the other. There are 5 circlets with punch-holes arranged crosswise in the one half and 4 (originally perhaps also 5) in the other. For this type of ornamentation see no. 223.

225. Pl. 135, Fig. 1,16 (see Pl. 138, Fig. 1,5). A plaque with two perforated projections on the back, where there is also a third perforation near the base, by means of which it could be fastened to another object. On the front a vine with leaves (possibly also flowers) is faintly outlined.

226. *Reg.* 550 b. An imitation coin or medal found in the late tombs among the ruins above the sanctuary of the basilica along with the Ottoman coins (see p. 285, nos. 98 ff.). In form it resembles the Ottoman coins; in size it occupies a position midway between metallics and half metallics; it is 16 mm. in d.; it was perforated near the edge in order to be worn as a pendant. On the one side a scroll border surrounds a circle of half moons and triangles in whose center there is a 5-pointed star formed of dots; the other side has a similar ornamentation, with this exception that the star is incised and enclosed by some indistinct design.

227. Pl. 135, Fig. 1,13. Elephant with a large hump or rider cut out of a thin flat strip.

228. Ib. 14. Rabbit cut out of a thin flat strip like no. 227.

229. Ib. 15 (see Pl. 139, Fig. 3,1). Figure on a throne. The throne is 38 mm. h. and 21 mm. w.; the arm-rests are 18 mm. h.; the back has 3 crossbars, the sides 2. The seated figure has lost most of its head; it is dressed in close-fitting garments draped over the knees; the r. arm rests on the arm-rest, the l. hand holds a club or scepter; the feet are drawn back beneath the seat; it is the traditional pose of Zeus.

230. Pl. 137, Fig. 2,1. Figure on a stand; from 82. The pedestal is 20 mm. h. and 32 mm. in d. The figure is incomplete; the upper part is broken away and lost; the lower part — still about 5 cm. h. — represents a large foot with 4 claws; the expanded part above the foot may represent wings, as in the case of a similar figurine in the Flagellation Museum, which is still complete; if so, an eagle may have been represented originally. In back of the figure there is a ring. The interior of the stand and figure are not hollow but filled with metal, probably lead.

231. Ib. 3. Head and antlers of a deer. The spread of the antlers is 71-79 mm.; the pointed head is about 39 mm. l.; behind the head there is a projection 35 mm. l. by means of which it could be attached to some other object.

232. Ib. 5. Handle consisting of a metal strip, 10 × 4 cm., and a ring attached to the former; above and below the attachments and on the center of the ring there are knobs.

233. *Reg.* 541. A case with a handle contains a bluish-red stone. The handle, describing a loop 16-21 mm. in d., is attached to the top of an oval case 23-33 mm. in d. and 8-10 mm. h.; around the sides half-circles are incised; they form 13 loops arranged in

1 *QDAP* 2 (1933), p. 182 & Pl. XLVIII, 6.
2 See *QDAP* 3 (1934), p. 16,6 & Pl. VIII, 5; this is an exact parallel.
3 Preserved in the museum of the Flagellation Monastery, Jerusalem; see *Guida*, p. 57, no. 64.
4 Bliss, *Excavations at Jerusalem, 1894-7*, London, 1898, p. 266, no. 39, reports the discovery of a mold for making such metal crosses.

3 groups of 2, 4 and 7 loops respectively. It comes from a late tomb (19th century) which had been arranged among the stones above the southern sacristy of the basilica. The case and stone were probably carried both as an ornament and as a charm; as a matter of fact, magical power is attributed to stones of the type contained in the case.

234. *Reg.* 542. A case and stone like no. 233 but smaller; the case is 21 mm. l., 17 mm. w. and 5 mm. h.; the sides are decorated with 11 loops; the blood-red stone has a slight shading of blue; it was found with no. 233.

235. Pl. 138, Fig. 2,15. A heavy ring, open on one side, is 45-65 mm. in d.; the band, about 12 mm. w. and 6 mm. thick, is flat on the inside and at the ends, but rounded on the exterior, on which there are a number of incised lines as ornaments. It comes from a 19th century tomb. It is perhaps a bracelet.

236-239. Pl. 135, Fig. 1,28-9, 31-2. Rings for fingers (4); from late burials.

240-249. *Reg.* 529-532, 560d-g, 578a. Ten rings for fingers; from 19th century tombs.

250. Pl. 135, Fig. 1,26. Half of a capsule or small case, 26 mm. l., 17-19 mm. w. and 12 mm. h., has 3 perforations through the flanged edge by means of which it could be attached to the other missing part; the ridge across the back is also perforated.

251. Pl. 138, Fig. 2,7. A medal without ornaments; from the basilica.

Bells.

252. Ib. 16. A bell with linear incisions; from a 19th cent. tomb.

253-254. Ib. 17 & 18. Two small bells from the basilica; date uncertain.

255. Pl. 137, Fig. 2,6. A bell from 56, which is 50 mm. h. and 37 mm. in d. at the base, has traces of rust inside which may point to an iron clapper. A similar bell has been reported from a 4th century tomb at Tarshîhâ.[1]

256. Ib. 7. A bell from 56 has preserved its clapper; it is 66 mm. h. and 23 × 50 mm. at the base.

257. *Reg.* 747. A bell from 38; date uncertain.

Rods, nails, spatulae, thimble, buckles, chains.

258-260. Pl. 135, Fig. 1,21,22,25 (see Pl. 137, Fig. 1,4). Three (or 4) rods; the last is 15.4 cm. l., 4 mm. in d. and reeded in the center.

261. Pl. 138, Fig. 2,10. Nail found in baptistery; it is 6 cm. l.; its dome-shaped head is 4-5 mm. h. and 15 mm. in d.; its shank is square in section, about 4 mm. w. on each side.

262. Pl. 135, Fig. 1,30. Pin or nail (incomplete). The head is 7 mm. in d.; the shank 2 mm. in d.; one piece is 55 mm. l., the other 19.

263. Pl. 138, Fig. 2,9. Spatula, 12.8 cm. l., 3-4 mm. in d., has a shallow bowl 10 × 14 mm.; it comes from a 19th cent. tomb above the southern sacristy.

264-266. Pl. 135, Fig. 1,20, 23-4. Three spatulae from recent tombs among the ruins.

267. Pl. 138, Fig. 2,8. A thimble from 29; it is 14 mm. l., 14 mm. in d. at one open end and 16 mm. in d. at the other.

268. Ib. 19. Buckle from a 19th cent. tomb above the southern sacristy.

269. Pl. 137, Fig. 2,4. Buckle from 56.

270. *Reg.* 536. Ring and 8 links of a chain from a 19th cent. tomb above the southern sacristy.

[1] See *QDAP* 3 (1934), p. 13, 25 & Pl. VIII, 12. — Also other bells are reported from that same place.

Vessels, metal strips, a weight, clamps, etc.

271. Pl. 137, Fig. 3, left. A flask-shaped can with a handle. The vessel is 21 cm. h. and 16 cm. w. across the shoulders. The concave base, 13 ½ cm. in d., has the umbilicus characteristic of 6th-century vessels made also of other materials. The splayed sides, 9 cm. h., are slightly ribbed; the sloping shoulders, 2 cm. high, are decorated with a herring-bone motif. The neck, 10 cm. l., 7 ½ cm. in d. at the base and 47 mm. in d. at the mouth, is ribbed. The surface of the vessel was blackened by fire, which seems to indicate that it was used as a kettle for boiling water or the like. Around the neck there is a separate piece which served as a handle. It consists of a band and a bar; the former averages 6 mm. in width; in 3 places it expands to form discs of which one is 35 mm. in d. and the others 14 mm. in d.; it terminates in wires attached to a bar which served as the handle. The can was found in 63 (see pp. 163 f.). A similar vessel found at Corinth is reported in *AJA* 39 (1935), p. 88.

272. Ib. right. A pan and loop-handle. The former has a flat base 23 cm. in d. and straight sides 7.5 cm. high. The handle, found with the pan, consists of a bar and wire; the bar is bent to form 3 sides, whilst 2 strands of wire, wound around the extremities of the bar, form the fourth side. It was found upside down on the shelf of room 63 with no. 271 (see pp. 163 f.); at that time the cracked base was still in its proper place.

273. *Reg.* 1946. A pan like no. 272 from room 82, but in a much more fragmentary condition.

274. Pl. 135, Fig. 1,1. A thin disc, 9 cm. in d., is pierced by 6 holes; from 56.

275. Ib. 11. A broken cup 76 mm. in d. and 20 mm. h.; a part is lost; from 56.

276. Ib. 12. A small crushed vessel.

277-279. Ib. 2-4. Three strips thickened along one edge and sharp along the other.

280. Ib. 18. A thin flat strip with expanded ends and a perforation in the center.

281. Pl. 138, Fig. 1,3. A small weight with rounded edges, whose surface measures about 12 × 20 mm., comes from the southwest corner of room 36.

282. Ib. 2 (see Pl. 133, Fig. 2,4, for another view of this same piece). A metal strip, 6 cm. l. and 2.8 cm. w., terminates in thin wires. The strip serves to unite 2 pieces of a steatite bowl as described on p. 300, no. 195. It is folded over the rim to cover the joint between 2 pieces; the wires were inserted in small holes in the side of the vessel and twisted so that both the band and the parts of the bowl were held firmly in place.

283-290. *Reg.* 1872, 2365, 2367-9, 2550, 2639 & 2835. Eight pieces of steatite bowls in which pieces of metal clamps (either bands or wires) are preserved; see no. 282.

N. B. — Some bolts used to join the bases and shafts of columns were probably of this metal; see pp. 51 and 94. — The coins were of bronze; see pp. 278-285. — There is a small quantity of scrap.

CHAPTER XIII

GLASS

A. GENERAL SURVEY

Glass was used for a number of cubes of the wall mosaics, for windows of the basilica and possibly also of the chapels but not for those of the monastery, for a weight, for some personal ornaments and for vessels.

The glass cubes used for the wall mosaics were described on p. 35.

The glass used for windows was treated on pp. 64-66. Such glass has been reported from Jerash, [1] from an early Byzantine basilica at Tell Hassân near Jericho, [2] from el-Mefjer, [3] Khan el-Ahmar, [4] Ophel, [5] etc.

The weight with an Arabic inscription was discussed on p. 276, inscription XXXVIII.

The personal ornaments consisted of colored bracelets and beads; they all come from the late tombs among the ruins. Seven bracelets were complete and a few others were represented by fragments. The rings vary in diameter between 41-75 mm.; the band is 3-9 mm. wide. On a blue or green background they have spots, stripes and bands colored black, white, yellow, red, brown, green and blue. The paste is opaque. The size of the rings indicates that some were worn by small girls, others by women. Such bracelets represent an ancient tradition still preserved among Bedouin women today. [6] — About 60 beads were found in the same context as the bracelets; they are not all of glass and have a variety of forms and colors. They serve to illustrate the modern history of the site.

Of the numerous glass vessels which were at one time used at Siyâgha only 3 small flasks are still complete, all the rest were broken or crushed to pieces

[1] See *Gerasa*, p. 546.
[2] See *QDAP* 5 (1936), p. 85.
[3] See *QDAP* 5 (1936), pp. 134 f., 137 & Pl. LXXXVIII, 1.
[4] See *QS* 1932, p. 198.
[5] See *PEF Ann.* 5, p. 99.
[6] See *Kisa* I, p. 100.

and it is on these pieces that we must base our conclusions regarding the number, form and purpose of the vessels. The body of the vessels was generally the most fragile part and suffered more than the others; bases, rims and handles were stronger and better preserved. Among the fragments we noted 390 bases or parts of the same, 341 fragments of rims and 298 handles; roughly speaking, between 300-400 vessels are represented; among them there are lamps, wine glasses, bowls and flasks. The glass generally has a light blue color, but there were also some green, brown, yellow, black and purple pieces; there was only one multi-colored vase; we abstract here from the irridescence produced by decay and from filaments of a different color noticed in a few pieces. Similar fragments of glass vessels occur on all the numerous Byzantine sites of Transjordan and Palestine; a comparison with that material will be instructive.

In the catalogue further details are given only regarding those pieces which represent vessels; typical pieces are illustrated in Pls. 138, Fig. 1, 6-10; 139, Fig. 3, 2; 140-142; they were all recovered in the monasteries during 1935 and 1937; but similar fragments were also found in 1933, as we pointed out elsewhere (see p. 20, note 5).

B. THE CATALOGUE

I. LAMPS

Tumbler-shaped lamps with a wick-tube.

1. Pl. 140,1. Base, part of sides and wick-tube; green; the best specimen found at Siyâgha. The concave base is 75 mm. in d.; the broken sides 40 mm. h.; on the interior of the vessel the concave base comes to a point which is crowned by the stump of a hollow wick-tube. This vertical glass tube in the center of the vessel is fixed to the pointed base with molten glass; it is still 38 mm. l. and 12 mm. in d.; its diameter diminishes gradually towards the top. The glass wick-tube is the distinguishing feature of this and the other lamps of this group. See nos. 2-17.

2. Ib. 2. A wick-tube like that of no. 1, 40 mm. l. and 14 mm. in d.; the expanded part at the lower end is a vestige of the molten glass at the point of attachment; green glass.

3. Ib. 3. A small piece of a green wick-tube 20 mm. in d.; see no. 1.

4. Ib. 4. A part of a base with a piece of the wick-tube attached; the latter is 29 mm. l. and 17 mm. in d.; blue glass; see no. 1.

5. Ib. 5. A part of a base with traces of the wick-tube; blue glass; see no. 1.

6. Ib. 6. As no. 5.

7-17. Eleven other fragments of bases of blue glass resemble the last few.

Nos. 1-17 represent a type of lamp that does not seem to have been used at Jerash. A complete lamp of this type was found in a tomb at Gezer dated to the 5th or 6th century A. D.; it is supposed to be the oldest example of this type of lamp known until now. A base of another was found during the excavations at Ophel in 1928-9; it comes from a drain under a Byzantine street and may be of the same date as the one from Gezer. The wick-tube characteristic of these lamps is also found in early Arabic lamps; it becomes quite common about the 12th century A. D. and has continued in use uninterruptedly in Egypt and Syria until the present day. [1]

Tumbler-shaped lamps without a wick-tube.

18-22. Ib. 7-11. Bases and parts of the sides of blue glass.

23-24. Ib. 12-13. As nos. 18 ff., but of green glass.

25-26. Ib. 14-15. As nos. 18 ff., but of black glass.

27-124. Some 98 other fragments like nos. 18 ff. were found.

In all well over 100 tumbler-shaped vessels without wick-tubes are represented by bases at Siyâgha; in other words, they are more than 5 times as numerous as the vessels with wick-tubes. The same type of vessel is very common at Jerash, where, according to Crowfoot and Harden, [2] it appears first in deposits of the 6th and 7th centuries; Baur [3] assigns the same type to the 5th-7th centuries and Kisa [4] dates some of these vessels to the 4th century. For complete forms see the sources indicated. In general this form of vessel seems to have been used earlier and much more extensively at Siyâgha than the vessels with wick-tubes. It does not necessarily follow that all these vessels without wick-tubes were used as lamps, some may have served other purposes, but when they were used as lamps, the wick was no doubt inserted into the oil and kept there by means of metal wick-holders of which a number was found on the site (see p. 310, nos. 188-222). [5]

Bowl-shaped lamps with a plain hollow stem.

125-130. Ib. 16-21. Six stems with a part of the bowl; blue glass. The stems vary in length between 50-80 mm.; they average about 20 mm. in d.; as a rule they taper slightly from the cup downwards; in one or the other case the stem has almost straight sides (see l. c. 17). The fragments of the bowls still attached to the stems vary from 34-65 mm. in d.; see *Gerasa*, Pl. CXL, a, top row, 2nd, for the appearance of a more or less complete bowl of this type.

131-133. Ib. 22-24. Three stems found near the oven in 93; they are covered with a white coating of decay concealing the original color; in form they differ from nos. 125 ff. by the bulging center and the contraction of the stem directly below the bowl. This variety is not so common at Siyâgha as nos. 125 ff.; it probably belongs to a slightly later date. Similar stems found at the chapel of the Beatitudes show a more marked tendency to bulge in the center and to contract both above and below the bulge. [6]

134-135. Ib. 25 & 26. As nos. 125 ff., but the glass is green and the sides are straighter.

1 See G. M. Crowfoot and D. B. Harden, *Early Byzantine and Later Glass Lamps*, in *JEA* 17 (1931), pp. 201 ff. passim.

2 *JEA* 17 (1931), p. 201.

3 *Gerasa*, pp. 521 ff.

4 *Kisa*, p. 343.

5 See *Gerasa*, p. 517, regarding such metal wick-holders found at Jerash.

6 See *RAC* 14 (1937), pp. 28 f., Figs. 26, 1-4; 27, 1-3. — Father Bagatti found similar stems during excavations at the church of the Visitation at ʿAin Kârim.

136. Ib. 27. As nos. 125 ff., but the glass is green-brown.

137-243. Some 107 stems or fragments of stems like those described in nos. 125-136; in the majority of cases the glass is blue and the form is similar to that of nos. 125-130. Similar stems have been reported from Jerash,[1] Beisan,[2] et-Tâbghah,[3] Ophel,[4] etc.

Bowl-shaped lamps with a beaded solid stem.

244. Ib. 28. A solid stem consisting of 2 beads and a fragment of the bowl. The bottom of the bowls is convex on the interior; of the sides only a few stumps remain; the glass is blue; found northeast of the basilica. — See *Gerasa*, p. 520, Fig. 17, no. 368, for the form of a complete vessel of this type; the bottom of our bowl resembles no. 369 l. c.; see ib. Pl. CXL, a, top row, 4th and Pl. CXLI, a, 3rd.

245. Ib. 29. A bead of a stem like no. 244.

246-254. Nine other beads were found; all probably formed parts of stems like no. 244.

Bowl-shaped lamps with beaded stems were found also at Jerash, where they were very numerous,[5] whilst the lamps with plain stems were rare there; at Siyâgha, on the contrary, the beaded stems were rare, whilst the plain hollow stems were numerous.

The bowl-shaped lamps with stems were supported on candelabra or polycandila;[6] these have holes into which the stems could be inserted, whilst the candelabra themselves were suspended by means of triple chains; good specimens were found at Beisan.[7] The tumbler-shaped lamps with wide bases could stand without any support; but both these and those with narrow bases most probably had three handles by means of which they could be suspended. The 298 glass handles found at Siyâgha no doubt belonged to lamps which were suspended. Only in a few cases were the handles still attached to a part of the vessel; in these cases one end of the handle is attached to the top of the rim and the other to the side of the vessel. The lower end of the handle is a disc of molten glass from which the roughly round band extends to the rim to which one side is applied, whilst the tip is folded back onto the handle. Generally the tip is short, but in a few cases it reaches back all the way to the lower attachment. The loop formed is generally oblong. In a few cases the handle itself forms a complete loop of which the one side is applied to the side of the vessel, the rounded part is on top and the 2 ends meet below. In exceptional cases the band is notched or wavy or flat and ribbed. The common form of the handles is that illustrated by Kisa II, p. 317, nos. 7-9; what we mean by a loop may be seen there in nos. 1-6; no. 22 ib. illustrates notching; the lower end of no. 25 ib. illustrates the wavy band and nos. 32-46 on p. 319 illustrate ribbing.

For complete vessels with 3 handles see *Gerasa*, p. 525, Fig. 20, no. 376; p. 527, Fig. 21, no. 382; p. 529, Fig. 22, no. 380; Pl. CXLI, c.

A comparatively good specimen of a triple chain by means of which such a lamp was suspended was found at Siyâgha; see pp. 309 f., no. 179.

We are not certain what rims should be associated with the lamps which we are considering, but in this connection we may observe that over half of the rims found (about 200)

1 See *Gerasa*, p. 521, nos. 4-6; *JEA* 17 (1931), pp. 198 & 202-5.
2 See *Beth-Shan* III, p. (43).
3 See *BVK* p. 30, Fig. 16.
4 See *JEA* 17 (1931), p. 203.
5 See *Gerasa*, pp. 515 ff. & 519 ff.
6 See *Gerasa*, p. 520.
7 See *Beth-Shan* III, Pls. XXVII, 4 & XXXVII, 1-4; these candelabra had either 4 or 6 holes for such lamps.

are double, that is, a hollow fold is produced by folding the rim outwards and down; the rest of the rims are simple, generally somewhat thickened and rounded, but now and then straight and plain and in a few cases everted and flaring.

II. WINE GLASSES

255. Ib. 30. Base, stem and part of bowl or cup; blue glass; this is one of the best specimens found, though also this is incomplete. The base or foot is a slightly concave disc 36 mm. in d. The plain solid stem is 15 mm. l. The fragment of the cup which is still preserved comes to a point near the stem; originally it must have been ovate in form and widest near the mouth; at present the cup is 47 mm. in diameter.

256. Ib. 31. Foot, stem and piece of bowl; green glass. The foot is a concave disc 37 mm. in d.; the plain stem, hollow at both ends, is 15 mm. l.; the fragment of the ovate cup is 43 mm. in diameter.

257. Ib. 32. As no. 256, but the glass is blue, the foot 50 mm. in d., the stem 18 mm. l. and the cup 30 mm. in diameter.

258. Ib. 33. Fragment of foot and stem; blue glass. The disc which served as the foot was formed by 2 layers of glass folded together leaving a hollow thickened ring around the edge. The stem was formed of 2 layers like the foot; its center is hollow.

259. Ib. 34. As no. 256, but the glass is blue, the foot 42 mm. in d., the stem 15 mm. l. and the fragment of the cup 30 mm. in diameter.

260. Ib. 35. As no. 256, but the color is obscured by decay, the foot is 38 mm. in d., the stem 11 mm. l. and the fragment of the cup 20 mm. in diameter.

261. Ib. 36. As no. 256, but the glass is blue; the foot, 44 mm. in d., is without the thickened edge characteristic of the preceding discs; the plain stem, 22 mm. l., is solid, that is, no hollows appear at either end; the fragment of the ovate cup is 36 mm. in diameter.

262. Ib. 37. A fragment of a foot (40-46 mm. in d.) and a stem (25 mm. l.) like no. 261; but the bottom of the cup is flat and its sides seem to have been straight; the surviving fragment is 50 mm. in diameter.

263. Ib. 38. Part of the base, 52 mm. in d., has a thickened hollow edge; the stem differs from all the rest in this that it has a knob in the center; its center is hollow and its upper end protrudes into the base of the cup; the cup is ovate and still 40 mm. in d.; the glass is green.

264. Ib. 39. As no. 263.

265-354. At least 90 fragments like nos. 255-264. No two are exactly alike in every respect.

The foot is always a disc; this differs in diameter, thickness and form of the edge, bottom and top. In diameter the discs vary between 38-52 mm.; in thickness they vary even on the same foot and of course the different feet differ from one another, generally between 2-8 mm. The disc may consist of a single or a double layer of glass; in the former case the edge is thinner than the center, in the latter the edge is thickened and hollow; in both cases the disc is not perfectly flat, but as a rule slightly concave below and convex above.

The stem is generally plain, but in a few cases it has a knob in the center. The plain stems are 11-25 mm. l. and 8-12 mm. in d.; they may be solid or hollow; in the latter case there is a plug somewhere in the center.

The cup is never complete; the surviving fragments still attached to the stem suggest that the ovate form, with the pointed end below, predominated; a cylindrical form is suggested by a few specimens. On the interior the bottom of the cup may be concave and pointed, or flat and straight, or slightly convex.

The wine glasses are either blue or green; the former color predominates; the latter is associated with vessels having knobbed stems.

Such wine glasses have been reported from Jerash [1] and Beisan; [2] fragments of the same have been noticed on a number of other Byzantine sites.

III. BOWL

355. Fig. 35. Two fragments representing about half of a dark green bowl which was originally about 35 mm. h. and had a diameter of about 105 mm.; the glass is 7 mm. thick near the base and diminishes in thickness towards the rim where it is 1½ mm. thick. The base is concave and the sides rounded. A few other fragments of blue glass suggest much larger bowls or plates, but their form is not so certain as that of this one, which should be compared with the dishes or shallow bowls treated in *Gerasa*, pp. 527 ff., nos. 32-48.

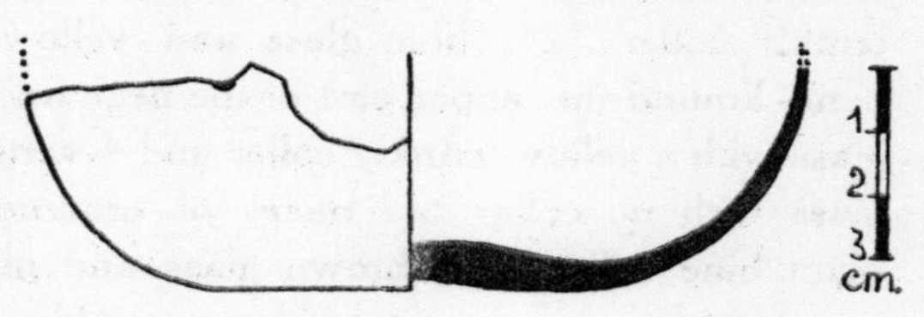

Fig. 35. Bowl.

IV. BOTTLES

Complete.

356. Fig. 36; Pl. 138, Fig. 1,7. A green bottle found in 62. It has the form of a flattened sphere with a concave base and a slightly flaring mouth; it is 52 mm. h. and 62 mm. in diameter. This type of bottle occurs also at Jerash. [3]

357. Pl. 141,1. A blue bottle found in 97; it is 45 mm. h.; its flattened body measures 15 mm. along the narrow side and 35 mm. along its wider side. The wavy ruffle at the base of the neck is brown. The flattened form of the body suggests a pilgrims' flask.

358. Ib. 2. A blue bottle found in 22; it is 42 mm. h.; its globular body is 26 mm. in d.; the rim is broken; around the neck are 2 wavy brown ruffles.

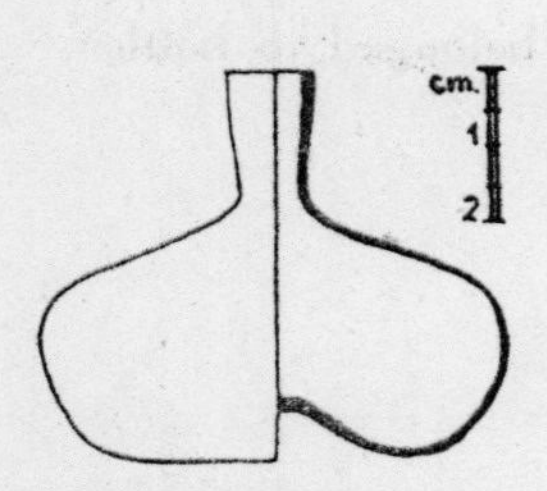

Fig. 36. Bottle.

Fragments of the body, neck and base.

359. Ib. 3. A fragment with a bulging body, constricted at both ends and flaring beyond them, is coated with white decay and decorated with a few golden-white threads.

1 See *Gerasa*, pp. 624-6, nos. 16-28.
2 See *Beth-Shan* III, Pl. XXXIX, 9, 16, 23.
3 See *Gerasa*, p. 540, no. 87; Pl. CXLI, a, 4th & Fig. 28, 4.

360. Ib. 4. A part of a green bottle with a flat base and a knob near the center; the upper part is missing.

361. Ib. 5. A fragment with a few knobs is covered with dark flakes obscuring the original color.

362. Pl. 142,36. A purple bottle with a flat base 33 mm. in d. has a rounded body on which there are traces of the lower attachment of a handle; the upper part of the bottle and the handle are missing.

363. Ib. 37; Pl. 138, Fig. 1,6. A blue bottle thickly coated with white decay has a cylindrical body whose straight sides are ribbed vertically; its base is concave; the upper part is missing; it may perhaps be restored like the one illustrated in *QDAP* 1 (1932), Pl. V, 19, or like another in *Gerasa,* p. 543, Fig. 30, no. 721 & Pl. CXLI, b, right.

364-368. Pl. 141, 19-23. Five blue fragments of the necks of large bottles with crinkly bands around the base of the necks; the wavy collars or ruffles are blue in all cases except the 1st and 5th, which are brown.

369-375. Ib. 24-30. Seven necks and pieces of the shoulders of bottles with crinkly or plain bands as ornaments: the piece numbered 24 is made of blue glass and has a blue crinkly collar; 25, blue glass and yellow crinkly collar; 26, blue glass with a plain blue band around the upper part of the neck and below it 3 vertical yellow crinkly bands; 27, green glass with a yellow crinkly collar and 4 vertical yellow crinkly bands on the shoulders; 28, black glass with no collar but traces of ornaments in relief on the shoulder; 29, blue glass and plain blue collar; 30, brown glass and plain collar of the same color.

Bottles, whose necks have crinkly or plain ornaments in relief, have been reported also from Jerash, [1] a Byzantine synagogue near Jericho assigned to the 8th century A. D., [2] etc.

376-387. Ib. 6-15, 31,32. Twelve fragments of the sides of vessels with crinkly ornaments like those on the necks of bottles: 6, blue glass and brown vertical band; 7, as 6; 8, blue glass and band; 9, double knob or ledge; 10, green band; 11, white band; 12, 2 disc-shaped projections; 13, blue band; 14, blue band with indentations above and below; 15, green band. — A bottle with similar ornaments around the body was found at Jerash. [3]

388-404. Pl. 142, 1-17. Seventeen fragments of bottle-necks whose outer surface is decorated with threads in relief; the threads are white, blue, green and brown; they differ somewhat in thickness. Similarly decorated bottle-necks have been reported from Jerash, [4] a rock-cut tomb at el-Jish dated to the 4th and 5th centuries A. D., [5] etc.

N. B. — Some of the bases mentioned in nos. 415 ff. no doubt belonged to bottles.

V. MISCELLANEOUS PIECES

Rims and sides of colored and decorated vessels.

405. Pl. 139, Fig. 3,2. Fragments of a multi-colored vessel found in a layer of ashes below the stone floor of room 78. The thickened rim is rounded; below it there is a broad

1 See *Gerasa*, p. 543, Fig. 30, passim; p. 545, Fig. 31, above.
2 *QDAP* 6 (1937), p. 75; Pl. XXI, 1, the bottle in the middle.
3 See *Gerasa*, p. 539, no. 80; Fig. 27, no. 2672; Pl. CXLI, b, left.
4 See *Gerasa*, p. 545, Fig. 31, passim; Pl. CXL, a, above, center.
5 *QDAP* 8 (1939), pp. 47 ff.; Pls. XXXII f.

brown band; then come 3 narrow stripes colored red, white and red respectively; the rest of the surface was divided into panels by vertical red lines on a light blue background; the panels were filled in with motifs executed in red and yellow; the few lobed and serrated designs which are still preserved are strongly reminiscent of the motifs on Nabatean pottery.[1]

406. Pl. 142,21. Fragment of a brown vessel whose surface is decorated with a single blue looped cord.

407-409. Ib. 22-24. Fragments of no. 406.

410. Ib. 18. Fragment with a brown rim like 16 & 17 ib.

411. Ib. 19. Fragment with gray and white stripes in the glass itself.

412. Ib. 20. Fragment with yellow-gray and white stripes.

413. Ib. 25. Fragment with a black rim decorated with 5 brown threads; another thread looks black.

414. Ib. 26. Fragment with a blue rim and blue threads on white glass.

Bases.

415. Ib. 27. Blue base, prob. of a bottle; the edge has a hollow ring; the center is slightly concave; this form is rare; only 2 others like this one were found.

416. Ib. 28. Blue, slightly concave base.

417. Ib. 29. Blue disc-base with fragments of the body attached.

418. Ib. 30. As no. 417.

419. Ib. 31. Flat base coated with decay.

420. Ib. 32. A base with a flat edge and a concave center has pieces of the straight-sided body attached; black-brown.

421. Ib. 33. A brown flat base.

422. Ib. 34. A brown round base which probably had legs.

423. Ib. 35. A brown round base and a fragment of the straight sides decorated with 2 vertical wavy brown bands.

424. Ib. 38. The bottom of a black vessel with a ring-base having 5 grooved legs or knobs.

425. Ib. 39. The bottom of a black vessel with 3 legs or knobs (originally probably 4); on the sides of the vessel there are traces of ornaments in relief.

Varia.

426. Pl. 138, Fig. 1,8. Pieces of traceried ornaments in relief.

427. Ib. 9. Ring, possibly a handle of a vase.

428. Ib. 10. Bead.

429. Pl. 141,16. Band with ribbed surface, probably a piece of a handle.

430. Ib. 17. A rod from room 14; broken; 52 mm. l.; it tapers to a point.

431-432. Two other fragments of rods are 52 and 21 mm. l. respectively and 5 mm. in d.; they have a spiral groove on the exterior and a blue spiral filament on the interior of the transparent glass.

[1] Regarding the same see, v. g., J. H. Iliffe, *Nabatean Pottery from the Negeb*, in *QDAP* 3 (1934), pp. 132 ff. & Pls. XLV ff.

CHAPTER XIV

CLAY LAMPS

A. GENERAL SURVEY

At Siyâgha lamps made of stone, bronze, glass and clay were used; the former two types were rare, the latter were abundant. Only 2 stone lamps were found; these were mentioned on p. 299, nos. 184 f.; the only bronze lamp discovered was referred to on p. 309, no. 177, but a bronze lid seems to indicate a second one (see ib. no. 178); the numerous glass lamps were treated on pp. 315 ff., nos. 1-254. Both lamps and lanterns were made of clay; the latter will be treated elsewhere; here only lamps made of clay are to be treated; some 120 are represented by more or less complete specimens and by fragments; none of them were found inside the basilica or chapels; they all come from the monasteries; typical pieces are illustrated in Pl. 143.

The clay lamps found at Siyâgha, with one exception (Pl. 143,9), belong to the familiar class of closed molded lamps whose oval form has been compared with an egg, a pear or a slipper.[1] Varieties have been distinguished according to the kind of ornament which characterizes the nozzle, that is, the section of the upper part of the lamp between the two openings. This part of the lamp is not always preserved; of 42 examples which have preserved the nozzle either entirely or in part, 21 belong to the so-called candlestick variety, 14 to the variety which has a channel on the nozzle, 3 have a cross on the spout and 4 a linear ornament. There was one mold for the base of such lamps. One lamp found in the southern monastery is of the boot-shaped type and without ornaments.

Within each variety further groups can be distinguished according to the ornamentation used for the rest of the surface around the central opening. Thus, for example, the candlestick variety comprises groups with inscriptions, with straight or slightly curved lines radiating from the central opening, with zigzag

[1] See *Gezer* 2, p. 227; *Samaria*, p. 317; Galling in *ZDPV* 46 (1923), pp. 1-50 passim: Type a; *PEF Ann*. 4, pp. 194 ff.; ib. 5, pp. 89 ff.; *Beth-Shan* III, p. (40); *QDAP* 3 (1934), pp. 84 ff.; ib. 4 (1935), pp. 174, 177 f.

lines, with arches having vertical lines or circlets enclosing dots, with a wavy line or with a vine. The channel-nozzle variety comprises specimens having a variety of linear ornaments either alone or combined with others, such as circlets, pellets and floral motifs; round arches with a pellet in the center are also used. At Siyâgha these specimens are too varied to permit us to distinguish real groups within the channel-nozzle variety. On the other hand the ornaments of lamps belonging to the channel-nozzle variety are often so similar to those of the candlestick variety that they cannot be used as a safe norm for classifying fragments exhibiting only one or the other detail. This fact should also serve as a warning against stressing the difference between the two varieties too much; in form and decoration the two varieties are so similar that they must have been in use at the same time, at least there must have been a considerable overlap in the periods during which they were used; the same holds good of the other varieties, such as those with the cross or other linear motifs on the spout.

The handle also serves, to a certain extent, to distinguish between the different varieties. The candlestick variety, as a rule, does not have a handle; the channel-nozzle variety, as a rule, has a small pointed knob-handle, though 2 lamps of this variety are also without a handle; the lamp with a cross on the spout has a handle which is not pointed but has a rather broad sharp edge; another lamp which has a handle in the form of an animal's head has the spout missing, but similar complete examples from other sites generally have a linear motif, reminiscent of the channel, on the spout (see, v. g., *QDAP* 3 [1934], p. 85, Fig. 2, top). The undecorated boot-shaped lamp had a loop-handle extending from the lip to the angle between the shoulder and the body.

The slight differences in form, ornamentation and handles, which exist between the different varieties of lamps found at Siyâgha have become the foundation for assigning the lamps to slightly different periods; thus, for example, the candlestick lamp was quite generally considered to be characteristic of the sixth century A. D., whilst the channel-nozzle lamp was considered to be characteristic of the seventh century. Quite recently, however, Iliffe and others have been able to adduce good evidence in favor of the theory that all the varieties which occur at Siyâgha, except the boot-shaped one, were in use already during the fourth century of the Christian era. Thus, for example, the tomb at el-Bassa, dated to about 396 A. D., contains a few lamps of the candlestick type, many of the channel-nozzle type and one with a handle in the form of an animal's head. Along with this group there was a lamp which shows a close relationship with lamps in vogue during the second and third centuries.[1] At Siyâgha, on the other hand, not a single fragment was found which would indicate any connection with the types of the second and third centuries; from this it seems to follow

[1] See *QDAP* 3 (1934), pp. 84 ff.; ib. 4 (1935), pp. 177 f.

that the lamps found at Siyâgha, taken as a whole, are slightly later than the group found in the el-Bassa tomb. But since we know from other sources that the site was occupied as early as the fourth century A. D. we would expect the earliest period of occupation to be represented by one or the other sherd of a lamp; in other words, the theory which holds that this slipper type of lamp was in use already in the fourth century of our era receives at least some indirect support from the evidence of the Siyâgha lamps. In short, the latest evidence seems to indicate that all the varieties of lamps found at Siyâgha were in use from the fourth century to the eighth or even a little later. These general statements may be supplemented in the catalogue, where each lamp will be considered more in detail.

B. THE CATALOGUE

I. CANDLESTICK LAMPS

With inscriptions.

1. Pl. 143,3 & Pl. 121,6. Fragment of upper half; red ware. On the incomplete spout is preserved a good example of the design from which this variety has derived its name: "the candlestick lamp;" [1] around the mouth of the reservoir is the Greek inscription discussed on pp. 270 f., no. XXII. The context at Siyâgha seems to confirm the view of FitzGerald [2] "that inscriptions are a somewhat late feature," but 2 lamps inscribed with the formula in question were found in the shaft tombs of the Nablus Road, Jerusalem; this discovery seems to lend support to the view that a date between the 3rd and 5th centuries is possible for such inscribed lamps. [3]

2. Pl. 143,4 & Pl. 121,8. A fragment of the upper half with a few letters of an inscription like that on no. 1 (see p. 271, no. XXIII). The piece has not preserved any part of the ornament on the spout, nevertheless the piece is classified with the candlestick lamps both on account of its relation to no. 1 and because the majority of the inscribed lamps seem to belong to this variety, but there are some that belong to the channel-nozzle variety.

3. Pl. 143,2 & Pl. 121,7. The greater part of a lamp whose spout is missing; around the mouth of the reservoir there is the inscription discussed on p. 271, no. XXIV; it is classified with the candlestick lamps for the same reason as no. 2.

4. *Reg.* 2227. Frag. of upper half like no. 3; see p. 271, no. XXV.

5. *Reg.* 1350. Frag. of lower half with a ring-base and of the upper half on which there are ornaments suggesting an inscription like that on nos. 3 and 4.

[1] See *Gezer* 2, p. 227.
[2] See *PEF Ann.* 5, p. 92.
[3] See *QDAP* 4 (1935), pp. 173 f.

Oblique lines around the mouth of the reservoir.

6. *Reg.* 1441. Complete; red ware; from 59.

7. *Reg.* 1921. Complete (restored from 5 fragments); red ware; from southern monastery.

8. *Reg.* 2021. Complete; about half as large as the average lamp; found inside the drain in 79 & 83.

9. *Reg.* 1464. Complete; found in a crushed condition in 62.

10. *Reg.* 1920. Two fragments representing part of lower and upper half; red ware; from 96.

11. *Reg.* 1999. Part of nozzle missing.

12. *Reg.* 691. Part of upper half; red ware; from 43.

13. *Reg.* 1922. Lower half complete; part of upper half missing; surface white; from 56.

N. B. — Since a number of channel-nozzle lamps are also decorated with oblique lines around the mouth of the reservoir, it is better to mention among the miscellanea fragments which exhibit only such ornaments; see nos. 63-79.

Zigzag line around the central opening.

14. *Reg.* 1348. Complete; gray ware; from area around 116.

N. B. — One more specimen with a zigzag line probably belongs to another variety; see no. 54.

Round arches with a vertical line or with a circlet enclosing a pellet.

15. *Reg.* 1463. Two pieces; fragment missing; cement color. The ornamental arches with a vertical line in the center resemble the rounded form of inverted Greek Omegas or of inverted plant motifs; the transition from one to the other was easy. See, v. g., *Gezer* 2, pp. 227 f. From 62.

16. *Reg.* 1466. Frag. of upper half as no. 15; from 62.

17. *Reg.* 2223. Frag. of upper half as nos. 15 f., but between the 2 surviving arches there is a cross whose arms end in 2 prongs; since the spout is missing the classification of this and the preceding fragment with the candlestick variety is doubtful; no channel-nozzle lamps have the vertical line in the arch, though some have the arch.

18. Pl. 143,1. Complete; black ware; the lower half has a ring-base enclosing a cross; the upper half has rounded arches linked together, each containing one circlet with a pellet in its center. These last 2 elements and the fact that the arches are linked together distinguish the ornamentation of this lamp from that of nos. 15 ff. From 32.

19. *Reg.* 1919. Complete; cement-colored ware; rest as no. 18; from 96.

20. *Reg.* 695. Fragment of lower and upper halves; red ware; decorated like nos. 18 f.; that is, the ring-base contains the arm of a cross and the upper half has arches with circlets and pellets, which have not been found on the channel-nozzle lamps; hence classified here as a candlestick variety. From 37.

21. *Reg.* 606. Half of a lamp like nos. 18 ff.; from 29.

Wavy lines and vine around the central opening.

22. *Reg.* 690. Piece of upper half; red ware; 2 wavy lines around the mouth; from 45.

23. *Reg.* 1461. Almost complete; vine motif; from 56.

24. *Reg.* 1918. Complete; vine ornament; from 96.

II. CHANNEL-NOZZLE LAMPS

Rectilinear ornaments only or combined with circlets, pellets, etc.

25. Pl. 143,15. Upper half with a pointed knob-handle; red ware; white outer surface; the channel is empty but the rest of the upper surface is decorated with oblique lines like nos. 6-13; see note after no. 13. From 53.

26. Ib. 16. Incomplete; gray-yellow ware; ornamentation as no. 25.

27. Ib. 20. Two fragments of the upper and lower halves; part of the spout is missing; on the upper half a pointed knob-handle; in the channel several tiny circlets; around the mouth diagonal lines divided into 2 groups by a vertical line in the center of each side. On the base 4 lines intersect at a central point inside a ring. From 75.

28. Ib. 21. Part of upper half missing; brown ware; on upper half a small knob-handle; the channel is formed by double lines on each side; each pair has a series of transverse lines; in the channel there is a row of pellets; between the channel and the knob on each side there are 3 horizontal lines and between them 2 series of transverse lines. On the base there is a circle subdivided by a straight line in the center and a curved line on either side of it. The straight line has a pair of pellets on each side of its extremities; inside each curved line there is a row of 3 pellets. From 77-78.

29. Ib 17. Complete; on its upper half there is a knob-handle; in the channel, a star; around the central opening, first a series of pellets and then a series of diagonal lines between 2 others; in the ring-base, 5 lines. From 98.

30. Ib. 18. Part of upper half missing; in the channel a motif suggesting a branch with 3 twigs; around the central opening 2 series of transverse lines between 3 horizontal ones, as on no. 28. From 117. For a parallel see *QDAP* 4 (1935), Pl. LXVII,12.

31. Ib. 24. Fragment of the upper and lower halves; red ware; in the channel 3 lines extend from a central pellet to the 2 lateral lines and the wick-hole respectively; in each of the 3 resulting subdivisions there is 1 pellet; around the central opening first a series of pellets, then a series of short diagonal strokes, as on no. 29. From the western monastery.

32. *Reg.* 1345. Frag. of the upper half; black ware; decorated like no. 31.

33. Pl. 143,25. Frag. of the upper half decorated like no. 31.

34. *Reg.* 1346 b. Frag. of the upper half with a small knob-handle and decorated like no. 33, to which it very probably belongs.

35. Pl. 143,22. Complete; red ware; surface has color of cement; small knob-handle; in channel a spear-shaped motif; around the central opening latticework.

36. Pl. 143,19. Complete; gray ware; small knob-handle; in channel 2 pellets; around central opening first a band consisting of small diagonal strokes then a band filled with circlets. In the wick-hole there was still a piece of the wick; the interior was filled with green oily earth. From 12.

37. Pl. 143,23. Complete; slightly more elongated than the other lamps. In the channel there is an indistinct design which may have been intended as a plant with a few roots, a stem flanked by 2 motifs and foliage. The rest of the upper surface is divided into 7 panels with distinctive ornaments: the 2 panels flanking the channel contain palm motifs executed in very fine lines; the next 2 panels contain circlets; the third pair has latticework and the last, between the horseshoe-shaped central opening and the small upright handle, diagonal lines. From the filling beneath the platform in 11. — This is a typical Late Byzantine and Early

Arabic lamp; that is, it originated in the Byzantine period and continued in use during the early Arabic period (seventh century A. D.). The palm design is a favorite motif of these lamps.[1]

Round arches with only a circlet or with only a pellet.

38. *Reg.* 1412. Frag. of the lower and upper halves; on both sides of the channel diagonal lines; around the central opening round arches containing a circlet. This ornament differs from that of nos. 18-21 in this that the circlet does not contain a pellet. From the western monastery.

39. Pl. 143,13. Complete; yellow ware; the narrow channel is flanked by diagonal lines; around the central opening there are round arches containing only pellets; there is no handle. — The lamp represents a transition from the candlestick to the channel-nozzle variety. It resembles the candlestick variety in this that it has no handle; whilst its narrow channel with the diagonal lines closely resembles the so-called candlestick. The round arches occur also on nos. 18-21, but there the pellet is enclosed in a circlet. From 96.

40. Ib. 14. As no. 39, but there is in addition a wavy line around the central opening; regarding this motif see no. 22. From 61.

41-45. *Reg.* 636, 1409, 1473, 2027-8. Five fragments of the upper half of lamps decorated with round arches containing only pellets; since this is a characteristic of the channel-nozzle lamps (see nos. 39 f.) at Siyâgha these fragments are mentioned here.

46. *Reg.* 658. Frag. of the upper half; the channel is subdivided into numerous smaller sections. Around the central opening there is a vine ornament forming medallions containing clusters of 6 fruits and buds or rosettes.

47. *Reg.* 699. Frag. of upper half with diagonal lines along the channel.

48. *Reg.* 2031. As no. 47.

49. *Reg.* 1411. Frag. of upper half with a latticed panel next to the channel.

50. *Reg.* 2222. Frag. of the channel-spout.

III. LINEAR ORNAMENTS SIMILAR TO THE CHANNEL ON THE SPOUT

51. Pl. 143,8. Frag. of upper half having 5 lines and pellets on the spout between the 2 openings. The pellets are arranged along both sides of the central line and around the central opening. This variety very probably originated from the channel-nozzle variety. From 61.

52. *Reg.* 2032. Frag. of upper half having 7 lines and pellets as no. 51; besides the pellets on both sides of the central line, there are 2 rows of pellets along the edge at each side, one above and the other below the joint. From 60-63.

53. *Reg.* 632. Frag. of upper half; a line in the center of the channel, parallel to its sides, divides the latter into two.

54. Pl. 143,7. Frag. of upper half with a zigzag ornament and pellets around the central opening seems to have had a number of lines on the spout. From 62.

55. *Reg.* 762. Frag. of upper half with 4 lines between the 2 openings and traces of a ladder-motif around the central opening. From E.

56. Pl. 143,6. Frag. of the upper and lower halves; black ware; red surface. The handle has the form of an animal's head; on the throat there is a cross in relief. It can be

[1] See Galling in *ZDPV* 46 (1923), pp. 16 ff., 19; see *Beth-Shan* III, p. (41); *PEF Ann.* 5, p. 92.

classed with this variety since it usually has a linear ornament on its spout. It comes from a trench along the southern wall of 59. It is the only lamp of this kind found at Siyâgha. It must have been quite common in Palestine; most museums in Jerusalem contain complete specimens of the same. In the el-Bassa tomb, dated about 396 A. D., this kind of a lamp was found associated with the candlestick and channel-nozzle varieties.[1] It may, therefore, have been in use as early as the fourth century A. D., though, as a rule, a much later date has been assigned to this variety. The cross on the throat of the animal's head is a fairly common feature and indicates the Christian character of the lamp.

IV. CROSS ON THE SPOUT

57. Pl. 143,5. Complete; small knob-handle with flat sides; around central opening oblique lines, as on many lamps of both the candlestick (nos. 6-13) and channel-nozzle (nos. 25 ff.) varieties. From 39.

58. *Reg.* 2019. As no. 57; a ringlet on two sides of the cross. From 56.

59. *Reg.* 631. A frag.; black ware; gray surface; cross flanked by circlets.

V. BOOT-SHAPED LAMP

60. Pl. 143,9. Complete, except for the fact that the loop-handle is broken off and missing; red ware. The form is rounded, the upper half and central opening are higher than the average slipper-shaped lamp found at Siyâgha. In contrast, this may be compared to a shoe or to a boot. It has no ornaments; also in this respect it differs from all the other lamps on the site. It was found in 82 and is the only lamp of this kind found at Siyâgha. It recalls the boot-shaped lamps of the Hellenistic period[2] revived in the early Arabic period.

VI. MISCELLANEOUS FRAGMENTS OF LAMPS

Upper half (and at times also a piece of the lower half).

61. Pl. 143,29. Frag. with slightly curved lines around the central opening. From 53.

62. *Reg.* 1410. Frag. with a relatively high stump-handle, flat in back; circlets on both sides of the handle; around the central opening diagonal lines. From 57.

63-79. *Reg.* 633-5, 637, 639-41, 692, 697, 1397, 1408, 1465, 2029-30, 2225-6, 2228. Seventeen fragments with diagonal lines around the mouth of the reservoir; but 692 has the lines on both sides of the stub-handle; 697 has preserved also a part of the lower half with a ring-base; 1408 has also a frag. of the lower half; 1465 has lost only the spout and in the place of the handle has a pellet; 2225 has also a piece of the lower half.

1 See *QDAP* 3 (1934), p. 85, Fig. 2.

2 See Galling in *ZDPV* 46 (1923), Tafel II, 3; *Beth-Shan* III, Pl. XXXVI, 25.

80. *Reg.* 659. Frag. of the lower and upper halves both of which are higher and more sharply splayed than the average lamp found on the site; it was found in 7; gray ware; in the position of the handle there is a cross with a bifurcation at the end of each arm; on each side of the cross there are round arches with a vertical line in the center, as nos. 15-17.

81. Pl. 143,28. Frag. with 2 narrow bands of ornaments around the central opening; the inner band contains a series of pellets; the outer band is decorated with a wavy line whose curves are filled in with small half-moons.

82. Ib. 27. Frag. of lower and upper halves; the latter is decorated with a vine.

83. *Reg.* 2025. Frag. with a vine ornament; from 110-5.

84. *Reg.* 694. Frag. with traces of a plant and circlets.

85. *Reg.* 1343. Frag. with a design consisting of 2 curved lines, each terminating in a circlet or a spiral enclosing a pellet.

86. *Reg.* 1352. Frag. with an ornament in the channel similar to that in the channel of no. 31.

Lower half either with or without ornaments.

87. Pl. 143,10. A ring-base encloses a cross.

88. Ib. 11. A part of a ring-base encloses a piece of a floral motif.

89. Ib. 12. A mold for the lower half of a lamp with a ring-base found in 34. — All the Byzantine lamps consist of two halves, a lower and an upper one, formed in separate molds. The two parts often became separated.

90-97. *Reg.* 686-9, 1353 a-b, 1414-5. Fragments with ring-bases.

98-104. *Reg.* 968, 1045, 1467-8, 1923, 2033-4. Fragments of bases.

105-118. *Reg.* 632 b, 638 (linear ornament), 642 (mouth), 643 (3 lines), 693 (lines), 696 (3 lines on spout), 698 (spout), 1046 (lines), 1474 (lines), 1162 & 1349 & 1351 (handles), 1431 (possibly a tiny lamp), 2443 (knob). All small pieces.

119. Another lamp found in 1939 was reported to the writer; it is supposed to be similar to the rest.

N. B. — All the other objects of clay illustrated in Pls. 144-158 are being treated by Father Hilary Schneider, O. F. M.; see pp. 21 f. and the preface.

CHAPTER XV

THE LITERARY SOURCES

A. INTRODUCTORY REMARKS

The memorial of Moses on Mount Nebo is mentioned by Aetheria, by the biographer of Peter the Iberian, by Thietmar and by Pantaleon d'Aveiro; vague references to the same may be found in the itinerary of Antoninus and in the Aramaic Targumim.

1. *Aetheria.* — The first mention of a memorial in honor of Moses on Mount Nebo is made in an ancient description of a visit to the Holy Land preserved in a codex discovered in 1884 at Arezzo by J. F. Gamurrini. The discoverer published the text in the year 1887[1] and since then several other editions of the same have appeared. This discovery has given rise to a rather extensive literature dealing with the text, its contents, the person of the pilgrim, the date of the pilgrimage, etc. For details we refer to A. Bludau.[2] We follow this author in calling the pilgrim Aetheria and adopt his view that the pilgrimage was made towards the end of the fourth century, more precisely about the year ±394 A. D. This date is in full accord with the results of the excavations. The Latin text was translated into English for the Palestine Pilgrims' Text Society by John H. Bernard. That part of the English translation which treats of Aetheria's visit to Mount Nebo will be reproduced below; summaries of that part of the text with explanations have been given by various scholars, so, v. g., by Bludau,[3] Leclercq,[4] and others; our own experiences will enable us to add a few observations.

2. *Peter the Iberian.* — A detailed account of the origin of the memorial of Moses at Mount Nebo and a number of other interesting facts regarding the

1 *S. Silviae Aquitanae Peregrinatio ad Loca Sancta* (*Biblioteca dell'Academia Storico-giuridico*, IV), Rome, 1887.

2 *Die Pilgerreise der Aetheria* (*SGKA* XV, 1./2.), Paderborn, 1927, pp. 1-294. — In the text we have referred to P. Geyer's edition in *Itinera Hierosolymitana Saeculi IIII-VIII* (*Corpus Scriptorum Ecclesiasticorum Latinorum*, *XXXVIIII*), Vindobonae, 1898, pp. 35-101.

3 See l. c., pp. 21-26.

4 *DAC* 12,1, cols. 1065-1070.

same are to be found in the biography of Peter the Iberian, written towards the end of the fifth or the beginning of the sixth century. The Greek original is no longer preserved; two Syrian translations of the same are preserved in Berlin and London respectively. The Berlin Syrian version, supplemented by the London Syrian version, together with a German translation, introduction and notes, was published in 1895 by Richard Raabe.[1] This edition is the basis of the English version given below; only that part of the biography is given, which has a direct bearing on the memorial of Moses on Mount Nebo. Abel,[2] Leclerq[3] and others have already drawn on this biography for information regarding Mount Nebo.

3. *Thietmar.* — Few visitors to the Holy Land, either in ancient or modern times, crossed the Jordan to visit places of Biblical and historical interest there; one of those few was a crusader called Thietmar or Thetmar. On his way from Engaddi[4] to Monréal Scobach[5] in 1217 he visited Mount Abarim where Moses died and was buried; there, according to the edition of Laurent, he found a beautiful monastery inhabited by Greek Christians with whom he spent a night. This text led Abel to the conclusion that the monastery at Siyâgha was still inhabited in the 13th century (see p. 113). The same text enabled de Luynes, the first modern explorer of Siyâgha, to identify the ruins which covered the site as those of a monastery and church (see p. 11). Other editions of Thietmar make no mention of the monastery or of any other monument in honor of Moses.[6]

4. *Pantaleon d'Aveiro,* a Portuguese Franciscan, visited Mount Nebo in 1564 A. D.; at his time the buildings on the top of the mountain were completely ruined and apparently abandoned; the small church at ʿAyûn Mûsa, however, was still tolerably well preserved and the traditions originally associated with the church on the hill had wandered down there (see p. 113, 5).

5. *An Anonymous Work* entitled: *A Relation from Constantinople, how the Sepulchre of Moses was lately found at Mount Nebo, and what was done thereupon.*[7] According to this work, an earthquake produced a wide crevice in the side of Mount Nebo; through this crevice some Maronite shepherds were able to penetrate into the heart of the mountain; there they discovered a cave with a tomb, which upon investigation proved to be the tomb of Moses. An attempt to remove the remains of Moses and the tomb was frustrated by the civil authorities who caused the entrance to the cave and the tomb to be closed. The events which are related are supposed to have taken place in October 1655. This story throws

1 *Petrus der Iberer, ein Charakterbild zur Kirchen- und Sittengeschichte des fünften Jahrhunderts*, Leipzig, 1895.
2 See Abel, *Géog.* I, pp. 381 ff.
3 *DAC* 12, 1, cols. 1070 f.
4 On the western side of the Dead Sea; see Abel, *Géog.* I, p. 107; Meistermann, *Guide*, p. 382.
5 Far to the southeast of the Dead Sea; see Meistermann, *Guide du Nil au Jourdain*, pp. 240 ff.: Chôbak.
6 See Titus Tobler, *Magistri Thetmari Iter ad Terram Sanctam Anno 1217*, St. Galli et Bernae, 1851, p. 30.
7 See *QS* 1904, pp. 142-148, 274-279; *Ugolinus*, 33, cols. 1802 ff.

no direct light on the memorial of Moses on Mount Nebo; in the entire story there is no reference to the buildings on top of the hill; but it is precisely this fact which seems to have some significance for one who has followed the history of that monument up to the 17th century. The complete silence which envelops those ruins seems to indicate that their true meaning was gradually forgotten; already above we noted that in the 16th century the monument was completely ruined and that the memories associated with it had wandered to the chapel in the valley; when that chapel also was ruined, men once more reverted to the tradition which originally gave rise to the monuments on the hilltop; they imagined the tomb of Moses in a cave in the very heart of the mountain; the present story is a witness of that belief.

6. *Antonini Placentini Itinerarium*. See p. 112, 3. The pilgrim in question mentions that many hermits lived at the place where Moses died; this statement implies the existence of some buildings at that place, but no express mention is made of them, much less of their memorial character. Antoninus has so many details in common with Theodosius that one must suspect that he places the death of Moses at Livias, just as Theodosius did.[1] Neither of the two seems to have crossed the Jordan; their information was either inaccurate or they misunderstood certain details. At any rate, there were monks at Mount Nebo at the time of Antoninus, as we know from the excavations.

7. *The Targumim*. — The Aramaic versions of the Bible are called *Targumim;* these do not merely give literal translations of the original text, but at times they paraphrase it; this was done even in the case of proper names, so, for example, in the case of the word "Nebo," which is paraphrased 5 times; the different renderings are indicated on pp. 115 f. In one case "Nebo" is paraphrased "the burial of Moses," in 4 cases "the house of the burial of Moses." The first reading is found in the *Targum* of Onkelos, which originated about the 2nd century of our era; at that time the memorial of Moses did not yet exist on Mount Nebo; that may account for the fact that Onkelos speaks merely of the place of the burial of Moses. The second reading is found in 3 places in the *Targum* of Pseudo-Jonathan and in a variant of Onkelos; all these readings are most probably not older than the 6th century of our era; at that time the memorial of Moses existed on Mount Nebo and the addition of the word "Beth," that is, "house" to the original paraphrase may be taken as an allusion to that monument.

The references to the memorial of Moses on Mount Nebo by Thietmar, Pantaleon, Antoninus and the Targumim are interesting, but those by Aetheria and the biographer of Peter the Iberian are more important; all acquire new significance when reviewed in the light of the recent clearances at Mount Nebo.

[1] See Geyer, p. 145, lines 19 f. & pp. 165 f.

B. TEXTS AND COMMENTARY

I. AETHERIA

From Jerusalem to ʿAyûn Mûsa.

"Having spent some time there,[1] God commanding me again, I had the wish to go as far as Arabia,[2] to Mount Nebo, where God commanded Moses to go up,[3] saying to him: 'Get thee up into the mountain Arabot,[4] unto Mount Nebo, which is in the land of Moab, over against Jericho; and behold the land of Canaan, which I give unto the children of Israel for a possession: and die in the mount whither thou goest up.' And so Jesus our God, who will not fail those who trust in Him, vouchsafed to bring into effect this my wish. Starting from Jerusalem, and journeying with holy men, with the priest and deacons from Jerusalem, and some brethren — that is, monks — we arrived at that place of the Jordan where the children of Israel had crossed . . .[5] Crossing the stream,

[1] Namely, in Jerusalem, after returning from Sinai.

[2] The Roman province of Arabia is meant; its boundaries are indicated by Abel, *Géog.* II, Carte X & pp. 184 ff.; Mount Nebo is near the western boundary line.

[3] The command of God is recorded in *Num.* 27, 12-14; *Deut.* 3,27; 32, 48-52.

a. *Num.* 27, 12-14: "The Lord also said to Moses: Go up into this mountain Abarim, and view from thence the land which I will give to the children of Israel. And when thou shalt have seen it, thou shalt go to thy people," etc.

b. *Deut.* 3,27: "Go up to the top of Phasga, and cast thy eyes round about to the west, and to the north, and to the south, and to the east, and behold it, for thou shalt not pass this Jordan."

c. *Deut.* 32, 48-52: "And the Lord spoke to Moses the same day saying: Go up into this mountain Abarim, (that is to say, of passages,) unto mount Nebo, which is in the land of Moab over against Jericho: and see the land of Chanaan, which I will deliver to the children of Israel to possess, and die thou in the mountain. When thou art gone up into it, thou shalt be gathered to thy people," etc.

[4] Aetheria gives us a variant reading of *Deut.* 32,48 ff.; hence it is clear that Arabot must be identical with Abarim. — It is evident that Aetheria is using the Bible as her guide; some think that for the identification of Biblical sites she used Jerome's Latin translation of the *Onom.* written by Eusebius in Greek. Neither Jerome nor Eusebius speak of a mountain called Arabot; according to them Moses died either on Abarim (*Onom.* 16,24) or on Nabau (*Onom.* 136,7).

[5] See *Josue* 3,16 f. — Somewhat further up stream the place was pointed out where the children of Ruben, of Gad and of the half tribe of Manasses built an altar; see *Josue* 22,10 ff.

we came to the city called Livias[1] which is in the plain . . . The plain itself is very large, under the mountains of Arabia above Jordan . . . Then, that the works we had begun should be accomplished, we began to hasten in order that we might arrive at Mount Nebo. As we went the priest of the place, i. e., of Livias, whom we had persuaded to move with us from the station, because he knew the places better, gave us advice. And this priest said to us: If you wish to see the water which flowed out of the rock, which Moses gave to the children of Israel when they were athirst, you can see it by imposing on yourself the fatigue of going about six miles out of your way (better: *of leaving the road at about the sixth milestone;* Latin: *ut de via camsemus forsitan miliario sexto*).[2]

[1] It is commonly identified with Tell er-Rameh; see p. 6; Meistermann, *Guide du Nil au Jourdain,* pp. 307 f.; Abel, *Géog.* II, p. 174: oasis of Tell er-Rameh and Tell Hammâm; the *Onom.* 48,13 ff. identifies Betharam or Bethramtha with Livias. — At Livias and in its immediate surroundings Aetheria was shown the place where the Israelites camped, where they mourned for Moses, where Josue was filled with the spirit of wisdom, where Moses wrote Deuteronomy, recited the canticle and blessed the children of Israel individually before his death. At that place Aetheria's party said a prayer, read a section of Deuteronomy, the canticle and the blessing pronounced over the Israelites and concluded its devotions with another prayer, as was the custom at all places visited.

[2] At Livias Aetheria's party procured as a guide a priest who knew the region thoroughly. He informed the pilgrims that if they wished to see the springs of Moses they could do so by *leaving the road at the sixth milepost.* The Latin text: "ut de via camsemus miliario sexto," as rendered by Bernard and others (v. g., also Bludau, op. cit., p. 23), is not only misleading but wrong; "miliario sexto" is not "6 miles" but "the 6th milestone." The party was evidently following the Roman road between Livias and Esbus; this road does not touch Mount Nebo but runs along the el-Mushakkar ridge immediately north of Mount Nebo; the 2 ridges are separated by the deep Wady ʿAyûn Mûsa. Owing to the precipitous cliffs on both sides of the wady it was difficult to cross unless one had an experienced guide who knew the paths which led along the sides of the cliffs. As a rule travellers between Livias and Esbus did not go to the trouble of crossing the wady to visit Mount Nebo; they were content to have the place pointed out to them; this is clear from the *Onom.* 16,26 f.; 136,6 ff. Even the spot from where Mount Nebo was usually pointed out to travellers is indicated by the *Onom.* 136,7 f., namely: "from the sixth milestone to the west of Esbus (ἀπὸ ἕκτου σημείου Ἐσβοῦς εἰς δυσμάς)." The Roman road had milestones; those which marked the 5th, 6th and 7th miles from Esbus have been found; the stones with the inscriptions mentioning the sixth mile from Esbus are near a place known today as Mehattah; there a path actually branches off from the main road and runs down to ʿAyûn Mûsa (see pp. 6 f.); that is most probably the path which the priest from Livias advised Aetheria to take. It did not lead the travellers "6 miles out of their way" as the translation suggests; on the contrary, it was actually the shortest and directest route to Mount Nebo, though somewhat more difficult than the main road; had the pilgrims continued along the main road, travelling would have been somewhat more convenient but the distance to be covered would have been greater; in this case they would have continued along the main road up to the 5th milepost from Esbus; there they could have taken the road to the right which led to Madaba via Kefeir

When he said this we eagerly wished to go, and immediately diverging from our road [1] we followed the priest who led us. In that place there is a little church under a mountain — not Nebo, but another inner mountain not far from Nebo; [2] many truly holy monks live there, whom they here call ascetics.

Abu Bedd; at this village they could have turned westwards following the ridge as far as Siyâgha along a tolerably convenient road. As stated, this road would have been longer than the one via ᶜAyûn Mûsa.

The sixth milepost seems always to have been a place of special significance along the road; this seems to follow not only from the narrative of Aetheria, but also from the remarks of Eusebius and Jerome and from our own experiences. Eusebius and Jerome merely state that Mount Nebo was usually pointed out to travellers from the 6th milestone; this was not due to the fact that it was the first place from which travellers coming from the west could see Mount Nebo, neither was it due to the fact that from there one obtained the best view of Mount Nebo; — Mount Nebo is visible from many other points along the road; the chief reason why Mount Nebo was pointed out from that spot seems to be indicated by Aetheria; that was the place where travellers, who wished to visit either ᶜAyûn Mûsa or Mount Nebo or both, would have to leave the main road and take a side path; that was the point where the traveller had to decide what he would do; there was time for deliberation, for the 6th milepost seems to have been a resting place in ancient times just as it is today. Near the place there is today a large tree; beneath it travellers who wish to escape the midday heat may pause and rest; if they are in need of water the side path enables them to reach ᶜAyûn Mûsa where they are always certain of an abundant supply both for themselves and their animals. This information was given us by the local Arabs and our own experience confirmed it. Travelling one day along the section of the road which leads from Madaba to Mehattah we found it convenient to rest under the tree at Mehattah (see Pl. 11,1); upon enquiring whether we would have to return by the same way by which we had come in order to reach Siyâgha, we were informed about the path that leads to ᶜAyûn Mûsa and from there to Siyâgha; we took this path on our way back to Siyâgha; the section leading to ᶜAyûn Mûsa was easy to negotiate; the steep climb from ᶜAyûn Mûsa to the top of Siyâgha, however, was rather difficult, but the experience was worth while, for it brought home to us the true meaning of Aetheria's words. — Pl. 5,2 is a view of Mount Nebo from Mehattah; Pl. 6,2 is another view of Mount Nebo taken on our way from Mehattah to ᶜAyûn Mûsa. — See also pp. 6 f.

[1] These words seem to confirm our view that the priest made the suggestion near the sixth milepost; the pilgrims decided to follow the suggestion and "immediately" left the main road to take the path to ᶜAyûn Mûsa.

[2] In Wady ᶜAyûn Mûsa there are three groups of ruins, as we indicated on p. 7. Among these ruins it would be natural to look for the remains of the chapel mentioned by Aetheria. The ruins around the caves next to the springs (see Pls. 12, right & 13, right) seem to be excluded by the express statement of Aetheria who declares that the mountain under which the chapel was located was not Mount Nebo, therefore, not the mountain on the south side of the wady with the caves and the springs, but another mountain, which is described as an "inner mountain" and "not far from Nebo." Aetheria could have meant a mountain either towards the east or the north; towards the east, however, Wady ᶜAyûn Mûsa (under the name: Wady Abu en-Naml) extends for a considerable distance causing a sharp and deep

At Ayûn Mûsa.

"These holy monks deigned to receive us very kindly; they permitted us to pay them a visit.[1] When we had entered and had offered prayer with them, they deigned to give us gifts of blessing, which they are accustomed to give to those whom they receive kindly. But, as I was saying, in the midst there, between the church and the monastery, there flows out of a rock a great stream of water very fair and limpid, and with a very good taste.[2] Then we asked the holy monks who lived there what was this water which was so good, and they told us that it was the water which holy Moses gave to the children of

division between the Nebo ridge on the south (see Pl. 12, right) and the el-Mushakkar ridge on the north (see Pl. 12, left); since, moreover, according to Aetheria, the mountain is "not far from Nebo," she probably meant some part of the ridge north of Wady ᶜAyûn Mûsa. Actually the small hill directly opposite or immediately north of the springs is covered with ruins; but these also seem to be excluded by the statement of Aetheria that the small church was "under the mountain," not on top of it. Further west, however, in the neighborhood of a tree (see Pl. 6,2) there are very extensive ruins which are used today as a cemetery. These ruins lie beneath the northern ridge and are not far from Mount Nebo; they seem to correspond remarkably well to the description given by Aetheria of the place where the chapel stood; as at the other two groups of ruins mentioned above, so here no traces of a chapel can be seen today. But also at Siyâgha it was difficult to recognize a church or chapel among the ruins before the clearances were made; the difficulties were increased by the fact that at Siyâgha late tombs were arranged directly above the sanctuary of the basilica, thus concealing the apse; the same may be the case at ᶜAyûn Mûsa and since the cemetery there is still being used by the local Arabs it is more difficult to carry out explorations there than at Siyâgha. — In this connection it should be noted that the ruins mentioned last actually consist of two groups; the one group is near to the tree referred to above, the other is somewhat further to the northwest on slightly higher ground. The two groups could represent a church, monastery and a hospice; between the two groups the water from the springs was flowing on the occasion when the writer visited the ruins.

[1] Very probably Aetheria and her party spent the night at ᶜAyûn Mûsa.

[2] As stated on p. 7 the springs are near the base of the northern slope of Siyâgha or Mount Nebo (see Pls. 12-15); if one would take the words of Aetheria in their strictest sense and refer them to the source of the springs, one would have to look for both the church and the monasteries at ᶜAyûn Mûsa near the foot of the slopes of Siyâgha, the one to the east and the other to the west of the springs; this is, however, contrary to the description given above of the location of the church. Actually the water from the easternmost spring precipitates itself over a precipice facing west (see Pls. 14-15, the stream of water is weak, because most of the water is now collected in a cistern and pumped to Madaba; see p. 7) and flows through the wady westwards, so that if some of the monks were living in the caves at the foot of Siyâgha (see Pl. 13, right) and if the church was among the ruins further west, as suggested above, then the water of the springs would have flowed "between the church and the monastery," exactly as Aetheria stated. — These are mere suggestions; the discovery of that ancient chapel would immediately clarify the text.

Israel in this wilderness.[1] Then, according to custom, a prayer was offered there, and the lection read from the books of Moses, and one psalm was said; and so with these holy monks and clergy who had come with us we went out to the mountain. Many, too, of the holy monks that lived there near the water, who were able and willing to endure the fatigue, deigned to ascend Mount Nebo along with us. So then, starting from that place, we arrived at the foot of Mount Nebo, which though very high, could yet be gone up for the most part sitting on an ass, but there was a bit slightly steeper which we had to go up laboriously on foot.[2]

On the summit of Mt. Nebo.

"So we arrived at the summit of the mountain, where there is now a small church on the summit of Mount Nebo.[3] Inside this church[4] at the place where the pulpit[5] is, I saw a place slightly raised containing about as much space as is usual in a grave.[6] I asked the holy men what this was, and they answered:

[1] See Meistermann, *Guide du Nil au Jourdain*, pp. 50-52, 237, 303-305, regarding the traditions associated with springs named after Moses in the regions between Sinai and Nebo. It was natural to place important springs under the protection of him who already during his earthly career had proven his power to provide his clients with water even in the desert. — See Abel, *Géog.* I, p. 460, regarding the springs near Mount Nebo named after Moses. — Most of the explorers who visited Siyâgha also visited ʿAyûn Mûsa and gave more or less enthusiastic descriptions of their impressions; see the references given on pp. 11 ff.

[2] The northern slope of Siyâgha is steepest near the foot (see Pl. 12, right; Pls. 5, 6, 13 f.); above the steep walls next to the wady there is today a winding road which makes the ascent quite convenient; already in ancient times there was a road between ʿAyûn Mûsa and the crest of the Nebo ridge; its course corresponded more or less to that of the modern road (see pp. 8 & 9 & Fig. 2). Aetheria could have followed either that road or a path which is also indicated in Fig. 2; in either case her description fits perfectly.

[3] For general views of the summit of Mount Nebo see Pls. 1 ff.; 22; 38,1; 159 & 160. — The "small church on the summit of Mount Nebo" is the cella trichora described on pp. 23 ff. Aetheria merely mentions the size of the church, not its form; the excavations have determined more precisely both the size and the form of the small church.

[4] On the interior the small church had three apses: one on the north, a second on the east and a third on the south.

[5] The cella trichora contained a pulpit; this is a fact regarding which we could not have been certain if Aetheria had not mentioned it (see, however, the following note); the later basilica contained a pulpit which we discovered (see pp. 66 f.); it probably marks more or less the position of the pulpit in the cella trichora. But Aetheria does not mention the pulpit for its own sake; it is mentioned only accidentally, — since its position was supposed to be known to her readers, — in order to indicate the position of another monument inside the church which attracted her special attention and is the center of the discussions which follow.

[6] Near the pulpit or, as some suppose, in the place where a pulpit usually stood (see Bludau, op. cit., p. 23: "an der Stelle, wo sonst das Lesepult [pulpitus] sich befindet;" — in this case the cella trichora did not necessarily contain a pulpit), Aetheria saw a monument

'Here holy Moses was laid by the angels, since, as it is written, "No man knows how he was buried," since it is certain that he was buried by angels. For his grave where he was laid is now shown to-day; as it was shown to us by our ancestors who lived here, so do we point it out to you; our ancestors said that it was handed down to them as a tradition by their ancestors.'[1]

which she describes as follows: "vidi locum modice quasi altiorem tantum hispatii habentem quantum memoriae solent habere." The comparative "altiorem" becomes clear if we presuppose a comparison with a pulpit referred to by Aetheria; the place or monument which Aetheria saw was "a little higher" than the pulpit in the church (or a little higher than an ordinary pulpit). On pp. 67 ff. we pointed out that near the pulpit in the last basilica we actually found a monument which is not only "a little higher" than the pulpit, but in every other respect resembles the monument described by Aetheria. If that is not the identical monument which Aetheria saw and described, then it is at least very similar to it.

[1] After Aetheria has directed the attention of her readers to the place or monument inside the church which had attracted her attention and aroused her curiosity and after describing it in such a way as to arouse their interest and curiosity, she informs them of its real meaning; it was nothing less than the tomb of Moses. This information she obtained from the holy men who accompanied her; their exact words are reproduced; there is not the least sign that their statements were doubted or questioned. The original text, as it has come down to us, produces some difficulty, but this has been removed to some extent by the translation of Bernard. Since this text is of the greatest importance for understanding the true meaning of the monuments at Siyâgha, a more detailed analysis of the same is not out of place here.

1) When Aetheria inquired about the meaning of the place or monument which she saw inside the church, the holy men who accompanied her replied: "Hic positus est sanctus Moyses ab angelis." — The context and usage suggest that the word "positus est" means the same as "sepultus est," that is, "was buried;" see Geyer, p. 410. From the words which follow we learn that the burial of Moses was ascribed to angels; this Christian tradition may be illustrated by referring to Jewish traditions, to *The Epistle of St. Jude,* verse 9 and to the work called *The Assumption of Moses.*

a. The Jewish traditions regarding the part played by angels at the death of Moses are summed up in *The Jewish Encyclopedia,* 9, pp. 53-54; see also J. Rabbinowitz, *Deuteronomy,* in *Midrash Rabbah,* VII, London, 1939, pp. 180-188. — They deal with the part played by angels at the death of Moses, not with the manner of his burial.

b. *Jude,* verse 9: "When Michael the archangel, disputing with the devil, contended about the body of Moses, he durst not bring against him the judgment of railing speech, but said: The Lord command thee." — The commentators are not in full agreement regarding the object of the dispute; some think that it was a question about the place and manner in which the body of Moses should be buried; others think that there was question of preserving the body of Moses from corruption or of causing it to see corruption. Regarding these and other views the reader may consult, v. g., Henrici Hulsii, *Disputatio de corpore, velo et sepulchro Mosis* in B. Ugolini, *Thesaurus Antiquitatum Sacrarum,* 33, Venetiis, 1767, cols. DCCLXXI-DCCCIV.

c. R. H. Charles, *The Apocrypha and Pseudepigrapha of the Old Testament in English,* II, Oxford, 1913, pp. 407-424, deals with the work known as *The Assumption of Moses.* From there (p. 408, note 2) we quote the following: "On pp. 105-110 of my edition I have shown by an examination of the existing Greek fragments of the Assumption proper, that the order of action in it was probably as follows:

(1) Michael was commissioned to bury Moses.

(2) Satan opposed the burial on the ground: (a) that he was the lord of matter (ὕλη) and that accordingly the body should be rightfully handed over to him; (b) that Moses was a murderer, having slain the Egyptian.

(3) Michael having rebutted Satan's accusations proceeded to charge Satan with having instigated the serpent to tempt Eve.

(4) Finally all opposition having been overcome, the assumption took place in the presence of Joshua and Caleb, and in a very peculiar way. A two-fold presentation of Moses appeared: one was Moses in company with angels, the other was the dead body of Moses, being buried in the recesses of the mountains.

"The passages in support of "(1)" will be found in Severus, Patriarch of Antioch (A. D. 512-519). See Cramer, *Cat. in Ep. Cathol.*, p. 160; likewise the two anonymous passages op. cit. on pp. 161, 163; two scholia from Oecumenius (c. 990). — In support of "(2)": *Jude* 9; Clem. Alex., *Adumbrat. in Ep. Judae;* Didymus Alex. (309-394); Severus of Antioch; *Acta Synodi Nicaen.* II, 20; anonymous passages in Cramer's *Cat. in Ep. Cathol.*, pp. 160, 161, 163 and the scholia of Oecumenius. — In support of "(3)" Origen, *De Prin.* III, 2, 1. — In support of "(4)" Clem. Alex., *Strom.* VI, 15; Origen, *In Jos. Hom.* II, 1; Euodius, *Ep. ad August. 258.*"

Granted that Moses was buried by angels, then it is easy to understand why men should not know how he was buried or where he was buried. If the informants of Aetheria point out the place where Moses was buried, then we must assume that they considered the manner of his burial unknown. The explanation given by the men themselves must clear up the problem.

2) "Quoniam, sicut scriptum est, sepulturam illius nullus hominum scit: quoniam certum est eum ab angelis fuisse sepultum." — The fact that angels buried Moses explains why no man knows his "sepultura." According to Bernard "sepultura" means the mode or manner of his burial, "how he was buried." — If this is true and if, with Bernard, we omit the negative particle in the following sentence, then we can understand why the informants of Aetheria are able to point out the place where Moses was buried; their contention would be that only the mode of burial was unknown, not, however, the place of burial; this latter fact, according to them, was always known; it was handed down by an ancient and reliable tradition, and this is why they are able to point out the place of burial to the pilgrims.

Others maintain that "sepultura" means the same as sepulcrum; so, v. g., Geyer, p. 415: "Grab;" so also Bludau, op. cit., p. 24. In this case the place of the burial of Moses or, in other words, the tomb of Moses would be unknown. — If this is true, then how was it that the informants of Aetheria were able to point out its whereabouts to the pilgrims? It is true that they appeal to an ancient tradition, but this does not yet explain when and how their forebears found out about the whereabouts of the tomb; this is not indicated; of course it could be taken for granted that in some way or other their forebears discovered this fact. But apparently not everyone took this for granted and so we find that in the following century the pilgrims are informed that the whereabouts of the tomb was revealed to a shepherd in a vision. See Peter the Iberian.

3) "Nam memoria illius, ubi positus sit, in hodie [non] ostenditur." — This sentence is translated by Bernard as follows: "For his grave, where he was laid, is now shown to-day." Bludau, on the other hand, translates: "Even if until today no monument indicates where

And so presently a prayer was offered, and all things which we were accustomed to do in order in the several sacred places were also done here, and then we began to go out of the church." [1]

he lies buried." According to Bernard this sentence is affirmative, whilst according to Bludau it is negative; according to the former "memoria" means "grave," according to the latter it means "monument." The former takes the indirect question: "where he was buried" as synonymous with "memoria" and translates: "his grave, where he was laid;" according to the latter "memoria" means one thing and "ubi positus sit" another; by "memoria" he understands "a monument" which indicates the position of the grave; and "ubi positus sit" means the place "where he was buried," that is, "the grave" itself. To make the sentence fit into the context Bernard suppresses the negative particle and accordingly reads: "For his grave, where he was laid, is . . . shown . . . ;" consequently we are able to point it out to you, etc. Bludau, however, retains the negative particle and reads: 'His monument is not shown (at the place) where he was buried,' nevertheless we are able to point out to you the place of his burial, etc. In the first case it seems that some violence is done to the text, in the second case to history, for there was actually a monument at the place where Moses was buried; but in spite of the fact that one or the other word and construction is not quite certain, the general tenor of the sentence is clear and both Bernard and Bludau, as well as others, agree that local tradition claimed to know the exact place where Moses was buried. This fact is emphasized by the words which follow.

4) "Sicut enim nobis a majoribus, qui hic manserunt, ubi ‹positus sit› ostensum est, ita et nos vobis monstramus." — Likewise in interpreting and translating this sentence there are various views. Before going into details it may be well to note that Aetheria's informants evidently wish to explain how they found out where Moses was buried, since this knowledge seemed to be at variance with the commonly accepted view based on *Deut.* 34,6, where it is stated that "no man hath known of his sepulchre until this present day." As if anticipating objections on the part of Aetheria the holy men immediately add the explanation that they have derived their information from their forebears, that is, from tradition; it is, moreover, a tradition based on the authority of persons who have lived on the spot. So far all agree.

Difficulties concern minor details; so, for example, the phrase: "ubi ostensum est." Bernard seems to ignore the relative "ubi" in his translation. Bludau refers the relative "ubi" back to the demonstrative "hic" and supplies the same verb after it, so that the meaning is: "where (they lived) was indicated (above);" — in this case the sentence would be parenthetical. Geyer supplied "positus sit" after "ubi;" according to him we must read: "For as it was shown to us by our ancestors who lived here, where *he was buried*, so do we point it out to you."

5) "Qui et ipsi tamen majores ita sibi traditum a majoribus suis esse dicebant." — The tradition regarding the place where Moses was buried did not originate with the immediate ancestors of the holy men, it was much older; in fact, it went back to their remote ancestors. — Aetheria does not question the correctness of that information. As at other places so also here Aetheria caused the text dealing with the event in question to be read; very probably the last chapter of *Deuteronomy* was read; prayers were also said before the party left the shrine.

[1] When Aetheria and her party were on the point of leaving the church the priests and holy monks who knew the place well called their attention to another very interesting tradition associated with the place; it was the final vision of Moses. The Biblical text (*Deut.* 34, 1-3) is greatly amplified by Aetheria. Her very interesting description was referred to

II. PETER THE IBERIAN

The visit to the hot springs at Livias and to the church and monasteries on Mount Nebo.

"On one occasion the blessed (Peter) was pleased to go into the regions of Arabia,[1] by reason of his infirmity, in order to use the hot baths at Livias,[2] named after Saint Moses[3] . . . On the following day we travelled to Ma-

on pp. 15 f., no. 11; the text itself has already been given on pp. 150-152 and there also some observations have been made, which it is not necessary to repeat here; her references to Balak and Balaam were treated on pp. 205-206; in speaking of her return from Mount Nebo to Jerusalem, Aetheria not only expressly states that she returned by the same road by which she had come, but she also adds that she passed through Jericho; in other words, she followed the Roman road mentioned above.

From Aetheria's account it seems to follow that all the events mentioned in the last chapter of *Deuteronomy* were commemorated at Mount Nebo, that is to say, not only the tomb of Moses was shown there but also his final vision and his death were commemorated there. A number of other events mentioned in the Bible were located in the immediate vicinity; such as the arrival of the Israelites, their camp and the story of Balak and Balaam.

[1] The Roman province of Arabia is meant; also Aetheria spoke of going to Arabia when she set out to visit Mount Nebo; see p. 333, note 2.

[2] Aetheria also stopped at Livias on her way to Mount Nebo, but she makes no mention of hot springs there. Livias is in Palaestina Prima; see p. 334, note 1 and the following note.

[3] Aetheria recalls many Biblical events associated with Livias and the immediate vicinity, but she does not mention springs named after Moses at that place; the only springs or waters associated with the name of Moses by Aetheria are those at the foot of Mount Nebo. — Hot springs at Livias associated with the name of Moses are mentioned also by Theodosius and Antoninus; see Geyer, p. 145, 16-21; p. 166,2 ff.; Abel, *Géog.* I, p. 155: el-Hammâm. At the times of Theodosius and Antoninus (about 530 and 570 respectively) the waters were still famous for their curative qualities. In the case of Peter the Iberian, however, the waters were ineffective; in fact he tried them only once and declared that he found them cold. Thereupon people who had come from Arabia persuaded him to proceed to Baʿar or Baaru in the nearby regions of Arabia and try the hot baths there. See Raabe, pp. 81 f.

The introductory sentence leaves the impression that Livias is in the Roman province of Arabia, but this first impression is removed by a number of clearer statements made later on. From them it becomes clear that the territory of Livias and that of the Province of Arabia are really adjacent to one another; in other words, the latter does not include the former. Thus, for instance, we are told that when Peter reached Livias many came from the neighboring land of Arabia to see him; the people of Madaba are spoken of as people coming from Arabia; this last phrase implies what was expressly stated in the preceding one, namely, that the two territories are distinct. For the limits between the Regio Livias and the Roman province of Arabia see Abel, *Géog.* II, Carte X & pp. 174, 186 f.

daba.[1] And at midway we came to the holy hill of Moses,[2] whose name is Abarim, i. e., Fasga (Pisga),[3] where God said to him: Go up and die. On it there is a venerable and very large temple,[4] named after the prophet,[5] and many monasteries, which are built around it.[6] And full of joy on account of our arrival at this place, we together with the aged man offered up prayer and thanksgiving to God, who honored us with the blessing and veneration of such a prophet. And whilst we were there, after prayer and adoration, the old man caused us to enter a cell about 5 cubits long and wide and not very bright,[7] and related the following[8]...

[1] Regarding Madaba see Abel, *Géog.* II, pp. 186 f.; Meistermann, *Guide du Nil au Jourdain,* pp. 270-277; *DAC* 10,1, cols. 806-885.

[2] "The holy hill of Moses." — This expression reminds us of one of the names applied to Siyâgha even in our own times; it was recorded by Luynes (see p. 11, no. 1) and by Merrill (see pp. 12 f.).

[3] Aetheria called the place "Arabot" and "Nabau;" Peter the Iberian, or rather his biographer, calls the place "the holy hill of Moses," "Abarim" and "Fasga" or "Pisga;" he adds that it is the hill "where God said to him (to Moses): go up and die." If the names would have left room for doubt regarding the identity of the place in question, then the reference to the event which occurred there removes all doubt; in both Aetheria and in Peter the Iberian it is the mountain on which Moses was to die. See p. 333. The location of that mountain is fixed quite accurately; it is "midway" between Livias and Madaba; this indication corresponds perfectly to what we know from Aetheria. See pp. 334 ff.

[4] Both Aetheria and the biographer of Peter mention a monument on top of the hill; the monument which Aetheria saw seems to have consisted of only a chapel and that was "small;" the one which Peter's party saw consisted of a group of buildings with a church and this was "very large." Evidently a change had taken place since the days of Aetheria; this fact was confirmed by the excavations; we found the cella trichora, which Aetheria had visited, incorporated in a large basilica (see pp. 45 ff.).

Incidentally, both the literary evidence and the excavations prove that Aetheria must have been at Mount Nebo before Peter the Iberian; if the latter visited the place in the fifth century then Aetheria could not have come in the sixth, as some scholars have endeavored to show; on the contrary, the fourth century theory receives confirmation from these facts. See p. 330.

[5] Moses is meant; both the hill and the monuments on top of the hill were named after Moses.

[6] From this text we know that the buildings around the church were monasteries and that they existed already in the fifth century; see pp. 109 ff. The excavations have proved that the words must be taken literally.

[7] We are not sure which cell is meant, but cell 98 corresponds so well to the measurements and other details given here that, if it was not the very cell in question, it at least serves to illustrate the kind of cell meant. See pp. 179 ff.

[8] The narrative which follows was given completely on pp. 110 ff.; there some observations regarding its significance were also made.

The origin of the memorial of Moses on Mount Nebo.

"There on that occasion we learned from the inhabitants of that mountain, how the builders of that temple became convinced that the body of holy Moses was lying there [1] and how, over it the temple was built [2] and the table and altar stand, and under the altar the vessel of oil and of grace,[3] although holy Scripture clearly and unmistakably states: Moses, the servant of the Lord, died in the land of Moab according to the word of the Lord, and they buried [4] him in the land [5]

[1] Both Aetheria and Peter's biographer speak of visiting the place where Moses died; both find there a monument which claims to mark primarily not the place of his death but the place of his burial. Since this latter fact was supposed to be a secret, it was only natural to ask when and how the secret was divulged. Aetheria did not give us an answer to that question; that is the purpose of the story which follows.

[2] Aetheria saw a monument inside the church which was supposed to mark the place where Moses was buried. Here we are informed that the church at Mount Nebo was built over the tomb of Moses. The traditions of the fourth and fifth centuries do not conflict with one another.

[3] Inside the church, those who were with Peter the Iberian saw "a table" and "an altar;" beneath the latter they saw a lamp with oil. No explanation is given of these objects; at first thought they seem to be the ordinary furnishings of a church; but the fact that they are expressly mentioned may be significant; especially the reference to a lamp with oil beneath the altar may imply that the tomb of Moses was venerated there. At the place where the altar must have stood we actually found a tomb built of masonry, which was described on p. 36. Had that been the only tomb found inside the church, we might have suspected that it represented the tomb venerated by pilgrims; but, as a matter of fact, four other tombs were discovered within the limits of the basilica (see pp. 35-39). Since, then, there is nothing in the biography of Peter the Iberian, which obliges us to look for the tomb of Moses beneath the altar, it is better to hold fast to the explicit and clear statement of Aetheria that the tomb was pointed out to her at the place where the pulpit is; since, moreover, even in the last basilica we found a monument near the pulpit which corresponds perfectly with the description of the tomb of Moses given by Aetheria, it is only reasonable to assume that it represents the place inside the church venerated by the pilgrims as the tomb of Moses (see pp. 67 ff.). This monument resembles a table and may be the object meant by the "table" of the biography. Regarding tombs in the form of tables see *HCA* pp. 122 ff.

[4] *Deut.* 34,5 & 6, is quoted according to the Greek text, where the plural form: "ἔθαψαν, they buried (him)," is used. In the original text and other versions the singular form was used: "he (namely, God) buried (him)." The meaning of the Greek text is most probably the same as that of the original text; the use of the plural form may have been influenced by the tradition that God used angels as his ministers in burying Moses; some scholars think that the plural form may have the same impersonal force as the German phrase: "man begrub ihn."

[5] This phrase can easily be harmonized with the tradition which locates the tomb of Moses on the top of a mountain; it differs, however, somewhat from the Greek text of the *LXX* which has come down to us; there we do not read: ἐν γῇ, as the text of the biography ("in the land") suggests, but Γαΐ, which is a mere transcription of the word used in the original text (גיא), not a translation of the same. Since in other places, v. g., in *Deut.* 3,29; 4,46, the Hebrew word, which is generally assumed to mean "valley," was rendered in

near the house of Fogor,[1] and no one up to the present day found out about his end.[2] They told us: A shepherd from the village of Nebo (Nabu), which

Greek by words which are equivalent to the English word "valley," we should have expected the same here; if in this case the word was not translated but merely transcribed, there must have been some special reason for it. What was that reason? That we do not know. If originally Γαΐ was not taken in the same sense as γῇ, then, to judge from the biography of Peter, it was at least the occasion for those who used only the Greek text of taking Γαΐ in the same sense as γῇ, and not in the sense of "valley." This deserves to be noted, since it removes a difficulty which immediately rises in the minds of those who are accustomed to versions which take the Hebrew word to mean "valley." How is it, we ask, that the tomb of Moses was pointed out on top of a mountain, when the Bible informs us that he was buried in a valley? The answer is given by the text which we read in Peter the Iberian; there we do not read that Moses was buried in a valley, but "in the land;" nevertheless, according to the rest of the Biblical text as given in the biography, "no one up to the present day found out about his end."

1 "Near the house of Fogor." — The place where Moses was buried was not a complete secret. Holy Scripture itself gives some indications. One clew was the phrase considered in the preceding note; a second indication is given here. "The land" in which Moses was buried was "near the house of Fogor." This is the same phrase as that used in the *LXX* and in the *Onom*. 64,21 f. According to the *Onom*. 48,3 (see also Abel, *Géog*. II, p. 278: Beth Peʿor) the house of Fogor or Bethphogor was located on the mountains overlooking Livias about 6 miles from that town. In other words, it was near Mount Phogor, which was probably identical with the el-Mushakkar ridge, north of Wady ʿAyûn Mûsa, opposite Siyâgha. See pp. 6 f.

2 "His end." — The thing which no man knew is expressed here by the words: "his end." From what follows it is clear that the precise place of his burial was unknown. According to Jewish tradition that place always remained unknown; according to Christian and Mohammedan traditions, that was not the case.

a. The Jewish traditions regarding the tomb of Moses were indicated briefly by J. C. Lauterbach in *The Jewish Encyclopedia*, 9, p. 54, as follows: "Although Moses died in the territory of the tribe of Reuben, he was buried in that of Gad at a spot 4 miles distant from the place of his death. He was carried this distance by the Shekinah, while the angels said to him that he had practiced God's justice (*Deut*. 32,22). At the same time the bat kol cried out in the camp of the people: "Moses, the great teacher of Israel is dead." (*Sotah* 13 b).

"God himself buried Moses (*Sotah* 14 a; *Sanh*. 39 a) in a grave which had been prepared for him in the dusk of Friday, the sixth day of creation (*Pes*. 54 a). This tomb is opposite Beth-peor (*Deut*. 34,6), in atonement for the sin which Israel committed with the idol Peor (*Sotah* 14 a). Yet it cannot be discovered; for to a person standing on a mountain it seems to be in a valley; and if one goes down into the valley, it appears to be on the mountain."

N. B. — The last words sound almost like an attempt to reconcile the tradition which locates the tomb of Moses in a valley with the one which located it on the top of a mountain.

See also *Enc. Jud*. 4,418: Bet Peor; Neubauer, *GT* p. 252: Beth-Peor; *Siphri*, v. g., in Ugolini, 15, col. DCCCCXCIJ.

b. Mohammedan traditions know of several places where the tomb of Moses is supposed to be and where it is venerated today. The most important of those places is the one in

Alinari, no. 30138.

Fig. 37. Death of Moses on Mount Nebo, right (mosaic in St. Mary Major, Rome).

is situated on the south side of the mountain,[1] whilst leading his flock to pasture, brought it to this place.[2] On arriving here, he saw, as in a vision,[3] a very large cave,[4] filled with much light, pleasing odor and splendor. Filled

the desert of Judea, between Jerusalem and Jericho. Regarding that shrine there is a rather voluminous literature indicated by L. A. Mayer in *QDAP* 2 (1933), pp. 27 f.; that writer gives further details, ibid. pp. 27 ff. Recently G. R. Berry, *Old and New in Palestine*, Hamilton, New York, 1939, pp. 63-65, expressed the view that the traditions originally associated with Mount Nebo were transferred to the shrine of Nebi Mûsa near the Jericho road, because this place was more conveniently reached by pilgrims. See p. 113,4.

c. The Christian traditions regarding the location of the tomb of Moses at Mount Nebo are recorded by Aetheria and by the biographer of Peter the Iberian; only the latter explains how that fact became known.

[1] This notice enables us to identify the village of Nebo with the ruins at el-Mekhayyat; see p. 8; Abel, *Géog.* II, pp. 397 f.

[2] The Arabs of the Nebo region prefer to live on the plateau during the summer months. Daily the flocks are brought to the springs either in Wady ʿAyûn Mûsa or in Wady el-Keneiyiseh (see p. 9); on the way to and from the springs the flocks are permitted to graze; the shepherds who accompany them (see Pl. 21,2) have ample time to think and dream; the mystery which surrounded Mount Nebo must have exercised some influence on them; as a matter of fact, we hear that one of them was favored with a vision in which the place where Moses was buried was made known to him. From what follows it is evident that Moses was buried in a cave in the heart of the mountain; the text gives further details both regarding the cave and regarding Moses himself.

[3] The vision. — It must be emphasized that according to this account the whereabouts of the tomb was seen only in "a vision." After the vision the shepherd himself no longer saw the cave; he even feared that afterwards he himself might not find the exact spot where he had the vision; to make sure that he would find it again he marked the place with heaps of stones. The visionary character of the cave is proven by the fact that the people, who heard of the vision and came to look for the cave, could not find it; neither was the shepherd able to show them the cave itself, but merely the place where he had the vision of the cave; the exact spot of the vision was guaranteed by the heaps of stones which he had made and which all could see; the church was built on the spot where the shepherd had the vision.

[4] The cave. — In the vision the shepherd did not merely see from a distance the cave in which Moses was buried, but he actually descended into it. The only other place in which mention is made of a cave is the 17th century account of the discovery of the tomb of Moses (see pp. 331 f.); in that case the tomb was reached by a crevice in the side of the mountain; there too sweet odors were said to fill the cave; those details sound like faint recollections of the story of the shepherd as recorded in the biography of Peter the Iberian.

In excavating the churches at Siyâgha we had to be realistic and take into consideration the possibility that a cave really existed inside the church and was actually pointed out to pilgrims as the tomb of Moses. Accordingly in 1935 extensive explorations were made beneath the level of the floor within the area of the original cella trichora; the results are described on pp. 35 ff.; no real cave was found; the closest approach to a cave was the trench in which tombs **a-c** were constructed (see pp. 37 ff.). We must, therefore, hold fast to the visionary character of the cave.

with astonishment — for never before had anything of the kind been seen at that place — he, strengthened by divine power, ventured to descend into that cave, and saw a venerable old man whose face was brilliant and beaming with kindness, and who was reposing on a luminous bed resplendent with glory and grace. And since he realized that this was holy Moses,[1] he immediately ran with great fear and joy to the village and hastened to inform those who lived there of the vision. Enlightened by God he collected small stones and made many stone heaps at that place, where he had the vision, since he bore in mind the possibility that after his departure, it might again become impossible

[1] Moses. — The shepherd does not say that inside the cave he saw a tomb which contained the remains of Moses, as is stated, v. g., in the account of the 17th century (see p. 331, 5); but his reference to the couch or bed reminds one of the arrangement inside of tombs or caves which became quite common since the end of the Bronze Age, in other words, since the time of Moses (see *BRL* col. 244, 8); this arrangement consisted of a stone bench on which the body was placed; Moses is represented as reclining on such a bench, which is luminous with glory. Moses himself has the appearance of a venerable old man, whose face is beaming with an extraordinary brilliance and with kindness. In this entire description one cannot detect a single trace of the darkness and gloominess of a tomb; there is only light and brightness, as at the Transfiguration of our Lord on the high mountain, where Moses appeared together with Elias (see *Mt.* 17,3; *Mc.* 9,4; *Lc.* 9,30). Possibly the present description was influenced by that scene. If so, then a number of other questions immediately arise, due principally to the association of Moses with Elias. The latter, for example, did not die; does it then follow that Moses also did not die? According to a commonly accepted view, Elias is one of the two witnesses mentioned in *Apoc.* 11, 1-13; is perhaps Moses the other witness?

There are some who believed that Moses is not dead; that belief may be illustrated by the following passage of St. Augustine, *Tract. in Joan. CXXIV*, 2, cited by H. Pope, *The Catholic Student's Aids to the Study of the Bible,* II, London, 1918, p. 250: "If we can believe," he says, "that Moses is not dead, since his tomb no man can find (*Deut.* 34,6), and he appeared at the Transfiguration with Elias, why should we not believe the same of John of whom it was said: 'So will I have him remain till I come.'" Other details given in that same legend may throw further light on the views which were probably current also regarding Moses. "According to a persistent tradition," Pope adds, on the authority of St. Augustine, that "John does not lie dead at Ephesus but merely sleeps in his tomb there, and that his breath as he sleeps gently stirs the soil above." "It seems to me idle," concludes Augustine, "to fight against an opinion like this. Let those familiar with the spot go and see if it is true that the earth is thus stirred; and as a matter of fact I have heard the story from responsible men."

There are also some who believe that Moses will be one of the two witnesses mentioned in *Apoc.* 11,1-13. See, v. g., D. Haugg, *Die zwei Zeugen, eine exegetische Studie über Apok. 11,1-13,* in *Neutestamentliche Abhandlungen,* XVII, 1, Münster in W., 1936, especially pp. 102-105.

The shepherd at Mount Nebo may have recognized Moses in the same way as the Apostles did at the Transfiguration, namely, either by a supernatural inspiration and illumination or by the fact that his face was radiant or "horned," as described in *Exodus* 34,29 ff. See also the commentaries dealing with the passages indicated.

to recognize the spot — and this actually happened. For when the inhabitants of that village heard it, they all came in great crowds to the (place of the) vision and looked for that cave. And that shepherd calling God to witness declared: At this place where these heaps of stone are, I beheld that vision and I went down into that cave and saw the holy prophet. And for this very reason I made these heaps of stones, in order that, if the prophet at God's command should again conceal himself, nevertheless the heaps of stone would indicate the place. And so, since they and besides many saints were convinced that the vision was a true one, and all the inhabitants of that region together hurriedly brought building material, this temple was built in the name of the great prophet and lawgiver,[1] and he proclaims publicly to every man and so that no doubt is possible his goodness and power by means of signs and wonders and cures, which since that time have occurred at this place without interruption. For it is a place of cure both for the souls and for the bodies, and a place of refuge for all those, who come here from all places and are afflicted in soul and affected with many kinds of sufferings of the body.[2]

"After we had prayed there and as a viaticum had received the prayers of the great prophet, we reached the town mentioned above" (namely, Madaba) . . .[3]

[1] The vision was the occasion for building the church in honor of Moses at that spot.

[2] In confirmation of the tradition which locates the tomb of Moses in a cave inside Mount Nebo, at the spot indicated by the church, the people appeal to the signs and wonders worked there at the intercession of the saint.

[3] An event which occurred on the way from Mount Nebo to Madaba was referred to on p. 249. — The entire biography deserves to be studied by those who are interested in the history of monasticism and in the problems uppermost in the minds of men at that time.

* * *

The texts of Aetheria and the biography of Peter the Iberian are the two most important literary sources which we possess regarding the monuments at Siyâgha; principally from them do we know to whom those monuments were dedicated and that they served to commemorate an event of outstanding importance not only in Biblical and religious history but also in the history of mankind as such. The other texts contribute so little to our knowledge of the site and its monuments that it is not necessary to reproduce them here; their substance was indicated above. Regarding the description of Abarim given by Thietmar (p. 331,3) the writer feels obliged to add that it makes the impression of one who was not at Siyâgha at all or of one who is accustomed to use very extravagant language. He is also the only pilgrim who in some way associates the ark with the Nebo region; the details which he gives suggest that he was dependent for his information, regarding the place of the ark, not on *2 Mach.* 2,4 ff. but on the *Vitae Prophetarum*; see p. 188, note 2.

CHAPTER XVI

THE SIGNIFICANCE OF THE MONUMENTS ON MOUNT NEBO

The monuments at Siyâgha serve to fix the traditional location of Mount Nebo; they mark the spot where Moses died and was buried and represent a flourishing center of monasticism in the Byzantine period and a goal of Christian pilgrims for several centuries; these are the principal facts to be borne in mind in order to appreciate the true significance of the monuments on Mount Nebo.

1. *The location of Mount Nebo.* — The Bible indicates that Mount Nebo is somewhere to the northeast of the Dead Sea; Eusebius and Jerome inform us that the place was usually pointed out from the sixth milestone to the west of Esbus; Aetheria reached this mountain from springs near its foot; the latter were associated in some way with Moses; the biographer of Peter the Iberian states that the mountain is about midway between Livias and Madaba. All these indications lead us to the neighborhood of Siyâgha; but, if it were not for the monuments on the site, the precise ridge or peak, which, according to tradition, was called Mount Nebo, would always have remained somewhat doubtful for us. As it is, it would actually be difficult to pick out another mountain in that region to which all the indications given in the literary sources fit so perfectly as they do the peak known today as Siyâgha.

2. *The name.* — In Early Byzantine times the place at which the memorial of Moses was located seems to have been called indiscriminately Nebo or Nabau, Abarim, Phasga or Fasga or Pisgah and the holy mountain of Moses. Three of those names are found in the Bible; the fourth is an extra-Biblical name. The name Siyâgha is found neither in the Bible nor in pilgrims' texts; it originated after the monastery had been built on the site; then people began to refer to the place as "the monastery," in Aramaic: "Siyâgha," as we pointed out on pp. 115 ff.; that name eventually supplanted all others and it is the only one which local tradition preserved down to our own times.

3. *The traditions.* — Only an extra-Biblical tradition is explicitly associated with the monuments at Mount Nebo; but it seems reasonable to assume that the monuments served to commemorate also other events associated with that spot in the Bible; this seems to be implied clearly enough in one or the other case.

a. The Bible associates the following events with Mount Nebo or its immediate vicinity: the passage and camp of the Israelites (*Num.* 21,20 ff.; 33,47 f.), the story of Balak and Balaam (*Num.* 23,13-26), the final vision and death of Moses (*Deut.* 34,1-5), the dispute about the body of Moses between Michael and Satan (*Jude* 9) and the concealment of the tabernacle, the ark and the altar of incense in a cave (*2 Mach.* 2,4-8).

Aetheria claims to have seen traces of the camp of the Israelites on the northern side of Siyâgha; see p. 151. The dominant position of Siyâgha, the ancient paths passing it on both sides (see Pls. 159 & 160) leading from the plateau to the valley of the Jordan (see Pl. 8) and the abundant supply of water in the valley immediately to the north (see Pls. 12 ff.), make it comprehensible why an army advancing from the southeast towards the Jordan should endeavor to occupy such a point until its rear was secure.

The story of Balak and Balaam is located by Aetheria to the southwest of the church at Siyâgha; see pp. 151 & 205 f. The fact that Balaam erected altars there, offered sacrifice and blessed Israel from that spot imparts to the place a certain religious significance, if it did not possess this character already before.

The vision of Moses is recalled by Aetheria in connection with her visit to the church at Mount Nebo; see pp. 150 ff. & 205 f. Aetheria's description should be compared with the account in *Deut.* 34,1-4 and with the facts given on pp. 5 ff. The vision was, no doubt, associated with the monument of Moses at Mount Nebo in some way, though Aetheria does not state this expressly.

Mount Nebo became a center of interest primarily by the fact that Moses died there; see *Deut.* 34,5. This is the only event associated with the site by Eusebius and Jerome; see *Onom.* 16,24; 136,7. When Aetheria was planning on going to Mount Nebo, she seems to have been prompted to do so on the one hand by the hope of enjoying the view from there and on the other hand by the desire of seeing the place where Moses died (see p. 333). The biographer of Peter the Iberian at first mentions only the death of Moses at Mount Nebo and his first impression seems to have been that the monuments on the site served to commemorate this event (see p. 342); later on he informs us of the local tradition regarding those monuments.

The death of Moses at Mount Nebo forms a part of the education of so many that there is an almost universal interest in Mount Nebo and all that concerns it.[1]

[1] All who have studied the Bible know that Moses died on Mount Nebo; but very few of us have ever heard that a memorial was erected in honor of Moses at that place. The excavations have revealed the character of that memorial.

This event has influenced art (see Fig. 37) [1] and its memory is perpetuated by the liturgy.[2] In spite of the fact that we have no document which directly and expressly associates the death of Moses with the monuments on the site, we have personally no doubt that the monuments served to commemorate also this event. The pilgrims emphasize the point which was practically unknown and thus seem to overlook the events which were well known.

The dispute about the body of Moses between Michael and Satan is not explicitly mentioned as associated with the memorial of Moses on Mount Nebo, but the insistence of the informants of Aetheria on the fact that angels buried Moses (see pp. 338 f.) seems to imply the connection clearly enough.

Finally, as regards the story dealing with the place of the concealment of the tabernacle, the ark and the altar of incense in a cave at Mount Nebo, one can readily detect a tendency of associating the ark and the other objects with their author; in other words, this tradition presupposes that those articles are very close to the place where Moses was buried; in so far they may be said to have some connection with the memorial of Moses on Mount Nebo, but this connection was not expressly stated by any one; in fact, the only pilgrim who makes any mention of the ark in this region seems to locate its place of concealment at some distance from the memorial. See pp. 17, note 2; 21,18; 187 f.; 347.

b. According to *Deut*. 34,6, as it is commonly understood, the place where Moses was buried remained unknown; but, according to a local tradition recorded by the biographer of Peter the Iberian (see pp. 343-7), its whereabouts was revealed to a shepherd and the monuments on Mount Nebo mark the spot where the shepherd had the vision; the cave in which Moses lies is in the heart of the mountain below the church; hence the monument which Aetheria saw inside the church could not have been the real tomb but merely a cenotaph. Both Aetheria and the biographer of Peter the Iberian are so intent on recording the rather unexpected new fact, namely, that the monuments on Mount Nebo mark the tomb of Moses, that they forget to mention whether other facts were also

[1] The scene in the basilica of St. Mary Major, at Rome, was executed either in the fourth century (at the time of Pope Liberius, 352-366 A. D.) or the fifth (the time of Sixtus III, 432-440 A. D.); see *HCA* p. 428; Marguerite van Berchem et Etienne Clouzot, *Mosaïques Chrétiennes du IVme au Xme Siècle*, Genève, 1924, pp. XXXII & 35 f., Figs. L & 39; *DAC* 11,2, cols. 1687 f., Fig. 8267. At the extreme right the death of Moses is represented; he is reclining on his left side; in spite of his 120 years, he is represented as a youth, still fresh, hale and vigorous, as is suggested by *Deut*. 34,7. The rock on which he is reclining and the mountains in the background resemble very closely the appearance of Siyâgha when viewed from the southwest; compare, v. g., Fig. 37 with Pl. 3,1.

[2] As early as the 7th cent. of our era the feast of Moses was commemorated in the church of Gethsemane on September 4th; see Heinrich Goussen, *Über Georgische Drucke und Handschriften die Festordnung und den Heiligenkalender Jerusalems betreffend* in *Liturgie und Kunst*, IV, 1923, p. 31. — The *Roman Martyrology* for September 4th still commemorates the death of Moses on Mount Nebo. — For further details regarding the day on which Moses is supposed to have died see, v. g., Cornelius a Lapide, II, Parisiis, 1866, pp. 534 f.

commemorated there; they probably took for granted that other events, expressly associated by the Bible with Mount Nebo, were also commemorated there or, at any rate, we may take it for granted. See chapter XV. The character of the monuments which mark the tomb of Moses was indicated very briefly by Aetheria and Peter's biographer; many more facts regarding those monuments were revealed by the excavations; they were reported in detail in chapters III-XIV.

4. *A brief history of the monuments.*

1) The time of Aetheria (± 394 A. D.). — The monument which Aetheria saw was "a small church" with a cenotaph inside; it corresponds to the cella trichora described in chapter III. Some suspected that the temple of Yahweh destroyed by Mesa in the middle of the 9th century B. C. stood on this spot and that remnants of the same are incorporated in the present church (see pp. 14,8; 236 ff.). This cannot be demonstrated.

2) The time of Peter the Iberian (5th cent. A. D.). — The cella trichora was transformed into a large basilica. On the interior at least the eastern apse was decorated with mosaics (see pp. 34 f.); the furnishings were made of marble and other rare stones (see pp. 286 ff.). If the mosaics of the apse would have been preserved more completely, they would probably have thrown some light on the event commemorated by the church; as it is, we can only surmise that either the death or the burial of Moses was represented; the more or less contemporaneous mosaic representation of the death of Moses in the church of St. Mary Major in Rome (see Fig. 37) may serve to convey some idea of the manner in which the death of Moses may have been represented; the description of the cave given by the shepherd and the appearance of Moses in the vision may possibly correspond to the scene which was depicted in the apse (see pp. 345 f.). — Around the atrium and on the north, west and south of the central group there were monastic buildings and a hospice for pilgrims. The place had become a flourishing center of monasticism and pilgrimages.

3) The Samaritan occupation (date uncertain; possibly in the first part of the 6th cent. A. D.). — Evidence of the same are marble slabs with Samaritan inscriptions (see pp. 271 ff.).

4) The time of the abbot Alex. (date uncertain; probably some time before the end of the 6th cent. A. D.). — He carried out restorations (see pp. 262 ff.).

5) The time of the abbot Martyrius and bishop Sergius (end of the 6th and beginning of the 7th centuries A. D.). — Work on the basilica and the baptistery was completed in 597 A. D. (see pp. 45 ff., 84 ff., 247 ff.).

6) The time of the abbot Theodore and bishop Leontios (beginning of the 7th century). — Work on the Theotokos chapel was completed (see pp. 91 ff., 255 ff.).

7) The end of the Byzantine period and the Umayyad period (7th and 8th centuries). — Coins suggest that the occupation of the site was fairly continuous

throughout the latter part of the Byzantine period and during the Umayyad period (see pp. 281 ff.); clay lamps suggest the same (see pp. 322 ff.); other evidence is less clear (see pp. 46,2; 106; 275 ff.; 297, no. 168; 300; 303; 316).

8) From the 8th to the 19th century. — The buildings at Siyâgha were neglected, fell to ruins and eventually their significance was completely forgotten. Travellers continued to pass by; some squatters lived in the ruins for a short time (see pp. 46, 113, 275 f.), even pilgrims continued to go there, so, for example, in the 13th and 16th centuries (see pp. 46 & 113). But the 16th century pilgrim, a Franciscan (see pp. 46, 113, 331), found the monuments completely ruined and the traditions transferred to a chapel at ʿAyûn Mûsa (see p. 331). In the 17th century the tomb of Moses was no longer associated with a building, but exclusively with a cave (see pp. 331 f.). The ruins were converted into a modern cemetery (see pp. 5, 46, 285, etc.). Soon the very location of Mount Nebo was forgotten and scholars sought to identify it with a variety of ridges and peaks (see the references in Abel, *Géog.* I, pp. 379 f., note 4). But the names and ruins survived; a peak continued to be called Neba; springs and the ridge overlooking them were named after Moses; the ruins continued to be called Siyâgha, "the monastery." The principal explorers who were instrumental in rediscovering and making known the site and its monuments were mentioned on pp. 11 ff.; the first one was Luynes in 1864. Then in 1884 the account of Aetheria was found; its publication in 1887 paved the way for a better knowledge of the monuments at Siyâgha; in 1895 the biography of Peter the Iberian was translated into a modern language and rendered accessible to a wider circle of readers; it served to lead scholars a step closer to the proper understanding of the monuments at Siyâgha (see pp. 330 f.).

9) The 20th century. — Since the beginning of the 20th century more and more scholars began to identify the ruins at Siyâgha with the monuments visited by Aetheria, Peter the Iberian and his biographer (see pp. 14 f.); doubts which remained were cleared up by the excavations. As a result, Siyâgha must be identified with the place which in Byzantine times was considered Mount Nebo; the Byzantine tradition, in turn, agrees so perfectly with the information regarding Mount Nebo contained in the *Onom.* of Jerome and Eusebius and in the Bible that we cannot reasonably call into question the identity of the Byzantine and Biblical Mount Nebo.

* * *

The chief significance of the monuments at Siyâgha, therefore, does not consist in the character of their architecture and art, but in their association with a Biblical site and person of more than usual interest. Those churches, chapels and monasteries exhibit more or less the same form of architecture, the same art in their mosaics, decorations, etc. as most other Christian buildings of the Byzantine period, not only in the Roman province of Arabia [1] but in the greater part of the Christian world; this is interesting enough; but it is not peculiar to the monuments at Mount Nebo. One thing, however, is peculiar to those monuments and to this they owe their chief significance; it is the fact that they serve to indicate, so to say, the stage on which was enacted the last scene in the earthly career of the greatest prophet of the Old Testament; they mark the place of the death and burial of Moses; this was the fact which attracted monks and pilgrims to Mount Nebo in ancient times; it is also today the chief attraction of Mount Nebo.

[1] Regarding the Roman province of Arabia in general see *PA* I-III; regarding Christianity in that province see *DHGE* 3 (1924), cols. 1158-1339; see also Abel, *Géog.* II, pp. 162 ff.; *HPT* especially pp. 457 ff.; *Gerasa*, passim.

The end.

I. GENERAL INDEX

(A star [*] indicates illustrations in the text; heavy print refers to plates.)

II. INDEX OF GREEK WORDS

III. INDEX OF ARAMAIC AND HEBREW WORDS

IV. INDEX OF ARABIC WORDS

V. INDEX OF BIBLICAL TEXTS